IMAGES OF W

THE LIBERATION OF THE PHILIPPINES 1944–45

RARE PHOTOGRAPHS FROM WARTIME ARCHIVES

Jon Diamond

Pen & Sword
MILITARY

First published in Great Britain in 2021 by
PEN & SWORD MILITARY
An imprint of
Pen & Sword Books Ltd
47 Church Street
Barnsley
South Yorkshire
S70 2AS

ISBN 978-1-52678-872-6

A CIP catalogue record for this book is available from the British Library.

Typeset by Concept, Huddersfield, West Yorkshire, HD4 5JL.
Printed and bound in the UK by CPI Group (UK) Ltd, Croydon, CR0 4YY.

FSC www.fsc.org MIX Paper from responsible sources FSC® C013604

Pen & Sword Books Limited incorporates the imprints of Atlas, Archaeology, Aviation, Discovery, Family History, Fiction, History, Maritime, Military, Military Classics, Politics, Select, Transport, True Crime, Air World, Frontline Publishing, Leo Cooper, Remember When, Seaforth Publishing, The Praetorian Press, Wharncliffe Local History, Wharncliffe Transport, Wharncliffe True Crime and White Owl.

For a complete list of Pen & Sword titles please contact
PEN & SWORD BOOKS LIMITED
47 Church Street, Barnsley, South Yorkshire S70 2AS, England
E-mail: enquiries@pen-and-sword.co.uk
Website: www.pen-and-sword.co.uk

Contents

Acknowledgements

This archival photograph volume in the 'Images of War' series is dedicated to the Allied Armed Forces service members who fought, were wounded and perished during the hellacious land, air and naval combat to recapture the Philippines from Imperial Japanese rule. General Douglas A. MacArthur had vowed to return to the Philippines after he was ordered to leave Corregidor for Australia in early 1942 to assume command of the Australian-American counteroffensive against the Japanese in the South-West Pacific Area (SWPA).

Lest we forget, we ponder, upon viewing these photographs, about the heroic sacrifice made to maintain freedom over military aggression, hegemony and brutality. The author is indebted to the able assistance of the archivists at both the United States Army Military History Institute (USAMHI) at the United States Army War College in Carlisle, Pennsylvania and the Still Photo Section of the National Archives and Records Administration (NARA) in College Park, Maryland. Their diligence is much appreciated as they maintain and safeguard these superb historic images for the present tome as well as for future viewers.

Abbreviations

AAA – Anti-Aircraft Artillery
AIF – Australian Imperial Force
AP – Armour-piercing
APC – Armoured personnel carrier
AT – Anti-tank
CAP – Combat Air Patrol
C-in-C – Commander-in-Chief
COMINCH-CNO – Commander-in-Chief and Chief of Naval Operations
COS – Chief of Staff
CPA – Central Pacific Area
FA – Field Artillery
FEAF – Far East Air Force
HE – High explosive
HMG – Heavy machine gun
HQ – Headquarters
IIIAC – III Amphibious Corps
IJA – Imperial Japanese Army
IJN – Imperial Japanese Navy
IMB – Independent Mixed Brigade

IR – Infantry Regiment
LMG – Light machine gun
MG – Machine gun
MMG – Medium machine gun
NCO – Non-commissioned officer
NEI – Netherlands East Indies
PoW – Prisoner of War
SNLF – Special Naval Landing Force
SPA – South Pacific Area
SPA – Self-propelled artillery
SWPA – South-West Pacific Area
TB – Tank Battalion
TD – Tank Destroyer
USA – United States Army
USAFFE – US Army Forces of the Far East
USN – United States Navy
USS – United States Ship
WP – White phosphorus
WPO – War Plan Orange

Chapter One

Imperial Japan's Conquest of the Philippines 1941–42

American Presence in the Pre-War Philippines

On 30 April 1898, Commodore George Dewey's nine-ship squadron passed Corregidor Island and entered Manila Bay. At dawn the next day, Spanish shore batteries opened fire as the American ships headed towards the Spanish base at Cavite. At nearly 0600 hours on 1 May, Dewey ordered Captain Charles V. Gridley, the commander of USS *Olympia* (Dewey's flagship), 'You may fire when you are ready, Gridley.' Spain's twelve-ship force was obliterated during the seven-hour battle, with only one American sailor dying. What began as the American frenzy, fanned by politicians and the press, to liberate Cuba from Spanish oppression and avenge the sinking of the USS *Maine*, a cruiser, on 15 February 1898 now led President William McKinley's administration to oust Spain from the Philippines with Dewey's domination of Manila Bay and Cavite.

American infantry, dispatched under Major General Wesley Merritt (a Civil War-era cavalry officer), in its initial action outside the Western Hemisphere, moved on Spanish-controlled Manila contemporaneous with a growing Filipino insurgency against the Spanish that spread across the archipelago and of which, in the spring of 1898, McKinley was almost unaware. Also, American soldiers – both US Army regulars and volunteers – were wholly unprepared for war in the Philippines from logistics and training standpoints. Filipino independence was declared by Emilio Aguinaldo, chief of the Filipino nationalists, on 12 June 1898 in his home town of Cavite along the southern shores of Manila Bay.

By the early summer of 1898, before Merritt's infantry arrived, 30,000 Filipinos had laid siege trenches around Manila as the Spanish troops were also prohibited a sea exit by Dewey's squadron in Manila Bay. One of Merritt's subordinates was another Civil War veteran Brigadier General Arthur MacArthur, the father of Douglas A. MacArthur. Brigadier General Thomas H. Anderson, another Civil War veteran, was to seize Guam, Spain's first Pacific colony after its discovery by Ferdinand Magellan in the early sixteenth century. Anderson sailed from San Francisco on 25 May 1898 with 2,500 American troops and once at sea was diverted to Guam, which after its seizure became the first US Pacific possession during this initial military expedition outside American continental limits. Late in June, Anderson's contingent came ashore at Cavite, prior to a move more proximate to Manila, naming the area Camp Dewey.

Dewey's informal intelligence convinced him incorrectly that the Filipinos, under their leader Aguinaldo, did not want independence, despite Filipino rebels seizing armaments and ammunition in addition to Spanish prisoners at Cavite. With only 2,000 men under him, Dewey waited for Brigadier General MacArthur and also Greene's detachments arriving in July 1898 and Merritt's troops at the end of the month to commence an American offensive on Manila. However, the Filipino rebels wanted to capture Manila from the Spanish without American help, thereby straining the relationship between the two armed actions. Then, on 31 July, Spanish forces shelled and attacked the Americans, killing a dozen, the first US troops to be killed in action in the Philippines.

With some sporadic fighting amid the siege lines of Manila, leaving a few more American soldiers killed in action, US Army infantry entered the city in August 1898. The Treaty of Paris between the US and Spain was signed on 10 December which granted independence to Cuba and made Guam, Puerto Rico and the Philippines American possessions. Nonetheless, US and Aguinaldo's forces were ready to combat one another as the American occupation force was to soon approach 22,000 troops in the vicinity of Manila. On the night of 4 February 1899, fighting erupted along a 10-mile front separating Nebraska volunteers and Filipino forces near Manila's Santa Mesa suburb where the Pasig and San Juan Rivers join flowing west-ward towards the *Intramuros* or 'Walled City'. The 'Philippine Insurrection' had commenced between the United States and Filipino nationalists, ultimately becoming guerrilla warfare as Aguinaldo left the Manila area for northern Luzon.

On 1 September 1900, William Taft, a future twenty-seventh American president (1909–13) and a Supreme Court Chief Justice (1921–30), along with his fellow commissioners assumed the functions of a legislative body in the Philippines, raising taxes, enacting laws and establishing judicial courts. In July 1902, then President Theodore Roosevelt proclaimed victory over the Filipinos with Aguinaldo's capture in March 1902 by a contingent of Kansas volunteers led by Colonel Frederick Funston. However, fighting dragged on in other parts of the archipelago with Filipino resistance to American occupation forces, notably on Samar and Luzon. The fiercest resistance came from Muslim rebels on the southern Philippine islands of Mindanao and Jolo. The Spanish referred to the Muslim Filipinos as Moros after the Moors of North Africa. The Moros comprised more than a dozen ethnic groups, each led by a local sultan. The Moros launched massive attacks against the Americans, often wielding only spears and knives.

John J. 'Black Jack' Pershing, a cavalryman and regimental quartermaster for the 10th Cavalry comprising African-American 'Buffalo soldiers' that fought on Kettle and San Juan Hills in Cuba, gained fame fighting the Moros. He was promoted from captain to brigadier general by President Theodore Roosevelt after his initial battles against the Moros. Pershing subsequently administered the region after a bloody action in 1913. Another senior officer gaining distinction fighting the Moros was Brigadier General Leonard Wood, a Harvard Medical School graduate who earned the Congressional Medal of Honor for his role in the capture of the Apache warrior Geronimo. One of Wood's lieutenants in the Philippines was another cavalryman, George S. Patton.

The casualties among the American forces in the Philippines were numerous as of 4 July 1902 when Roosevelt proclaimed that the war was over. There were more than 4,000 Americans killed and almost 3,000 wounded, while many became afflicted with lingering tropical diseases. More than 20,000 Filipino soldiers were killed, as well as 200,000 civilians who died from war, famine and atrocities.

Douglas MacArthur was the central military individual in the Philippines before the outbreak of war in the Pacific during the Japanese conquest of the archipelago and throughout the islands' liberation by US forces in 1944–45. MacArthur graduated from West Point in 1903. His late father was Arthur MacArthur, Jr, who was the commander of US forces in the Philippines from 1898 to 1901. In 1904, Douglas MacArthur was deployed to the Philippines where he first met a prominent lawyer, Manuel Quezon. During the First World War, MacArthur served as a 42nd Infantry Division's brigade commander and its COS, ending the conflict as a brigadier general with many decorations for valour. In 1930, MacArthur was appointed Army Chief of Staff, a job his famous father never received. In 1935, while remaining on active duty in the US Army, he arrived in the Philippines again to take up President Quezon's paid position to train the Filipino army with the rank of field marshal. As war with Japan loomed in 1941, the Filipino armed forces remained unprepared for a major war due to inadequate armaments, as well as language and cultural differences among the various native troops.

Outbreak of the Pacific War

Japan was embroiled in a protracted conflict with China since the invasion and annexation of Manchuria in 1931. Japan and the Soviet Union were also involved in an undeclared border conflict in north-east China from 1932 to 1939. A second Sino-Japanese War erupted in early July 1937 after the 'Marco Polo Bridge Incident' at Wanping, 15km from Peking. From 1937 to 1939, Japan was on a war footing with more than 1 million troops on the Asian mainland and, thereby, primed for their blitzkrieg across the Pacific and throughout southern Asia, the Philippines, Malaya, Singapore and the Netherlands East Indies (NEI) after the surprise Imperial Japanese

Navy (IJN) attack on US military installations at Pearl Harbor, Hawaii, on 7 December 1941, which ceded temporary naval supremacy to the IJN in the Pacific Ocean.

Contemporaneous with Admiral Chūichi Nagumo's aerial assault on the United States Navy's (USN's) Pacific Fleet and army installations on Oahu, both the IJN and Imperial Japanese Army (IJA) conducted offensive operations across Asia and the Pacific spanning 7,000 miles from Singapore to Midway Island (see Map 1). Malaya and Singapore were early targets in Japan's major southern thrust, with additional operations to seize the Philippine archipelago, Hong Kong and parts of British Borneo. Guam was occupied on 8 December and Wake Island fell on 23 December. When Allied resistance was encountered by the IJA, notably on the Bataan Peninsula and Corregidor Island in the Philippines, these American bastions were simply cut off and bypassed until a lack of supplies and food compelled surrender.

Since US Army and Navy planners believed that the Philippine Islands were not defensible if the Japanese mounted a full-scale attack, military preparations were wholly incomplete before General Douglas A. MacArthur's arrival in 1935 to command the archipelago's Filipino-American forces as a field marshal. Over the next six years, the build-up of forces under his leadership was still tardy and unfinished. Pre-war American Pacific strategy in 1941 was code-named War Plan Orange (WPO-3). US war planners surmised that the Japanese were intent on landing their assault troops at sites of their choosing along Luzon's coastline and among other Philippine islands. The planned Filipino-American response was to take up strong defensive positions on the Bataan Peninsula and in fixed fortifications around Manila. WPO-3 envisioned a stockpiling of foodstuffs, ammunition and medical supplies within the Bataan Peninsula to enable MacArthur's Filipino-American force to hold out until the USN arrived with reinforcements after a theorized victory over the IJN somewhere in the Pacific Ocean.

General Douglas MacArthur, now the commander of United States Army Forces in the Far East (USAFFE), scrapped WPO-3 and unsuccessfully prepared to repel the Japanese invasion at the waterline. American stockpiles were scattered throughout Luzon, leaving the Bataan Peninsula bereft of supplies for a long siege after the Filipino-American force retreated into that locale. MacArthur's strategy of scrapping WPO-3 and contesting Japanese amphibious assaults at the shoreline became a disaster.

Hours after the Pearl Harbor attack, MacArthur and his Chief of Staff (COS) Major General Richard K. Sutherland vacillated about a preemptive attack by US Air Corps B-17s on the Japanese airfields based on Formosa. Regardless of the unlikelihood of success if the Americans attacked the Formosan fields, keeping the B-17s at Clark Field rather than moving them to Del Monte airfield on Mindanao proved disastrous as neither the non-dispersed nor non-concealed US planes proved easy targets for the Japanese Formosa-based bombers, which destroyed MacArthur's air strength

MONGOLIA
MANCHUKUO (Manchuria) (Japan)
U.S.S.R.
Vladivostok
Sea of Japan
Bejing
KOREA (Japan)
JAPAN
Tokyo
Osaka
CHINA
PACIFIC OCEAN
INDIA
Wuhan
Shanghai
Hangzhou
East China Sea
Fuzhou
Okinawa
Ryukyu Islands (Japan)
Bonin Is.
Iwo Jima
Marcus Is.
Midway Is.
French Frigate Shoal
Hawaiian Islands
Pearl Harbor
Canton
Formosa (Japan)
Hong Kong (Br.)
Hanoi
FRENCH INDOCHINA
Philippine Sea
Mariana Is.
Asuncion
Wake Is.
Johnston Is.
SIAM
Luzon
Manila
South China Sea
PHILIPPINES
Saipan
Guam
Bikini
Rongelap
Marshall Islands
Enewitok
Kwajalein
Maloelap
Majuro
Jaluit
Ulithi
Yap Is.
Caroline Islands
Truk
Palau Islands
Peleiu Is.
Mindanao
BRUNEI (Br.)
NORTH BORNEO (Br.)
MALAYA (Br.)
SARAWAK (Br.)
Singapore (Br.)
Sumatra
Borneo
Celebes
Palmyra Is.
Tarawa
Gilbert Islands
Howland Is.
Baker Is.
Christmas Is.
Bismarck Archipelago
Nauru
Ocean
Hollandia
New Guinea
NORTHEAST NEW GUINEA
Rabaul
Solomon Islands
Canton Is.
Phoenix Islands
DUTCH EAST INDIES
Java
PAPUA (Aust.)
(Aust.)
Ellice Islands
Timor
Arafura Sea
Port Moresby
INDIAN OCEAN
Darwin
Coral Sea
New Hebrides
Samoa
Fiji
AUSTRALIA
New Caledonia
Tonga Islands

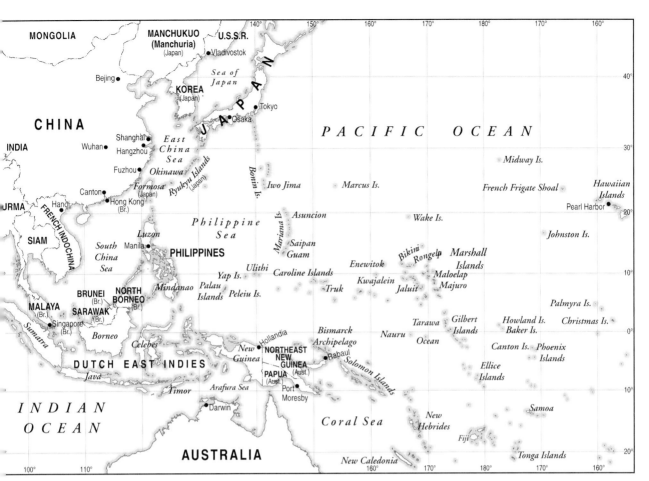

Map 1. Strategic Overview of the Pacific War, 1941–42. Soon after the 7 December 1941 Pearl Harbor aerial attack, Malaya and the Philippines were invaded. Singapore fell to Yamashita's 25th Army on 15 February 1942. Filipino-American forces surrendered at Bataan on 9 April 1942 followed by the capitulation of the Corregidor garrison on 6 May. Other American possessions such as Guam and Wake Island were captured by the Japanese juggernaut in December. The Dutch East Indies fell to Japanese forces in their drive towards the SWPA and Indian Ocean. Rabaul on New Britain Island in the Bismarck Archipelago was invaded in February 1942 with the Australian forces there having retreated or been captured. Rabaul, at New Britain's north-eastern tip, became the main bastion for the IJA and IJN in the SWPA. Japanese outposts were established in North-East New Guinea and along Papua's northern coast. Port Moresby on Papua's southern coast and northern Australia were saved from invasion during early May's Battle of the Coral Sea. The IJN was decisively defeated by a USN carrier-based aircraft victory, the Battle of Midway, in early June, eliminating a potential threat to the Hawaiian Islands. *(Meridian Mapping)*

mostly on the ground. Most of the B-17s and nearly a score of P-40 fighters were destroyed at Clark Field. Simultaneous Japanese air attacks at nearby Nichols and Iba Fields cost the Americans many more fighters destroyed on the ground. The remnants of the American air presence in the Philippines quickly succumbed to the enemy's air superiority.

IJA Lieutenant General Masaharu Homma and his 14th Army were denied a quick victory in the Philippines, despite their air and naval dominance, as MacArthur's

Filipino-American troops retreated into the Bataan Peninsula and held out there until 9 April. It was not until 6 May that the neighbouring island fortress of Corregidor in Manila Bay capitulated following a Japanese invasion (see Map 2).

Darwin, a port and administrative seat in Australia's North-West Territories, was now under direct threat after the Japanese established bases along the northern coast of North-East New Guinea and soon Papua. The Australian government, with most of its army in the Middle East, could only spare modest reinforcements for Darwin's garrison, which was initially bombed by the Japanese on 19 February, just four days after Singapore's surrender, with a large contingent of Australian Imperial Force (AIF) troops, which figured largely in Australia's pre-war defence planning. In early March, Port Moresby had only the 30th Infantry Brigade, a field artillery regiment and coastal AAA units, totalling between 6,000 and 7,000 men.

Australian Prime Minister John Curtin wanted his AIF divisions returned from the Middle East for home defence. Two brigades of the AIF 6th Division were transferred to Ceylon, while the division's remaining brigade and the AIF 7th Division were returned to Australia, the leading elements arriving in mid-March. With the AIF 9th Division remaining in the Middle East, Curtin was mollified by the 'green' US 32nd and 41st Infantry divisions, both National Guard units, being hastily deployed to

Map 2. Japanese Invasion of the Philippines, December 1941. General Homma's IJA 14th Army's main assembly area was located on Formosa, the Pescadores Islands **(1)** (off Formosa's west coast) and in the Ryukyu Islands **(A)**. An IJN Task Force from Formosa seized Batan Island **(2)**, well to Luzon's north, on 8 December. Two days later elements of this same Task Force seized Camiguin Island **(3)** off Luzon's north-eastern tip, while an amphibious force (the *Tanaka* Detachment, part of the IJA 48th Division) from the Pescadores Islands landed at Aparri **(4)** on Luzon's northern coast that same day. Also on 10 December, another portion of the 48th Division (the (*Kanno* Detachment) also from the Pescadores Islands, landed on Luzon's north-western coast at Vigan **(5)**. The 48th Division's main body, under General Tsuchibashi, landed at the Lingayen Gulf sites **(6)** of Baung, Caba, Agoo and Damortis on 22 December. Two weeks earlier, on 8 December, MacArthur's FEAF was neutralized on the ground at Luzon's Clark **(7)** and Iba **(8)** Fields. Nichols Field and Cavite Navy Yard, both just south of Manila, were pulverized by unmolested Japanese aerial attack on 10 December. These IJA 48th Division forces then moved against the US 26th Cavalry Regiment near Rosario on 24 December before attacking southwards down the Central Luzon Plain **(9)** against serial Filipino-American defensive lines of Major General Wainwright's Northern Luzon Force before approaching the 'open city' of Manila on 2 January 1942.

On 24 December, a portion of the IJA 16th Division (*Morioka* Force) from Amami Ōshima **(A)** in the northern Ryukyus, landed at Lamon Bay **(B)** along Luzon's eastern mid-portion to combat Brigadier General Parker's Southern Luzon Force. Portions of the units of the IJA 16th Division's 33rd Regiment separately left Koror **(C)** in the Japanese-mandated Palau Islands, more than 600 miles directly east of Mindanao, to land at Legazpi **(D)** (*Kimura* Detachment) on the south-eastern tip of Luzon's Bicol Peninsula on 12 December and at Davao **(E)** on Mindanao (*Miura* Detachment) on 19–20 December. The Davao assault force was reinforced with the IJA 16th Army's 146th Regiment (*Sakaguchi* Detachment). *Miura* Detachment units broke off to attack Jolo **(F)** Island in the Sulu Archipelago south-west of Mindanao on 24 December. (*Meridian Mapping*)

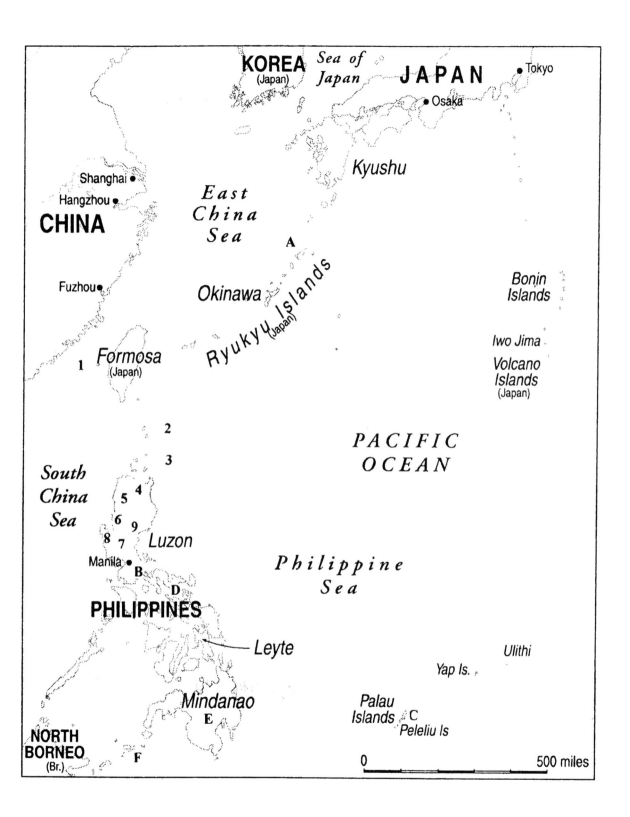

KOREA
(Japan)

Sea of Japan

JAPAN

• Tokyo

• Osaka

Kyushu

Shanghai •

Hangzhou •

CHINA

East China Sea

A

Fuzhou •

Okinawa

Ryukyu Islands
(Japan)

1   Formosa
(Japan)

Bonin Islands

Iwo Jima

Volcano Islands
(Japan)

PACIFIC OCEAN

2

3

South China Sea

4

5

6   9

8   7   Luzon

Manila •

B

D

Philippine Sea

PHILIPPINES

Leyte

Ulithi

Yap Is.

Mindanao

E

Palau Islands   C

Peleliu Is

NORTH BORNEO
(Br.)

F

0   500 miles

Australia's defence in April and May 1942 under MacArthur, now the C-in-C, South-West Pacific Area (SWPA).

Japanese staging moves to take New Guinea began on 8–11 March when IJA and IJN elements landed at Salamaua, Lae and Finschhafen on the Huon Peninsula in North-East New Guinea. By April 1942, Allied air attacks were causing extensive damage to Japanese air capacity and naval movements in the Solomon Sea, so between 1 and 20 April Imperial Special Naval Landing Force (SNLF) troops were also landed at multiple sites along the northern coast of both North-East and Netherlands New Guinea to assist in airfield construction. Strategically, the Pacific War was to be determined by either capturing enemy airfields or nearby suitable terrain to construct new ones for aerial umbrellas to control the sea lanes as well as to support future amphibious landings for expansion.

The Japanese planned to isolate Australia's Northern Territories, along with Darwin and its harbour, by occupying Port Moresby on the southern coast of Papua. Initially, rather than taking Port Moresby by an overland route, the IJN was to capture it in an amphibious operation, which was mitigated by a US carrier task force at the Battle of the Coral Sea on 4–8 May. Despite the tactical loss of the USS *Lexington* and damage to the USS *Yorktown*, the Japanese invasion force strategically retreated after losing a carrier and having another one damaged. Additionally, many experienced IJN pilots died in the sea battle, the first fought solely by carrier-based planes. This naval battle was Japan's first major setback and nullified this initial Port Moresby amphibious invasion.

New Guinea possessed no cities or towns, with the exception of the smaller ones at Port Moresby, Milne Bay, Lae and Finschhafen. There were a few coconut plantations, trading posts and small Christian missions, such as at the villages of Buna and Gona on Papua's northern coast. Port Moresby, on Papua's south coast, had a population of 3,000 before the war comprising mostly native Papuans. Emanating from Port Moresby, only native paths connected the northern and southern Papuan coasts, the most famous being the Kokoda Trail (or Track to the Australians), named after the village situated in a narrow mountain valley 1,200ft above sea level in the northern foothills of the Owen Stanley Range. Kokoda also had a small airfield, which was a main Japanese objective as they planned a future overland advance from new beachhead garrisons established at Buna and Gona. Allied and Japanese engineers were separately busy evaluating either extant airfields or suitable Papuan terrain for the construction of new ones.

The Japanese faced another strategic dilemma after strategically losing at the Battle of the Coral Sea as well as losing four large IJN carriers at Midway in early June. Since the Japanese were committed to new landings along Papua New Guinea's northern coast for an overland attempt to seize Port Moresby, Lieutenant General Harukichi Hyakutake's 17th Army (headquartered at Rabaul) gathered its divisions from Davao (in the Philippines), Java and Rabaul to prepare for a summer Papuan offensive. Japanese General Headquarters agreed to a two-pronged approach on Port Moresby: one route would be along the coast from Papua's easternmost Milne Bay which would be taken by an assault from the sea, while the other route would be overland from Buna and Gona along the rugged Kokoda Trail.

In June 1942, MacArthur dispatched additional 'green' Australian militia units to Port Moresby as the US 32nd and 41st Infantry divisions (both American National Guard units) arrived in Australia. The Australian Militia's 39th Battalion, already deployed at Port Moresby, was ordered north to defend Kokoda.

By the end of July 1942, Lieutenant General Hyakutake had landed 13,500 troops at Buna and Gona and had forced the Australians, mainly militia, back south beyond Kokoda. The fighting was mostly guerrilla-style with fire-fights and ambushes in both wet jungle and tall kunai grasslands. To the chagrin of Japanese planners, there was no possibility of taking any vehicle along the track since it was only a few feet wide and could only be traversed, through its ridges, valleys, jungles and streams, by foot-slogging marches through calf-high thick mud.

The Australian militiamen were attacked by the Japanese on 29 July and steadily retreated. Eventually reinforced by Middle East veteran AIF formations, the Australians combated IJA units across the Owen Stanley Range via the Kokoda Trail as the Japanese tried an overland route to seize Port Moresby. By mid-September 1942, a stiffening Australian defence and orders for the Japanese advance to cease saved Port Moresby again. Also, a second amphibious Japanese invasion at Milne Bay during late August-early September aimed at seizing Port Moresby was turned back by Australian ground and air forces. Now it was to become the Americans' and Australians' turn to begin their offensive up the Kokoda Trail and through the Papuan jungle to drive the Japanese from Buna, Gona and Sanananda.

On 10 September 1942, MacArthur ordered Lieutenant General Robert L. Eichelberger's I Corps headquarters (HQ) to deploy Major General Edwin Harding's 32nd Infantry Division to capture the 11-mile-long group of Japanese installations at Buna. After a few months of arduous marching and combat against a bunkered Japanese foe, the unprepared American former National Guardsmen, with the aid of battle-hardened Australians, evicted the Japanese from their installations by January 1943. However, a steep Allied 'butcher's bill' was incurred and MacArthur vowed, 'No more Bunas.'

Meanwhile, in early May 1942 in the South Pacific Area (SPA) across the Solomon Sea from Papua, the IJN established the Japanese 25th Air Flotilla seaplane base on Tulagi, a tiny island in the Florida group across the Sealark Channel from Guadalcanal in the southern Solomon Islands. Tulagi's seizure was part of a larger Japanese military plan for further south-eastward strategic moves against New Caledonia, the New Hebrides, Fiji and Tonga islands, with its IJN 8th Fleet (the Outer South Seas Force

Tokyo
JAPAN
Osaka
East China Sea
Shanghai
Wuhan
Hangzhou
CHINA
Fuzhou
Okinawa
Ryukyu Islands (Japan)
Bonin Is. (Japan)
Volcano Islands
Iwo Jima
Marcus Is.
PACIFIC OCEAN
Canton
Formosa (Japan)
Hong Kong (Br.)
BURMA
Hanoi
FRENCH INDOCHINA
Wake Is.
Asuncion
Philippine Sea
Mariana Is.
Saipan
Tinian
NIMITZ/SPRUANCE
SIAM
Luzon
Manila
South China Sea
PHILIPPINES
Guam
Marshall Islands
Leyte
Ulithi
Caroline Islands
Eniwetok
Wotje
Yap Is.
Palau Islands
Kwajalein
Maloelap
Majuro
Jaliuit
Truk
Mindanao
Peleliu Is
BRUNEI (Br.)
NORTH BORNEO (Br.)
HALSEY
MALAYA (Br.)
SARAWAK (Br.)
Makin
Tarawa
Gilbert Islands
Singapore (Br.)
MACARTHUR
Sumatra
Borneo
Hollandia
Bismarck Archipelago
Nauru
Ocean
Celebes
New Guinea
NORTHEAST NEW GUINEA
New Britain
Rabaul
Bougainville
DUTCH EAST INDIES
PAPUA (Aust.)
(Aust.)
New Georgia
Java
Solomon Islands
Guadalcanal
Ellice Islands
INDIAN OCEAN
Timor
Arafura Sea
Port Moresby
Milne Bay
Darwin
AUSTRALIA
Coral Sea

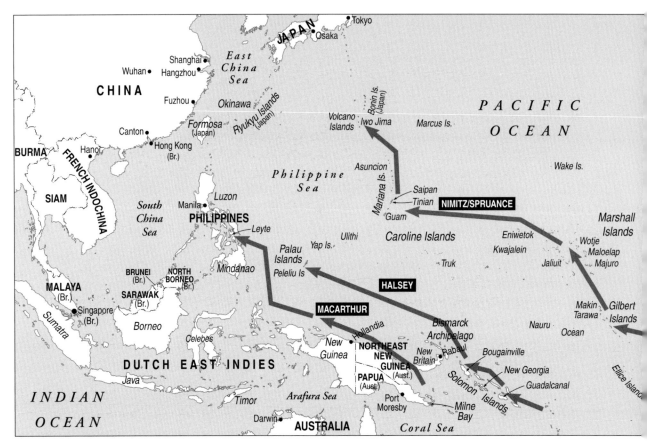

Map 3: Allied Counteroffensive Axes in the CPA, SPA and SWPA, 1943–44. In the CPA, Admiral Nimitz assigned, in August 1943, his COS Vice Admiral Raymond Spruance to command the Central Pacific Force (later redesignated the Fifth Fleet in April 1944). This USN, Marine and army force advanced and separately conquered the Gilbert Islands (November 1943), the Marshall Islands (January to February 1944) and the Marianas (June to August 1944). Then Nimitz and Spruance's staffs drew up plans to seize Iwo Jima in the Volcano Islands south of the Bonin Islands and north-west of Saipan. The IJN naval bastion of Truk in the eastern Caroline Islands was bypassed.

In the SPA, Vice Admiral William Halsey commanded his Third Fleet up the Solomon Islands with the capture of the New Georgia group (July to September 1943) and Bougainville (November 1943).

In the SWPA, General Douglas MacArthur with Australian-American ground forces and US Navy's Seventh Fleet vessels drove up the northern coast of North-East and Dutch New Guinea (1943–44). The southern end of New Britain was invaded by Marine and US Army amphibious forces in December 1943, while Rabaul was neutralized in an aerial campaign. MacArthur's ultimate goal was a return to the Philippines in the latter half of 1944.

At the Allied Cairo Conference in November 1943, Nimitz proposed an invasion of Japanese-controlled Formosa and, perhaps, seizure of East China coast bases as a prelude to a CPA advance on the Ryukyu Islands and then Japan's Home Islands. With this CPA offensive, the Philippines would be bypassed.

At a conference at Pearl Harbor on 26 July 1944 between Roosevelt, MacArthur, Nimitz and Admiral William Leahy, MacArthur persuaded Roosevelt and the JCS that returning to the Philippines would sever Japan's conquests in two and honour his promise of 'I shall return' to the Filipino citizenry. The JCS instructed MacArthur's SWPA forces to liberate the Philippine archipelago, beginning with the southern island of Mindanao, as focus on a CPA invasion of Formosa halted. In order to protect MacArthur's flanks, Morotai in the Moluccas ('left flank'), situated 300 miles from the Philippines, was assaulted by the US 31st Infantry Division and some Australian forces. To secure MacArthur's

under Vice Admiral Gunichi Mikawa) to eventually close the sea lanes from the United States to the Antipodes' Allied counteroffensive staging areas. USN Admiral Ernest J. King, C-in-C US Fleet and Chief of Naval Operations (COMINCH-CNO), marshalled his forces to interdict the enemy's expansion after a local coastwatcher, District Officer Martin Clemens (a captain commissioned in the British Army), discovered that a Japanese airfield construction party had landed on Guadalcanal on 28 May.

On 7 August, the bulk of the US 1st Marine Division (Reinforced), under the command of Major General Alexander A. Vandegrift, amphibiously landed on Guadalcanal, while other Marine specialist units quickly seized Tulagi and Gavutu-Tanambogo. Along Guadalcanal's northern coast, a six-month gruelling Marine defence of the almost-completed enemy airfield's perimeter (captured and renamed Henderson Field) ensued amid near-constant Japanese aerial and naval bombardment, deadly surface ship action in Sealark Channel (now called 'Iron Bottom Sound') and sporadic major IJA ground assaults. The US Army's America1 and 25th divisions arrived piecemeal to assist the Marines as reinforcements and then eventually moved westward against remaining enemy strongpoints through jungles and over mountains. By the first week of February 1943, Japan evacuated Guadalcanal, ending their south-eastern Pacific strategy to isolate the Antipodes.

After the bittersweet successes of Guadalcanal and Papua, three separate axes of Allied advances were conducted in the SWPA, SPA and the Central Pacific Area (CPA) (see Map 3). Beginning in January 1943, MacArthur's Australian-American forces seized strategic locales along the North-West New Guinea's northern coast and among nearby islands (e.g. Woodlark, Kiriwina, Goodenough) in the Solomon Sea. MacArthur dispatched the US Army's 112th Cavalry Regiment and the 1st Marine Division to invade New Britain's southern end at Arawe and Cape Gloucester at New Britain's southern end on 15 and 26 December respectively.

'right flank', Halsey's Third Fleet's amphibious force attacked Peleliu and Angaur in the Palau group of the western Caroline Islands, directly due east of Mindanao, in mid-September. Nimitz decided not to attack the well-defended Yap Island to the north-east of the Palau Islands, but planned on assaulting Ulithi Atoll, further to the north-east in the Caroline Islands, with an 81st Division IR to obtain favourable fleet anchorage. As events unfolded, MacArthur's Sixth Army landed at Leyte on 20 October 1944 as Mindanao was to be initially bypassed.

After the seizure of the Marianas, Nimitz ordered Spruance's Fifth Fleet to eventually seize Iwo Jima, a heavily-fortified island with two well-constructed air bases, which enabled Japanese fighter squadrons to interdict the advancing American LOC further westward across the CPA towards the East China Sea. Also, once captured, these airfields could base P-51 fighter escorts to accompany the Mariana-based B-29 Superfortress bombers that were suffering heavy losses on their 2,500-mile round trip over Japanese cities and military targets. Iwo Jima's airfields were also envisioned as emergency landing sites for damaged B-29 Superfortress bombers on their return leg from the Japanese Home Islands to their Mariana Islands bases.

American commanders were also planning an assault on Okinawa in the Ryukyu Islands as a prelude to and staging area for the final invasion of the Japanese Home Islands. (*Meridian Mapping*)

Strategically, the Allies seized extant enemy airfields or built new ones for future Allied aerial operations (Operation CARTWHEEL) to neutralize Rabaul by air. After Buna, MacArthur's new strategy was to bypass Japanese strongholds along New Guinea's northern coast in his campaign westward to capture the entire island mass in preparation for a return to the Philippines.

MacArthur's SWPA 1943–44 New Guinea Campaign

The Japanese built up the pre-war airfield and harbour at Lae in North-East New Guinea into a major base and anchorage on the Huon Peninsula. Japanese planners proposed an advance from Lae onto Wau with the intent of yet another attack on Port Moresby along a different geographic axis rather than via the Kokoda Trail. However, the Allied air forces prevented Japanese reinforcements from landing at Lae and a combined Allied offensive was launched during the summer of 1943 to capture the enemy bastion.

Elements of the US 41st Infantry Division pushed along the coast while the Australians advanced on a western axis from Wau through the Markham Valley. The Australians continued in the Allied offensive on the Huon Peninsula at Lae, Salamaua, Finschhafen and in the Markham River Valley. Here, the terrain and climate were daunting, as well as this area being rife with tropical diseases.

Japanese losses in their prolonged defence of Salamaua against the American and Australian advance left Lae exposed to an Allied envelopment. On 4 September 1943, almost 8,000 troops of the 7th Australian Division landed 18 miles east of Lae in the rear of Japanese defences, the first step in General Sir Thomas Blamey's New Guinea Force to clear the Huon Peninsula. After capturing Lae, the 7th Australian Division advanced west into the upper Ramu Valley to secure airfields for Lieutenant General George Kenney's US Fifth Air Force. The 9th Australian Division landed near Finschhafen and, against strong opposition at Sattelberg, these veteran troops eventually cleared the western shore of the Vitiaz Strait.

Throughout the earlier part of 1944, MacArthur's SWPA ground forces, comprising the US Sixth Army's (under Lieutenant General Walter Krueger) 6th, 24th, 32nd and 41st Infantry divisions, with attached elite cavalry, parachute, engineer and scout units, along with the 1st Marine Division given to MacArthur for the southern New Britain Island campaign, were transported by the growing VII Amphibious Force (under Rear Admiral Daniel Barbey) of the US Seventh Fleet. These SWPA ground forces moved inexorably westward along the northern coast of Netherlands New Guinea and New Britain's Willaumez Peninsula with successful missions at Saidor (2 January), the Admiralty Islands (29 February), Talasea (6 March), Aitape (22 April), Hollandia (22 April), Tanahmerah Bay (22 April), Wakde Island (18 May), Biak Island at the entrance of Geelvink Bay (27 May), Middleburg Island (30 June), Sansapor on the Vogelkop Peninsula (30 June), and Noemfoor Island (2 July).

Strategic War Planning for the Philippine Islands Campaign (Map 3)

At the November 1943 Cairo Conference, Allied war leaders recognized that ultimate aims of the American Pacific offensives included the Philippines' liberation, a Formosa invasion and establishing East China coastal air bases during late 1944 into spring of 1945 to bomb the enemy Home Islands. However, with Allied Pacific victories accumulating throughout mid-1943, MacArthur persuaded Roosevelt and the JCS at Pearl Harbor on 26 July 1944 that repossessing the Philippines would sever Japan's conquests in two and solidify the SWPA commander's promise of 'I shall return' to the Filipino citizenry. Enthusiasm for Nimitz's CPA fleet invading Formosa and possibly seizing East China coast air bases dissipated, although an invasion of the Ryukyu Islands targeting Okinawa would fall in the CPA's domain prior to the Japanese Home Islands.

In order to protect MacArthur's flanks for a proposed Mindanao invasion, two other amphibious operations were required. First, Morotai in the Halmahera group of the eastern NEI's Molucca chain, situated 300 miles from the Philippines, would cover MacArthur's 'left flank', and was to be assaulted by the US Army's 31st Infantry Division and some Australian forces on 15 September 1944. Neutralizing the Palau Islands was deemed necessary to secure MacArthur's 'right flank'. American intelligence was aware that at the start of the Pacific War, Palau-based IJA planes struck the southern Philippines. Peleliu's airfield was only 500 miles west of Mindanao. Also, in the closing weeks of December 1941, Palau-based Japanese troops invaded the central and southern Philippine Islands. Thus, the US 1st Marine and Army 81st divisions were to assault the Peleliu and Angaur islands within the Palau Group commencing on 15 September 1944 to prevent Japanese aerial interdiction of MacArthur's attack on Mindanao.

Halsey's USN Third Fleet staff and that of the Joint Expeditionary Force of the 1st Marine Division and the Army's 81st Infantry Division troops, comprising III Amphibious Corps (IIIAC), was delegated by Nimitz in early April 1944 with the operational planning of an upcoming Palau Islands campaign with Peleliu's airfield the prime objective. Ulithi Atoll, north-east of the Palau group, was to be assaulted by an 81st Division IR in order to obtain suitable anchorages for the massive USN fleet.

Admiral Halsey, who was previously the joint commander of the SPA and was now in charge of the Third Fleet's operations in the CPA, had reservations that an assault on the heavily-defended Palaus was likely to be a bloodbath, despite securing the airfields and anchorages there. The Palaus were reinforced with the IJA 14th Division, veterans from the IJA's Kwantung Army in Manchuria, which was sent to Koror in mid-April 1944, augmenting that island group's garrison strength to 35,000 troops.

US aerial reconnaissance, during the initial few days of September 1944, showed that the Japanese airfields at Peleliu and Babelthuap had not been completely repaired after the USN Task Force 58's carrier strikes of March 1944. Also, the number of Japanese bombers in the Palau group was probably not a consequential force and probably could have been dealt with by further USN carrier strikes. Furthermore, during carrier-based air-raids over Mindanao and the central Philippines, American intelligence observed a weakness of Japanese air power there that had led Halsey to publicly question the direction of the projected invasions and timetable for the Philippine operation. On 13 September, Halsey's staff sent an urgent message to Nimitz recommending that the seizure of the Peleliu and Ulithi Atoll be abandoned as well as transferring those troops earmarked for the Palau Islands operations to MacArthur for a Philippine invasion. Also, Halsey suggested that the assault on Leyte be undertaken as soon as possible due to the weakness of Japanese air forces in the southern and central Philippines.

Leading the American expeditionary force volunteers to Cuba after the sinking of the USS *Maine* in 1898 was Civil War veteran Major General Joseph 'Fighting Joe' Wheeler (left) in charge of volunteers and second-in-command of the Fifth Army Corps. Brigadier General Leonard Wood (centre) led the 1st US Volunteer Cavalry regiment in Cuba and was superior to Colonel Theodore Roosevelt (right). Roosevelt achieved fame by leading his 'Rough Riders' in the capture of Spanish blockhouses atop San Juan Hill. After Cuba, Wood went to the Philippines to lead American troops fighting the Moros. Wood later returned to the United States to become the army's chief of staff, followed by appointment as governor of the Philippines in 1921. *(Author's collection)*

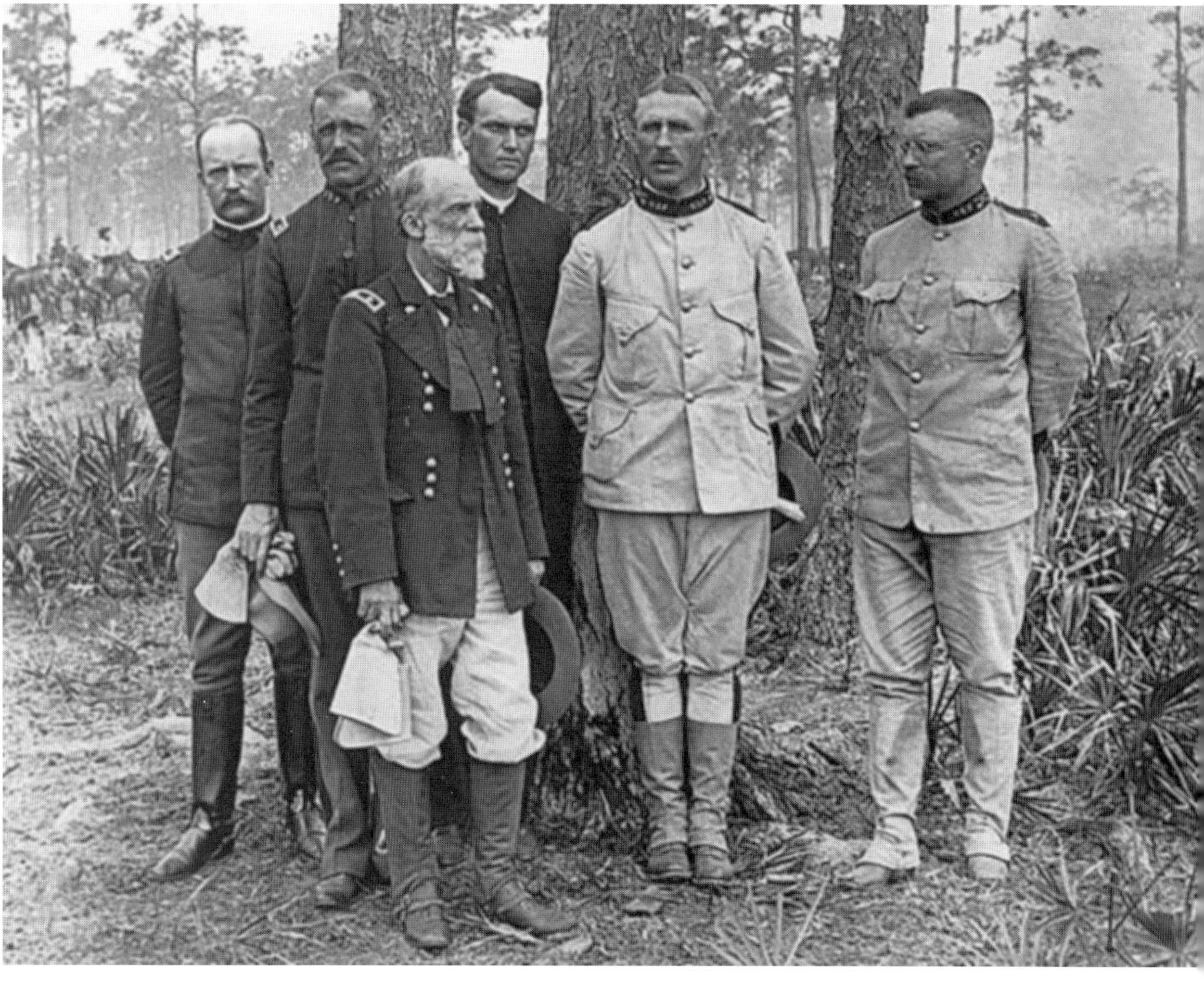

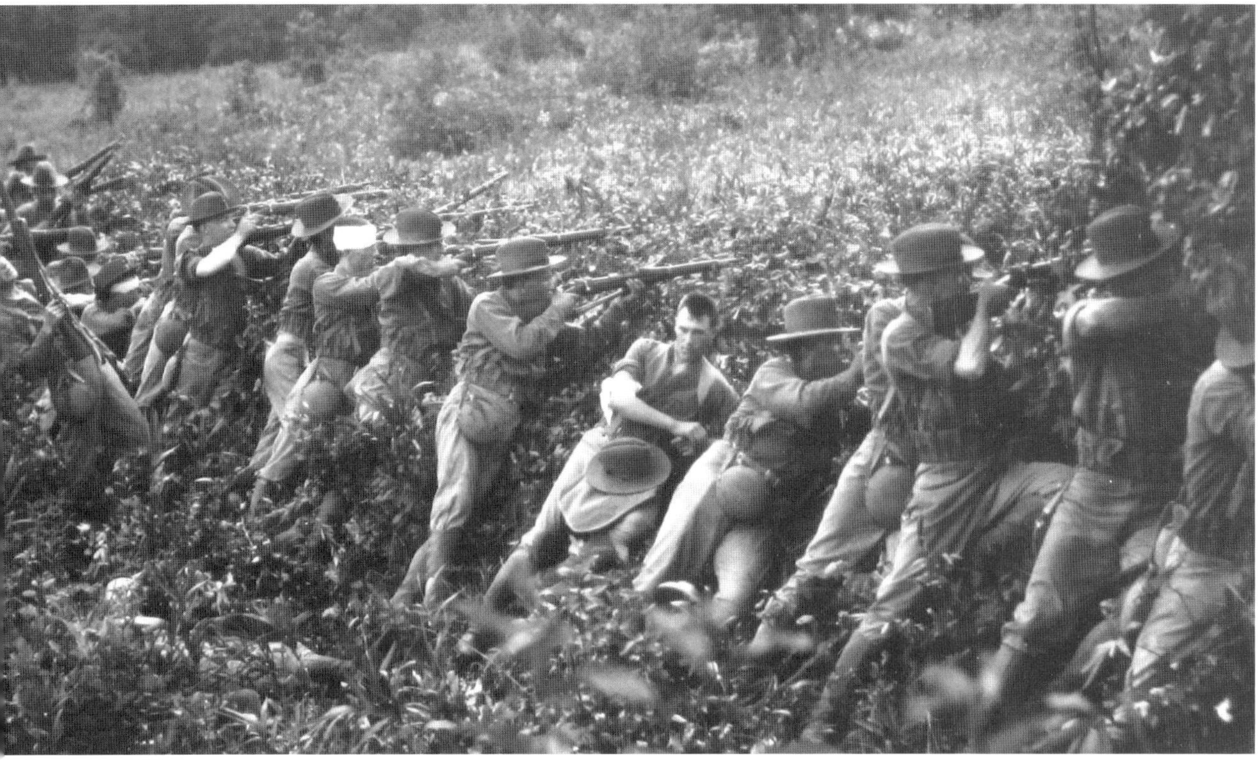

US Marines are shown here firing against and taking casualties from Filipino insurgents on Luzon in 1899. On 8 October 1899, a Marine battalion from Cavite under Lieutenant Colonel G.F. Eliot captured Noveleta, a small municipality in Cavite Province 16 miles from central Manila, incurring only two killed and fourteen wounded. *(NARA)*

A Battery's crew from Company B, 1st Nebraska Volunteers is shown here positioning their cannon to fire. Initially, the American troops took up positions outside Manila to aid Filipino rebels against the Spanish. However, after the Spanish surrender, Americans bitterly fought Filipino insurrectionists who had declared independence. *(Author's collection)*

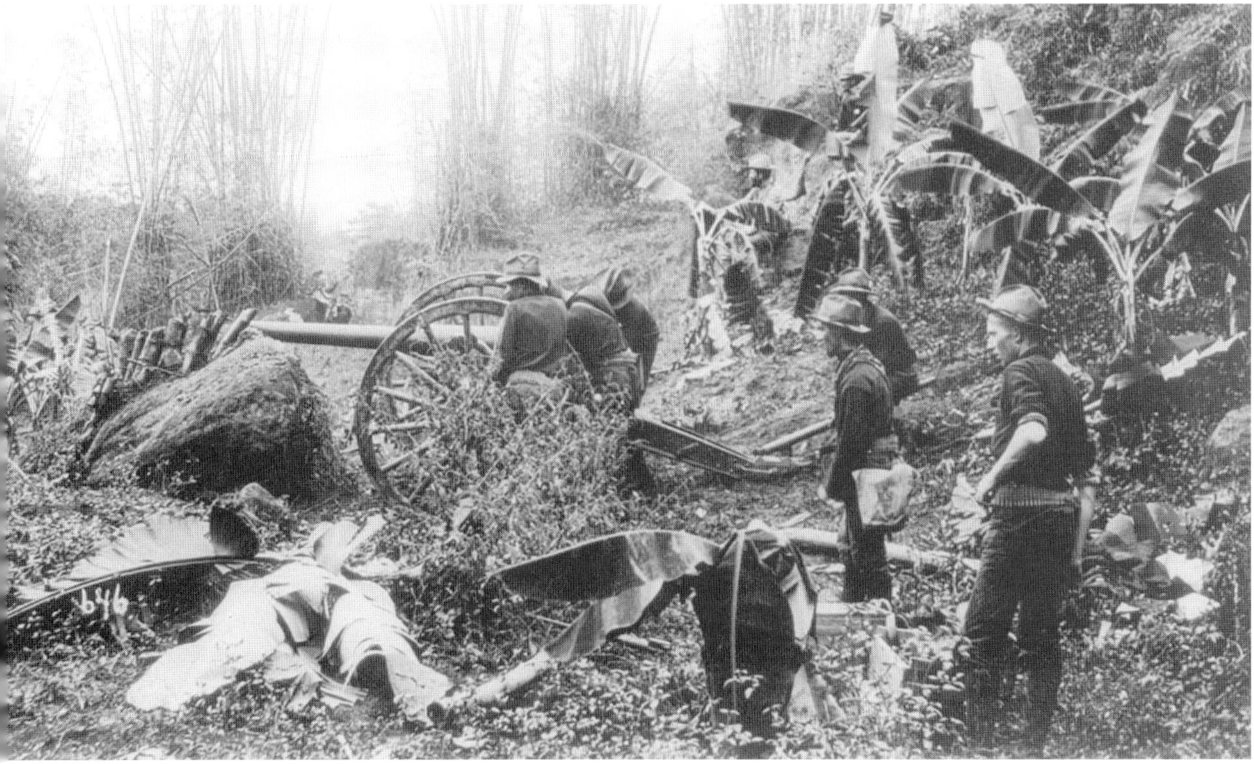

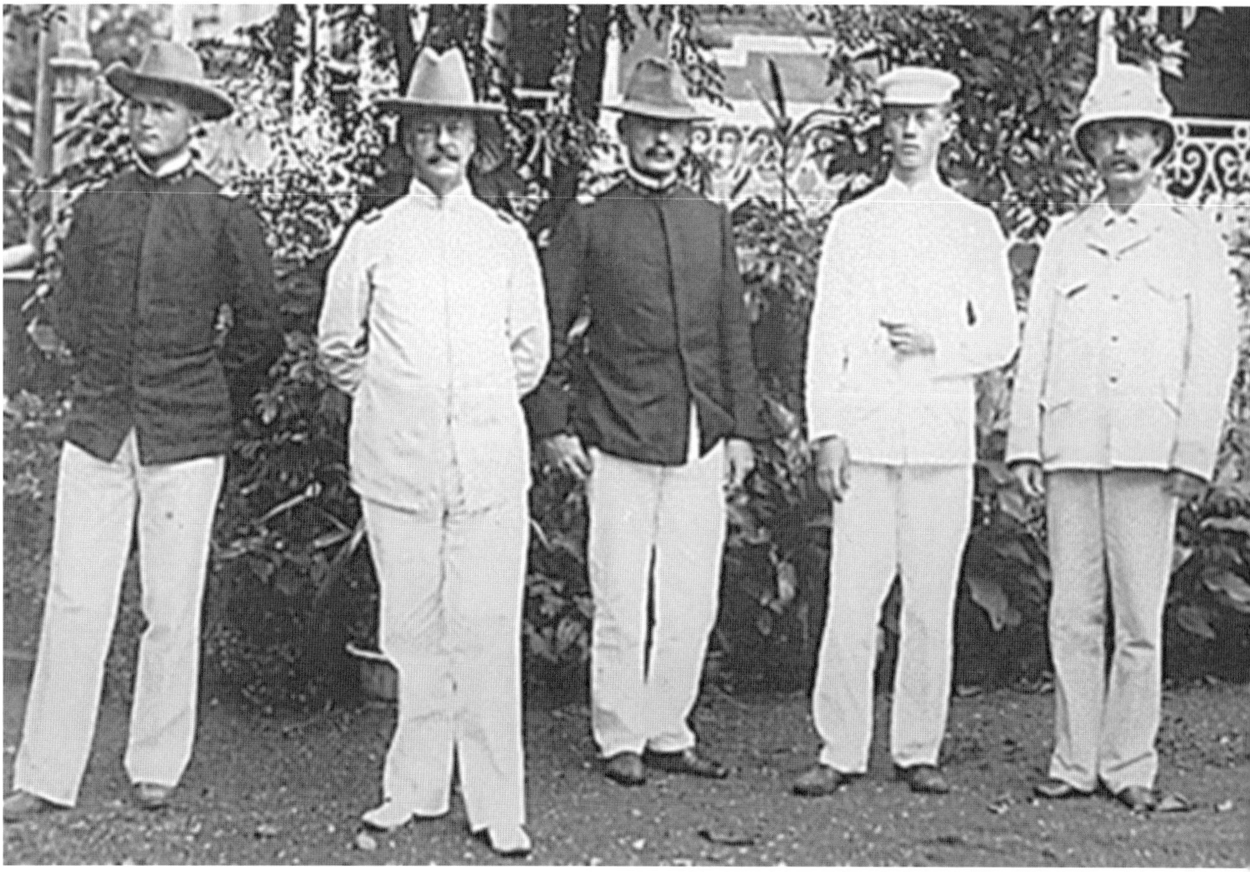

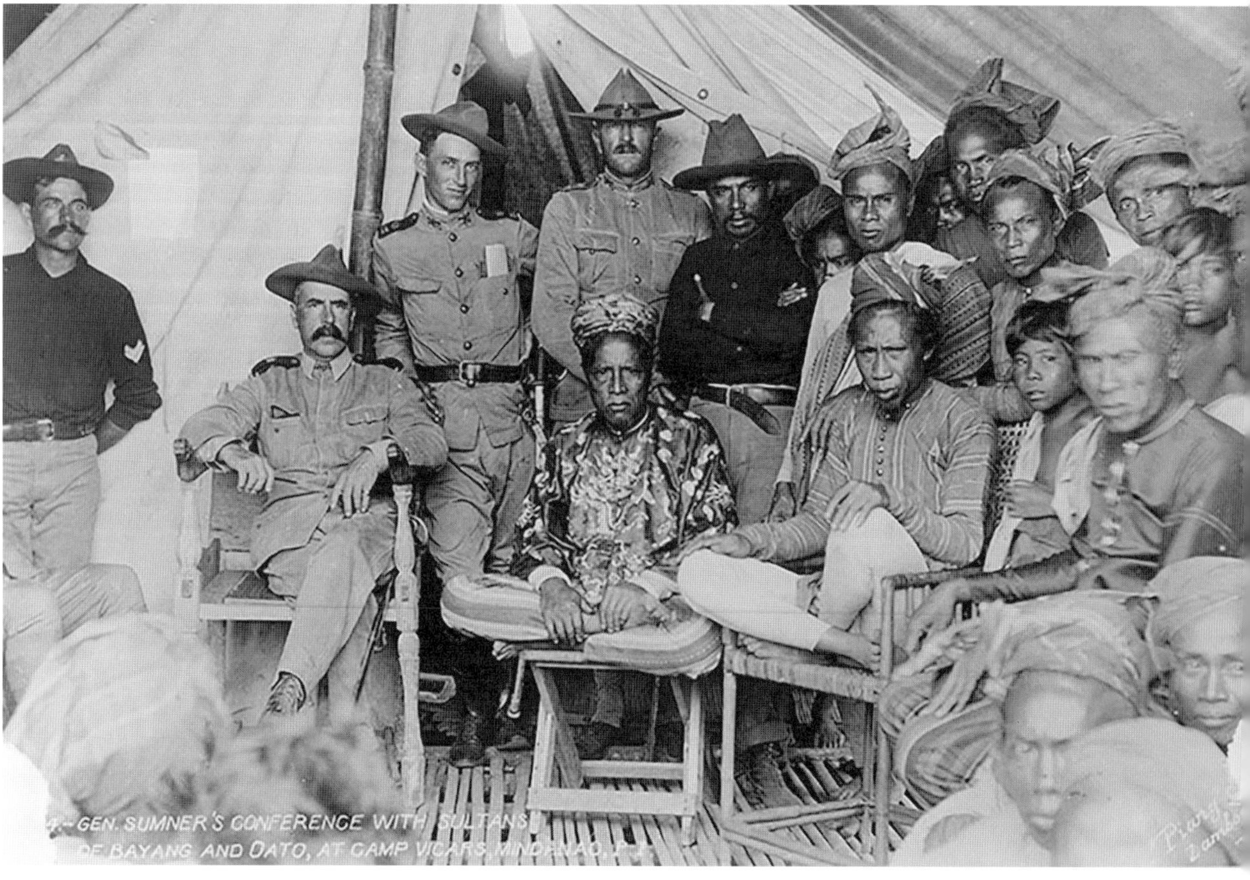
GEN. SUMNER'S CONFERENCE WITH SULTANS
OF BAYANG AND DATO, AT CAMP VICARS, MINDANAO, P.I.

Second Lieutenant Joseph W. Stilwell (right), a recent West Point graduate, is shown here with one of his fellow soldiers foraging for food in the Philippines. Stilwell requested to serve with the 12th Infantry during the 'Moro Insurrection' from 1904 to 1906 and had another tour with this same regiment in the Philippines in 1911. (*Author's collection*)

(**Opposite, above**) Lieutenant General Arthur MacArthur, Jr (second from left) is shown here standing with his staff officers in the Philippines. MacArthur was awarded the Congressional Medal of Honor for gallantry as a Union soldier during the Civil War. In 1899, he led a division north from Manila towards Malolos, where Aguinaldo's capital and insurgent government was situated. Before Malolos fell, Aguinaldo fled into northern Luzon, utilizing guerrilla warfare to prolong the 'insurrection'. MacArthur was appointed military governor of the Philippines at age 55. (*NARA*)

(**Opposite, below**) Captain John J. Pershing of the 15th Cavalry (middle of back row, standing) is shown here at General Sumner's conference at Camp Vicars on Mindanao with the sultans of Bayang and Oato in 1902. In 1901, Pershing started the first of four campaigns with the final one capturing the Moro stronghold of Lake Lanao. Pershing would go on to lead a punitive raid into Mexico after the brigand Pancho Villa. In 1917, he was commanding general of the American Expeditionary Force (AEF) to France during the First World War. From 1921 to 1924, Pershing became Chief of Staff of the US Army. (*Library of Congress*)

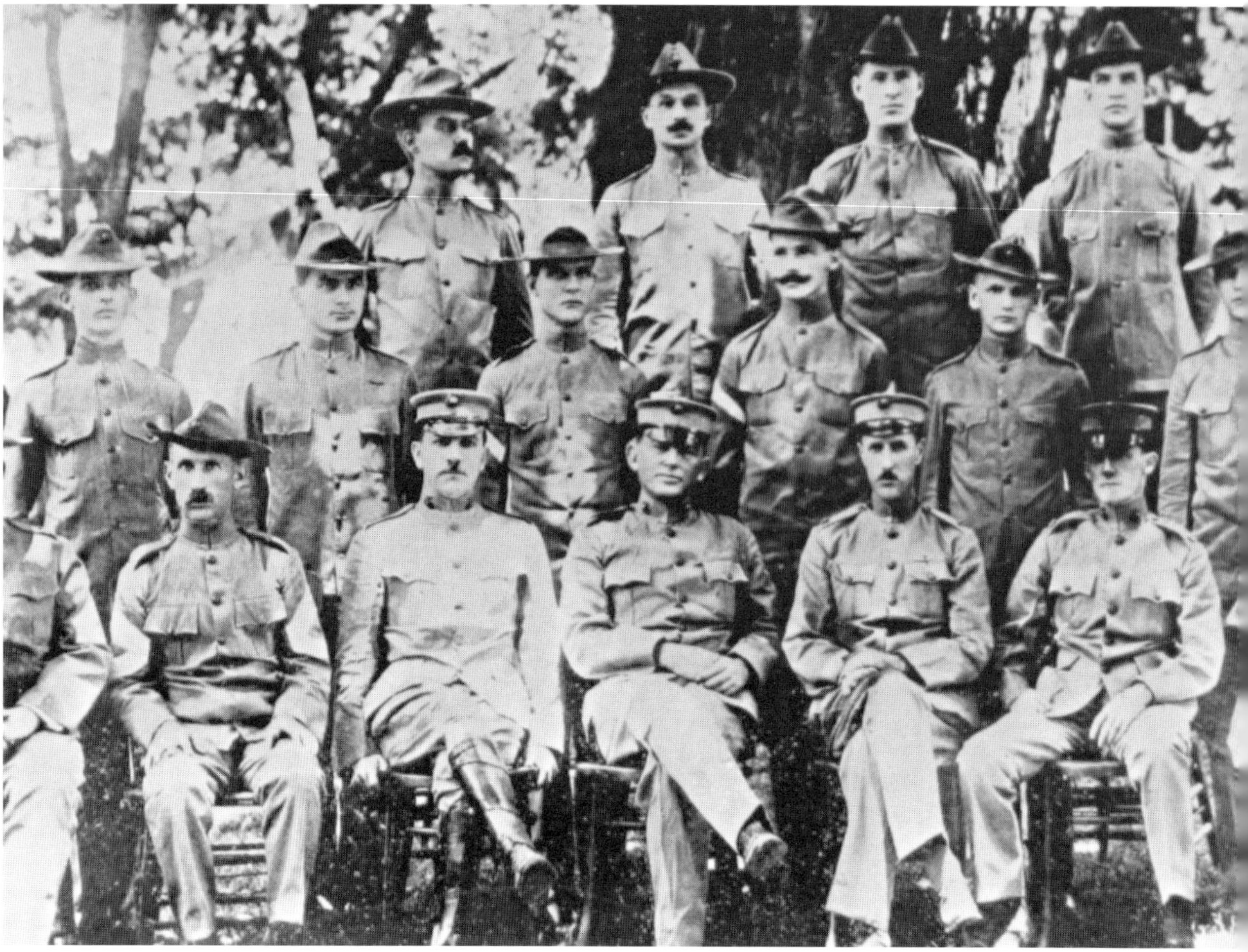

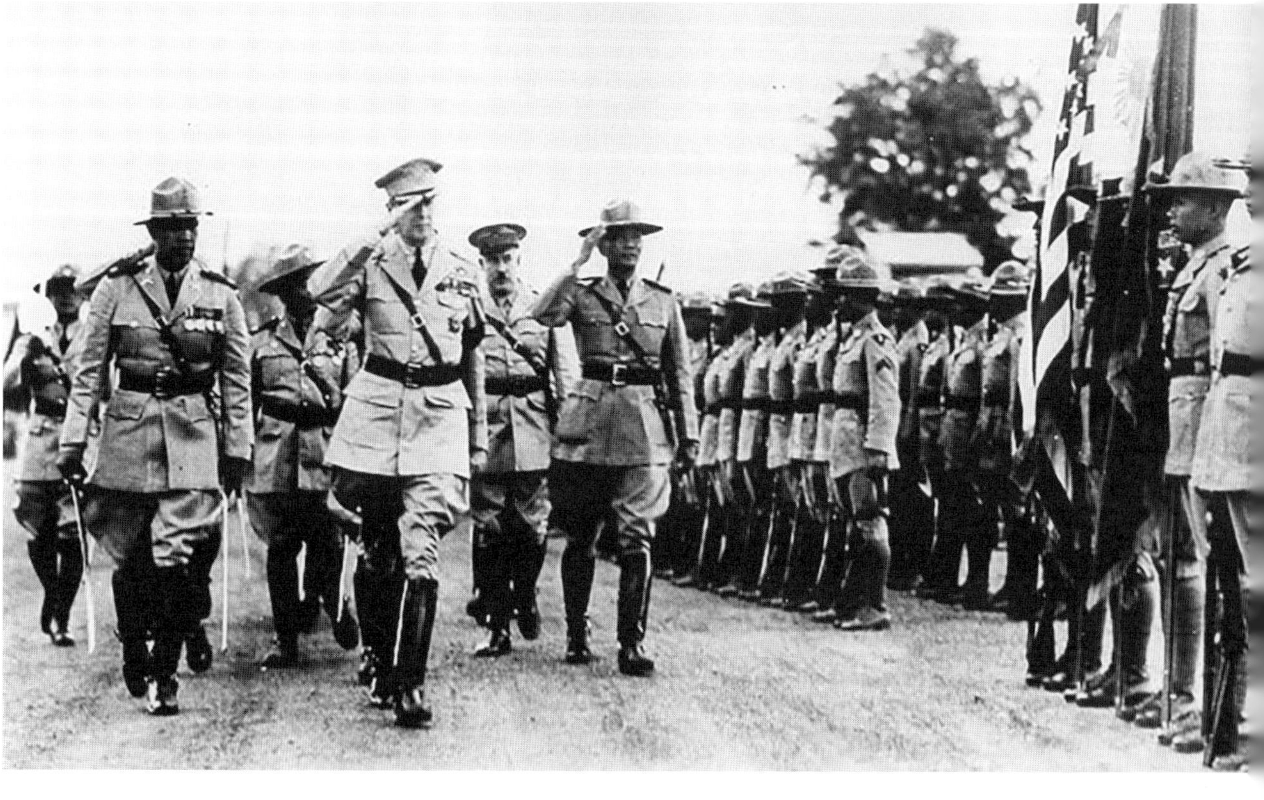

Major Dwight D. Eisenhower is shown here as General Douglas MacArthur's aide in the Philippines in 1935. Eisenhower had a turbulent relationship with his commander for many reasons, both Stateside and in the Philippines, including the disastrous 'Bonus Army' March in Washington, D.C. in 1932. Despite the prickly professional interaction between the two men, Eisenhower would have a meteoric rise with the advent of the Second World War. (*Author's collection*)

(**Opposite, above**) US Marine Corps Major John A. Lejeune (centre front row, seated) is shown here alongside his subordinate officers in the Philippines in 1908. Lejeune was the son of a Confederate States of America army captain as well as a graduate of the United States Naval Academy in 1888. Lejeune was deployed to Cavite on Luzon in 1907 as a major and then was promoted to command the First Marine Brigade the following year as a lieutenant colonel. After service in France in the First World War, Lejeune became a lieutenant general in the Marine Corps and its 13th Commandant. Camp Lejeune, a Marine Corps base in North Carolina, bears his name. (*NARA*)

(**Opposite, below**) Douglas MacArthur as a field marshal of the Filipino Army reviews an elite Filipino Scout unit in Manila in 1936. In March 1934, Congress legislated the Philippines' transition to Commonwealth status under its president, Manuel Quezon, with eventual independence in 1946. Quezon and the Roosevelt administration planned to build up an independent Filipino military force capable of defending the archipelago once independence occurred. In 1935, Quezon sought General Douglas A. MacArthur to oversee this process. (*Author's collection*)

A mule-mounted Japanese column is seen here advancing across a bridge during the Sino-Japanese War, which commenced in earnest in 1937 following the 'Marco Polo Bridge Incident'. During its peak, the IJA had more than 1 million troops fighting the Chinese on the Asian mainland. *(NARA)*

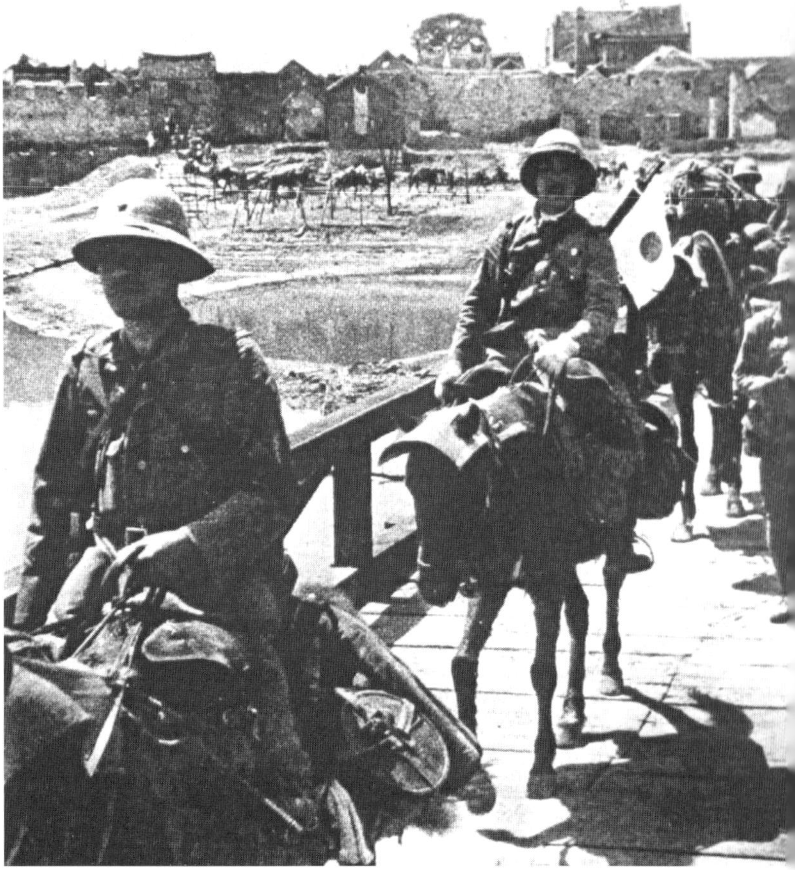

An IJA howitzer is shown here firing on Chinese positions. Unlike the Allies, the Japanese were honing their tactics and strategies against Generalissimo Chiang Kai-shek's Nationalist Chinese forces. When the Pacific War started, many veteran IJA units left China for deployment in other Asian and Pacific locales during the Japanese blitzkrieg of 1941–42. *(NARA)*

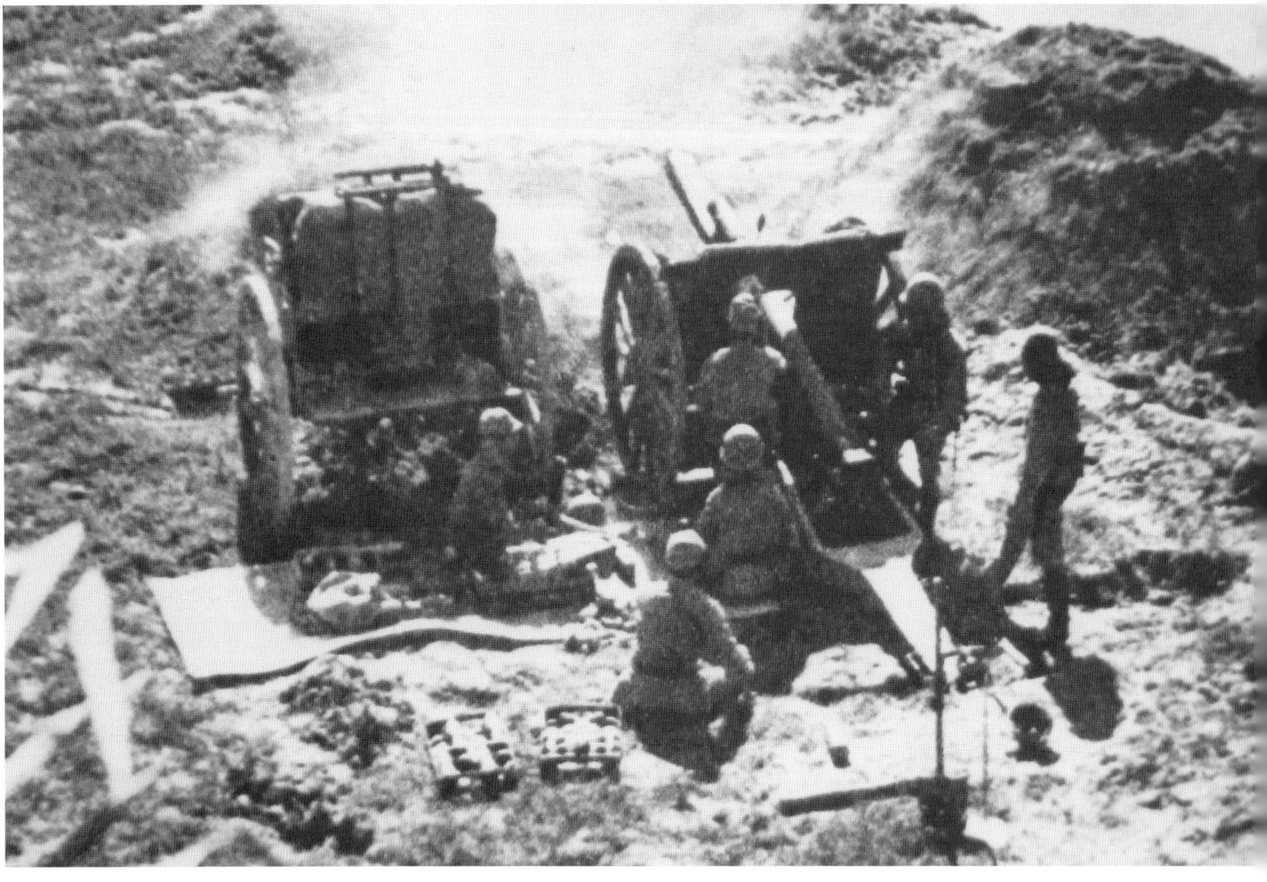

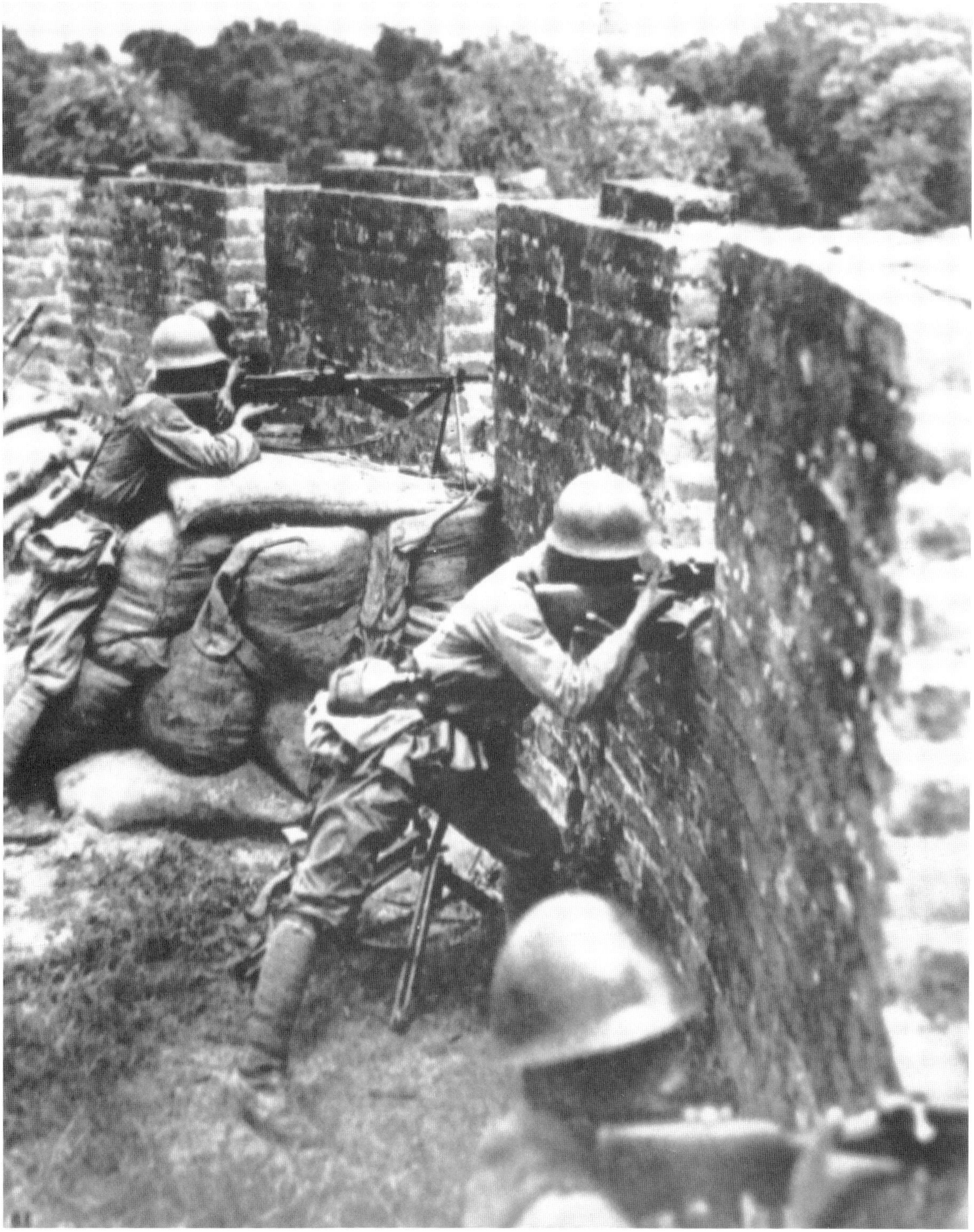

A Japanese naval landing party is shown here firing a 6.5mm Nambu light machine gun (LMG) from a brick turret's parapet in Shanghai. Not only were the well-armed Japanese Marines aggressive in their tactics, but these IJN elite forces also committed innumerable atrocities against civilian and other native populations. *(NARA)*

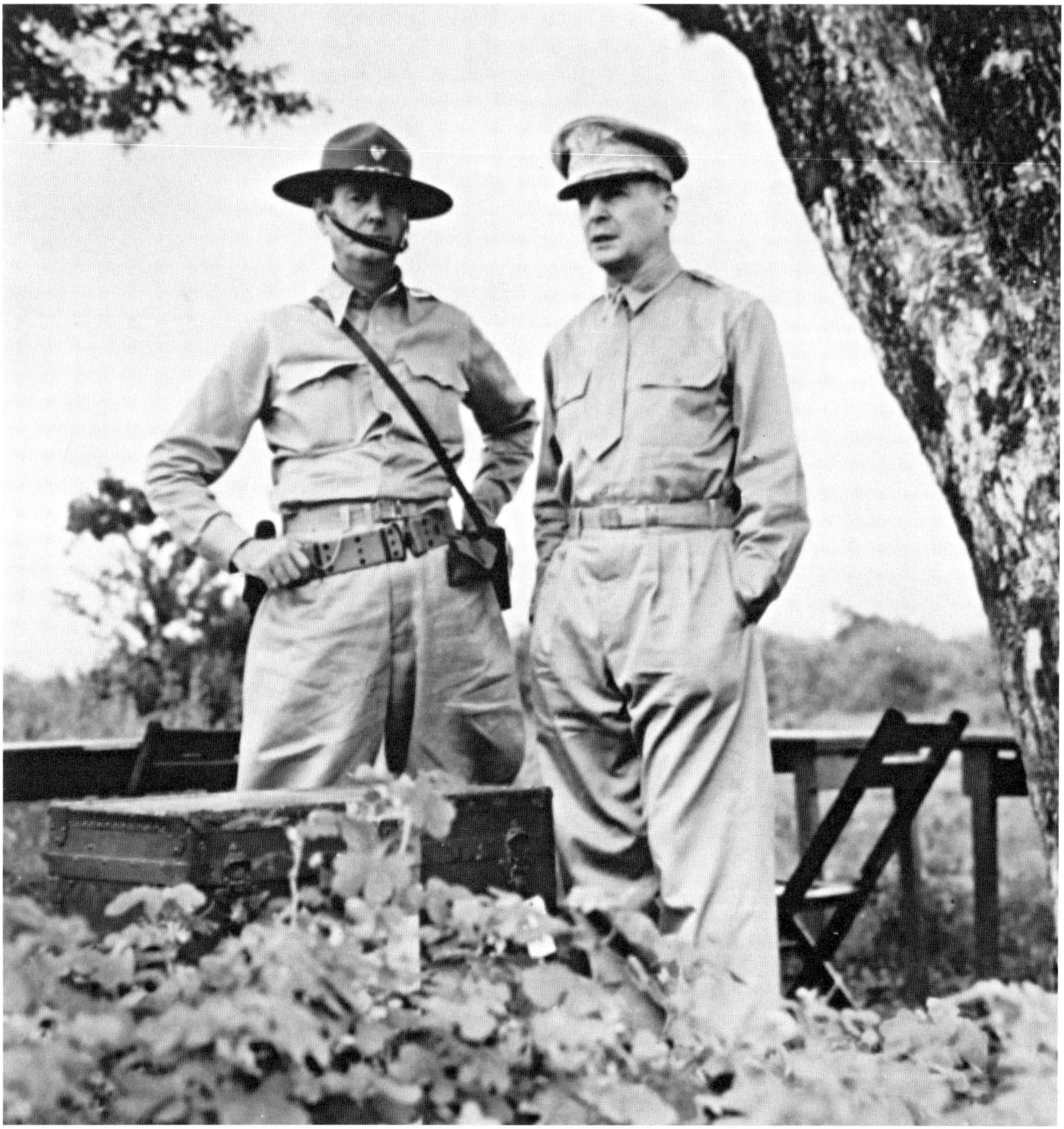

General Douglas A. MacArthur (right) and Major General Jonathan Wainwright on 10 October 1941 before the Japanese invasion are discussing defensive plans for the archipelago. On 26 July 1941 Roosevelt recalled MacArthur to active duty and named him commander of USAFFE, which included the army's Philippine Division and other Filipino infantry divisions. Wainwright was the commanding officer of the US Army's elite Philippine Division and then the North Luzon Force comprising four infantry divisions and the 26th Cavalry Regiment, a traditional horse-mounted elite unit of Filipino Scouts led by American officers. Brigadier General George Parker led the South Luzon Force's two infantry divisions, while a reserve force of two divisions remained in Manila's environs. Major General William F. Sharp had three infantry divisions among his Visayan-Mindanao Force in the southern Philippines. Wainwright, promoted to lieutenant general, replaced MacArthur as USAFFE Commander when the latter was ordered by President Roosevelt to leave Corregidor to become C-in-C, SWPA, with headquarters in Australia. *(NARA)*

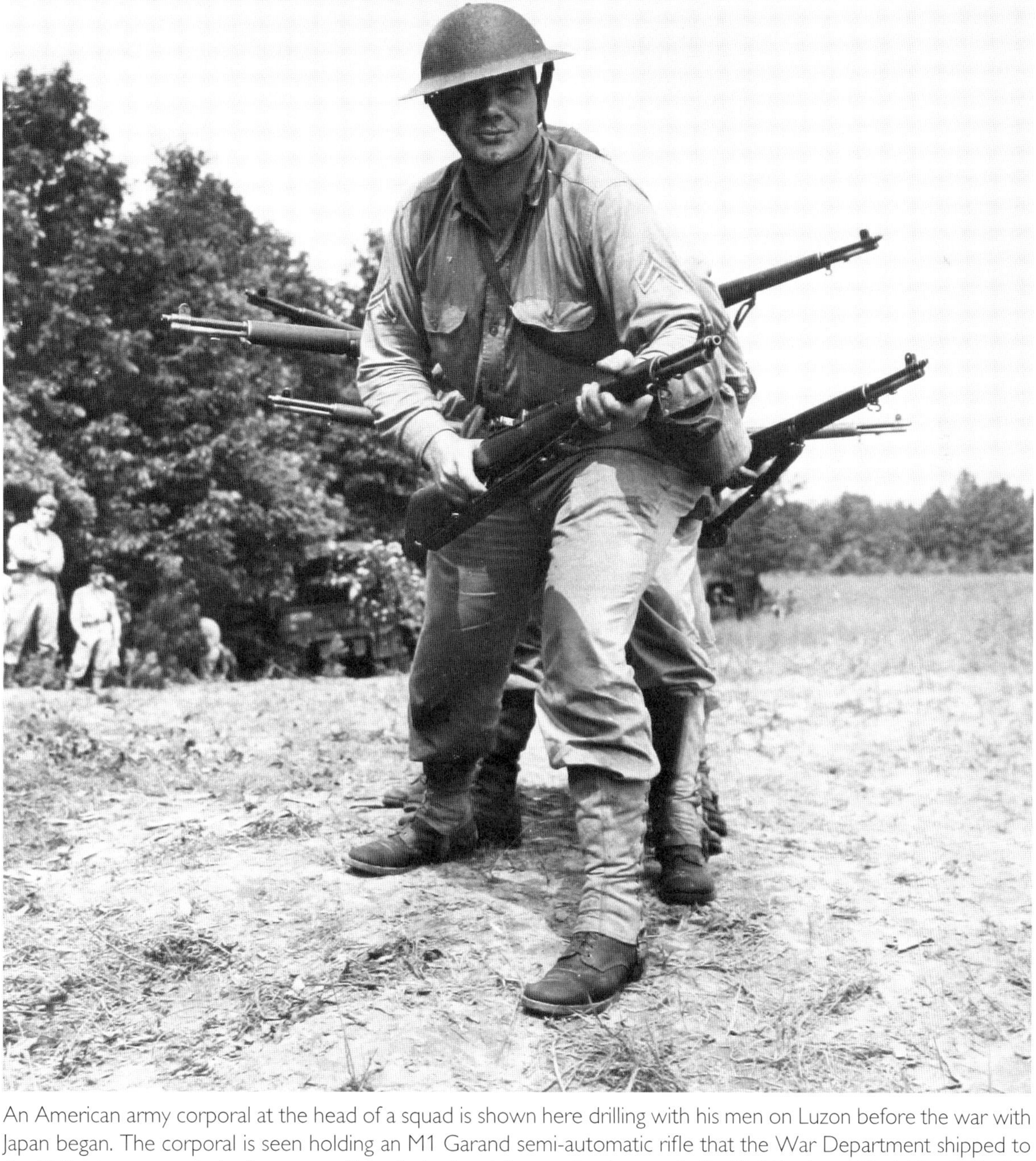

An American army corporal at the head of a squad is shown here drilling with his men on Luzon before the war with Japan began. The corporal is seen holding an M1 Garand semi-automatic rifle that the War Department shipped to the Philippines as a priority for some of MacArthur's soldiers as the threat of a Pacific War intensified. The Philippine Division's 31st Regiment was entirely American with the remaining 45th and 57th regiments comprising almost all Filipino Scouts. *(NARA)*

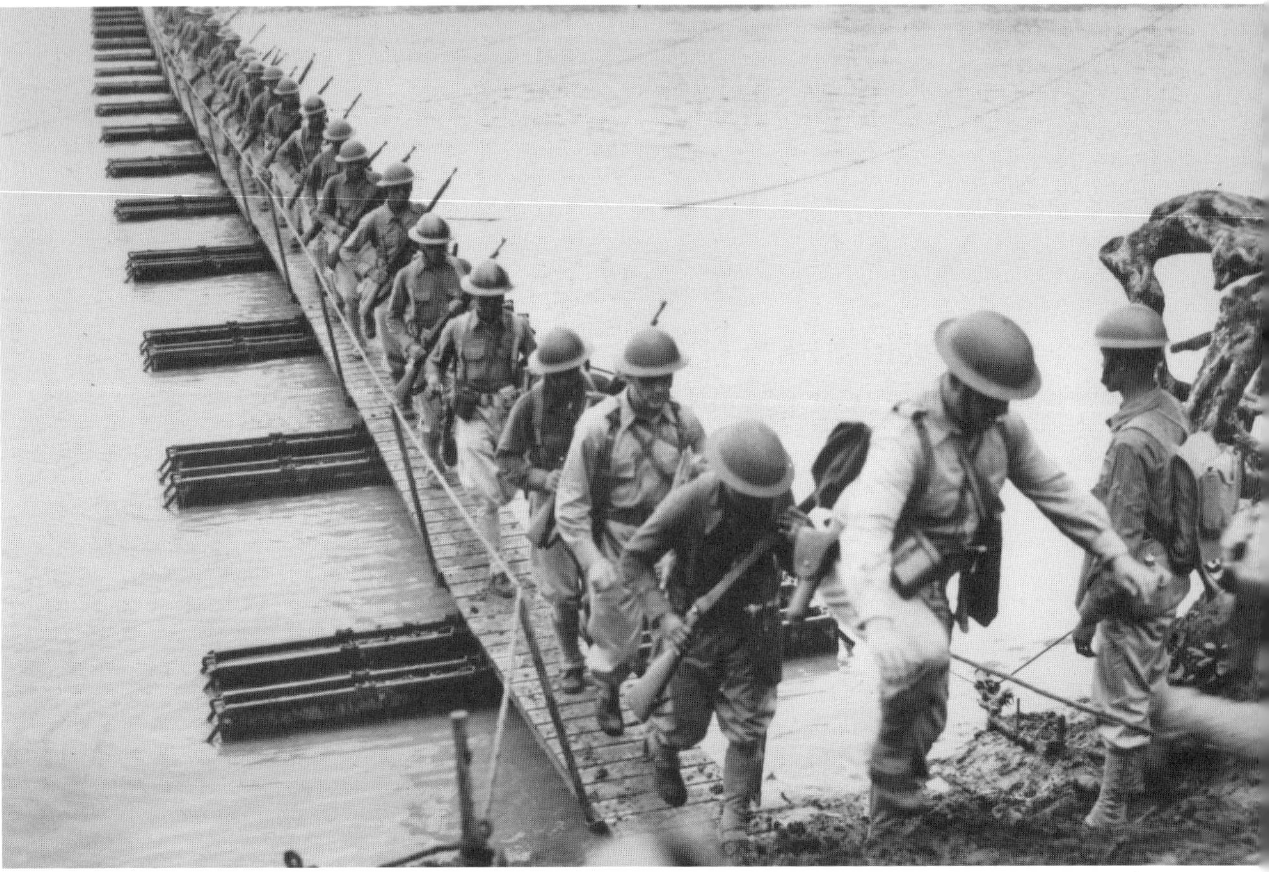

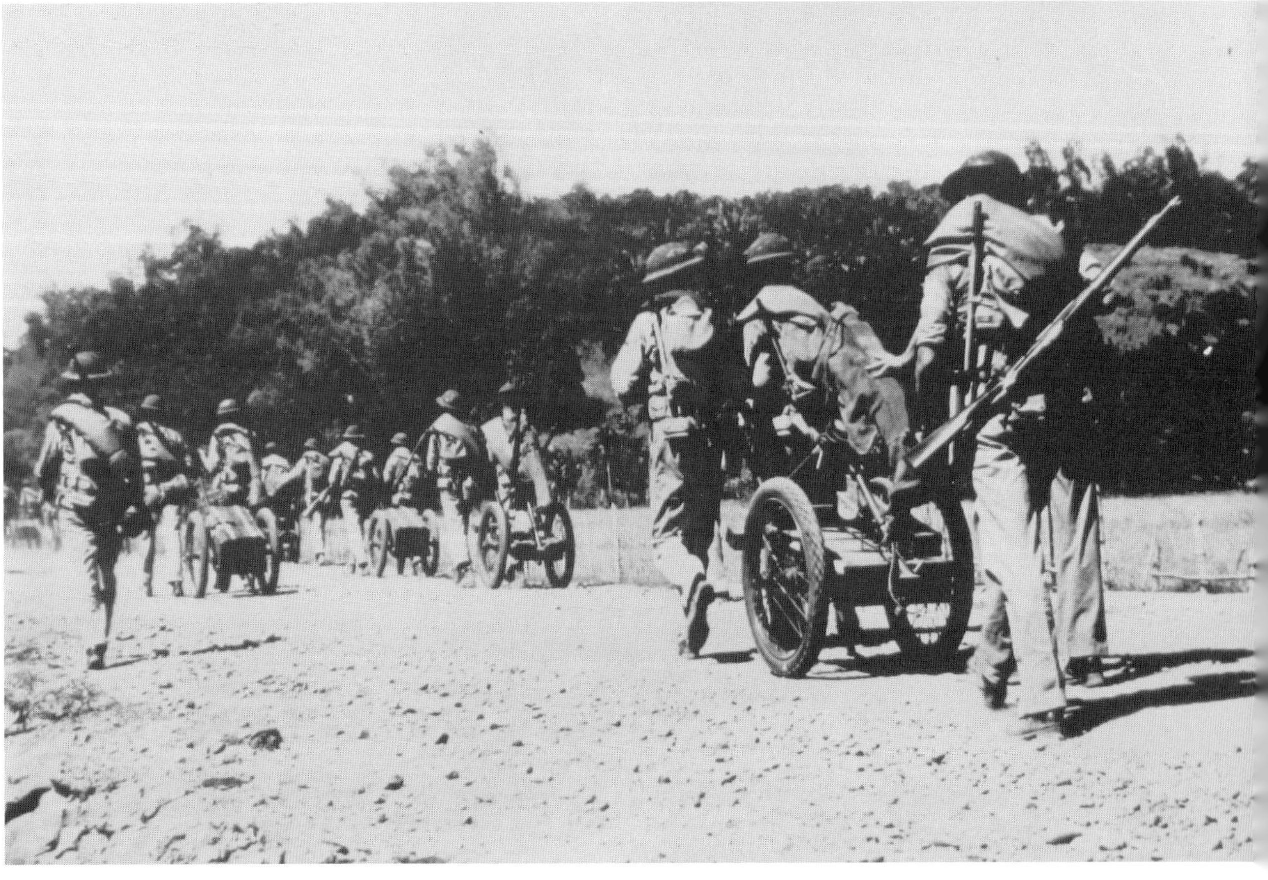

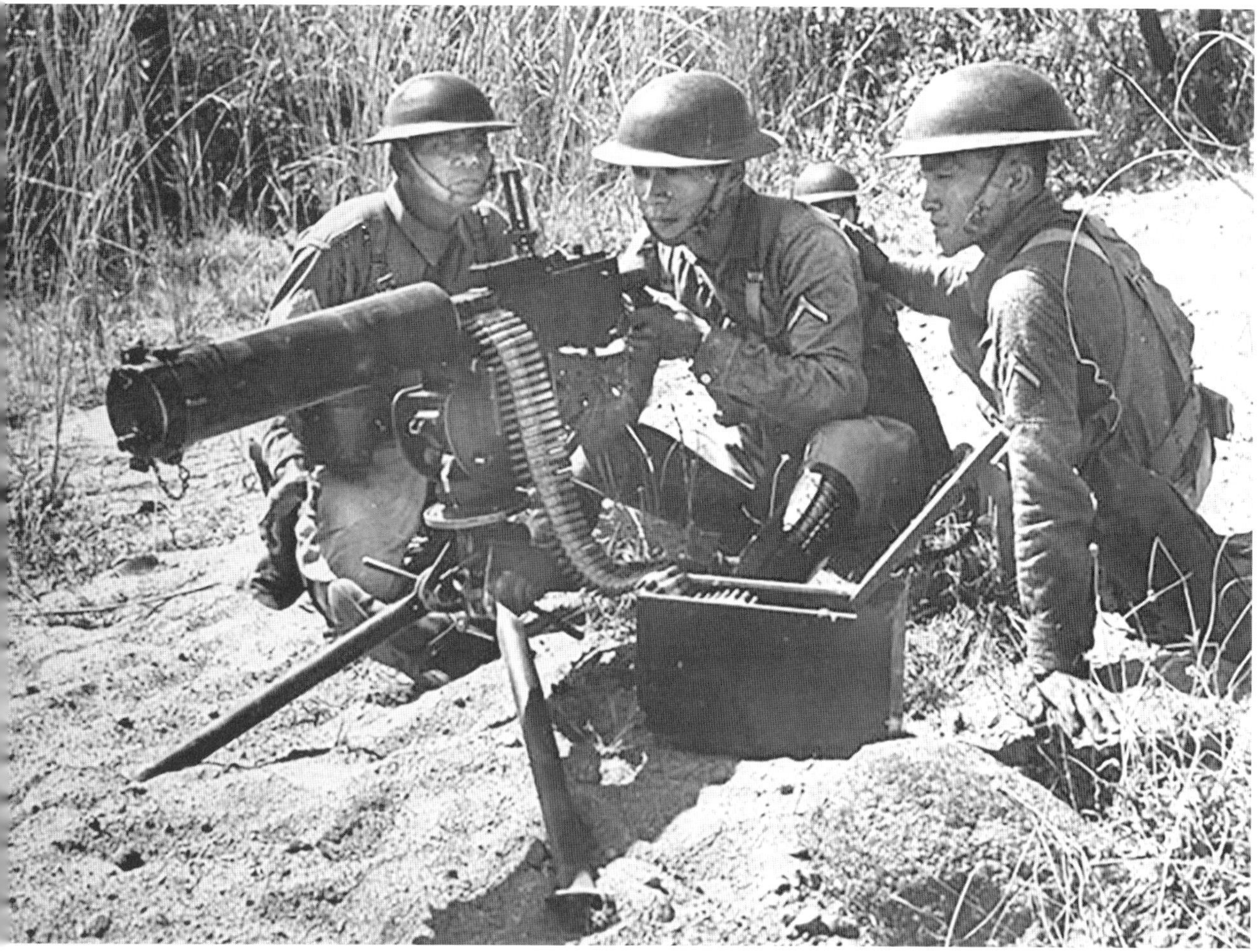

(**Opposite, above**) American officers and NCOs are shown here leading a Filipino detachment across a duckboard pontoon bridge during a training manoeuvre on Luzon before the war started. By December 1941, MacArthur's Filipino-American Army had 100,000 Filipinos speaking a myriad of languages and local dialects along with 32,000 American soldiers. Aerial strength also increased in the Philippines as war loomed. MacArthur had more than 200 aircraft comprising 35 modern B-17C heavy bombers and more than 100 P-40 fighter/pursuit planes stationed at Luzon's Clark, Nichols and Iba Fields. *(NARA)*

(**Above**) A posed propaganda photograph shows three Filipino soldiers in full kit wearing steel First World War-era helmets and manning their Browning M1917 0.30in-calibre water-cooled medium machine gun (MMG). In fact, MacArthur had inadequate arms for his Filipino troops. Eisenhower had returned Stateside in 1938 and attempted to garner support for his superior's developing army. Unfortunately, the US War Department in Washington sent MacArthur First World War-era artillery pieces, Browning machine guns, Browning Automatic Rifles (BARs) and assorted older issue army rifles with ammunition of poor quality. With war inevitable, additional guns, medical equipment, foodstuffs and fuel were dispatched to the Philippines to sustain a delaying action on the Bataan Peninsula if Japan invaded Luzon. *(NARA)*

(**Opposite, below**) The 4th Marines, having been redeployed from Shanghai, are seen here moving into their positions on Bataan before the outbreak of hostilities. In smaller units, this Marine regiment was gradually ferried to Corregidor for its defence in late December 1941 after Japan invaded the Philippines. *(NARA)*

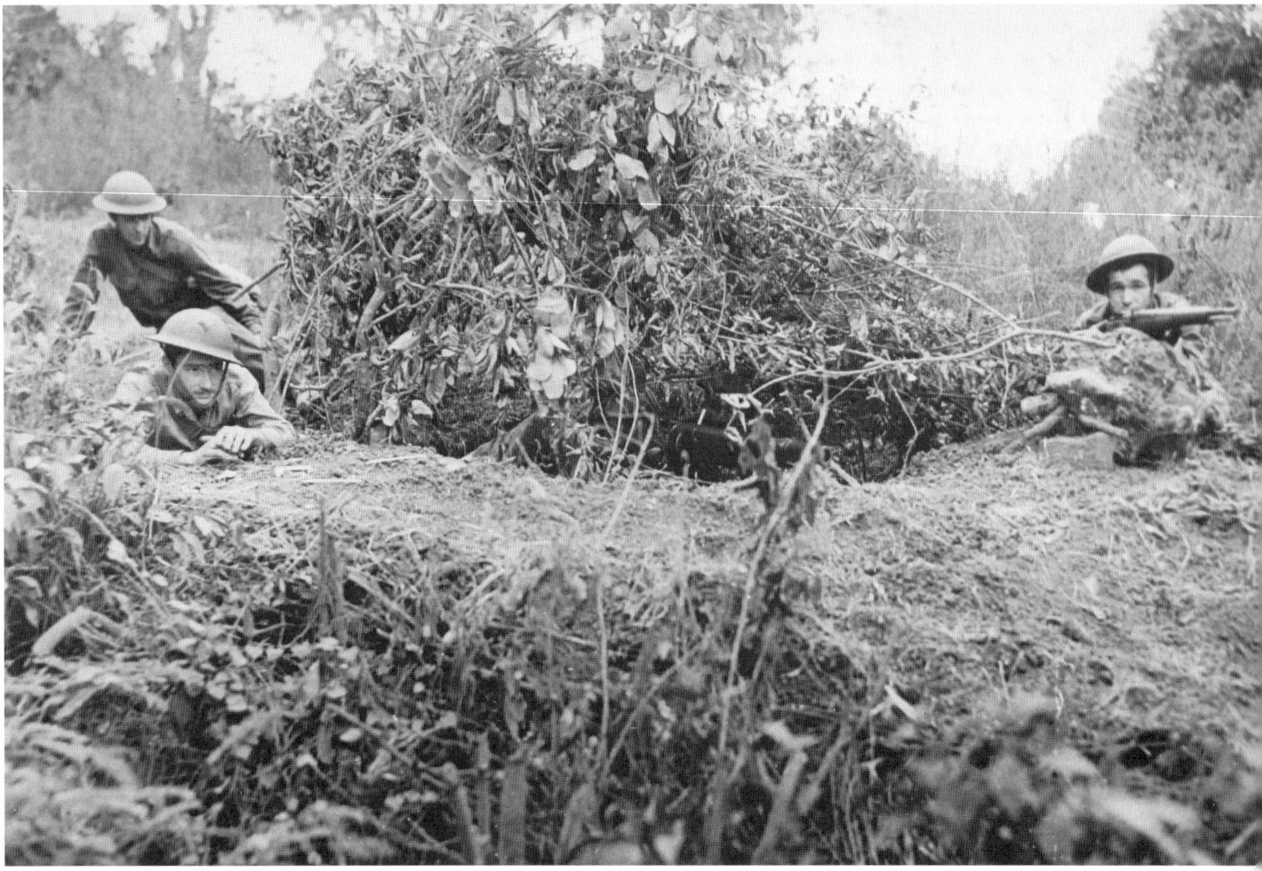

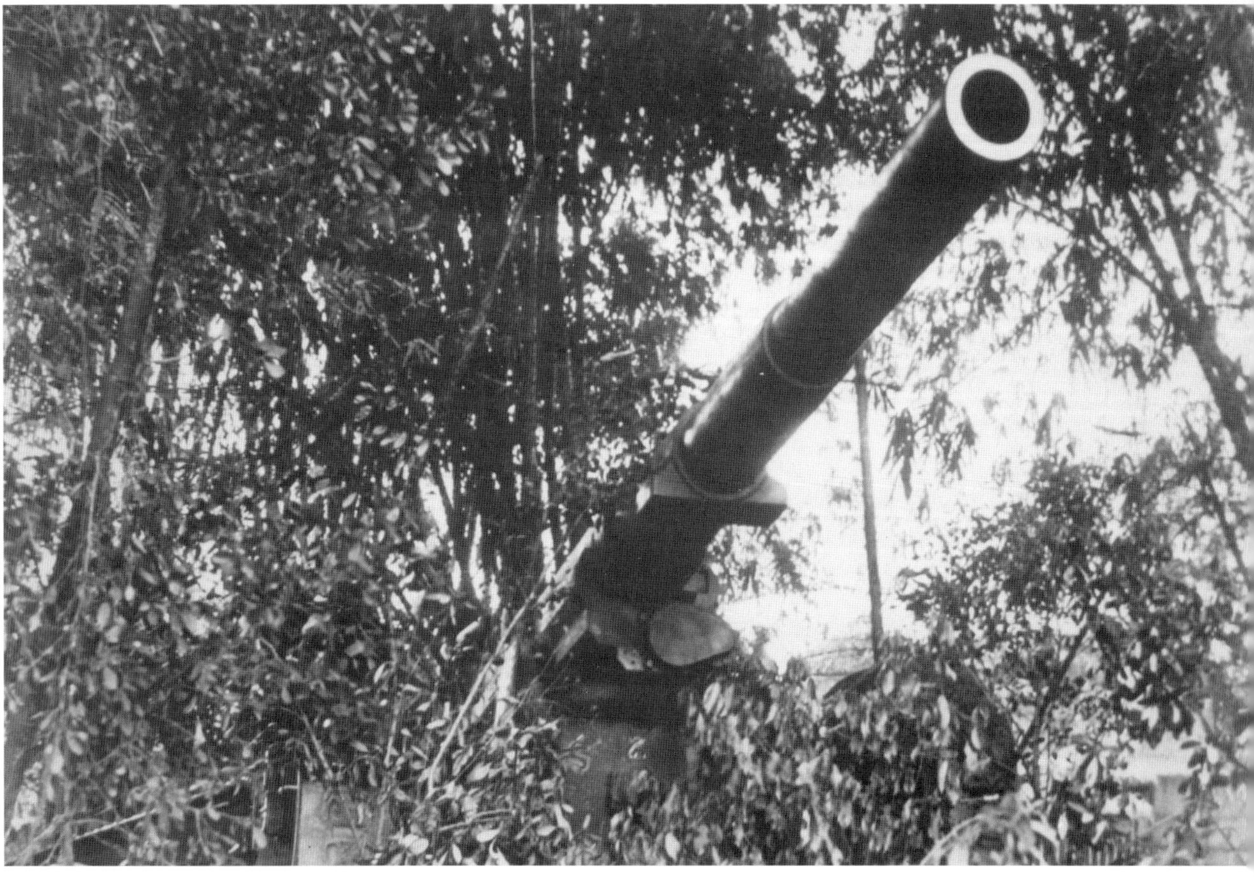

(**Opposite, above**) US Army soldiers are manning their camouflaged low-calibre anti-tank (AT) gun on Bataan after Luzon's invasion. The Americans also had a provisional tank group of more than 100 M3 Stuart light tanks in the 192nd and 194th TBs. The TBs also had 75mm self-propelled guns utilizing M3 half-tracks. American M3s fared poorly against IJA 95 light tanks with General Homma's 48th Division's landings along Lingayen Gulf on 22 December 1941 due to a lack of fuel and Japanese air cover. Another tank battle ensued on 31 December in the streets of Baliuag between IJA Type 89 medium tanks of the 7th Regiment which had a 57mm gun that fired only high-explosive (HE) and not armour-piercing (AP) shells. The IJA used their tanks mainly for infantry support and not for action against Allied armour. The Type 89 IJA tank had relatively thin armour that the American M3 tank's 37mm gun could easily penetrate. The American M3 light tanks and M3 half-tracks of the 192nd TB destroyed eight IJA tanks. (*NARA*)

(**Opposite, below**) A 3in gun of the 200th Coast Artillery (CA) Regiment, a New Mexico National Guard unit, is shown here under camouflage on Luzon. The 200th CA Regiment covered the retreat of the Northern Luzon Force into Bataan fighting against Japanese aerial and ground attacks. MacArthur also had the 17th Ordnance Battalion, the 86th Field Artillery (FA) Battalion (155mm guns) and the 88th FA Regiment (75mm guns) under his command on Luzon. (*NARA*)

(**Above**) A crude Filipino-American tank trap made of logs and barbed wire is shown here. When MacArthur's shoreline plan to stop the Japanese invasion failed, the Northern and Southern Luzon Forces retreated towards the more defensible Bataan peninsula. The tank trap was one of many attempts to delay the Japanese movement across Luzon to get both Filipino-American forces safely into Bataan. (*NARA*)

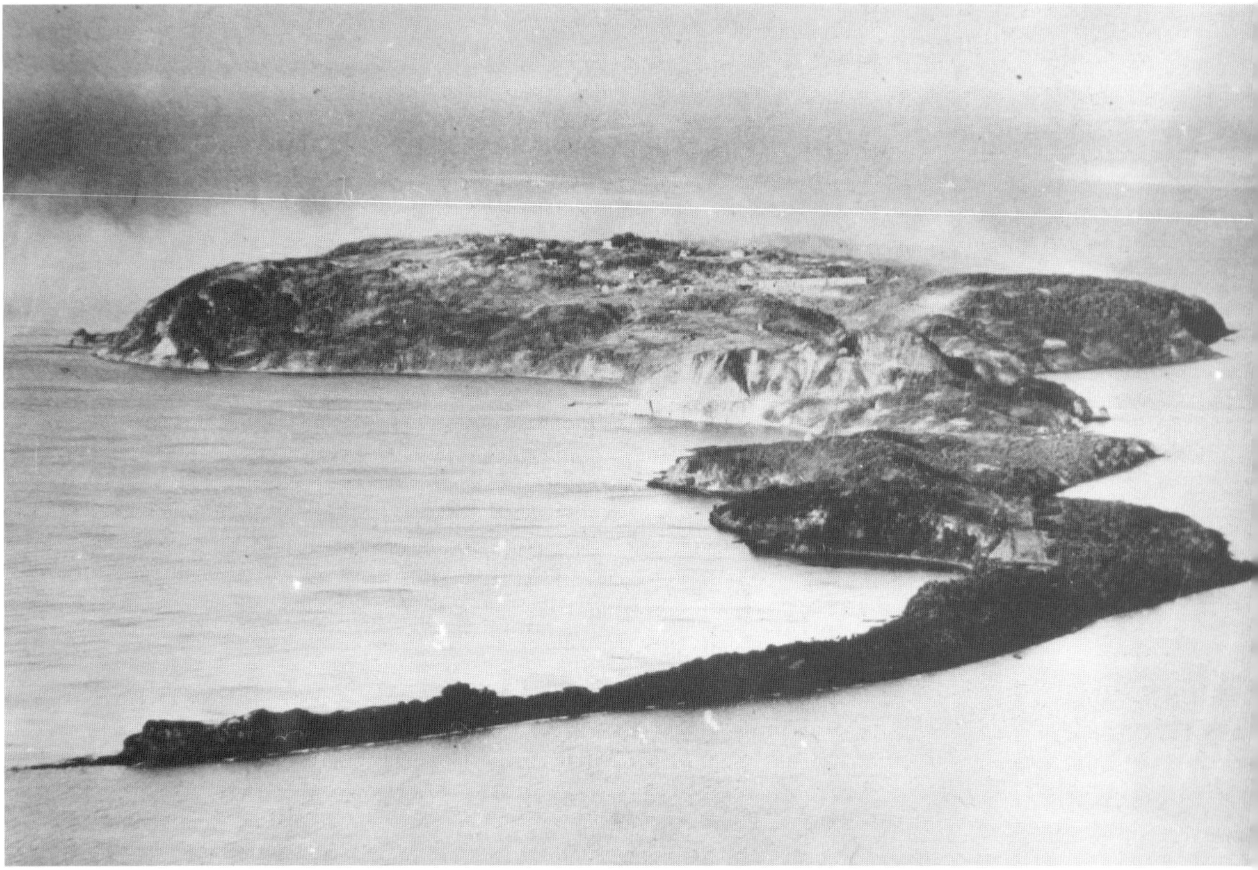

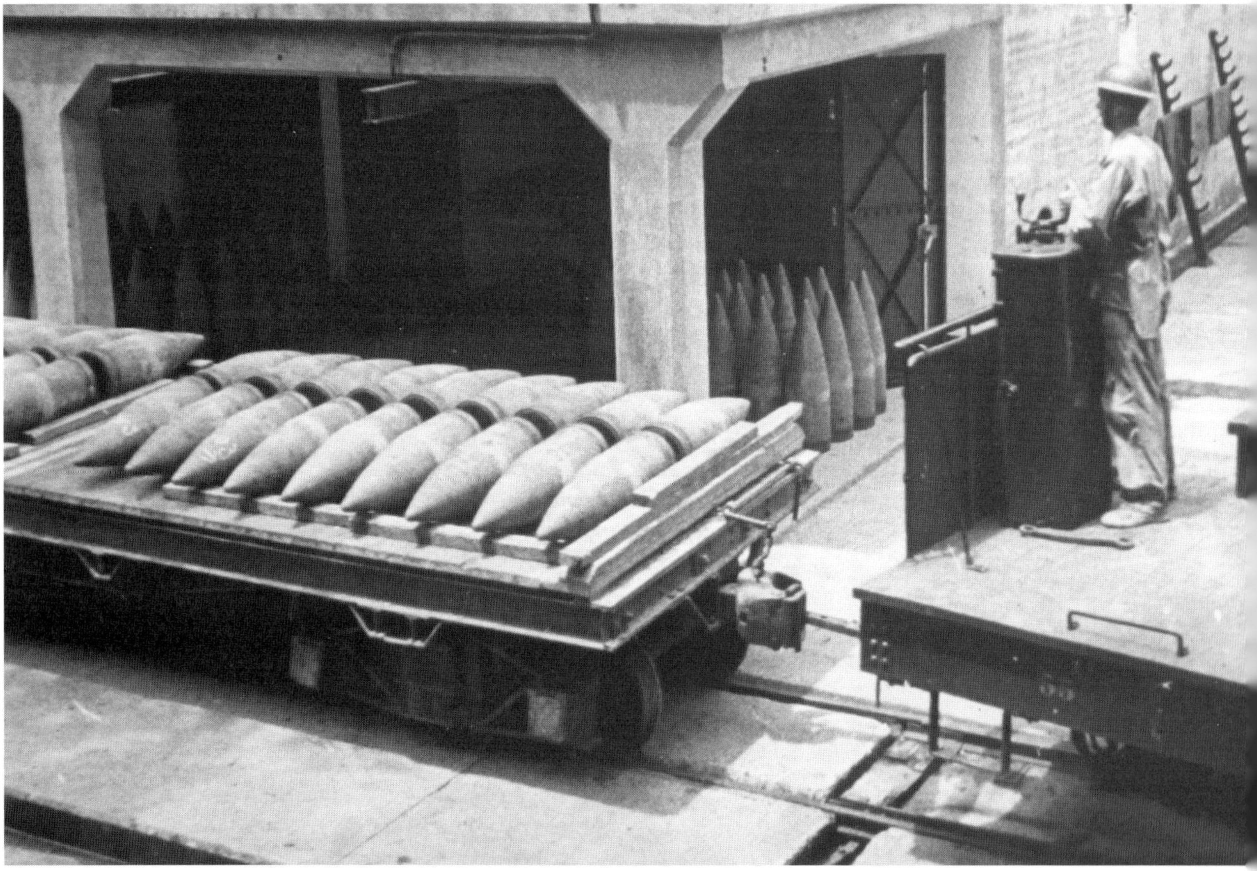

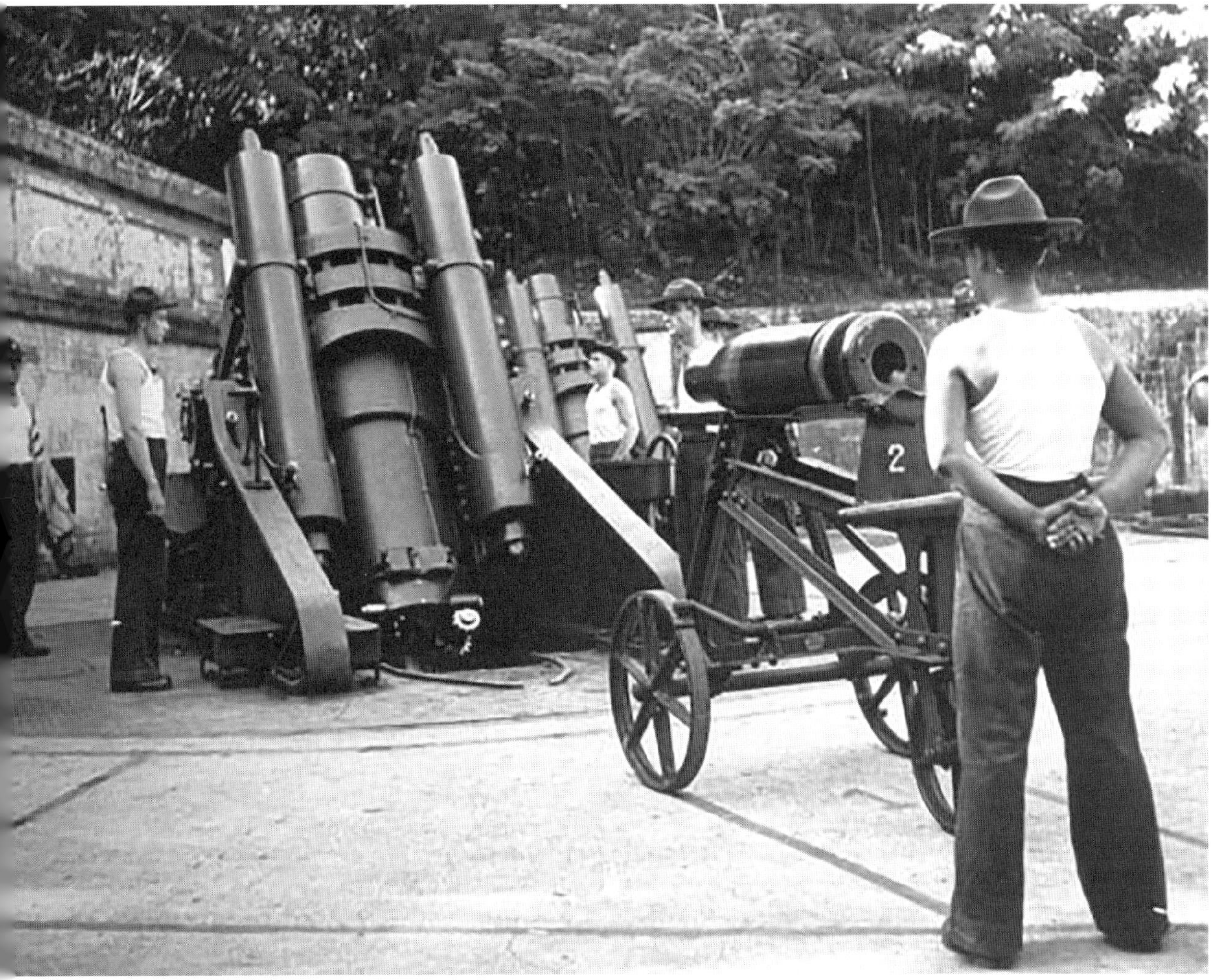

(**Opposite, above**) The comma or tadpole-shaped Corregidor Island, 3.5 miles in length and 1.5 miles in width, is seen here in an aerial view in Manila Bay situated to the south-east of Mariveles at Bataan's southern tip. Corregidor was subjected to Japanese land-based, twin-engined IJN bombing sorties that began on 29 December 1941. With Bataan's fall on 9 April 1942, IJA heavy artillery on the peninsula was employed against Corregidor's defenders before an amphibious assault. US coastal defence guns and heavy mortars, designed to repel large naval ships, were less effective against Japanese invasion craft. Almost 12,000 Filipino and American troops along with the 4th Marines 1,500 riflemen manned the beach defences for the IJA assault on 5 May. *(NARA)*

(**Opposite, below**) Artillery shells from an ammunition dump below ground are brought to the large-calibre guns of one of Corregidor's batteries via a narrow-gauge rail. When the Japanese attacked, American artillery batteries tore into Homma's landing force destroying a score of IJN vessels, but the Japanese landed nonetheless on 5 May 1942 as the 4th Marines' beach defences were unable to hold. *(NARA)*

(**Above**) A heavy 12in mortar crew of the US 59th CA is shown here standing at attention next to its ordnance at Battery Geary on Corregidor before the war in 1941. There were two batteries of 12in mortars totalling ten guns. This was in addition to eight 12in, two 10in, two 8in and five 6in heavy naval guns. Altogether, Corregidor had a total of fifty-three coastal guns and mortars among its twenty-three batteries. *(Author's collection)*

(**Above**) Two American servicemen are shown here in the Malinta Tunnel under the similarly-named hill. It consisted of a main east-west passage 1,400ft long and 30ft wide. The tunnel had twenty-five laterals, each approximately 400ft long, branching out at regular intervals from each side of the main passage. The underground hospital was housed in a separate system of tunnels north of the main tunnel and had twelve laterals of its own. Reinforced with concrete walls, floors and overhead arches, blowers to furnish fresh air and a double-track electric car line along the east-west passage, the Malinta Tunnel was to furnish bombproof shelter for the hospital, headquarters, shops and underground storehouse. (*NARA*)

(**Opposite, above**) USN seamen are shown here searching for survivors amid the smouldering, twisted wreckage of the USS *West Virginia* at 'Battleship Row' in the Pacific Fleet's anchorage at Pearl Harbor on 7 December 1941. Admiral Chūichi Nagumo's six carriers' surprise sunrise aerial assault ushered in the Japanese blitzkrieg across East Asia and the Pacific. Four USN battleships were sunk and another four damaged. The Japanese lost twenty-nine aircraft during the two-wave aerial assault. (*NARA*)

(**Opposite, below**) A wrecked B-17C four-engined bomber is shown here at Hickam Field. The plane was part of a flight of 'Flying Fortresses' from California that was caught amid the Japanese aerial attack on the Oahu airfield. Hickam Field had runways that were long enough (7,000ft) for the army's four-engined bombers. Other Army Air Corps airstrips, Wheeler and Bellows Field, along with the USN's air stations at Kaneohe Bay, Ford Island and Barbers Point, were also attacked on 7 December 1941. At Wheeler Field, most of the pursuit planes were destroyed on the ground; however, a dozen Army Air Corps pilots of the 15th Pursuit Group managed to get their P-36 and P-40 fighters aloft to down some of the attacking aircraft. More than 185 US aircraft were destroyed and 155 damaged on the ground at the army's fields and USN Air Stations. The Marine Corps Air Station at Ewa, 7 miles west of Pearl Harbor, was the first installation hit during the attack with all forty-eight aircraft destroyed on the ground. (*NARA*)

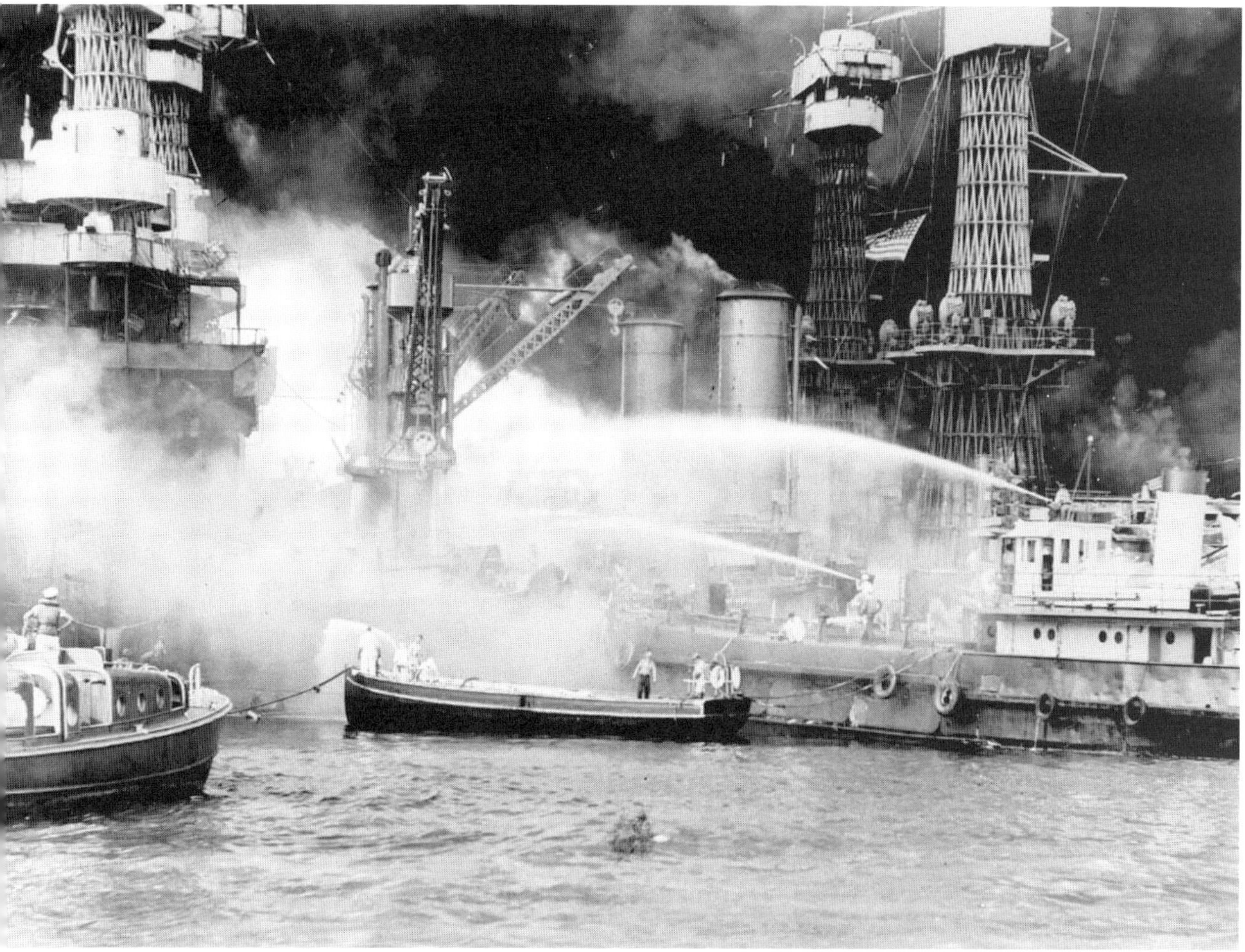

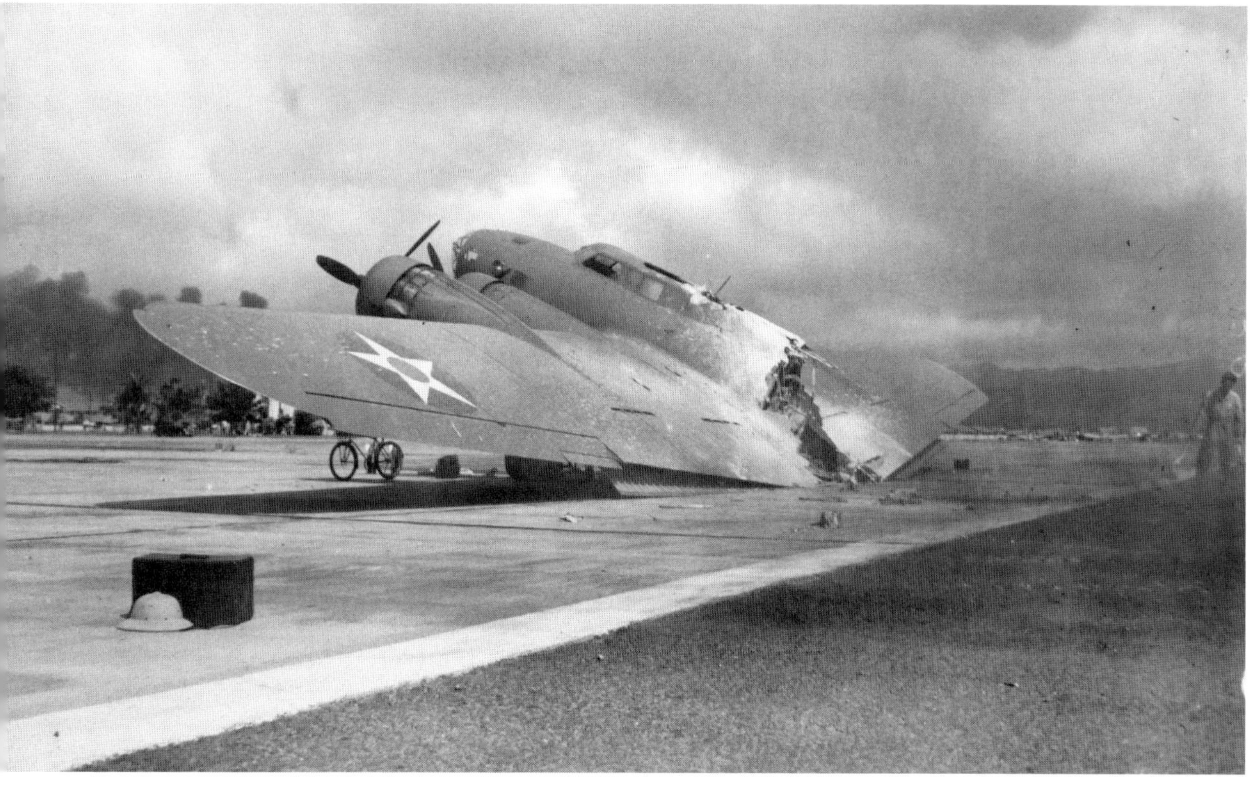

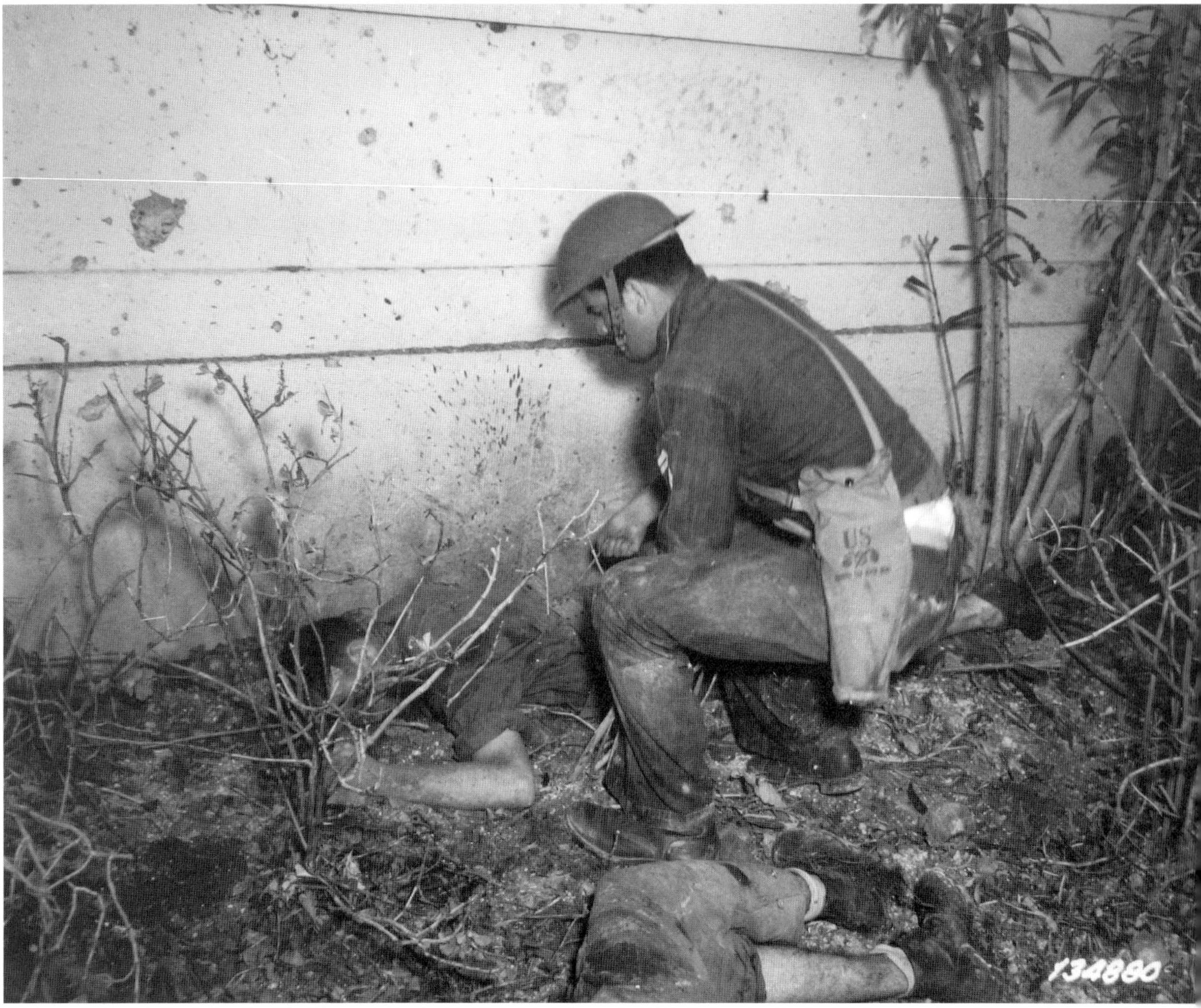
134880

(**Above**) An army soldier is seen here examining the corpses of two of his comrades at Hickam Field after the IJN attack, which killed 180 men and wounded more than 300. Many men were killed while eating breakfast within the barracks' 3,200-man mess hall. More than 2,400 Americans perished during the Oahu attack with more than 1,000 wounded. *(NARA)*

(**Opposite, above**) A row of P-40 'Warhawks', the Army Air Corps' most advanced fighter, is seen lined up at Luzon's Clark Field with older pursuit planes (left). Clark Field, situated 40 miles north-west of Manila, also housed B-17C aircraft of the Far East Air Force (FEAF). The IJN attacked the non-dispersed American aircraft on 8 December, destroying nineteen B-17s and sixteen P-40s. A handful of P-40s made it aloft to engage the enemy planes. The Japanese lost only seven planes in air combat and to AAA fire. On 17 December, the remaining FEAF's B-17s left Del Monte Field on Mindanao for Australia. *(Author's collection)*

(**Opposite, below**) Several destroyed US P-35 pursuit planes are shown here at Nichols Field, a fighter base located to Manila's south near Cavite Navy Yard on 10 December 1941. As the IJN aircraft enjoyed free rein over Luzon's skies with the elimination of the majority of the FEAF at Clark and Iba Fields (on Luzon's west coast) two days previously, the Japanese launched a new series of air-raids at Nichols Field and Cavite Navy Yard to clear the way for IJA amphibious landings. *(NARA)*

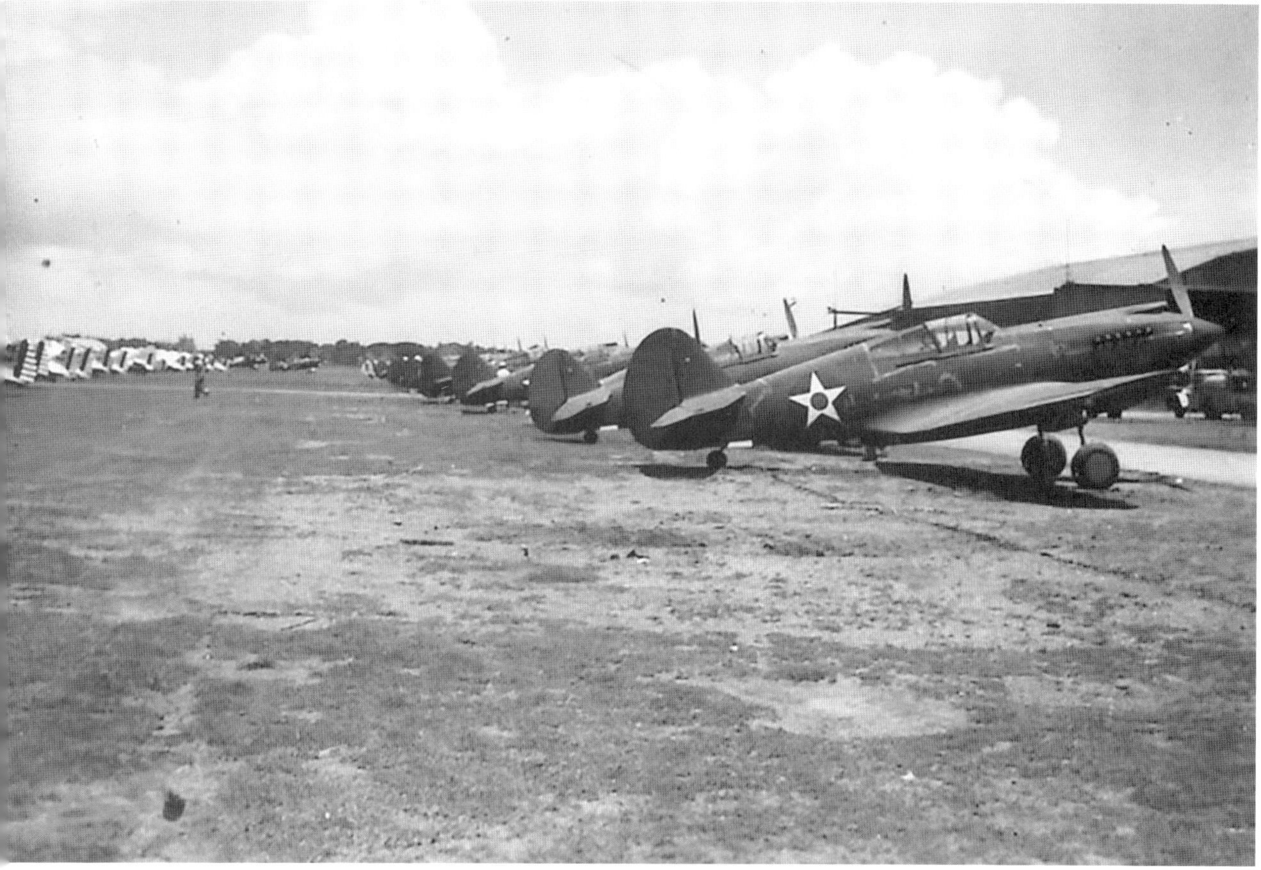

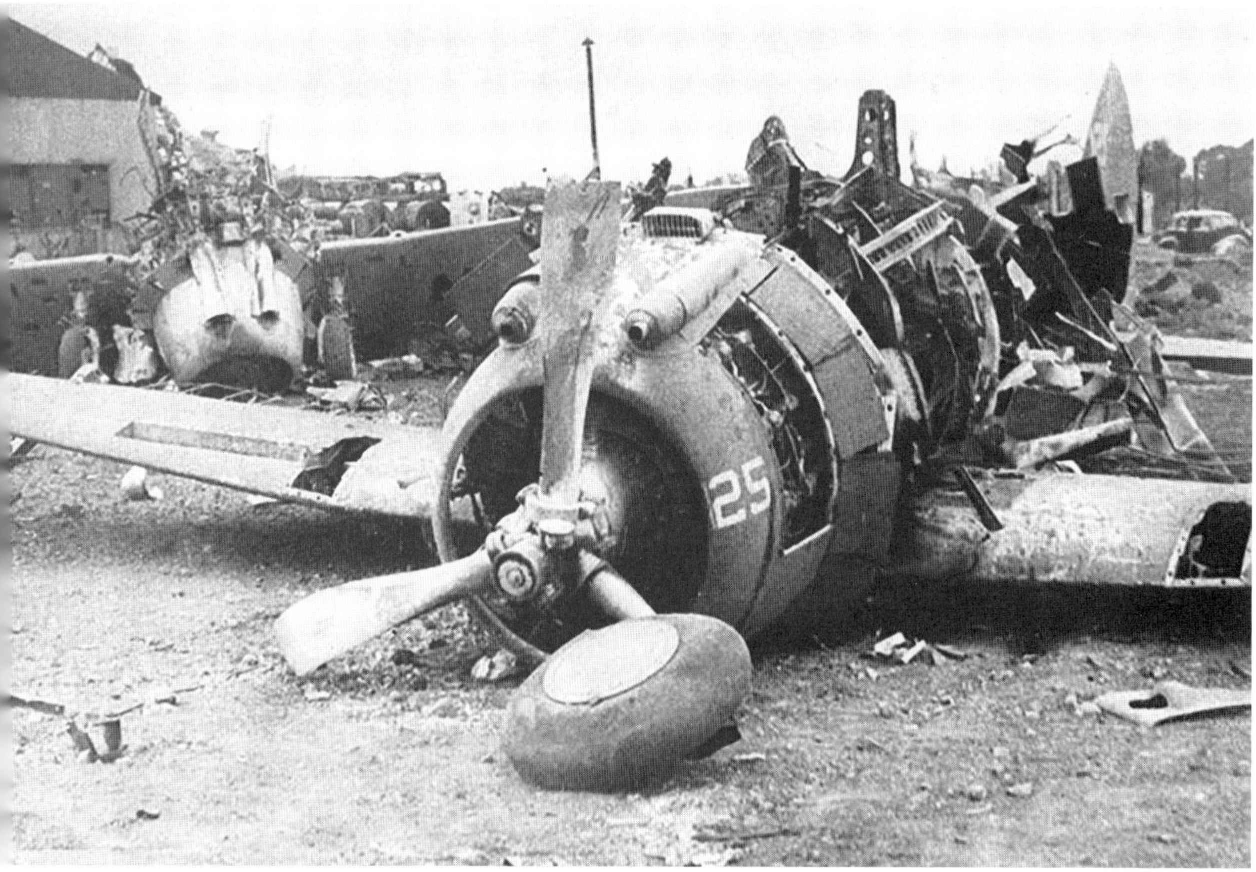
25

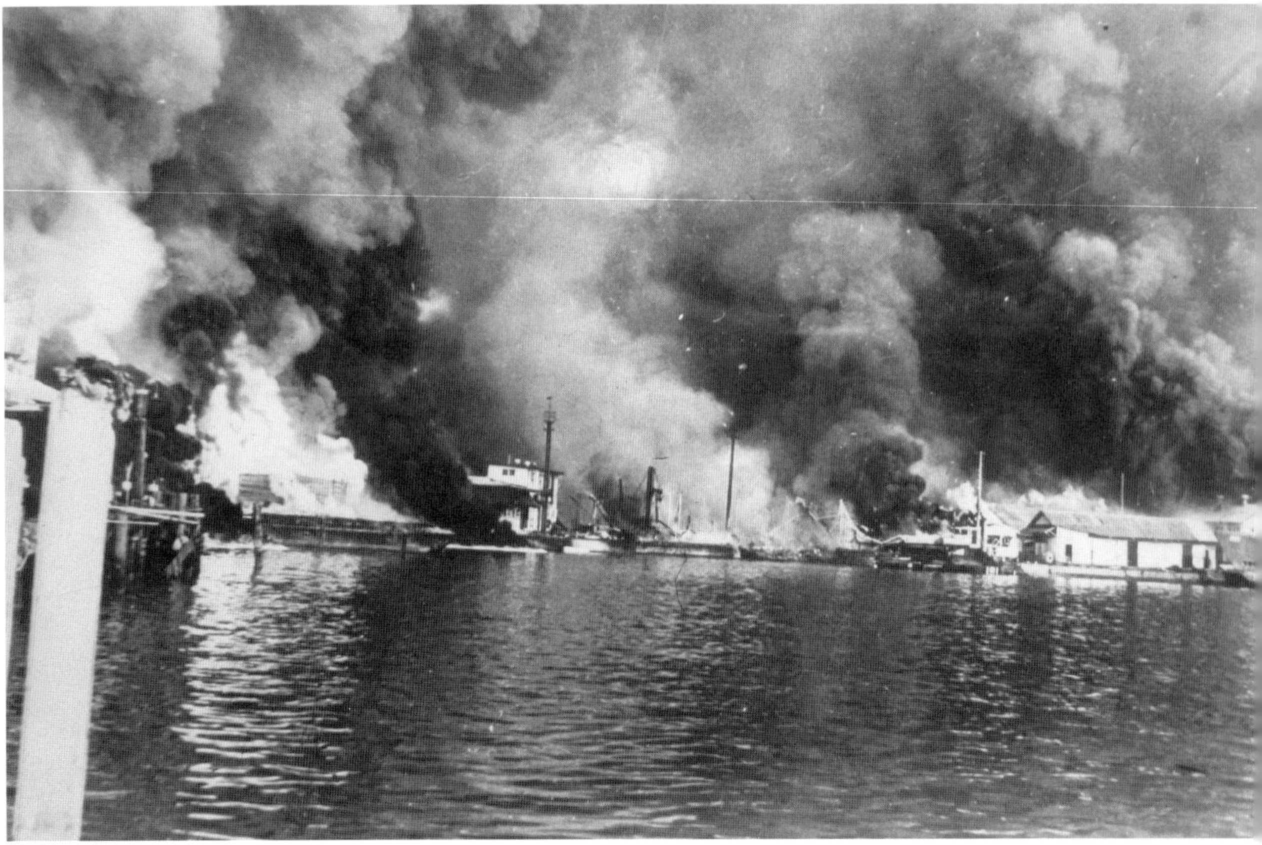

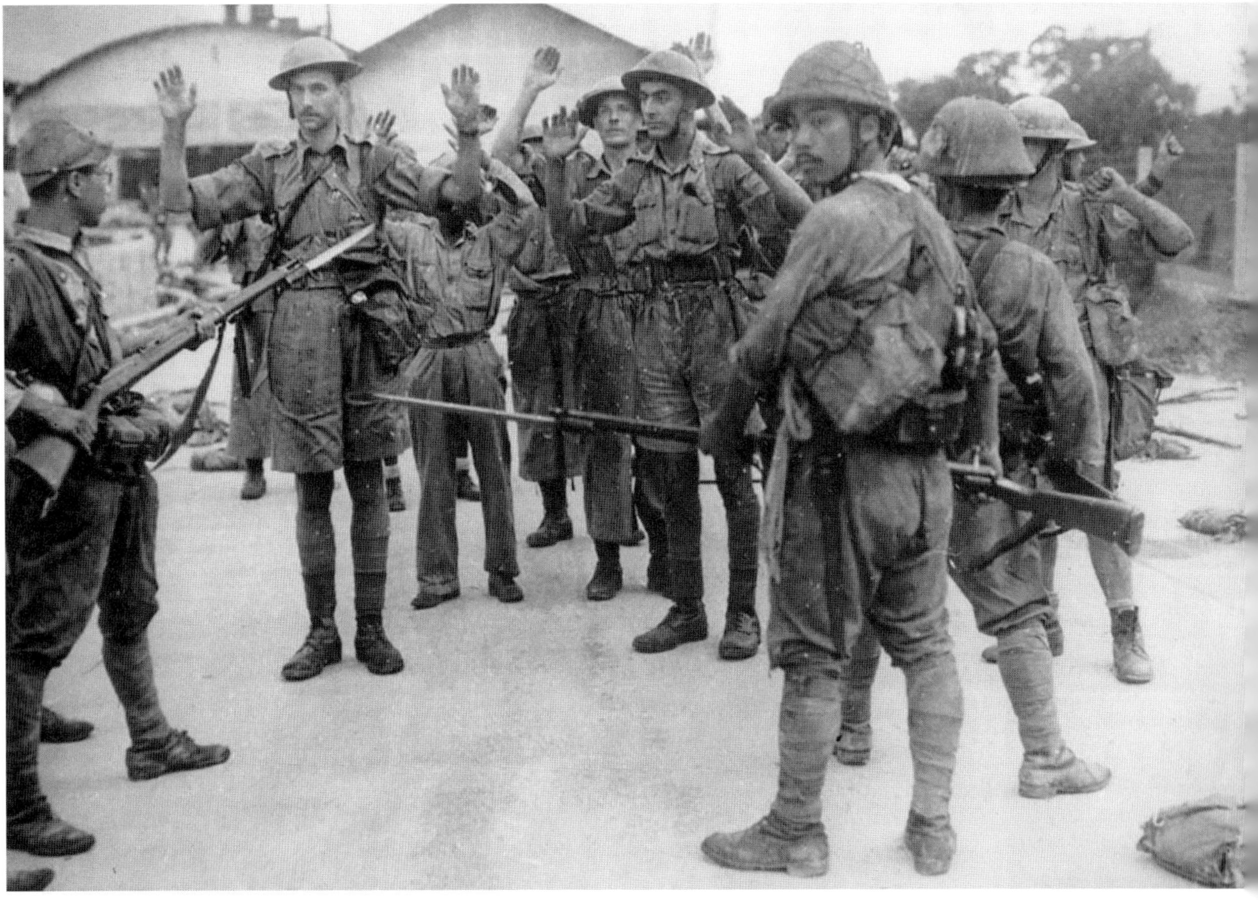

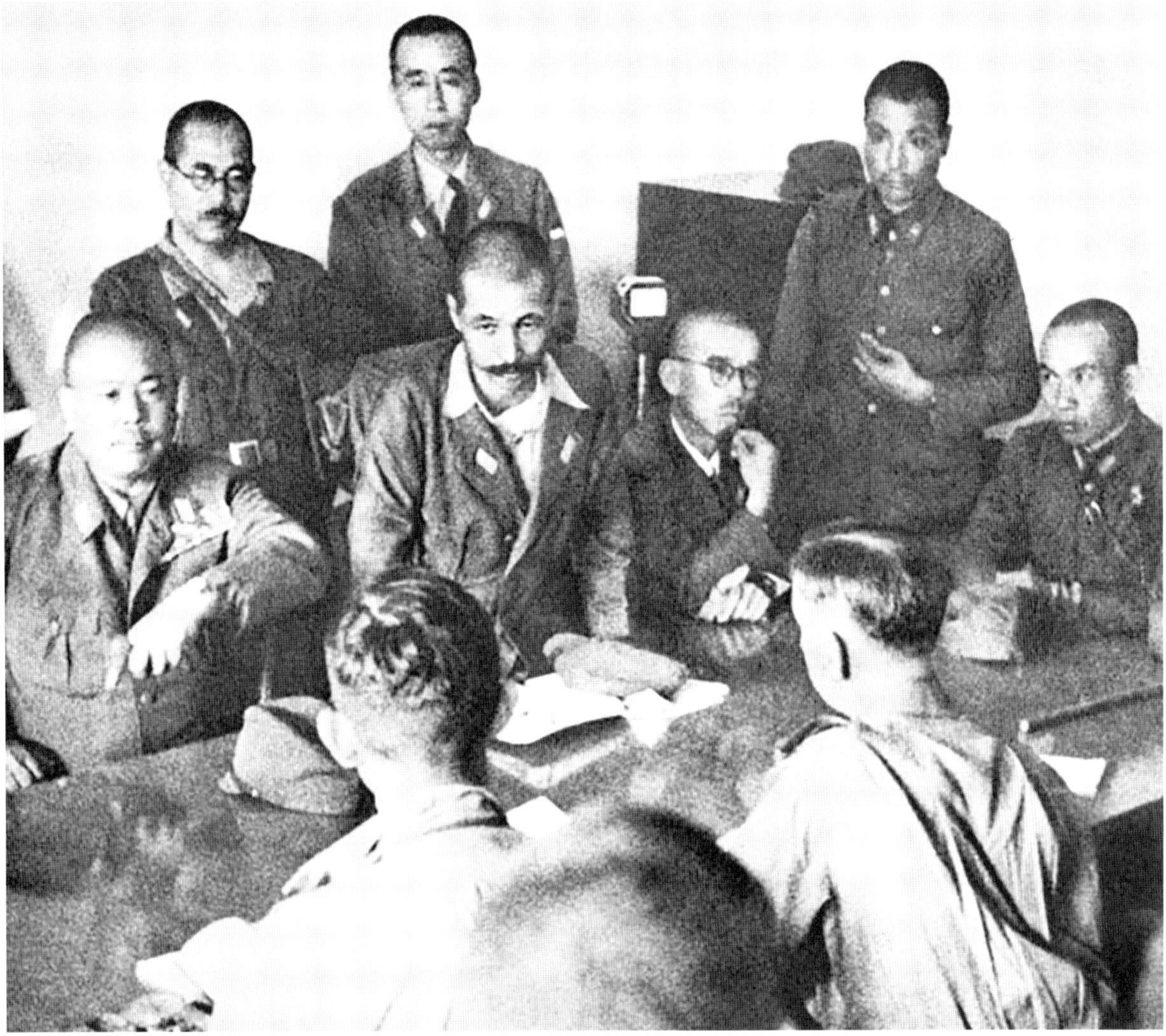

(**Opposite, above**) Barges and oil tanks are seen burning at Cavite Navy Yard after an uncontested IJN air-raid on 10 December 1941. Almost every Japanese bomb landed within the naval base or docks, detonating massive explosions and starting horrendous fires. *(NARA)*

(**Above**) Lieutenant General Arthur Percival, Singapore's commanding general (far right, back to camera) is seen here surrendering to the IJA 25th Army commander Lieutenant General Tomoyuki Yamashita (far left, seated) at Bukit Timah's Ford Factory on the city's outskirts on 15 February 1942. Percival's water reservoirs had been captured and Yamashita bluffed Percival that the Japanese had inexhaustible artillery ammunition to continue further bombardment. *(Author's collection)*

(**Opposite, below**) Victorious IJA 25th Army soldiers are shown here humiliating British and Commonwealth infantrymen for the camera while surrendering in Singapore City on 15 February 1942. It was the greatest capitulation of British arms in the Empire's history. Approximately 80,000 British, Indian and Australian troops in Singapore surrendered, in addition to the previous 50,000 who had become PoWs during the Malayan combat that commenced on 8 December 1941. *(Author's collection)*

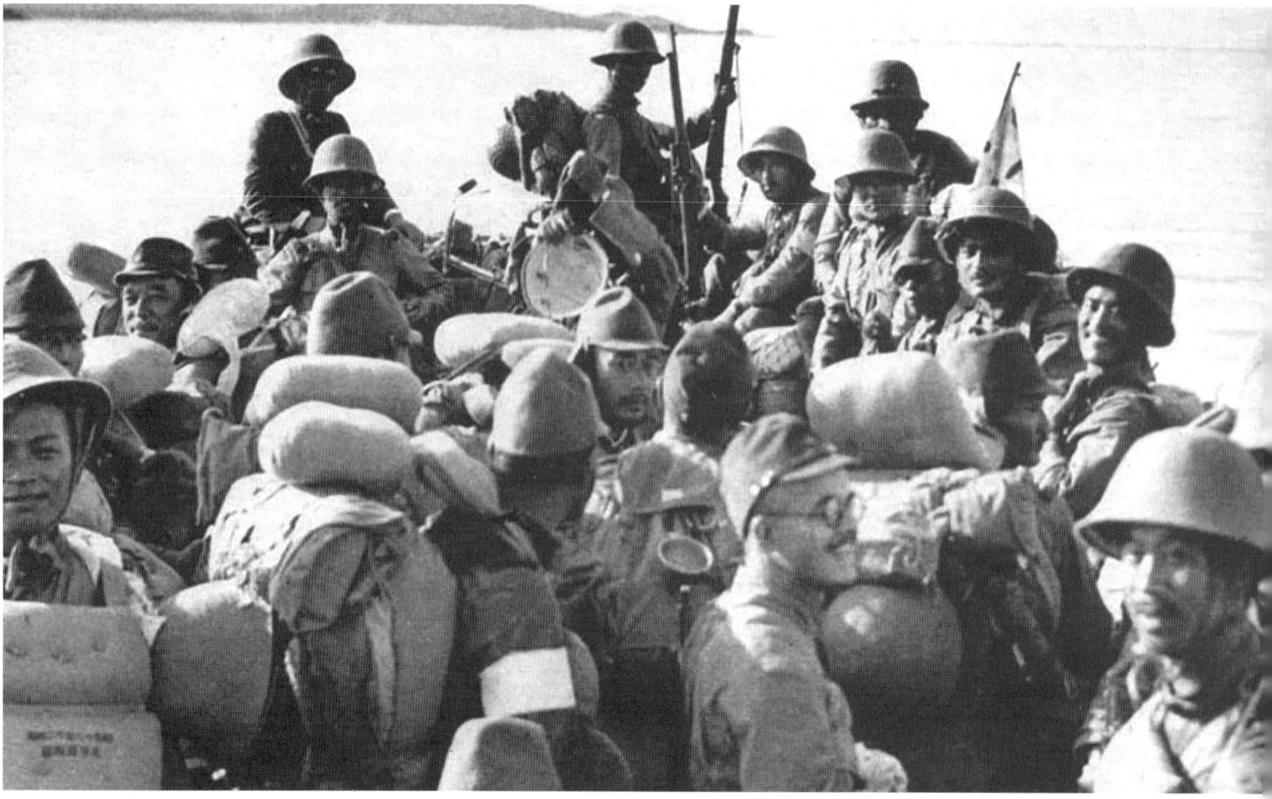

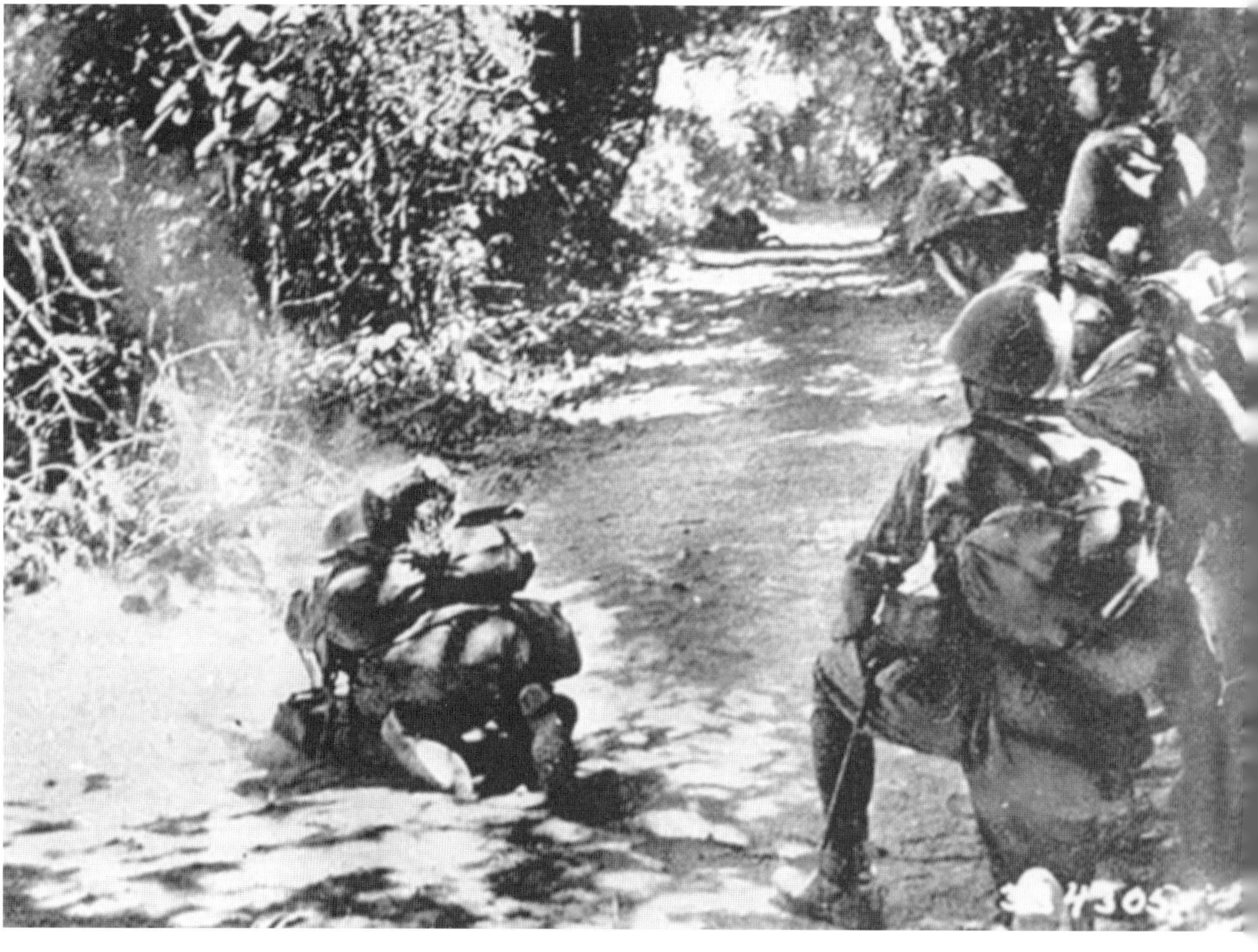

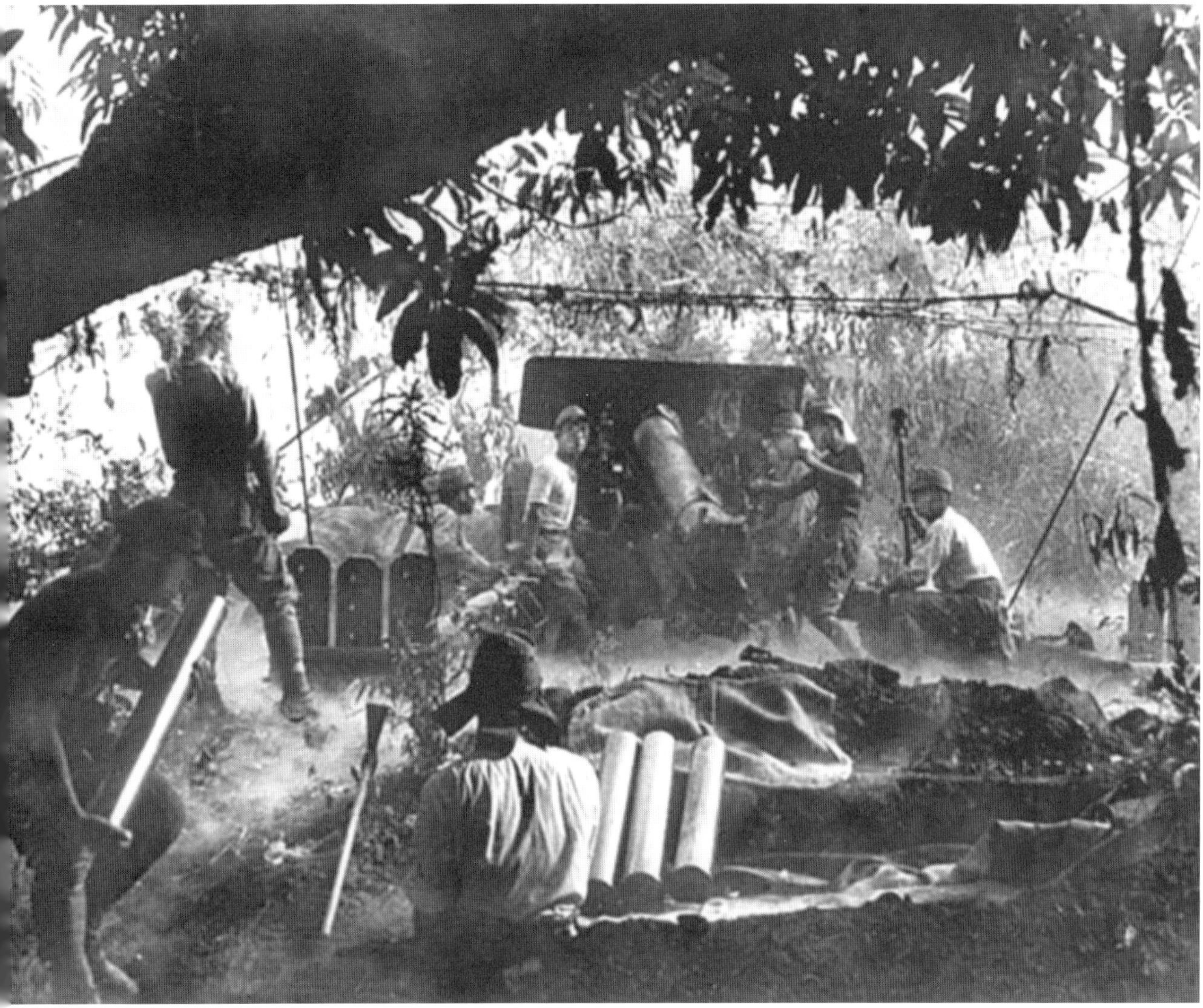

(**Opposite, above**) A Japanese landing barge is shown here approaching a Luzon landing zone in December 1941. MacArthur chose to scrap WPO-3 and contest all the landings at the beaches, which turned out to be a colossal blunder with the Japanese getting ashore easily at several points on Luzon's shoreline. *(Author's collection)*

(**Opposite, below**) Japanese infantrymen of Lieutenant General Masaharu Homma's 14th Army are shown here peering down a road as they approach Filipino-American positions on the Bataan Peninsula into which MacArthur's Northern and Southern Luzon Forces had withdrawn for a protracted defence. However, much of the Philippine army's ammunition, foodstuffs and medical supplies were abandoned throughout Luzon during the retreat to Bataan. *(NARA)*

(**Above**) An IJA heavy artillery battery fires at Filipino-American positions on Bataan. This heavy ordnance was brought in from Malaya and Singapore (after Percival's capitulation) to break through Bataan's Bagac-Orion Line. Japanese artillery fire coupled with aerial assaults demoralized the Filipino-American forces, lowering their capability to fight, especially with food, ammunition and medical supply shortages. *(NARA)*

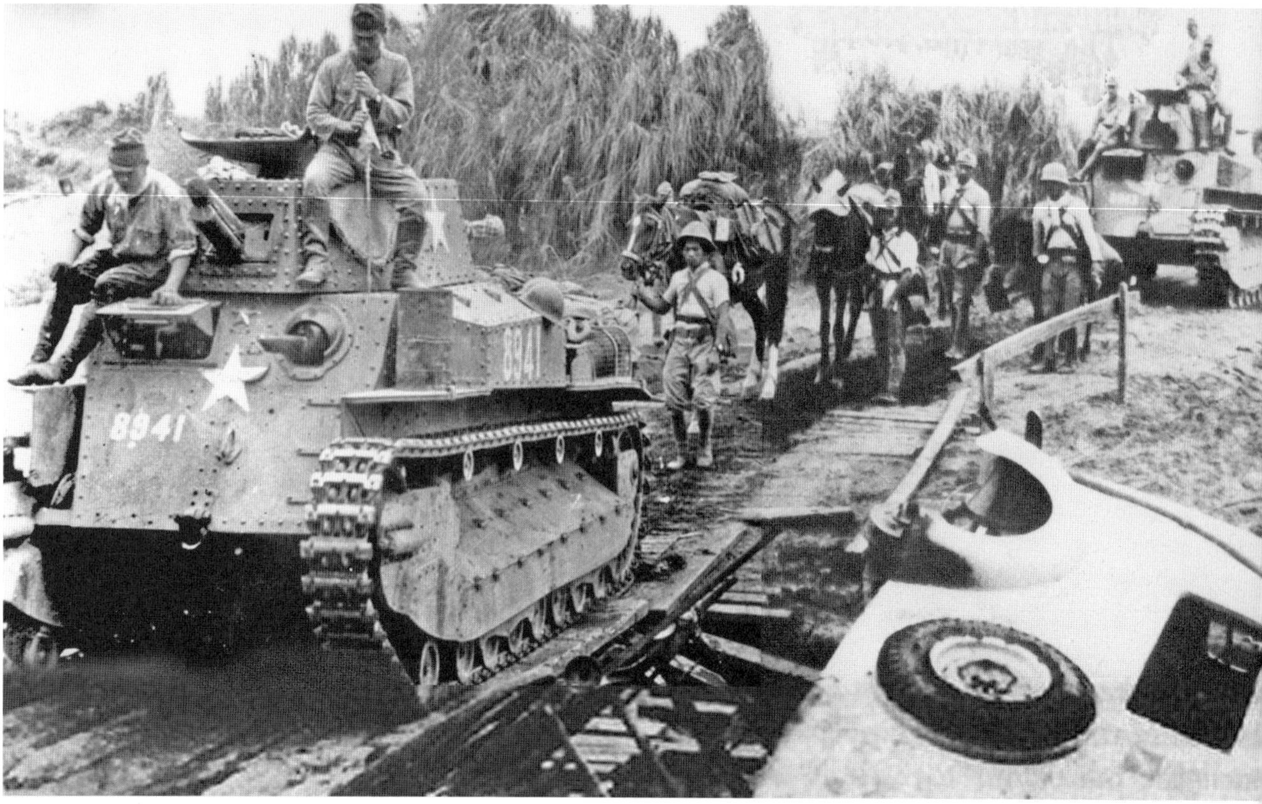
8941

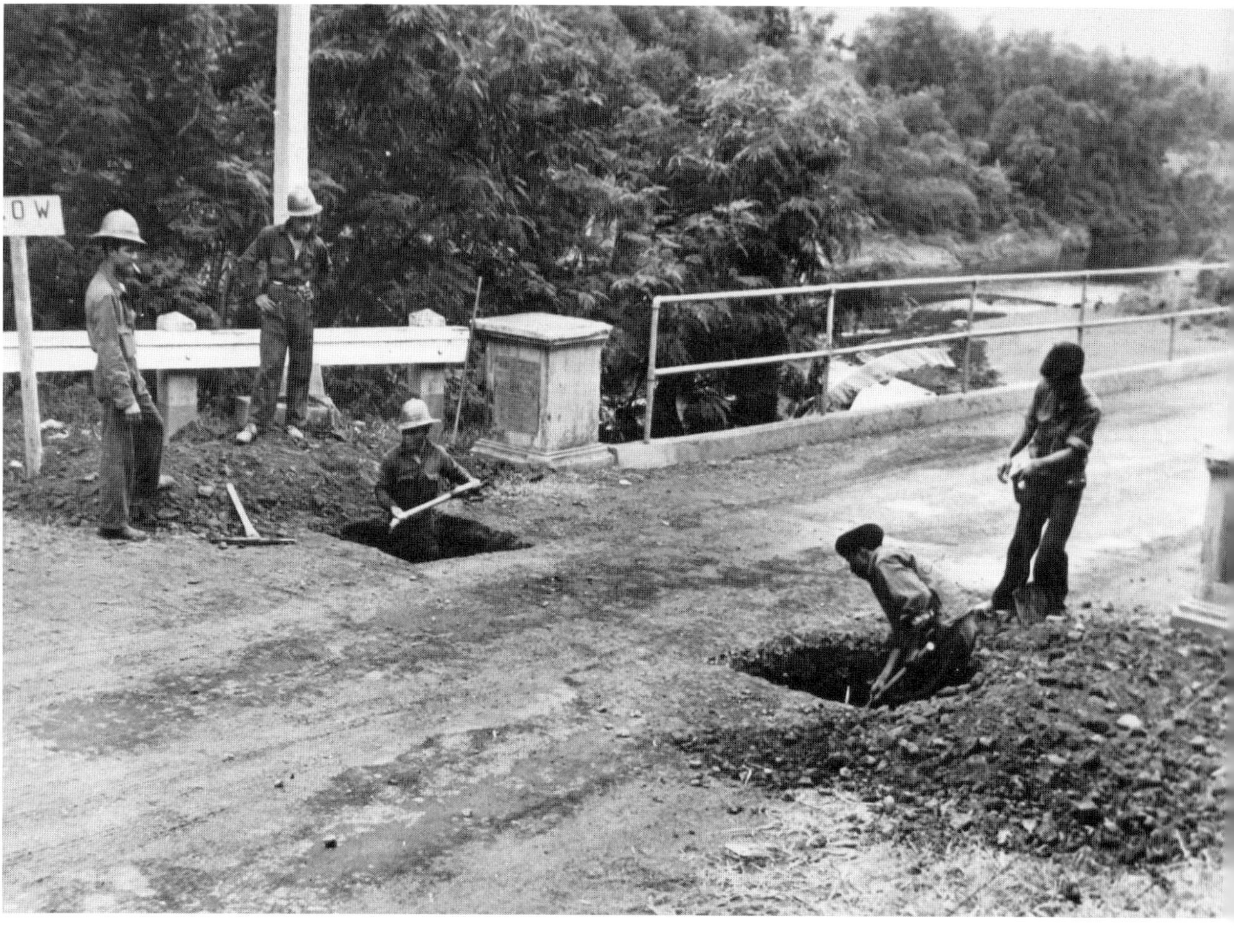

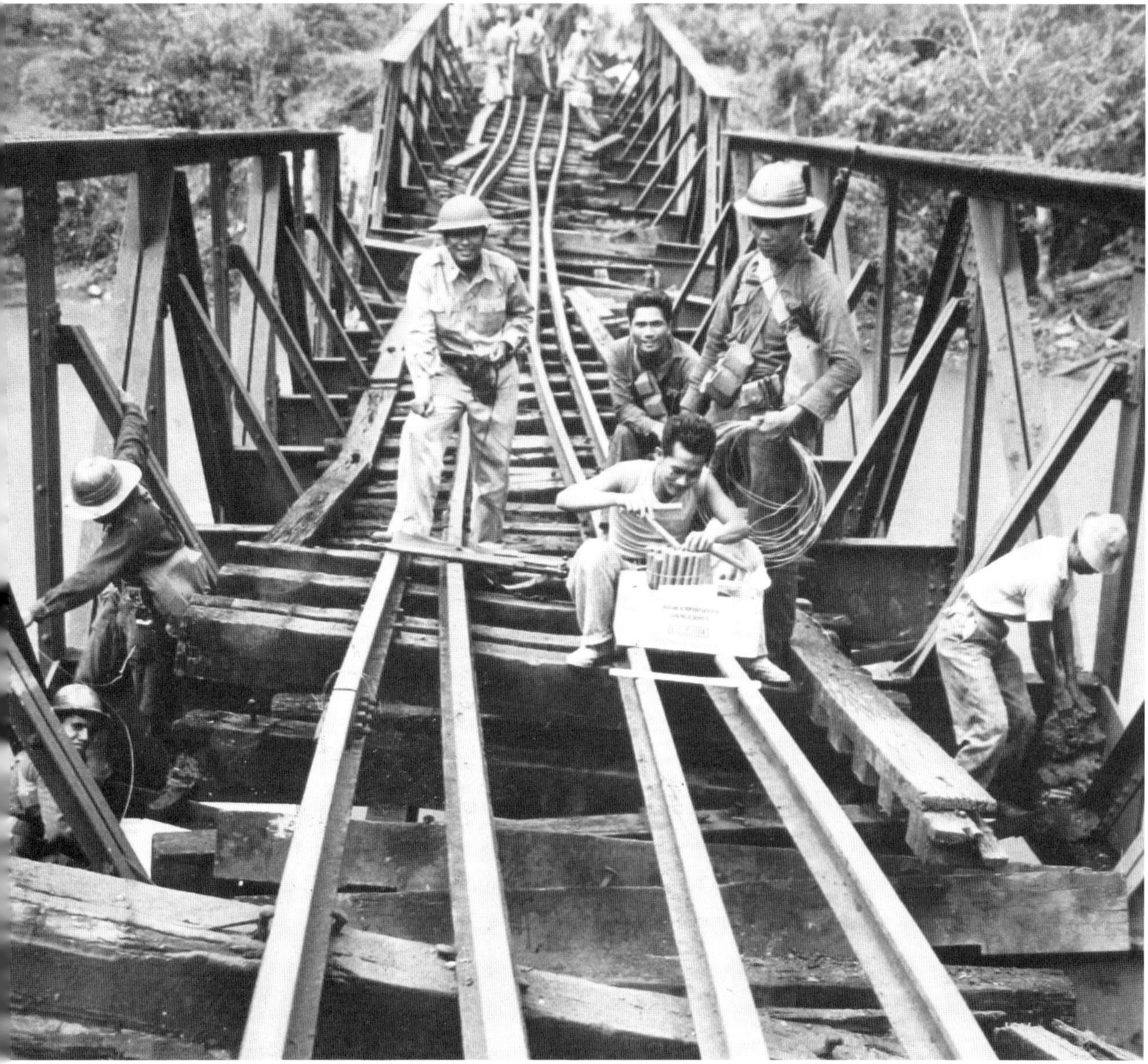

(**Opposite, above**) A column of IJA Type 89 *I-Go* medium tanks is seen here moving across a wooden bridge and passing an abandoned US Army staff car on the way towards Manila in January 1942. The Type 89 had a short-barrelled 57mm turret gun to destroy pillboxes and enemy fortifications as well as two 6.5mm Type 91 MGs. Manila was declared an 'Open City' by MacArthur to prevent destruction and civilian casualties. *(NARA)*

(**Above**) Filipino soldiers are shown here preparing to dynamite bridge remnants to retard the IJA southward advance down the Central Luzon Plain against a series of Wainwright's defensive lines. These delaying tactics were to also enable the Filipino-American Northern and Southern Luzon Forces to retreat into the Bataan Peninsula. *(NARA)*

(**Opposite, below**) Filipino engineers are seen here planting explosives to destroy a concrete road bridge (right). This demolition was to delay Japanese Type 89 medium and 95 light tanks moving southwards towards Manila within days after landing at sites along Lingayen Gulf. *(NARA)*

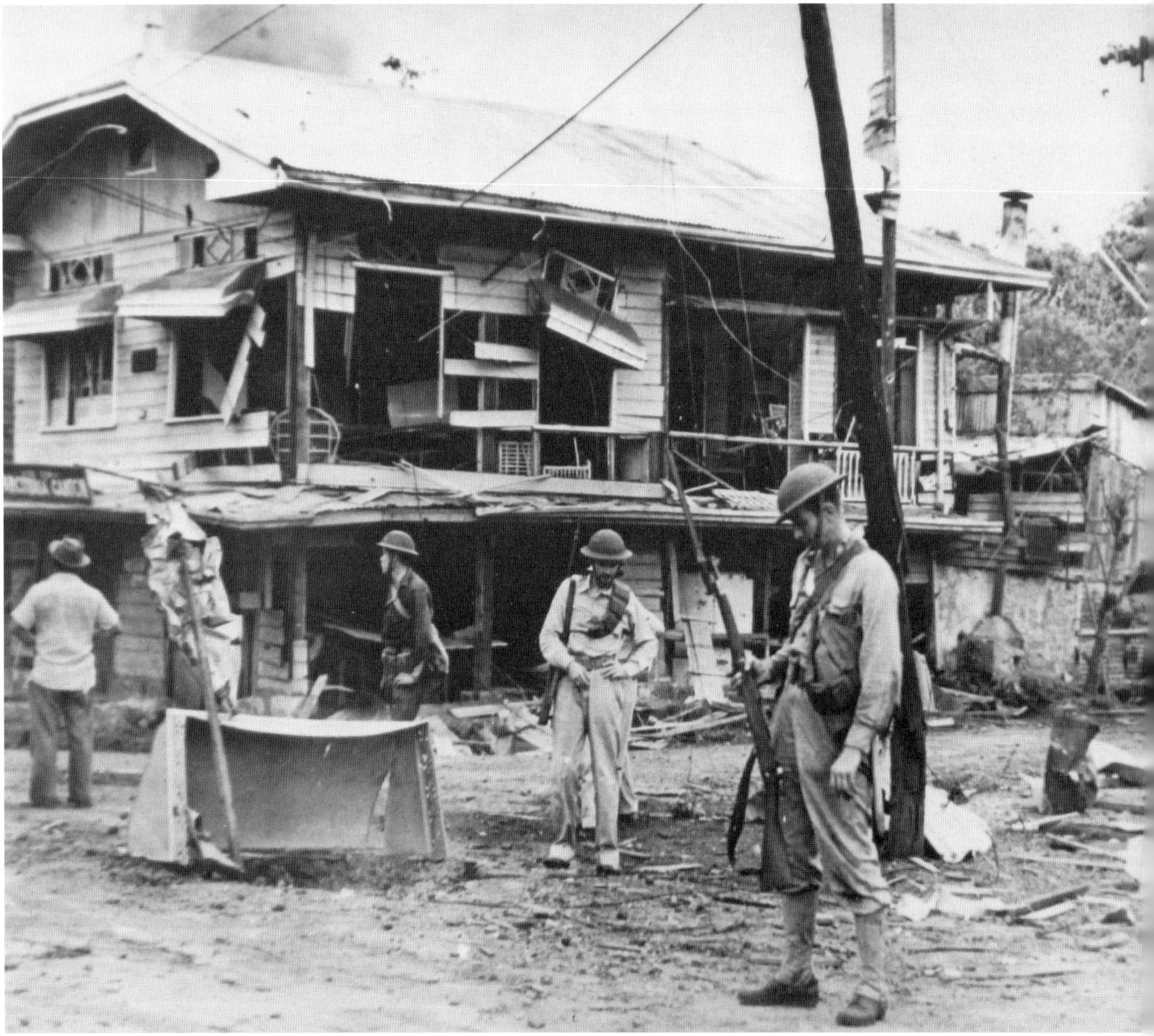

(**Above**) US Army regulars are shown here standing amid the ruins of a village in the Bataan Peninsula after Japanese forces moved on the Filipino-American positions following the capture of Manila on 2 January 1942. *(NARA)*

(**Opposite, above**) An M3 half-track of the 192nd TB of the Philippine army's 1st Provisional Tank Group is seen here moving towards the front lines in late December 1941 to contest Japanese armour near Baliuag in order to keep the lines of retreat open to the Bataan Peninsula. An air-cooled mounted MG is visible. These half-tracks also mounted 75mm howitzers as the US Army's principal tank destroyers (TDs) during the early part of the war. *(Author's collection)*

(**Opposite, below**) American and Filipino soldiers are shown here leading a group of blindfolded and undressed Japanese PoWs for interrogation. Blindfolds and uniform removal prevented the Japanese from seeing defensive dispositions and hiding weapons respectively. Although short on rations, ammunition and medical supplies, Filipino-American forces on the Bataan Peninsula put up a stout defence until finally surrendering on 9 April 1942. *(NARA)*

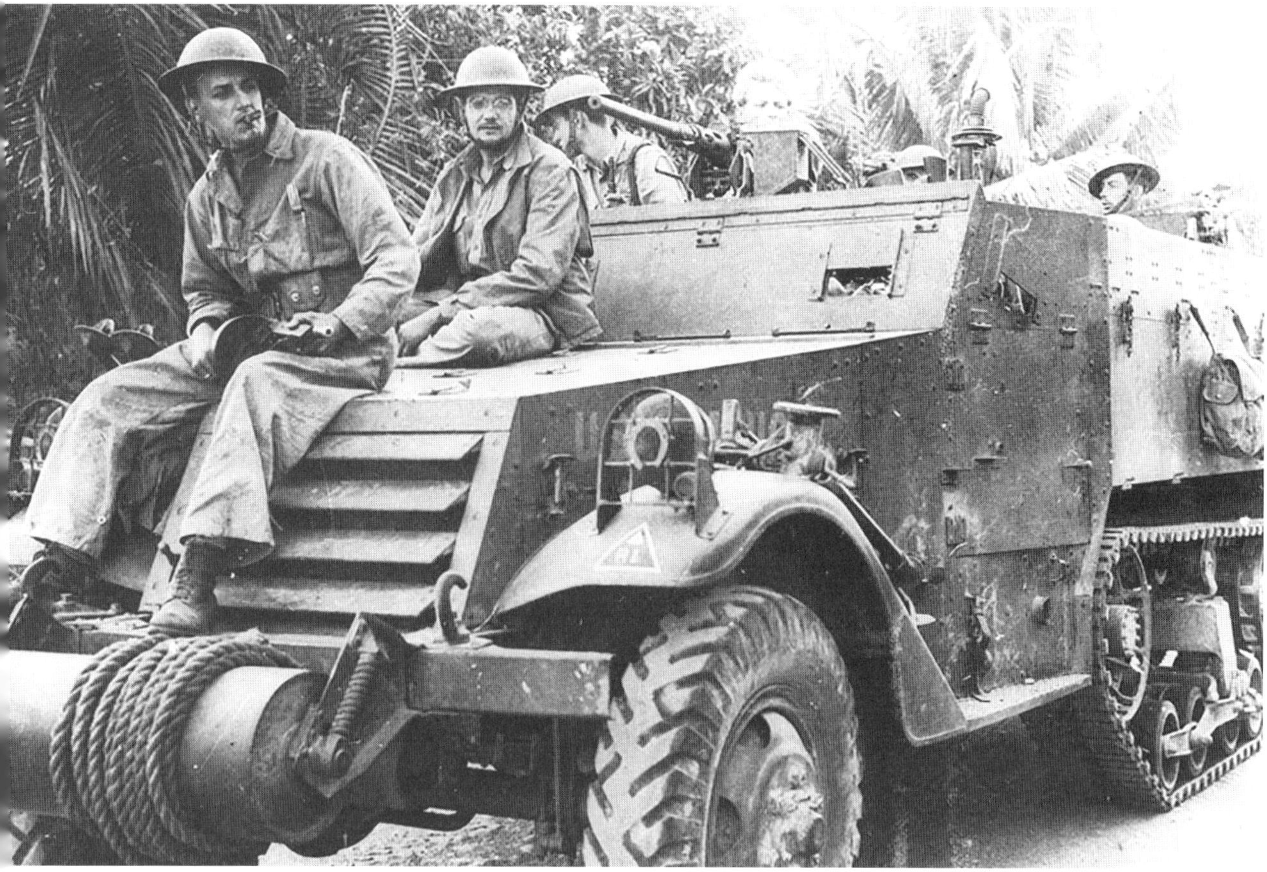

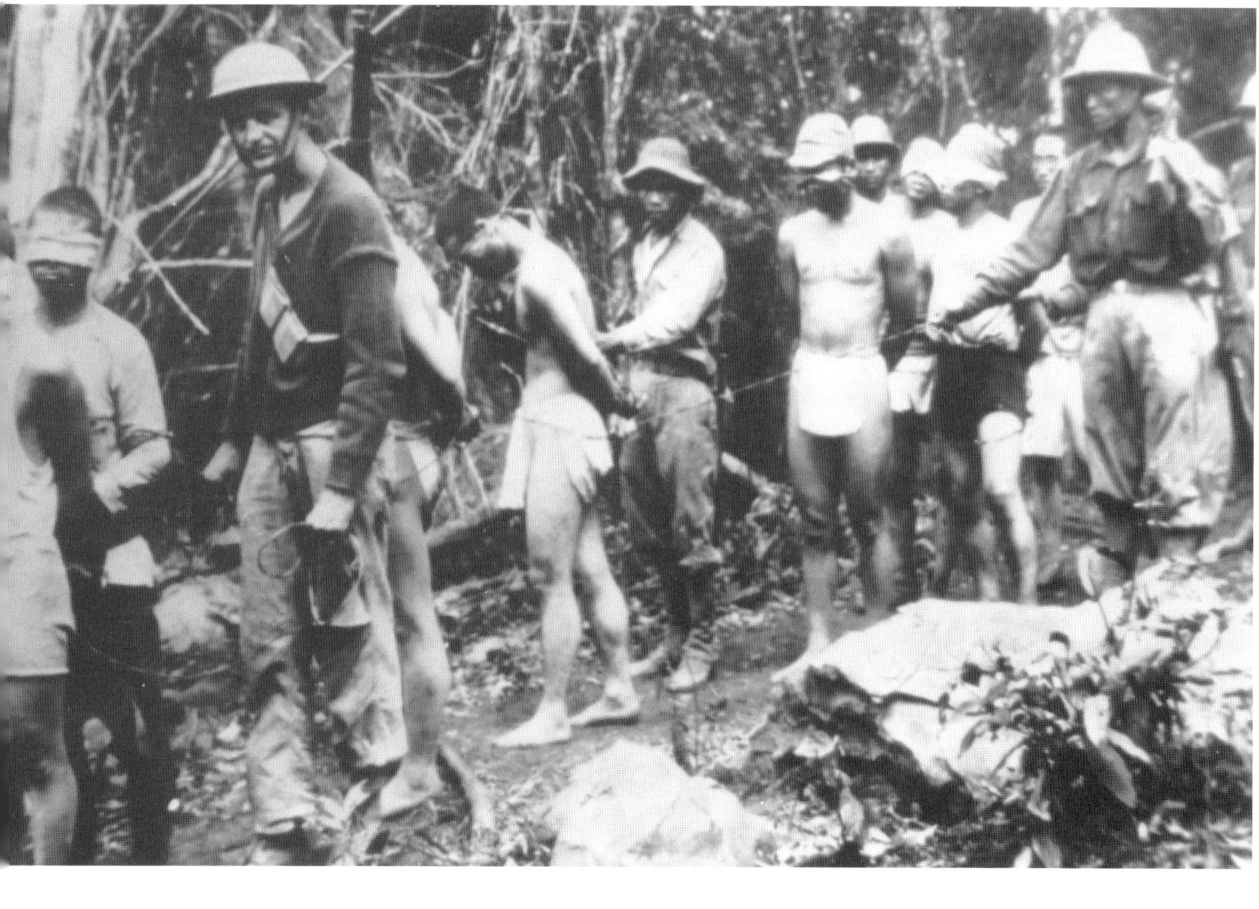

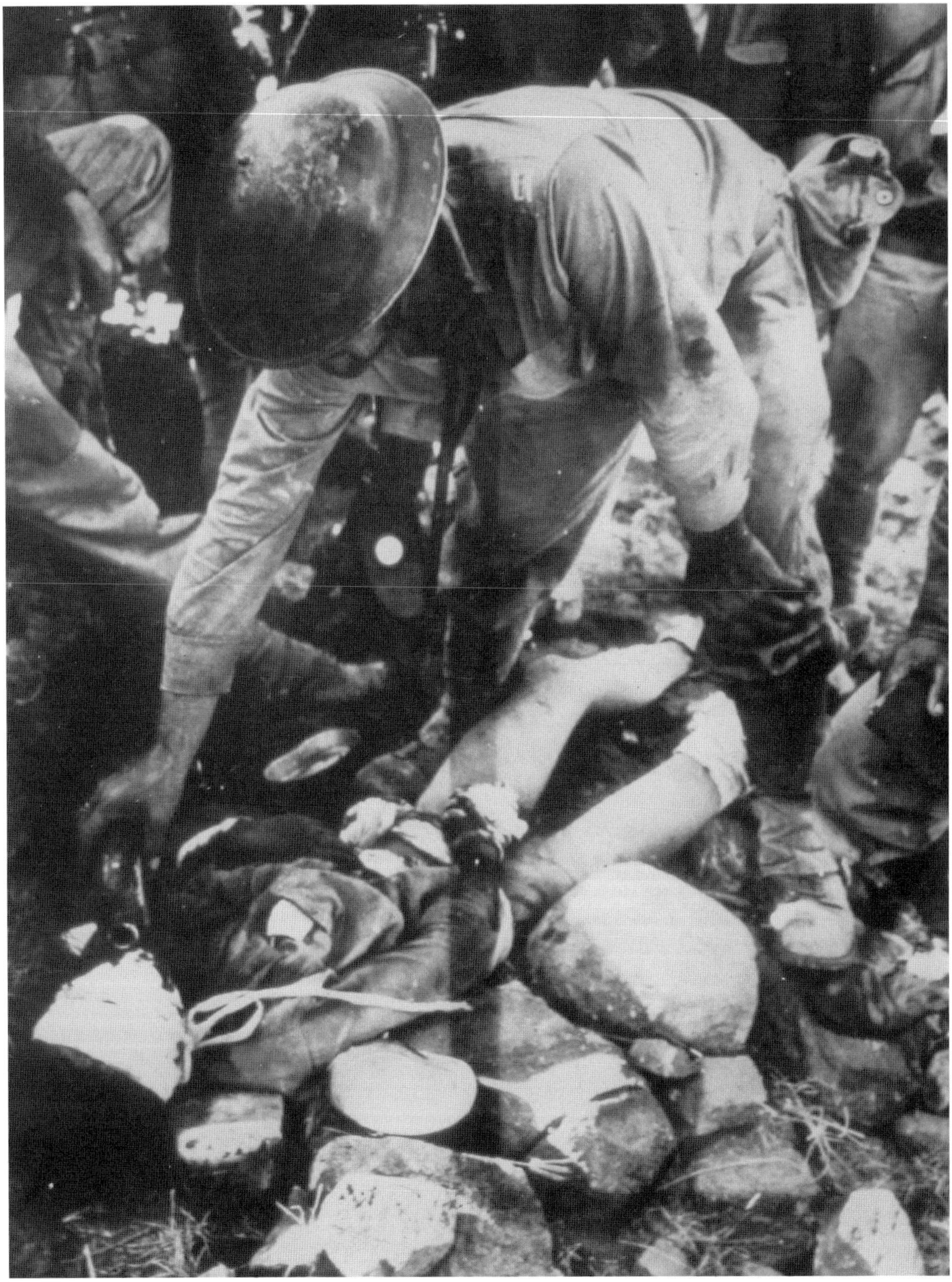

An American army officer is shown here giving some water to a dying Japanese soldier. Japanese PoWs were also fed, despite the defenders' dwindling rations. Reciprocal kind treatment was not rendered to the Filipino-American forces when Bataan capitulated on 9 April 1942. *(NARA)*

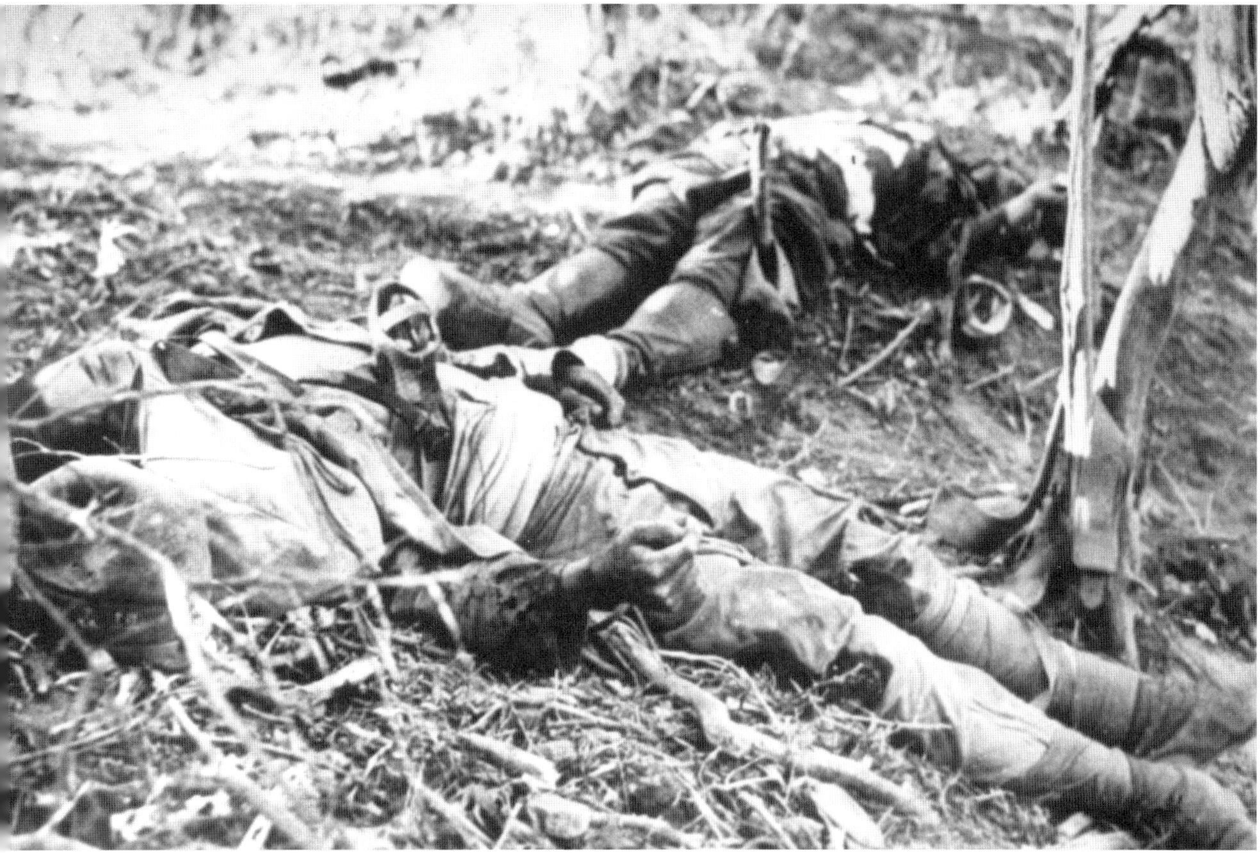

Two Japanese soldiers killed in action against Filipino-American forces defending Bataan are shown here. With the defence of the Filipino-American armed forces, Japanese General Homma was losing both time and mounting casualties to complete Luzon's conquest. *(NARA)*

Four US Army regulars, two officers and two NCOs of the Philippine Division's 31st Infantry are shown here in a slit trench after a Philippine army ammunition dump on Bataan blew up during a Japanese bombardment of the peninsula's defences in early 1942. *(NARA)*

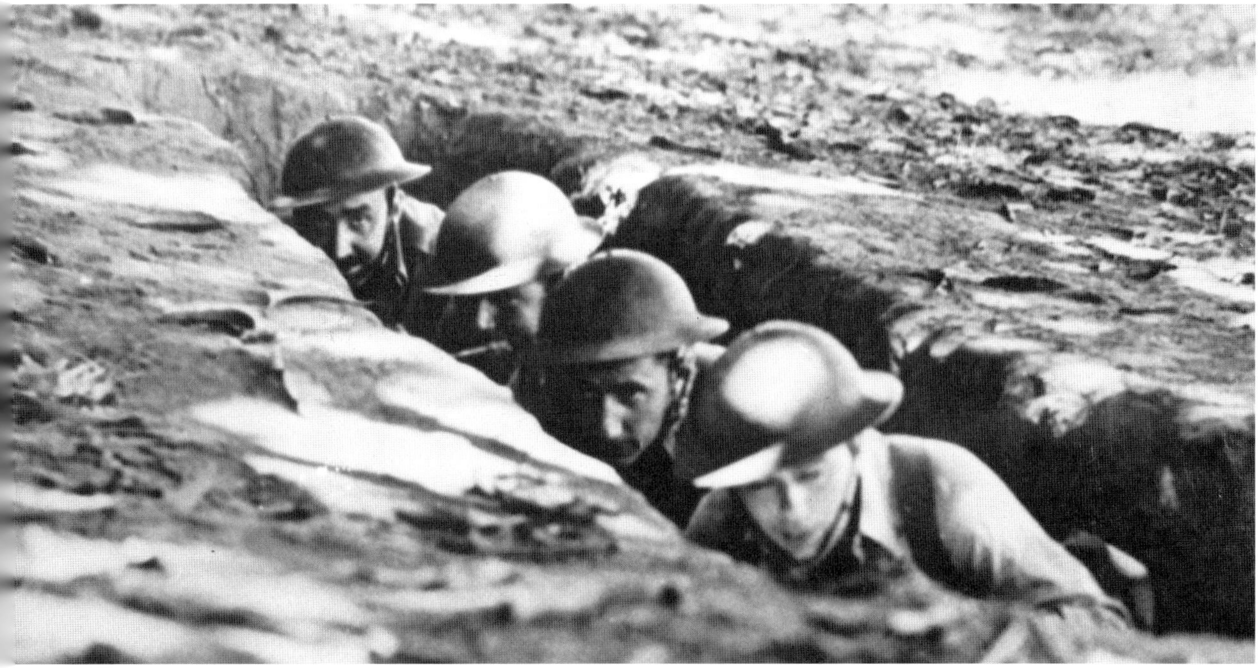

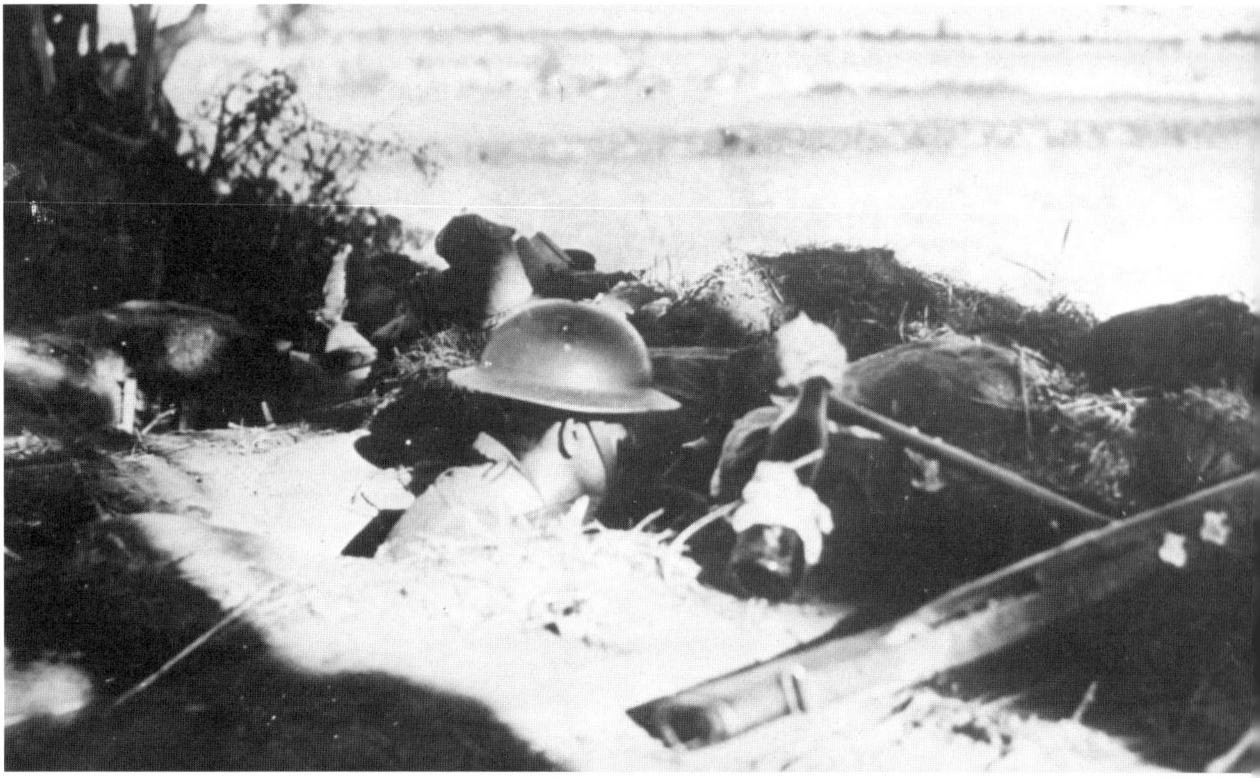

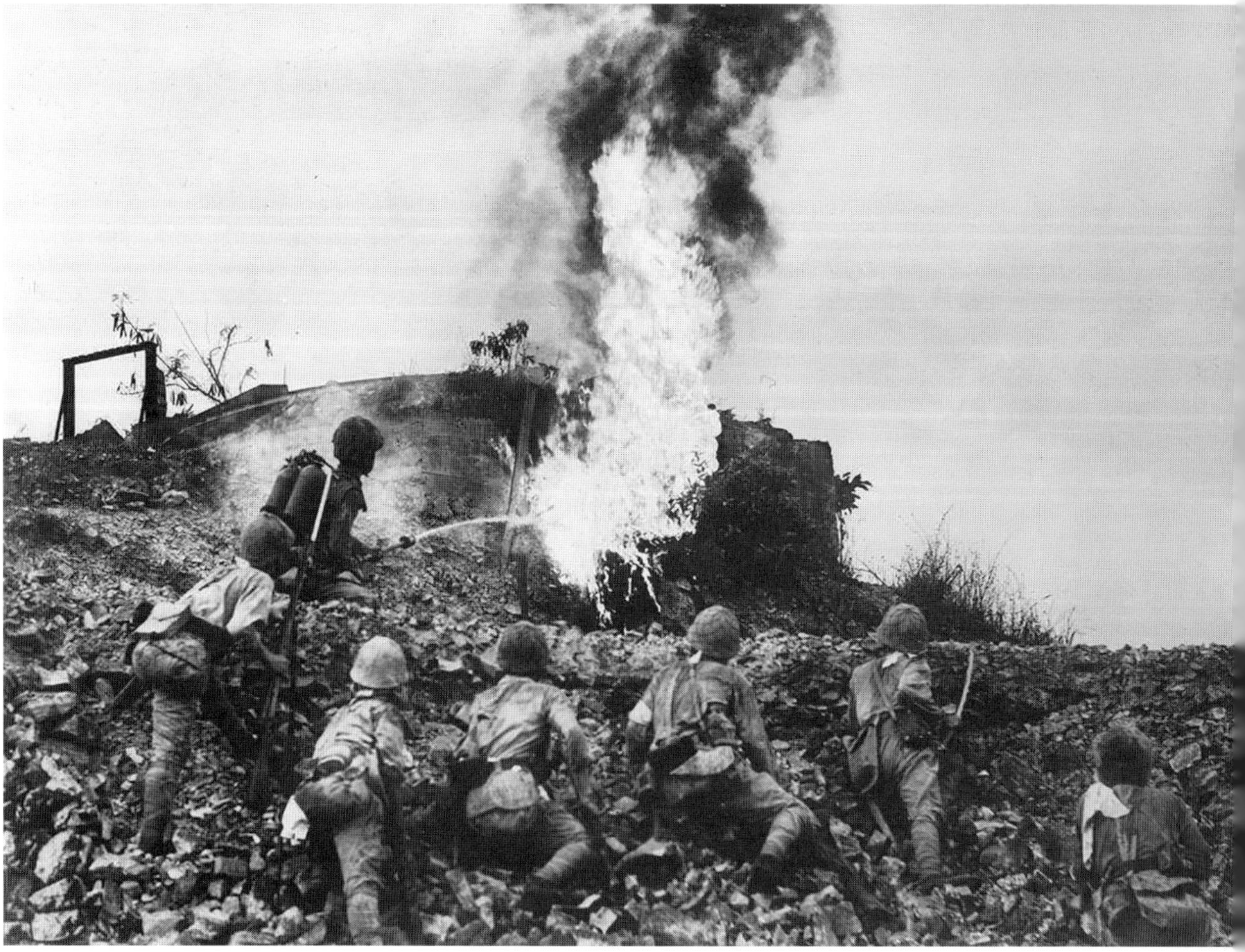

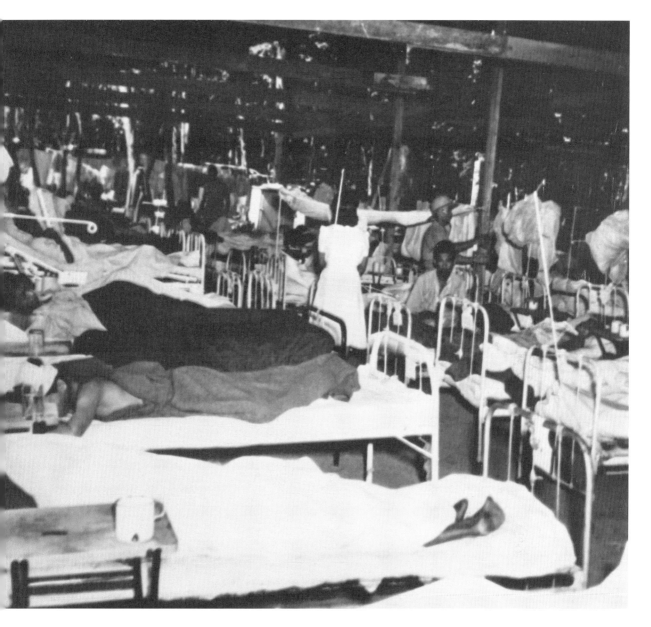

(**Opposite, above**) A US Army soldier on Bataan is shown here holding a gasoline-filled glass bottle with a cloth wick ('Molotov Cocktail') that he was going to use as a last-ditch AT weapon as Japanese tanks approached Filipino-American positions in early 1942. (*NARA*)

(**Opposite, below**) Japanese assault troops are shown here utilizing a flame-thrower against an American pillbox on the Orion-Bagac Line in late January 1942. This Filipino-American defensive line formed a continuous position across Bataan enabling physical contact between Wainwright's North and Parker's South Luzon Forces defending the peninsula. (*Author's collection*)

(**Above**) A Bataan hospital ward is shown here treating 'gas gangrene' cases caused by a bacterial skin infection that produced a progressive 'flesh-eating' illness in which the organism produced gas. These infections required antibiotics and extensive surgical debridement and/or amputation. (*NARA*)

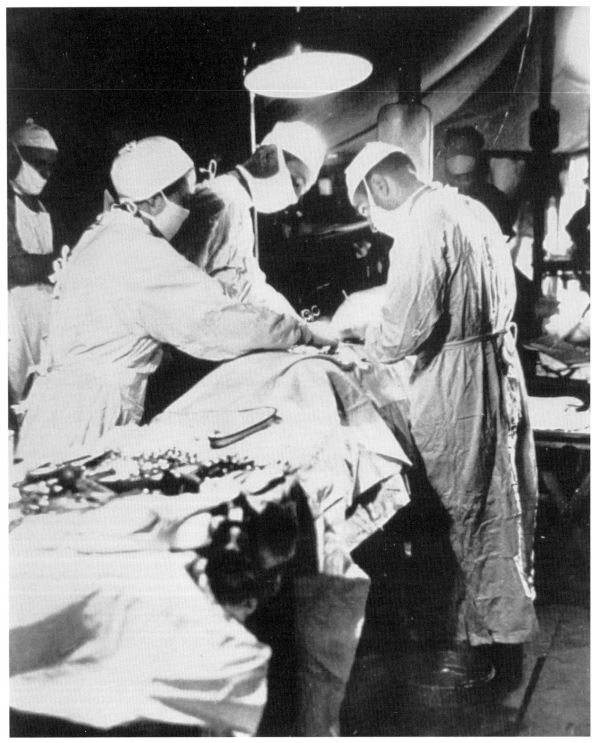

US Army Medical Corps surgeons and nurses are shown here operating in a makeshift surgical theatre behind the lines on the Bataan Peninsula. The medical personnel performed their duties during bombardments with a dwindling stock of medical supplies. *(NARA)*

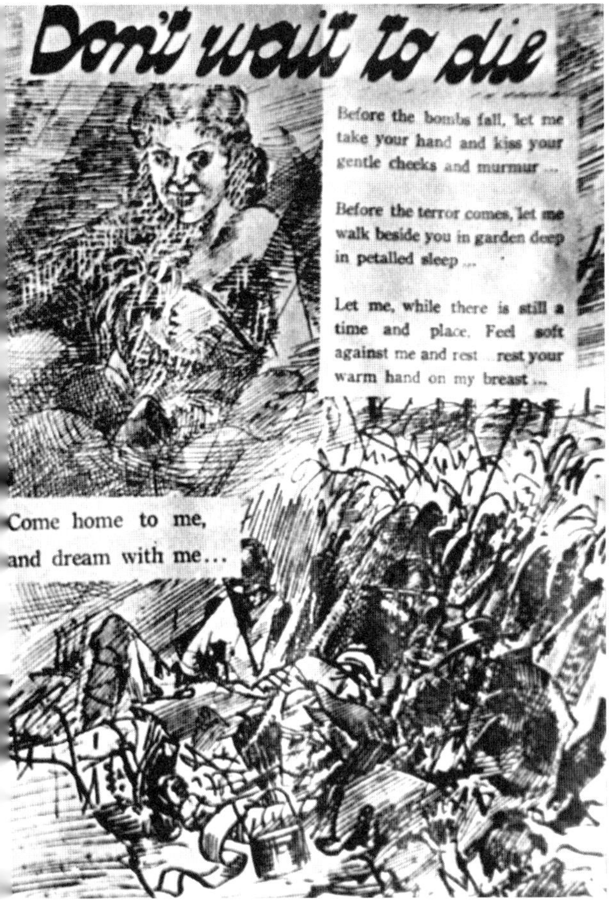
Don't wait to die
Before the bombs fall, let me take your hand and kiss your gentle cheeks and murmur ...
Before the terror comes, let me walk beside you in garden deep in petalled sleep ...
Let me, while there is still a time and place. Feel soft against me and rest ... rest your warm hand on my breast ...
Come home to me, and dream with me...

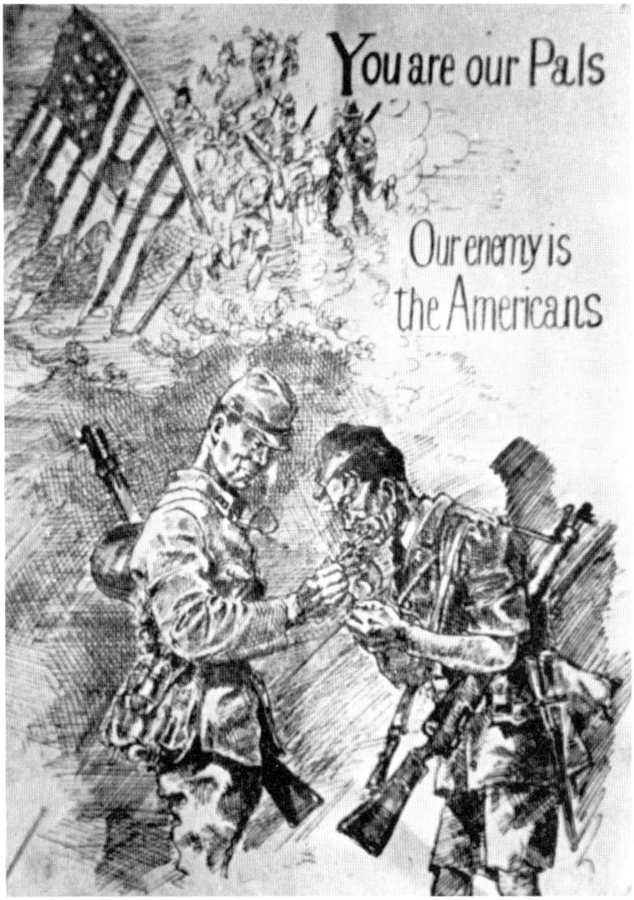
You are our Pals
Our enemy is the Americans

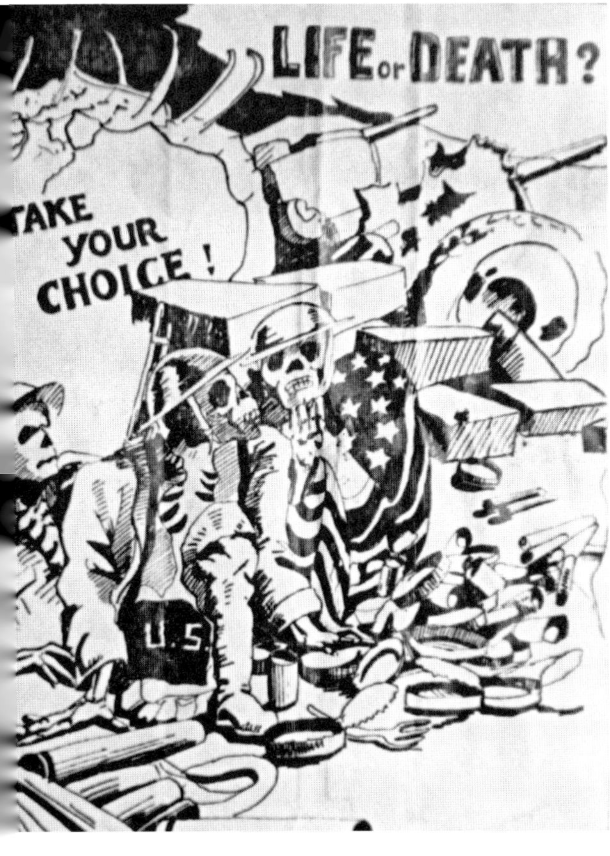
LIFE or DEATH?
TAKE YOUR CHOICE!
U.S

(**Above, left**) A Japanese leaflet that was circulated among American troops on Bataan in early 1942 is shown here appealing to US troops fighting far from their homes and loved ones. The psychological effect of this propaganda compounded starvation, ammunition shortages and dwindling medical supplies. *(NARA)*

(**Above, right**) A Japanese propaganda leaflet dropped into predominantly Filipino defensive positions on Bataan in early 1942 claims that both Japanese and Filipino soldiers are Asians. The rapidly-retreating American forces were the common enemy and the Philippine army's native contingents should surrender. *(NARA)*

(**Left**) This leaflet was dropped among American lines on Bataan on 20 January 1942 and shows destroyed American ordnance and the corpses of US soldiers. The message was that the Americans could choose between life and death, although this leaflet was dropped almost three months before the Filipino-American surrender of Bataan. *(NARA)*

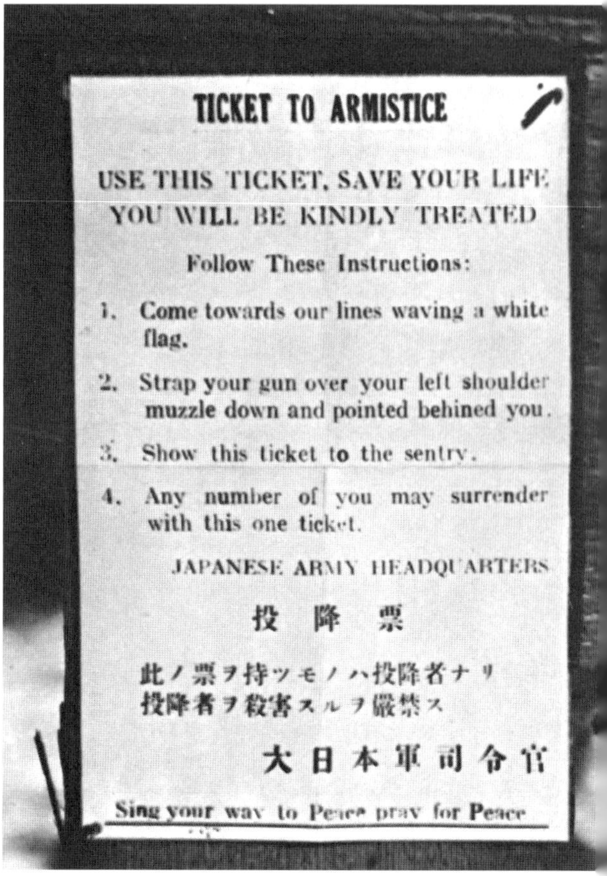

TICKET TO ARMISTICE

USE THIS TICKET, SAVE YOUR LIFE
YOU WILL BE KINDLY TREATED

Follow These Instructions:

1. Come towards our lines waving a white flag.
2. Strap your gun over your left shoulder muzzle down and pointed behined you.
3. Show this ticket to the sentry.
4. Any number of you may surrender with this one ticket.

JAPANESE ARMY HEADQUARTERS

投降票

此ノ票ヲ持ツモノハ投降者ナリ
投降者ヲ殺害スルヲ嚴禁ス

大日本軍司令官

Sing your way to Peace pray for Peace

The leaflet invited the Filipino and American forces on Bataan in early 1942 to surrender honourably. Without American reinforcements or replenishment of supplies along with near-constant aerial and artillery bombardment, a dispirited Philippine army was further subjected to Japanese propaganda. *(NARA)*

MacArthur and his COS Major General Richard K. Sutherland in Lateral Three of the Malinta Tunnel on Corregidor shortly before President Franklin D. Roosevelt ordered the USAFFE commander to Australia with his family and vital staff officers via a hazardous PT boat escape on 11 March 1942 followed by a B-17 flight to Batchelor Field in Australia. Other staff officers were evacuated by US Navy submarines from Corregidor or Bataan to Australia. MacArthur arrived in Melbourne on 21 March 1942 to become SWPA commander. In Australia, he proclaimed: 'I came through and I shall return.' While on Corregidor, MacArthur was called 'Dugout Doug' since he toured Bataan's front lines only once. This nickname infuriated MacArthur since he was known for his gallantry in past combat in Mexico and France during the 'Pershing Expedition' and the First World War respectively. *(NARA)*

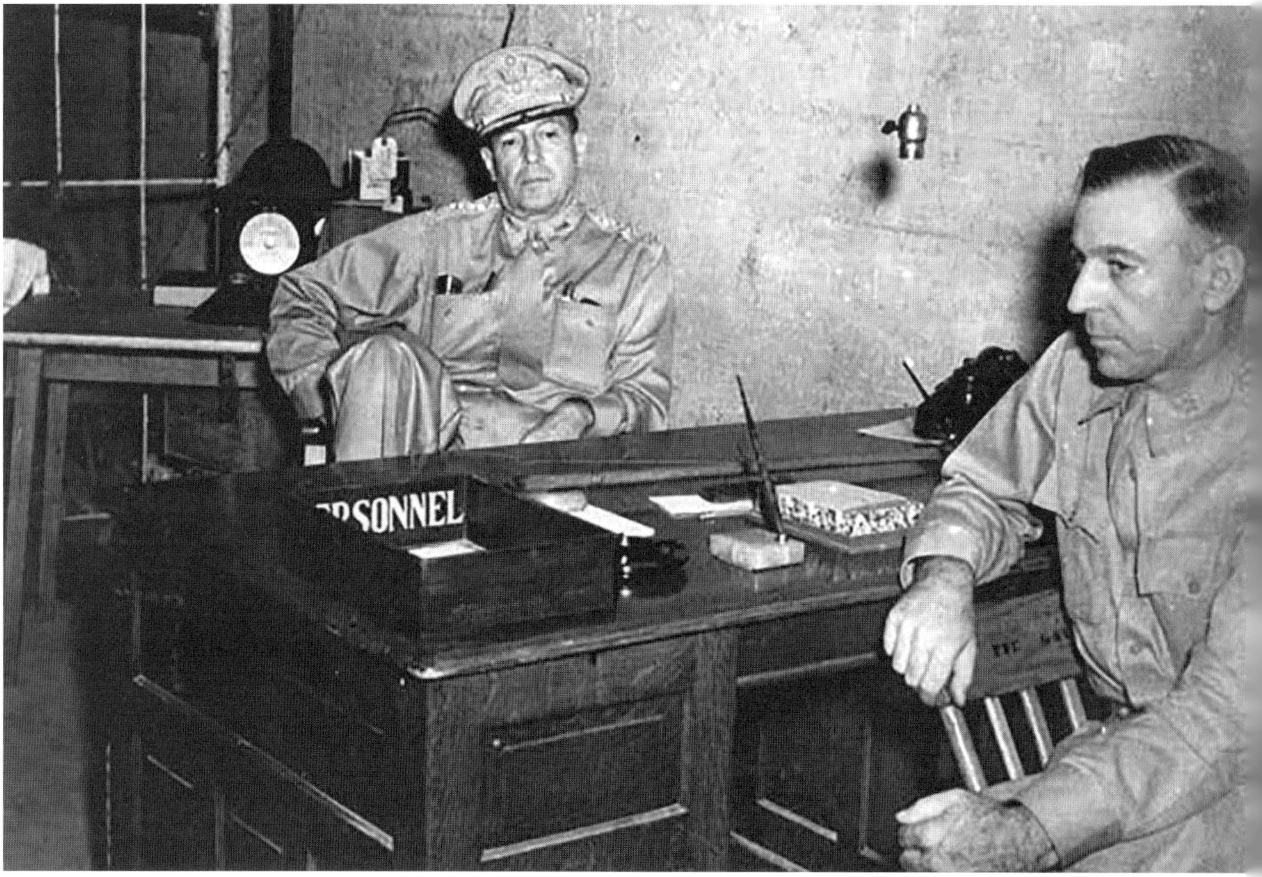
RSONNEL

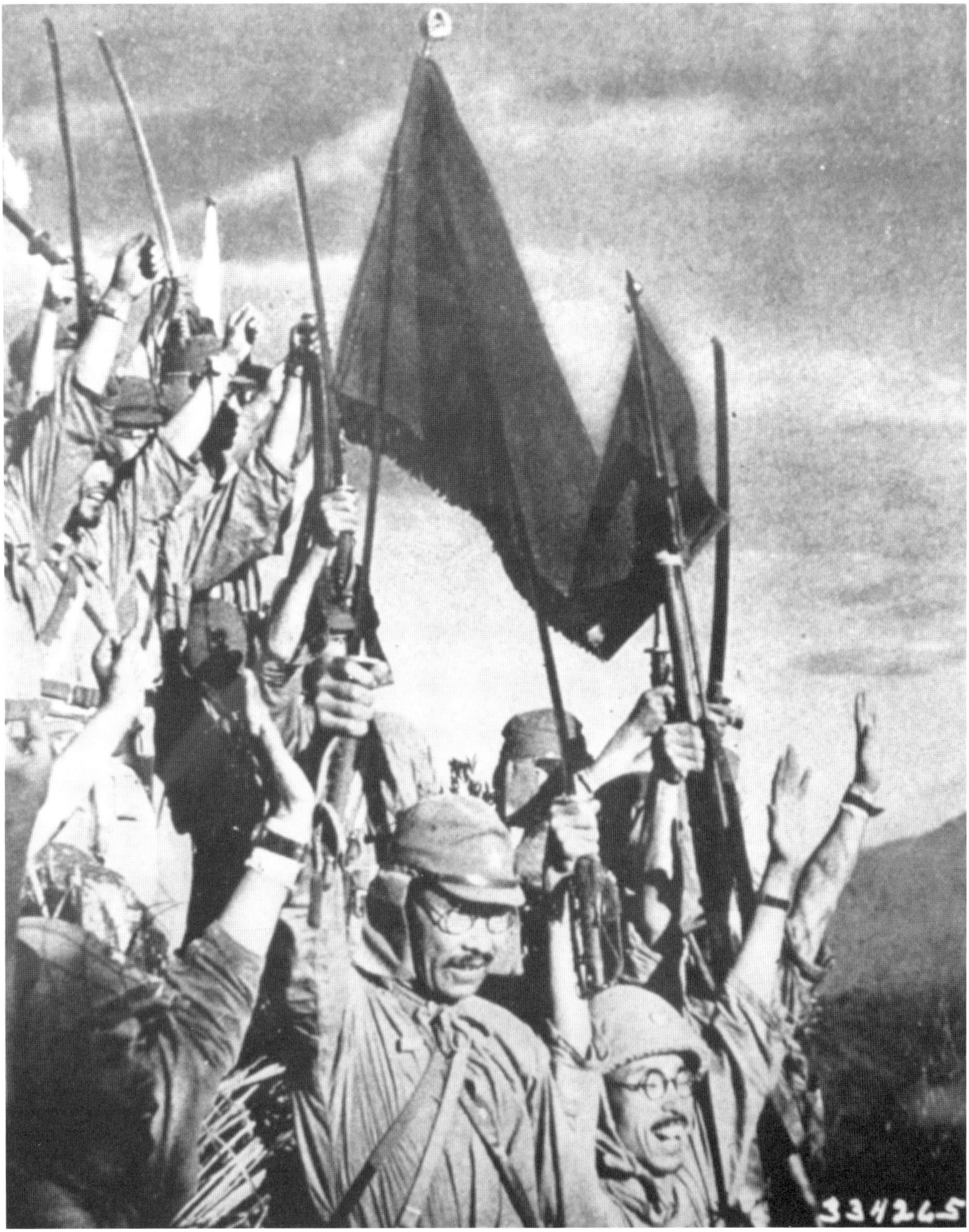
334265

IJA troops of the 61st Infantry Regiment are shown here shouting their traditional *banzai* salute to the emperor at Mount Limay on Bataan after the surrender of Filipino-American forces on 9 April 1942. (NARA)

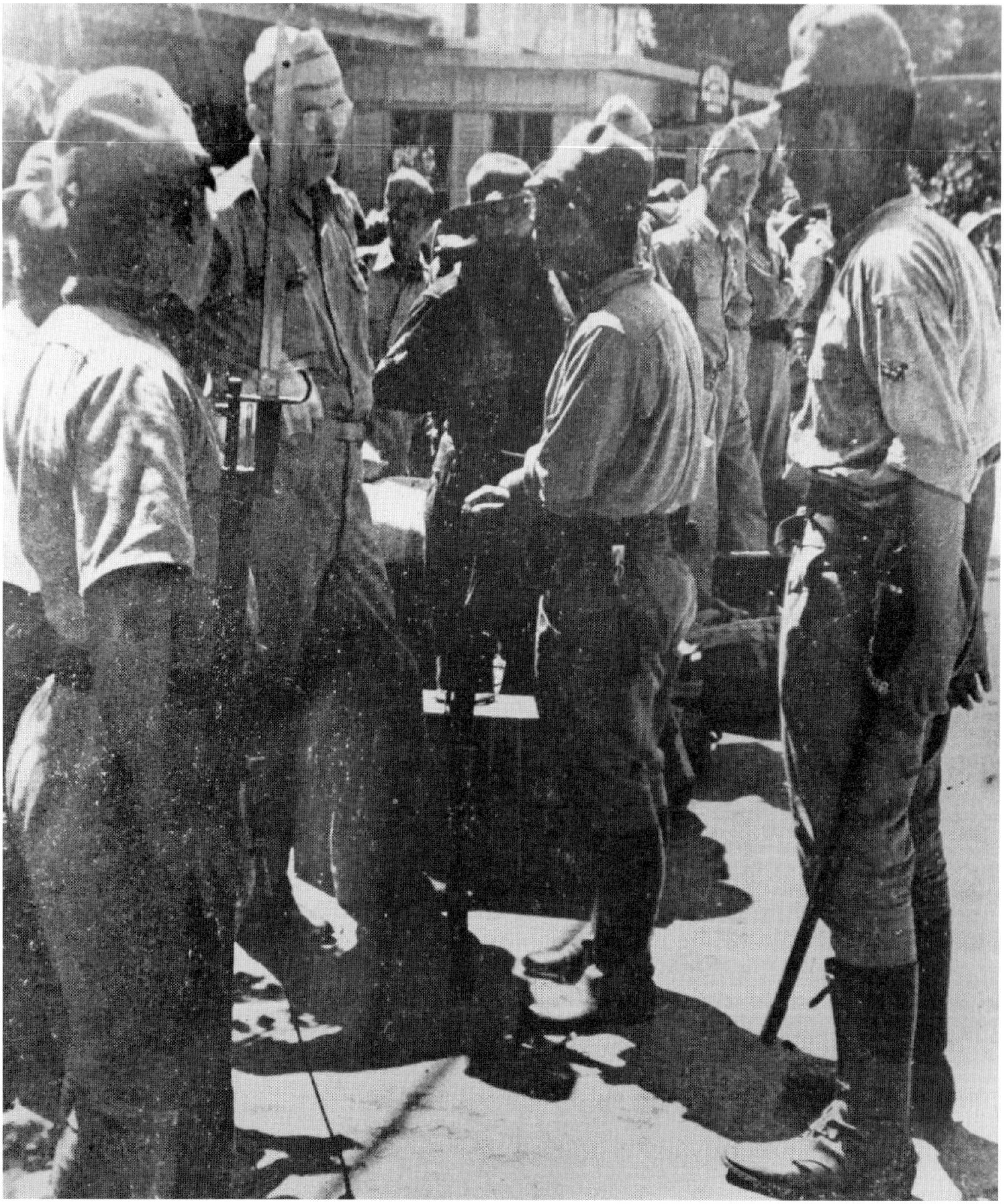

An American general is shown here discussing terms of surrender of his unit to IJA 14th Army officers on Bataan. On 3 April 1942, after refitting and reorganization, Japanese 14th Army commanding general Homma unleashed the most intense artillery shelling of the campaign, devastating the Philippine army's 41st Division, which after the bombardment offered little resistance to the Japanese advance. Note the American soldiers still have their personal possessions, which were often confiscated or discarded during their march into captivity. *(Author's collection)*

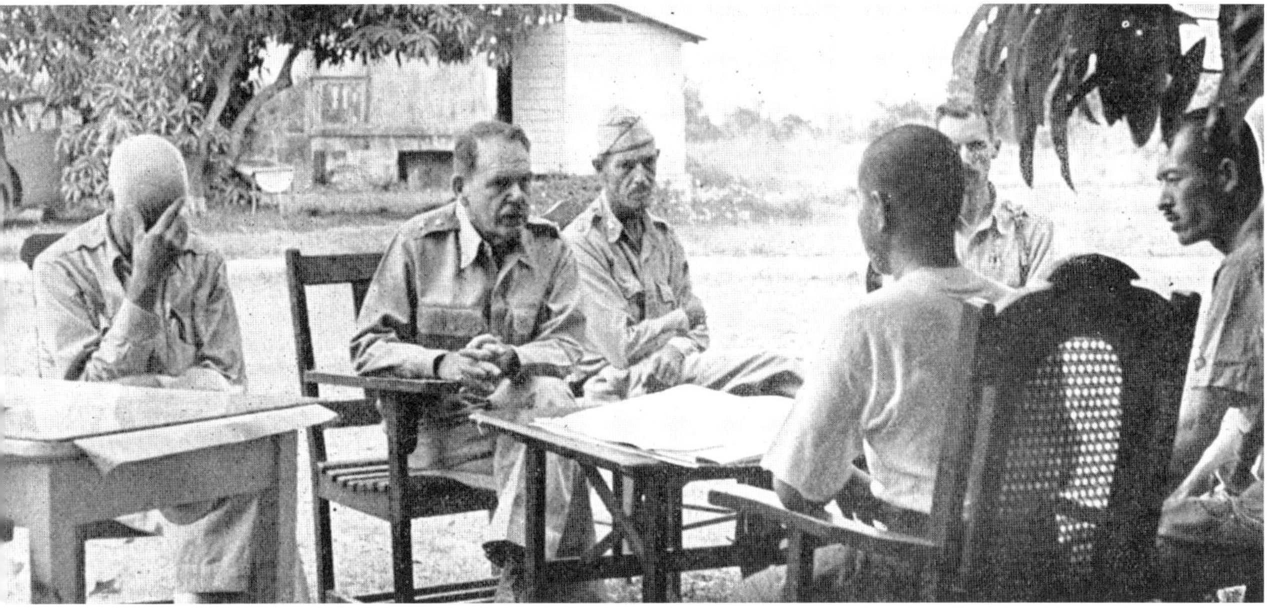

On 9 April 1942, about 12,000 Americans and 63,000 Filipinos became PoWs under the conquering Japanese 14th Army. Major General Edward 'Ned' P. King (seated second from left) is shown here discussing the terms of surrender of his Luzon Force with General Homma's designee, Colonel Nakayama Matoo. To the right of King were two other American majors, Wade Cothran and Achille Tisdelle. The Japanese never anticipated the staggering number of the Philippine army forces surrendering and did not have food or shelter for this large number of troops who were already half-starved and rife with disease. *(NARA)*

With the fall of Bataan on 9 April 1942, American and Filipino PoWs are shown here marching northwards into captivity. The survivors of MacArthur's Philippine army were ordered to pose with their hands up as Japanese guards smiled to the side of the Bataan 'Death March' column. The Japanese had a sense of urgency to move the PoWs out of Bataan so that the Corregidor offensive could commence. *(NARA)*

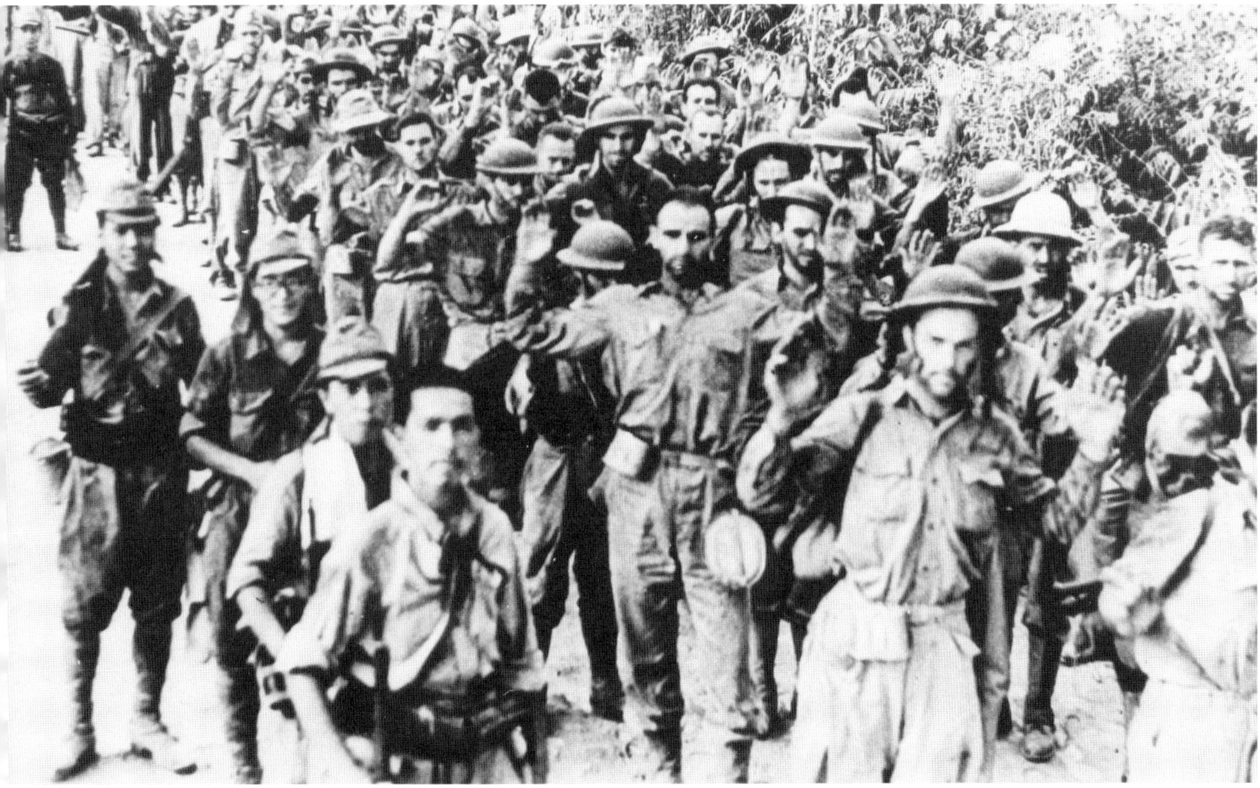

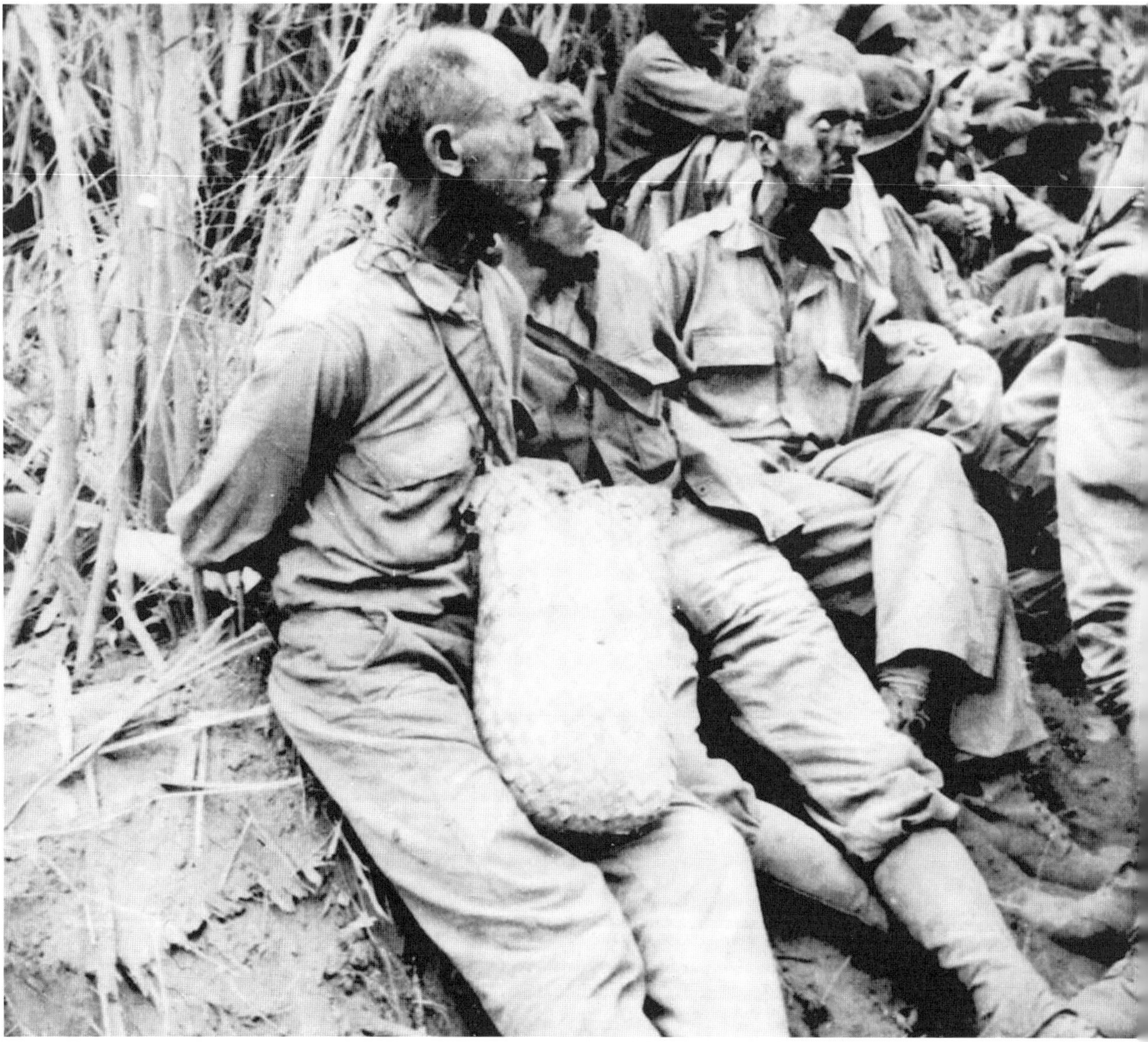

(**Above**) American PoWs, some with their hands tied behind their back, are allowed only a brief break during the infamous 60-mile northward Bataan 'Death March' in April 1942. The ordeal lasted several days, with thousands of Americans and Filipinos dying during the route as the Japanese committed atrocities too numerous to count. *(NARA)*

(**Opposite, above**) A large collection of mostly American troops that surrendered at Bataan are shown here getting a break before the Bataan 'Death March' began in earnest northward to stockades and concentration camps. Death and atrocities were all too common after the Japanese commanders accepted an 'honourable' Filipino-American surrender. *(NARA)*

(**Opposite, below**) American survivors of the Bataan 'Death March', most without any possessions as they were confiscated by the Japanese, are shown here arriving at one of the trek's termini, Camp O'Donnell. A Japanese photographer (right foreground) is seen filming the haggard column. American and Filipino soldiers arriving at the PoW camp were suffering from malaria and other diseases in addition to near-starvation from months of short rations while on Bataan. *(NARA)*

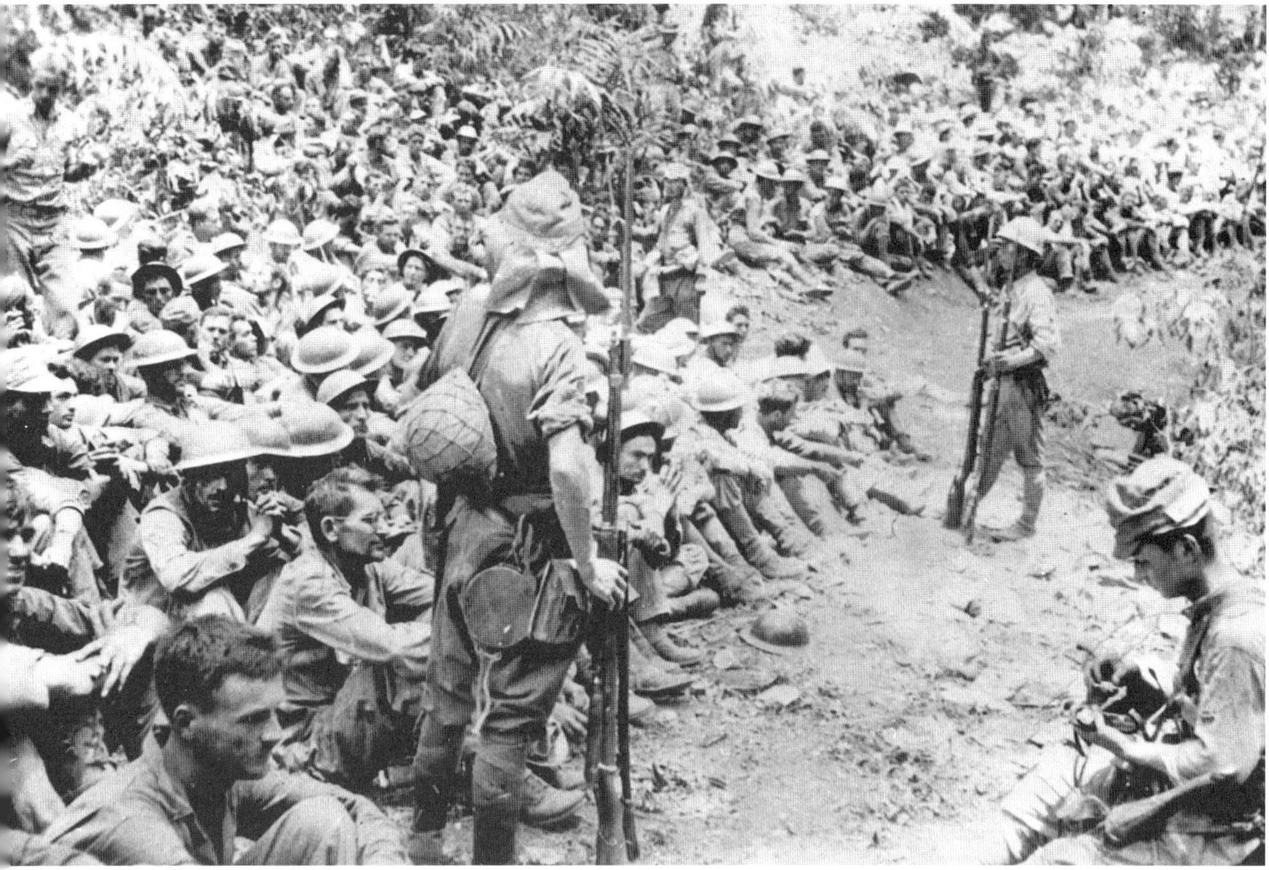

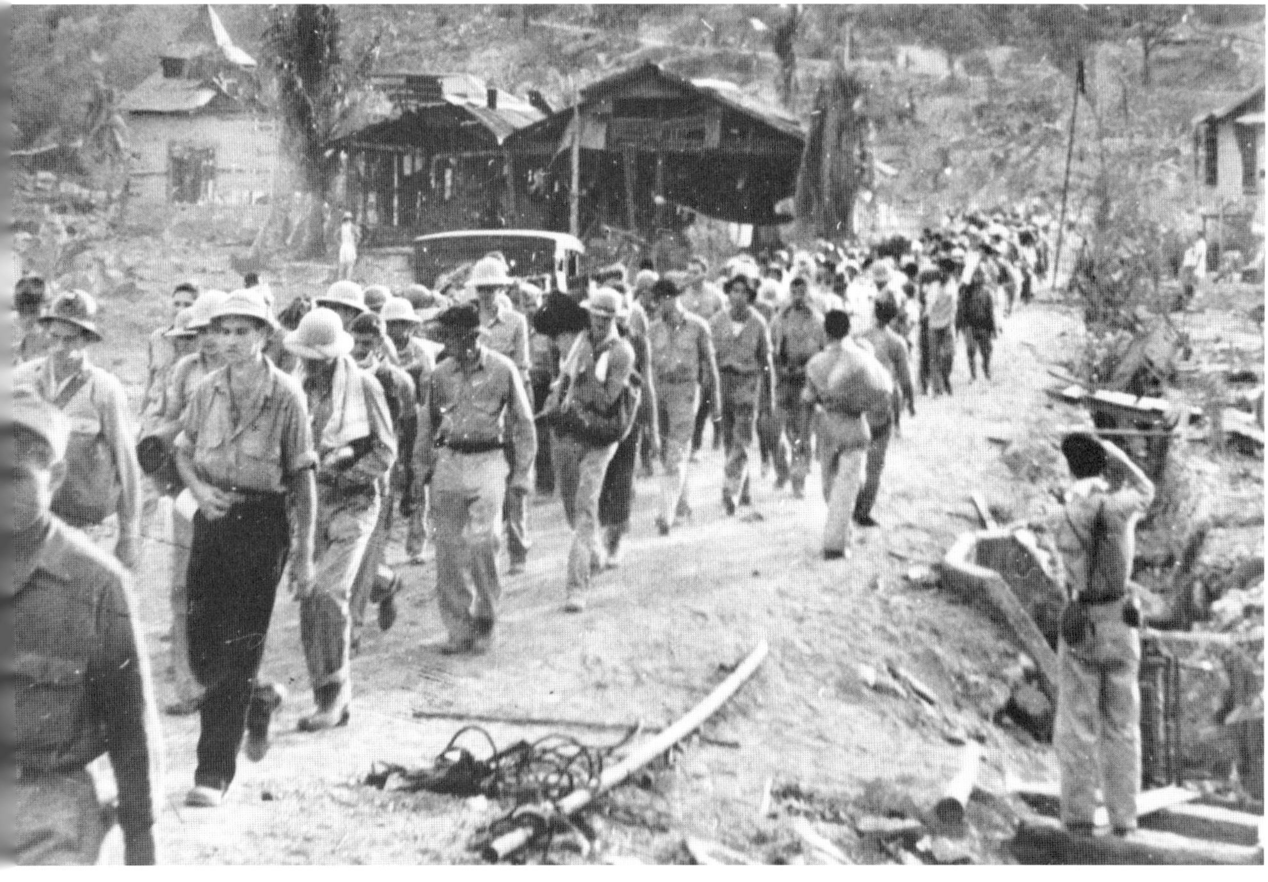

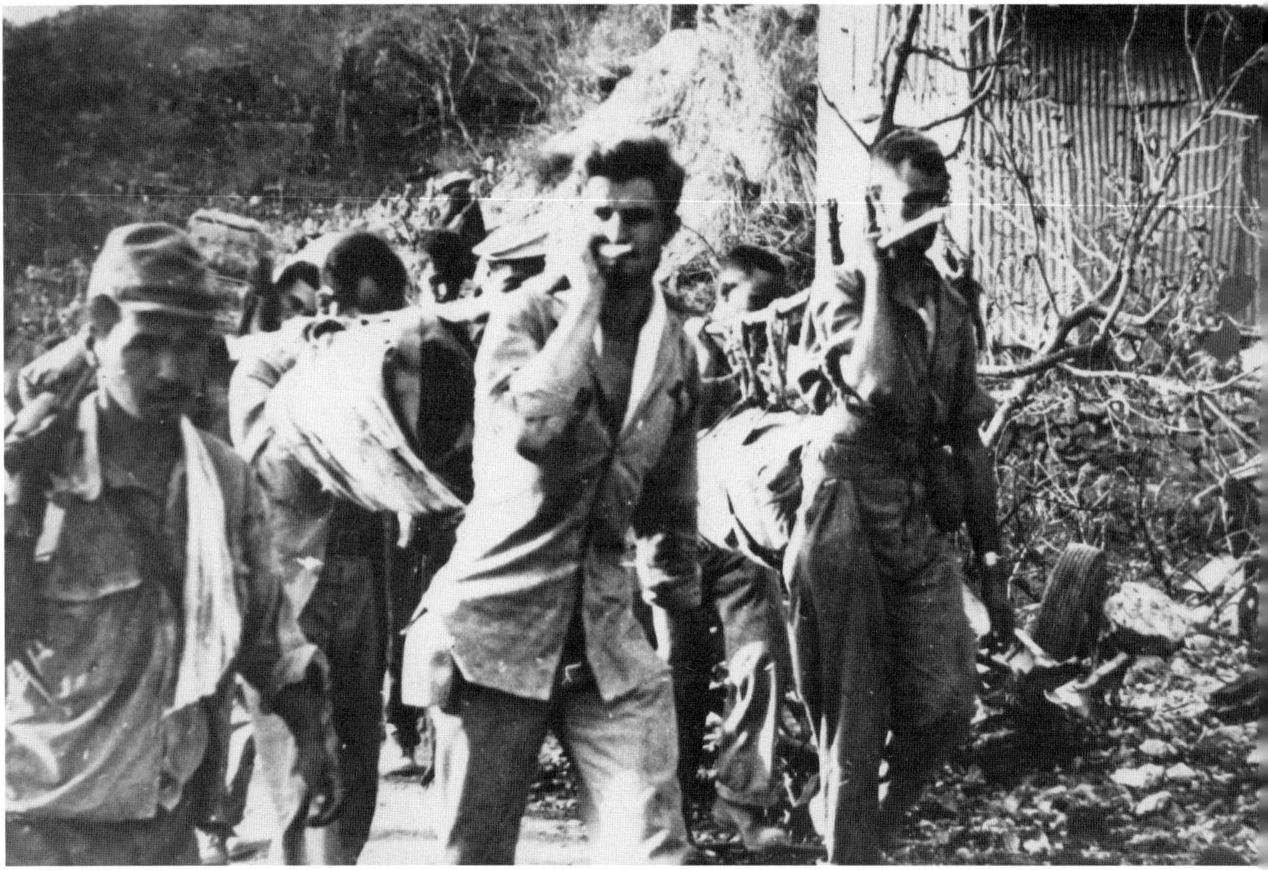

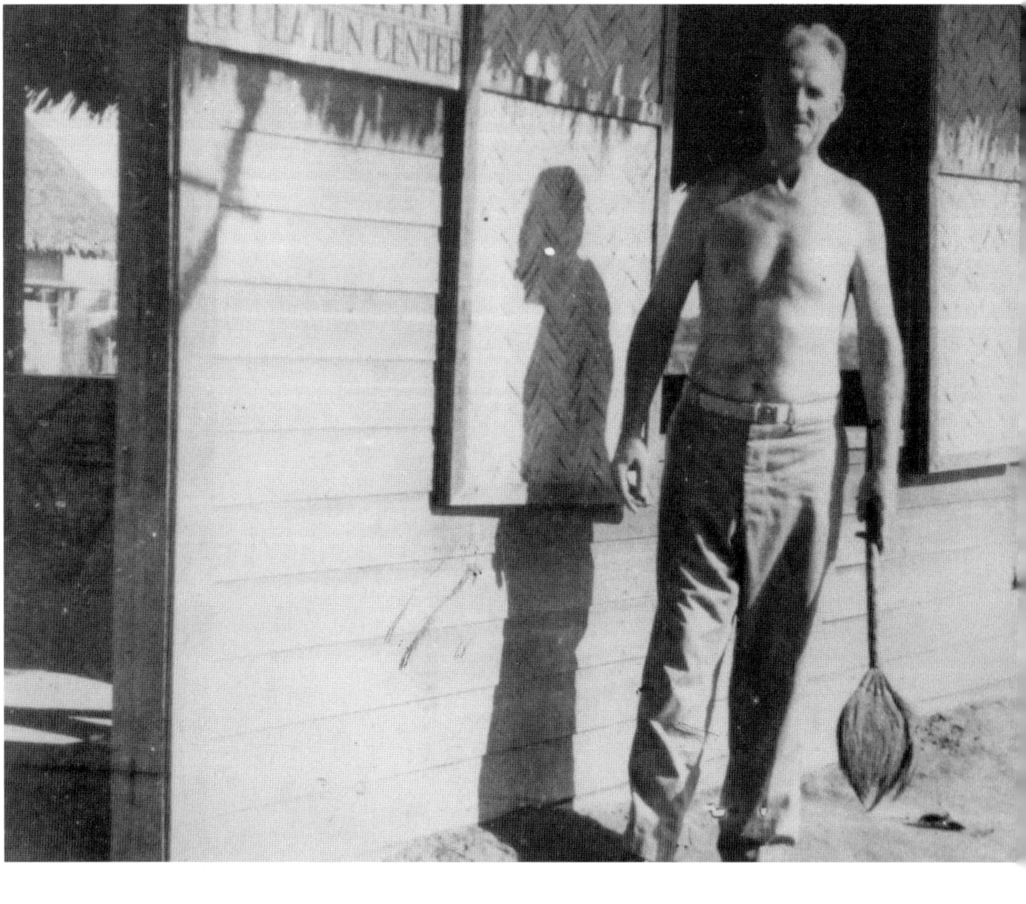

An IJA 14th Army officer is shown here reviewing a map of Corregidor Island during the assault planning phase in early May 1942. The island had been under tremendous artillery bombardment from Bataan, now in Japanese hands, and from aerial assault. *(Author's collection)*

(**Opposite, above**) At Camp O'Donnell, an American burial party is shown here carrying US soldiers for burial just outside the stockade's main gate north of the road to Capas. A Japanese soldier accompanies them in 1942. The first exhausted Filipino and American PoWs arrived at Camp O'Donnell on 11 April 1942 and the last on 4 June. The deadliest period for the Americans was the end of May 1942 with more than fifty prisoners dying daily. More than 1,500 American PoWs were recorded as dying at Camp O'Donnell, while an estimated 20,000 Filipinos perished. By the end of June, most of the American PoWs were sent to other stockades scattered around the Philippines such as at Cabanatuan, and ultimately to Japan and other countries. Japan closed Camp O'Donnell as a PoW camp on 20 January 1943 with many of the Filipino PoWs being paroled to their home towns as non-combatants. *(NARA)*

(**Opposite, below**) At Luzon's notorious Cabanatuan PoW camp in Nueva Ecija Province, US Navy Chaplain D.L. Quinn is shown here standing outside the 'Camp Library Recreation Center' in 1942. At one time the Cabanatuan camp housed as many as 8,000 American PoWs. By January 1945, the PoW population dwindled to about 500 Americans as the Japanese sent able-bodied men to work as forced-labour stevedores and in Home Island coal mines. Quinn was one of the healthier American PoWs that was transited from Cabanatuan to Japan for forced labour. Chaplain Quinn received a posthumous Purple Heart Award. When MacArthur invaded Luzon in January 1945, the Cabanatuan camp still had more than 500 Americans that had been earmarked for execution. *(NARA)*

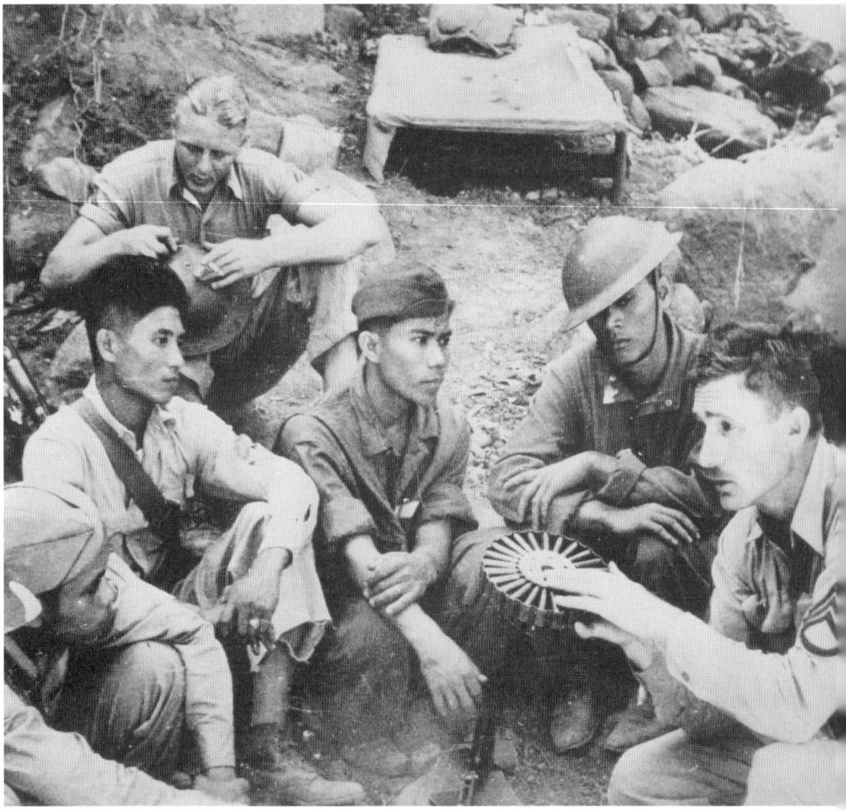

A 4th Marines sergeant that had arrived on Corregidor from Bataan at the end of December 1941 is shown here instructing Filipino soldiers regarding the drum magazine from a Lewis MG of First World War vintage. The 4th Marines were assigned to beach defence and to repel any Japanese amphibious assault; however, the early May 1942 enemy landings quickly overcame the American forces. *(NARA)*

Strung barbed wire at a Corregidor beach did not hinder the Japanese landing forces at all. Marine defensive positions were also quickly overcome, especially given the extensive pre-invasion bombardment of Corregidor's installations. *(NARA)*

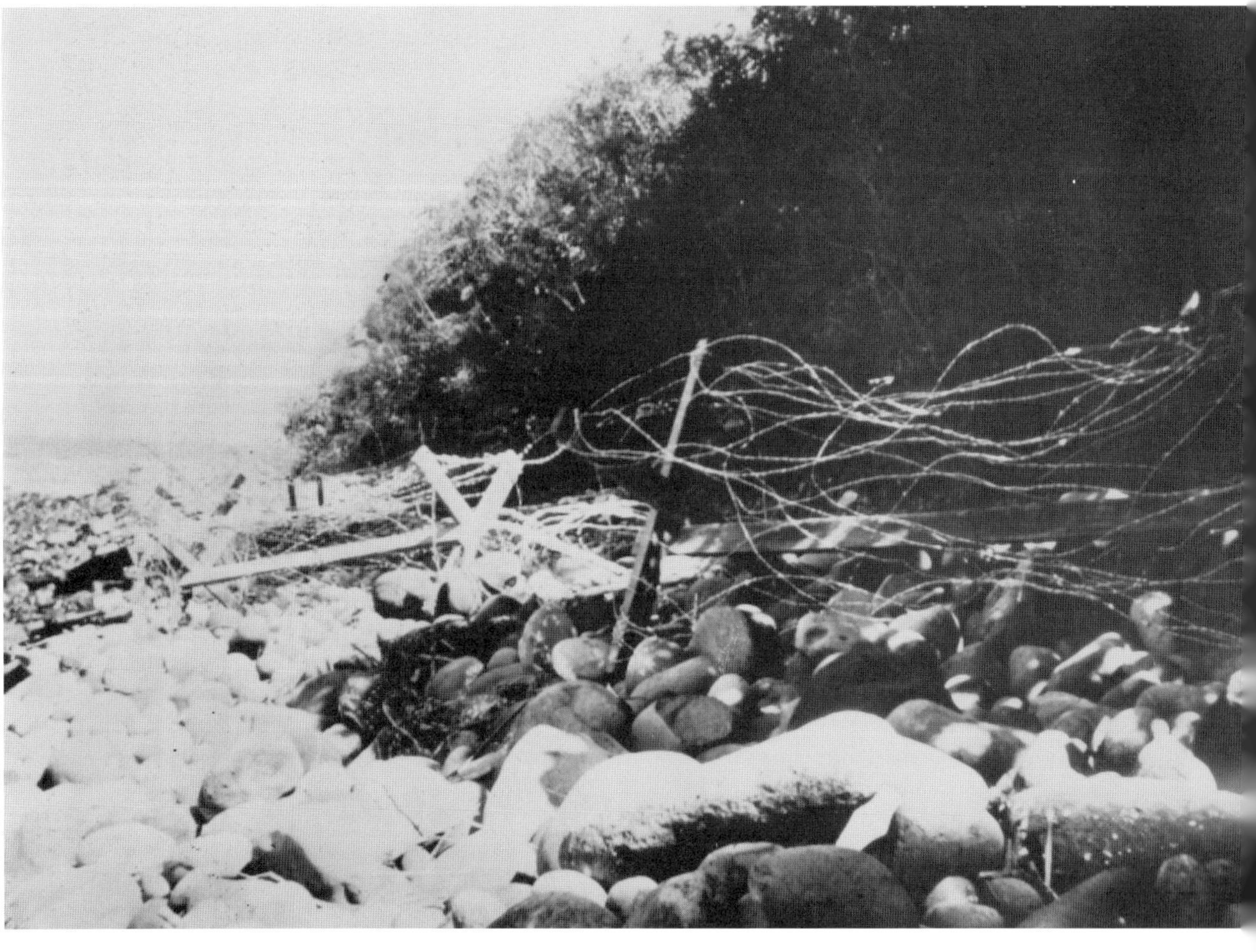

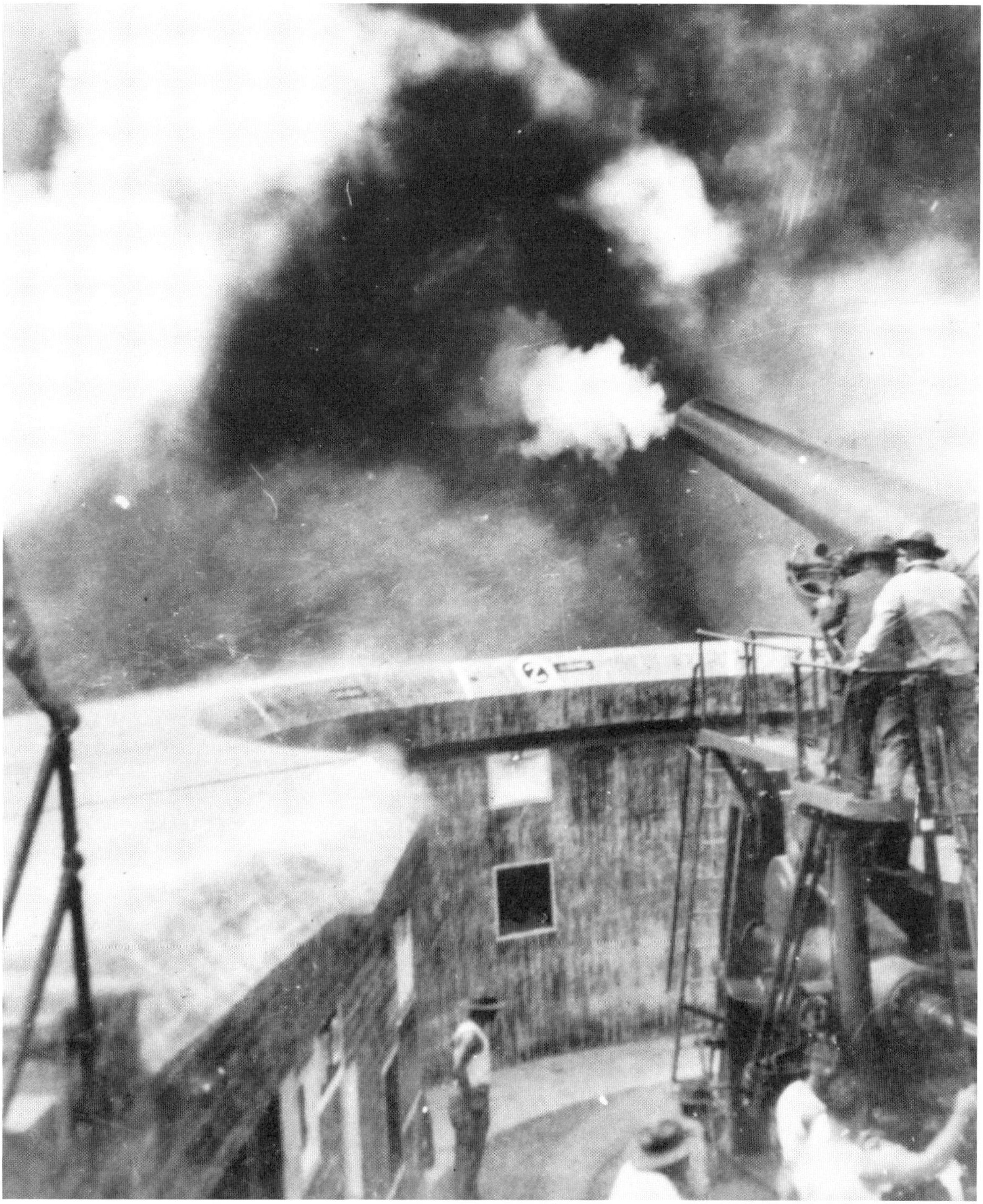

A huge 12in coastal defence gun at the Wheeler Battery is shown here during pre-war target practice. The purpose of these large-calibre weapons was to destroy large enemy ships entering Manila Bay. Although some small Japanese landing craft were destroyed by Corregidor's coastal guns during the early May 1942 invasion, these weapons were not used for their intended purpose. *(NARA)*

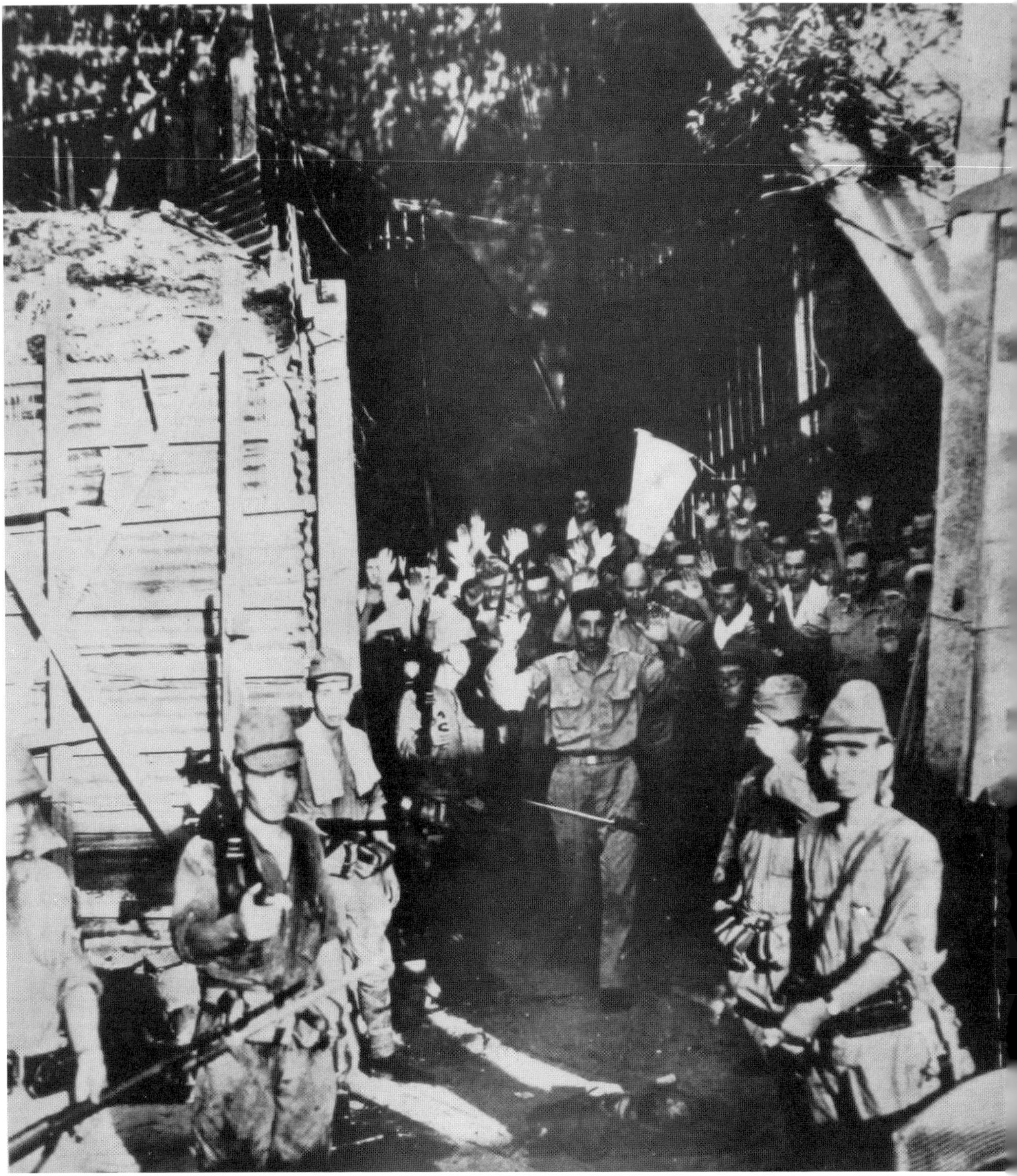

American and Filipino soldiers emerge from the Malinta Tunnel to surrender to the enemy on 6 May 1942. The tunnel was a warren of Allied activity, serving as a headquarters and a bomb-proof storage area, along with a 1,000-bed hospital and communication area. This surrender marked the nadir of American combat misfortune in the Pacific and heralded the Japanese high-water mark of their blitzkrieg. *(NARA)*

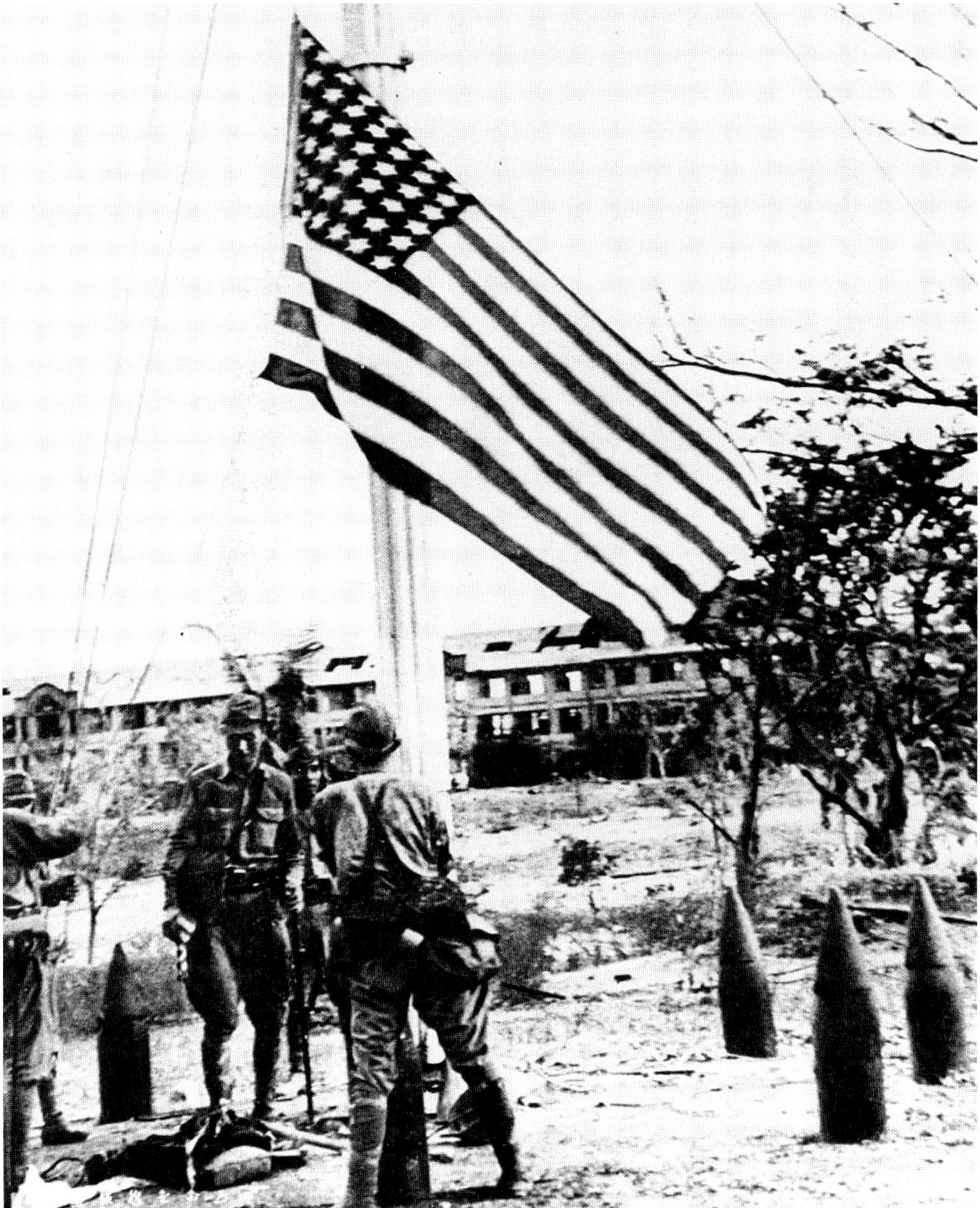

Japanese troops are shown here hauling down the 'Stars and Strips' in front of the Fort Mills barracks on Corregidor on 6 May 1942. The island fortress, which was constructed to withstand a naval assault with its heavy artillery and mortar batteries, was antiquated with regard to enemy air superiority and artillery on Mariveles and at Cavite pounding the garrison into submission. *(Author's collection)*

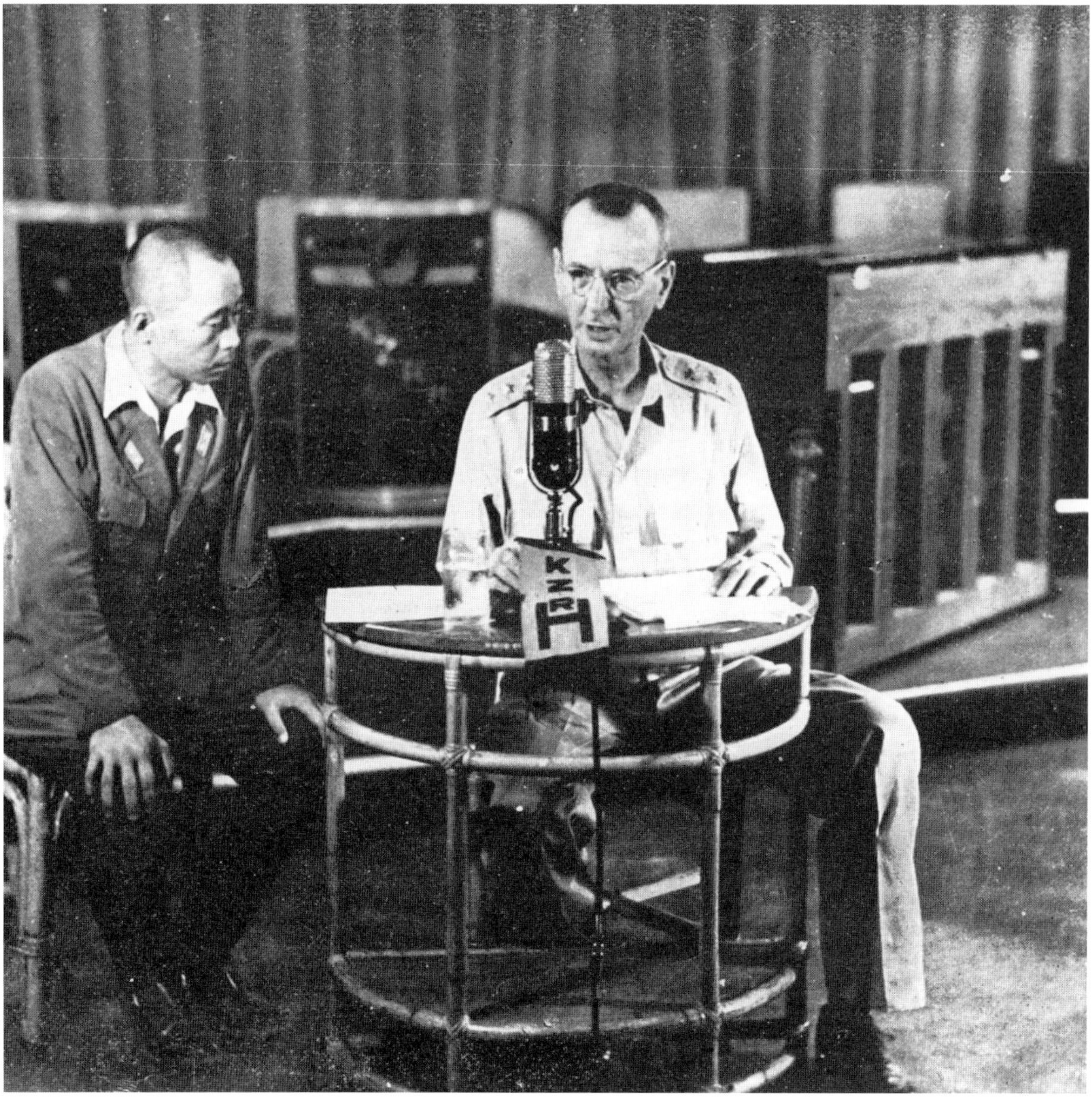
KZRH

Lieutenant General Jonathan Wainwright, commander of USAFFE after MacArthur's departure for Australia, is shown here broadcasting his surrender to all Philippine garrisons with a Japanese officer at his side. About 120 senior American officers including Wainwright were taken to a camp near Tarlac City after their surrender at Corregidor on 6 May 1942. He was transferred to PoW camps on Taiwan and then Manchuria, where he was liberated by Soviet troops on 16 August 1945. On his return to the United States after the September surrender ceremony aboard the USS *Missouri*, Wainwright received his fourth star and the rank of general. *(NARA)*

Chapter Two

Terrain, Weaponry and Fortifications

The Philippine Archipelago, approximately 1,000 miles from north to south, comprises some 7,000 islands with only 1,000 of them inhabited. The archipelago is divided into three main groups: Luzon and the northern islands; the Visayan Islands, principally Samar, Leyte, Panay, Negros, Cebu and Bicol in the centre; and Mindanao and the Sulu Archipelago to the south (see Map 4).

The Filipinos (pre-war population 16 million) are quite heterogeneous, speaking more than seventy dialects among eight different languages. The vast majority of the Filipinos are Christians, with a substantial Muslim minority living towards the south on Mindanao and in the Sulu archipelago.

Terrain of Leyte

Leyte, the eighth largest Philippine island of 2,800 square miles (115 miles in length and 15–45 miles in width), is situated in the north-eastern Visayan group. Its capital city Tacloban with its strategic airfield was less than 300 miles south of Manila. Leyte was a logical entry point for MacArthur's invasion forces to secure a base for future operations to the north as well as hasten control of the remaining islands in the Visayan group (see Map 5).

Topographically, due to Leyte's volcanic origin, the island's spine comprises a range of mountains with the southern portion of the island almost entirely mountainous and possessing limited military importance. However, two prominent valleys, Leyte and Ormoc, were important military targets that needed to be seized by Lieutenant General Walter Kruger's Sixth Army. A heavily-forested central mountain range separated the island's eastern and western coasts.

Leyte Valley's broad plain is situated along the north-eastern part of the island extending from Leyte Gulf and San Pedro Bay (the latter a northern extension of the former) to the east to Carigara Bay along its northern coast. Militarily, Leyte Valley possessed the island's main road network. Because of seasonal monsoons, July through to September was the best period for an amphibious invasion. Ormoc Valley, about 5 miles wide, extended 15 miles north from Ormoc Bay. Ormoc Valley was

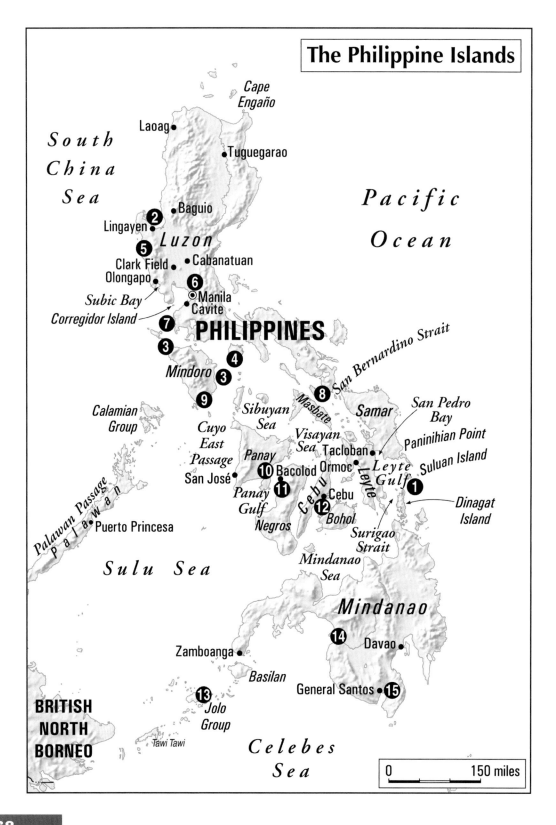

The Philippine Islands

South China Sea

Pacific Ocean

Cape Engaño

Laoag

Tuguegarao

Baguio

2 Lingayen

Luzon

5

Clark Field • Cabanatuan

Olongapo

6

Subic Bay

⊙ Manila
Cavite

Corregidor Island

7

PHILIPPINES

3

4

Mindoro **3**

San Bernardino Strait

9

Calamian Group

Sibuyan Sea

Masbate

8

Samar

San Pedro Bay

Cuyo East Passage

Visayan Sea Tacloban

Paninihian Point

Suluan Island

Panay

10 Bacolod

Ormoc

Leyte Gulf

1

San José

11

Cebu Cebu

Dinagat Island

Panay Gulf

12

Negros *Bohol*

Palawan Passage

Palawan

Puerto Princesa

Surigao Strait

Sulu Sea

Mindanao Sea

Mindanao

14 Davao

Zamboanga

Basilan

BRITISH NORTH BORNEO

13

Jolo Group

General Santos • **15**

Tawi Tawi

Celebes Sea

| 0 | 150 miles |

Map 4: The Philippine Islands' Liberation, 1944–45. (1) Leyte's amphibious invasion began as the US Sixth Army's X and XXIV Corps landed on 20 October 1944 to seize the island's vital Japanese airfields (e.g. Tacloban) defended by the IJA 16th Division. On 17 October, 6th Ranger Battalion units took Dinagat Island. After the beachheads were secure, the massive naval clashes comprising the overall Battle of Leyte Gulf ensued 23–26 October. **(2)** The US Sixth Army's Luzon invasion commenced at Lingayen Gulf on 9 January 1945 as XIV and I Corps amphibiously landed. Other Sixth Army units came ashore on 10–11 January, including the 6th Ranger Battalion, which liberated the Cabanatuan PoW camp on 30–31 January, freeing 512 imprisoned Americans. **(3)** Mindoro Island was amphibiously assaulted with brigade-sized units on 15 December 1944 and 1 January 1945 to capture airfields to enable SWPA Air Forces to bomb Luzon before that island's invasion. Another brigade-sized invasion occurred from elements of the US 24th Division on 21 March 1945. Mindoro's capture severed Yamashita's Luzon forces from IJA garrisons in the southern Philippines. **(4)** An American brigade-sized invasion of Marinduque, a small island between southern Luzon and eastern Mindoro, was conducted to secure more proximate American airfields for the Luzon campaign. **(5)** The US Eighth Army's XI Corps' invasion of Luzon's west coast north of Olongapo, situated north-west of the Bataan Peninsula and west of Clark Field, began on 29 January 1945. Objectives included Olongapo and Subic Bay, a former US naval base, which would open the Bataan Peninsula's west coast for shipping and logistical support as well as prevent IJA forces from retreating into the peninsula. **(6)** The Battle for Manila raged from 3 February to 3 March 1945. Yamashita ordered the bulk of his IJA forces to abandon the city; however, the IJN's Manila Naval Defence Force mounted a suicidal defence of the capital, resulting in thousands of Filipino deaths and the devastation of the 'Pearl of the Orient'. **(7)** The American amphibious and airborne invasion of Corregidor Island in Manila Bay was conducted on 16 February 1945. The American paratroop assault included elements of the 503rd PIR from air bases on Mindoro. The 3rd Battalion of the US 34th IR made its amphibious assault from Mariveles on the now-captured Bataan Peninsula. **(8)** A small-scale American invasion of Masbate by units of the 40th Division from Leyte occurred on 7 April 1945, although much of the island was controlled by Filipino guerrillas. This was the last island in the Visayan Passages that was liberated. **(9)** The southern tip of Mindoro Island was assaulted by elements of the US 24th Infantry Division on 25 March 1945. Four days earlier, other elements of the 24th Division landed at Mindoro's northern tip near Calapan. **(10)** The US Eighth Army's 40th Infantry Division landed on Panay Island on 18 March 1945 as part of Victor I to liberate the Visayas Islands group. The Japanese outposts in Iloilo City on the southern coast of Panay Island were overcome within two days. **(11)** As part of Victor I on 29 March 1945, other 40th Division units amphibiously assaulted Bacolod City on Negros Island's north-west corner with the coast plain captured by 2 April. On 9 April, all three 40th Division's IRs pushed east into Negros' mountainous interior against strong IJA defences. By 4 June, the Japanese had withdrawn further into the mountains. The 40th Division required eight weeks to overcome the enemy's final defences. **(12**) The Americal Division assaulted Cebu Island, Bohol and the south-eastern tip of Negros Island on 26 March 1945 as part of the Eighth Army's Victor II on 26 March 1945 as two IRs landed to Cebu City's west and east. The next day, American forces moved into an almost-destroyed Cebu City. The Japanese had 15,000 troops on Cebu, although more than 8,000 Filipino guerrillas isolated 2,000 IJA soldiers in northern Cebu. **(13)** Jolo Island was invaded on 9 April 1945 during Victor IV by units of the 41st Infantry Division with Filipino guerrilla assistance. Stiff Japanese resistance was encountered through 22 April with more than 2,000 Japanese killed. Prior to that, other 41st Infantry Division units invaded other Sulu Archipelago islands, which stretched from Mindanao's Zamboanga Peninsula to northern Borneo. Zamboanga City was assaulted by a 41st Infantry Division IR on 10 March, but it was opposed by a rigid Japanese defensive line, which finally broke on 23 March with more than 6,000 Japanese troops killed. Basilan Island and Tawi-Tawi were assaulted on 16 March and easily captured. **(14)** As part of the Eighth Army's X Corps' Victor V operation, Mindanao's west coast was invaded on 17 April 1945 by the US 24th Infantry Division, which quickly headed inland. On 22 April, the US 31st Division landed as well. The 24th Division was ordered to seize Davao, with the 31st attacking up the north of the island. On 3 May, units of the 24th Division entered a heavily-destroyed Davao, the last major Philippine city under Japanese control. **(15)** On 12 July 1945, the 24th Division's 21st IR arrived at the north-west shore of Sarangani Bay. Japanese forces retreated into General Santos City, where they made a last stand that continued until mid-August when organized enemy resistance on Mindanao ceased. (*Meridian Mapping*)

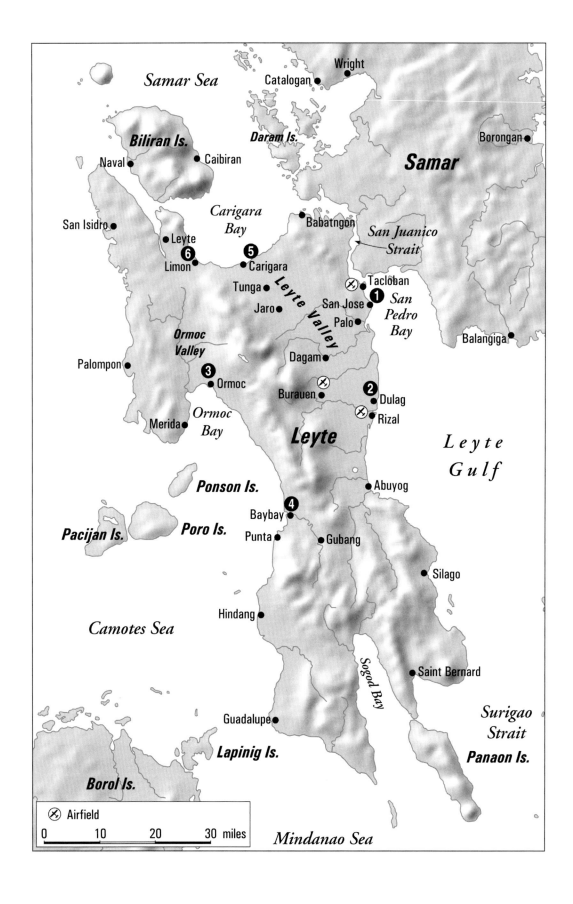

Samar Sea

Wright

Catalogan

Borongan

Daram Is.

Samar

Biliran Is.

Naval

Caibiran

Carigara
Bay

Babatngon

San Juanico
Strait

San Isidro

Leyte

⑥

Limon

⑤

Carigara

Tunga

Jaro

Leyte Valley

⊗ Tacloban

① San
Pedro
Bay

San Jose

Palo

Balangiga

Dagam

Ormoc
Valley

Palompon

③ Ormoc

⊗

Burauen

② Dulag

⊗

Rizal

Leyte Gulf

Merida

Ormoc
Bay

Leyte

Ponson Is.

Abuyog

Baybay ④

Pacijan Is.

Poro Is.

Punta

Gubang

Silago

Hindang

Camotes Sea

Sogod Bay

Saint Bernard

Surigao
Strait

Guadalupe

Lapinig Is.

Panaon Is.

Borol Is.

⊗ Airfield

0   10   20   30 miles

Mindanao Sea

wedged in between the central mountain range and the hill mass of the north-west coast of Leyte. The northern part of Ormoc Valley was separated from Carigara Bay by a narrow neck of the central spine of the island's ridges, which was to be heavily contested. Almost all of Ormoc Valley's southern part was cultivated land, forest or scrub growth.

Ormoc Bay on Leyte's western coast had good landing beaches, which the Japanese took advantage of in their reinforcing amphibious movements of late October–early November 1944, but was crossed by many streams, creeks and small rivers. Carigara Bay at the northern end of Leyte possessed shallow waters, but inland swamps and mountainous terrain negated it as an amphibious assault site. Leyte Gulf and San Pedro Bay on the island's eastern coast possessed good sandy beaches; however, the presence of only one parallel road adjacent to the shoreline made beach exiting problematic, which was compounded by inland rice paddies and swamps. Nonetheless, Leyte Gulf was the best anchorage in the Visayan group of islands, being approachable through only two major entrances: Surigao Strait to the south-west and San Bernadino Strait to the north-west.

San Juanico Strait, which separates Leyte from Samar to the north, connected Carigara and San Pedro Bays. Tacloban, lying at the head of San Pedro Bay, is the largest city and provincial capital on Leyte. Other important towns included Carigara on the northern coast and the ports of Ormoc and Baybay on Leyte's west coast. The locales of Palo and Abuyog are situated on the east coast.

Leyte has two coastal road nets: one southern and the other northern. The northern road net was designed to move vegetation and produce from the northern

Map 5: Sixth Army Invasion and Conquest of Leyte, 20 October to 25 December 1944. (1) X Corps' 24th Infantry and 1st Cavalry divisions invaded Leyte on 20 October 1944 near San Jose in San Pedro Bay. The 24th Division moved on Palo's highway junction leading into the Leyte Valley, while the 1st Cavalry Division seized Tacloban Airfield near the San Juanico Strait's entry into San Pedro Bay. **(2)** XXIV Corps' 7th and 96th Infantry Divisions landed on 20 October near Dulag The 7th Division was to seize Dulag Airfield, between Dulag and Rizal, and then capture other inland airfields at San Pablo, Bayug and Buri before moving on Burauen. **(3)** Luzon-departing Japanese troop convoys reinforce the IJA 35th Army through Ormoc from 23 October to 1 November amid devastating American aerial interdiction. The IJA troops that disembarked at Ormoc moved north towards Carigara Bay to bolster a defensive line from Jaro to Limon to contest the US Sixth Army's units' westward movement. **(4)** US 7th Division units arrived at Baybay on the island's west coast on 2 November after traversing Leyte's 'waist', beginning at Abuyog on 29 October. **(5)** US 24th Division forces arrived at Carigara on 2 November after westward movement along Carigara Bay against IJA forces moving north through the Leyte Valley. **(6)** The two X Corps' divisions, the 24th Infantry and 1st Cavalry, moved west from Carigara to combat IJA forces along a series of heavily-defended hill masses, 'Breakneck Ridge', during early November. The US 32nd Division relieved the battered 24th on 18 November. On 22 November, the 32nd Division captured Limon, enabling Sixth Army forces to control Breakneck Ridge. (*Meridian Mapping*)

interior areas to Tacloban, located on the Cataisan Peninsula. The southern network was poorly maintained. There was a winding trail that connected Baybay and Abuyog. Another winding trail meandered from Baybay to Ormoc and then through the Ormoc Valley to Carigara.

There was a principal Japanese airstrip at Tacloban. The Japanese constructed another airfield at Dulag, 2 miles to the west of that coastal locale. Three other small airstrips – Buri, Bayug and San Pablo – were situated near Burauen, located 5 miles west of Dulag. Another small enemy airfield was located at Valencia in the Ormoc Valley, 8 miles north of the port of Ormoc.

From a topographical/military perspective, control of the Leyte and Ormoc Valleys along with their ridges and mountains was a prerequisite for conquering the island. To accomplish this, the high ground near Palo had to be captured. The control of Ormoc Valley and Ormoc Bay was dependent on seizing the lowlands near the port of Ormoc and the hills above it to the east.

During the combat on Leyte, there were three typhoons and an earthquake. Extensive rainfall negated the early US Sixth Army capture of Leyte's airfields at a time when MacArthur's commanders needed land-based air support. The Japanese, having firm airfields on some surrounding islands in the Visayan group, were able to mount attacks against American targets. However, Halsey's Task Force 34 carriers remained offshore for an additional month, otherwise the Japanese would have had aerial superiority during the US Sixth Army's heavy ground combat period.

Luzon's Terrain as a Military Determinant

Lieutenant General Yamashita, commander of the IJA 14th Area Army, planned a protracted delaying action on Luzon. Defending the entire island was not feasible as he needed good natural defensive terrain as a force multiplier and food-producing areas for his troops. Yamashita abandoned any notion of defending Luzon's Central Plain or the Manila Bay area. Instead, he divided his Luzon forces into three groups and placed each in a mountainous area (see Map 6).

The mountainous region to the north-east and east of Lingayen Gulf were the strongest and strategically most important sectors and included the highly-cultivated area of the Cagayan Valley, which supplied most of Luzon's crops after the Central Plain. Yamashita personally defended this northern Luzon sector with the *Shobu* Group (see Chapter 3 for details), which had its 14th Area Army HQ at Baguio, the Philippines summer capital, with an elevation of 5,000ft above sea level and 25 miles north-east of San Fabian on Lingayen Gulf. The *Shobu* Group's defensive zone had its boundaries shaped as an isosceles triangle. The triangle's south-western anchor was Baguio with the baseline extending 35 miles eastward to Bambang situated on Route 5 north of the mountain pass exits from the Cagayan Valley. The apex of the triangle was Bontoc at the junction of Routes 4 and 11, 50 miles north-east of Baguio.

Yamashita's next defensive zone was the Zambales Mountains to the west of Luzon's Central Plain. This position overlooked Clark Field and Fort Stotsenburg. The *Kembu* Group (see Chapter 3 for details) was responsible for delaying American air forces from using Clark Field and also threatening the US Sixth Army's right flank as it moved south from Lingayen Gulf.

The third major Luzon defensive locale was to be defended by the *Shimbu* Group (see Chapter 3 for details). Although this Japanese force was to defend southern Luzon, it was principally situated in the mountains east and north-east of Manila. The *Shimbu* Group commander, Lieutenant General Shizuo Yokoyama, was under strict orders from Yamashita not to defend the capital city of Manila. In this defensive zone, the Japanese would still be in control of Manila's dams and reservoirs. Yamashita also stationed miscellaneous troop formations, under *Shimbu* Group control, in the Bicol Peninsula of south-eastern Luzon.

Fortifications and Weapons
Japanese Airfields
Lieutenant General George Kenney pointed out to MacArthur that until Japanese airfields on Leyte at Tacloban, Dulag, San Pablo, Buri, Bayug and Valencia were captured by US X and XXIV Corps troops, the Americans would be fighting 500 miles beyond the range of their land-based fighter cover.

Kamikaze *Planes and Suicide Boats*
The IJA Fourth Air Army, based in Manila, was responsible for the Philippines air defence prior to the Leyte invasion of 20 October 1944. This formation had received air reinforcements from Manchuria's Second Air Army as well as from southern Asian aerodromes. However, IJN Vice Admiral Takehiko Onishi, the First Air Fleet commander, first formed a *kamikaze* Special Attack Corps, which was launched against Vice Admiral Kinkaid's US Seventh Fleet in Leyte Gulf on 21 October. Initial sorties flown by the IJA 201st Fighter Attack Group were largely unsuccessful against the American fleet; however, they became more effective with time, hitting four USN carriers.

Much of the bulk of the IJA and IJN air strength based on Luzon had been destroyed in support of the US invasion of Mindoro in December 1944 to January 1945, leaving fewer than 150 Japanese aircraft. The Japanese did not mount a large-scale air effort on Luzon as the air defences of the Ryukyu Islands, Formosa and the Home Islands were augmented. Thus, *kamikaze* attacks were unleashed on the US Seventh Fleet on 2–9 January 1945 as it was approaching its destination of Lingayen Gulf and inflicted considerable damage on the US Fleet by 5 January including carrier escorts, heavy cruisers, destroyers and transports. This was in addition to December 1944 *kamikaze* attacks against Mindoro-bound convoys, which sank twenty-four

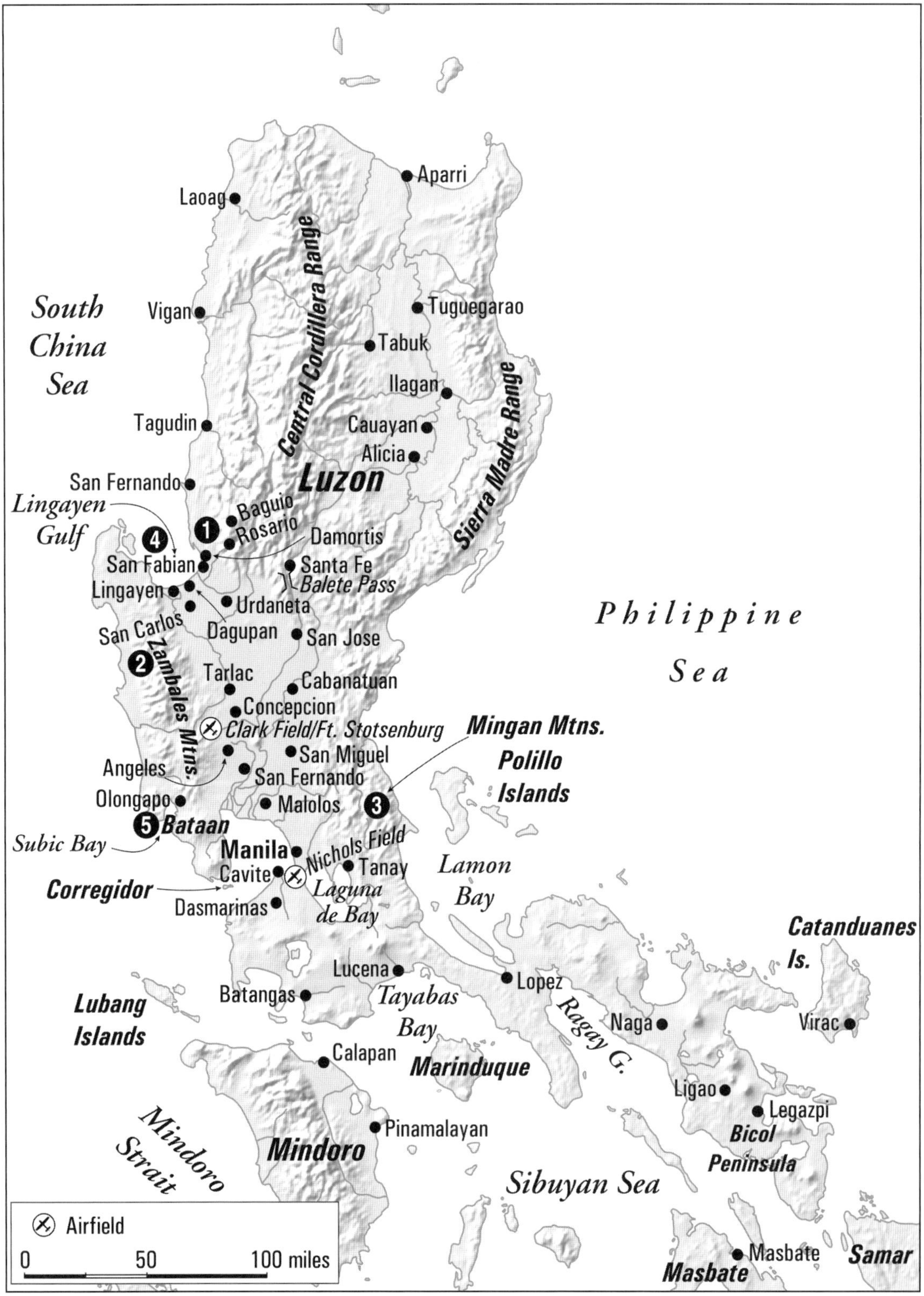
South China Sea
Laoag
Aparri
Central Cordillera Range
Vigan
Tuguegarao
Tabuk
Ilagan
Sierra Madre Range
Tagudin
Cauayan
Alicia
San Fernando
Luzon
Lingayen Gulf
1
Baguio
Rosario
4
Damortis
San Fabian
Santa Fe
Balete Pass
Lingayen
Urdaneta
Dagupan
San Carlos
San Jose
Zambales Mtns.
2
Tarlac
Cabanatuan
Concepcion
Clark Field/Ft. Stotsenburg
Mingan Mtns.
San Miguel
Angeles
San Fernando
Polillo Islands
Olongapo
Malolos
3
5 Bataan
Subic Bay
Manila
Nichols Field
Cavite
Tanay
Lamon Bay
Corregidor
Laguna de Bay
Dasmarinas
Philippine Sea
Catanduanes Is.
Lucena
Lopez
Batangas
Tayabas Bay
Ragay G.
Lubang Islands
Naga
Virac
Calapan
Marinduque
Ligao
Legazpi
Mindoro Strait
Pinamalayan
Bicol Peninsula
Mindoro
Sibuyan Sea
Airfield
0 50 100 miles
Masbate
Masbate
Samar

American ships and damaged sixty-seven others with more than 1,200 Allied seamen killed and another 1,800 wounded in action.

Many IJA suicide boats were stationed at various points along the south-western and southern coasts of Luzon. Ultimately the crews of these suicide boats were to fight as infantry under *Shimbu* Group control.

On Leyte, Lieutenant General Shiro Makino's IJA 16th Division, which had been involved in Bataan's 1942 capture, was concentrated at Dulag, a US Sixth Army landing zone. Since April 1944, Makino had constructed three defensive positions on the island. The first one was on Leyte's east coast near Dulag. The second was between Dulag and Leyte Valley, with mountainous storage depots at Jaro. A third one was in Leyte Valley near Dagami.

Japanese Armour

Lieutenant General Sōsaku Suzuki's IJA 35th Army, headquartered on Cebu in the Visayan Islands, comprised the 16th, 102nd, 30th and 100th divisions. The IJA 16th Division had as part of its strength the 7th Independent Tank Company. This Japanese tank company was part of the Southern Leyte Defence Force and opposed the US 7th Division of the 6th Army's XXIV Corps in a piecemeal fashion as the Americans moved to quickly seize the airfield at Dulag as well as other nearby inland airfields at Buri, Bayug and San Pablo in the vicinity of Burauen.

Map 6: Luzon Invasion and its Conquest, 9 January to 2 September 1945. (see Chapter Five for details of the campaign) **(1)** Yamashita's personally-commanded *Shobu* Group (150,000 troops) was situated throughout all of northern Luzon with headquarters at Baguio at the southern end of the Central Cordillera Range. The *Shobu* group comprised the IJA 10th, 19th, 23rd and 103rd Divisions, and the 58th IMB and elements of the 2nd Tank Division. **(2)** Lieutenant General Rikichi Tsukada's *Kembu* Group (30,000 troops) from IJA forces including the 39th IR from the IJA 10th Division and the 2nd Mobile IR used the Zambales Mountains to the west of Clark Field and Fort Stotsenburg in western Luzon as a redoubt. **(3)** Lieutenant General Shizuo Yokoyama's *Shimbu* Group (80,000 troops) mainly the IJA 105th and 8th Divisions as well as the notorious 16,000-strong IJN Manila Naval Defence Force. Yokoyama's *Shimbu* Group was to defend southern Luzon from Manila southwards to include the Bicol Peninsula. Their redoubt was in the Mingan Mountains northeast of Manila. **(4)** The US Sixth Army's XIV Corps' amphibious landing in Lingayen Gulf on 9 January 1945. The US 40th and 37th Divisions' IRs landed opposite Lingayen at the western side of the gulf. Troops of the 40th Division easily captured Lingayen, while 37th Division units approached Dagupan and then moved further inland. US I Corps' 6th and 43rd Divisions landed opposite San Fabian at the eastern end of Lingayen Gulf. Heavy Japanese resistance was met in the Ilocos Mountains to the east of the gulf. In all, 68,000 US troops landed early on 9 January, which figure was to soon exceed 200,000. **(5)** The US Eighth Army's XI Corps, comprising the 38th Division reinforced with units from the 24th Division, landed unopposed at San Antonio on Luzon's west coast on 29 January 1945 to seize the San Marcelino airfield for immediate restoration to conduct American air sorties. Then these Eighth Army troops attacked Olongapo and captured the former American naval base at Subic Bay. These actions were also to prevent the *Kembu* Group from entering the Bataan Peninsula to Olongapo's south. (*Meridian Mapping*)

Yamashita had the remainder of the IJA 2nd Tank Division on Luzon. He relocated the division's *Shigemi* Detachment from between Cabanatuan and San Jose to a new position at the road junction town of Urdaneta on Route 3 north of the Cabaruan Hills in order to either counterattack or to defend the Villa Verde Trail, which meandered north and east over rough mountainous terrain to join Route 5 north of the Balete Pass near Santa Fe.

American Naval Forces

The Japanese on Leyte were to be attacked by two huge US fleets: the Third under Admiral William Halsey, and the Seventh under Vice Admiral Thomas Kinkaid. Kinkaid was subordinate to the SWPA commander MacArthur, while Halsey, who led the faster and more powerful fleet, reported to Admiral Nimitz. Kinkaid's fleet, which had furnished the amphibious vessels for MacArthur's 1943–44 New Guinea campaign, had more obsolescent battleships and carrier escorts as opposed to the larger fleet carriers. MacArthur believed that by seizing the Visayan group islands, he was better positioned to liberate Luzon and Manila as well as the remainder of the archipelago.

Northern Luzon's mountainous terrain is demonstrated as the US Sixth Army's 3rd Battalion, 126th IR, 32nd Division descends a hill in the Santa Fe region on 1 June 1945 just north of Balete Pass and east of Baguio. The Japanese had 150,000 troops contesting five US Sixth Army divisions: 6th, 25th, 32nd, 33rd and 37th troops at locales such as the Villa Verde Trail, the Balete Pass and the Cagayan Valley throughout the spring of 1945. *(NARA)*

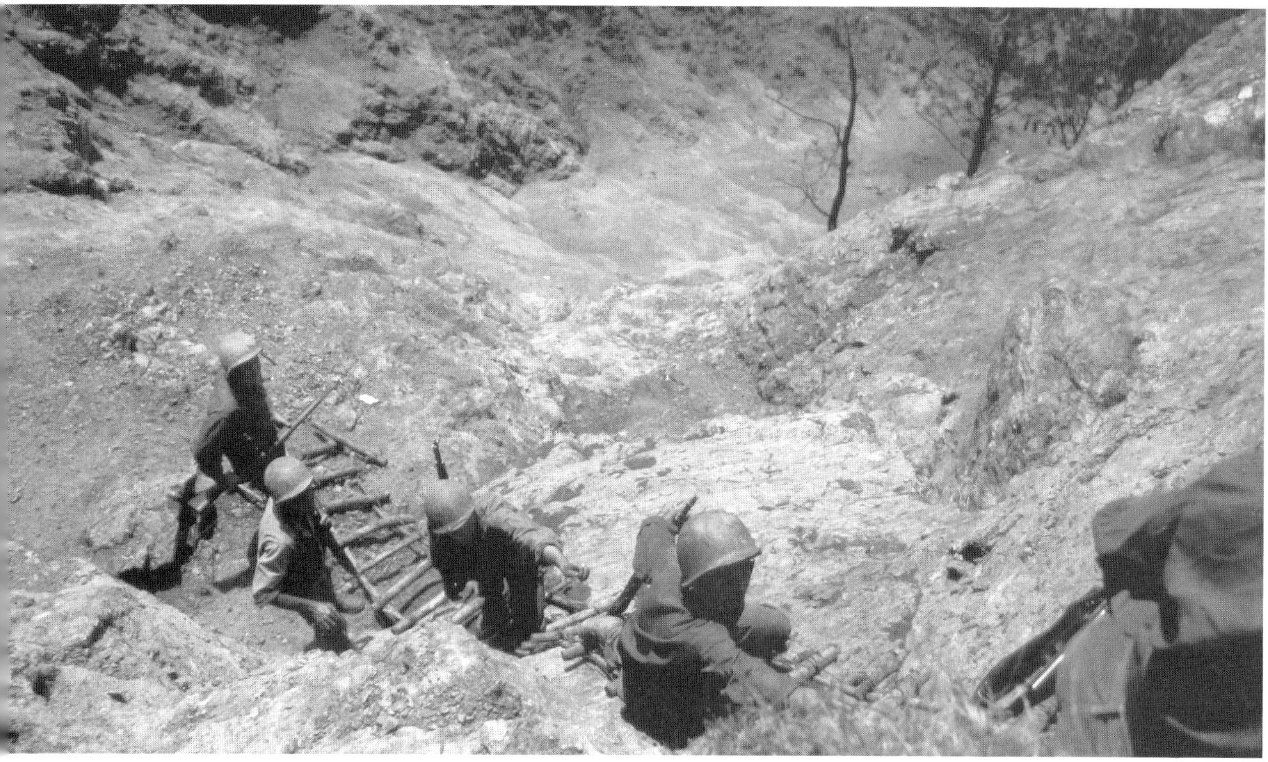

In Northern Luzon's hilly terrain, members of Company C, 1st Battalion, 123rd IR, 33rd Division used a crude ladder to climb a steep cliff onto Cervantes in the western part of the island on 15 June 1945. *(NARA)*

US Eighth Army soldiers of the 1st Battalion, 151th IR, 38th Division (the 'Avengers of Bataan') are shown here viewing Japanese defences atop a ridge on Carabao Island (Fort Frank) in Manila Bay on 16 April 1945. There was almost no resistance as the Japanese had evacuated. In early February 1942, Fort Frank surrendered to the Japanese after its freshwater source was interrupted. *(NARA)*

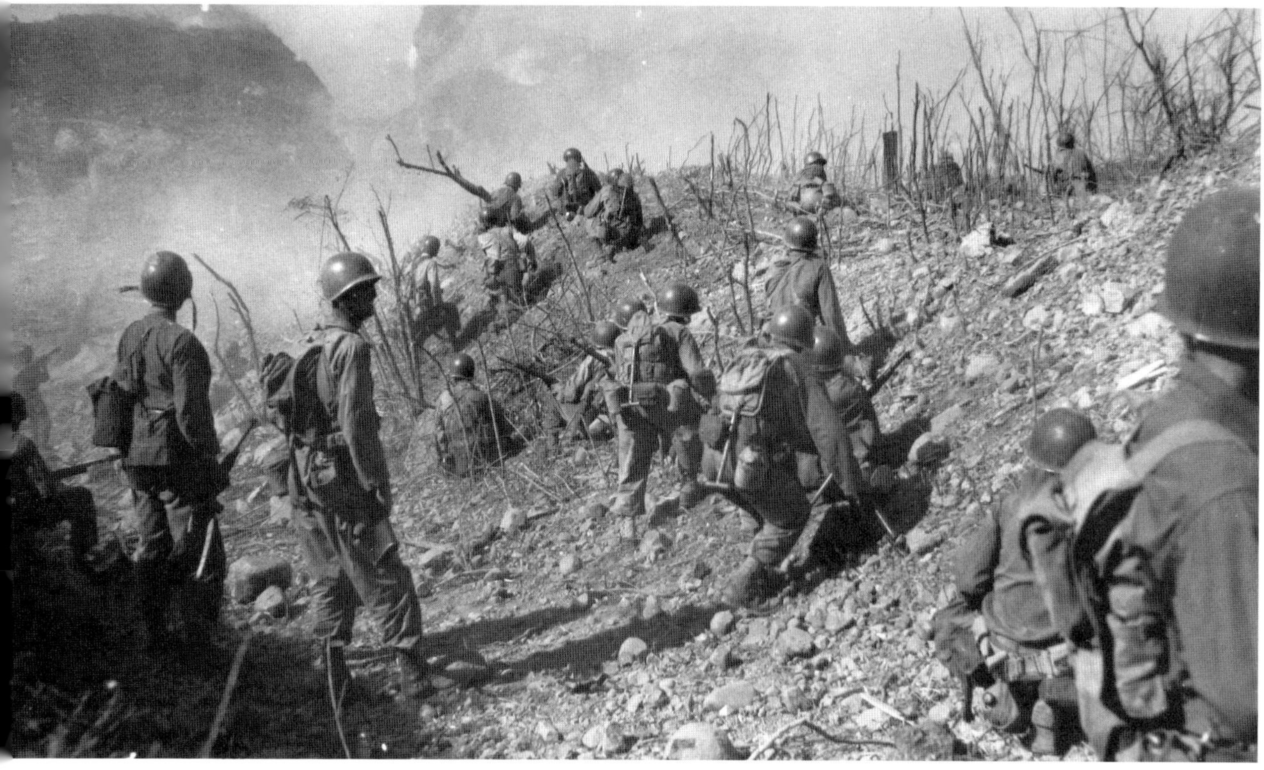

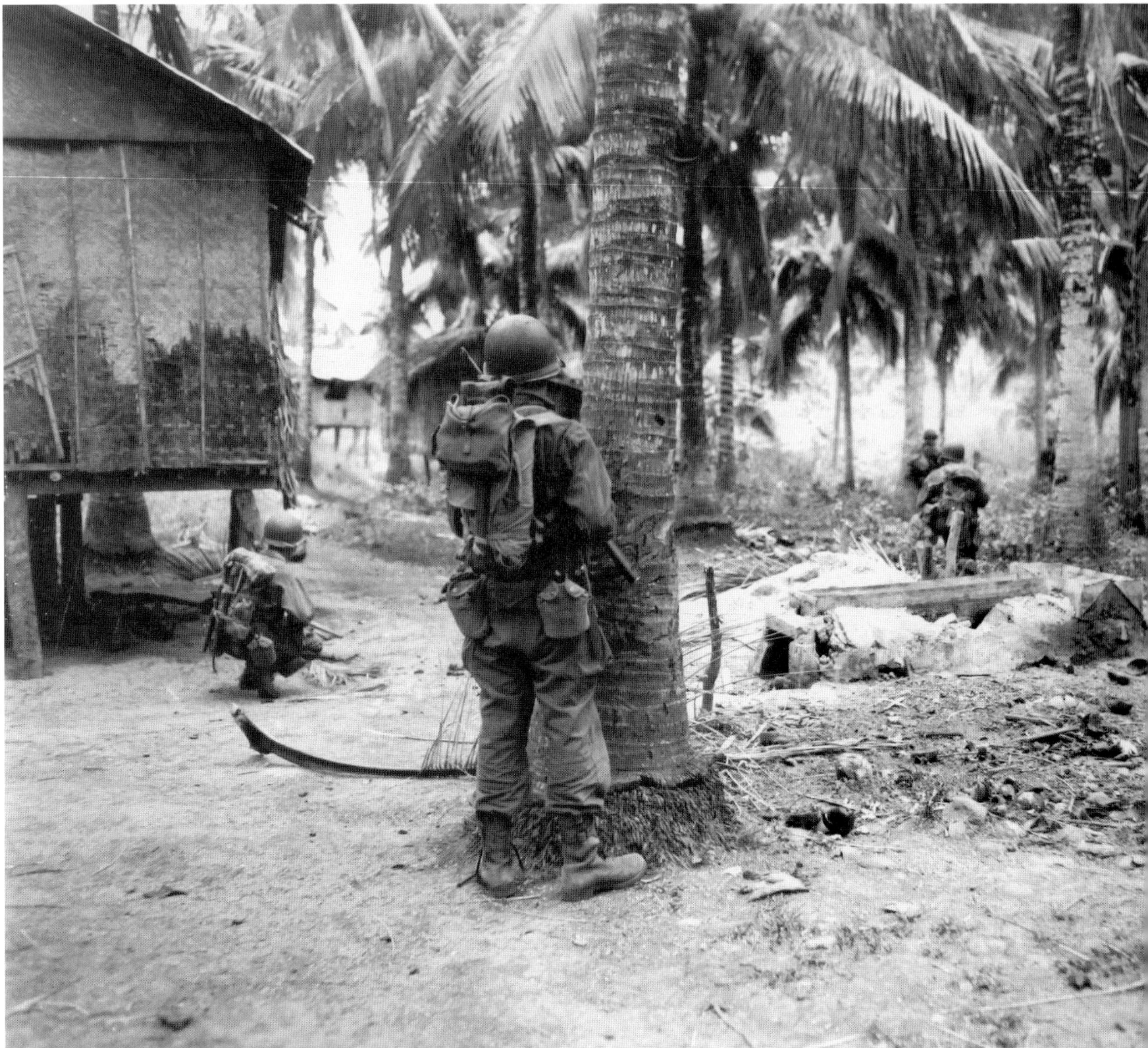

(**Above**) G Troop, 1st Cavalry Division patrol is seen here moving through a Filipino village on the way to Alaminos in Laguna Province on Luzon on 31 March 1945. The village huts were built on stilts with many palm trees making it a potential Japanese sniper or MG position against the advancing US Sixth Army cavalrymen. *(NARA)*

(**Opposite, above**) US Sixth Army soldiers from the 1st Battalion, 161st IR, 25th Division are seen here on 22 March 1945 moving through brush on a hill near the Balete Pass with a dead Japanese soldier (foreground). The Balete Pass was on the highway between San Jose and Santa Fe in Central Luzon's highlands. IJA forces retreated into this mountainous redoubt after the successful Lingayen Gulf invasion of 9 January 1945. *(NARA)*

(**Opposite, below**) US 25th Division soldiers from Company K, 3rd Battalion, 161st IR are shown here firing on the Japanese near San Jose amid dense scrub. From March to May 1945, US Sixth Army divisions fought the northwardly retreating Japanese up Highway 5. Atop the elevated terrain of Mount Imugan, the IJA rained heavy artillery fire on the advancing Americans amid the mountainous terrain towards Santa Fe. *(NARA)*

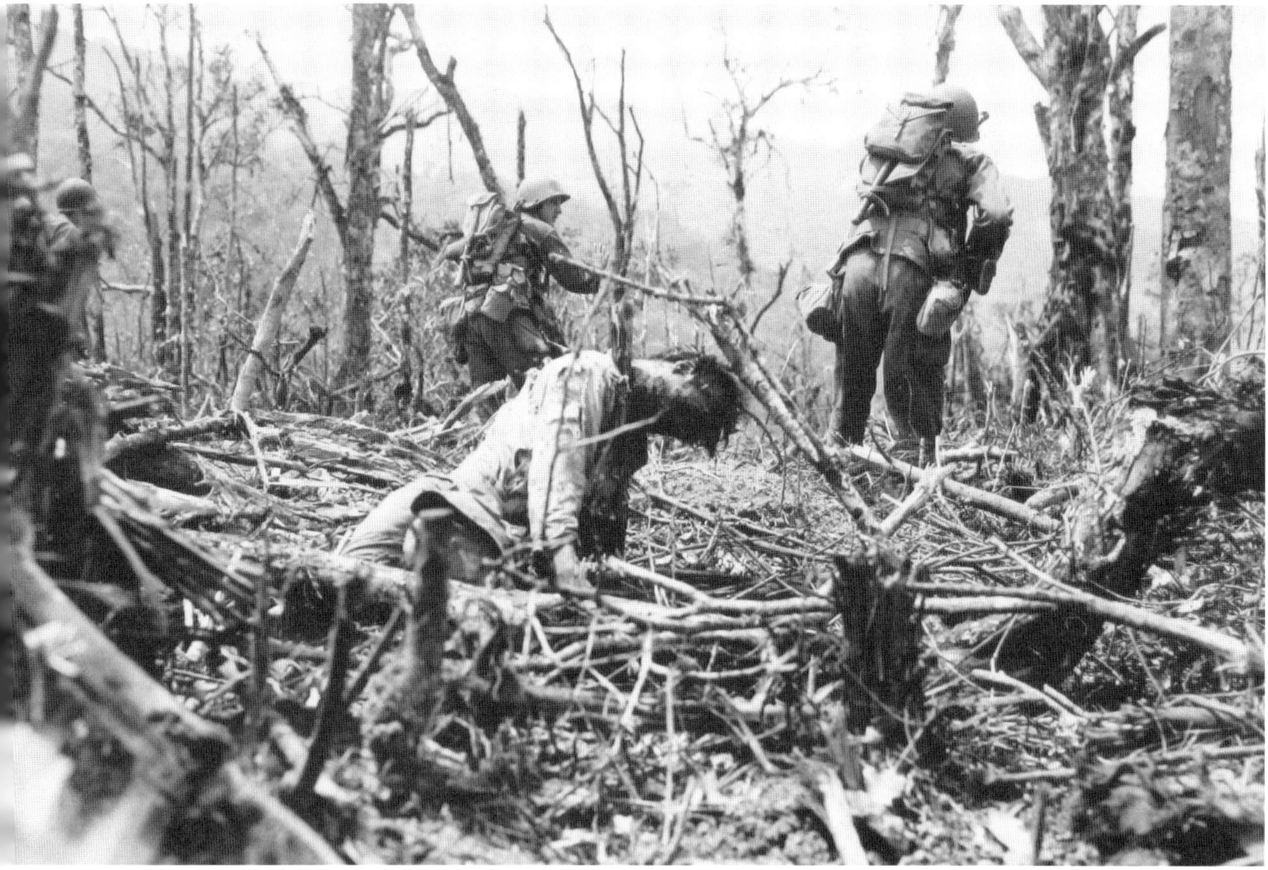

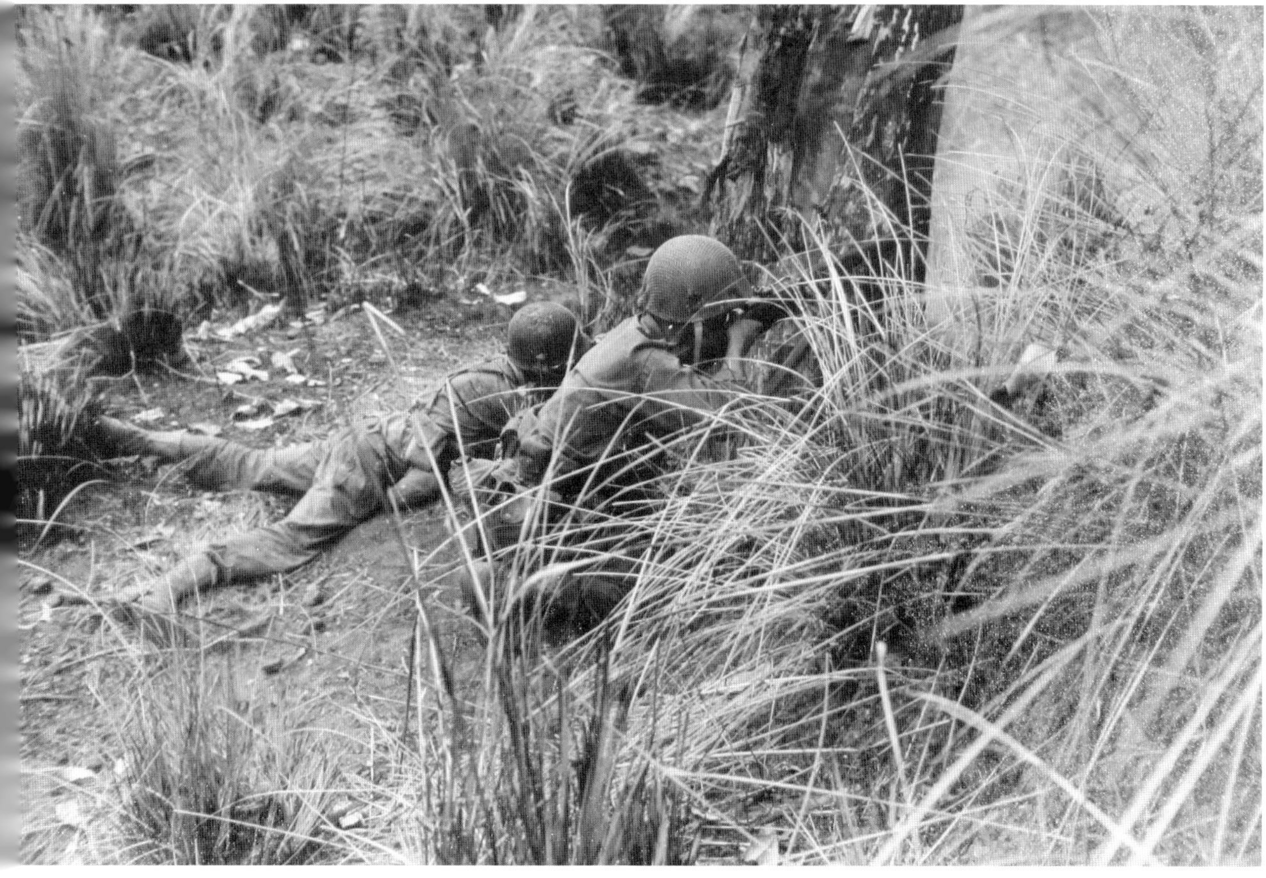

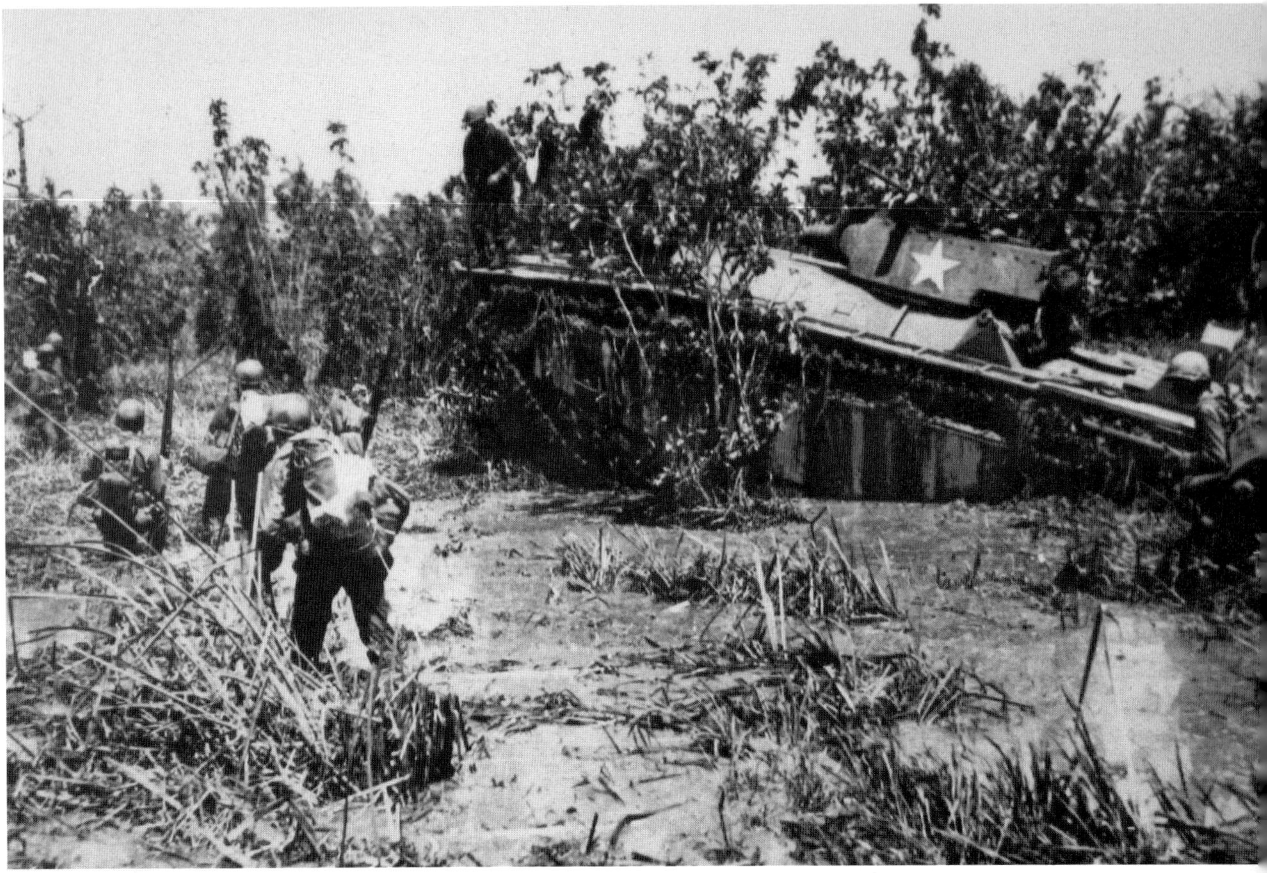

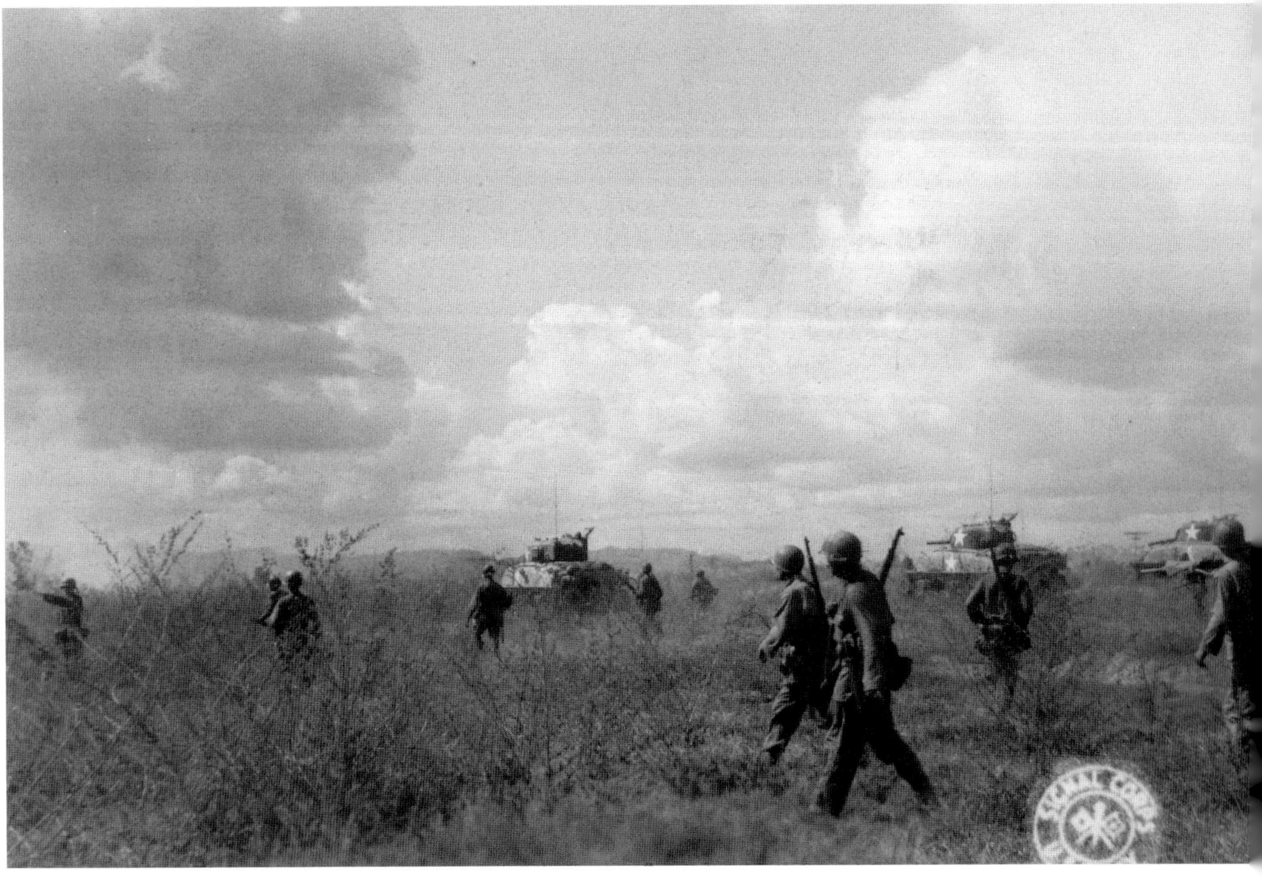
SIGNAL CORPS

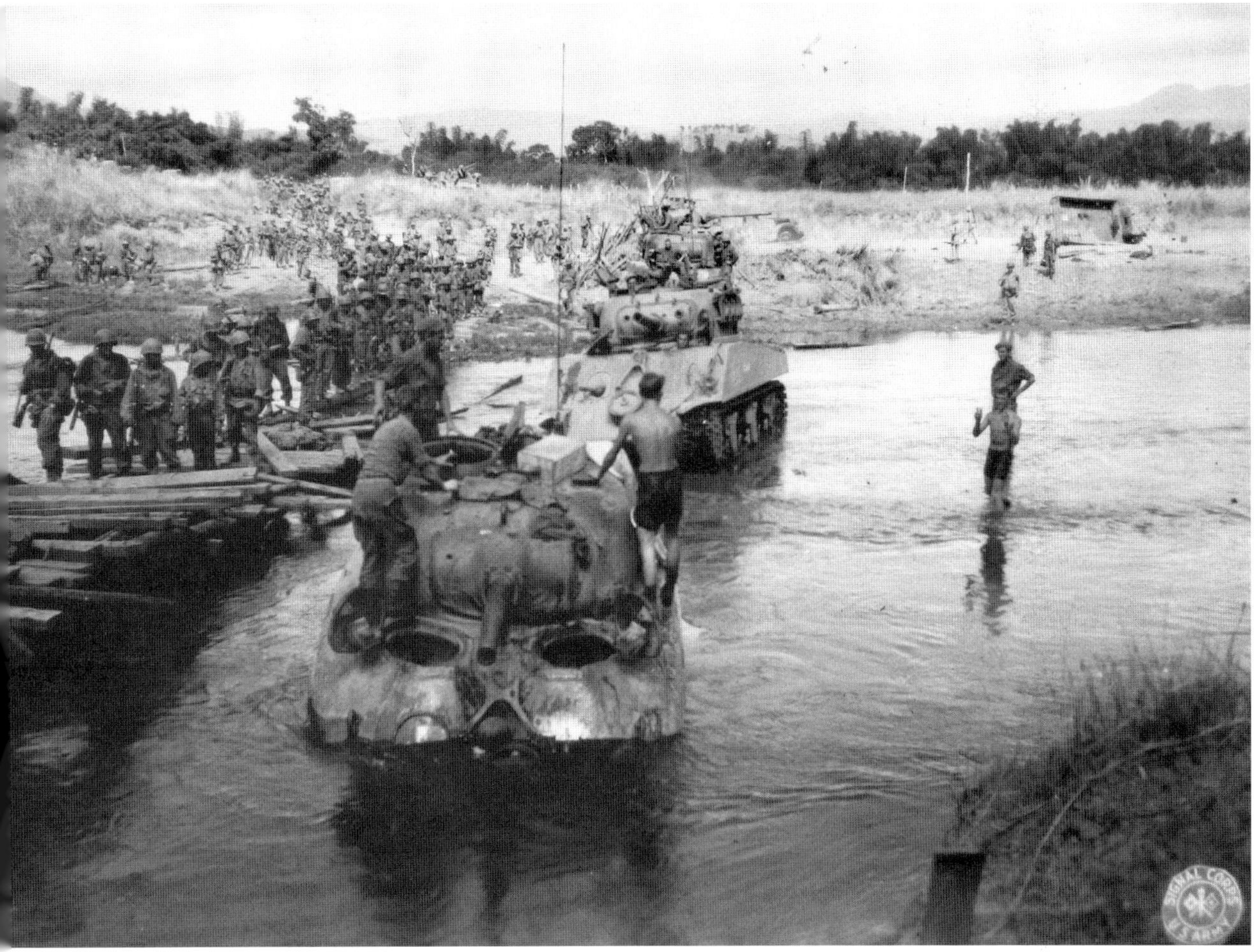

(**Opposite, above**) On Leyte, Sixth Army soldiers are seen here moving in swampy terrain past an LVT (A) with an M8 HMC turret on 3 November 1944. American forces were superior in heavy armour over the IJA. However, Leyte lacked road infrastructure for the Americans' full advantage as jungles, swamps, rivers and mountains also became obstacles to the US Sixth Army's advance, delaying the conquest of this island. *(NARA)*

(**Opposite, below**) The 129th IR, 37th Division is shown here following M4 medium tanks firing canister at Japanese snipers across the flat terrain among Clark Field's runways in Luzon's Central Plain on the island's west coast. Fort Stotsenburg, west of Clark Field, was defended by the *Eguchi* Detachment, a brigade-sized force of the larger *Kembu* Group positioned in the Zambales Mountains north-west of Clark Field during combat from 24 to 31 January 1945. The 40th Division advanced on the 37th's northern flank. The fort was named after Colonel John Stotsenburg, an officer in the Sixth US Cavalry and the First Nebraska Volunteers, who was killed during the Philippine Insurrection in April 1899. Before the Japanese invasion of December 1941, Fort Stotsenburg was garrisoned by the Philippine Division's elite 26th Cavalry and many FA regiments. *(NARA)*

(**Above**) A US M4 medium tank is pulled from a river south of Bambang in Nueva Vizcaya Province in Luzon's mountainous territory well to the north-east of Santa Fe on 6 June 1945. US soldiers crossed the river over an improvised wooden bridge. Just as MacArthur had hoped the many Philippine waterways would delay the 1942 Japanese offensive, American forces in 1945 were often slowed by these terrain features, especially in the IJA's redoubt of northern Luzon. *(NARA)*

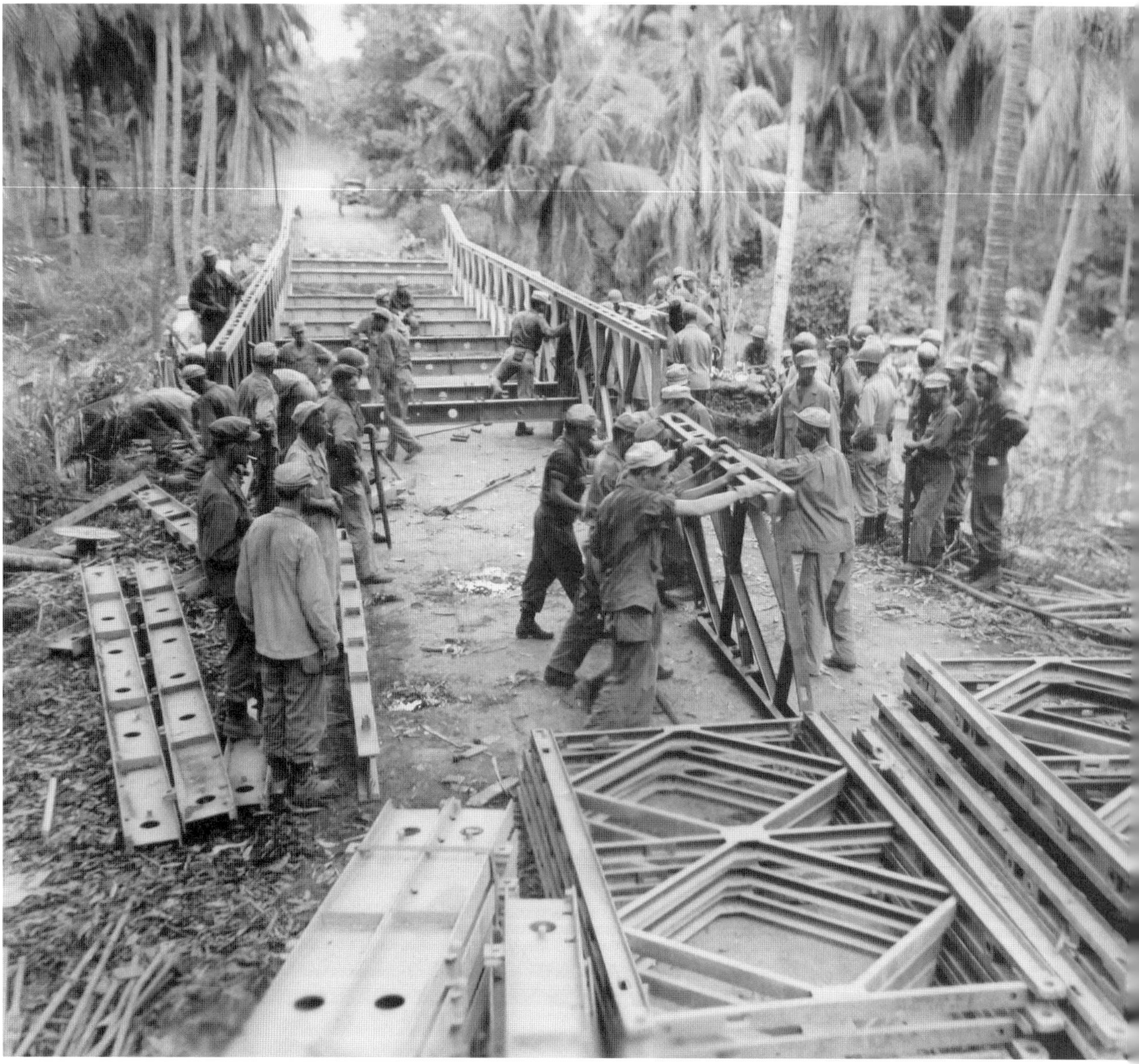

(**Above**) US Army engineers erected a Bailey bridge over a jungle ditch on 3 April 1945. This invaluable temporary structure, devised by Donald Bailey, a civil servant in the British War Office, was a pre-fabricated steel truss bridge transported in 10ft sections. Once sections were assembled with simple tools, wood planking was laid for a road surface. Bailey bridges were able to support a minimum of 20 tons of matériel across a waterway. *(NARA)*

(**Opposite, above**) On Luzon, 37th Division soldiers used a masonry wall and a tree across the road for cover from a Japanese MG that was holding up their advance to Quezon City, 6 miles from Manila, on 4 February 1945. *(NARA)*

(**Opposite, below**) On Leyte, 32nd Division soldiers are shown here entrenched in their 0.30in-calibre M1917 water-cooled MG position camouflaged by vegetation awaiting a Japanese counterattack on 24 November 1944. Surviving elements of the IJA 26th Division started the counterattack with an artillery bombardment that heralded several days of combat, the Battle of 'Shoestring Ridge' near Damulaan on Ormoc Bay on Leyte's western coast. The 32nd Division was relieved on 28 November. *(NARA)*

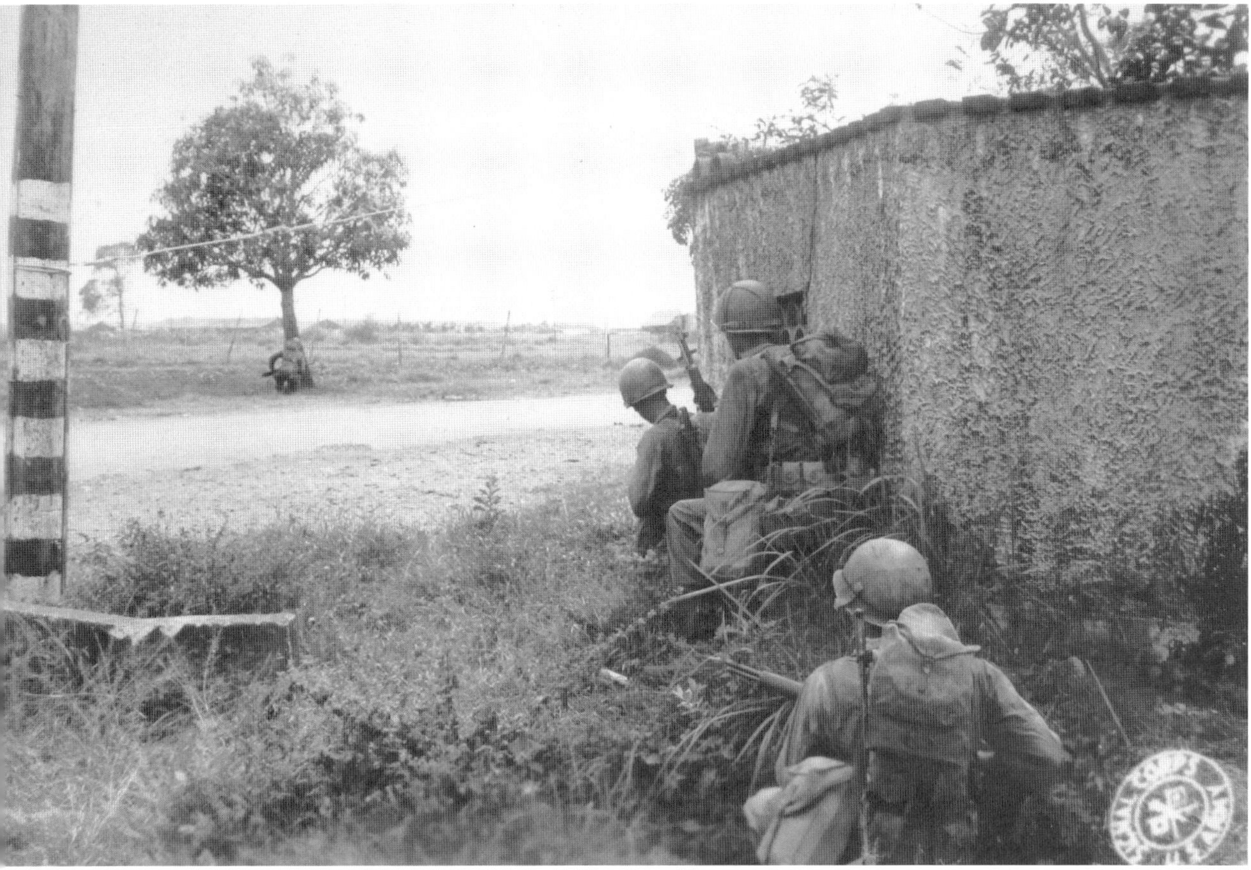

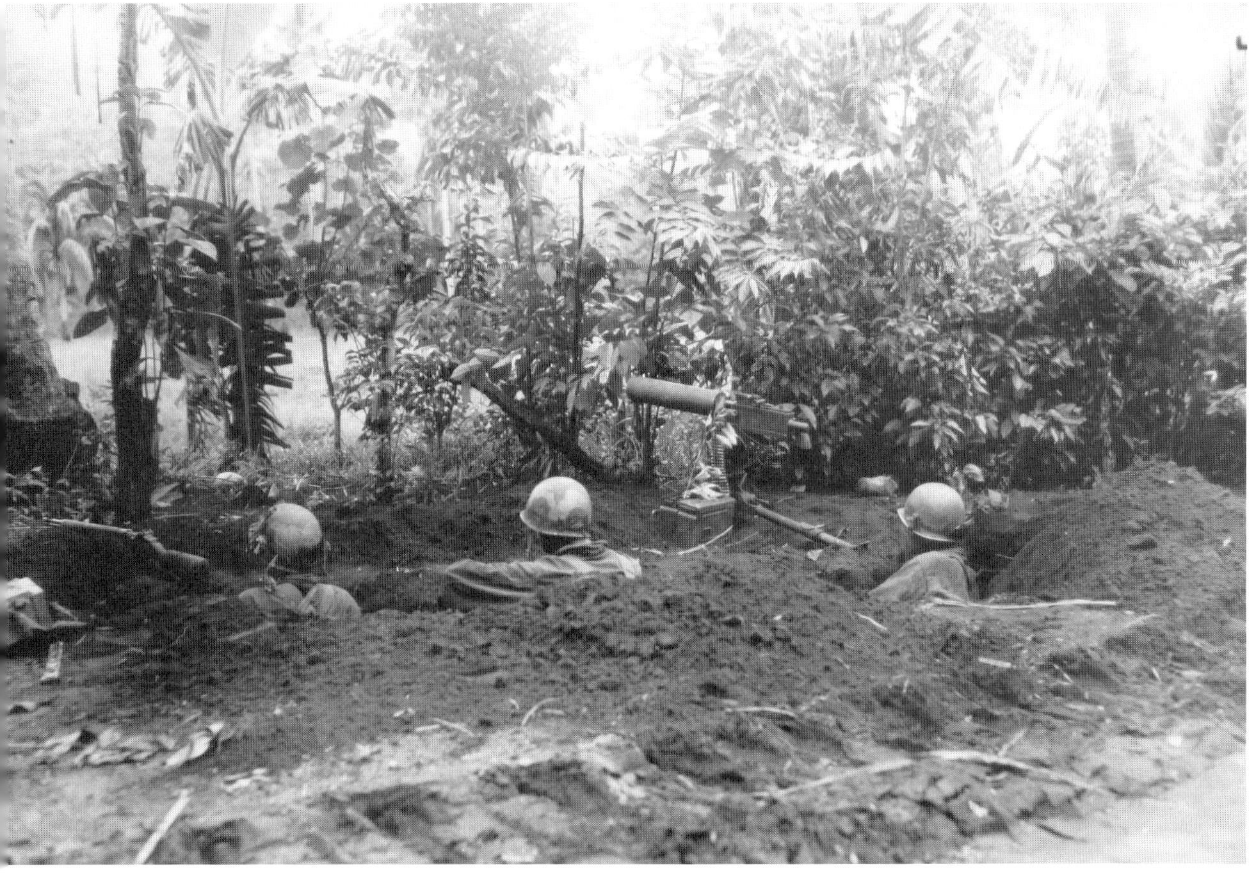

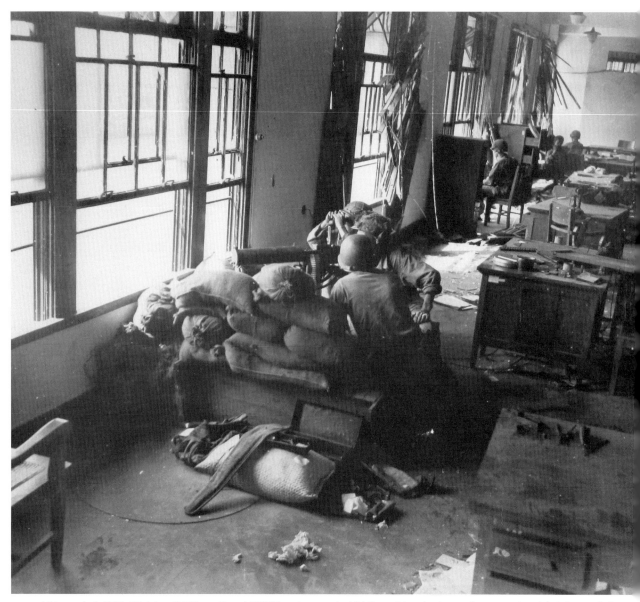

(**Above**) A 37th Division 0.30in-calibre M1917 water-cooled MG position is shown here on the third floor of the Philippines National Bank in Manila across the Pasig River from the *Intramuros* section or Manila's 'Walled City'. Remnants of the brutal IJN Naval Defence Force were holed up there, subjected to American heavy artillery, tank gunfire, MG fire and small-arms firing from sharpshooters of the 37th Division. (*NARA*)

(**Opposite, above**) Two riflemen from the 129th IR, 37th Division are dug in with their M1 Garand 0.30-06 semi-automatic weapons in a Baguio cemetery on 24 April 1945 as Sixth Army divisions moved against Yamashita's *Shobu* Group in northern Luzon's mountainous area near Baguio and east to Bambang. (*NARA*)

(**Opposite, below**) On Leyte, three 7th Division soldiers and a Filipino used a carabao (water buffalo) to haul signals equipment. Two M4 medium tanks are seen (background) with dense vegetation to the side of the mud track (right). Pack animals were useful on such rudimentary trails or when jungle interfered with mechanized vehicles. (*NARA*)

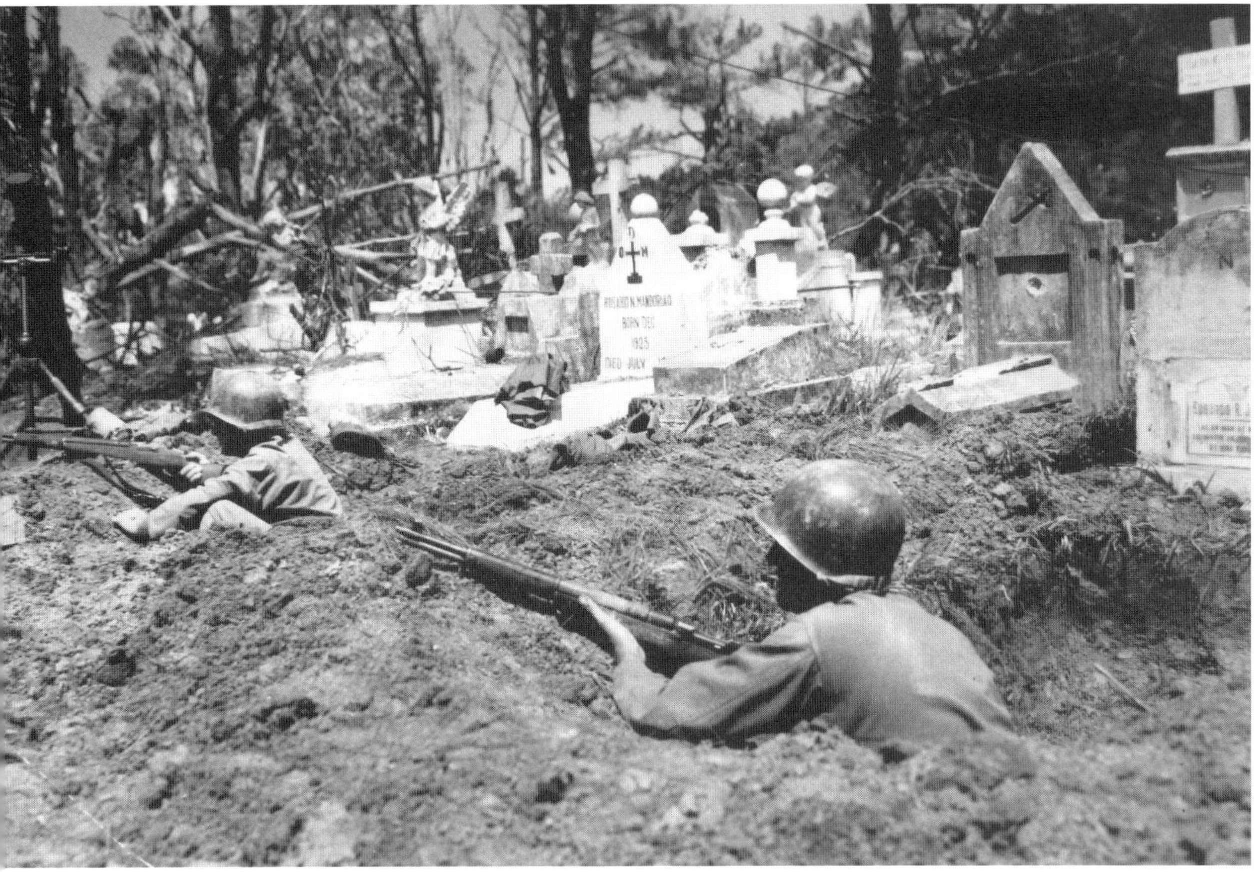
BORN DEC
1925
DIED JULY

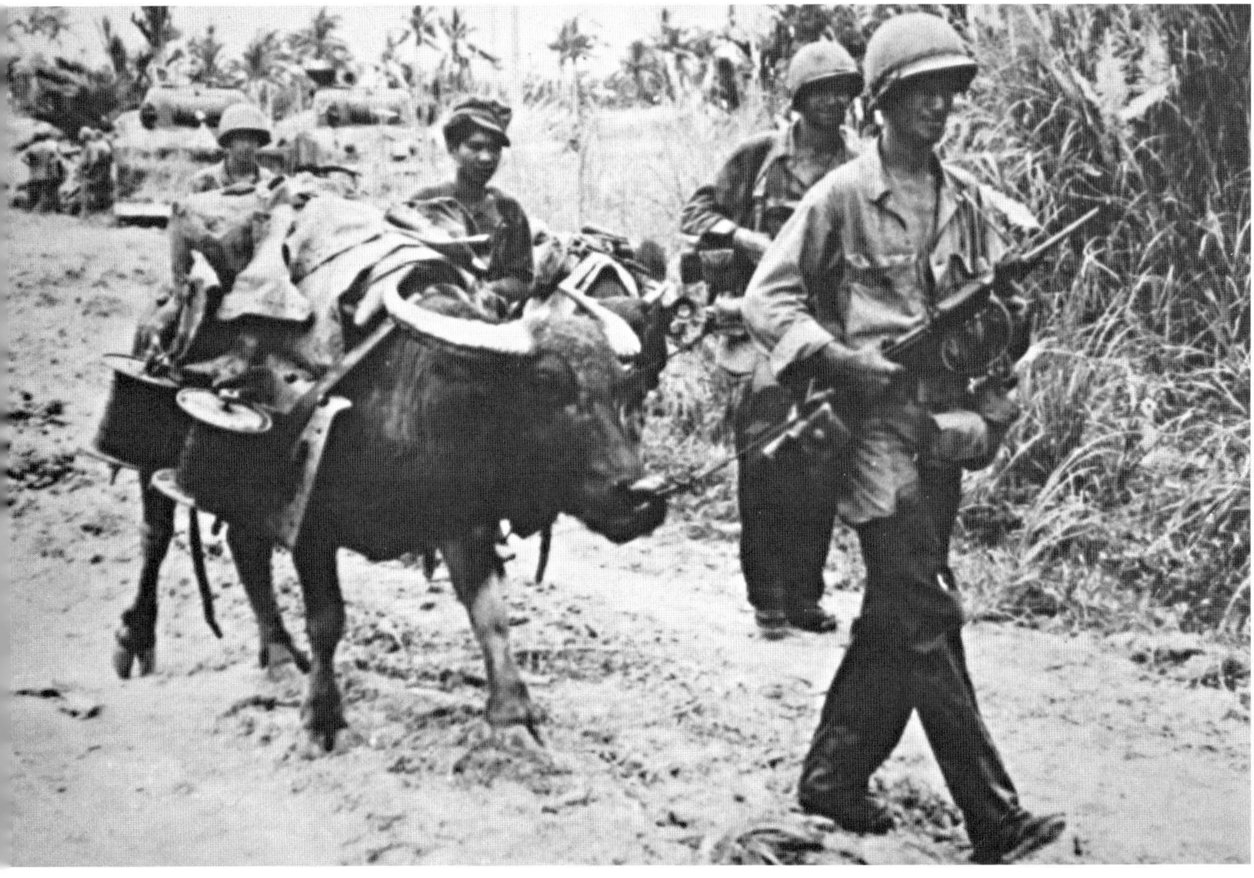

An 11th Airborne Division sergeant is shown here leading his mule with supplies for the front lines along a dirt road connecting Cavite to Manila on 3 February 1945. The 1st Cavalry Division, 37th Infantry Division and the 11th Airborne's 511th PIR and 188th GIR all converged on Manila with the airborne troops moving specifically towards Nichols Field south of the capital. *(NARA)*

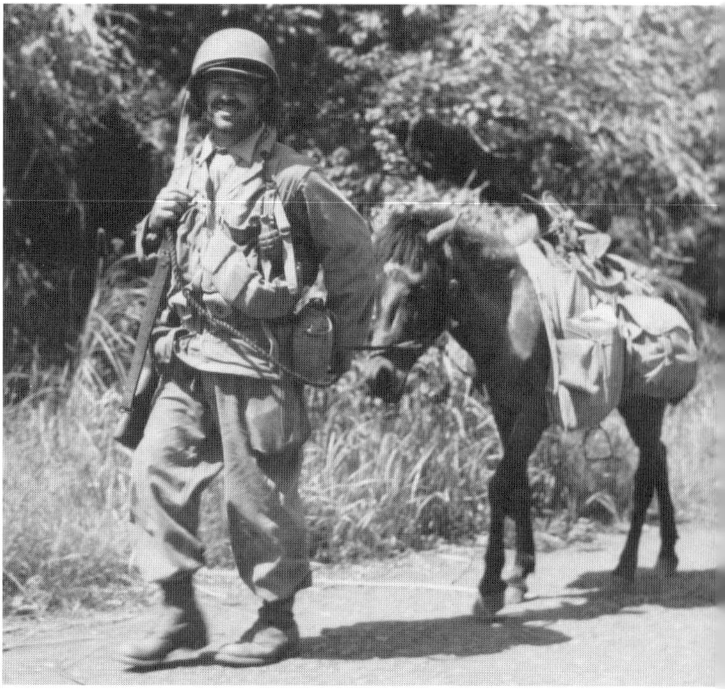

Three 96th Division infantrymen scaled a camouflaged log-reinforced Japanese pillbox on Leyte. The soldiers carried their M1 Garand 0.30-06 and M1 carbine 0.30in-calibre semi-automatic weapons. The IJA troops harvested palm tree logs for these 'defence-in-depth' fortifications to delay the American inland advance from the landing beaches. *(NARA)*

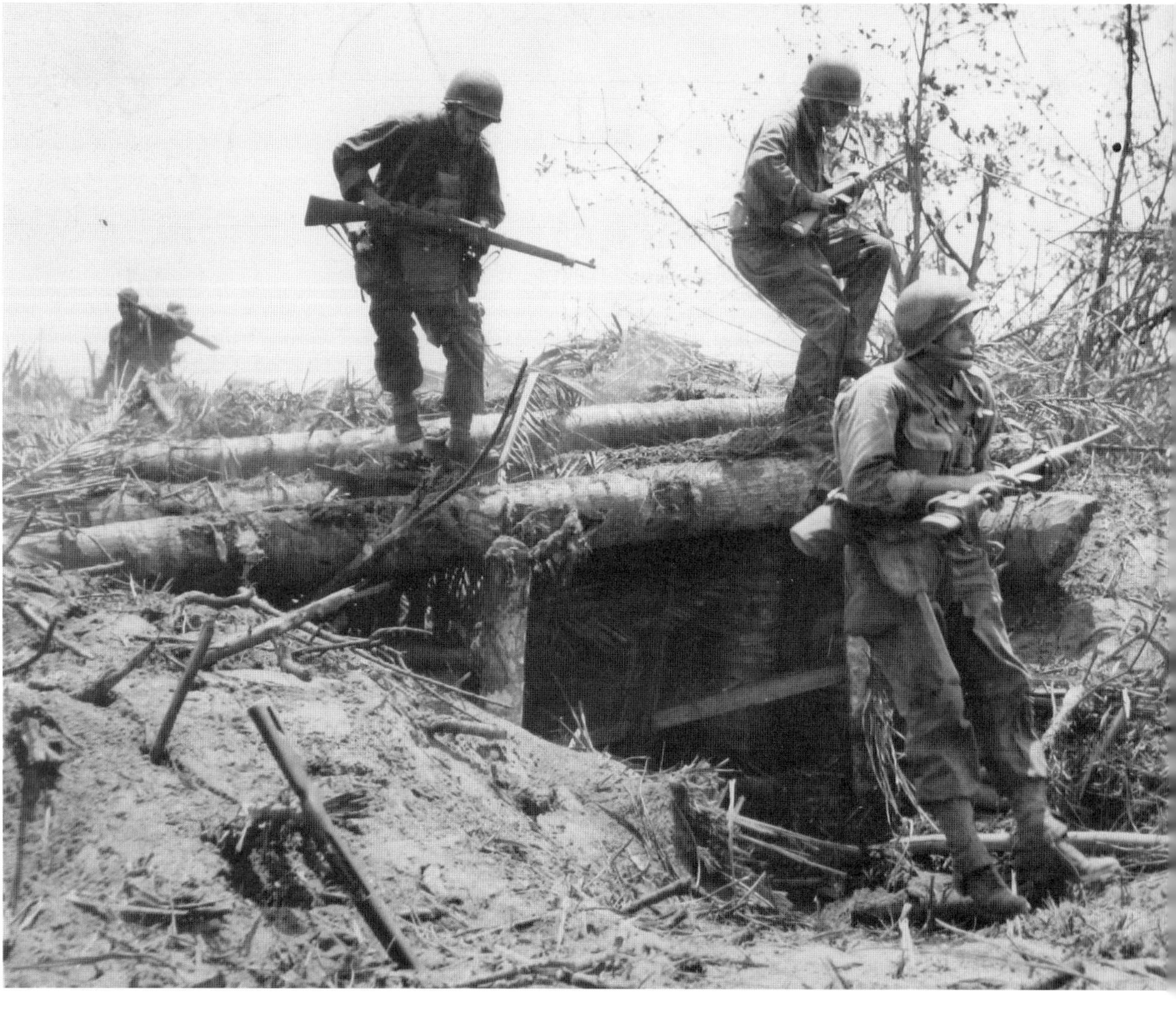

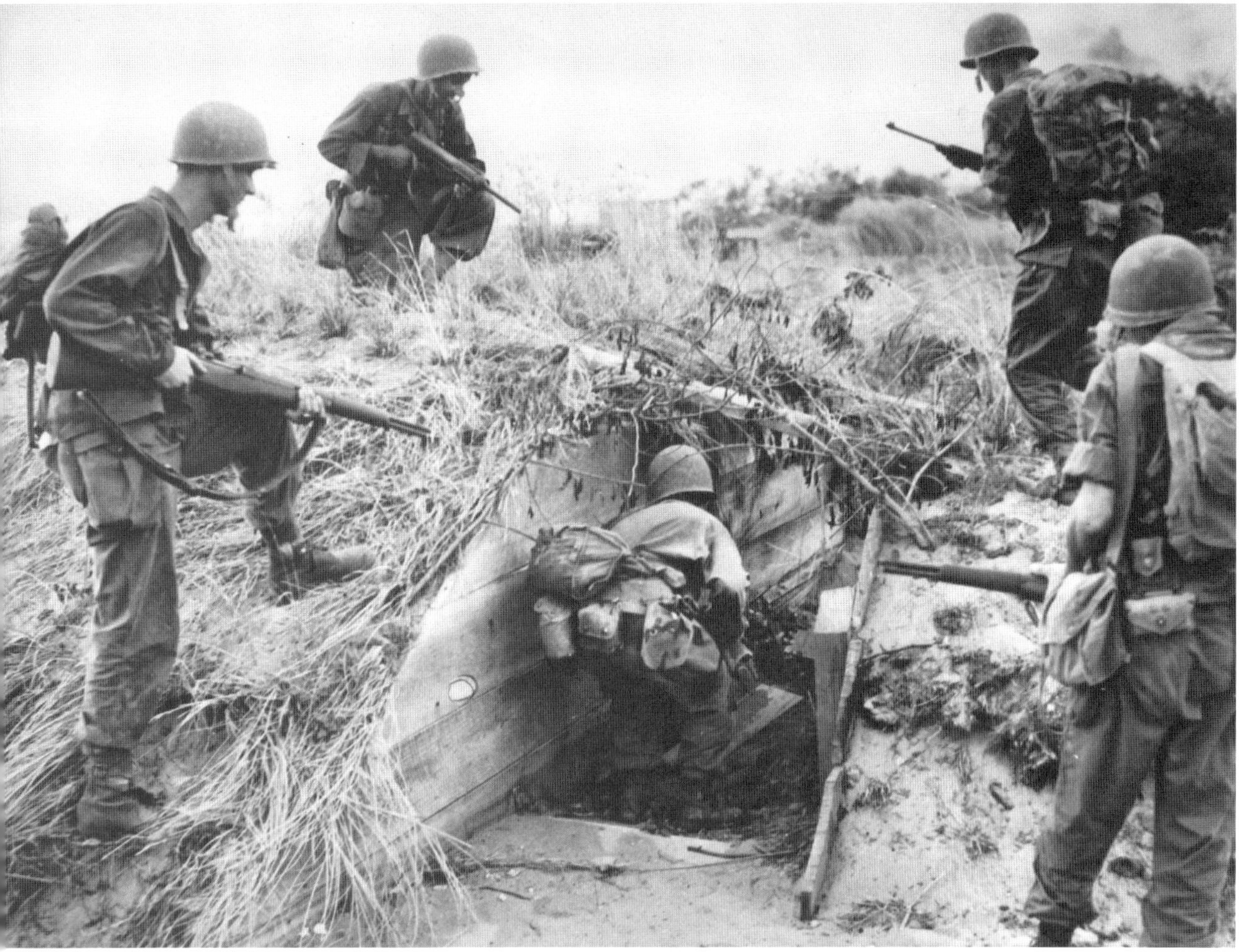

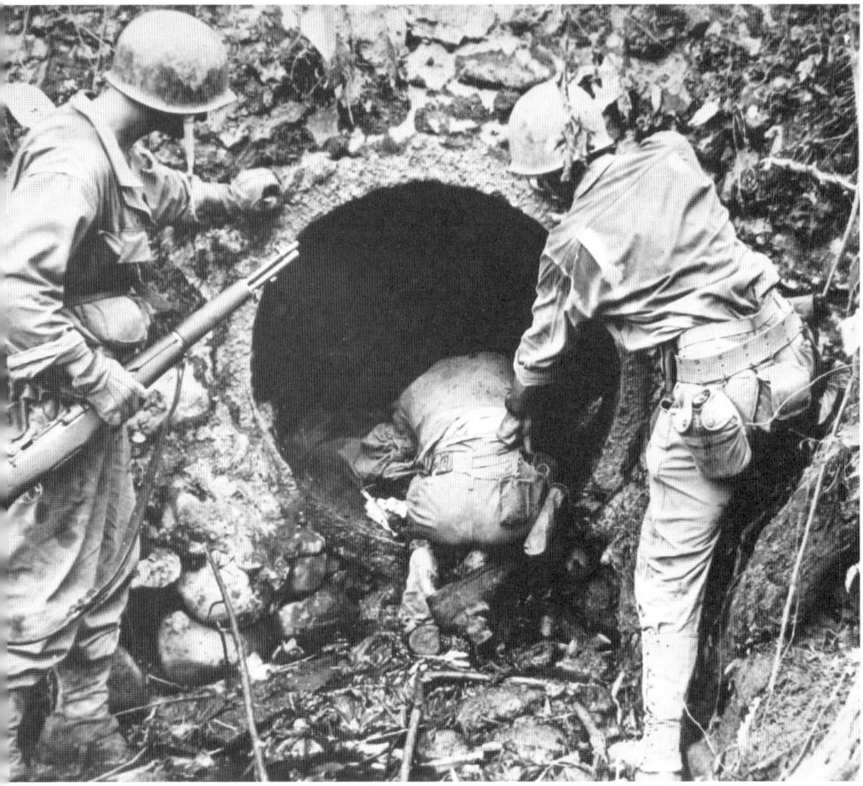

Five 38th Division infantrymen are shown here moving through a wood-reinforced rear entrance of a Japanese fortification. These IJA positions were expertly camouflaged with nearby vegetation to maximize lethal ambushes. *(NARA)*

A dead Japanese infantryman is pulled from a concrete culvert that served as his sniper position. Against often overwhelming local American infantry superiority of numbers, Japanese defenders resorted to stealth tactics of sniping during the daytime and infiltration of enemy lines at night. *(NARA)*

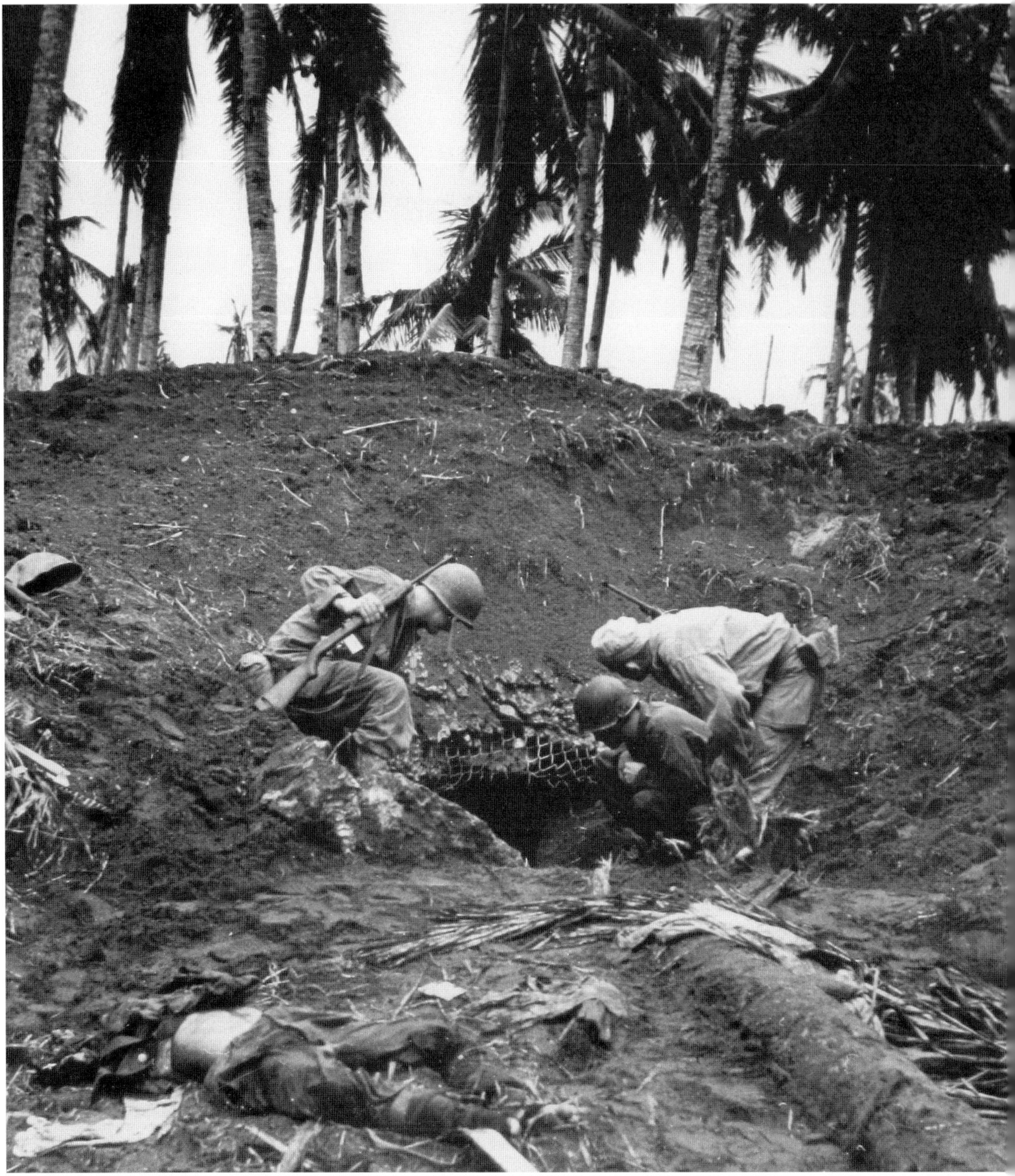

Three Sixth Army 96th Division soldiers are seen here peering through an entrance into a Japanese earthwork fortification on Leyte in the Catmon Hill vicinity that was cleared by 30 October 1944. The wire mesh at the opening of the earthen mound prevented hand grenades from being lobbed in by American troops. A dead IJA 16th Division soldier is seen on the left (foreground). *(NARA)*

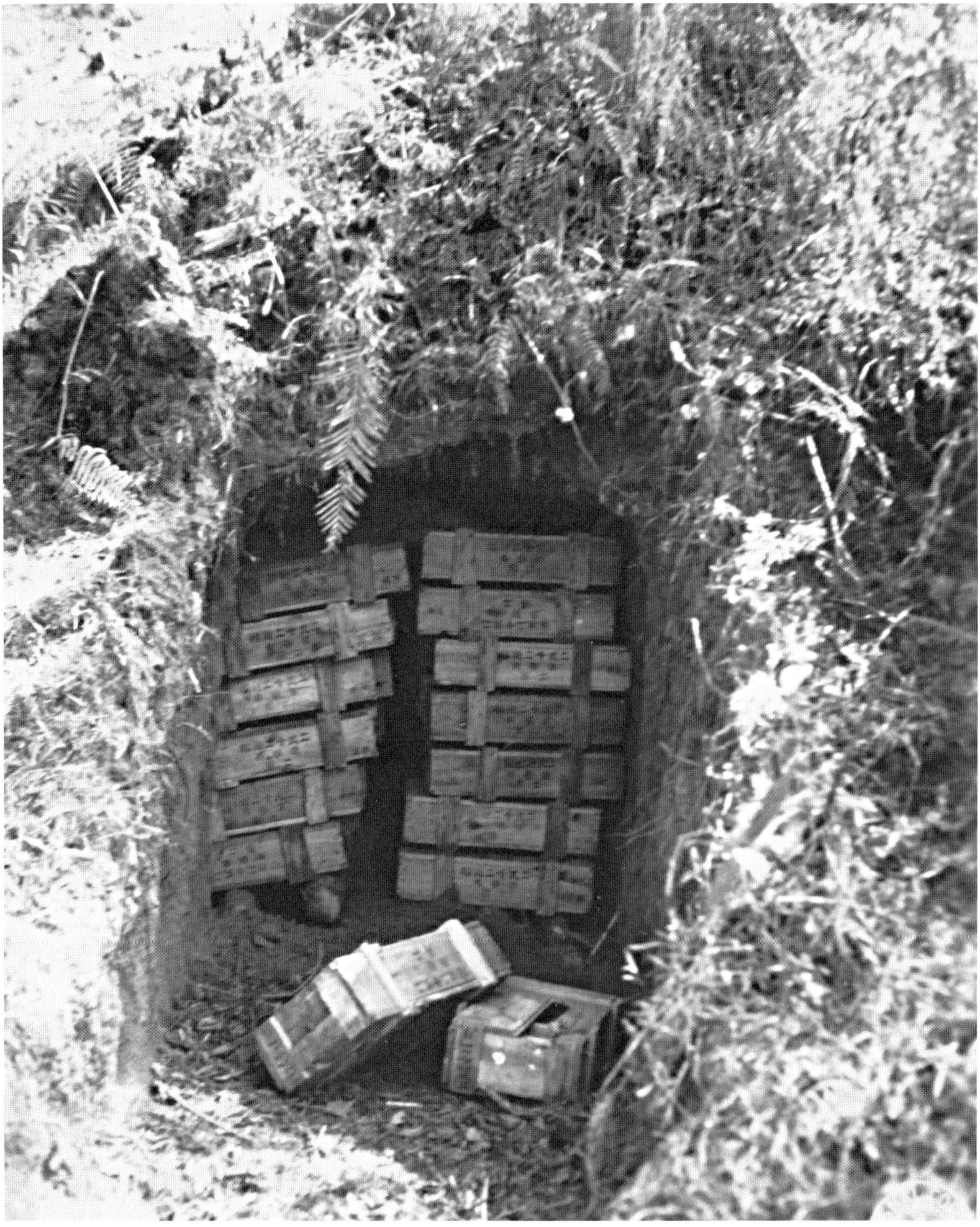

Japanese ammunition crates are stacked here in a hillside's excavated opening near Baguio on Luzon's western half to protect it from American artillery fire and aerial bombardment. American 33rd Division soldiers found this cave in late April 1945 after embarking northwards from Rosario up Route 11 in late March. *(NARA)*

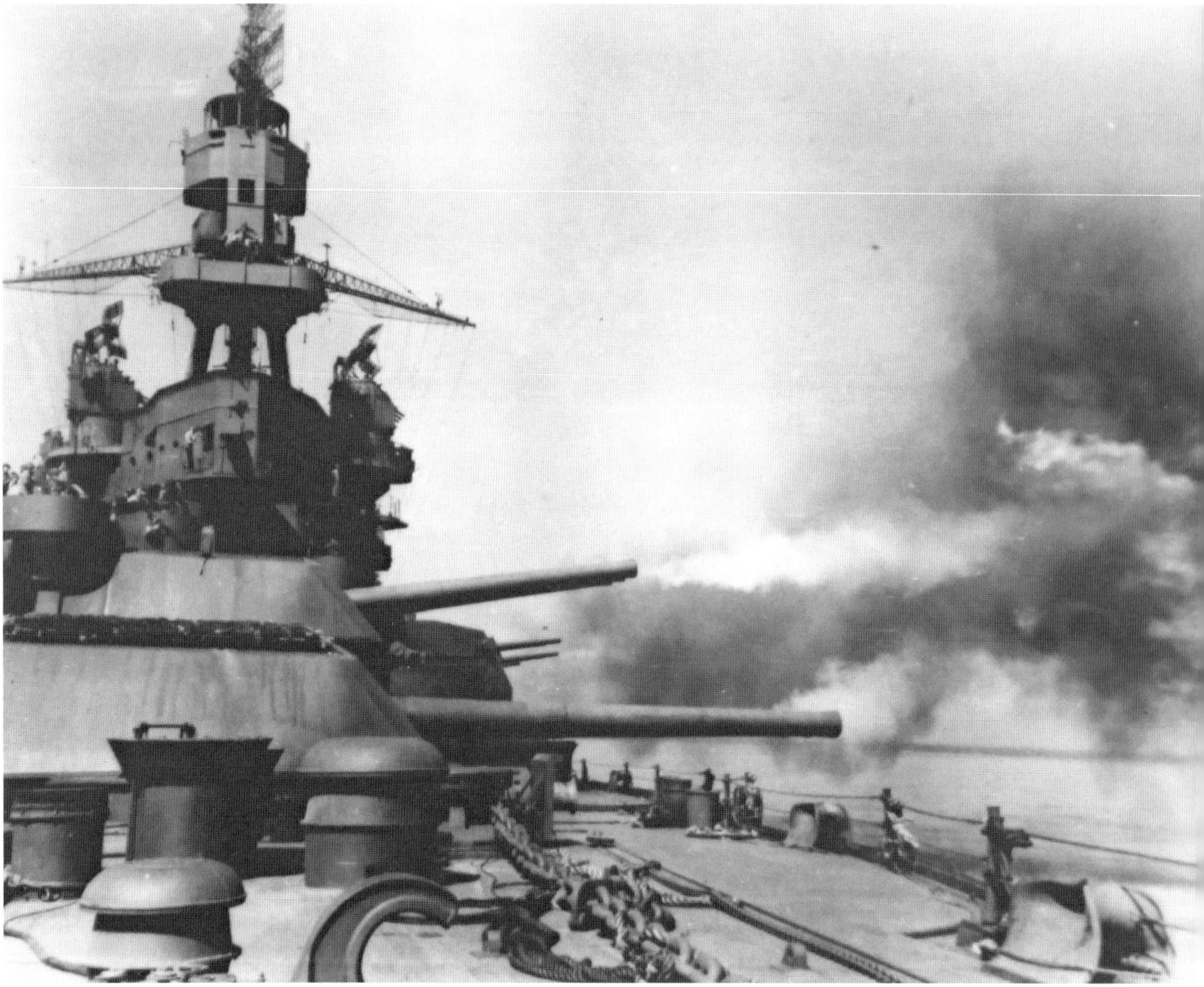

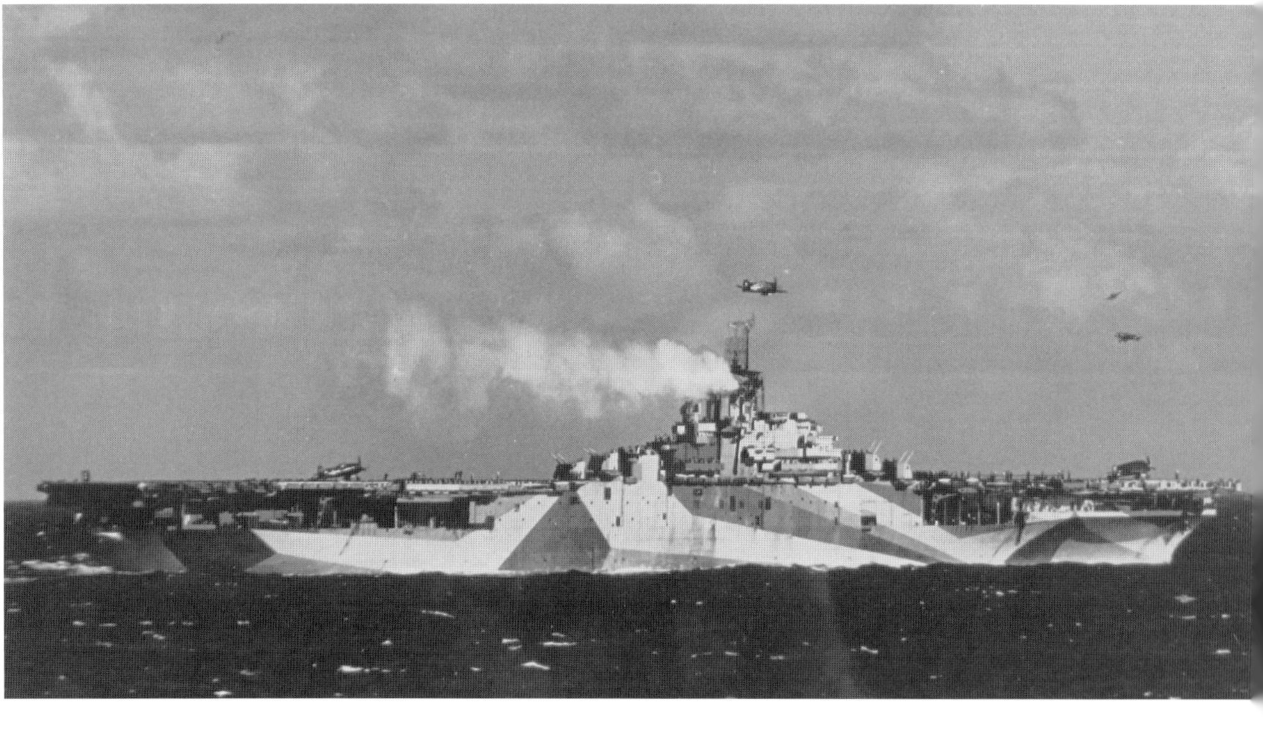

(**Opposite, above**) The USS *Pennsylvania*'s 14in guns fired a broadside salvo against Japanese positions on Leyte on 20 October 1944. The *Pennsylvania* was part of TG 77.2, the Bombardment and Fire Support Group under Rear Admiral Jesse Oldendorf that rained fire on Japanese beach defences. The *Pennsylvania* also participated in the Battle of Surigao Strait on 25 October. The American battleship line 'crossed the T' of the Japanese fleet, sinking two IJN battleships and three destroyers. (*NARA*)

(**Opposite, below**) Off Luzon's coast, an *Essex*-class fast carrier recovers aircraft from a sortie against Japanese airfields and positions during the January 1945 Lingayen Gulf invasion. The US Navy's camouflage scheme for carriers during this phase of the Pacific War is demonstrated here. As sufficient American air power was needed until Luzon airfields were readied, fleet carriers from the Third Fleet (under Halsey) and escort carriers from the Seventh Fleet (under Kinkaid) provided the landings' aerial umbrella. December's amphibious assaults on Mindoro also provided MacArthur with proximate airfields for the Lingayen Gulf assault. (*NARA*)

(**Above**) The fires on the flight deck of the USS *Essex* (background) are controlled by the carrier's crew after a Japanese *kamikaze* plane – a Yokosuka D4Y3 Model 33 *Suisei* or 'Comet' (code-named 'Judy' by the Allies), a two-seat carrier-based dive-bomber – exploded after crashing onto the flight deck and igniting the fuel tanks of USN planes being readied for take-off on 25 November 1944. Another downed Japanese plane burned in the water (far background). Fifteen US Navy personnel were killed and another forty-four wounded. After rapid fire control and flight deck repair, the *Essex* returned to combat to support the Mindoro invasions of mid-December 1944. The *Essex* (in TG 38.3) participated in the Lingayen Gulf invasion of 9 January 1945. (*NARA*)

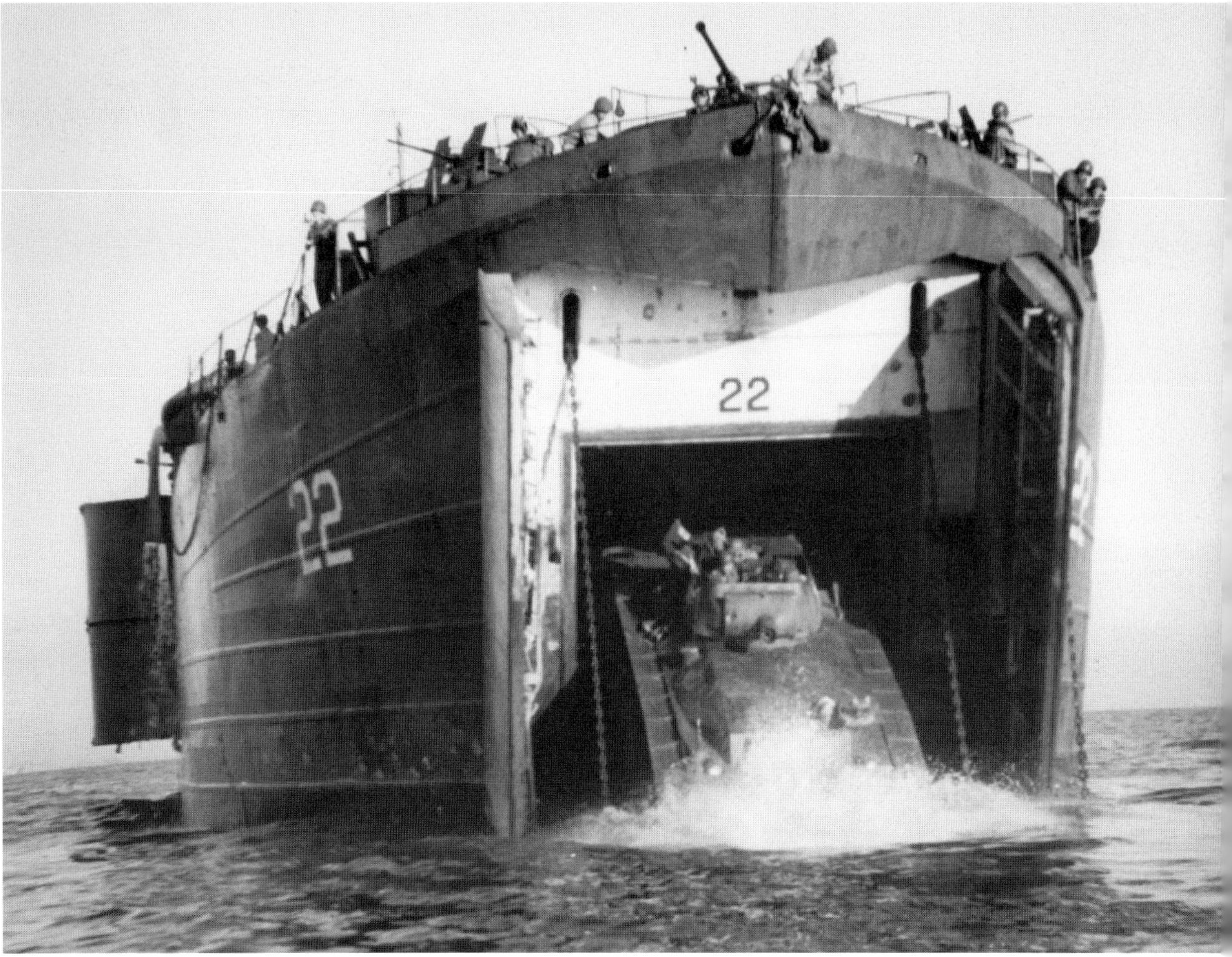
22
22

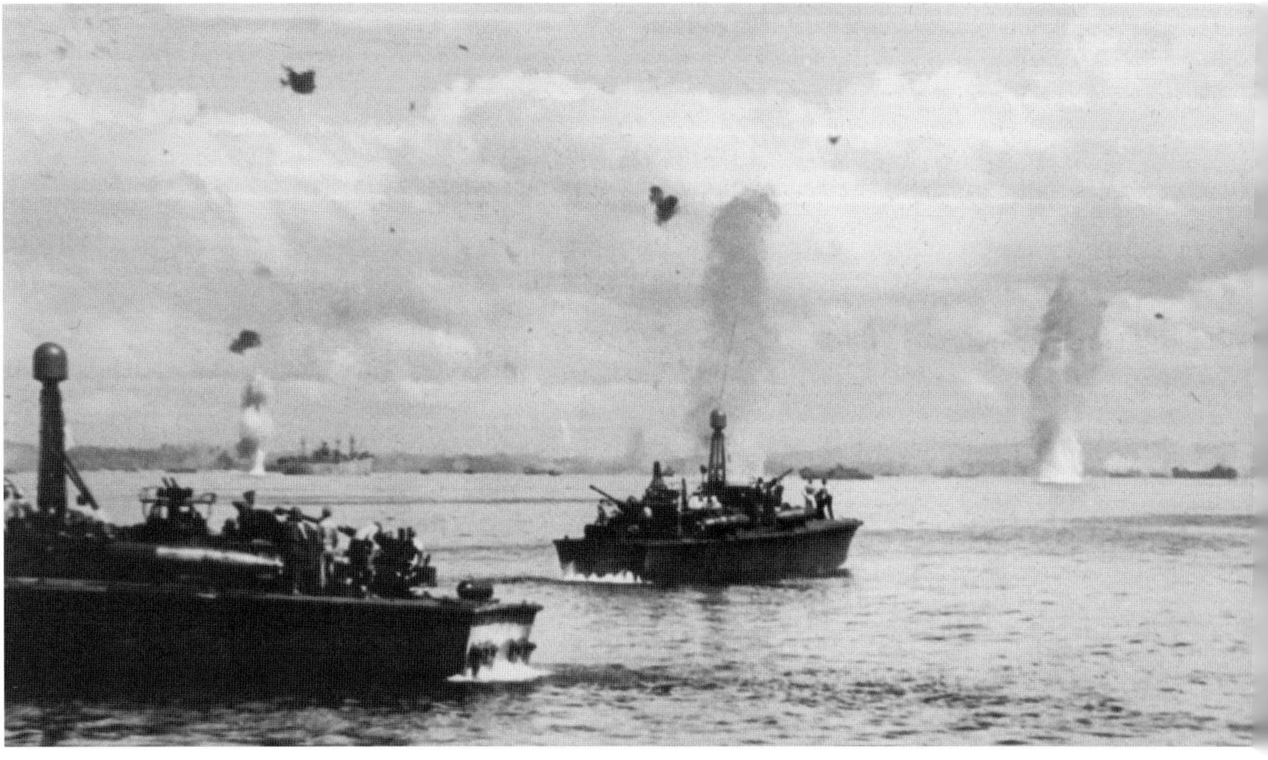

(**Opposite, above**) With its bow ramp lowered and hull doors opened, an LST releases an LVT (A) 4 amphibious tractor for the US Sixth Army's Lingayen Gulf invasion on 9 January 1945. As these shallow-draft attack transports closed in on the shoreline, amphibious tractors, tanks, jeeps, trucks, supplies and troops were landed with a brief run-in to the beachhead. This LVT (A) 4, with its M8 HMC turret housing a 75mm howitzer, was designed to lead non-armoured amphibious tractors carrying assault troops to the beaches and provide fire support with its 75mm gun ashore prior to the arrival of M4 medium tanks. Once ashore, the LVT (A) 4 had a maximum speed of 17 mph. A versatile tracked vehicle, the LVT (A) 4 could provide direct gunfire on enemy positions, serve as a troop or supply carrier and evacuate wounded to rear-area aid stations while ashore. (*NARA*)

(**Opposite, below**) PT boats are under way as *Liberty* transport ships are attacked by Japanese planes during the Leyte invasion of 20 October 1944. The IJA Air Force's (IJAAF's) 2nd Air Division in the Philippines was reinforced by air units in Manchuria, China, Formosa and the Home Islands before the American invasion; however, Halsey's Third Fleet fast carrier raids destroyed half the enemy's air strength in the Philippines before Leyte's invasion. Nonetheless, the IJNAF mustered 200 land and carrier-based aircraft to contest the invasion. Furthermore, the first *kamikaze* flights from Manila occurred on 21 October. (*NARA*)

(**Above**) Three Consolidated PBY Catalina flying boats patrol over Lingayen Gulf for the US Sixth Army's 9 January 1945 amphibious assault. The PBYs were utilized for reconnaissance and bombing as they could carry an external bomb load of 4,500lb in addition to several MGs. They were also used to detect any Japanese submarine presence in proximity to the invasion fleet. (*NARA*)

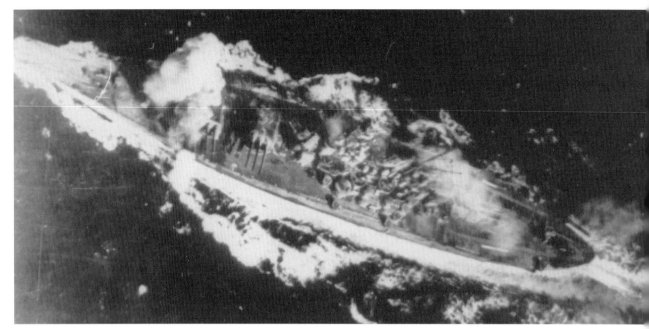

(**Above**) The IJN heavy battleship *Yamato* is under USN aerial attack at the Battle of the Sibuyan Sea on 24 October 1944. The *Yamato* was hit near her forward gun turret while her sister giant battleship *Musashi* was sunk and an IJN cruiser *Myoko* crippled by USN aircraft. The IJN Centre Striking Force (seven battleships, thirteen cruisers and nineteen destroyers) under Vice Admiral Takeo Kurita was ordered on 20 October to destroy Vice Admiral Thomas Kinkaid's amphibious support force of transports and escorts with a surprise attack at Leyte Gulf on 25 October, thereby stranding the US Sixth Army ashore. The larger portion of Kurita's force was to enter Leyte Gulf from the north through the San Bernadino Strait. A detachment of Kurita's Centre Striking Force (Southern Force) under Vice Admiral Shoji Nishimura, after crossing the Sulu Sea, was to enter Leyte Gulf from the south via the Surigao Strait to threaten Kinkaid's transports with two battleships, two cruisers and several destroyers. At the Battle of Surigao Strait on 25 October, Nishimura's Southern Force was dealt a decisive blow by USN battleships, cruisers and PT boats with only two IJN ships surviving. Kurita's Centre Striking Force managed to enter Leyte Gulf after steaming around Samar Island. This massive IJN fleet encountered only Taffy 3's six escort carriers, three destroyers and destroyer escorts. The melee that ensued on 25 October was the Battle off Samar Island with USN destroyers attacking the IJN surface fleet, enabling Rear Admiral Clifton Sprague to get his fighter- and torpedo-bombers aloft. These aircraft damaged three IJN cruisers and Kurita, who incorrectly thought he had engaged American capital ships, retired his force. (*NARA*)

(**Opposite, above**) The IJN light carrier *Zuiho*, which was converted from a submarine tender, is shown here with its deck pattern under aerial attack by USN aircraft from the USS *Enterprise* at the Battle of Cape Engaño on 25 October 1944. Coincident with the larger IJN Centre and Southern Force's surface ships, Vice Admiral Jisaburō Ozawa led a Northern Force comprising the IJN heavy carrier *Zuikaku*, three light carriers (*Zuiho* was one) and two converted carriers to lure Admiral Halsey's Third Fleet away from Leyte Gulf and north for American aerial attacks. The *Zuiho* was sunk by American naval aircraft during the Battle of Cape Engaño. (*NARA*)

(**Opposite, below**) A US Fifth Air Force twin-engined B-25 Mitchell medium bomber is making a low-level strafing attack on an IJN troop transport in Ormoc Bay on 9 November 1944. The IJA 26th Division sailed from Manila in two separate task forces on 8 November, intending to land at Ormoc on Leyte's western coast at the northern end of Ormoc Bay. The following day, the US Fifth Air Force's B-25s, A-20s, P-38s and P-47s as well as Admiral Halsey's Third Fleet carrier planes attacked the two Japanese task forces, sinking several of the Japanese transports and escorting destroyers. After losing 3,200 soldiers during the aerial assault, the remainder of the IJA 26th Division landed at Ormoc and proceeded south along Leyte's western coast to confront the advancing American units. (*NARA*)

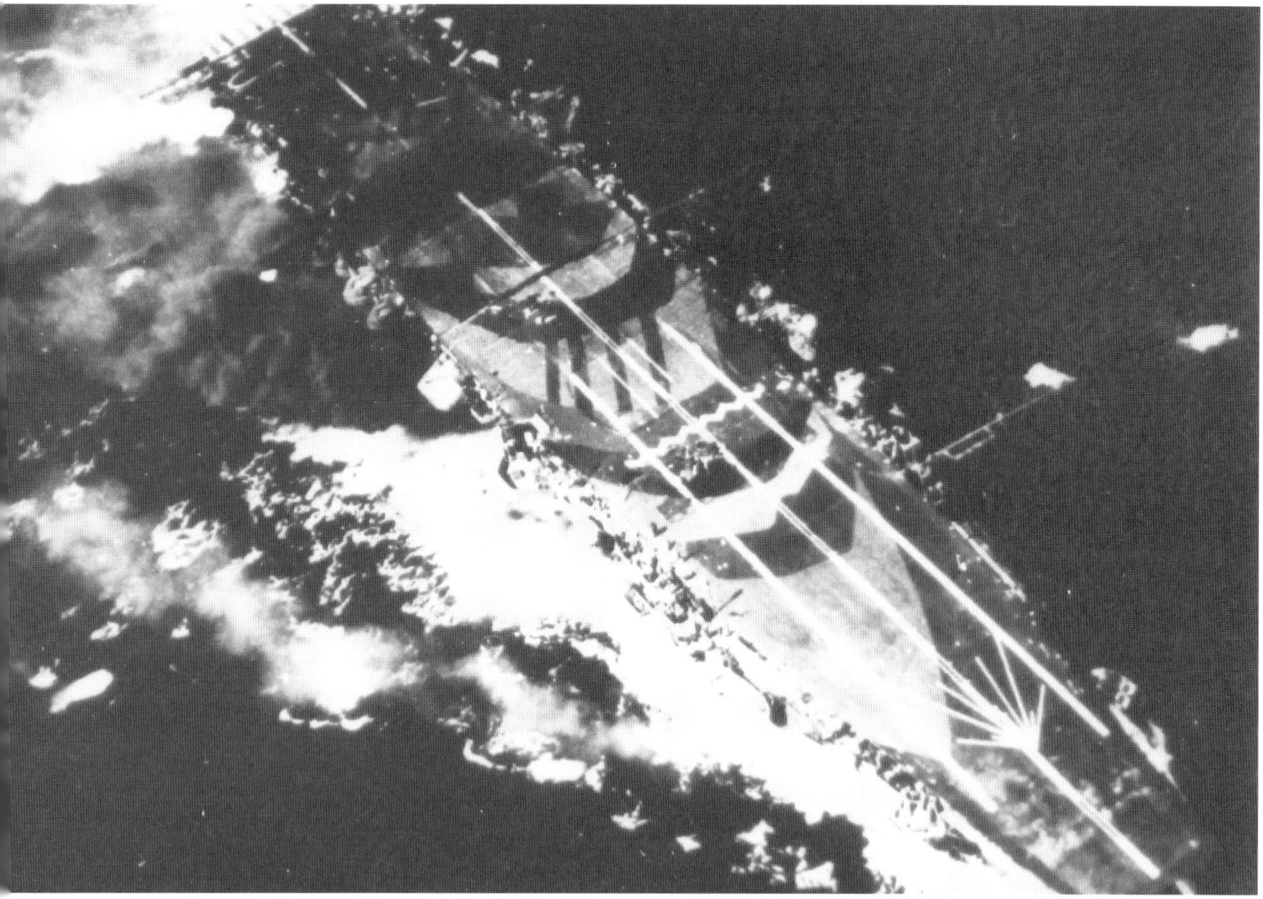

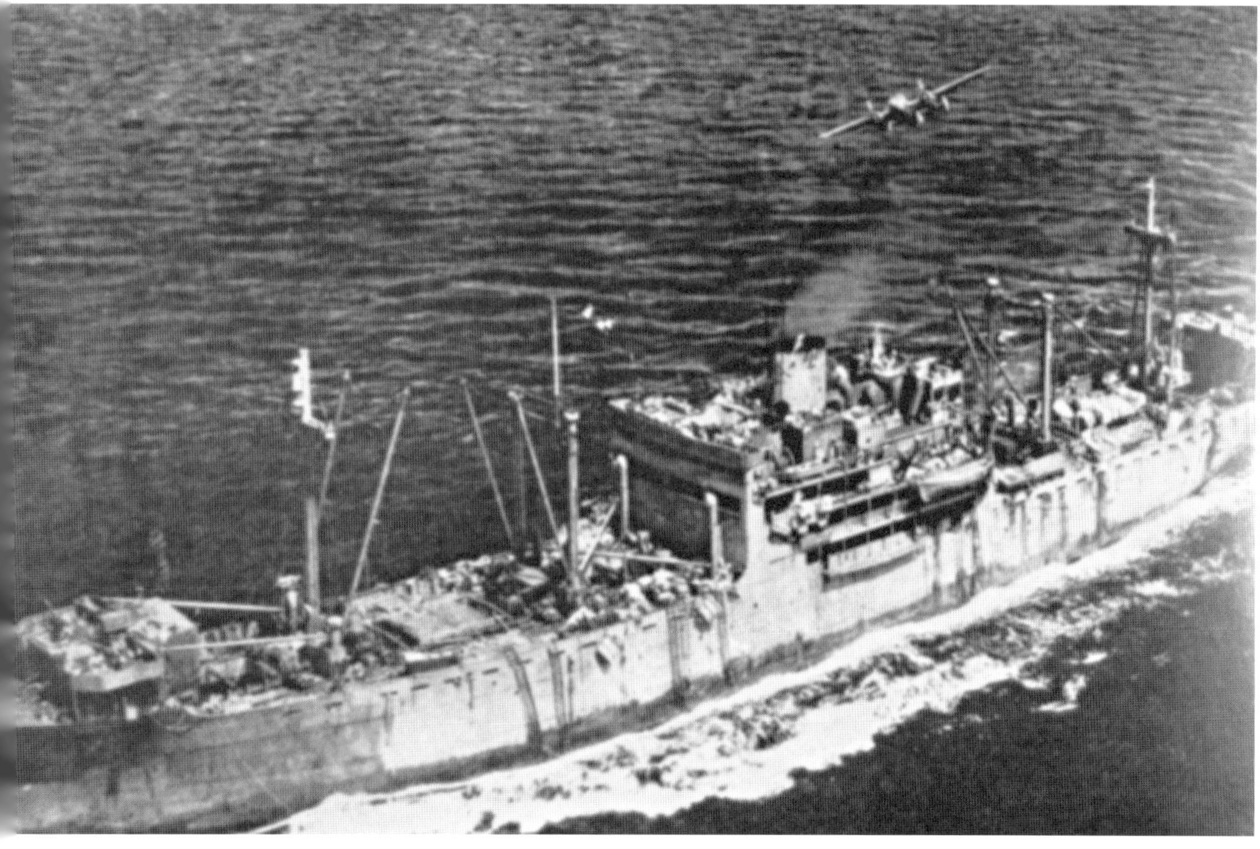

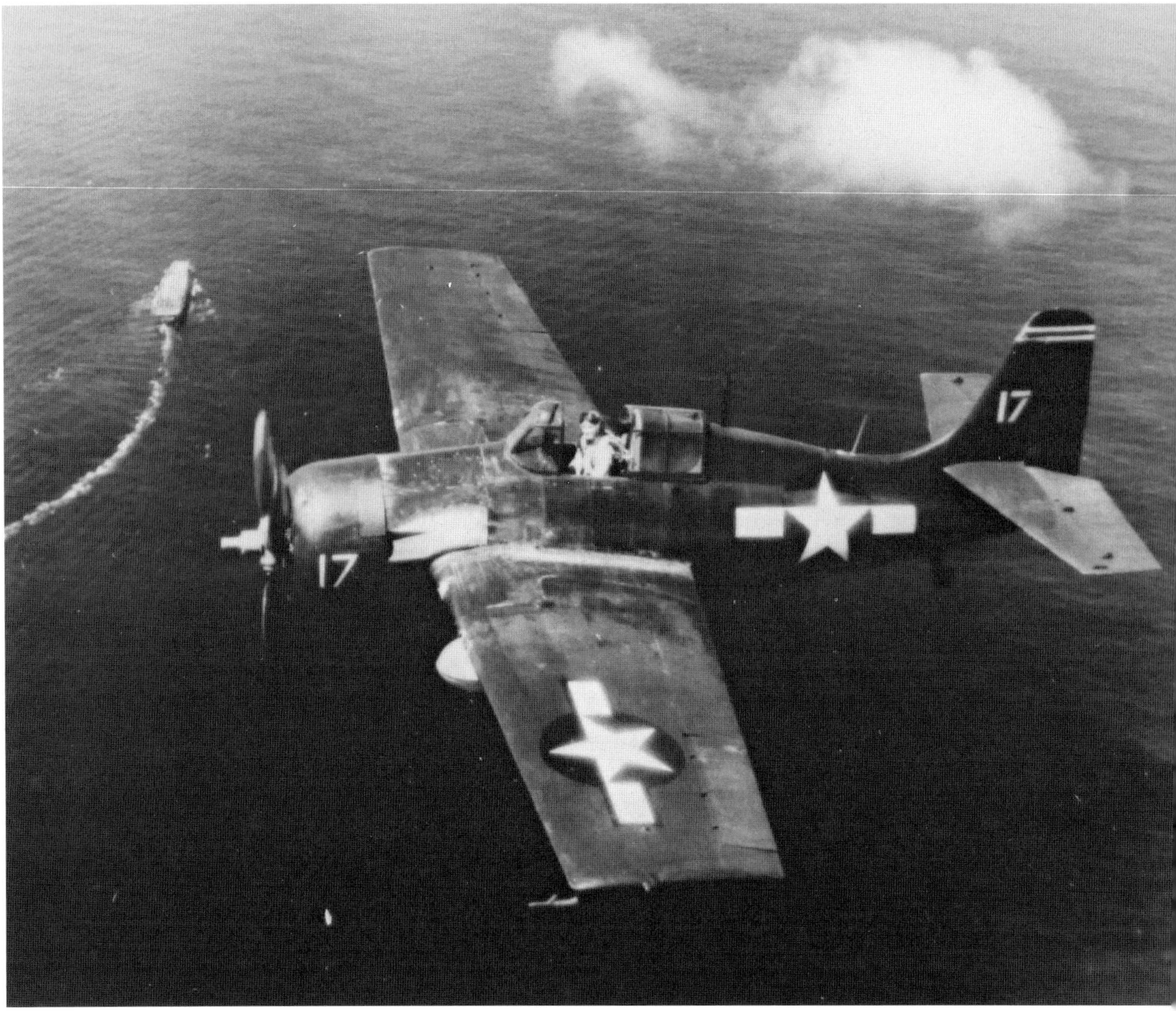

(**Above**) A Grumman F4F 'Wildcat' single-seat fighter is shown here above the USS *Santee*, an escort carrier, as Combat Air Patrol (CAP) during Leyte's invasion on 20 October 1944. After launching aircraft against Japanese surface ships just after dawn on 25 October, a *kamikaze* plane crashed through the *Santee*'s flight deck and damaged the hangar deck. Also that morning, a Japanese submarine torpedoed the *Santee* causing flooding, which was repaired, and the carrier returned to action. *(NARA)*

(**Opposite, above**) American sailors are shown here arming Grumman TBF 'Avengers' with torpedoes on the USS *San Jacinto*, an *Independence*-class light aircraft carrier, to strike Japanese carriers during the Battle of Cape Engaño on 25 October 1944. Previously the *San Jacinto* sent planes against Kurita's Centre Striking Force at the Battle of the Sibuyan Sea before heading north as part of Admiral Halsey's Third Fleet. *(NARA)*

(**Opposite, below**) A USN two-seat carrier-borne Curtiss Scout Bomber (SB2C) 'Helldiver' is shown here ready for launching from the USS *Hancock* for a strike on Manila Bay on 25 November 1944 as aerial interdiction prior to the US Sixth Army landing at Lingayen Gulf on 9 January 1945. The Helldiver was the successor to the Scout Bombing Douglas (SBD) 'Dauntless'. The Helldiver was capable of carrying either an internal or external torpedo as well as bombs and depth-charges with a maximal ordnance load of 3,000lb. *(NARA)*

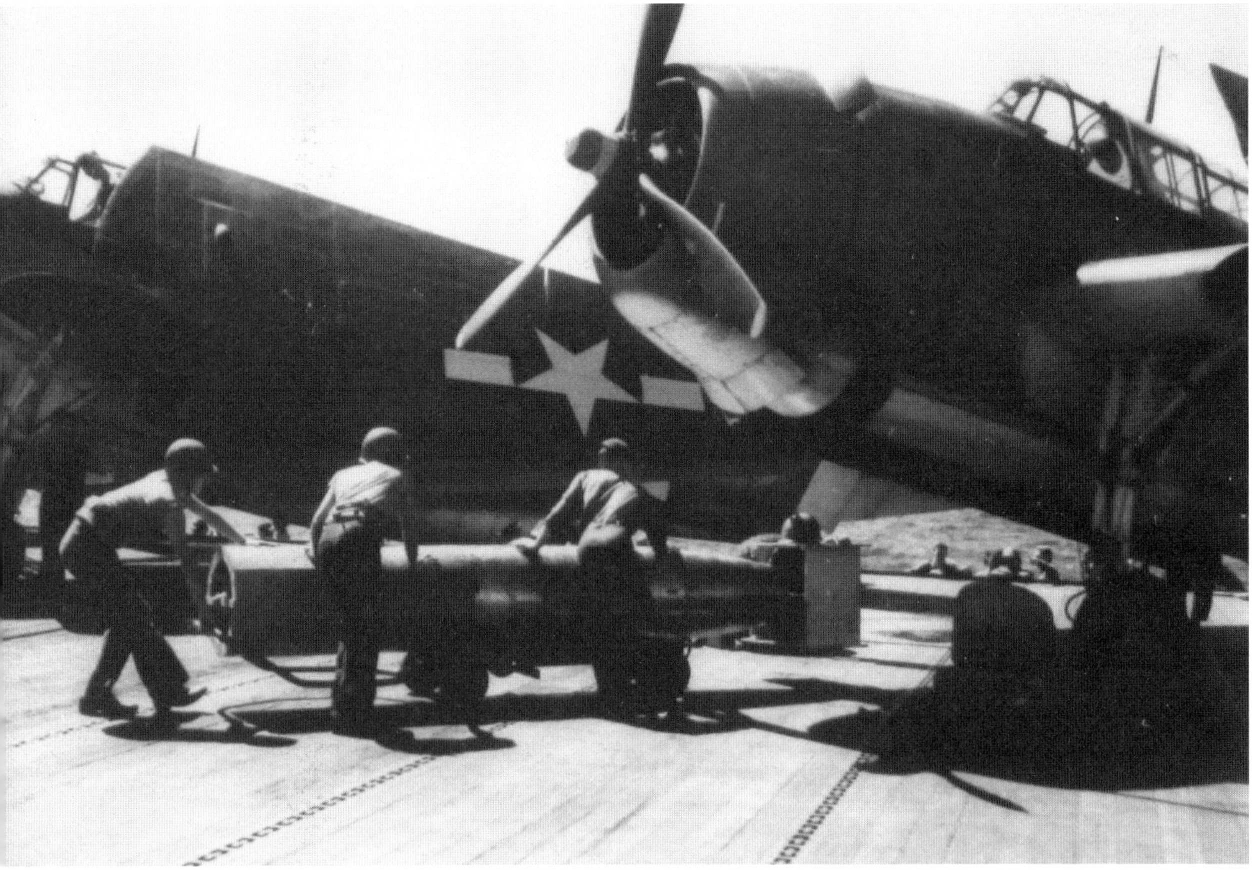

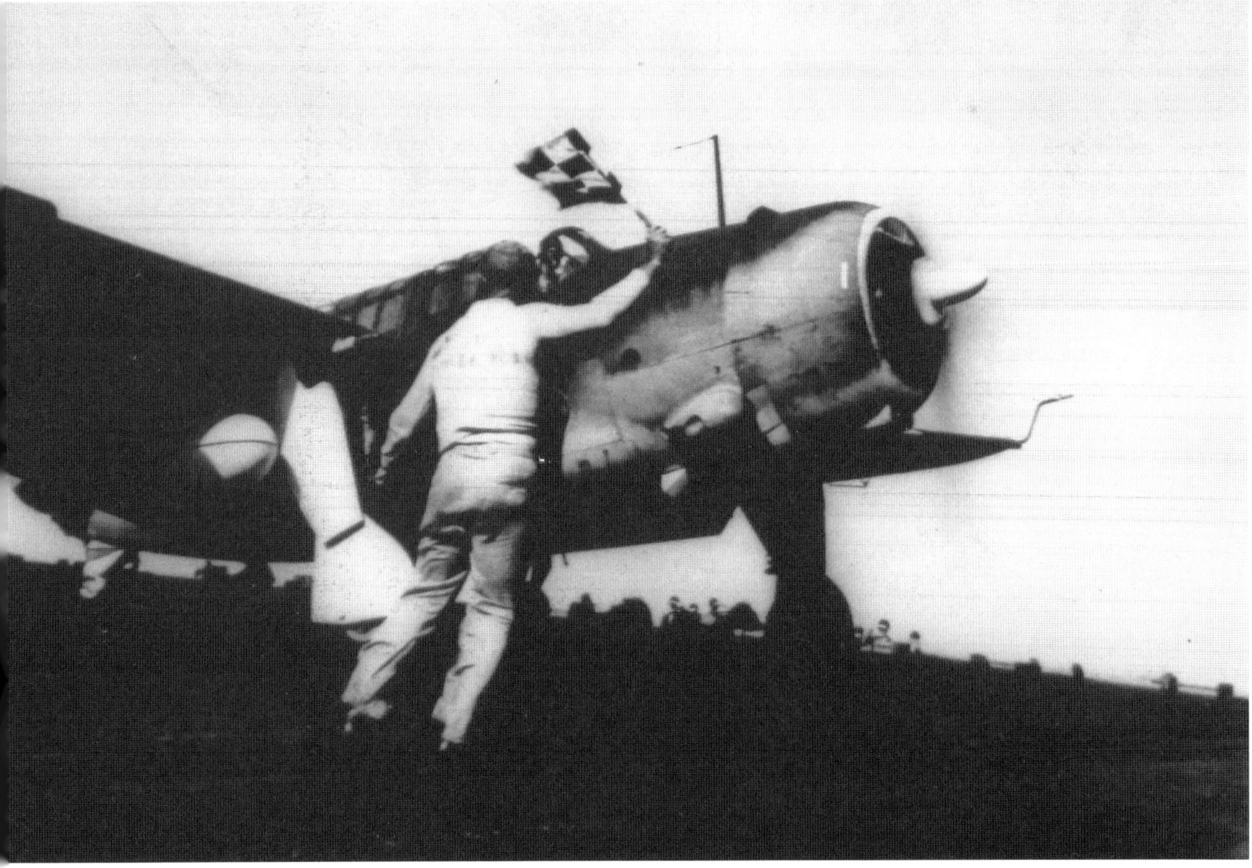

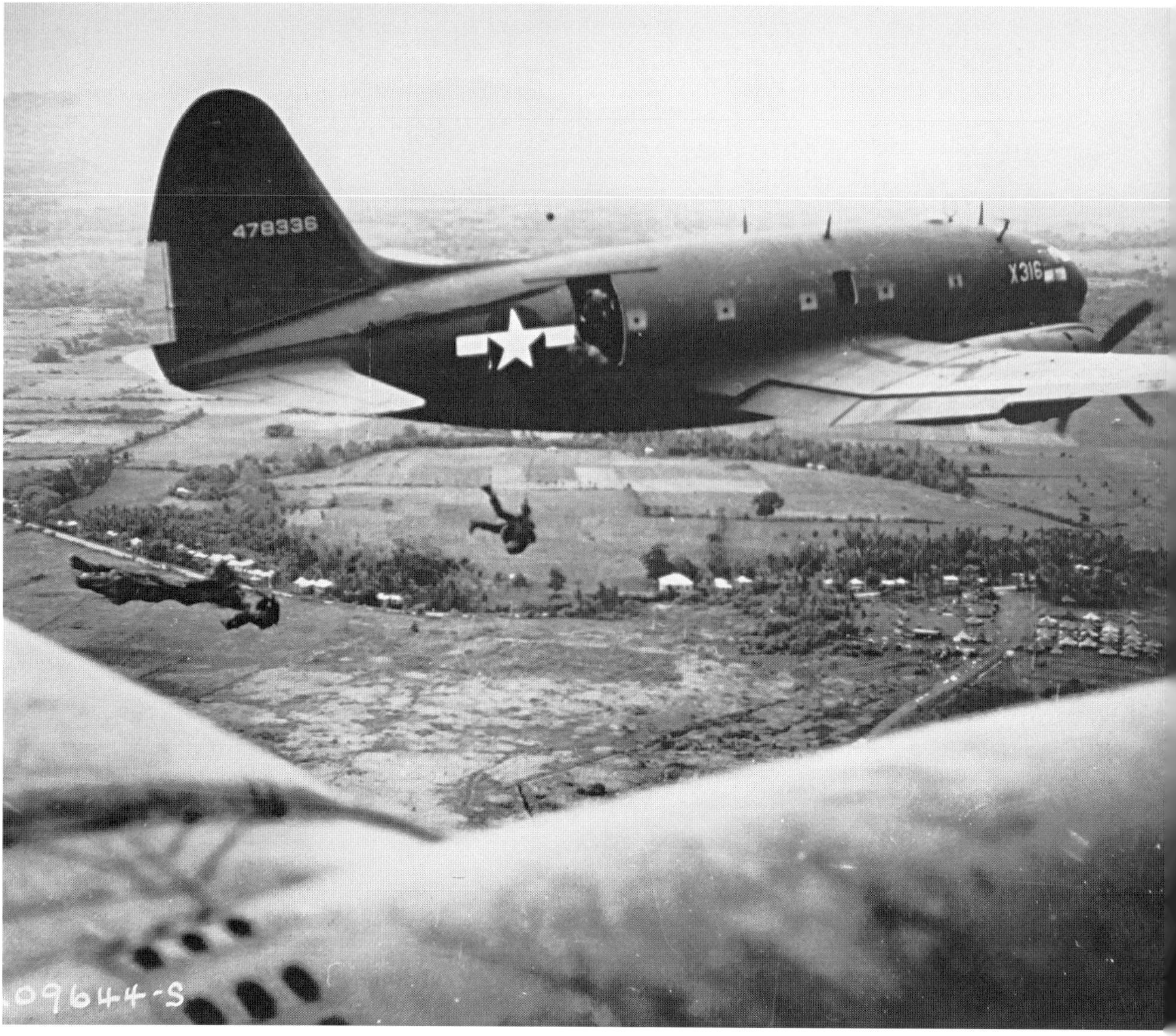
478336
X316
09644-S

(**Above**) A Curtiss twin-engined C-46 transport, 'Commando', is shown here releasing 11th Airborne Division paratroopers onto a Luzon landing field below in January 1945. When used by the USN or USMC, its designation was R5C. The C-46 served in a similar role to the Douglas C-47 'Skytrain' but it was not as extensively produced. *(NARA)*

(**Opposite, above**) Scores of destroyed IJA and IJN aircraft are seen here littering Clark Field on the western side of Luzon near Fort Stotsenburg, which was the site of the contentious battle to recapture the airfield by the American infantry from 24 to 31 January 1945. Mountainous terrain arose (background) from the flat Central Luzon Plain on which both bases were situated. The Japanese retreated into the Zambales Mountains after their loss of Clark Field at the end of January 1945 from which IJA artillery fire rendered the aerodrome unusable until late in the war. *(NARA)*

(**Opposite, below**) An M10 TD is seen here (left) as American soldiers on Luzon attempt to extricate a jeep from a ditch (right). Although the Americans had a numerical and quality superiority in their armour and mechanized vehicles, the lack of a road infrastructure in the Philippines made movement for even four-wheel-drive and tracked vehicles difficult. *(NARA)*

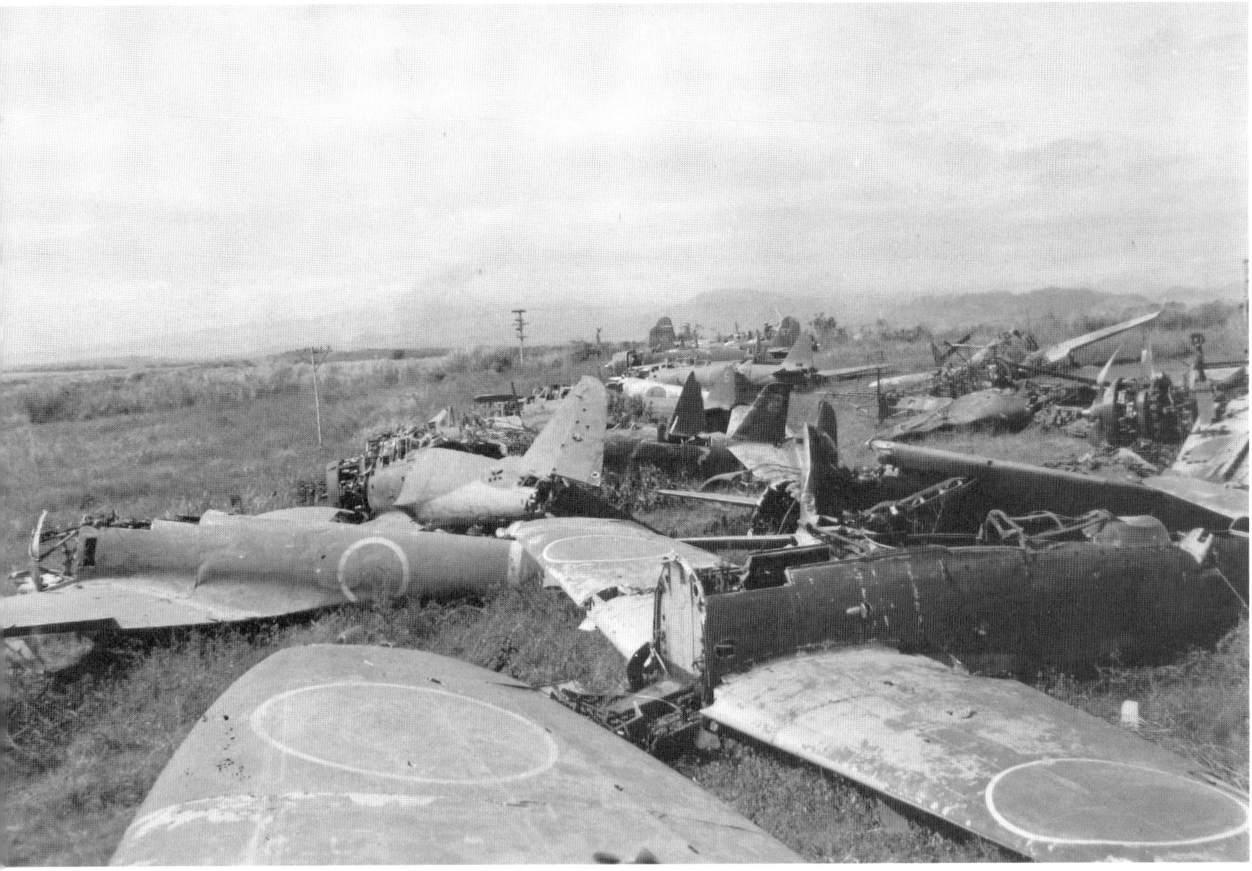

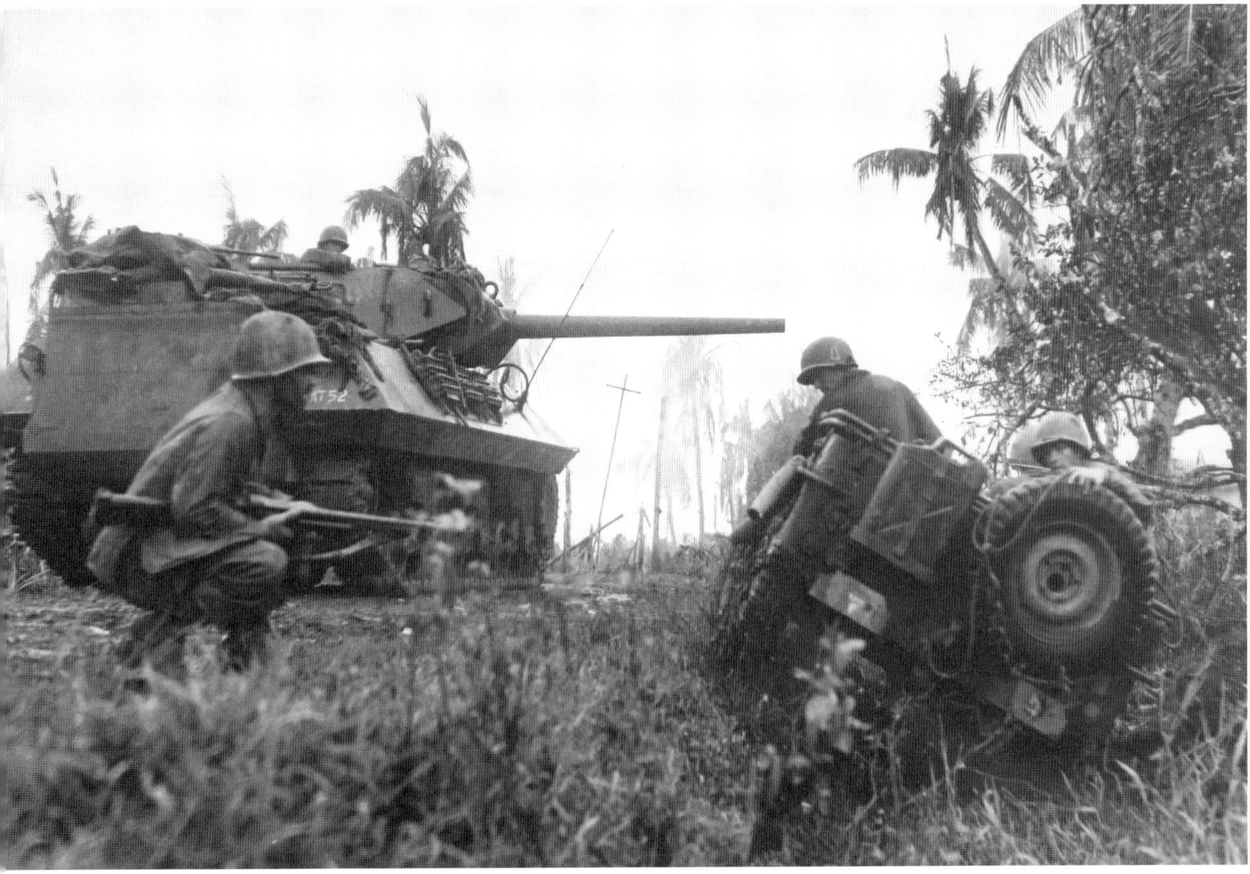

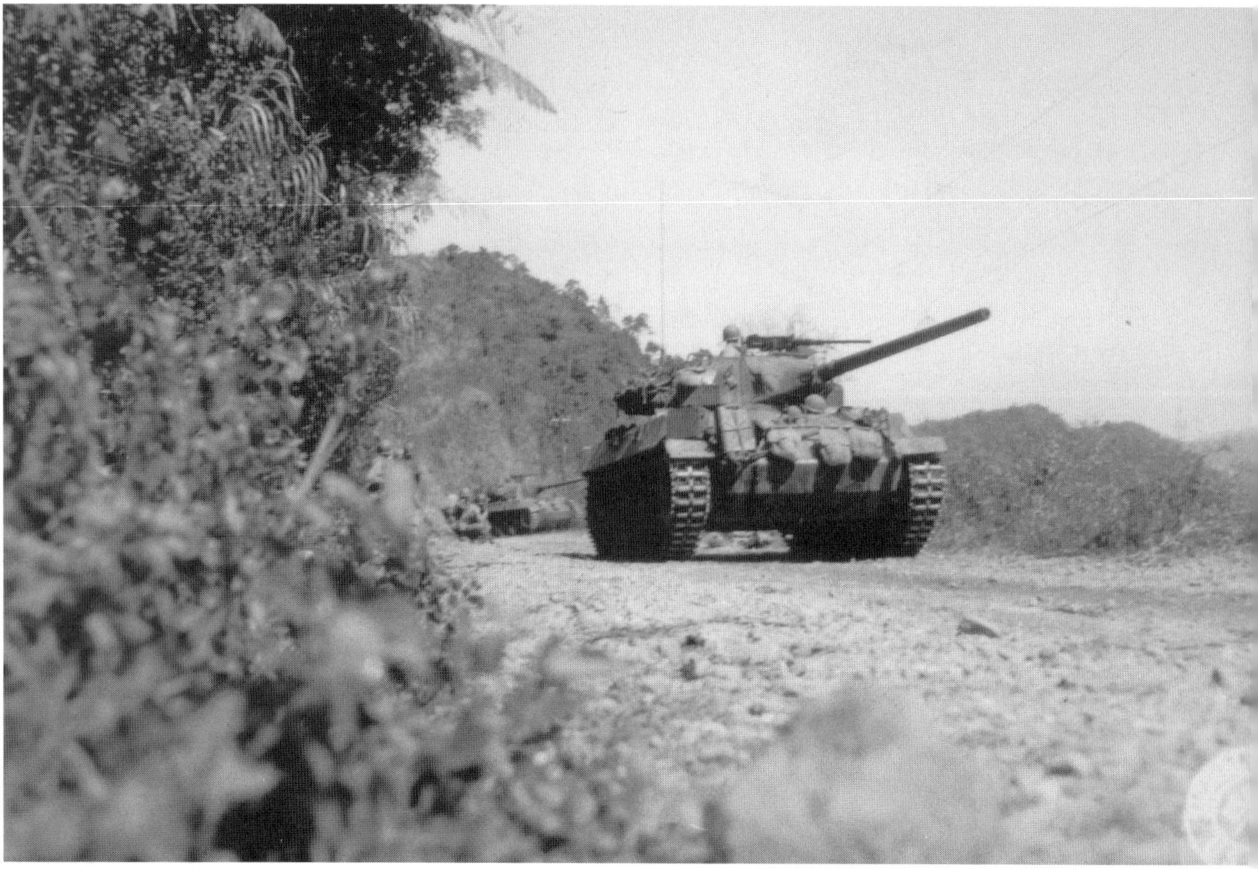

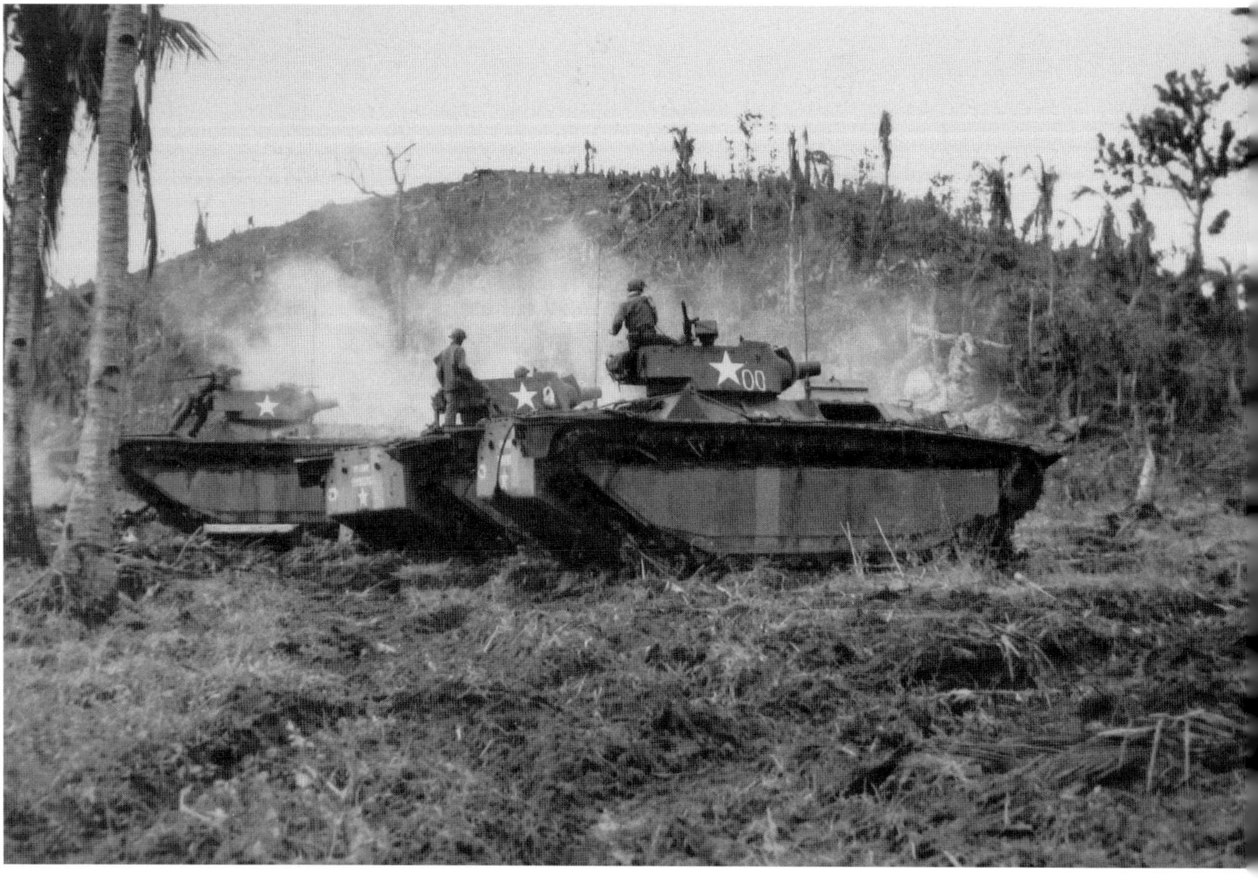
00

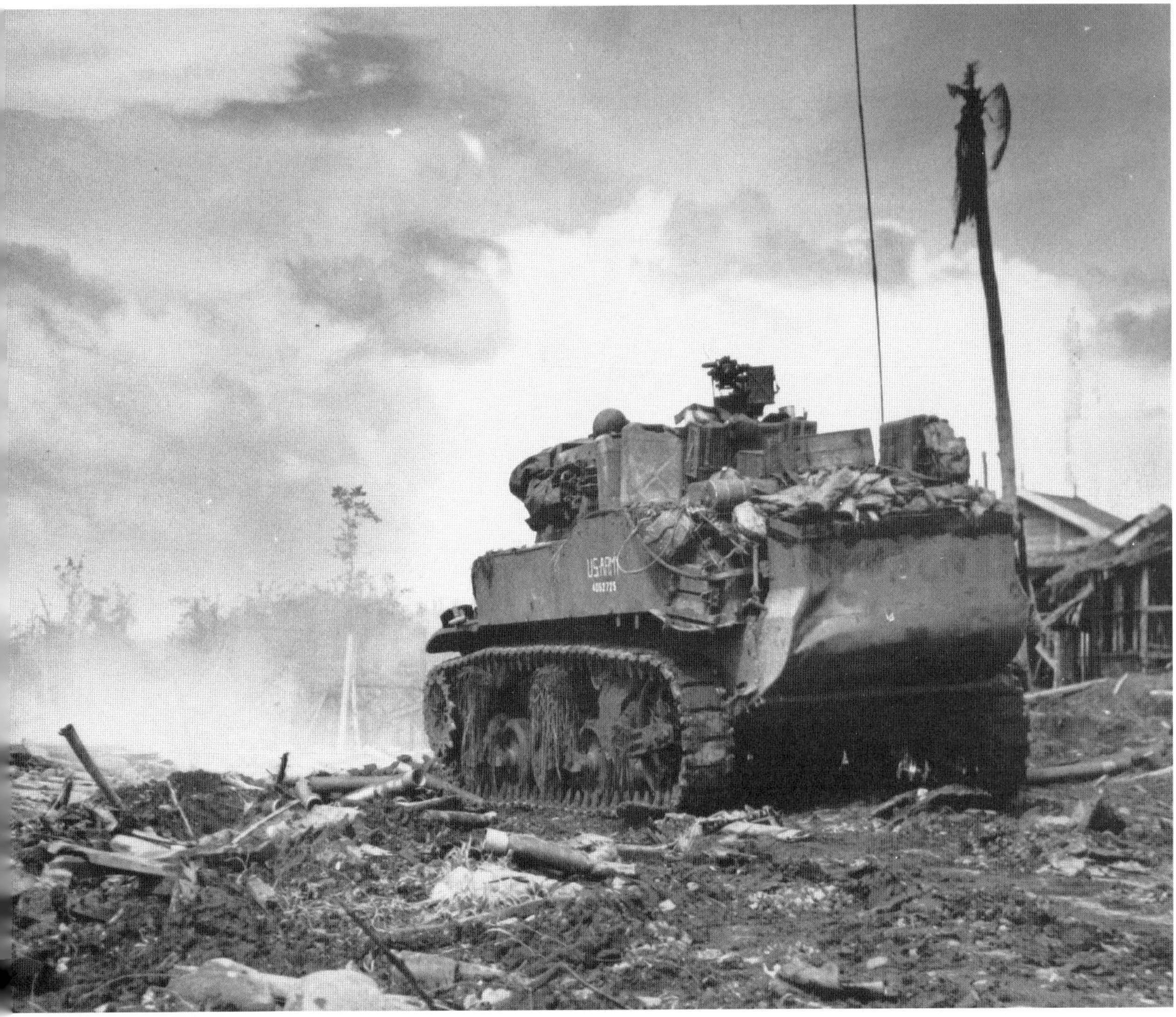

(**Opposite, above**) Two M18 'Hellcats' from Company B of a TD battalion are seen here on a dirt road with infantrymen as the TDs were to fire their 76mm guns on Japanese positions near Baguio in April 1945. The M18 was designed in 1943 and its 76mm M1A1 gun was more powerful than the M10 as well as being one of the war's fastest tracked vehicles. *(NARA)*

(**Opposite, below**) Three LVT (A) 4 amphibious tractors are shown here concentrating their 75mm howitzer gunfire from M8 HMC turrets on Japanese positions on Leyte's Hill 120 on 1 November 1944. Initially the LVT (A) 4 mounted a 37mm gun in an M3 light tank turret; however, this gun was too weak to demolish fixed enemy fortifications at the beachhead and inland. *(NARA)*

(**Above**) An M8 HMC is shown here firing its 75mm howitzer against a Japanese pillbox on Leyte on 2 January 1945. The high degree of elevation (40 degrees) that could be achieved by the turret's howitzer enabled it to reduce Japanese troops and gun emplacements that were bunkered on the sides of hills with plunging fire. This armoured tracked vehicle was developed on the chassis of the M5 Stuart tank. It had a crew of four and also a 0.50in-calibre Browning M2HB HMG. The M8 HMC had a speed of 36 mph. *(NARA)*

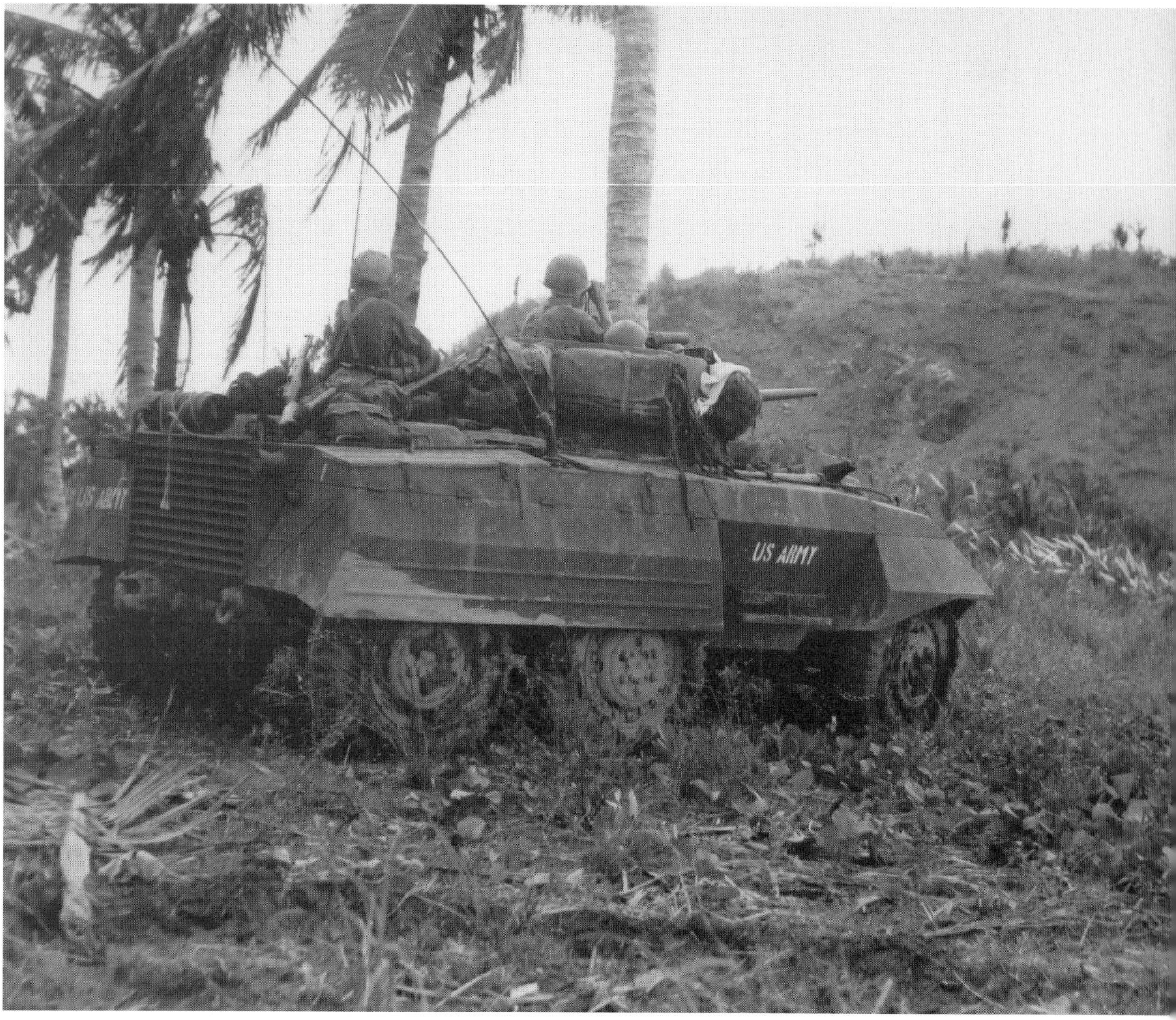
US ARMY
US ARMY

(**Above**) An M8 light armoured car with its crew commander holding binoculars (left turret) is shown here while on reconnaissance. Thinly-armoured, it was still a widely-used non-tracked vehicle with a crew of four. The M8 was noted for its cross-country mobility and low silhouette, affording it evasiveness and concealment. The M8 light armoured car had a 37mm turret gun and two MGs. Its maximum road speed of 55 miles per hour enhanced the M8's role as a versatile reconnoitring armoured car. *(NARA)*

(**Opposite, above**) Company F infantrymen, 2nd Battalion, 130th IR, 33rd Division are walking along a northern Luzon road and atop an M7 SPA tracked vehicle on the way from Bauang to Baguio in late April 1945. The M3 medium tank was modified to provide a fully-tracked carriage for its 105mm mounted howitzer. This vehicle made its debut in 1942 in North Africa and also functioned as an armoured personnel carrier. The M7 SPA had one Browning 0.50in-calibre HMG in its pulpit-shaped turret (left side of vehicle), hence its British moniker of 'Priest'. *(NARA)*

(**Opposite, below**) An M3 half-track is seen here with an M16 mounted quadruple 0.50in-calibre MG. The American soldiers are pouring fire on Japanese positions along the Villa Verde Trail's Caraballo Mountains on 8 May 1945. The US 25th and 32nd Infantry divisions tried to move through the Villa Verde Trail against stubborn Japanese resistance from March to late April to get to Santa Fe and then into the Cagayan Valley. *(NARA)*

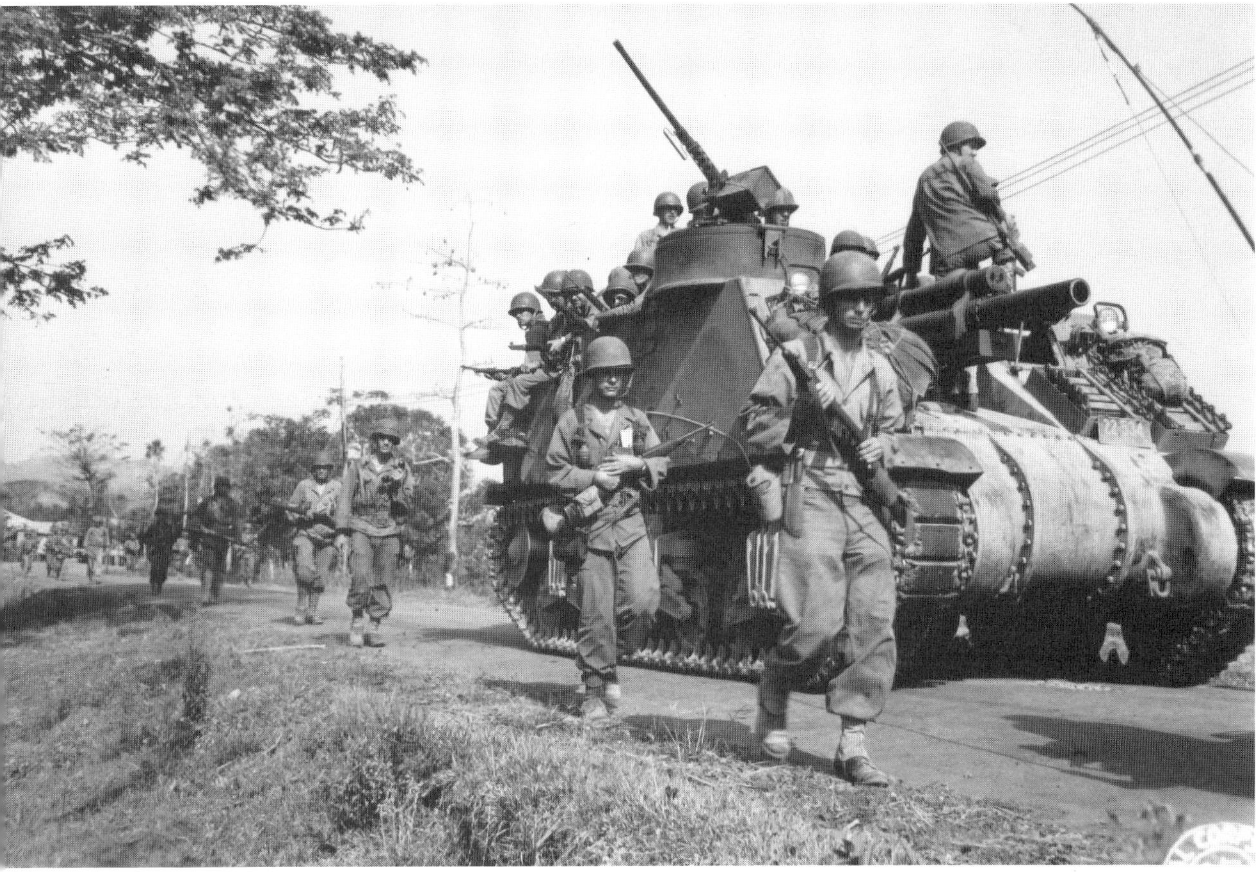

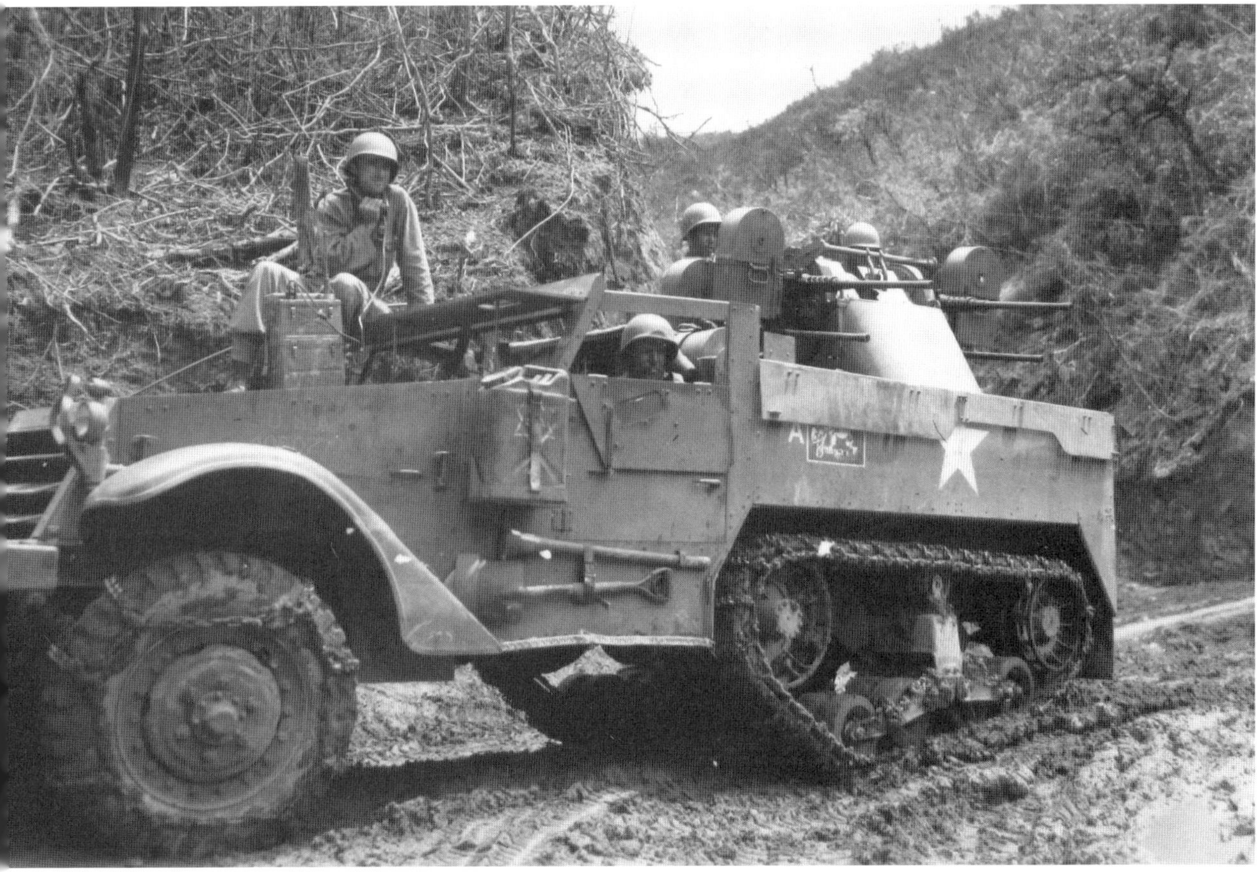

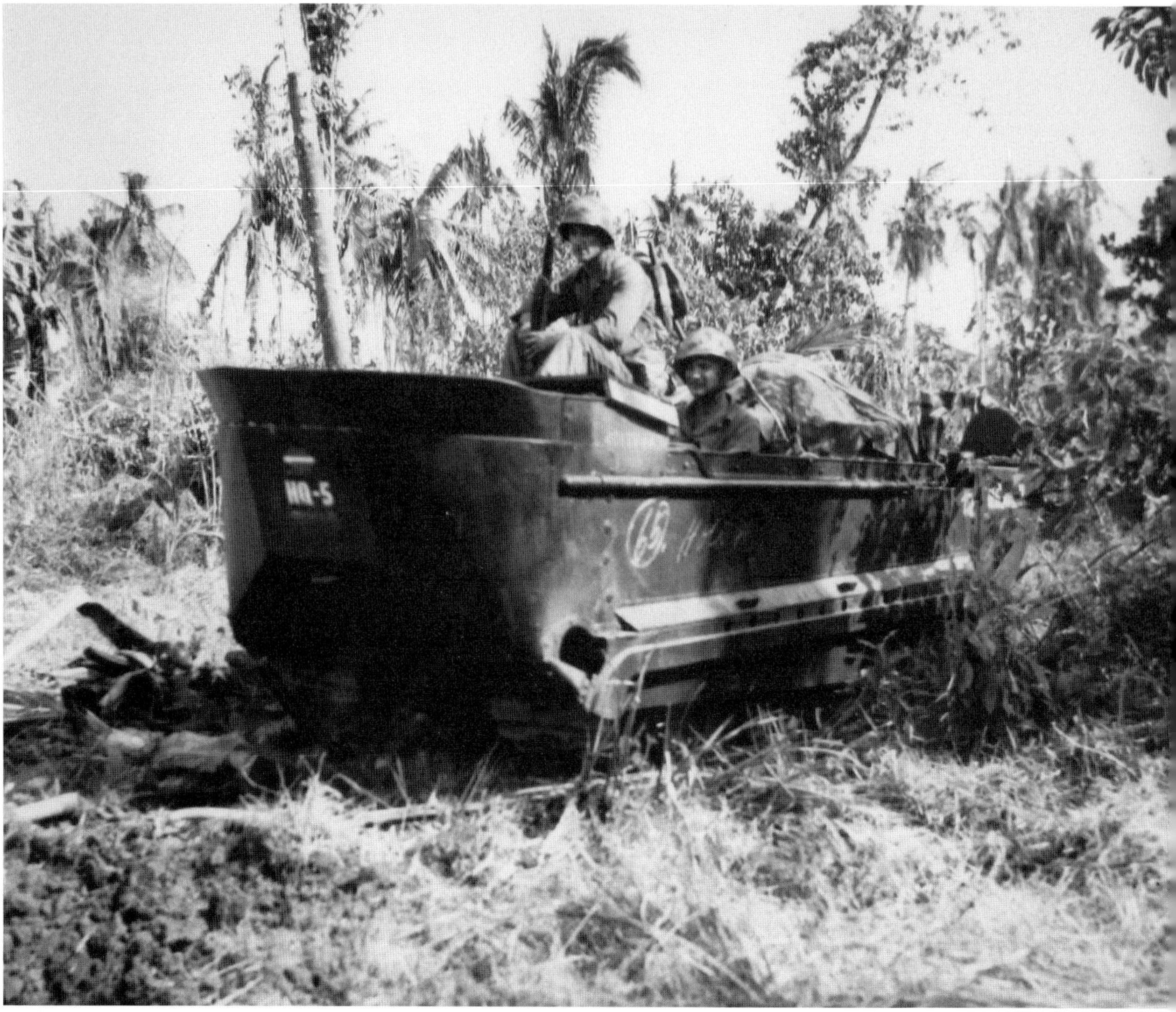

(**Above**) An M29 'Weasel' emerges from Leyte's dense underbrush to secure the airfield at Dulag in late October 1944. This tracked light vehicle (top speed 36 mph) was introduced for the First Special Services Force's proposed attack across Norway's snowy terrain to neutralize Nazi 'heavy water' plants. Although never used in Norway, it was adapted to carry arms, explosives and supplies as well as serve as an ambulance over muddy terrain. Due to its lighter weight, it was able to cross minefields and not detonate Japanese anti-tank (AT) mines. As it was also amphibious, it was able to traverse Leyte's swamps and rivers for the US Sixth Army's divisions on Leyte and elsewhere. *(NARA)*

(**Opposite, above**) An American DUKW is seen here passing a disabled IJA Type 89 *I-Go* medium tank on Leyte on 21 November 1944. The DUKW first appeared in 1942 and was a General Motors Corporation (GMC) 6 × 6 truck with a boat-shaped hull for buoyancy to enable it to carry supplies from offshore ships to the beachhead. In the water it had a maximum speed of 6 mph, but once ashore it could achieve 55 mph. *(NARA)*

(**Opposite, below**) A 40mm Bofors AAA gun is shown here mounted on an M3 half-track in northern Luzon along the Villa Verde Trail. The versatile 40mm Bofors would be fired over open sights at 120 rounds per minute to support infantry or reduce Japanese entrenched positions as shown. It weighed 2,000lb and needed to be either towed or mounted. *(NARA)*

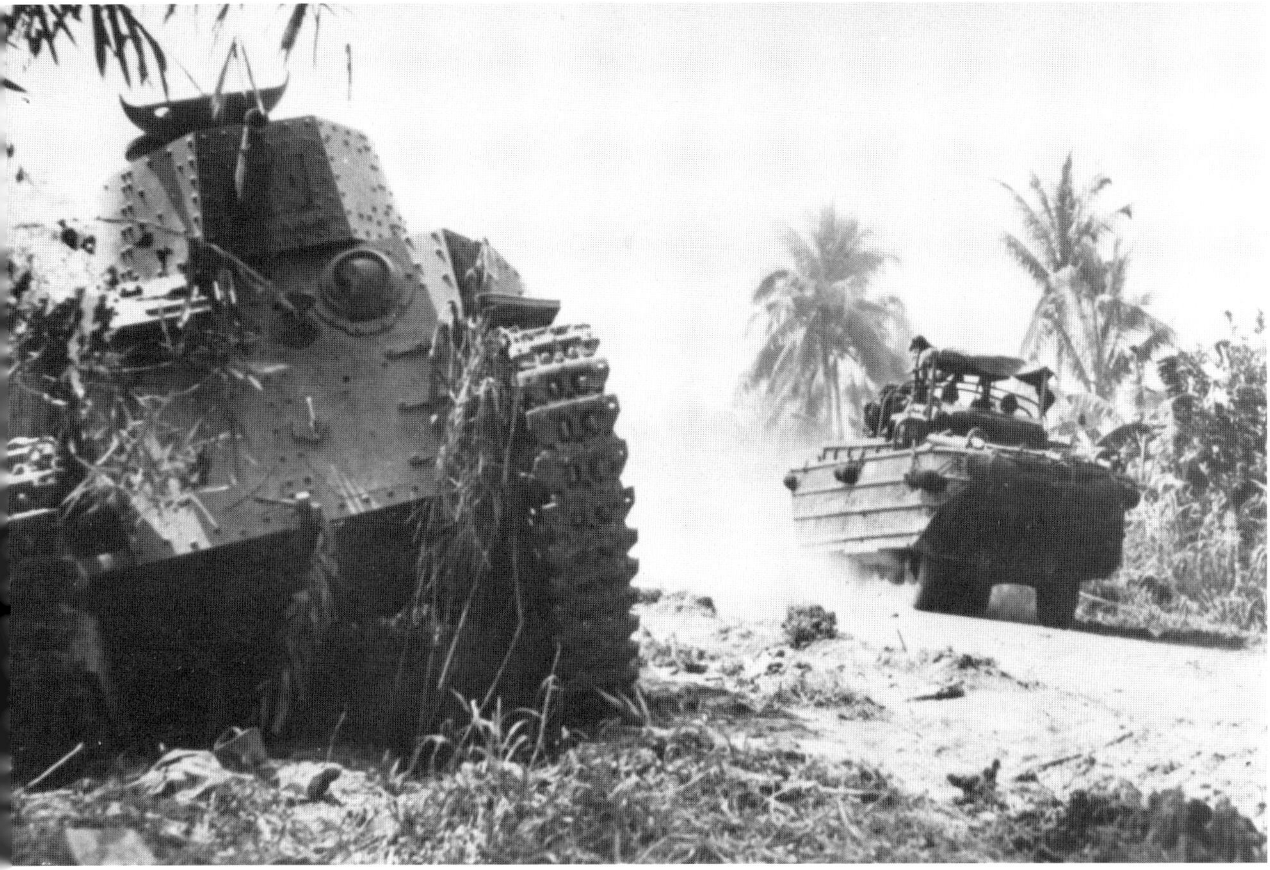

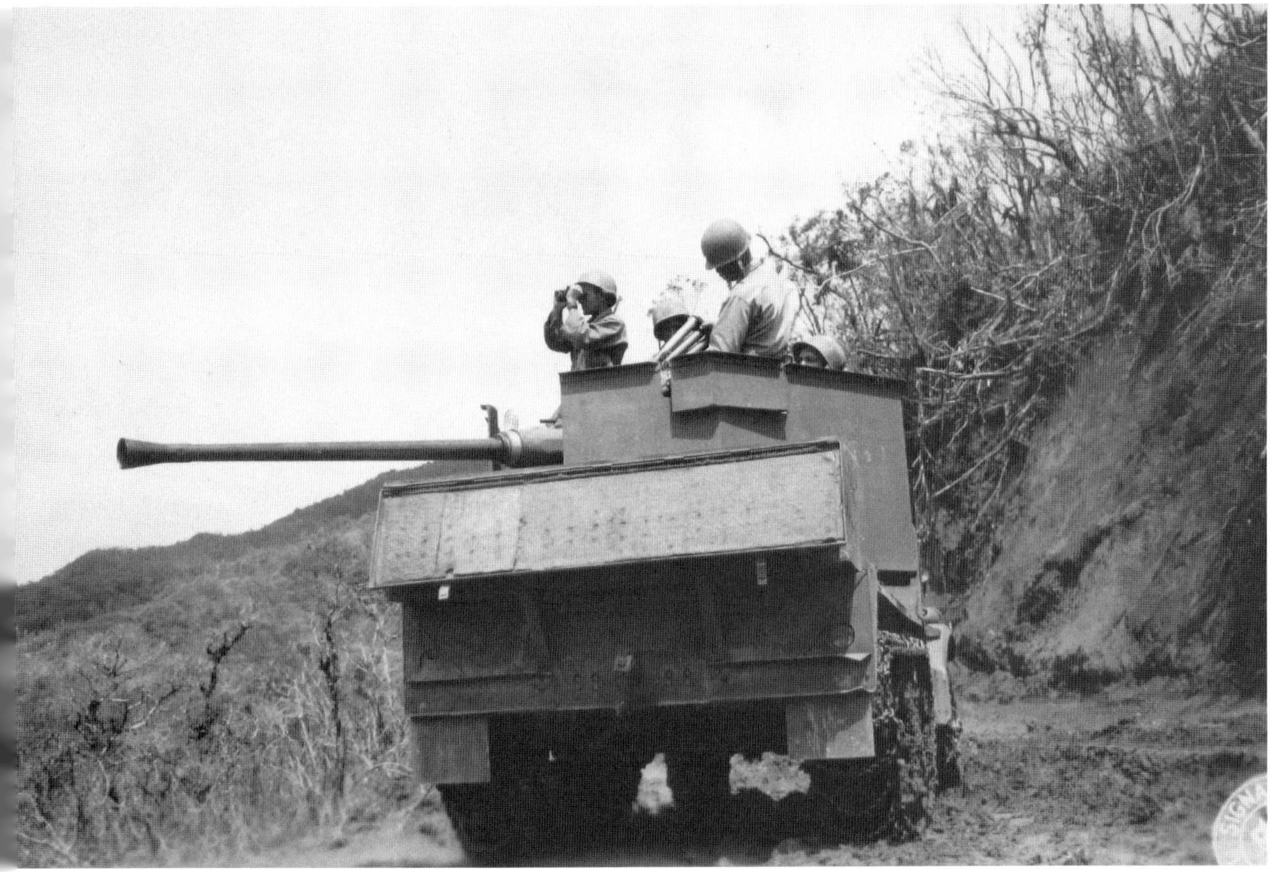

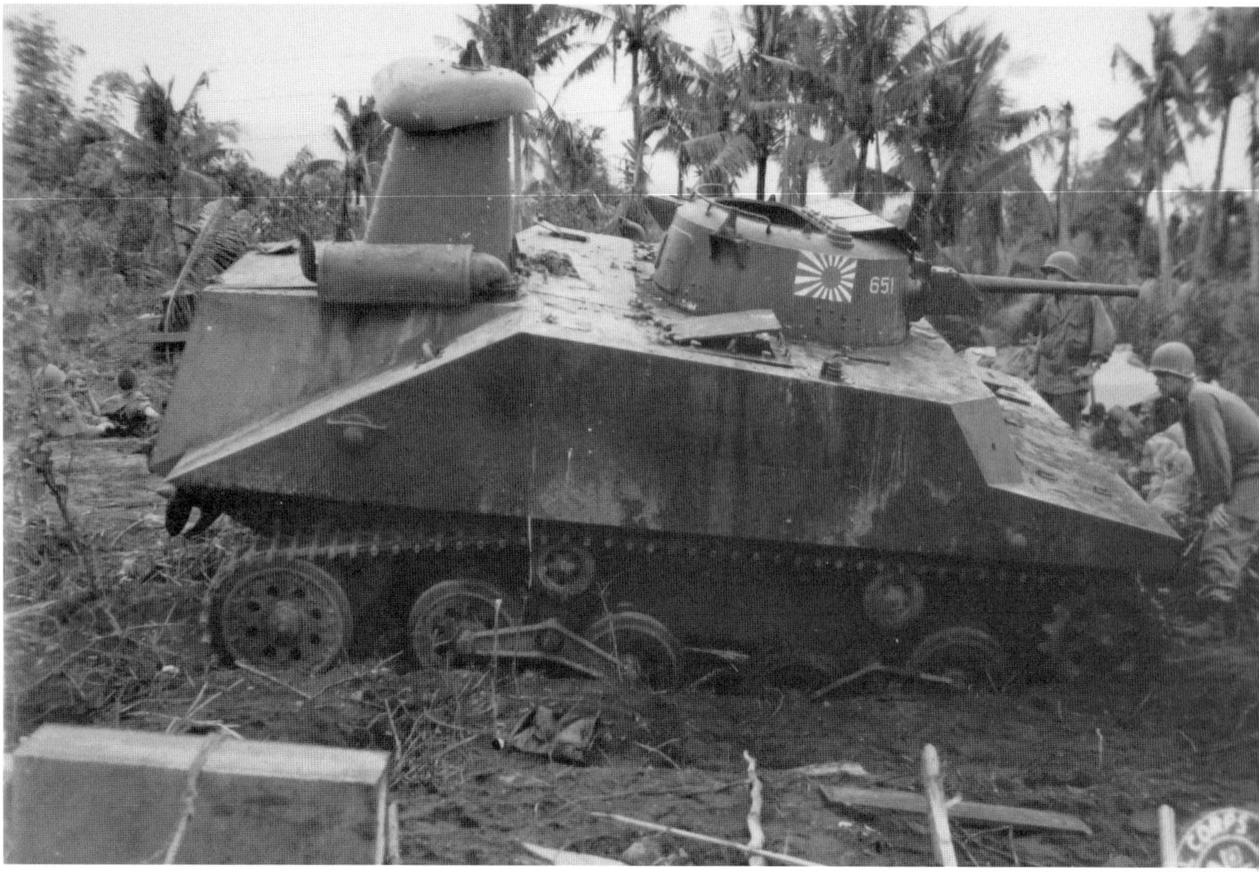
651
CORPS

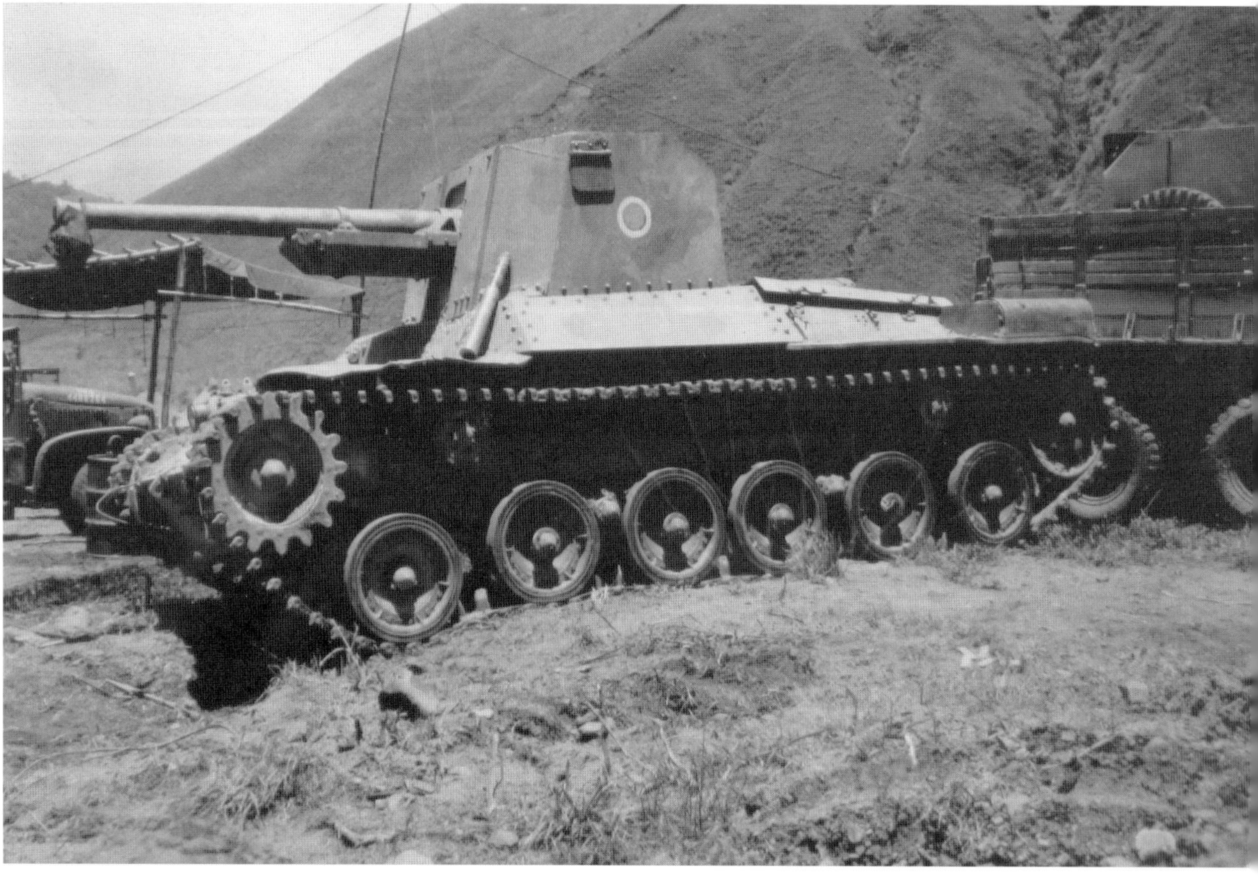

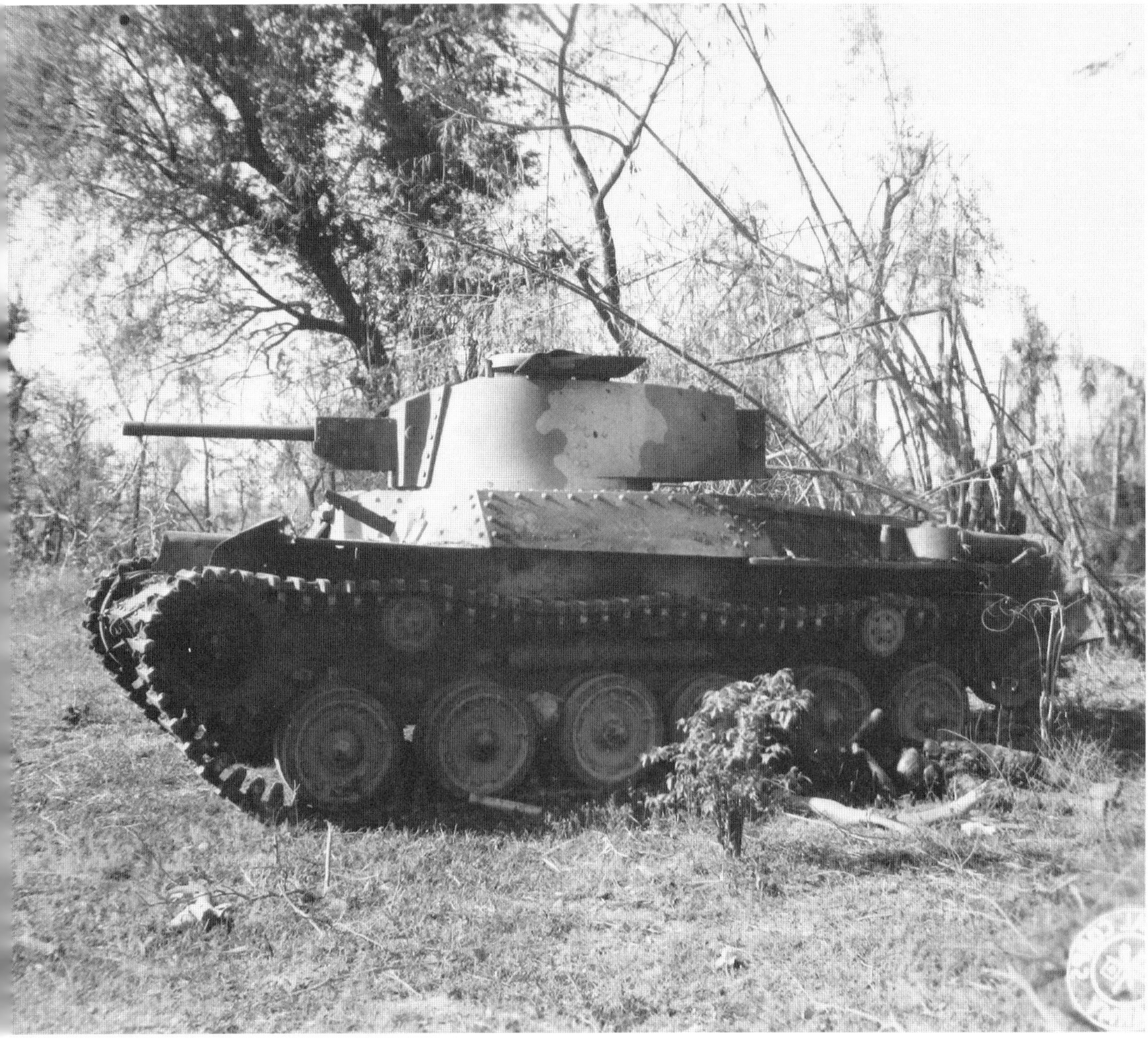

(**Opposite, above**) Two Sixth Army soldiers examine a Japanese Type 2 *Ka-Mi* amphibious tank at Ormoc on 6 January 1945. The tank had a 37mm turret gun and two MGs with a crew of five. This armoured vehicle was first used in the Guadalcanal campaign in late 1942. On Leyte in late 1944, the Type 2 *Ka-Mi* tanks supported the 101st SNLF at Ormoc Gulf on the island's western coast. *(NARA)*

(**Opposite, below**) A Type 3 *Chi-nu* Japanese medium tank mounting a high-velocity 75mm gun was captured by US 37th Division soldiers in Nueva Vizcaya Province in northern Luzon on 25 June 1945. This tank, based on the Type 97 *Chi-Ha* design, began development in 1943 to combat the Allied M4 medium tank; however, it did not enter production until 1944. *(NARA)*

(**Above**) A destroyed Japanese *Chi-Ha* medium tank with a 47mm gun at Luzon's San Manuel on 27 January 1945 is shown here. The *Chi-Ha* had a low silhouette and was designed for infantry support. A dead IJA crewman is seen (right) at the tank's rear. *(NARA)*

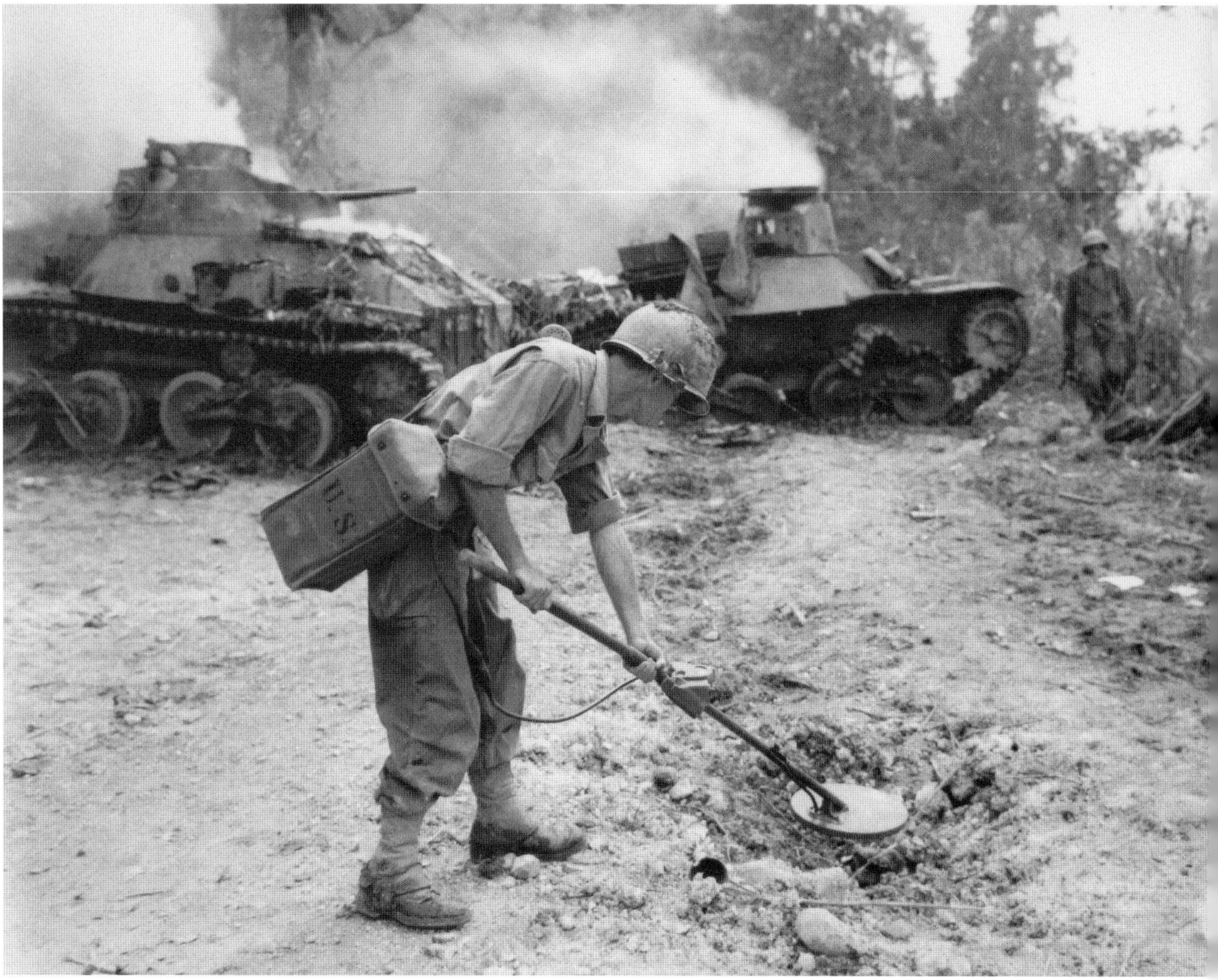

(**Above**) A US Army engineer searches for land mines with his SCR-625 metal mine detector, which weighed 8lb and consisted of a 6ft pole attached to an 18in diameter wooden disc with a cylindrical search coil underneath capable of detecting metal mines up to a foot below ground. However, the SCR-625 was ineffective against wooden or plastic mines, necessitating time-consuming bayonet-probing. Two disabled Type 95 *Ha-Go* (or *Ke-Go*) light tanks are in the background. The *Ha-Go*, adequate against infantry with its Type 94 37mm turret gun, was outclassed by modern Allied tanks. Nonetheless, it was the most numerous Japanese tank produced. In 1941–42, the *Ha-Go* saw action in Malaya, Burma and the conquest of the Philippines. On 22 December 1941, north of Damortis, during the retreat towards Bataan, American US M3 light tanks confronted *Ha-Go* tanks in the US Army's first armoured battle of the war. *(NARA)*

(**Opposite, above**) A battery of US 155mm cannons ('Long Toms') is shown here bombarding Ormoc on Leyte's western coast. The Long Toms could fire one 200lb shell every minute, with a maximum range of more than 25,000 yards. *(NARA)*

(**Opposite, below**) A 16th Provisional FA Battalion 90mm AAA crew, attached to the 25th Infantry Division, is shown here in a fortified emplacement with a shell to be breech-loaded for a direct-firing role. The shelling of Japanese positions at the Balete Pass was critical for the 25th Division advance towards Santa Fe in April to May 1945. *(NARA)*

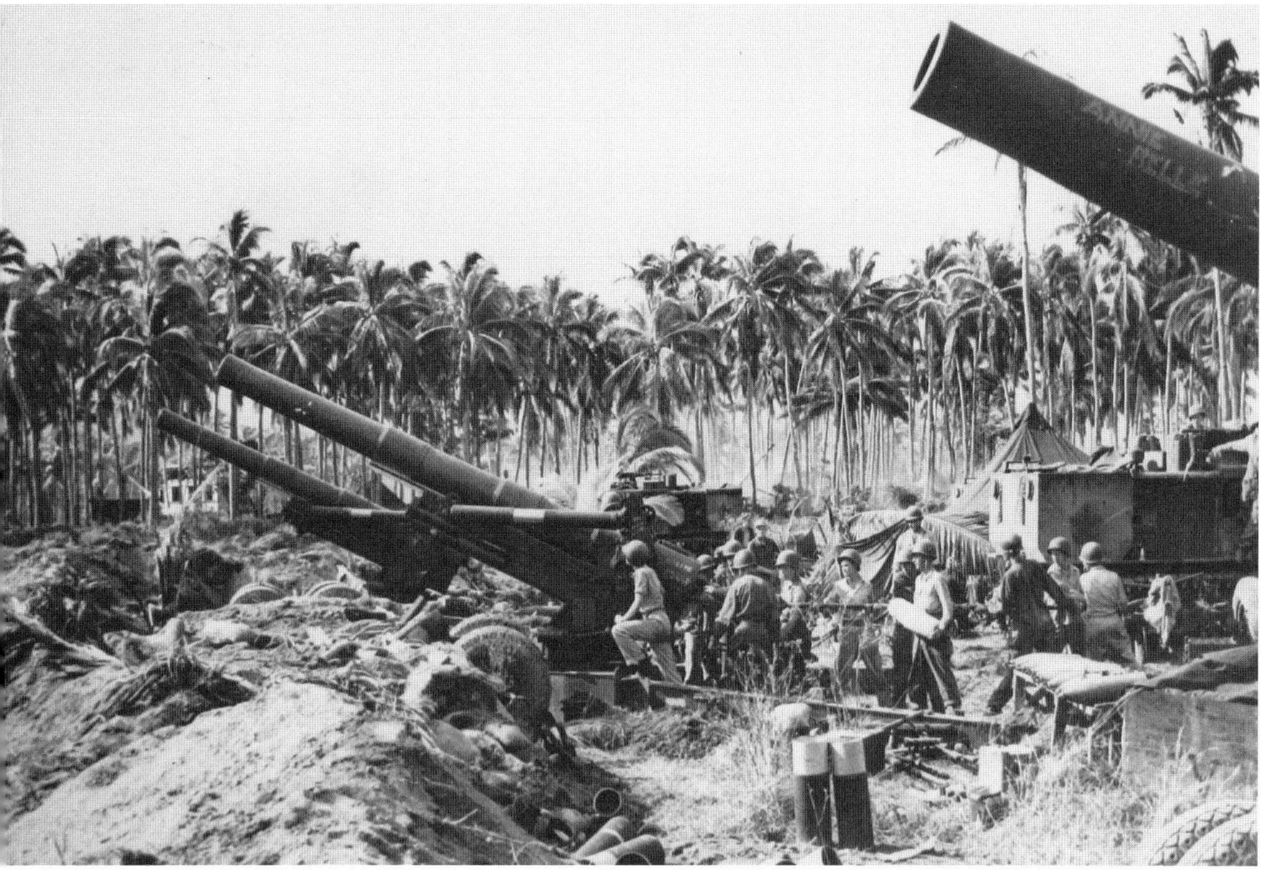

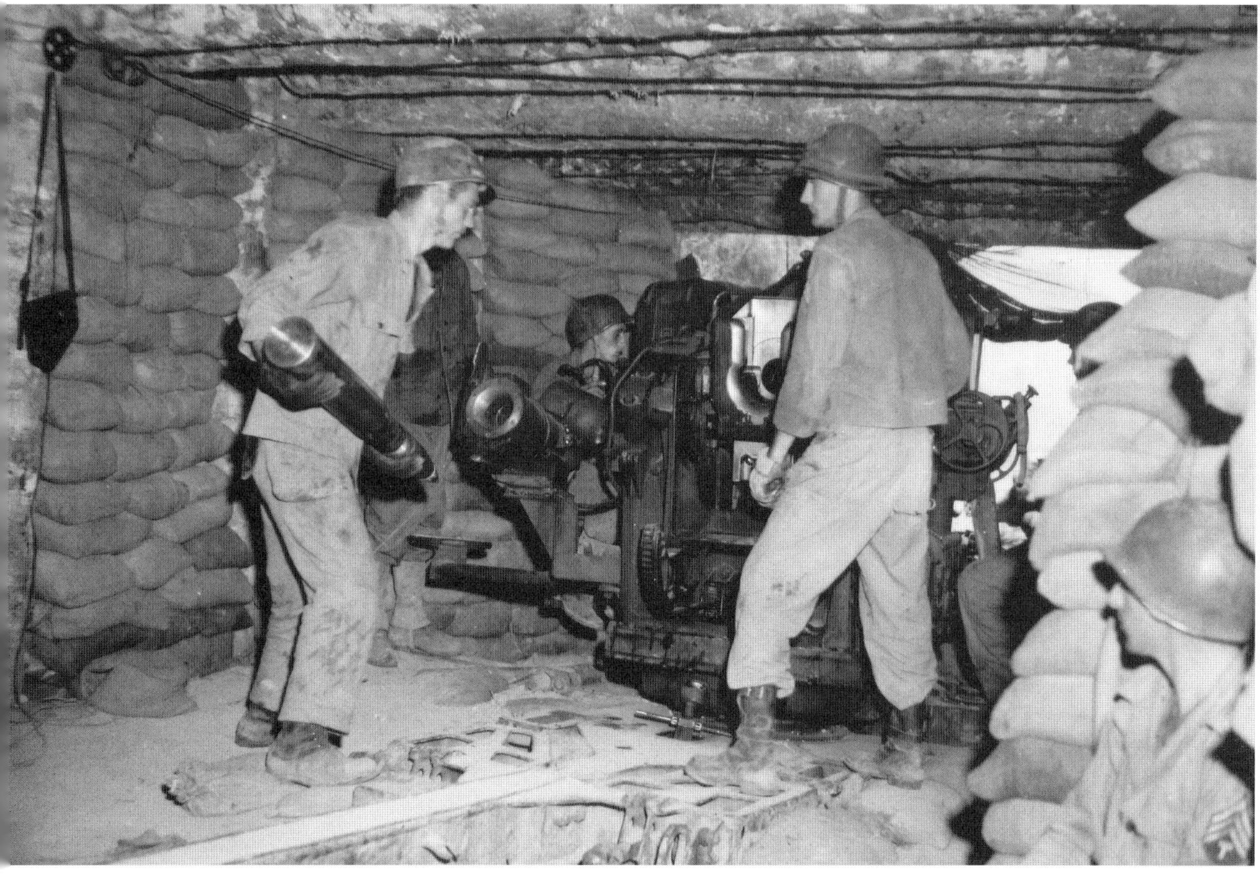

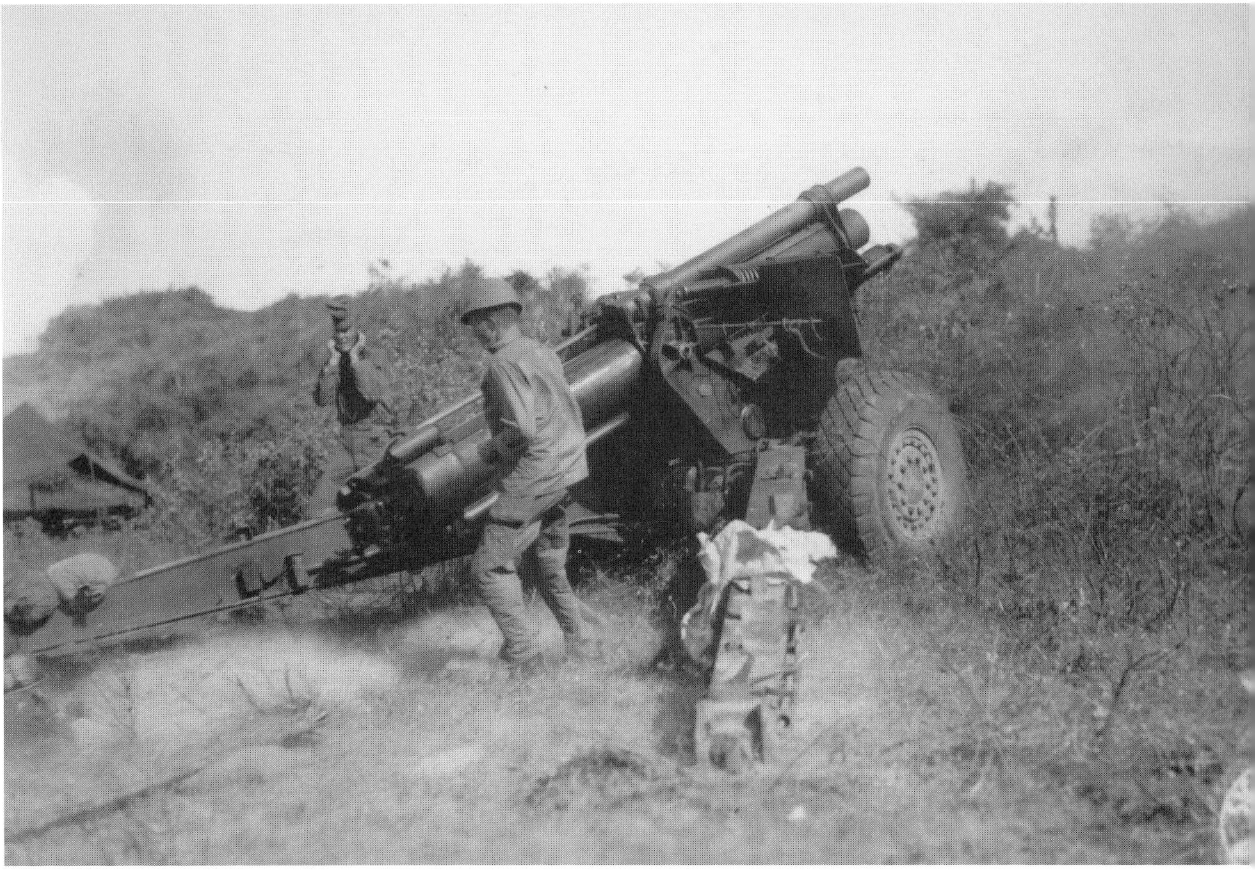

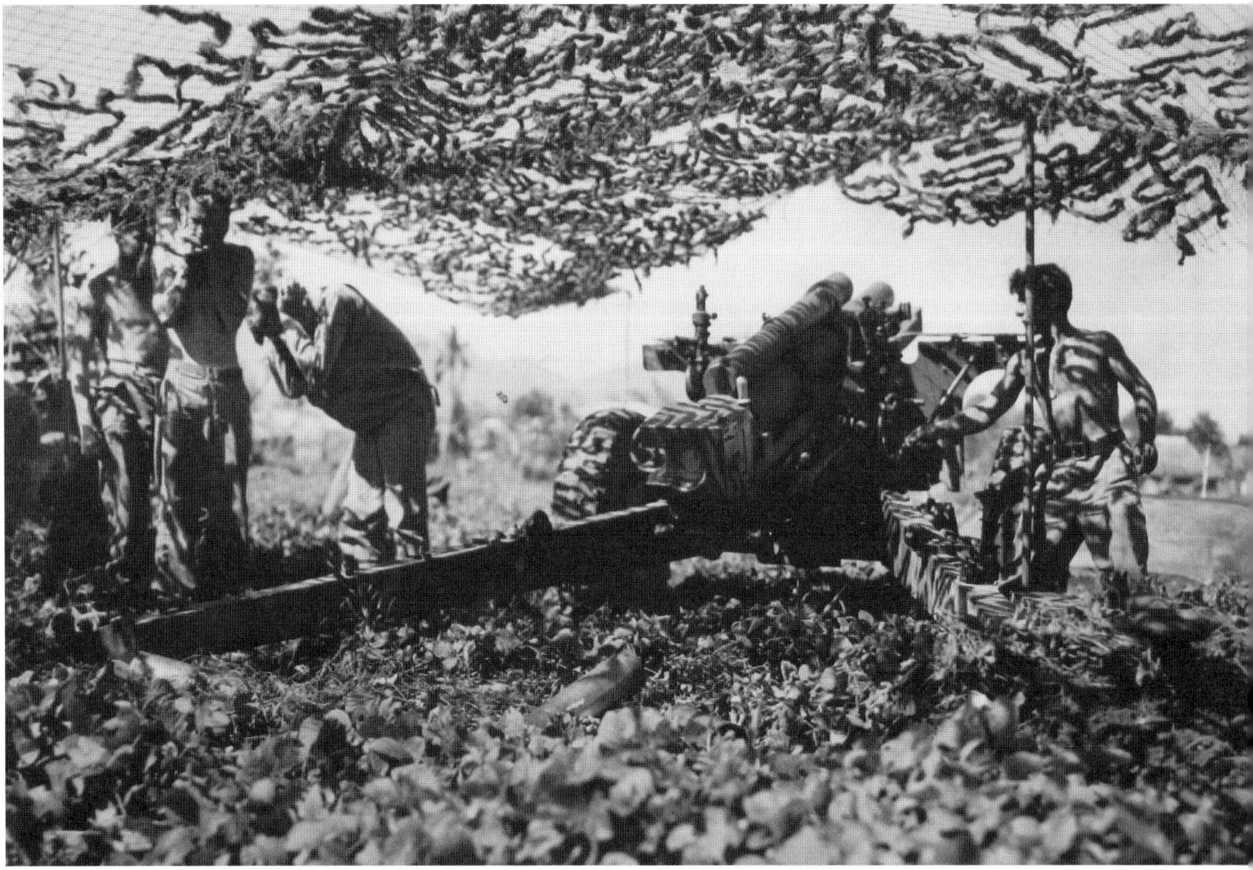

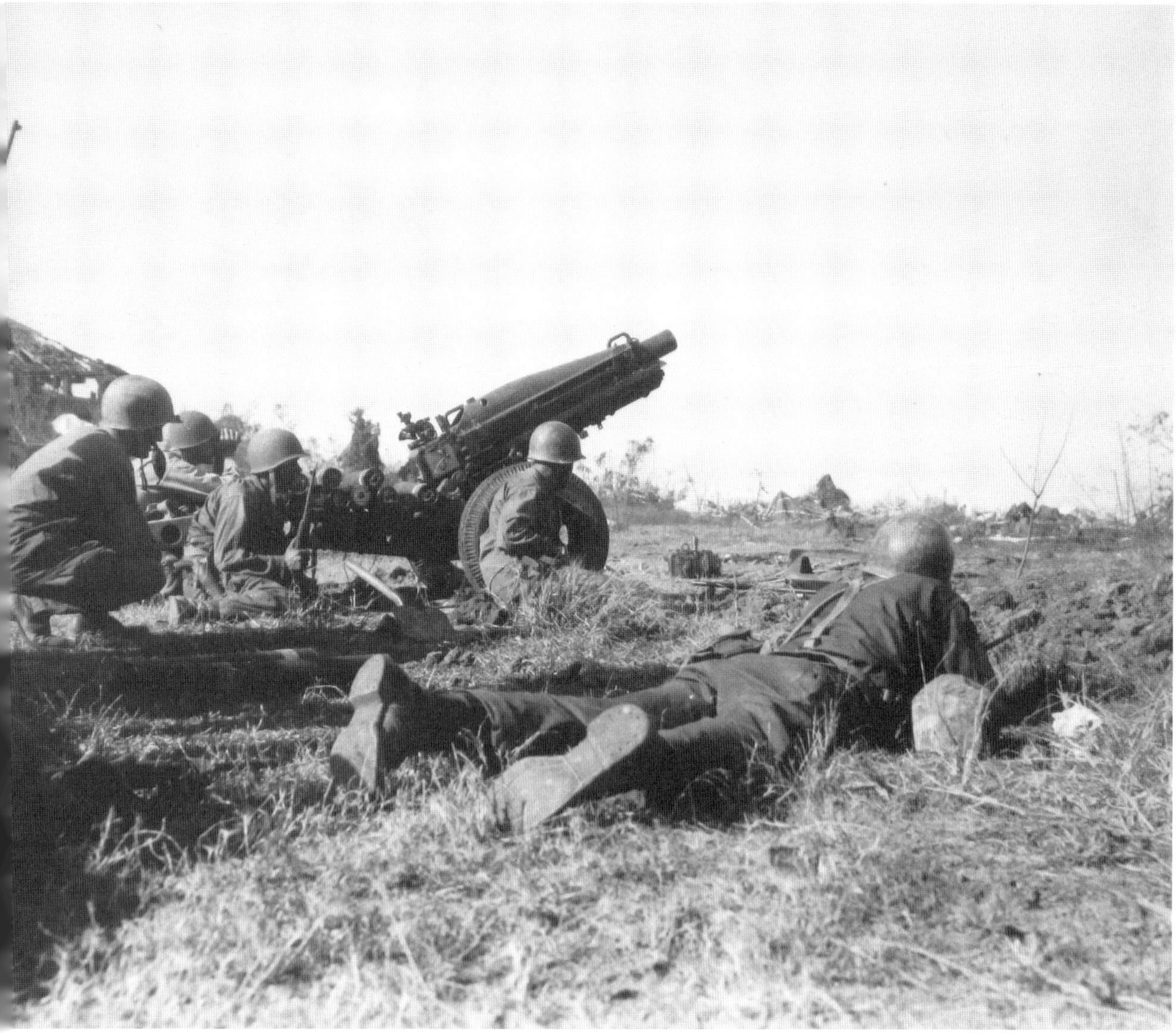

(**Opposite, above**) A 155mm howitzer is shown here firing a round 1,000 yards from the front lines at Urdaneta located south-east of the Lingayen Gulf invasion site on 16 January 1945, one week after the amphibious assault. This howitzer could fire a 95lb shell a maximum range of more than 16,000 yards. *(NARA)*

(**Opposite, below**) A 105mm howitzer crew under camouflage netting is shown here firing their weapon on Leyte on 4 December 1944. This ordnance was an army division's standard FA piece, although it was designed in 1928 but did not see extensive production until 1941. The 105mm howitzer could fire HE, AP and canister rounds, the latter against massive enemy formations. This howitzer's maximal range was 12,500 yards. *(NARA)*

(**Above**) An American 75mm pack howitzer gun crew is seen here taking cover from Japanese sniper and MG fire on Corregidor in February 1945. Originally developed for mountain troops in the 1930s, this gun's six components could be quickly disassembled and reassembled within three minutes as well as manhandled or carried by pack animals ('pack howitzer'). Because of the gun's versatile design, it was also incorporated into Allied paratroop units for airborne assaults with gliders. *(NARA)*

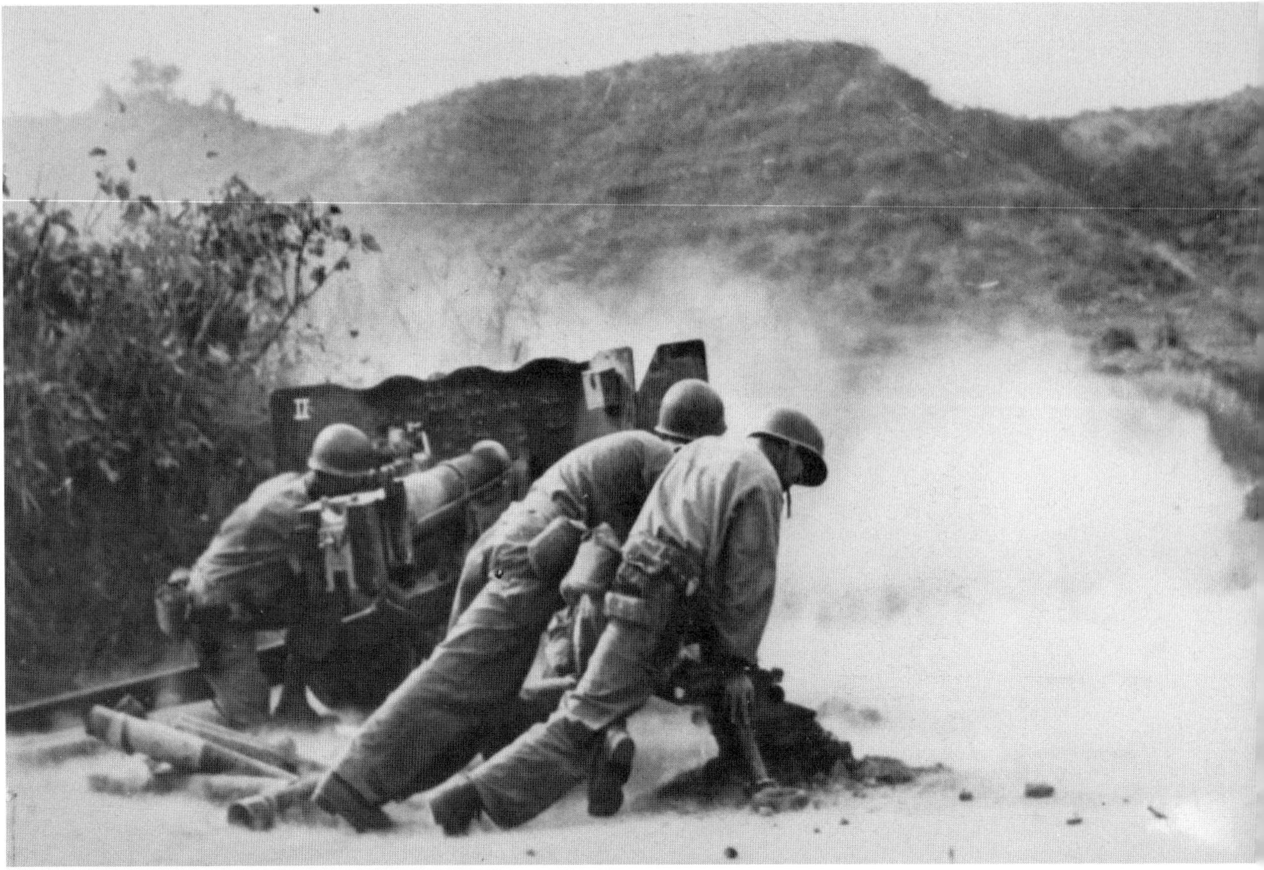

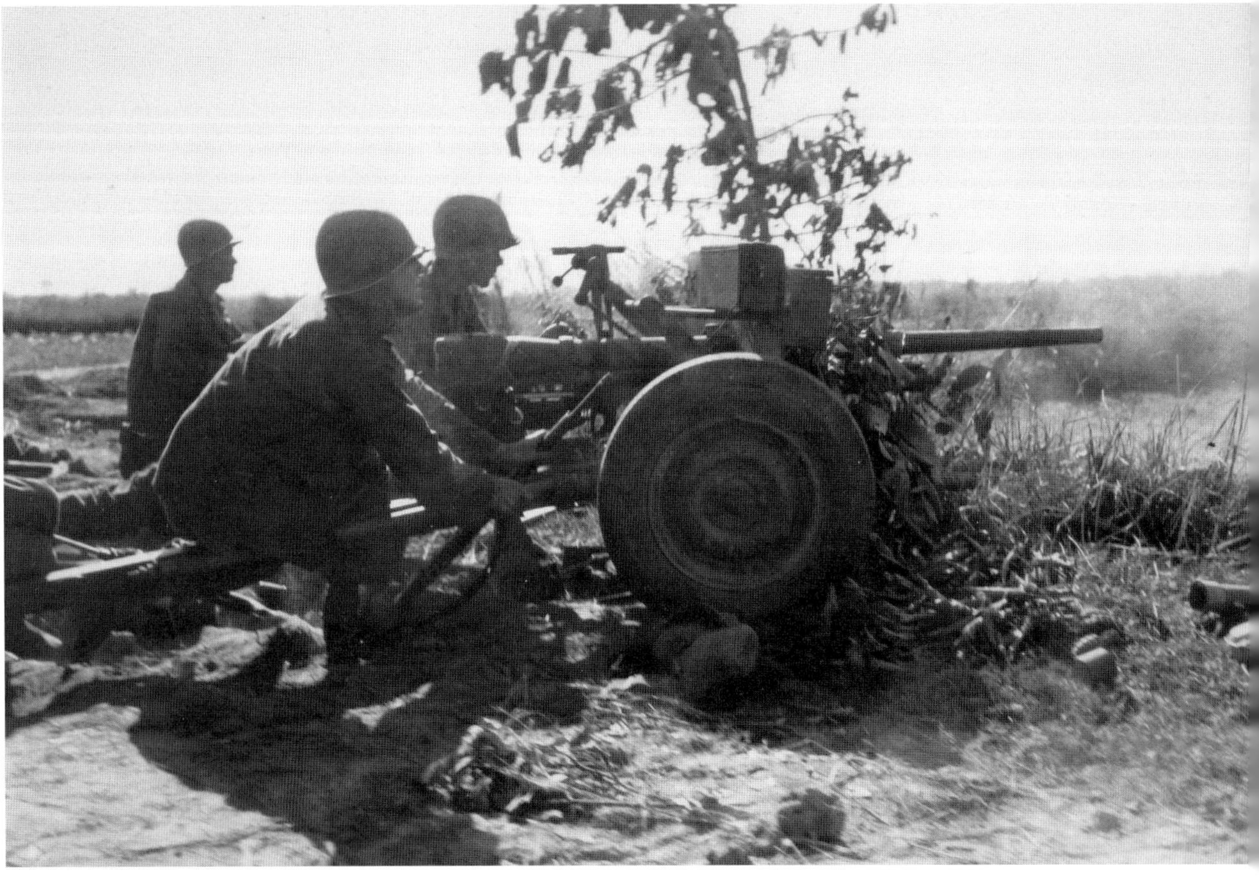

(**Opposite, above**) In early February 1945, American soldiers fire their 57mm AT gun against Japanese positions in the Cabusilan Hills, the most prominent section of the Zambales Mountains, approximately 5 miles from Clark Field. Elements from the US XIV Corps' 37th and 40th Infantry divisions initiated their attacks against Japanese-occupied Clark Field on 27–28 January. Clark Field was valued as a base for close US air support since it possessed several airfields; however, it was principally defended by the IJA *Kembu* Group's several thousand troops, which were positioned across the eastern approaches of the Zambales Mountains overlooking the runways for shelling. Thus, American air sorties were prevented for a long interval after Clark Field's capture. *(NARA)*

(**Opposite, below**) An American 37mm AT gun is shown here firing at entrenched Japanese positions in Luzon's Cabaruan Hills in January 1945. These near-obsolete weapons by ETO standards proved their utility with a short-range HE shell, which was effective against thinly-armoured enemy tanks. Against massed Japanese infantry assaults, the 37mm gun, when loaded with canister, acted like a 'giant shotgun' that decimated the enemy's ranks. *(NARA)*

(**Above**) A 4.2in chemical mortar crew of the 127th IR, 32nd Division is shown here firing either an HE or WP round against Japanese mortars 300 yards away along the Villa Verde Trail during the 'Battle of the Mortars'. The 32nd Division soldiers were in protracted combat in their drive to Japanese Fourteenth Area Army headquarters in Baguio in northern Luzon. This mortar could hurl a 20lb round from 560 to 4,400 yards as its 4ft tube was rifled. With difficult terrain prohibiting transport of cumbersome FA, the 4.2in mortar provided 'plunging' bombardment against enemy reverse slope positions. *(NARA)*

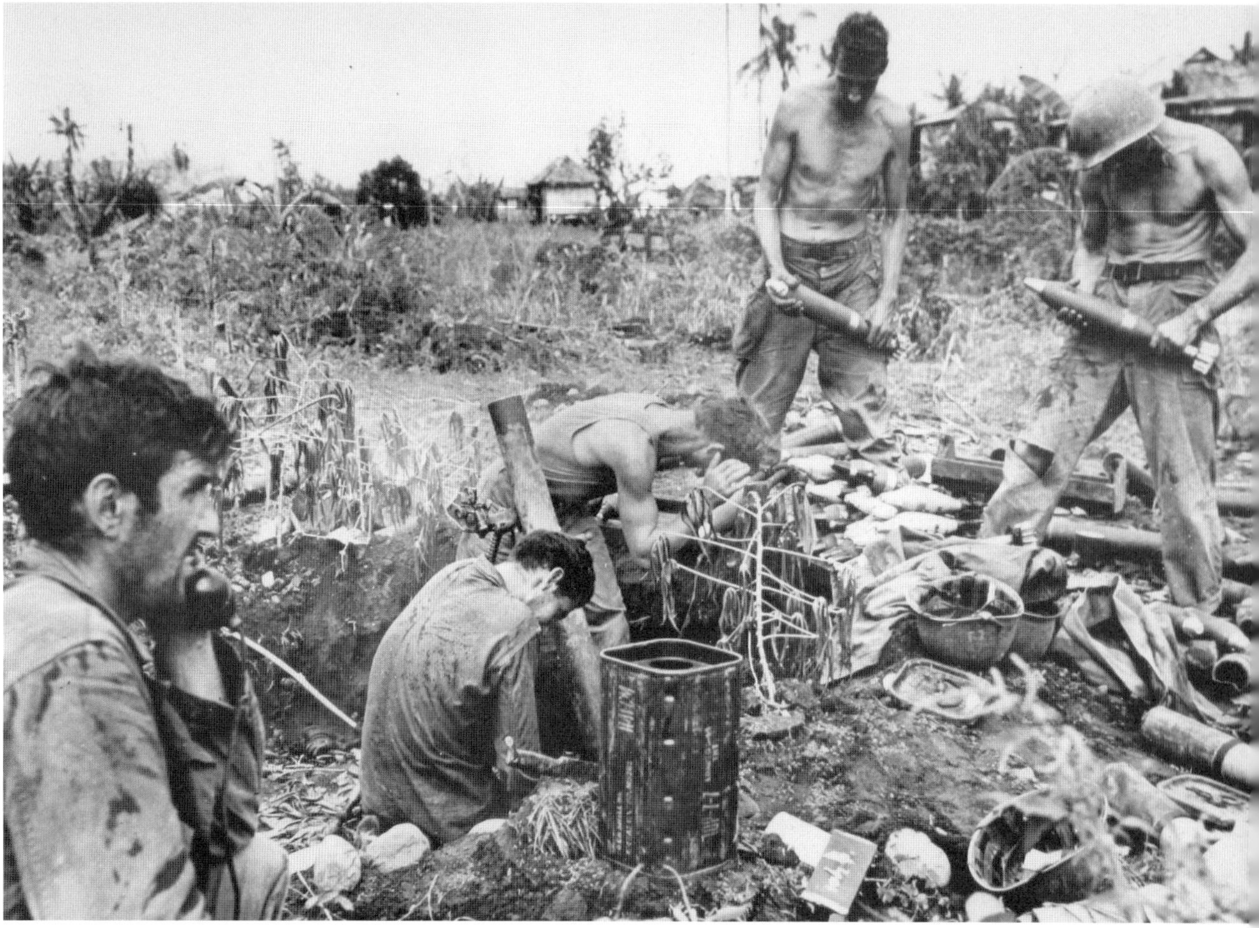

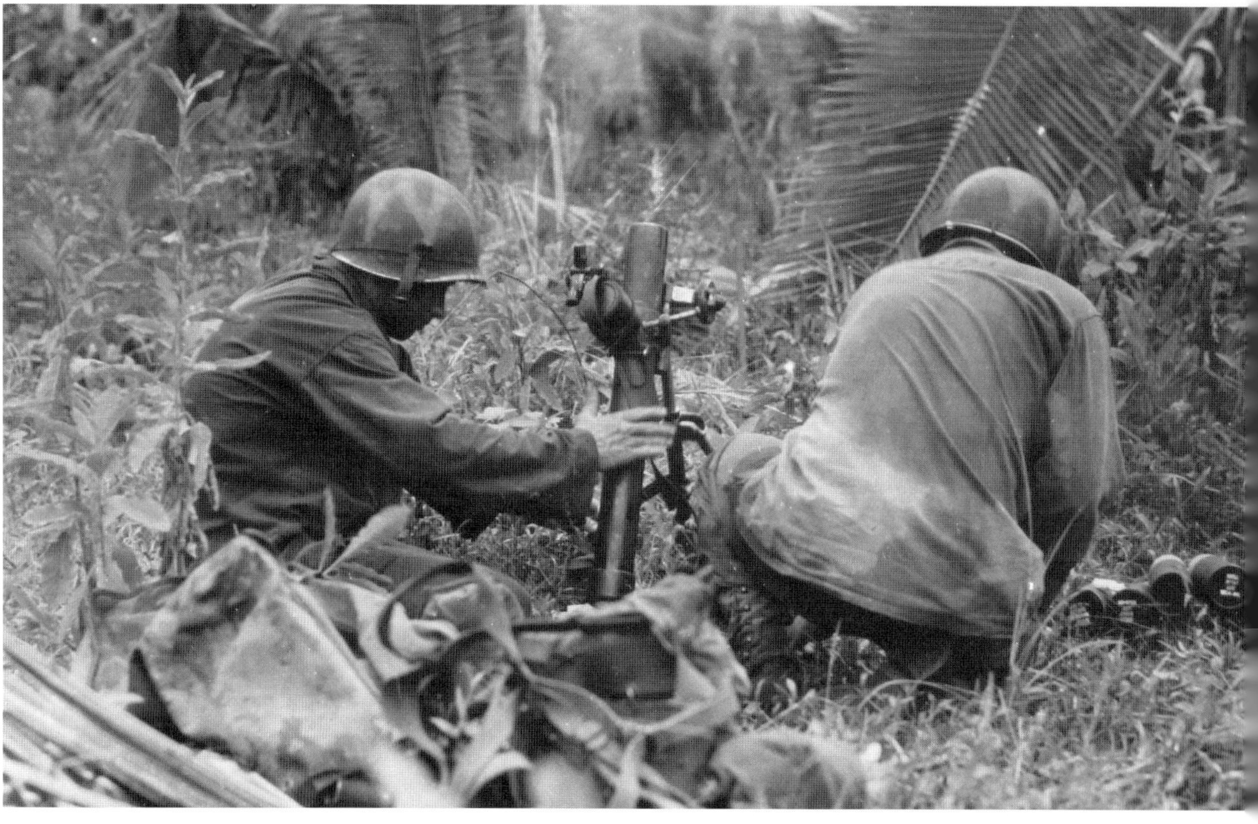

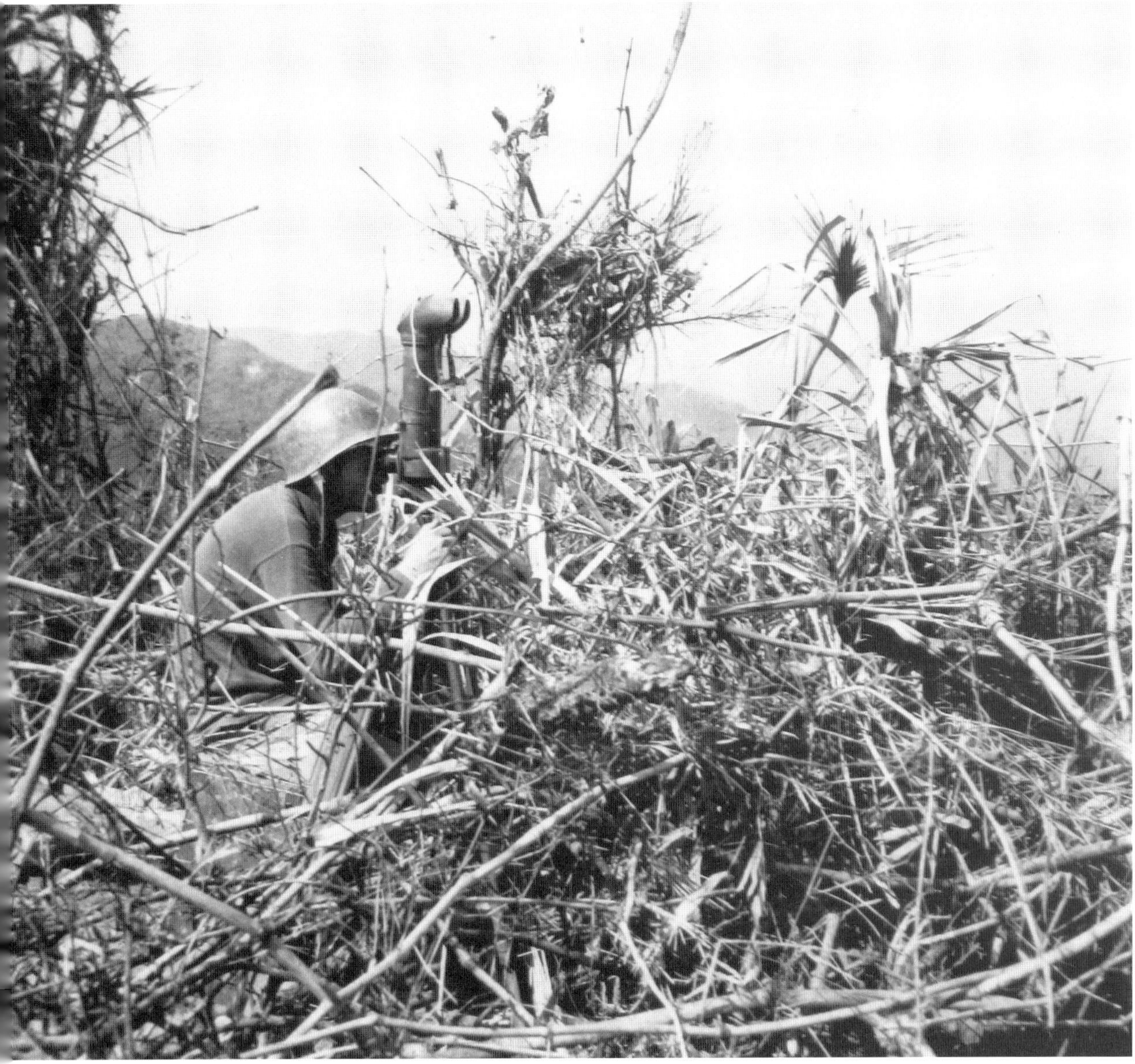

(**Opposite, above**) An 81mm M1 mortar crew is seen here firing an HE round from a shallow pit in relatively open terrain against Japanese positions near Ormoc on Leyte in late November 1944. The open terrain setting for this 81mm mortar crew attested to the rapid need to deploy this weapon against enemy positions and troop concentrations as it was the most powerful infantry weapon at battalion level. *(NARA)*

(**Opposite, below**) A 60mm M2 mortar crew is shown here firing rounds onto Japanese positions on Catmon Hill on 23 November 1944. This mortar fired HE, WP or illumination rounds at company and platoon level with a range of more than 1 mile. Experienced mortarmen could fire eighteen rounds per minute. *(NARA)*

(**Above**) An army artillery spotter uses a binocular periscope to gauge the accuracy of gunfire on Japanese positions on the Villa Verde Trail in northern Luzon on 2 May 1945. The spotter is situated in dense vegetation as cover from enemy snipers. *(NARA)*

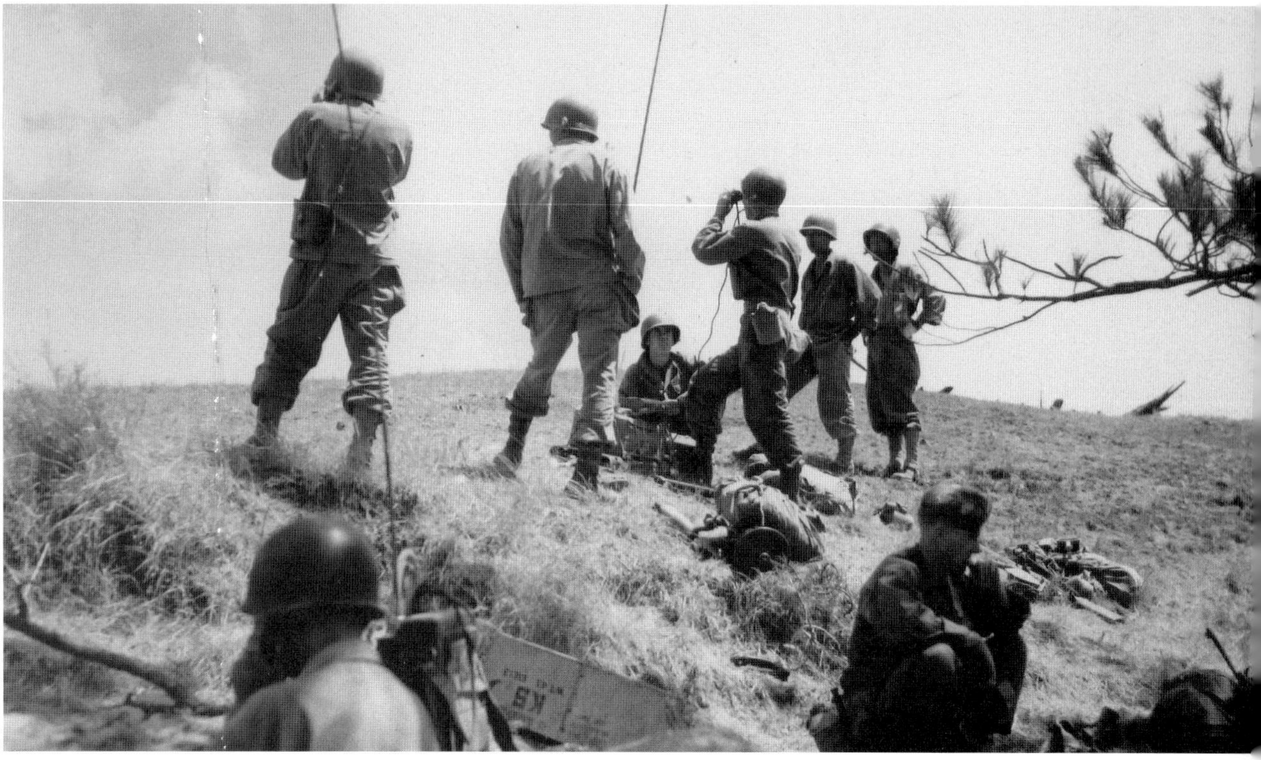

Army artillery observers on Luzon are marking corrections in gunfire coordinates for the FA battalion attached to the 127th IR near San Nicholas on 4 March 1945. The spotters are equipped with radio sets to relay their observation back to fire direction teams. *(NARA)*

Soldiers of the 151st IR are using a WP grenade against a suspected Japanese position on Carabao Island (Fort Frank) in Manila Bay on 16 April 1945. The M15 WP grenade, which had the moniker 'Willie Pete', was originally designed for screening infantry movements. However, upon detonation, the grenade emitted white phosphorus particles which, after coming into contact with enemy soldiers' skin, would burn their surface at an inordinately high temperature, making it impossible for the enemy to remain in their caves and the sides of ridges. *(NARA)*

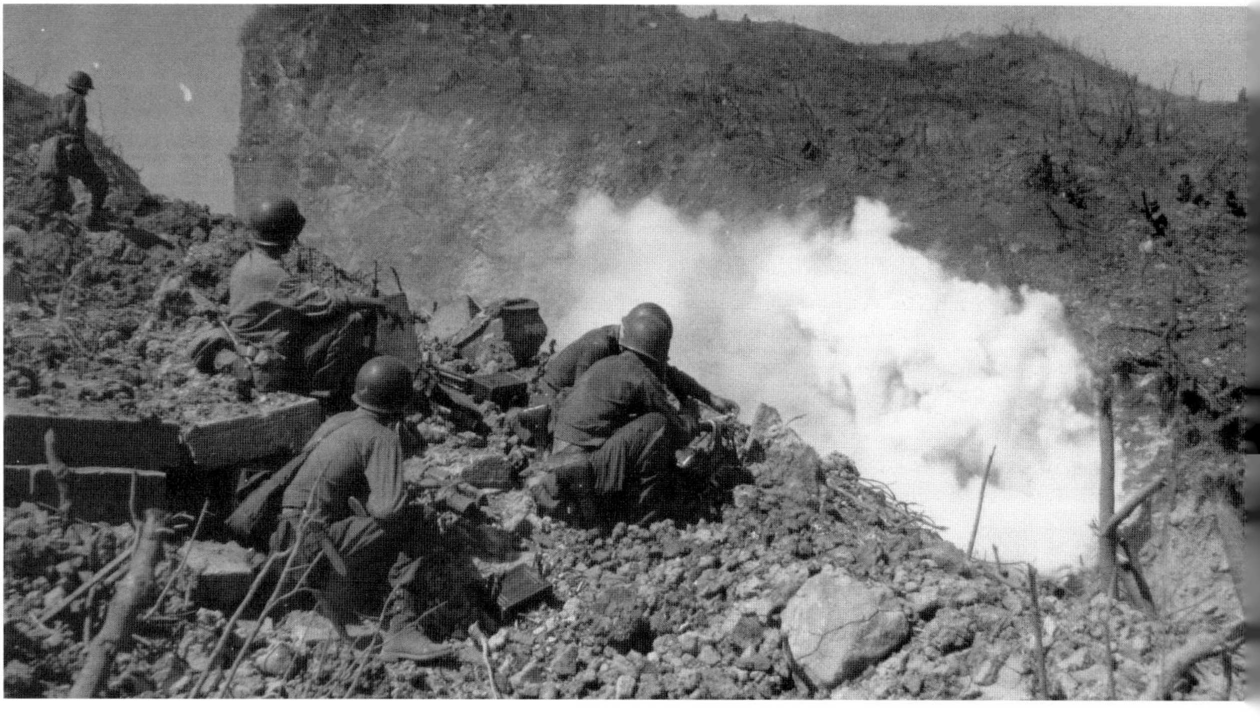

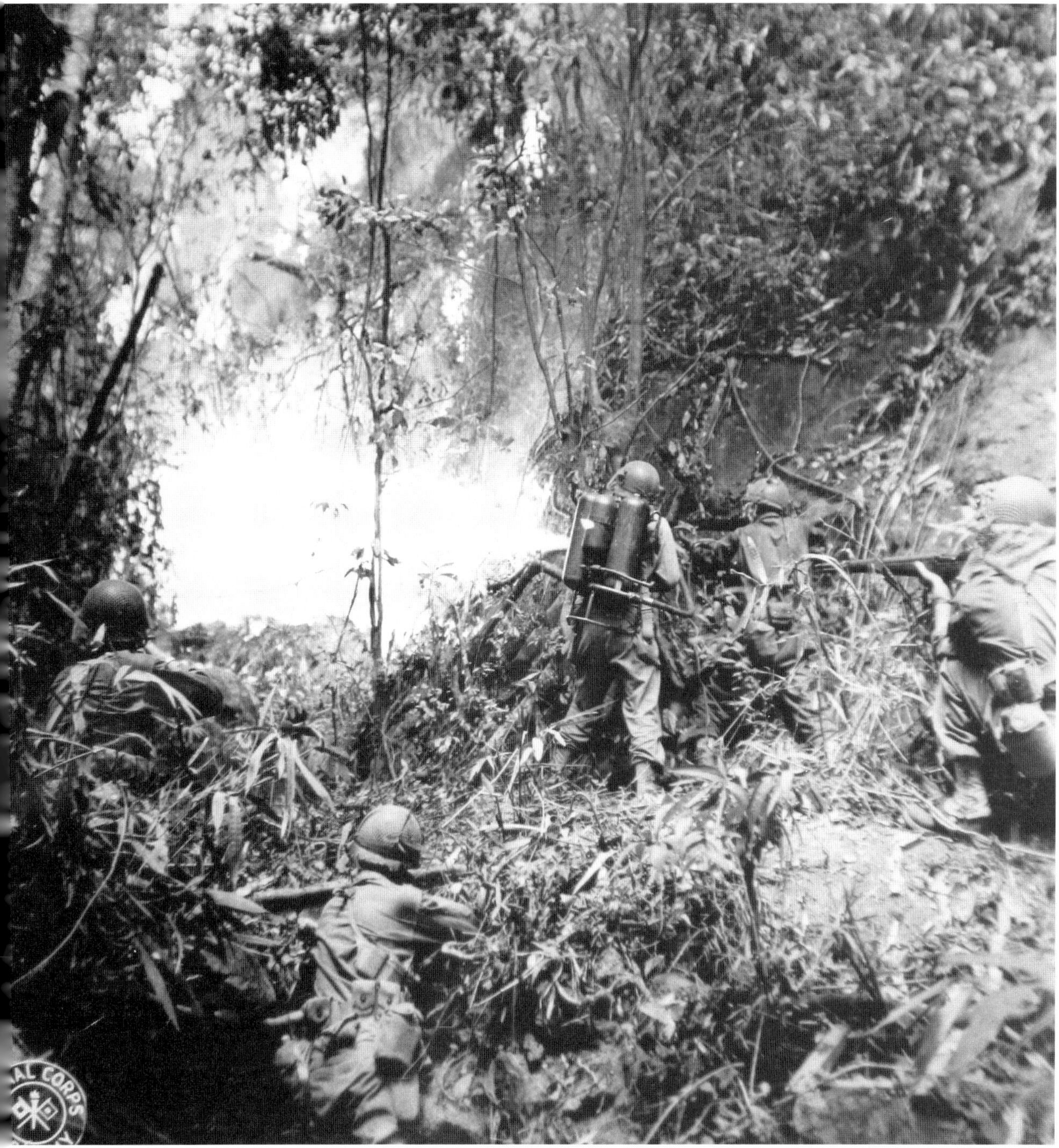

A patrol from Company K, 3rd Battalion, 161st IR, 25th Division is shown here using an M2-2 flame-thrower to burn out an enemy position near the Balete Pass in densely-vegetated mountains on 19 April 1945. The American soldiers were attempting to prevent the Japanese from retreating towards Baguio. The M2-2 weighed 70lb and entered service in 1943. The flame-thrower consisted of three tanks: two that housed 4 gallons of combustible fuel, while the third contained nitrogen propellant. Bursts of flame were fired for eight to nine seconds with a range of 70–130ft. Riflemen are shown protecting the flame-thrower as well as shooting at any Japanese soldiers trying to rush the patrol. *(NARA)*

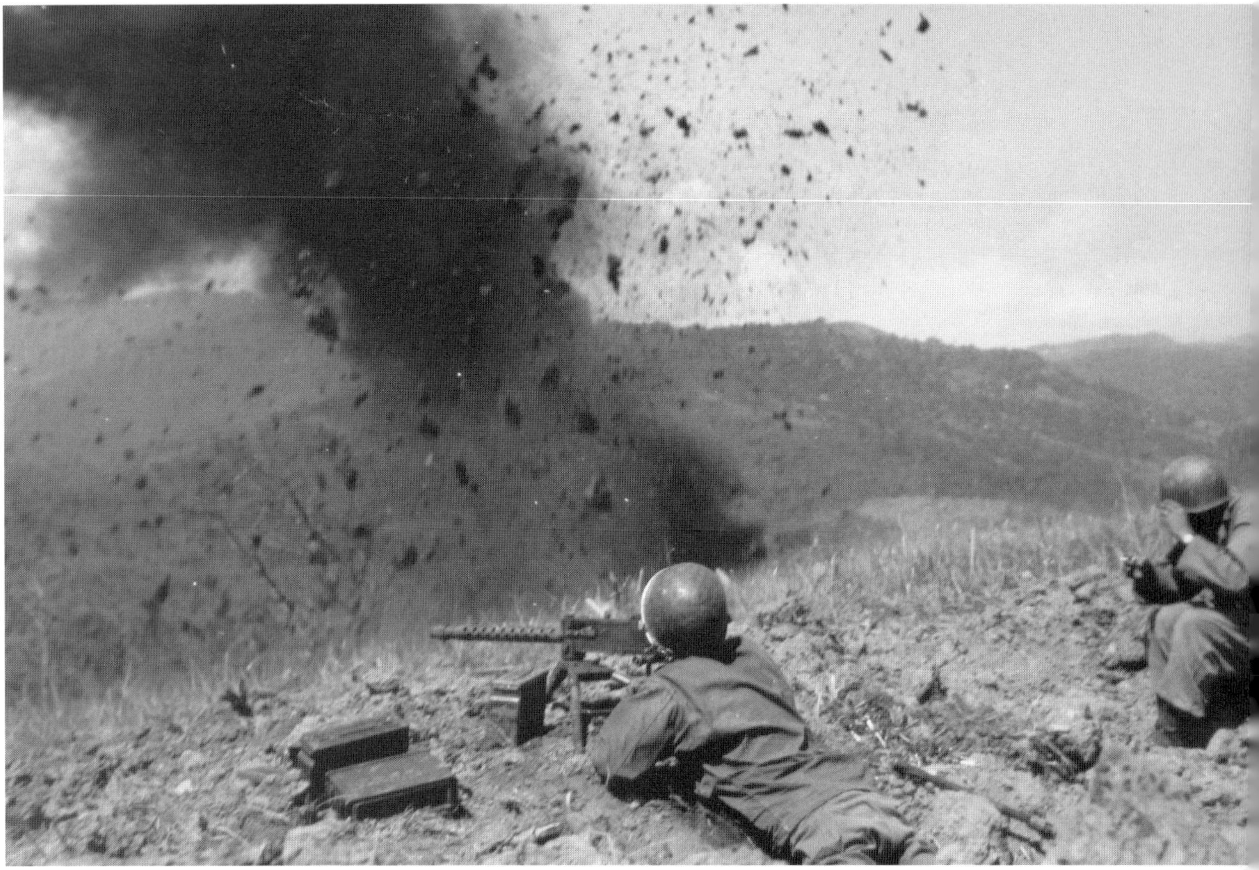

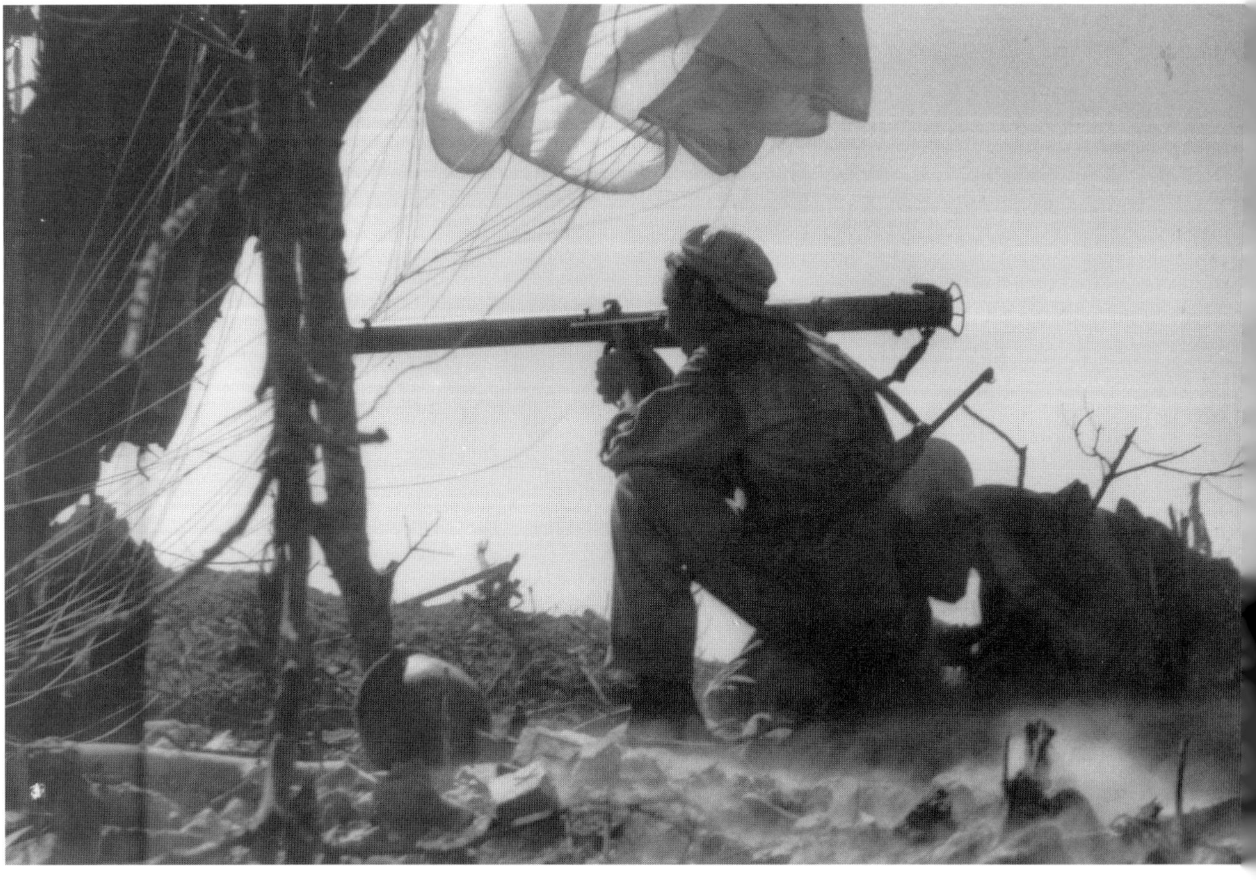

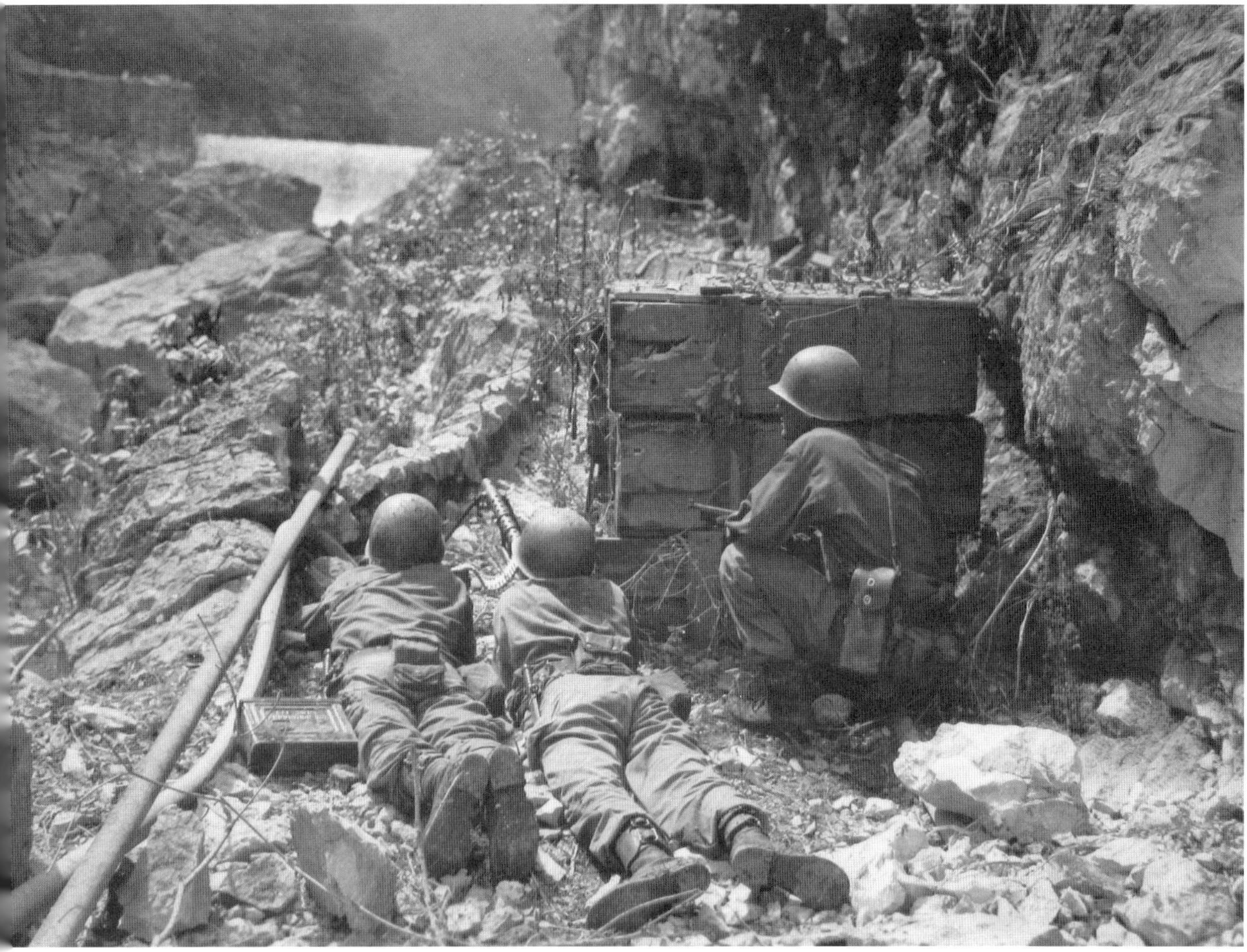

(**Opposite, above**) A 0.30in-calibre LMG crew from Company A, 152nd IR is seen here taking cover from a TNT satchel that exploded on a Japanese dugout in Rizal Province on Luzon on 25 May 1945. American demolition teams were deployed when direct fire or flame-throwers were ineffective at deeply-burrowed Japanese infantry. Rizal Province is located approximately 10 miles east of Manila and has mountainous terrain suitable for natural or man-made caves as it is perched on the western slopes of the Sierra Madre mountain range's southern face. *(NARA)*

(**Opposite, below**) A bazooka-firing paratrooper from the 503rd PIR discharges his rocket at a Japanese position on Corregidor in early February 1945. Two types of bazookas were used in the Pacific by this stage of the war. The M1A1 and M9 fired the M6 2.36in HEAT (high-explosive anti-tank) shaped-charge warhead at short range. Designed as an AT weapon against the treads and rear of armoured vehicles, in the Pacific War it was deployed to fire its 60mm HE projectile directly into Japanese caves and against reinforced MG and sniper positions. The M1A1 weighed 13.5lb. The M9 had the advantage that it could be disassembled into two halves for easier carrying. It weighed 15lb. The name 'bazooka' is due to its resemblance to a musical instrument developed and popularized by an American comedian in the 1930s. *(NARA)*

(**Above**) A 0.30in-calibre LMG crew from Company A, 1st Battalion, 149th IR, 38th Division is shown on a road covering an American infantry advance onto the Wawa Dam (background) on the Marikina River. Several Japanese caves, pillboxes and MG nests delayed the American advance. The Marikina River with its headwaters in the Sierra Madre Mountains is a tributary of the Pasig River which ran through the centre of the city of Manila. *(NARA)*

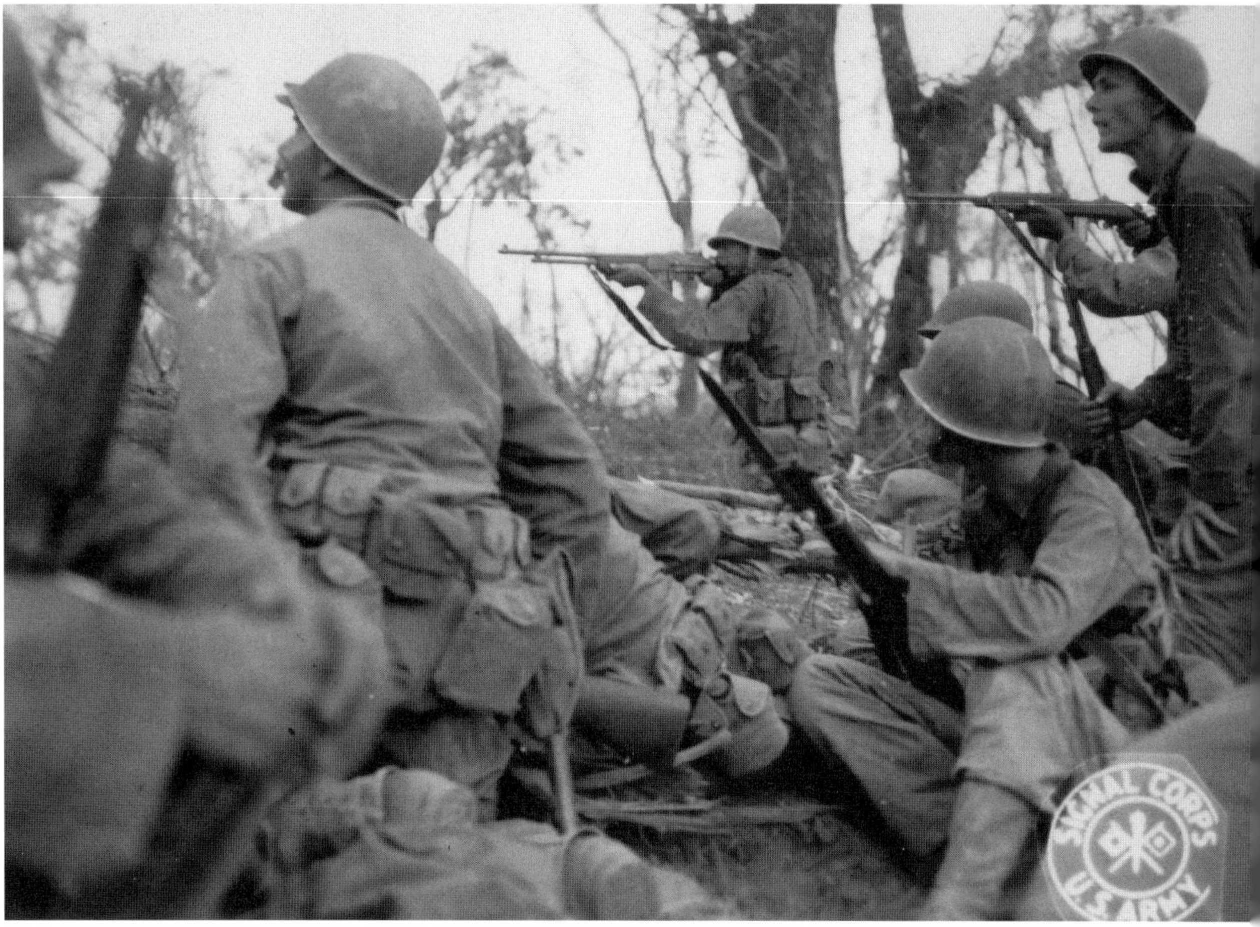
SIGNAL CORPS
U.S. ARMY

(**Above**) American infantrymen with a variety of personal weapons are shown here covering the advance of a flame-thrower unit against an enemy bunker in the Cabaruan Hills near Urdaneta on Luzon on 27 January 1945. Urdaneta is in Luzon's Pangasinan Province south-east of the US Sixth Army's 9 January amphibious landing zones at Lingayen Gulf. One soldier is firing his Browning Automatic Rifle (BAR) (background), while another (right, background) has his 0.30in-calibre semi-automatic M1 carbine ready to fire. The soldier in the foreground (right) has a bayonet attached to his 0.30-06 M1 semi-automatic Garand rifle. The BAR, a portable squad-level light automatic weapon, was not able to deliver a sustained fire rate from its twenty-round trapezoidal-shaped magazine. The M1 Garand replaced the Springfield Model 1903 bolt-action rifle with its distribution starting in 1940. The M1 Garand fired at a rate of forty to fifty rounds per minute. It weighed 9.6lb (unloaded), a disadvantage for jungle combats. The M1 Carbine semi-automatic 0.30in-calibre rifle was produced in late 1941 for non-front-line troops as it was more effective (fifteen- or thirty-round detachable magazine) than a pistol and lighter (5.2lb unloaded) and more compact than the M1 Garand. Its combat use was favoured at close quarters such as in urban streets or jungle. The carbine fired forty-five rounds per minute. *(NARA)*

(**Opposite, above**) Three Sixth Army soldiers are seen here neutralizing a crude but well-camouflaged Japanese excavated dugout on the Villa Verde Trail with percussion hand grenades on 29 May 1945. Riflemen were ready to shoot at any surviving Japanese soldiers trying to rush the trio. *(NARA)*

(**Opposite, below**) Several US 43rd Division soldiers are inspecting a captured Japanese 12in naval gun situated in a depressed weapon pit near Rosario near Lingayen Gulf in early February. Fortunately, the enemy defence of Lingayen Gulf shoreline was limited on 9 January 1945. *(NARA)*

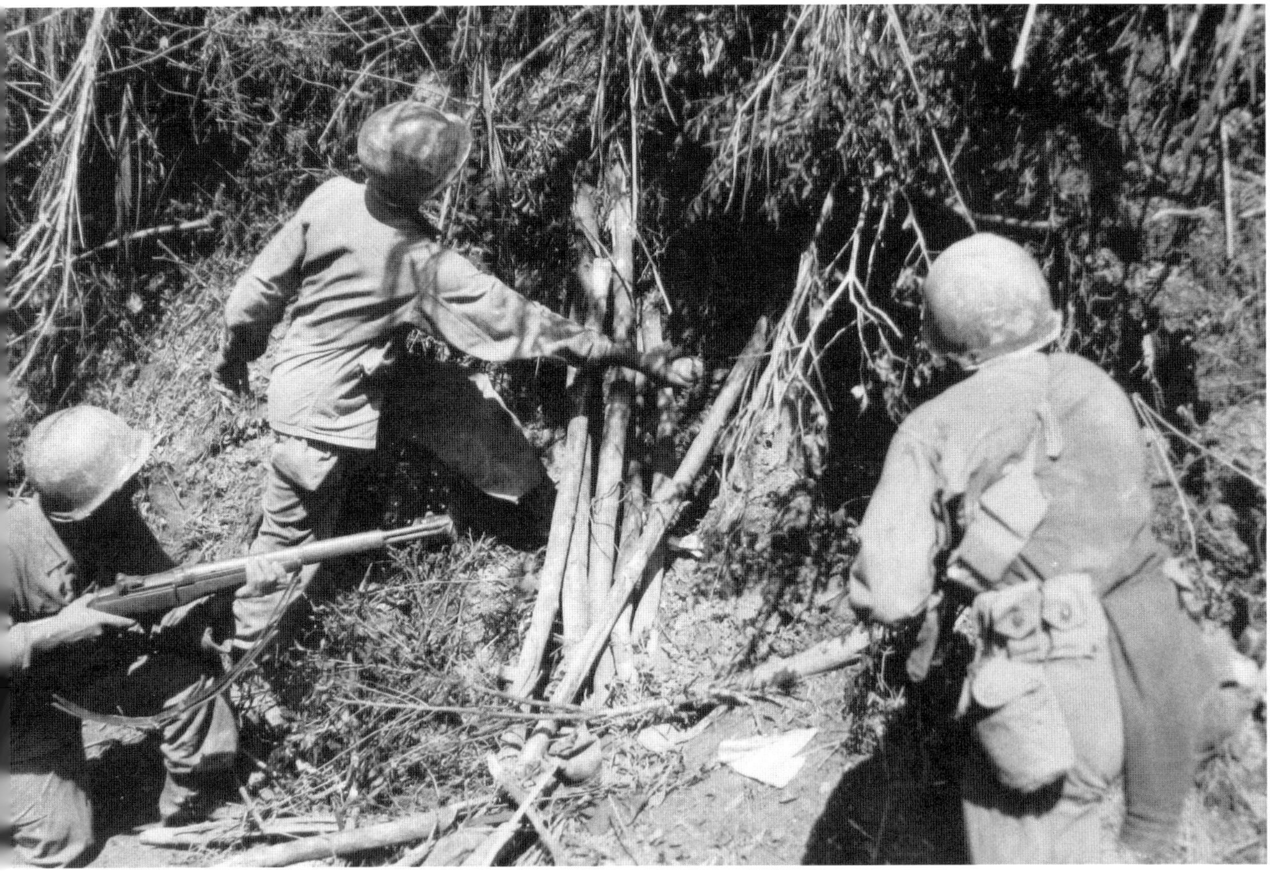

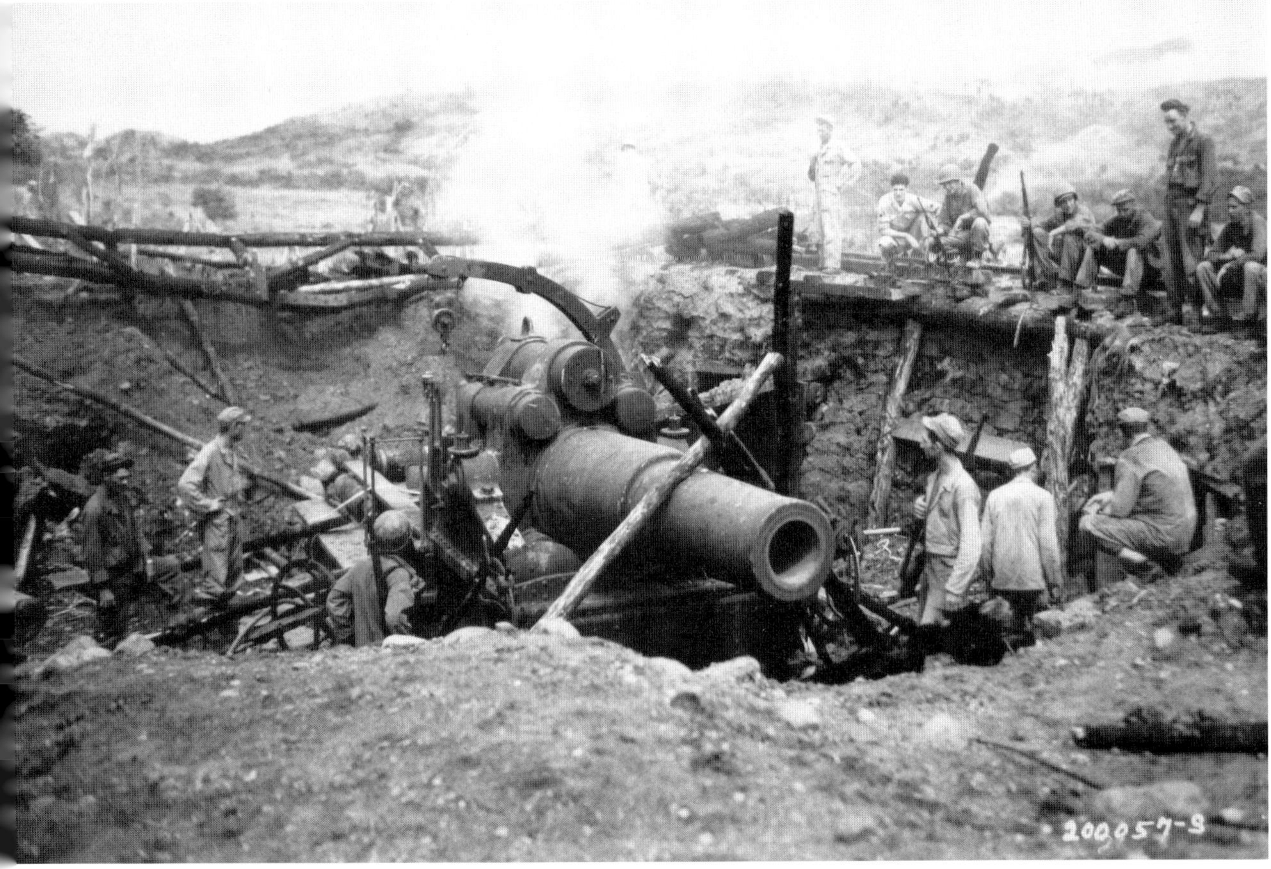
200057-S

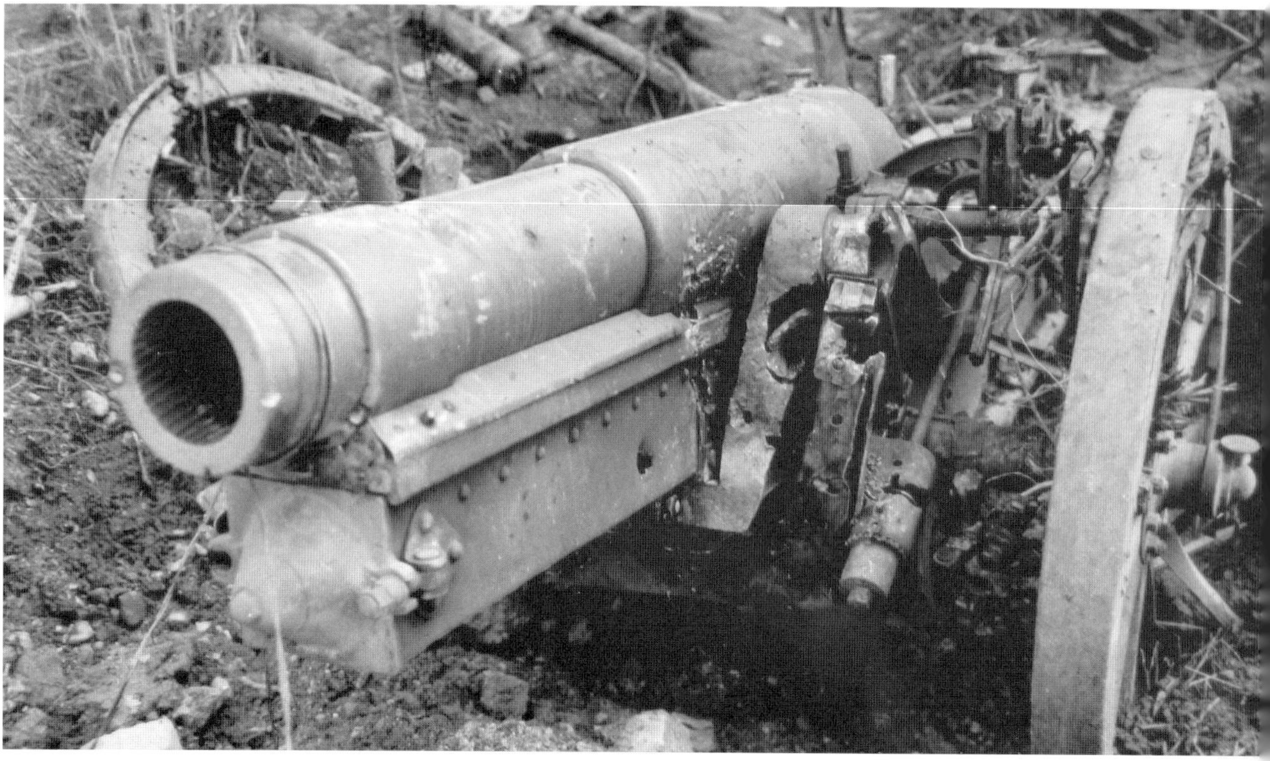

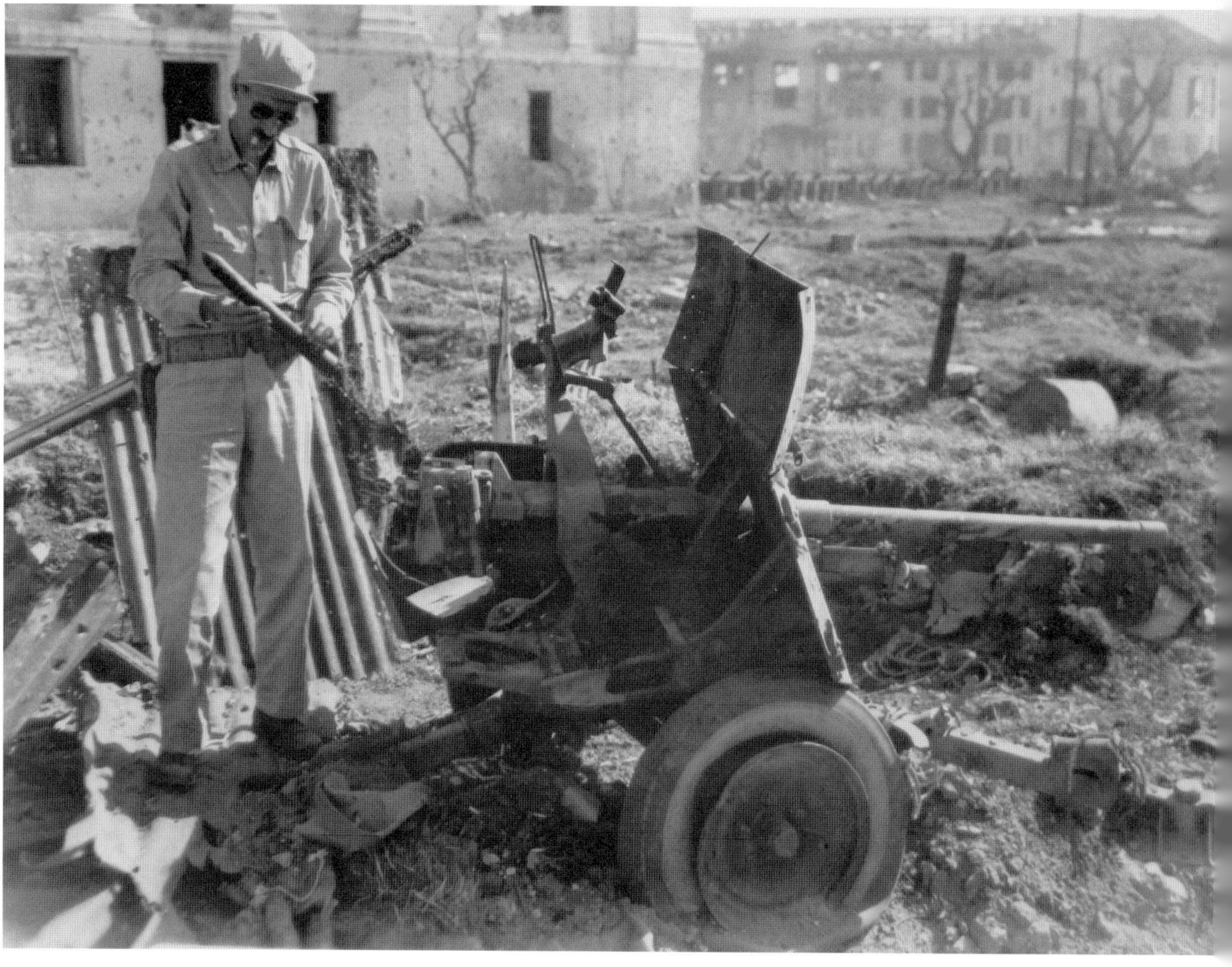

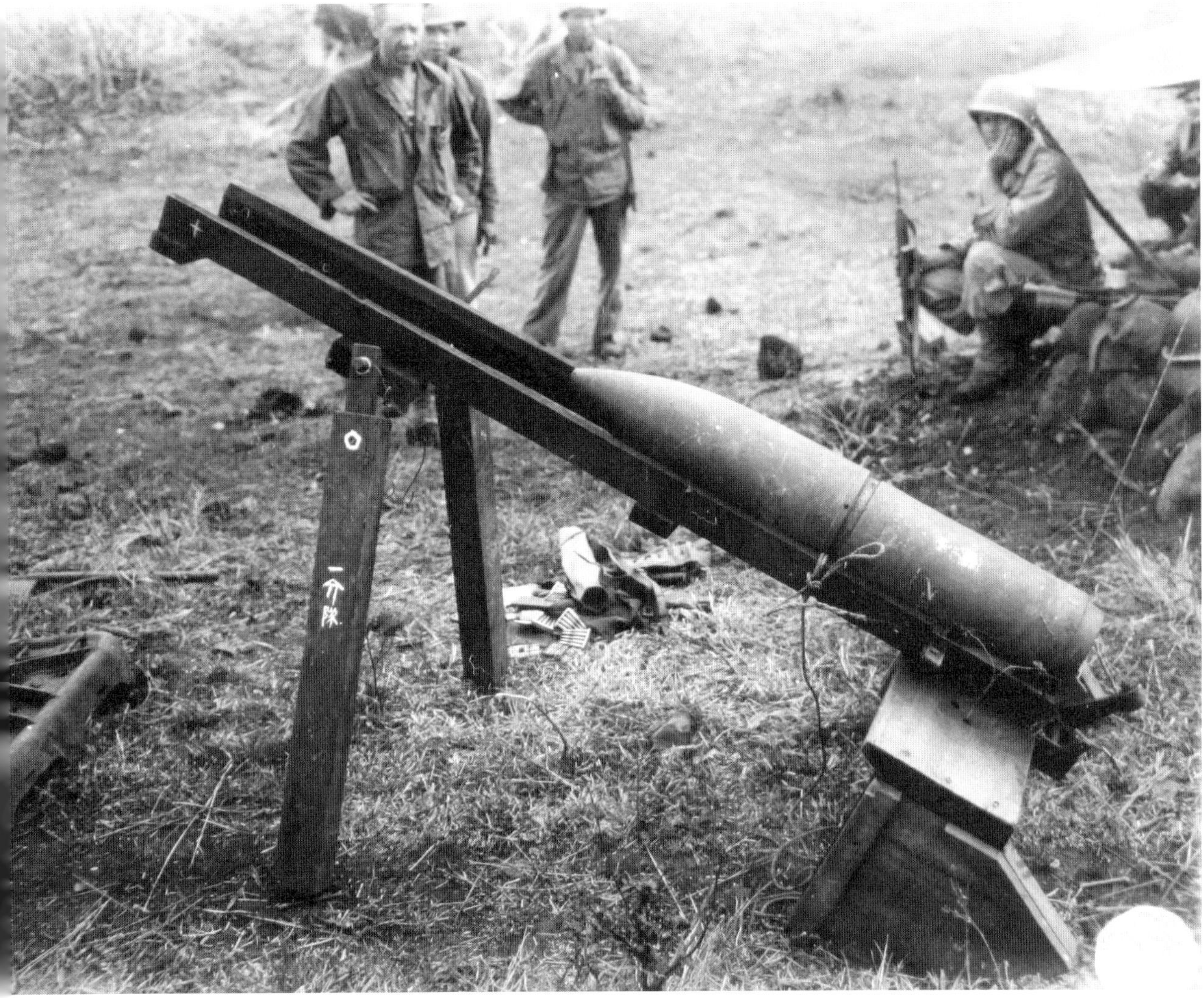

(**Opposite, above**) A Japanese Type 96 150mm howitzer is disabled with its gun shield and right wheel destroyed on Luzon after it was knocked out by Sixth Army soldiers near Highway 3. The IJA used this field piece in the 1930s against both the Chinese and Soviets. It was the main IJA howitzer until the war's end. *(NARA)*

(**Opposite, below**) An American soldier in Manila between the Legislature and Finance buildings is seen here holding a solid-shot AT shell for a British 2-pounder that was captured by the Japanese during their blitzkrieg throughout southern Asia in 1941–42. The British 2-pounder soon became obsolete in North Africa during 1940–41; however, Australian gunners did manage to destroy Japanese Type 95 *Ha-Go* light tanks in southern Malaya in early 1942. *(NARA)*

(**Above**) A Japanese 8in rocket on its launcher is shown here after capture by Company G, 2nd Battalion, 103rd IR, 43rd Division at Teresa in Rizal Province south-east of Manila on 17 March 1945. This rudimentary weapon, which made its debut on Iwo Jima, consisted of two narrow-gauge horizontal 15ft rails situated on a hill's reverse slope. The aiming and trajectory of these rockets was uncontrolled and directed by guesswork, limiting their accuracy. The rockets, once launched, made a screeching noise as the projectile's metal created friction along the rails. *(NARA)*

Chapter Three

Commanders and Combatants

US Army Commanders

General Douglas A. MacArthur was a larger-than-life military personality. His résumé included being a West Point graduate, a Congressional Medal of Honor recipient in April 1942 for valour during the Philippine invasion by Japan, COS of the 42nd ('Rainbow') Division in the First World War, Superintendent of the US Military Academy, Army Chief of Staff, Field Marshal of the Philippine Army and then commander of Filipino-American forces during the early months of the Second World War. He was recalled from Corregidor to Australia on 11 March 1942 by President Roosevelt. With seventeen of his staff officers and his family, MacArthur took a hazardous PT boat journey to Mindanao and then travelled via army B-17 bombers to Darwin, Australia. In Melbourne, he was appointed SWPA commander at the direct request of the Australian government. MacArthur vowed to organize the American offensive there against Japan and liberate the vanquished Philippine Islands. On 20 October 1944, he would wade ashore at Leyte not far from Tacloban where he had arrived in 1903 as a second lieutenant during the Moro Insurrection.

MacArthur left Corregidor with his staff officers, the 'Bataan Gang', which was presided over by his COS, Major General Richard Sutherland. On Corregidor, MacArthur recommended Sutherland as his successor. MacArthur had a number of first-rate ground, aerial and naval commanders (see Chapter 3 image captions for details). These included Lieutenant General Walter Krueger, commander of the US Sixth Army, which was to participate in both the Leyte and Luzon invasions. After the Papuan campaign had ended in early 1943, MacArthur requested Krueger, then the US Third Army commander, be sent to New Guinea for his 1943–44 campaign to defeat the Japanese on that massive tropical island.

Lieutenant General Robert Eichelberger commanded American and Australian soldiers during the Papuan campaign. After capturing Buna and the attention of the American press, Eichelberger was relegated back to Australia as I Corps commander to retrain and refit the American 32nd and 41st Infantry divisions for future operations in New Guinea. MacArthur wanted a field commander loyal to him and not to General George Marshall, as Eichelberger, the army chief of staff's protégé was deemed to be. During the Philippine Islands campaigns, Eichelberger led the

US Eighth Army, which relieved the Sixth Army at the end of the Leyte campaign. The Eighth Army then participated in the landing near Subic Bay and Olongapo on Luzon's west coast in an attempt to block Japanese troops from entering the Bataan Peninsula. After southern Luzon was liberated, the Eighth Army moved into the central and southern Philippine Islands.

Lieutenant General George Kenney, the SWPA Fifth Air Force commander, achieved aerial superiority over the skies of New Guinea and made several strategic and tactical innovations which were then continued during the Philippine Islands' liberation. Kenney transformed his Fifth Air Force into a multidimensional unit to include troop transport and supply; aerial artillery for troops who lacked field artillery; and, with innovations perfected by his B-25 Mitchell and A-20 Havoc medium bombers as the daytime interdiction of Japanese coastal shipping and reinforcements, which became vital to block the flow of IJA reinforcements into Leyte via the port of Ormoc.

US Navy Commanders

Admiral William F. Halsey, Jr was a veteran of anti-submarine destroyers in the First World War. He held assignments in naval intelligence and also served as naval attaché to the Weimar Republic in Berlin in 1922. He became intrigued by fleet aviation and in 1935, at the age of 52, he received his aviator's wings. He commanded the pre-war USS *Saratoga* and in 1940 he received the rank of vice admiral and took command of the Pacific Aircraft Battle Force. US Navy Task Force (TF) 16, built around the carriers USS *Hornet* and *Enterprise*, was under the audacious Halsey's command when at 0820 hours on 18 April 1942, USAAF twin-engined B-25B Mitchell medium bombers, under the command of Colonel James Doolittle, took off from the *Hornet*'s deck to bomb Tokyo.

Halsey arrived in Noumea to take command of the SPA during the height of the Guadalcanal campaign in the autumn of 1942. Halsey energized the troops on Guadalcanal by sending whatever supplies and reinforcements to the island that were at his disposal as well as vigorously contesting Japanese resupply and bombardment efforts with costly naval surface actions in terms of ships and sailors.

Rear Admiral Thomas Kinkaid assumed command of the Pacific Fleet's Cruiser Division in 1941 and defended the US carriers *Lexington* at the Battle of the Coral Sea in May 1942 and the USS *Hornet* at Midway in June 1942. During the Solomon Islands campaign he commanded TF 16, which was built around the carrier USS *Enterprise*, during the Battles of the Eastern Solomons and the Santa Cruz Islands. In June 1943, he was promoted to the rank of vice admiral. In January 1943, he commanded the Allied forces in the Aleutian Islands campaign prior to serving as Commander, Allied Naval Forces and the US Seventh Fleet in the SWPA under MacArthur beginning in November 1943 supporting the numerous amphibious assaults during the New

Guinea campaign. For the Philippine Islands assaults, Kinkaid commanded the Allied fleet during the Battle of Leyte Gulf on 24–25 October 1944 and planned and executed the invasion of Luzon at Lingayen Gulf on 9 January 1945. He was promoted to the rank of admiral on 3 April 1945 after supporting campaigns in the central and southern Philippine Islands and Borneo.

Rear Admiral Jesse Oldendorf commanded Task Group (TG) 77.2 at the Battle of Surigao Strait on 24 October 1944 and defeated IJN Vice Admiral Shoji Nishimura's Southern Force by 'crossing the T' of his opponent, thereby preventing the enemy surface flotilla from entering Leyte Gulf from the south through the Surigao Strait and decimating the US Sixth Army beachheads on Leyte. Nishimura was killed and the IJN battleships *Fuso* and *Yamashiro* were sunk. During the Lingayen Gulf invasion of Luzon on 9 January 1945, Vice Admiral Oldendorf (promoted in December 1944) was to lead Kinkaid's Bombardment Group. On 6 January while steaming towards Lingayen Gulf, Oldendorf survived a *kamikaze* attack on his flagship, the USS *New Mexico*.

Rear Admiral Daniel Barbey joined the MacArthur team in January 1943 to develop and implement a new naval unit, the Seventh Amphibious Force, which was to land American and Australian troops on New Guinea's hostile shores to wrest control from the Japanese.

Japanese Army Commanders

Field Marshal Count Hisaichi Terauchi was C-in-C of the IJA's Southern Expeditionary Army Group headquartered in Singapore during the Pacific War after having served as the leader of the North China Army from 1937–41. Becoming a field marshal in June 1943, his HQ was relocated to the Philippines in May 1944, but as the Allies approached the archipelago, he moved his command to Saigon. He incorrectly assumed that Mindanao would be the American target after New Guinea; however, the Japanese strengthened their garrisons throughout the entire archipelago.

Lieutenant General Tomoyuki Yamashita ('Tiger of Malaya') commanded the IJA 14th Area Army in the Philippines on 10 October 1944 with HQ on Luzon. In November 1941 Yamashita was given the command of the IJA 25th Army for the Malaya and Singapore campaigns when he was recalled as the Manchukuo army commander in northern China. With both Prime Minister Tojo and Terauchi being his political enemies, Yamashita knew he needed a swift and decisive victory to prevent demotion or worse. After his stunning IJA 25th Army victory on the Malayan Peninsula culminating in the capture of Singapore on 15 February 1942, Tojo shunted him to minor theatres of war out of jealousy.

Lieutenant General Sōsaku Suzuki was appointed commander of the IJA 35th Army in the Visayan Islands (headquartered on Cebu) in July 1944, three months before the Leyte invasion. Prior to promotion to lieutenant general in March 1941, Suzuki's commands were in China; however, with the outbreak of war, he served as Yamashita's

COS of the IJA 25th Army for the Malaya and Singapore invasions. Tokyo ordered Suzuki to send the bulk of his army, approximately 45,000 troops, to Leyte to combat the US Sixth Army's invasion on 20 October 1944. After his forces were defeated on Leyte and with the subsequent invasion of Cebu on 26 March 1945, Suzuki fled into that island's hills.

Japanese Naval Commanders
Details of IJN commanders can be found in this chapter's image captions.

Major American Combat Formations for the Leyte Campaign
The US Sixth Army, under Lieutenant General Walter Krueger, had two amphibiously assaulting infantry corps: X and XXIV. The X Corps comprised the 1st Cavalry and 24th Infantry divisions, while the XXIV Corps had the 7th and 96th Infantry divisions. Additional XXIV Corps units included the 20th Armoured Group and the 11th Airborne Division's 503rd PIR. Krueger also utilized the 32nd and 77th Infantry divisions for the campaign. As the campaign was winding down, Lieutenant General Robert Eichelberger's Eighth Army took over as the Leyte ground force while the Sixth Army prepared for the Luzon invasion. Both US armies were supported by the Fifth and Thirteenth Air Forces led by Lieutenant General George Kenney.

The USN armada for Leyte included Vice Admiral Kinkaid's Seventh Fleet and Admiral William F. Halsey's Third Fleet attached to the SWPA by Admiral Nimitz. The Seventh Fleet comprised a Northern Attack Force, Task Force 78 and a Southern Attack Force, Task Force 79.

Major Japanese Combat Formations for the Leyte Campaign
The IJA Order of Battle for Leyte included the 14th Area Army led by Yamashita. This Area Army was under the control of the IJA Southern Army led by Field Marshal Hisaichi Terauchi. In the Visayan Group of Islands, the IJA 35th Army was led by Lieutenant General Sōsaku Suzuki. This formation comprised the IJA 1st, 16th, 26th and 102nd Divisions and the 54th, 55th and 68th IMBs. An IJA Fourth Air Army comprising the 2nd and 4th Air Divisions defended Leyte. At the time of the American invasion, Leyte's principal IJA formation, the 16th Division, was led by Lieutenant General Shiro Makino.

Major American Combat Formations for the Initial Phases of the Luzon Campaign
Two US Sixth Army Corps, I and XIV, comprised the landing force for the Lingayen Gulf assault on 9 January 1945. I Corps had the 6th and 43rd Infantry divisions with the attached 163rd RCT. XIV Corps had the 37th and 40th Infantry divisions and the 108th RCT. The Sixth Army's reserve units were the 25th Infantry Division along with

the 158th RCT, the latter attached to I Corps' 43rd Division. The 6th Ranger Battalion, which was to prove valiant in the liberation of the Cabanatuan PoW camp, was also part of Krueger's reserve along with the 13th Armoured Group. The US 32nd Infantry and 1st Cavalry divisions were still on Leyte.

On 29 January, in an attempt to isolate the entrance into Bataan, thereby keeping Yamashita's *Kembu* Group from entering the peninsula, Eichelberger landed the Eighth Army's XI Corps' 38th Infantry Division along with the 24th Infantry Division's 34th IR on Luzon's western coast. The assault's immediate aims were to attack San Antonio and capture the San Marcelino airfield. Then Eighth Army troops were to move on Olongapo and Subic Bay. Seizing Subic Bay, the former US naval base, would open up another port for Kinkaid's transports.

Major Japanese Combat Formations for the Luzon Campaign

Yamashita divided his 14th Area Army troops into three groups, each situated in one of Luzon's mountainous redoubt areas rather than contest the Americans in force at the assault beaches. The *Shobu* Group, under Yamashita's personal command, numbered more than 150,000 troops and was situated throughout all of northern Luzon with HQ at Baguio at the southern end of the Central Cordillera Range. This group comprised the IJA 10th, 19th, 23rd and 103rd Divisions, the 58th IMB and elements of the 2nd Tank Division.

The *Kembu* Group, under Lieutenant General Rikichi Tsukada, numbered 30,000 troops from a variety of Japanese forces including the IJA 10th Division's 39th IR and the 2nd Mobile IR. The *Kembu* Group used the Zambales Mountains to the west of Clark Field and Fort Stotsenburg in western Luzon as a redoubt.

The *Shimbu* Group, led by Lieutenant General Shizuo Yokoyama, numbered 80,000 troops from mainly the IJA 105th and 8th divisions. However, it also possessed the 16,000-strong Manila Naval Defence Force, which was to perpetrate heinous atrocities on the capital city's civilian population during the month-long combat there. Yokoyama's *Shimbu* Group was to defend southern Luzon from Manila southwards to include the Bicol Peninsula. Their mountainous redoubt was in the Mingan Mountains north-east of Manila.

(**Above**) Admiral Nimitz, C-in-C Pacific Fleet, is shown here pointing at a map of the Far East at an Oahu conference on 26 July 1944, where he proposed bypassing the Philippines and instead invading Japanese-occupied Formosa and seizing East China coast bases as a prelude to a Central Pacific Area (CPA) advance on the Ryukyu Islands and then Japan's Home Islands. Nimitz is joined by (left to right) General Douglas A. MacArthur, C-in-C SWPA, President Franklin D. Roosevelt and JCOS member Admiral William Leahy. MacArthur won the debate as he reminded Roosevelt that this would betray the Filipino people as the SWPA commander promised an American liberation of their islands as soon as was feasible. Mindanao was targeted for invasion in the autumn of 1944. *(NARA)*

(**Opposite, above**) Lieutenant General Walter Krueger (centre), commander of the US Sixth Army, is shown here addressing three of his 21st FA Battalion officers in the hills of northern Luzon's Villa Verde Trail on 18 March 1945. Major General Innis Swift, the I Corps commander, stands behind Krueger. Krueger entered the US Army as a private soldier and fought on during the Philippine Insurrection for which he earned a commission in 1901. Krueger served during Pershing's Mexican Punitive Expedition in 1916 and with the American Expeditionary Force in France during the First World War. He attended Fort Benning's Infantry School and commanded the 55th Infantry Division. He served in the Army War Plans Division and was an excellent division and corps commander. Krueger commanded Sixth Army forces throughout the 1943–44 New Guinea campaign as well as the Leyte invasion of October 1944, Mindoro assault in December 1944 and the massive Lingayen Gulf amphibious attack on 9 January 1945, after which his units contested the Japanese defenders of Manila and Yamashita's troops in northern Luzon. *(NARA)*

(**Opposite, below**) Lieutenant General Robert L. Eichelberger (left foreground), US Eighth Army commander, talks to an 11th Army Airborne 511th PIR's jeep reconnaissance unit at Zapote, a few miles from Manila, in early February 1945. In addition to helping to secure victory in Papua in late 1942, Eichelberger had an illustrious army career as a 1909 West Point graduate, Secretary of the General Staff in 1935 and Superintendent of West Point in 1940. After the war erupted, he trained the 77th Infantry Division and was then given command of I Corps for the North African invasion. However, with the Japanese invading Papua, he took his I Corps staff, as a new lieutenant general, to Australia. At Leyte, his Eighth Army reinforced the Sixth Army. On Luzon, Eichelberger's Eighth Army invaded the western part of the island on 29 January prior to a series of amphibious assaults in the Central and Southern Philippine Islands. *(NARA)*

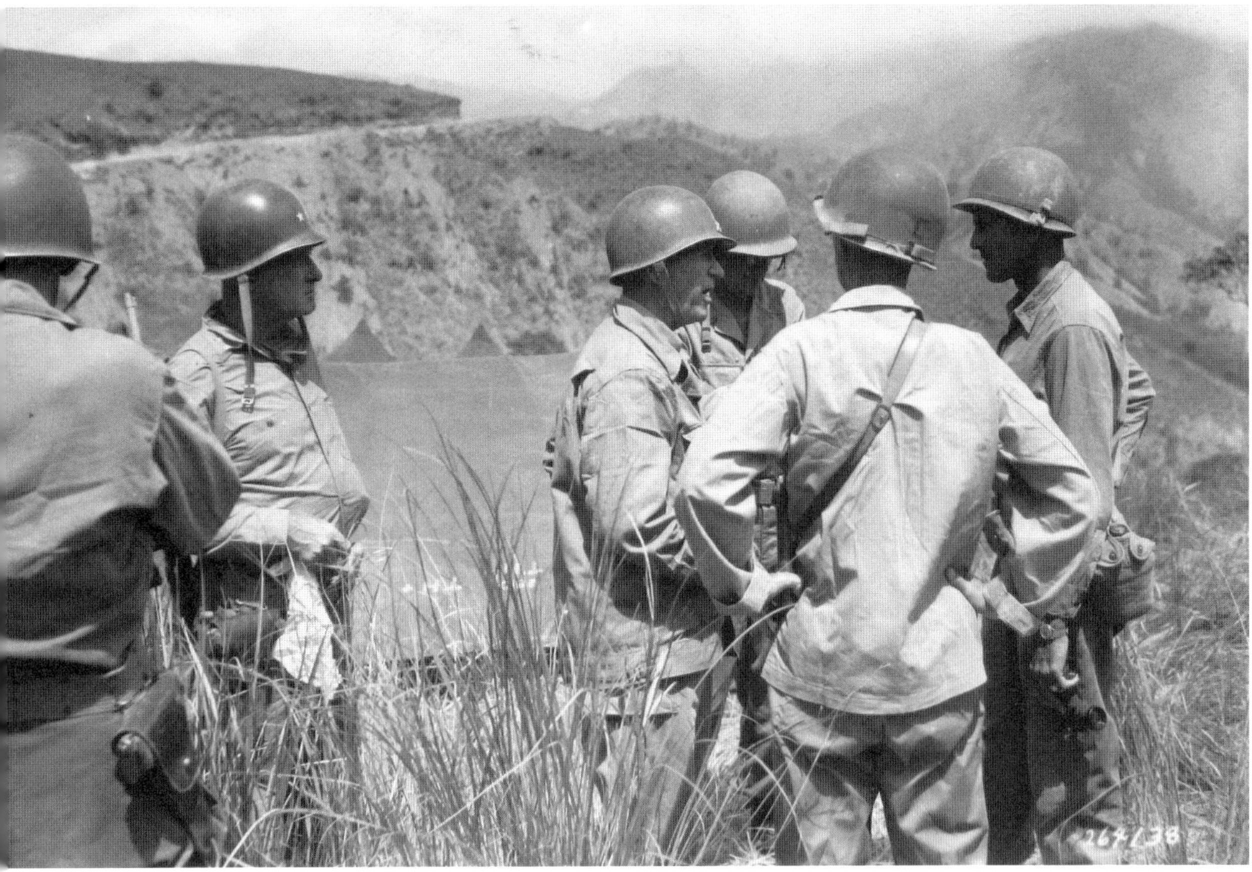
264138

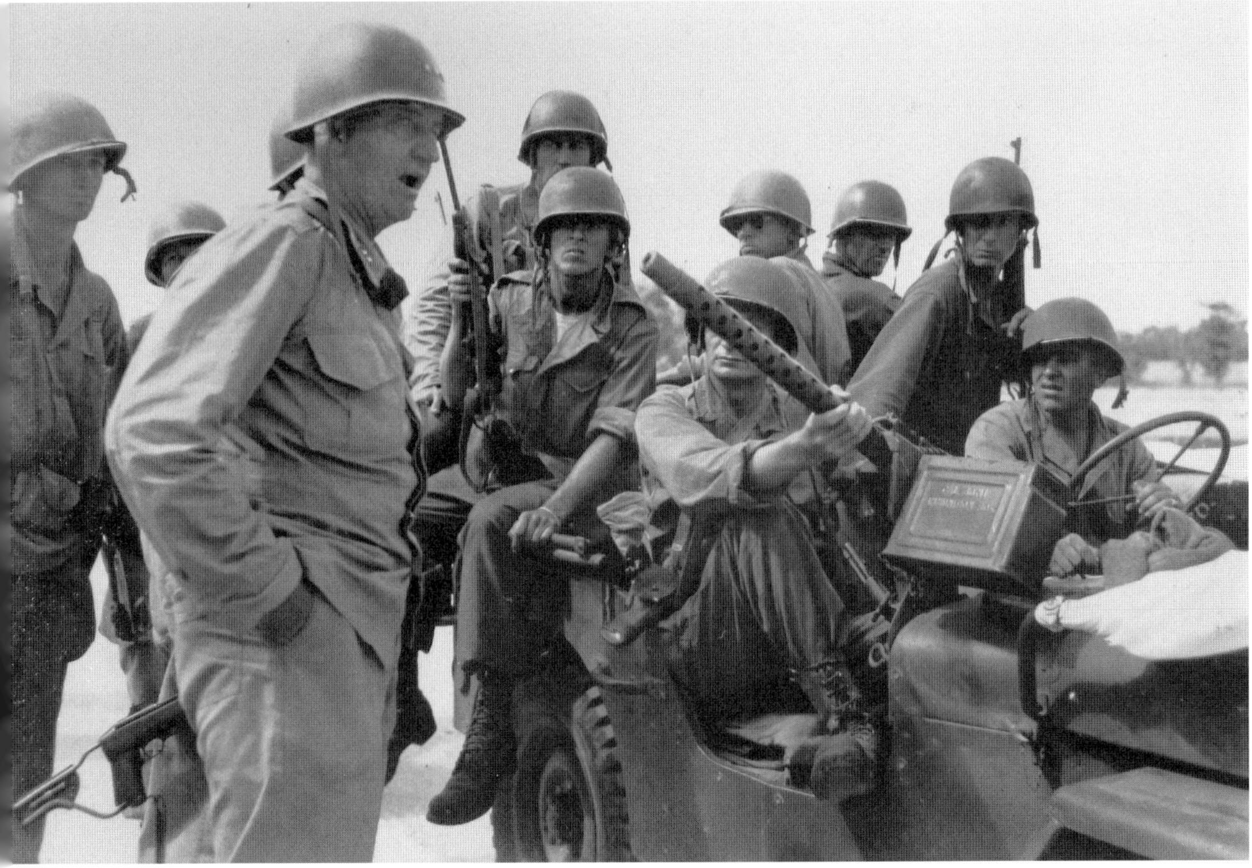

Lieutenant General George Kenney (left), commander of the Fifth and Thirteenth Air Forces, is shown here conferring with Brigadier General Paul Wurtsmith, the new leader of the Thirteenth Air Force for the Southern Philippines and Borneo campaigns. In 1942, Major General Kenney was dispatched to MacArthur's HQ in Australia when the Japanese capture of Port Moresby on New Guinea looked imminent. Kenney revolutionized the new Fifth Air Force with new tactics and strategies for enemy interdiction. In the Philippines, he would be in charge of numerous fighter, bombardment and air transport groups and continued to employ his well-honed aerial tactics against Japanese land and sea targets as well as neutralize any Japanese air presence. *(NARA)*

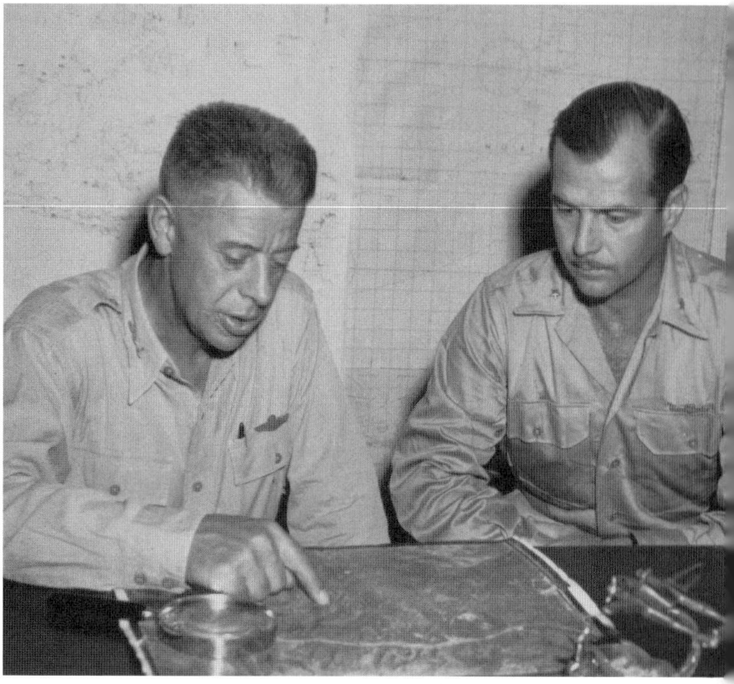

Major General William H. Gill (left), commander of the 32nd Infantry Division since February 1943, is shown here conferring with Major General Verne Mudge (right), commander of the 1st Cavalry Division on Leyte. The 32nd Division relieved Sibert's X Corps' 24th Infantry Division in mid-November 1944. The 1st Cavalry Division with the 32nd Infantry Division continued X Corps' offensive against the Japanese, driving south-westward across Leyte from 7 to 30 November. *(NARA)*

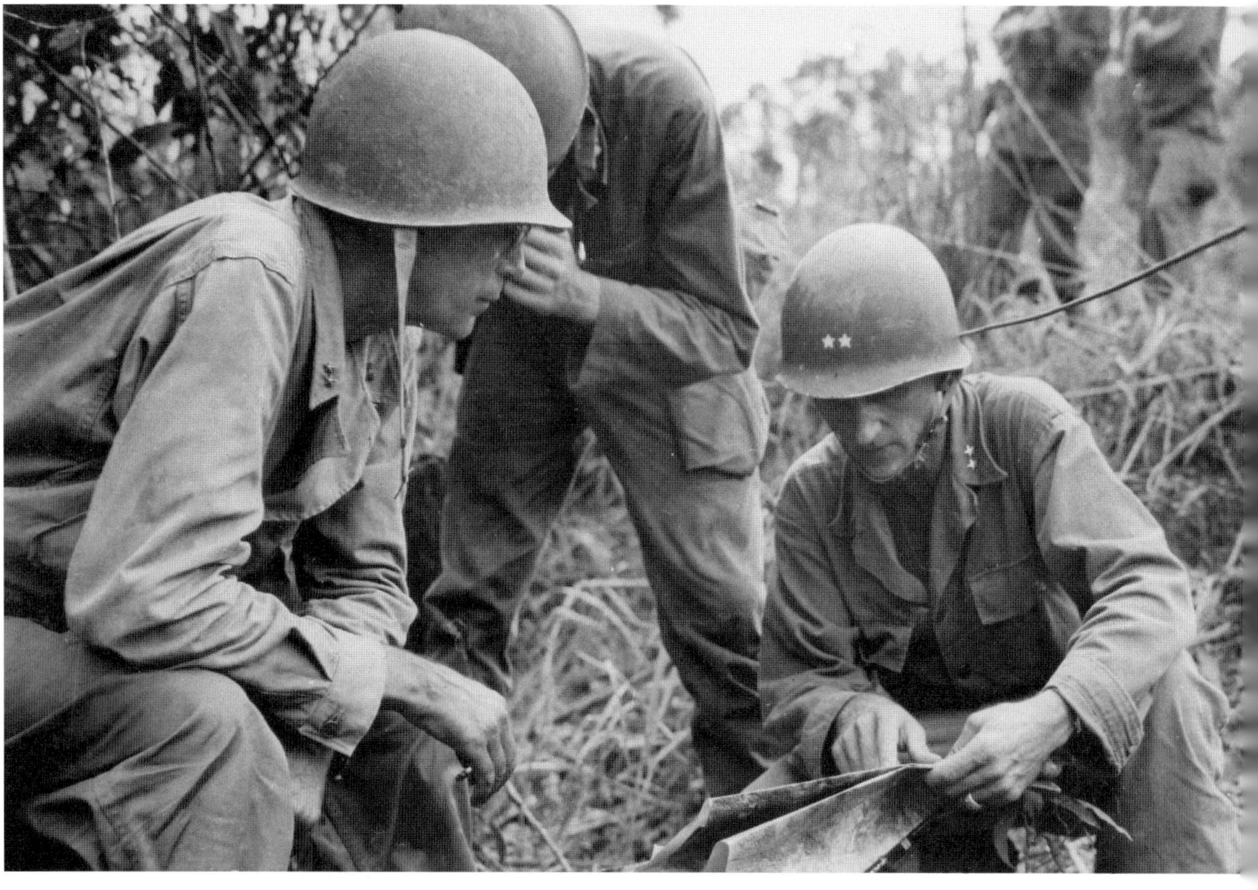

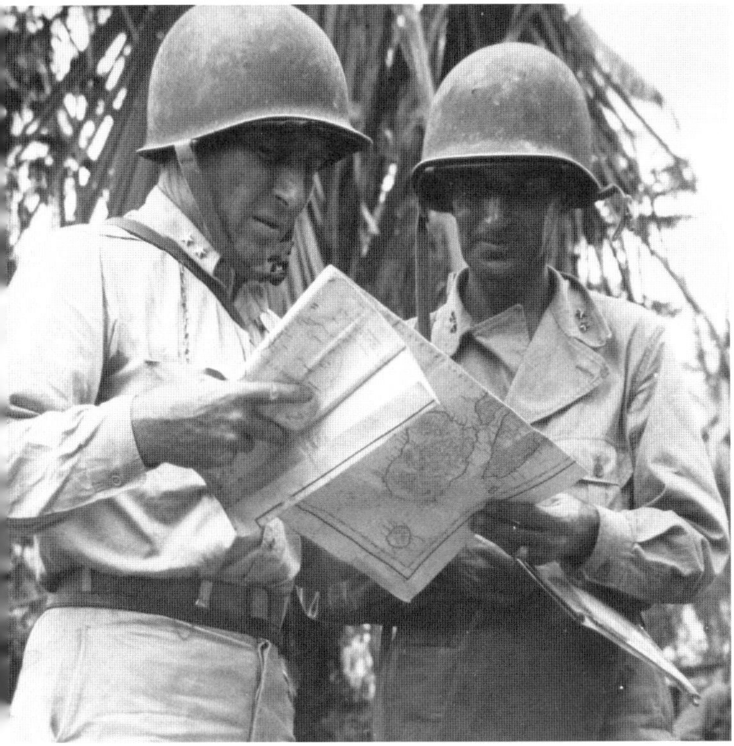

Major General Franklin C. Sibert (left), commander of the Sixth Army's X Corps on Leyte, is shown here with Major General Frederick A. Irving, commander of the 24th Infantry Division on Leyte. Sibert was Lieutenant General Joseph Stilwell's chief infantry officer in Burma and was a member of the 'Walkout from Burma' in the spring of 1942. In December 1942, he commanded Stilwell's Branch Office, New Delhi before being appointed commander of the 6th Infantry Division in New Guinea prior to promotion to X Corps' commander for the Leyte campaign. Irving was a West Point graduate of 1917 and saw action in France, being awarded a Silver Star. He led the 24th Infantry Division during the Sixth Army's invasion of Hollandia during the New Guinea campaign in April 1944. *(NARA)*

Major General Robert Beightler (far left), commander of the 37th Infantry Division, is shown here taking Lieutenant General Yamashita's surrender to American forces in the Kiangan Valley in northern Luzon on 2 September 1945. Sixth Army estimates were that by 30 June, Yamashita had lost more than 170,000 soldiers killed and 4,000 captured during the Luzon campaign. Beightler had served under MacArthur during the First World War in the 42nd 'Rainbow' Division. *(NARA)*

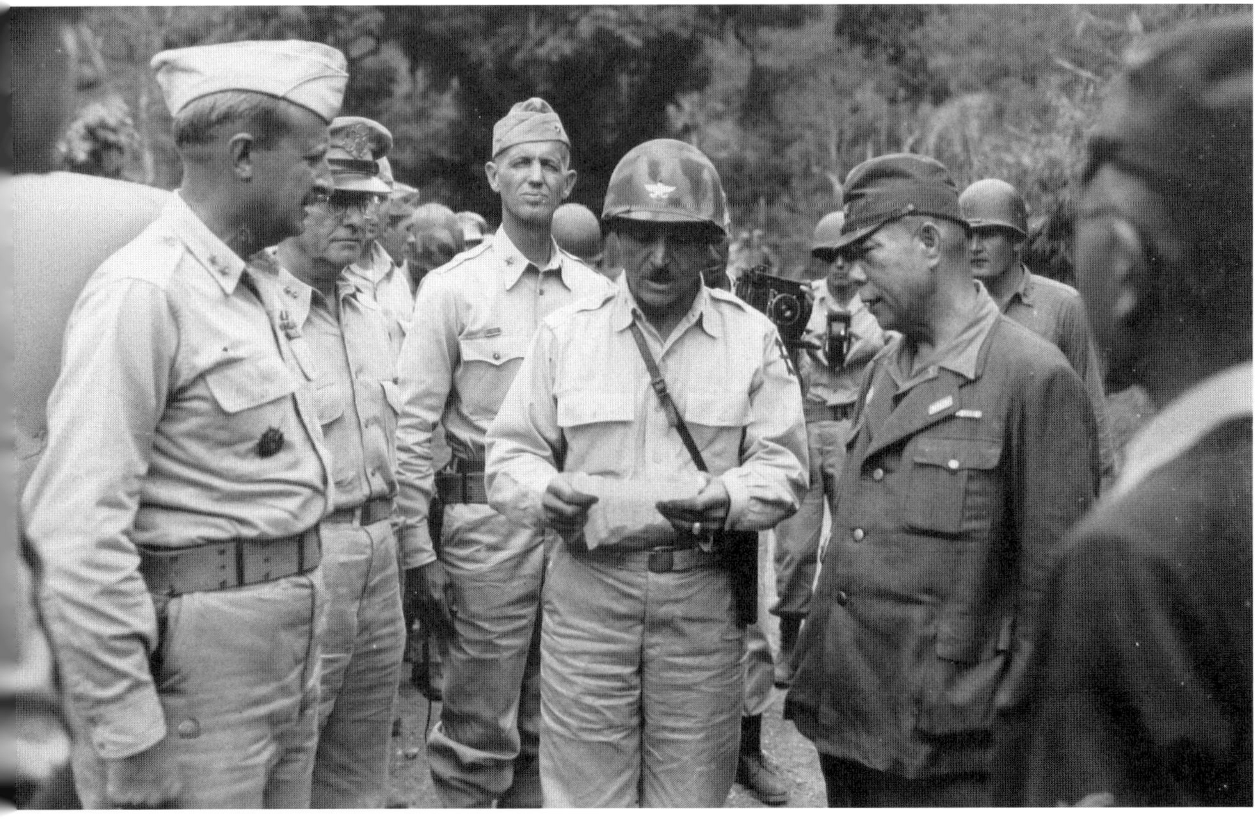

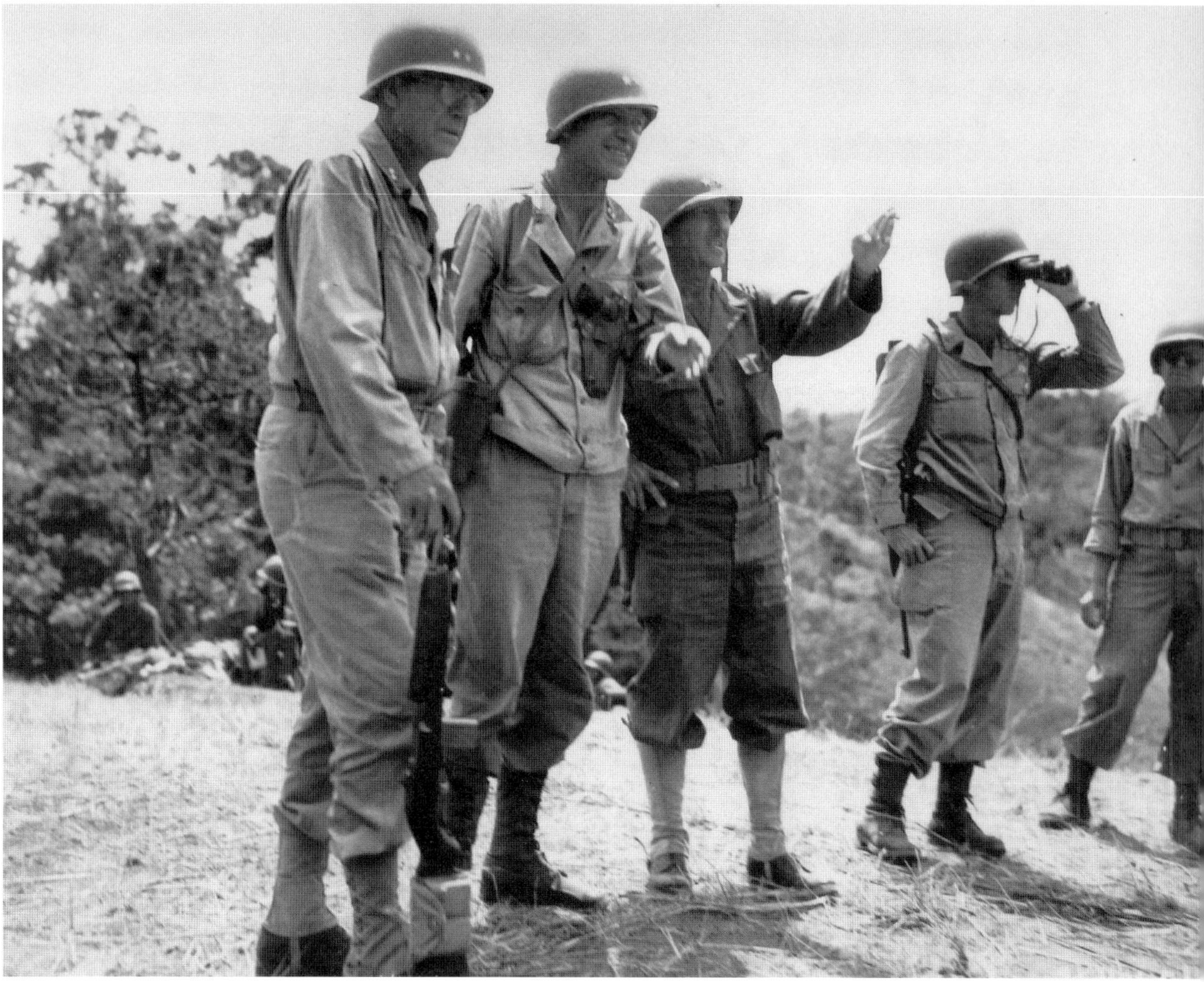

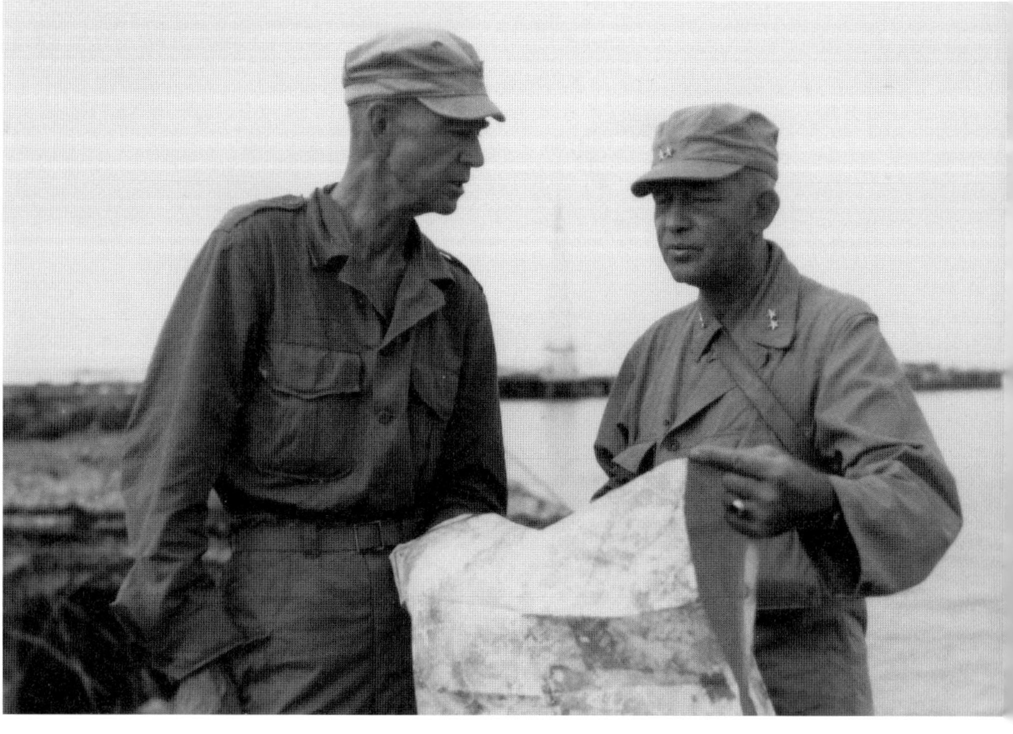

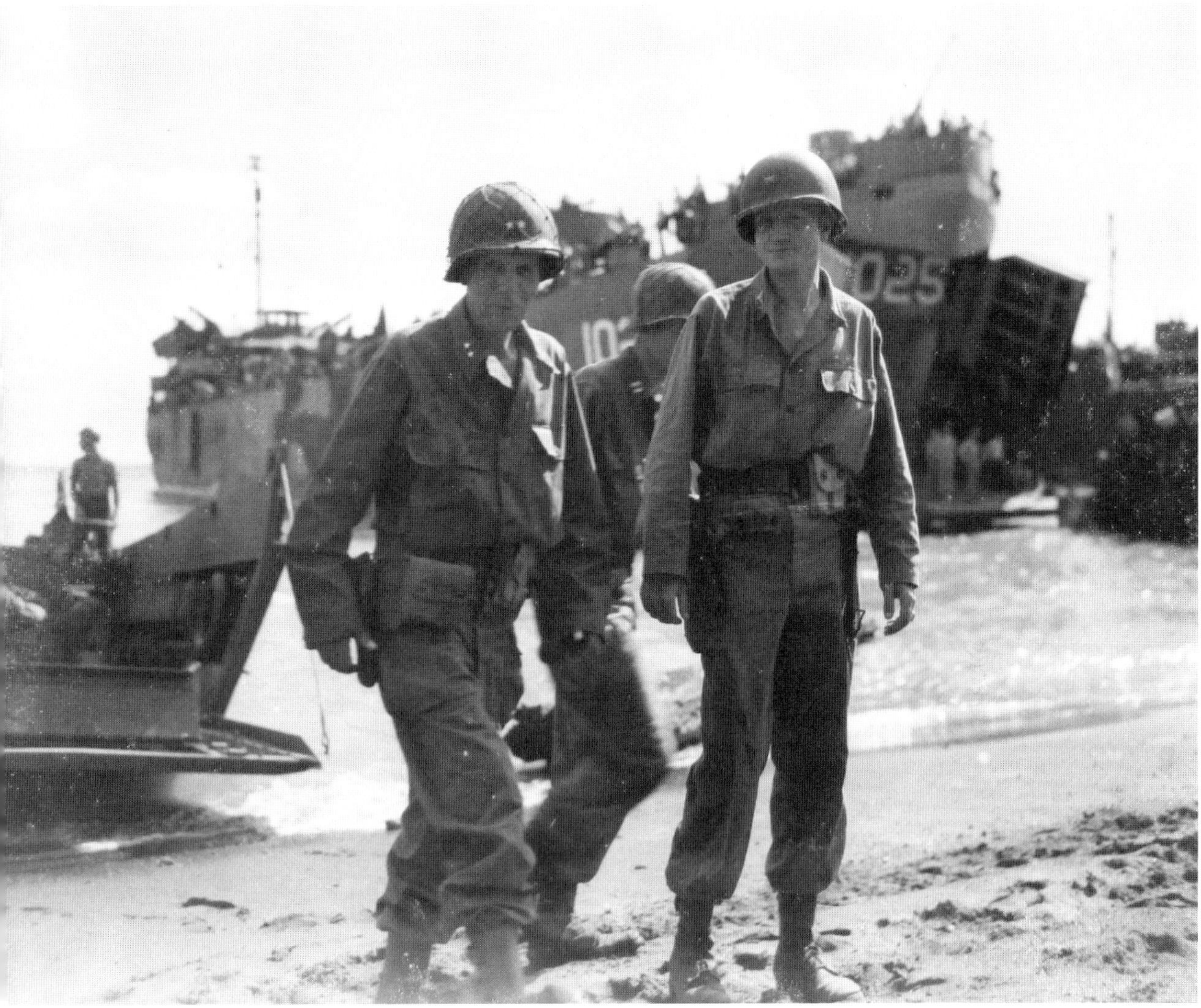

(**Opposite, above**) Sixth Army generals are shown here on Luzon weeks after the successful Lingayen Gulf invasion of 9 January 1945. They are Major General Oscar Griswold (right), XIV Corps commander, and Major General Edwin Patrick (middle), commander of the 6th Infantry Division, who was mortally wounded by a lurking Japanese machine-gunner near Rizal, Luzon on 14 March and died the next day. He was one of only three American division commanders that died in combat. On the right (pointing) is Major General Charles Hall, commander of XI Corps. Hall had previously commanded the 93rd Infantry Division. *(NARA)*

(**Opposite, below**) Major General Jens Doe, commander of the 41st Infantry Division, is shown here going over a map of Mindanao's Zamboanga Peninsula with the 163rd IR commander Colonel Moroney on 12 March 1945. The 41st Division, originally a National Guard unit from the north-western United States, landed on Mindanao, the twenty-first island in the Philippines to be invaded, as part of Eichelberger's Eighth Army. Doe previously led the 163rd IR before replacing Major General Horace Fuller. *(NARA)*

(**Above**) Major General Rapp Brush (left), commander of the 40th Infantry Division in Eichelberger's Eighth Army, is seen here on Panay Island with his COS, Colonel George Latimer, on 18 March 1945. Brush commanded the 21st IR prior to leading the 40th Infantry Division from 1942 to 1945. *(NARA)*

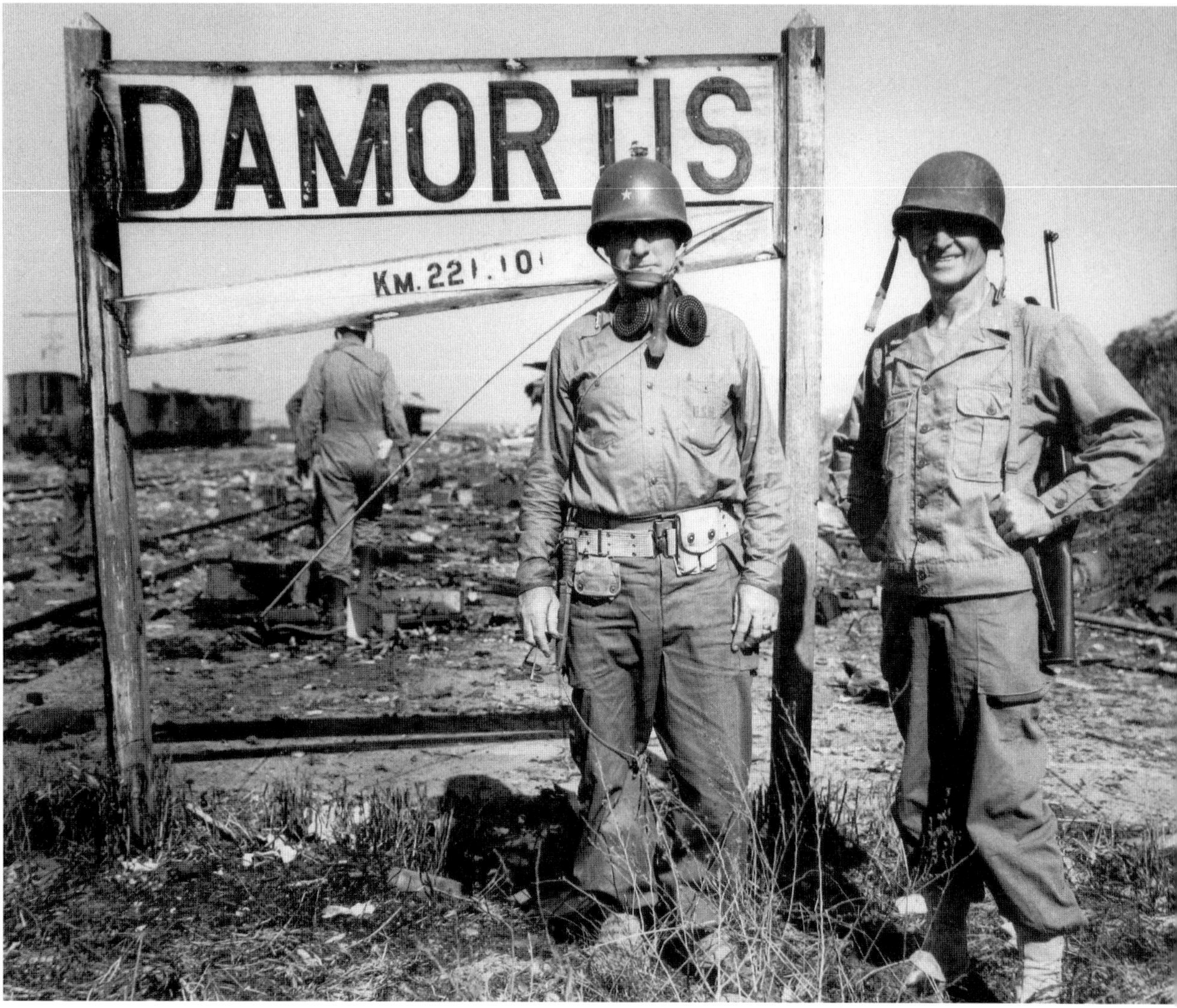
DAMORTIS
KM. 221.10

(**Above**) Major General Innis Swift (left), commander of the Sixth Army's I Corps, is seen here at the Damortis railway station with Brigadier General Hanford MacNider on 7 February 1945. MacNider, a wounded Buna veteran, led the 158th IR ('Bushmasters') during the New Guinea campaign. The 158th IR was attached to I Corps' 43rd Division under Major General Leonard Wing, and along with I Corps' other division, the 6th Division, landed at Lingayen Gulf. I Corps units then moved south to take up blocking positions to prevent Lieutenant General Yamashita from interfering with the Sixth Army's XIV Corps' advance towards Clark Field and Manila. The 43rd Division with its attached 158th IR closed in on the railroad at Damortis and the key road to Rosario. *(NARA)*

(**Opposite, above**) The US Navy commanders at the invasion of Leyte are shown here. From left to right are Vice Admiral Thomas Wilkinson, the Third Fleet Amphibious commander, Vice Admiral Thomas Kinkaid, the SWPA Naval and US Seventh Fleet commander, and Rear Admiral Daniel Barbey, the Seventh Fleet Amphibious commander. In the SWPA, Kinkaid participated in the New Guinea and New Britain campaigns. During the Battle of Leyte Gulf, the Seventh Fleet's Bombardment Group, under Rear Admiral Jesse Oldendorf, participated in the last major battleship engagement of the war as his capital ships held off the Japanese fleet at the Surigao Strait. Barbey directed MacArthur's amphibious assaults along the New Guinea coast. Wilkinson led the invasion of Bougainville's Empress Augusta Bay under Halsey's Third Fleet during the Solomon Islands campaign. *(NARA)*

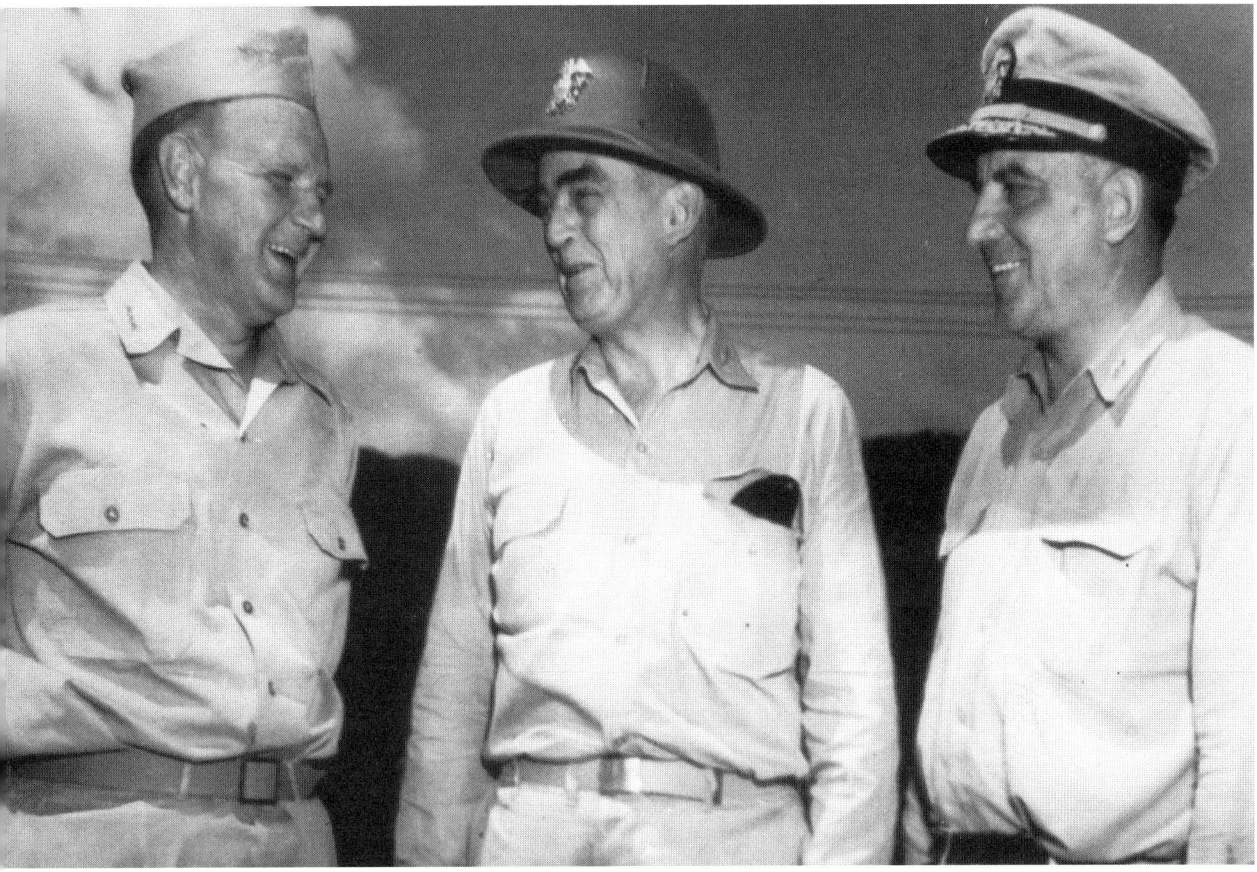

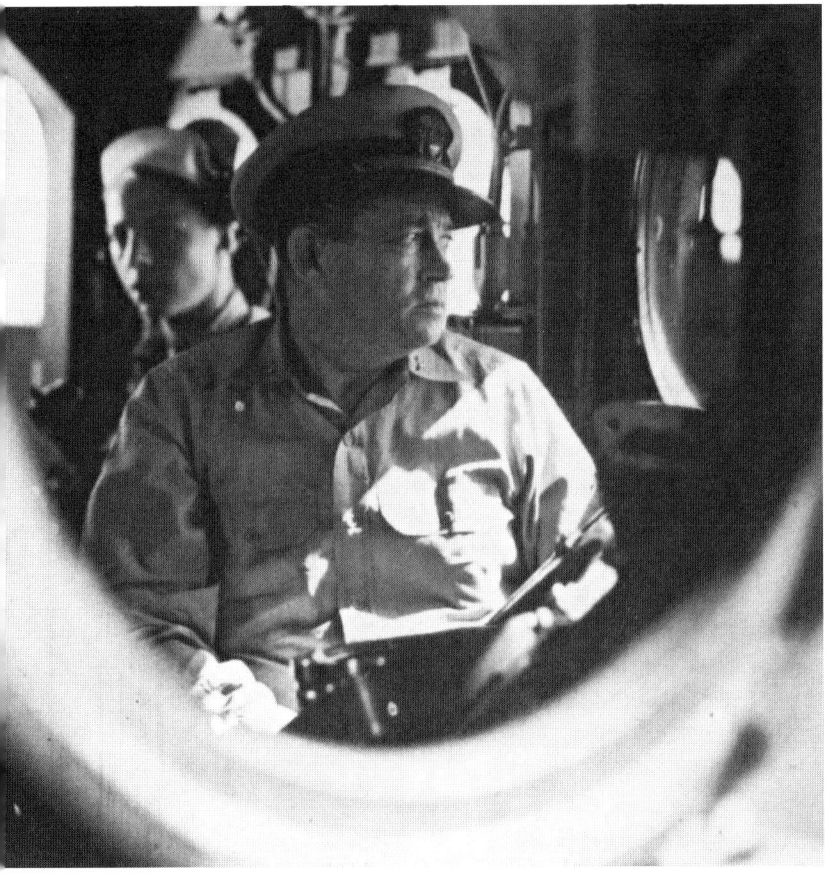

(**Left**) Rear Admiral Clifton A.F. Sprague is shown here through a porthole aboard the escort carrier USS *Fanshaw Bay*. In the Battle off Samar Island, Sprague won a Navy Cross for his leadership of Taffy 3 comprising six escort carriers, three destroyers and three destroyer escorts that fought off IJN Vice Admiral Kurita's much stronger Centre Strike Force during the sea battle there on 25 October 1944. *(NARA)*

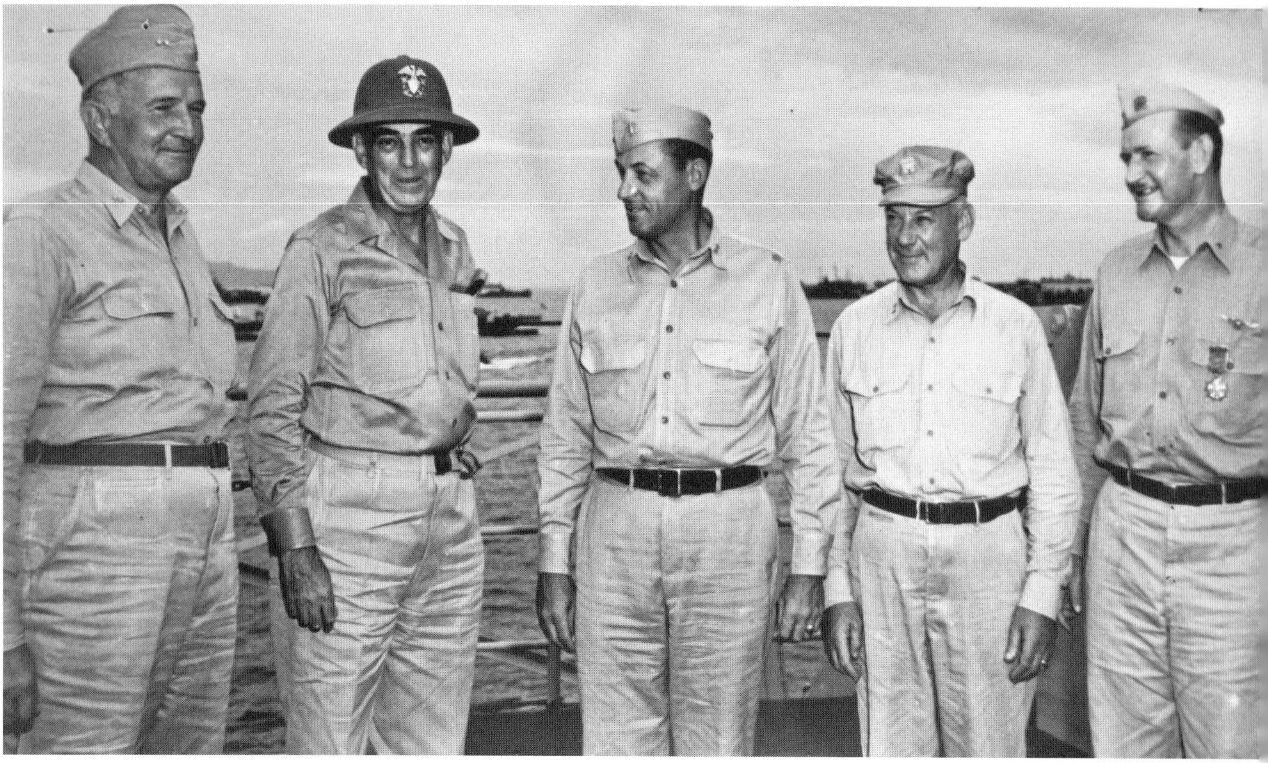

The USN commanders for Luzon's invasion on 9 January 1945, (left to right) Vice Admiral J. Oldendorf, commander of the Battleship Bombardment Group; Admiral T. Kinkaid, Seventh Fleet commander and planner of the Luzon landing at Lingayen Gulf; Rear Admiral T.E. Chandler, head of the cruiser division; and Rear Admiral R. Berkey, leader of the Close Covering Group Command. Commodore V.H. Schaeffer (far right) was Kinkaid's COS. *(NARA)*

Two liberating American soldiers are seen (background, left) among soldiers, sailors and Marines captured on Bataan and Corregidor in a section of Bilibid Prison in Manila. This facility was liberated on 4 February 1945. *(NARA)*

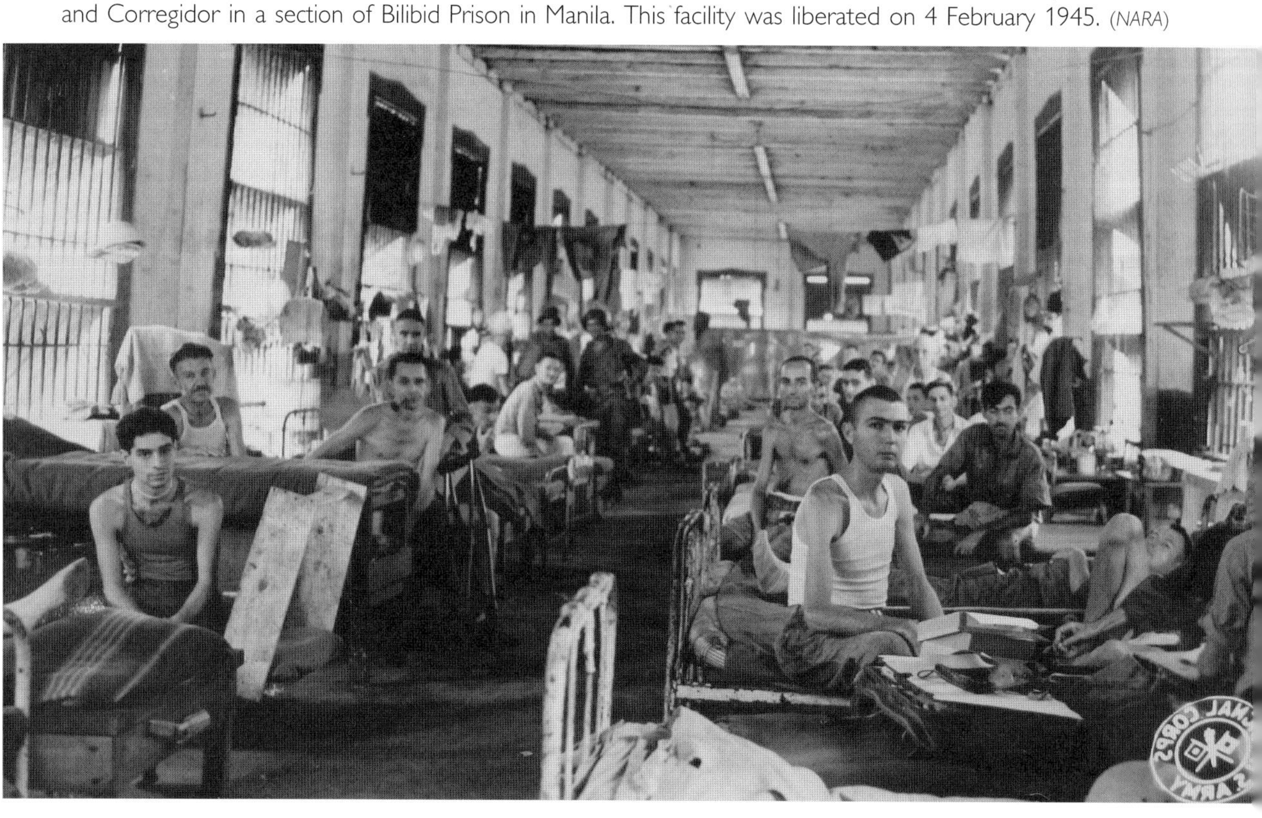

(**Above, left**) Lieutenant General Sōsaku Suzuki led the IJA 35th Army located in the Visayan Islands with HQ on Cebu. Suzuki was COS for the Central China Expeditionary Force and also COS for Yamashita's 25th Army during the invasion and capture of Malaya and Singapore in 1942. Suzuki survived Leyte's conquest but later died attempting to escape on Mindanao on 19 April 1945 after the US Eighth Army's invasion there. (*NARA*)

(**Above, centre**) IJN Vice Admiral Takeo Kurita commanded the Centre Strike Force during the Battle of Leyte Gulf on 25 October 1944. Kurita commanded the 7th Cruiser Division at the war's outbreak, participating in the invasions of Java and the Netherland East Indies. In July 1942, he was reassigned to the 3rd Battleship Division and bombarded Henderson Field on Guadalcanal on the night of 13 October 1942. In 1943, Kurita replaced Admiral Kondo as commander of the IJN 2nd Fleet (devoid of aircraft carriers), which he led as the Centre Strike Force during the Battle of the Sibuyan Sea (23 October 1944) and the Battle off Samar Island (25 October 1944). This force included the enormous battleships *Yamato* and *Musashi*, along with three other battleships, ten cruisers and thirteen destroyers. This larger, more powerful force turned back after being confronted by a much smaller and weaker force of American escort carriers, destroyers and destroyer escorts off Samar Island. (*NARA*)

(**Above, right**) IJN Vice Admiral Jisaburō Ozawa is shown above. He was the last C-in-C of the Combined Fleet. At the war's outbreak, he was C-in-C of the IJN 1st Southern Expeditionary Force, which was involved in the invasion of Malaya on 8 December 1941. In early 1942, his fleet was involved in the invasions of Java and Sumatra. After the disaster at Midway, Ozawa relieved Admiral Chūichi Nagumo as commander of Japan's carrier forces. On 25 October 1944, Ozawa's force with only one large carrier, *Zuikaku*, along with several smaller ones lured Halsey's TF 34 north as a decoy so Vice Admiral Kurita's Centre Striking Force could cross the San Bernadino Strait and attack the US Sixth Army on the Leyte beaches. (*NARA*)

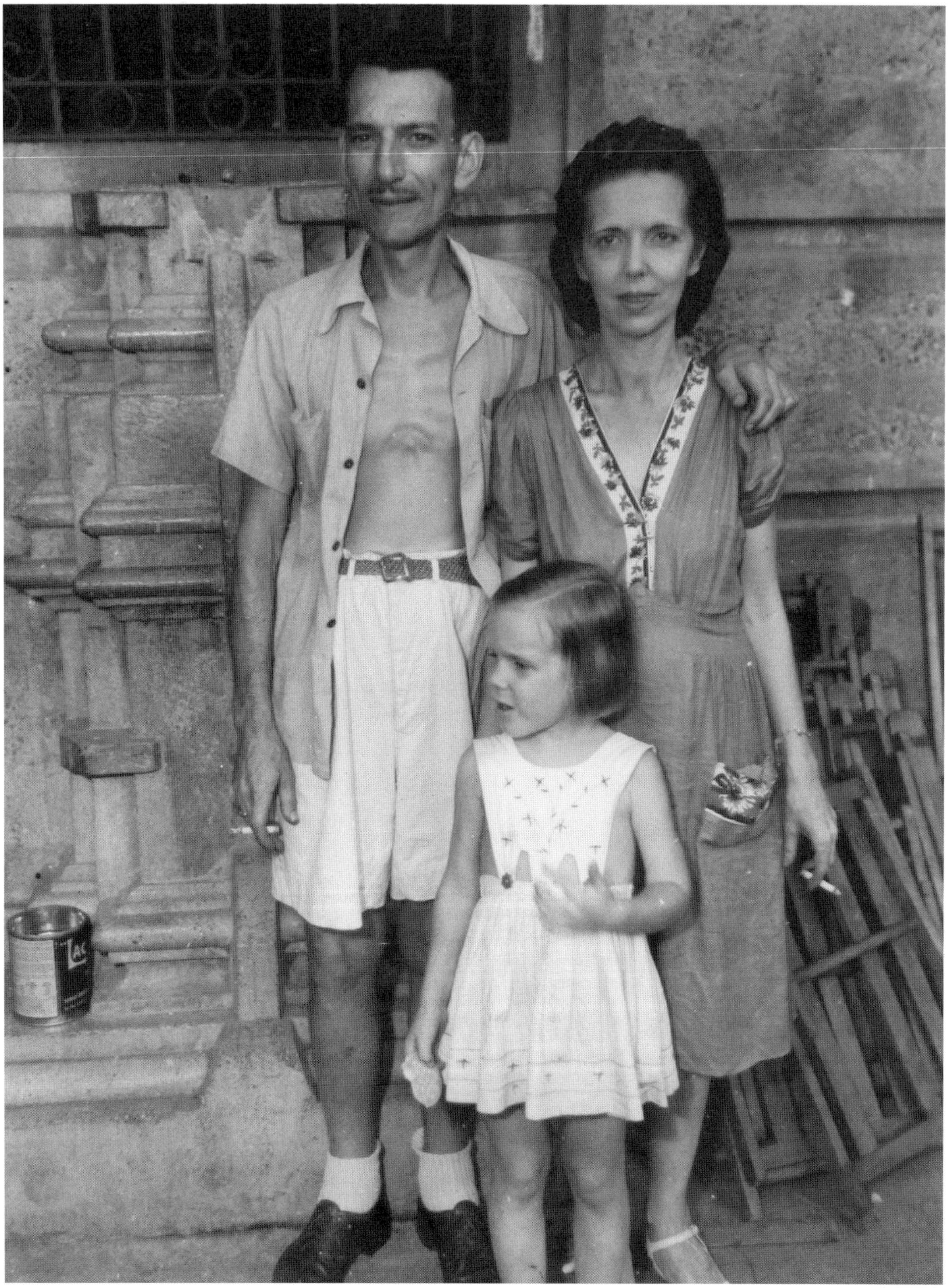

A family of American citizens is shown posing casually after their release from the Japanese internment facility at Bilibid Prison. Their cachectic [wasted] appearance with the man's ribs showing is apparent. Elements of the 37th Division's 148th IR reached Manila by 4 February 1945. By midnight on 5 February, the soldiers advanced through the city to the Bilibid Prison where they liberated more than 1,000 Allied internees before reaching the Pasig River with its demolished bridges. *(NARA)*

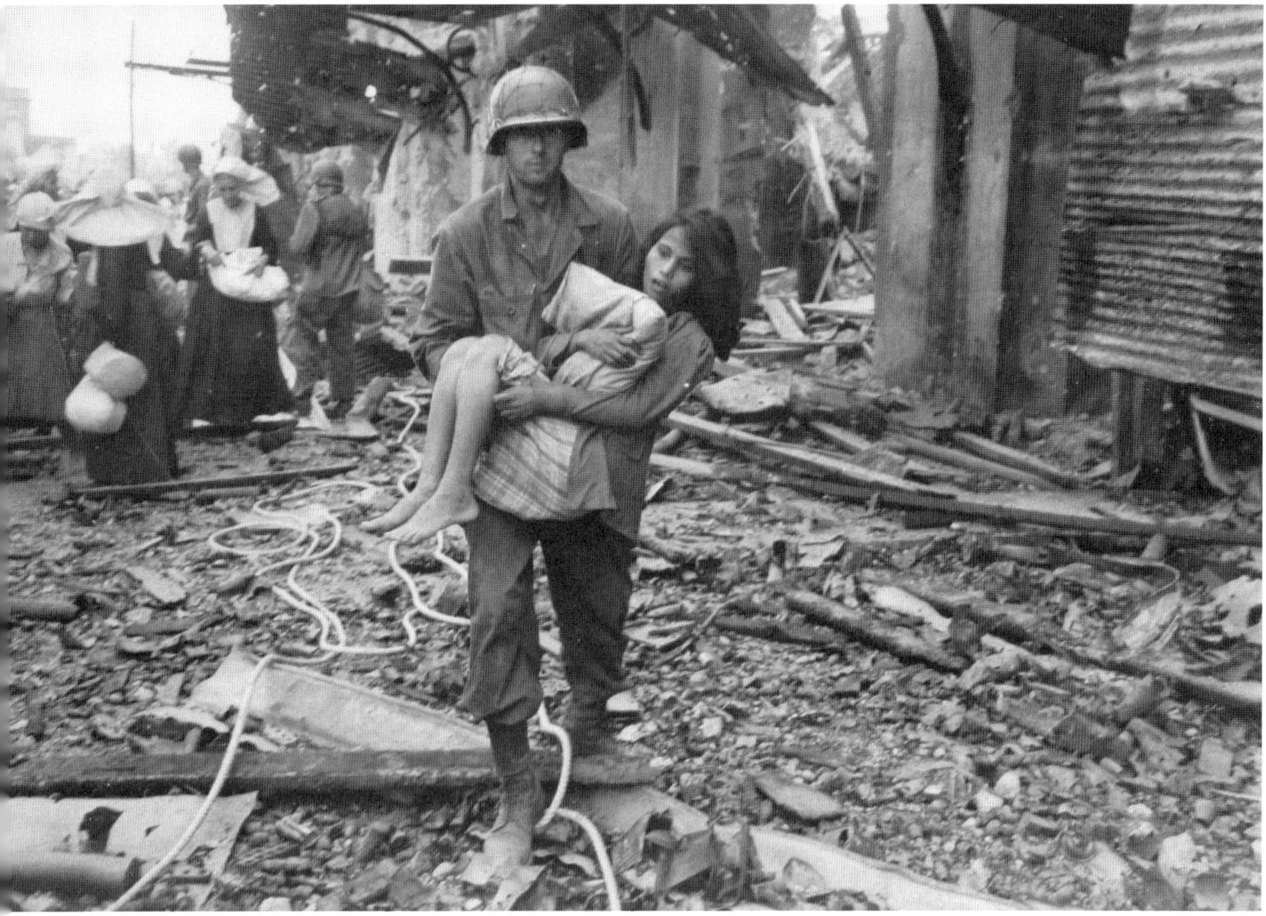

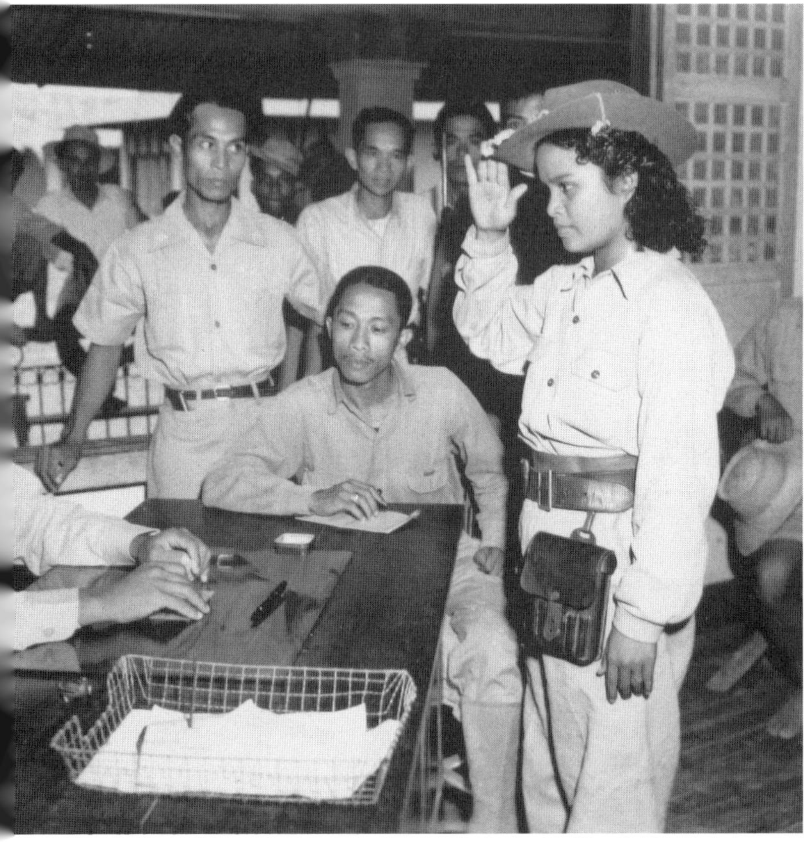

An American soldier is seen here carrying a shell-shocked Filipino girl through the ruins of a war-torn section of Manila. Other Filipinos, soldiers and nuns are present (background). American and Japanese troops fought bitter house-to house combat with the annihilation of much of the IJN's Manila Naval Defence force along with tens of thousands of Filipino citizens killed. *(NARA)*

Filipino guerrilla leader Florentina Punsalon, a 20-year-old, is seen here saluting Captain Marcel Payne at a Filipino guerrilla HQ on 17 January 1945 within days of the Luzon invasion. *(NARA)*

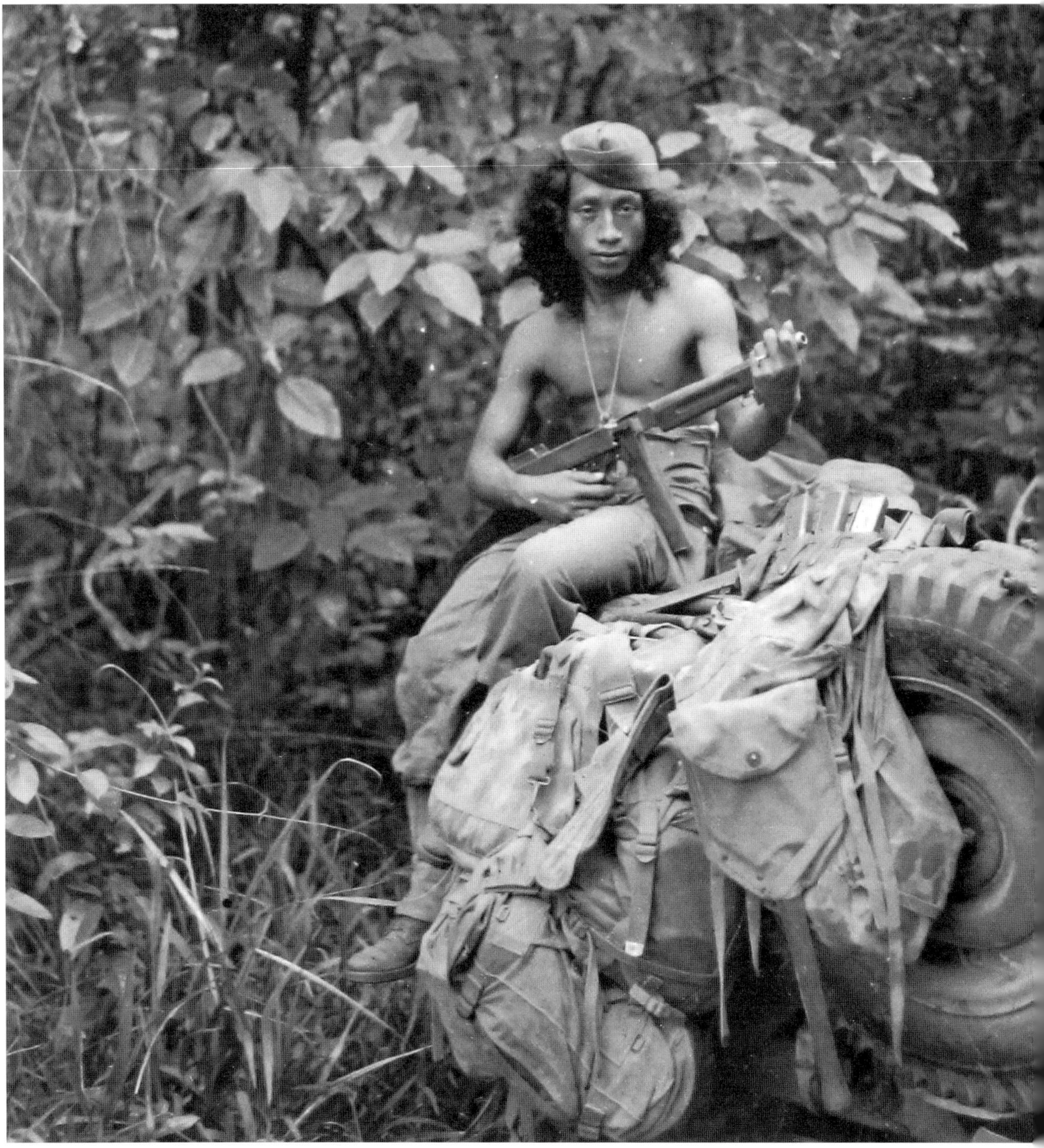

(**Above**) On Mindanao, a Philippine Scout, Amicedo Favola, is shown with his Thompson 0.45in-calibre SMG. Favola worked with the Eighth Army's 24th Division's Reconnaissance Squadron in April 1945. *(NARA)*

(**Opposite, above**) On Mindoro, two Filipino citizens are shown indicating to members of an American combat team the direction of a Japanese unit's retreat into the hills near San Jose. An American brigade-sized force landed on Mindoro's south-western coast near San Jose on 15 December 1944. *(NARA)*

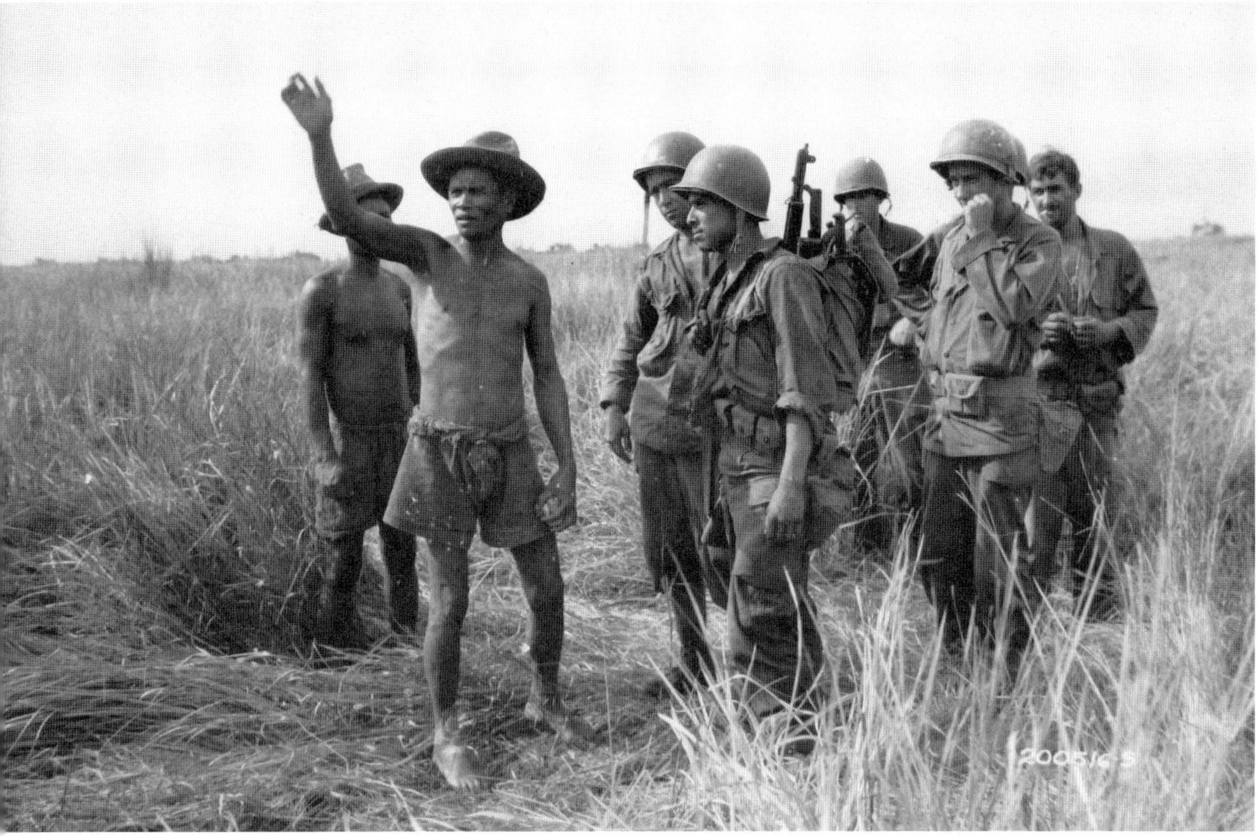

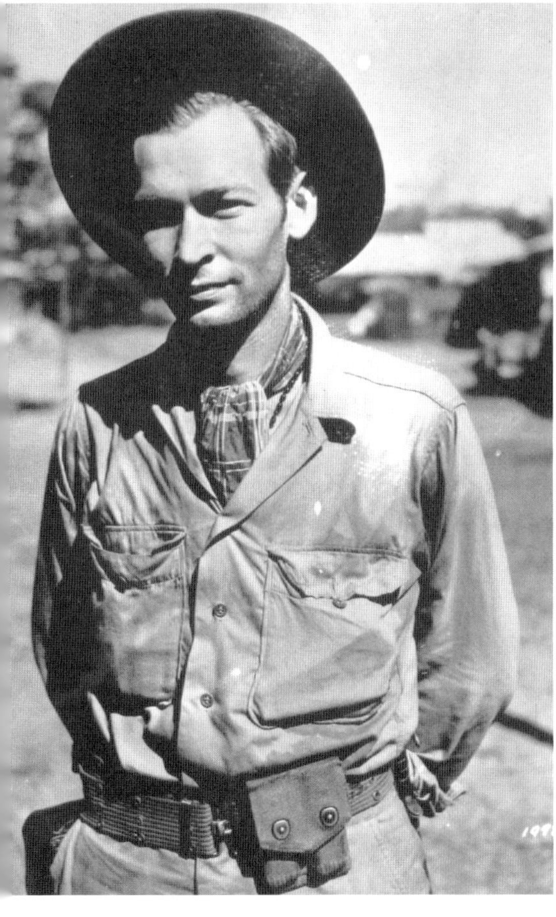

(**Left**) Major Robert Lapham, an Iowa native, was with the 45th Philippine Scouts on Bataan and led a band of Filipino guerrillas on Luzon in the province of Nueva Ecija in proximity to Cabanatuan City, the provincial capital, for three years. Cabanatuan City was located 4 miles from the PoW camp. Lapham rode his horse 40 miles to meet and inform Sixth Army G-2 (Intelligence) staff officers at Calasiao on 26 January 1945 of the mass murder of 140 American PoWs at the Puerto Princesa camp on the island of Palawan on 14 December 1944. The Cabanatuan PoWs had become aware of this atrocity too in early January, weeks after its diabolical occurrence, via the 'Bamboo Telegraph' (the Filipino 'grapevine') and feared that they too would be exterminated. Lapham conveyed that this potential terrible disaster was real. A few survivors of the Palawan massacre, including Private Eugene Nielsen of the 59th Coast Artillery that surrendered on Corregidor in 9 May 1942, gave first-hand accounts of the December atrocity to SWPA G-2 officers on Morotai on 7 January. After escaping the Puerto Princesa camp massacre, they were rescued by local Filipinos and turned over to US Army troops for Catalina flying boat transit to Morotai. Prior to that, no army intelligence officers had been apprised of this horrific incident. *(NARA)*

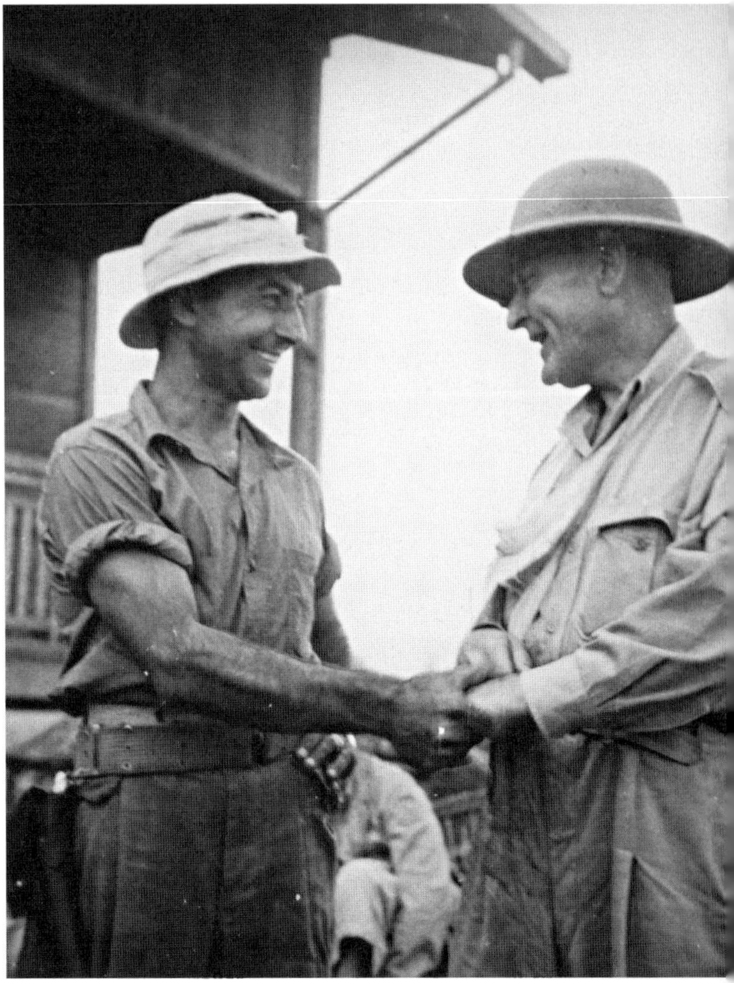

Lieutenant Colonel Henry Mucci (left), commanding officer of the 6th Raider Battalion, shakes hands with Colonel James Duckworth (right), a doctor and the senior PoW officer at Cabanatuan, on 31 January 1945 after the successful raid that liberated 512 captives. Duckworth was reportedly in disbelief when the Rangers burst into the Cabanatuan camp, killing the Japanese troops and urging the PoWs to move to the front gate during the late evening hours of 30 January. Mucci was assigned the task of conducting the raid and delegated his junior officer, Captain Robert Prince, to plan it. Mucci, a West Point graduate, was a born leader and revered by his Rangers for his fitness and ability to exhort his troops. Duckworth's right arm was in a sling as he had fallen in part due to the prevalence of 'night blindness' among the PoWs as he was urged to move quickly to the main gate for evacuation. *(NARA)*

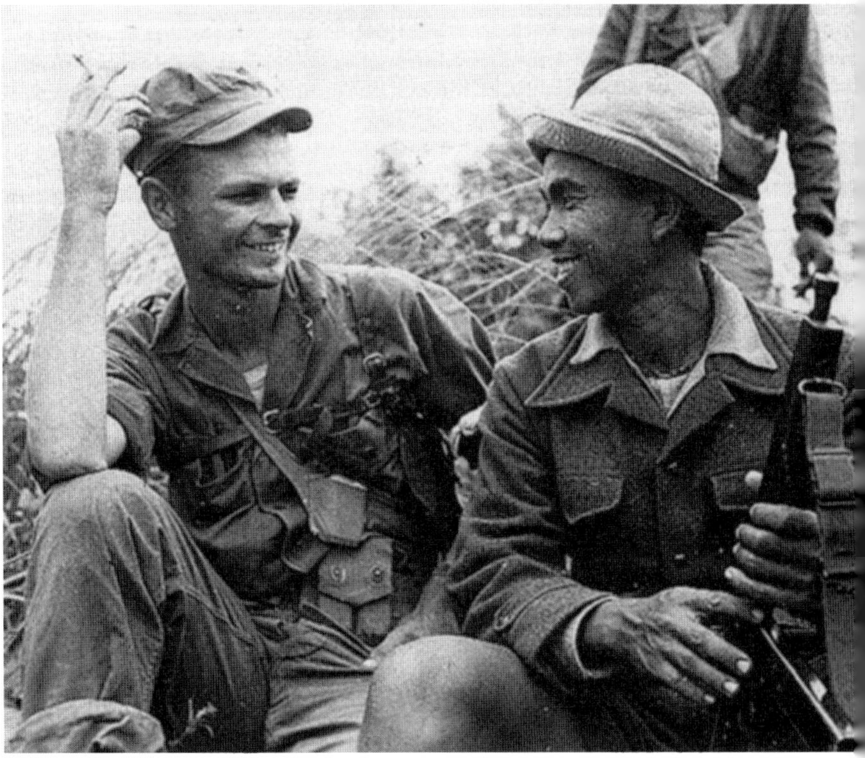

Captain Robert Prince, C Company commander, 6th Ranger Battalion, planned and led the Cabanatuan PoW camp assault, under Mucci, on the night of 30 January 1945. He is shown here with a Filipino guerrilla scout after the successful raid that freed 512 American PoWs who were slated for execution by the Japanese in the infamous Cabanatuan camp. Prince was known for his extreme composure in stressful situations. *(Author's collection)*

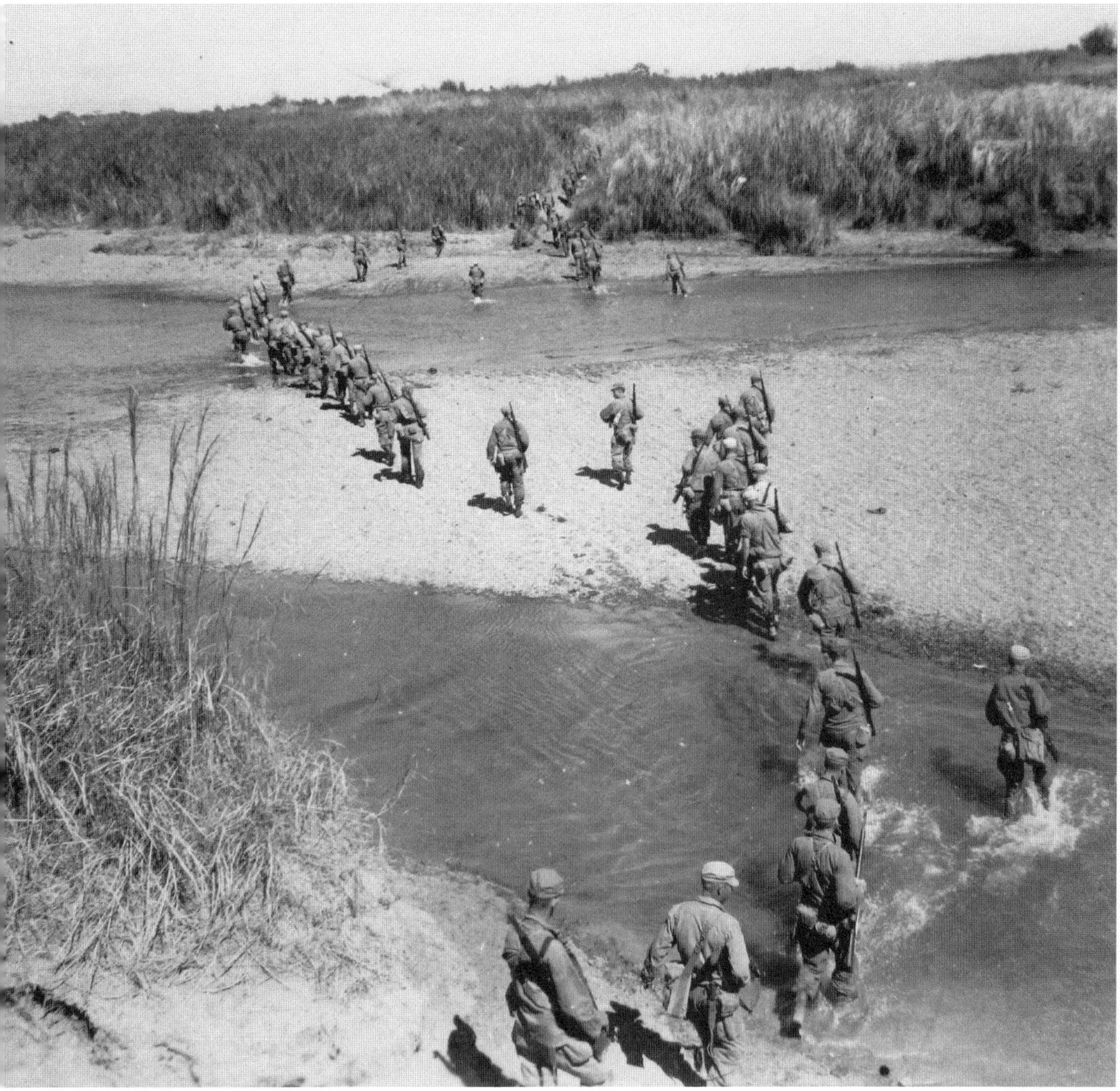

The 6th Battalion Rangers from C Company and a platoon from F Company are shown here crossing a river behind enemy lines near San Rosario on 27 January 1945 as part of their 30-mile clandestine march to the Cabanatuan PoW camp. The Rangers bivouacked for the night on 29 January at Platero to the north of the Pampanga River before their stealthy approach to the Cabanatuan PoW camp the following day. Krueger authorized 120 of them to assault the Cabanatuan PoW camp at dusk on 30 January. Before landing on Luzon, the Rangers were army mule-skinners that had been trained as a 75mm pack howitzer unit, the 98th FA Battalion in the mountains of Colorado for combat in Papua New Guinea's Owen Stanley Range. As Buna-Gona and Sananda had been captured by MacArthur's Australian-American force in early 1943, the mules were no longer needed and were sent to Burma. The 98th FA Battalion was disbanded and transformed into the 800 men of the 6th Raider Battalion under Mucci, who was a Pearl Harbor attack veteran as a provost marshal in Honolulu. On 17 October 1944, just prior to the main Leyte invasion of 20 October, elements of Mucci's 6th Battalion Rangers amphibiously assaulted Suluan and Dinagat Islands and met with no Japanese resistance. The next day they took Homonhon Island. *(NARA)*

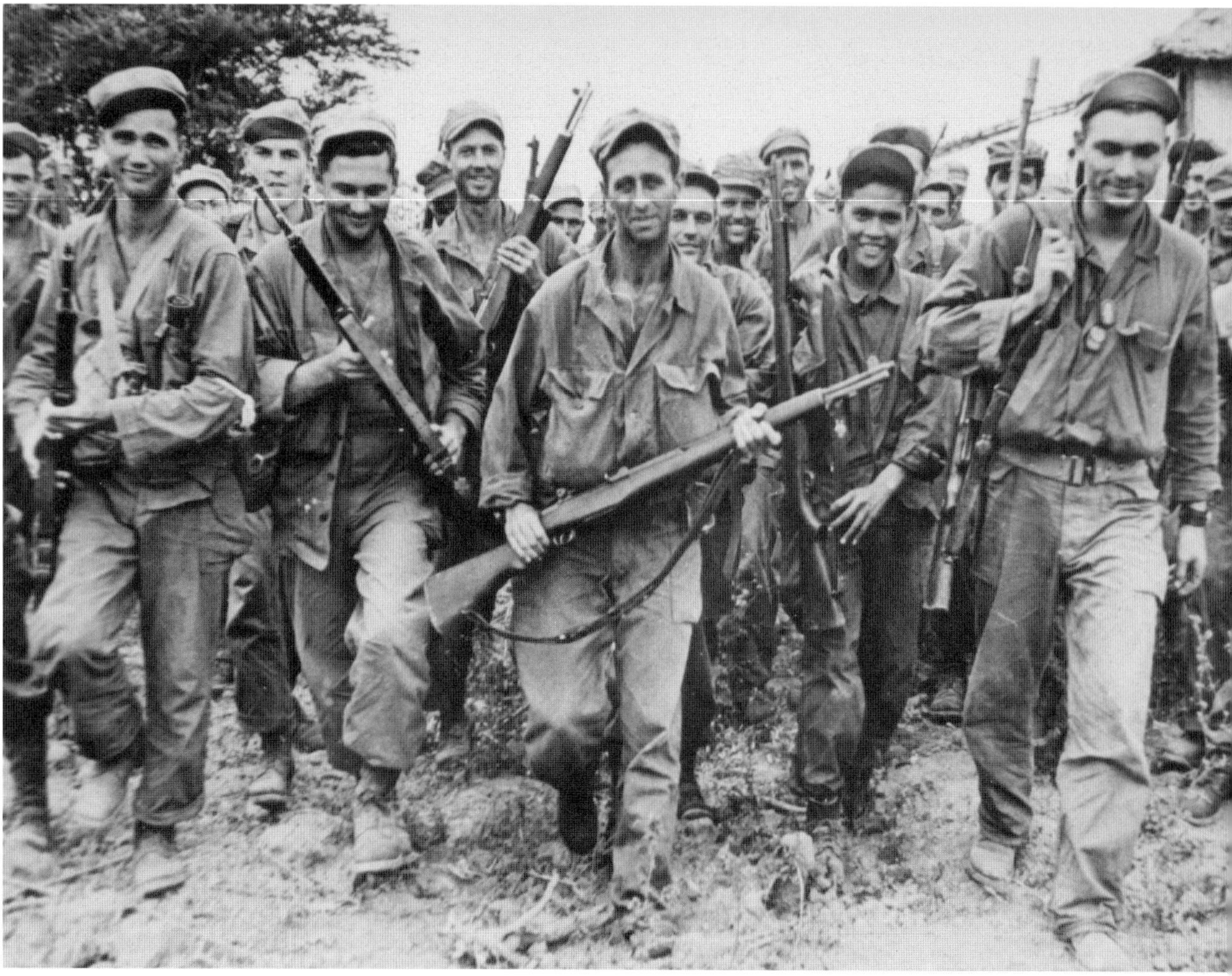

A platoon of F Company, 6th Battalion Rangers led by 1st Lieutenant John F. Murphy ('Murf') is shown here (centre) after their successful raid on the Cabanatuan PoW camp and the liberation of 512 American PoWs. C Company (ninety Rangers), under the command of Captain Robert Prince, led the raid with the attached platoon (thirty Rangers) from F Company under Murphy. The 120 Rangers were accompanied by three Alamo Scout lieutenants and an organized Filipino guerrilla force. *(NARA)*

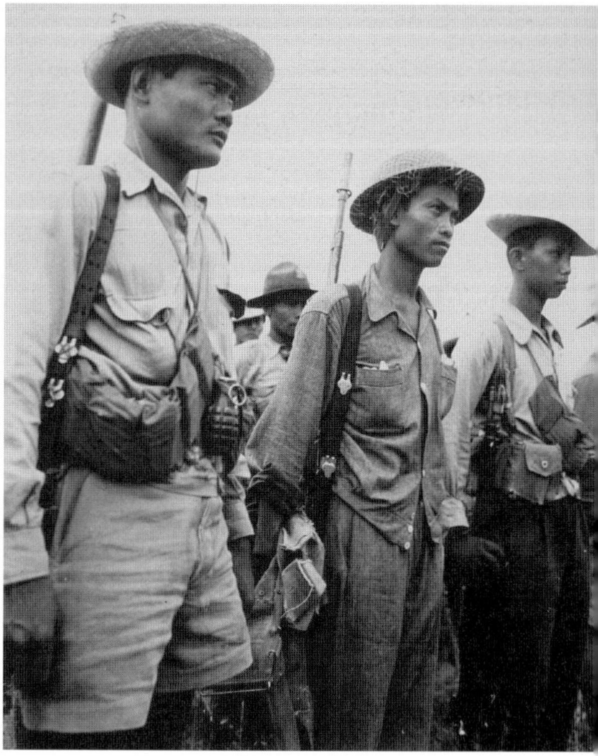

For the Cabanatuan PoW camp raid, approximately 200 Filipino guerrillas under Captain Juan Pajota were utilized. In addition to escorting the infirm PoWs in oxcarts after their liberation from the camp by the Rangers, Pajota's guerrillas manned an essential roadblock to confront approximately 1,000 Japanese troops stationed near the Cabu River Bridge situated 1 mile to the north-west of the PoW stockade. *(NARA)*

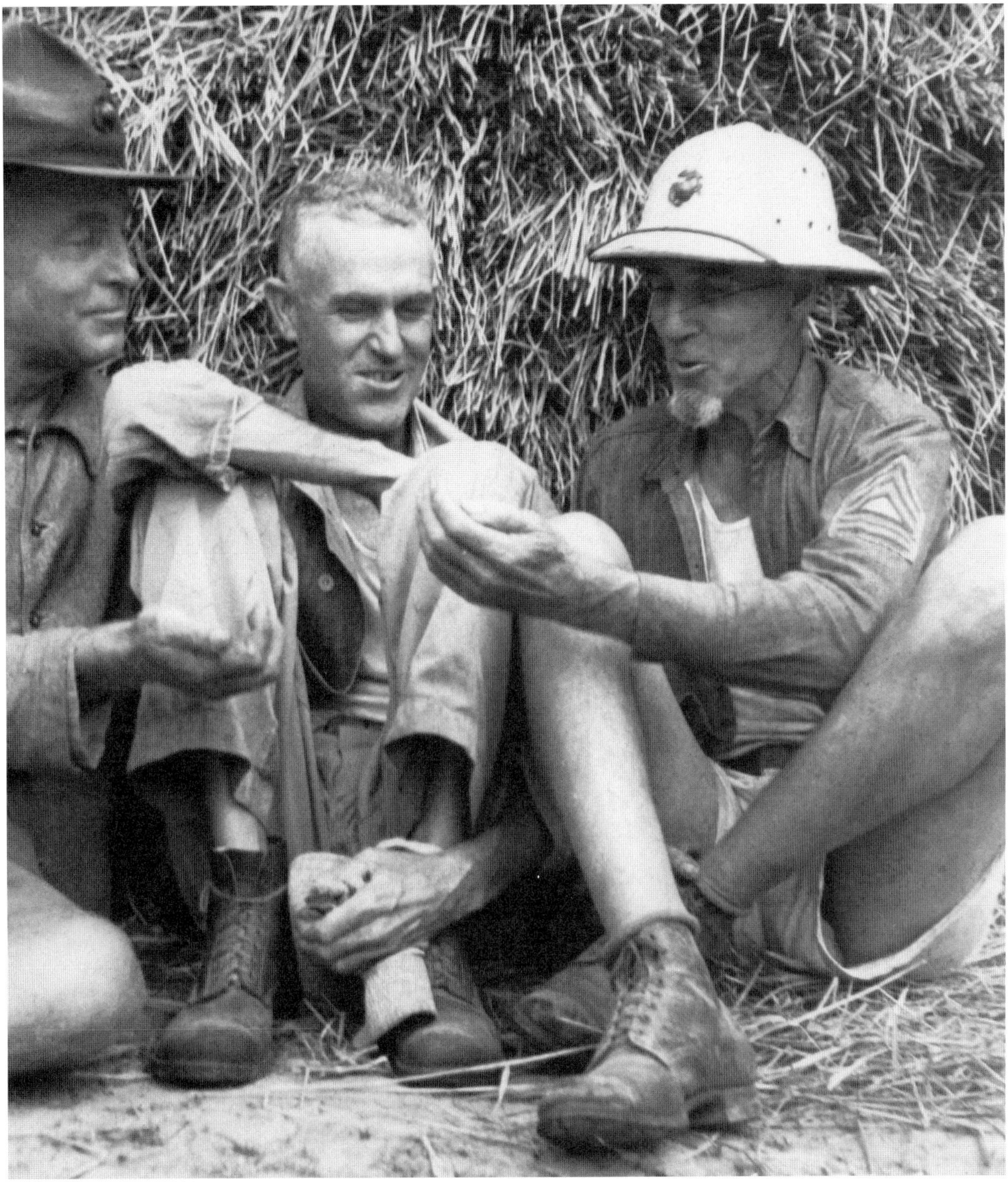

Three US Marines from among the liberated American PoWs from the Cabanatuan camp are shown after the raid on 31 January. From left to right are Sergeant John Kelly, Warrant Officer James Shinel and Master Technical Sergeant Eugene Commander. They had referred to themselves as the 'ghosts of Bataan' on account of them being the sickest and weakest of the soldiers, sailors and Marines captured at Bataan and Corregidor in April and May 1942 respectively. The 4th Marines had been on Corregidor since the end of December 1941 and attempted to stop the Japanese amphibious assault of that island in early May 1942. *(NARA)*

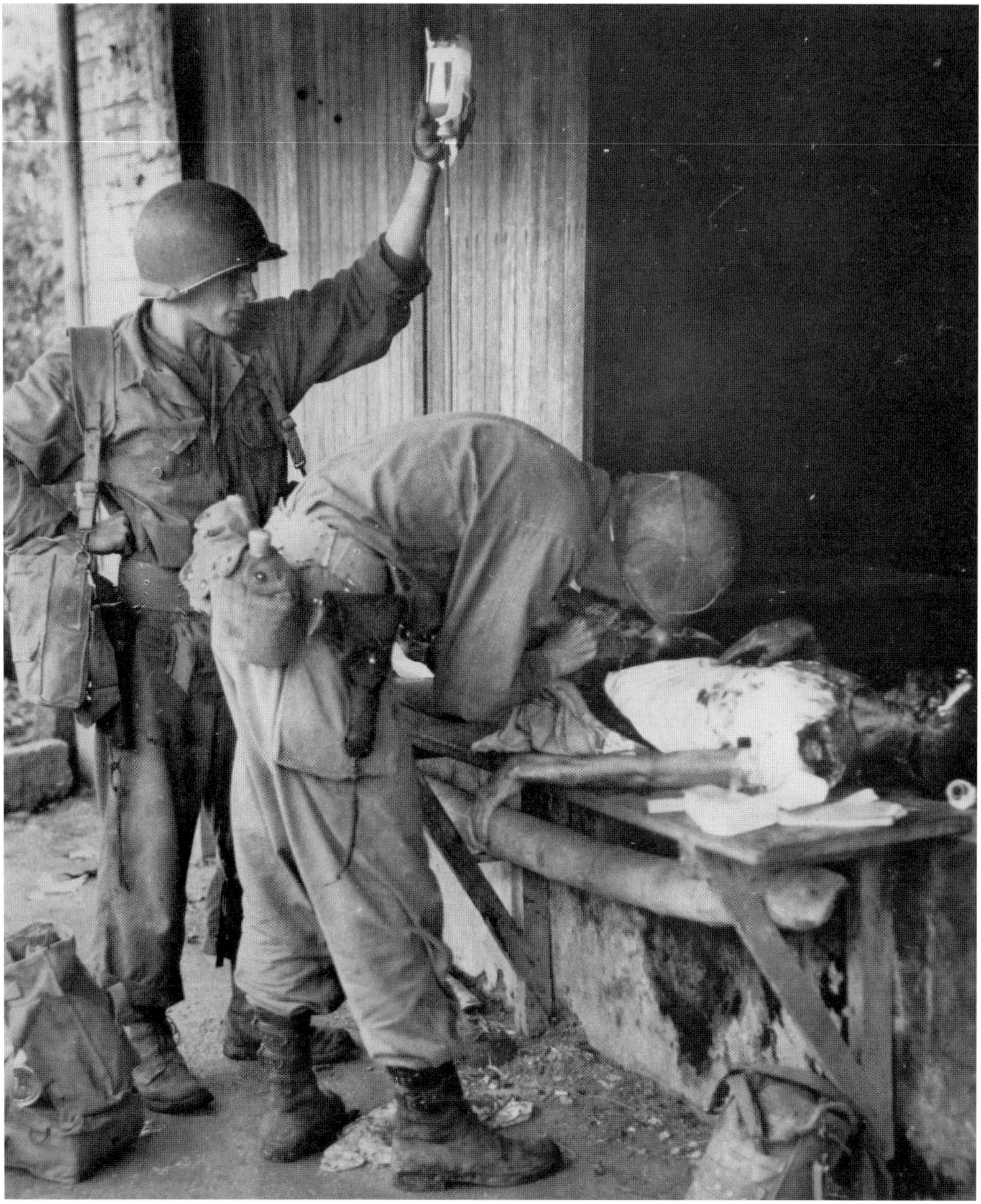

Captain John D. Watson, a doctor attached to the 37th Division's 148th IR liberating Manila, is shown here examining a wounded Filipino who suffered a Japanese officer's samurai sword slash. The medic (left) is seen holding a bottle of plasma to resuscitate the wounded civilian. Despite the Geneva Convention, some medical personnel wore sidearms as the Japanese regarded these Americans as choice targets. *(NARA)*

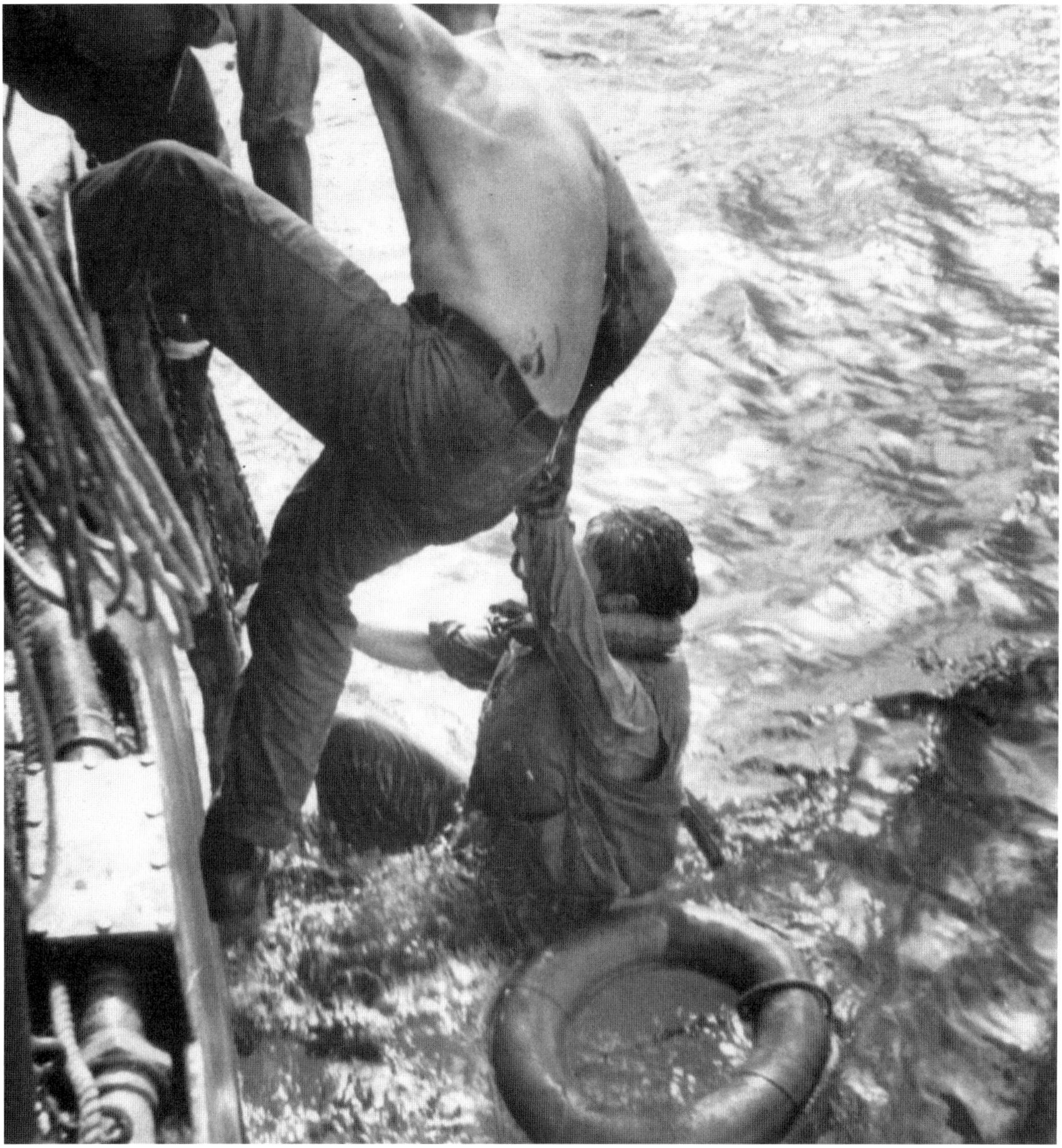

One of the 1,200 seamen that survived the carnage of the Battle off Samar Island (25 October 1945) is pulled from the sea by crew members of an intact destroyer escort on 27 October. The Battle off Samar Island was the centremost action of the Battle of Leyte Gulf. It was off Samar Island that American naval forces were most unprepared and undergunned. However, the American vessels made repeated attacks, convincing the Japanese that they were facing much larger capital ships than destroyers and destroyer escorts. The USS *Johnston* and *Hoel*, both destroyers, along with the *Gambier Bay*, an escort carrier, all part of Task Force 77.4 (Taffy 1, 2 and 3) were struck and sunk during the conflict by shells from Admiral Kurita's six heavy and two light cruisers as well as four Japanese battleships including the *Yamato*. A destroyer escort, USS *Samuel D. Roberts*, was also sunk by IJN gunfire, while another USN escort carrier, USS *St. Lo*, was sunk by a *kamikaze* aircraft during the battle. (*NARA*)

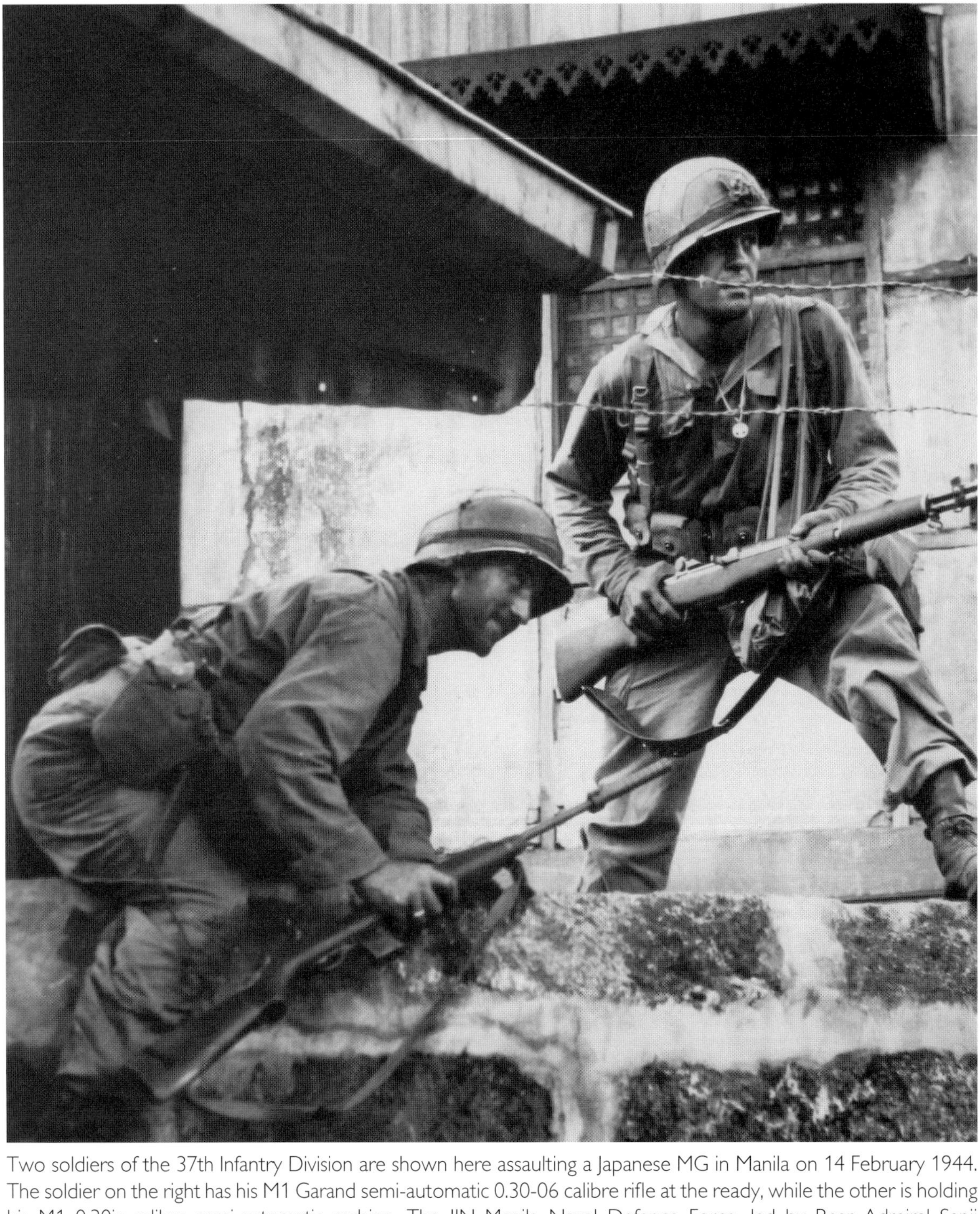

Two soldiers of the 37th Infantry Division are shown here assaulting a Japanese MG in Manila on 14 February 1944. The soldier on the right has his M1 Garand semi-automatic 0.30-06 calibre rifle at the ready, while the other is holding his M1 0.30in-calibre semi-automatic carbine. The IJN Manila Naval Defence Force, led by Rear Admiral Sanji Iwabuchi, decided to mount suicidal resistance to US Sixth Army forces along the Pasig River and from within the *Intramuros* ('Walled City') near the city's harbours. The 37th Division's 148th IR reached Manila on 4 February; however, demolished road bridges delayed their entry into the city proper. *(NARA)*

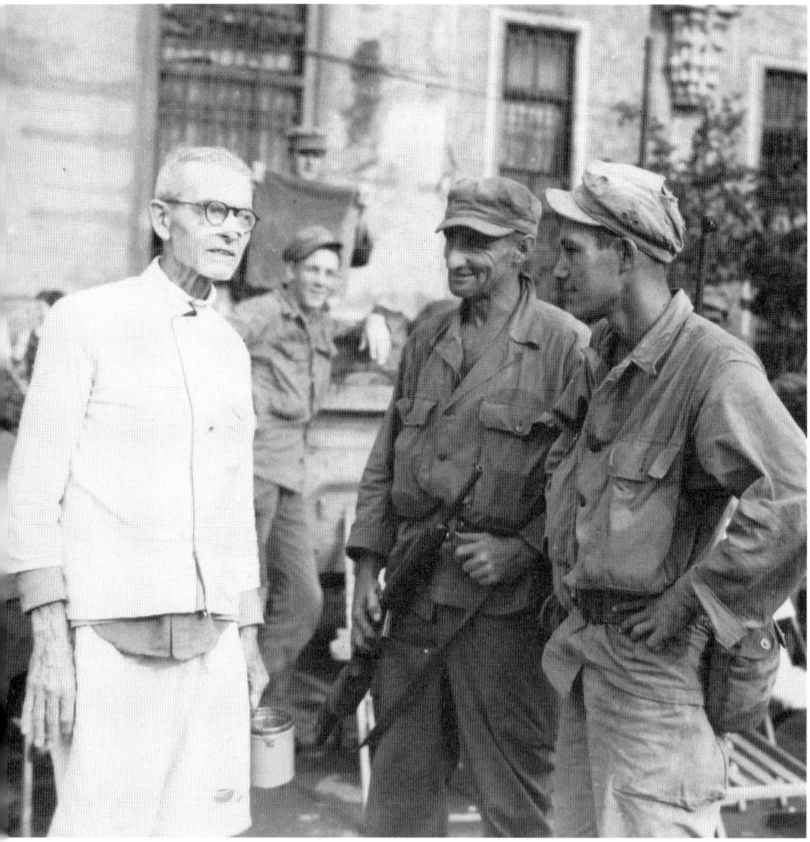

A 74-year-old internee from the Santo Thomas University prison camp is shown here talking to two of his 'liberators', both cavalrymen from the 1st Cavalry Division's 8th Cavalry Regiment, which was one of the first of Krueger's units to enter Manila on 3 February 1945 after a 100-mile trek over seventy-two hours. On 5 February, more than 3,500 internees at the prison camp were liberated. *(NARA)*

A trio of engineers attached to Krueger's Sixth Army is shown here trying to open wooden boxes of Japanese ammunition on a barricaded Manila street in February 1945. The engineers were paying keen attention to whether the boxes were wired to explode upon manipulation as the engineer (right) peers at a slight opening of one end. *(NARA)*

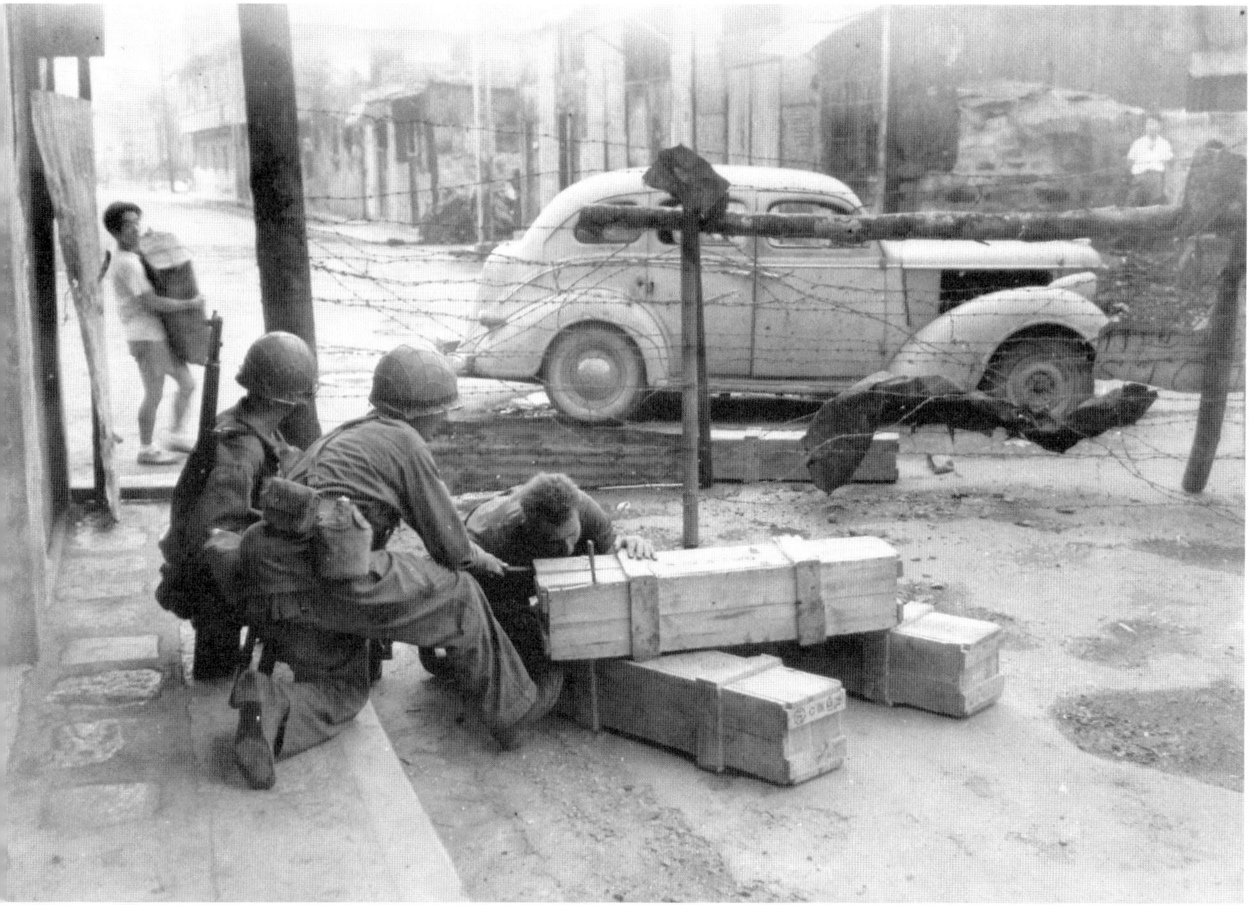

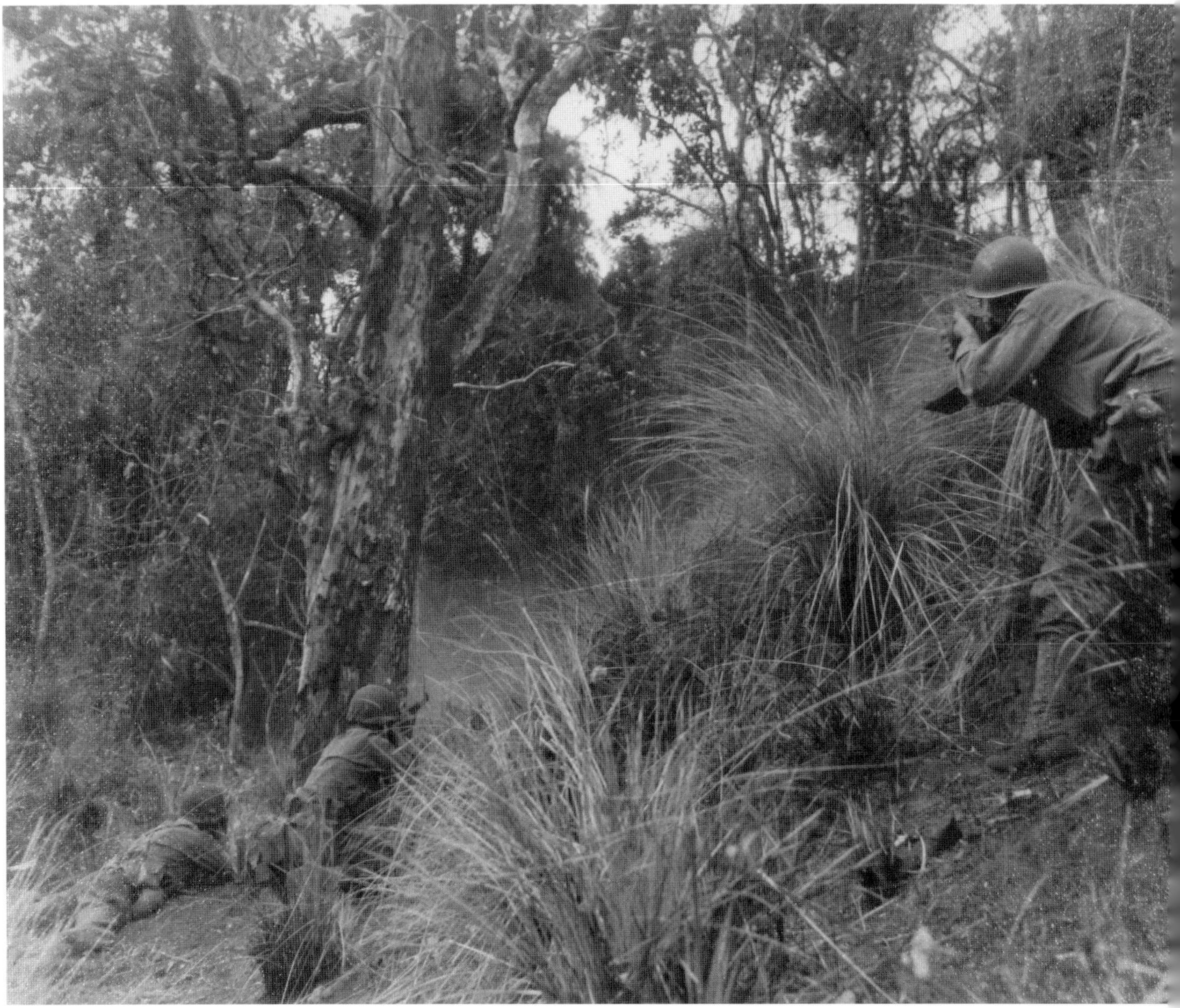

(**Above**) A US army combat photographer (far right) is shown here immortalizing the action of the 3rd Battalion, 161st IR, 25th Division near the Balete Pass near Santa Fe in the mountainous region of northern Luzon. This division heavily engaged Japanese troops from March through to late April 1945 in their attempt to break through the Villa Verde Trail and Route 5 to capture Santa Fe. Stout enemy resistance and steep hills and mountains slowed the Sixth Army advance to gain entry into the Cagayan Valley. *(NARA)*

(**Opposite, above**) Paratroopers of the 11th Airborne Division's 511th PIR are shown here putting on their parachute harnesses prior to boarding their C-47 transport for their airdrop. This PIR fought for several days south of Manila to overcome Japanese strongpoints and pillboxes. The 511th PIR was supported by elements of the 187th and 188th Glider Infantry Regiments (GIR) in combat against the IJN 3rd Naval Defence Battalion defending Nichols Field to Manila's south. After eight days of combat, Nichols Field fell to the US airborne forces on 12 February 1945. *(NARA)*

(**Opposite, below**) American wounded from the 158th IR ('The Bushmasters') are tended to on the Rosario-Luzon Highway on 1 March 1945. This IR, led by Brigadier General Hanford MacNider who was wounded at Buna in 1942, was attached to the 43rd Division. The Bushmasters landed at Lingayen Gulf on 11 January 1945 as a reserve unit, but saw extensive combat action afterwards during the Sixth Army's southern advance. *(NARA)*

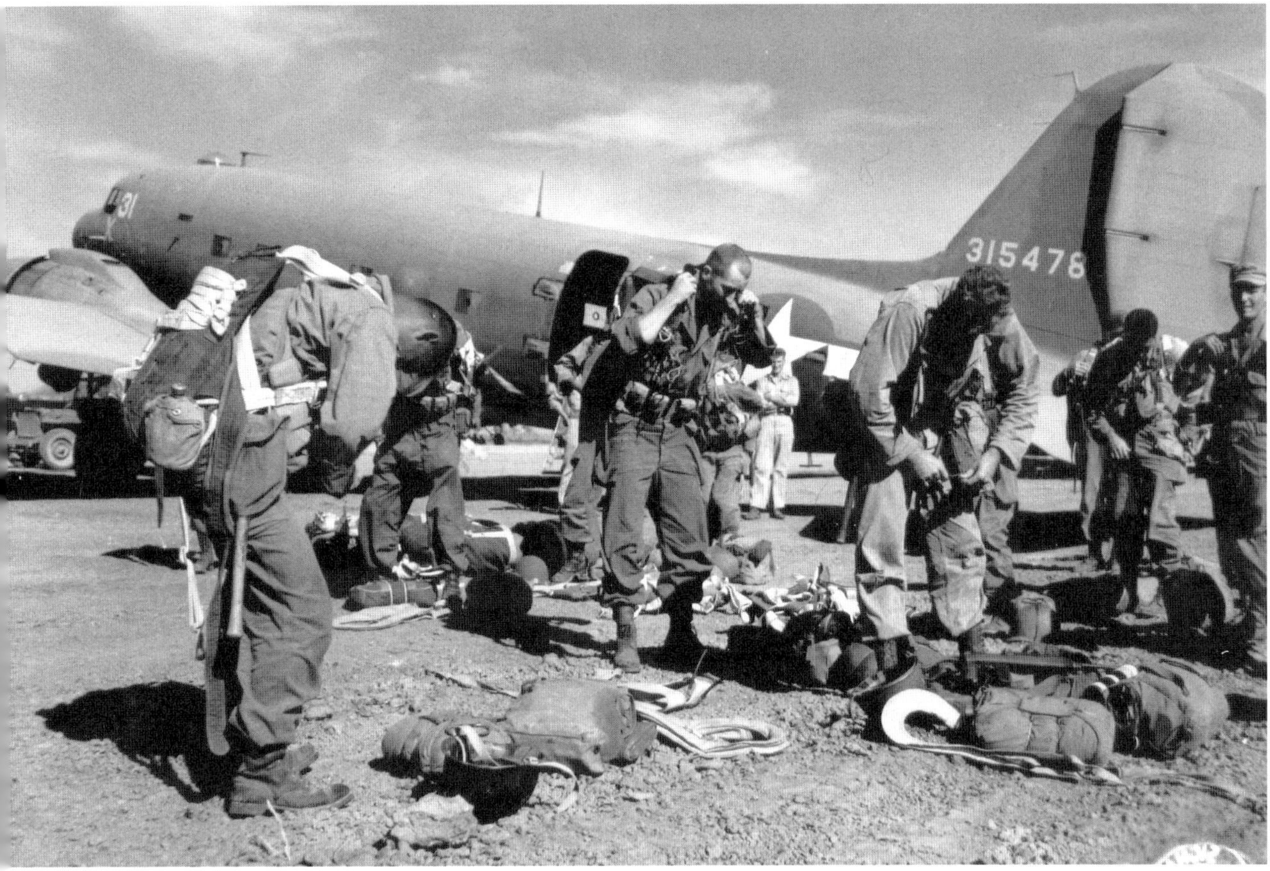
31
315478

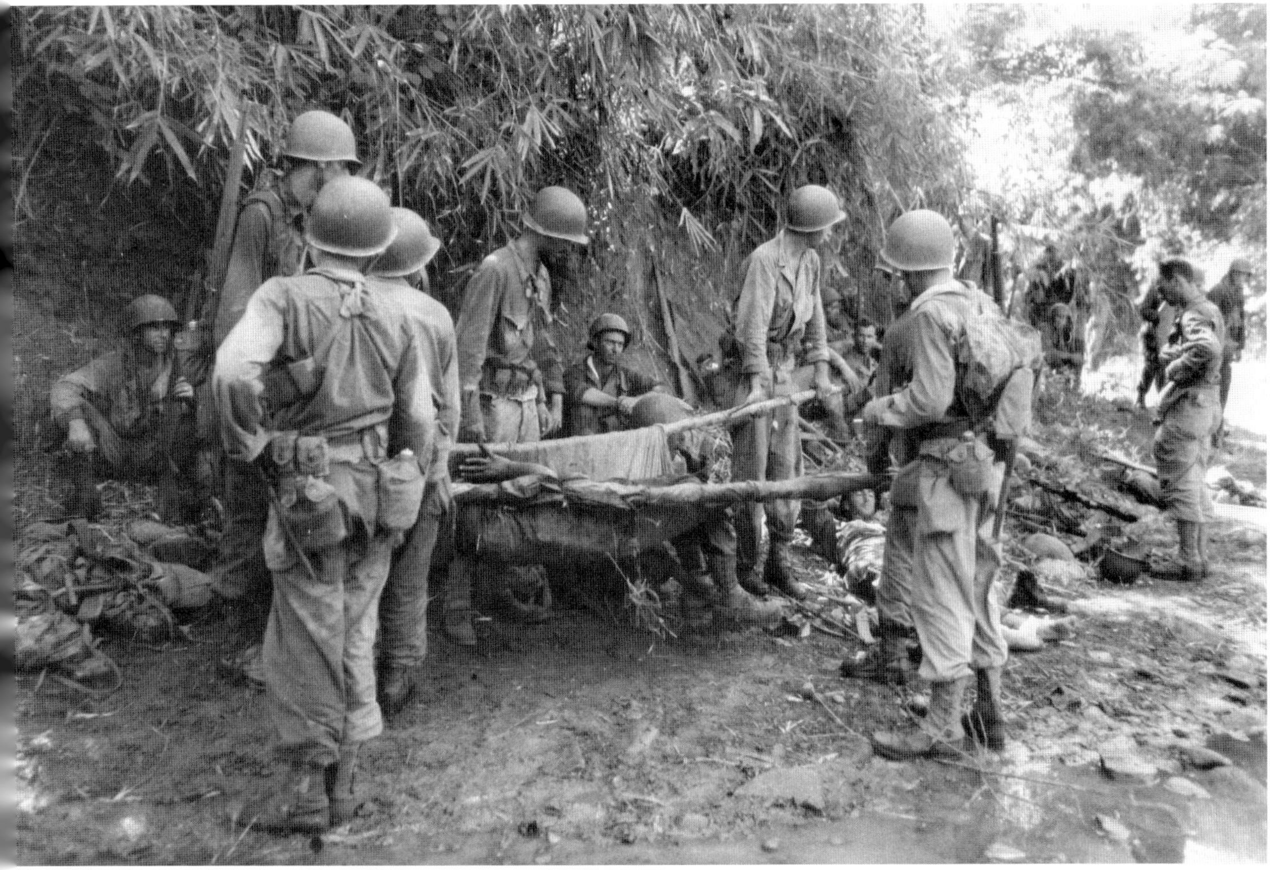

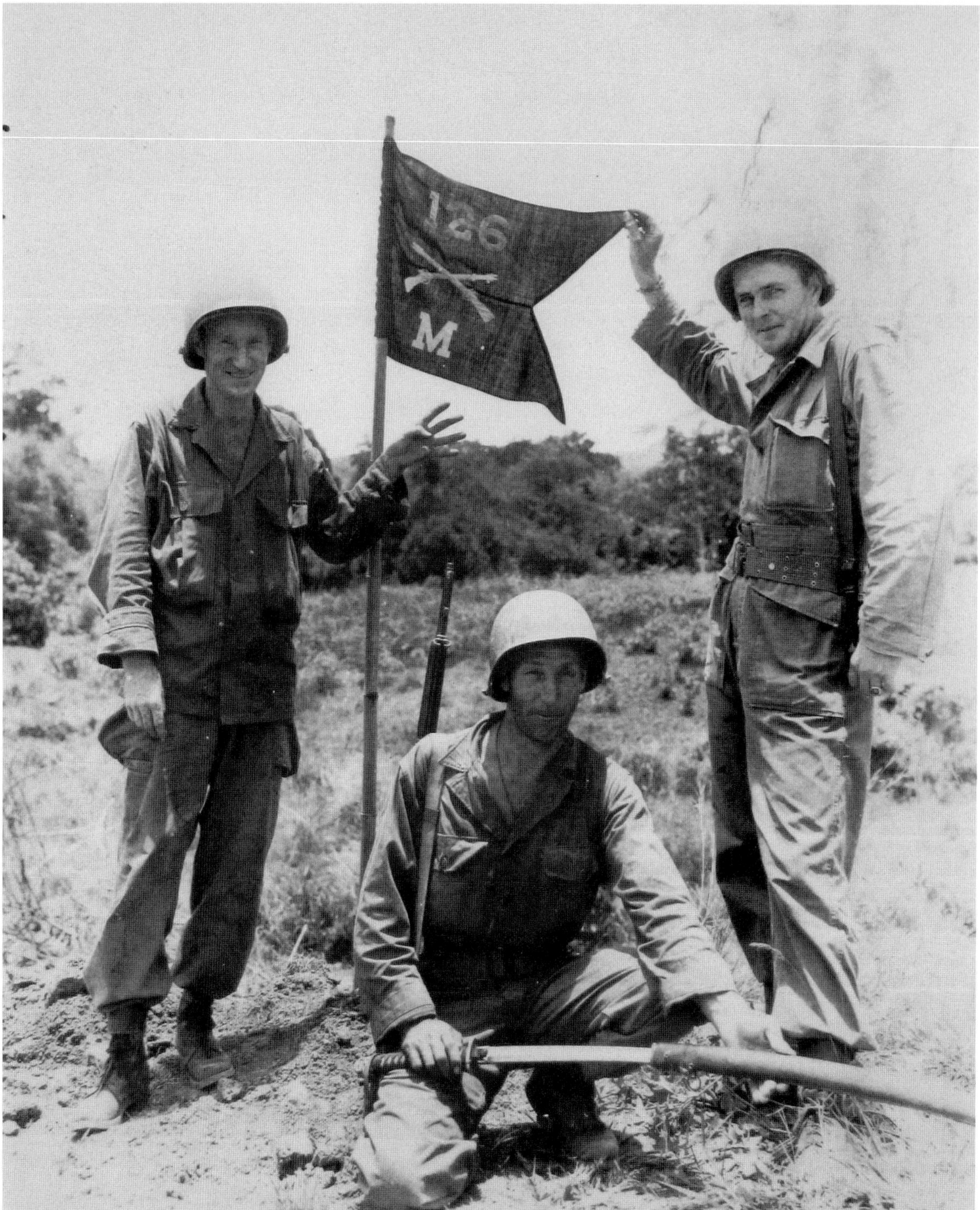
126
M

Soldiers from Company M, 126th IR, 32nd Division are shown here with their unit's pennant and a Japanese samurai sword in northern Luzon's Cagayan Valley during the summer of 1945. The 32nd Division fought along with the 25th Division across mountainous terrain to break through the Villa Verde Trail to get to Santa Fe. *(NARA)*

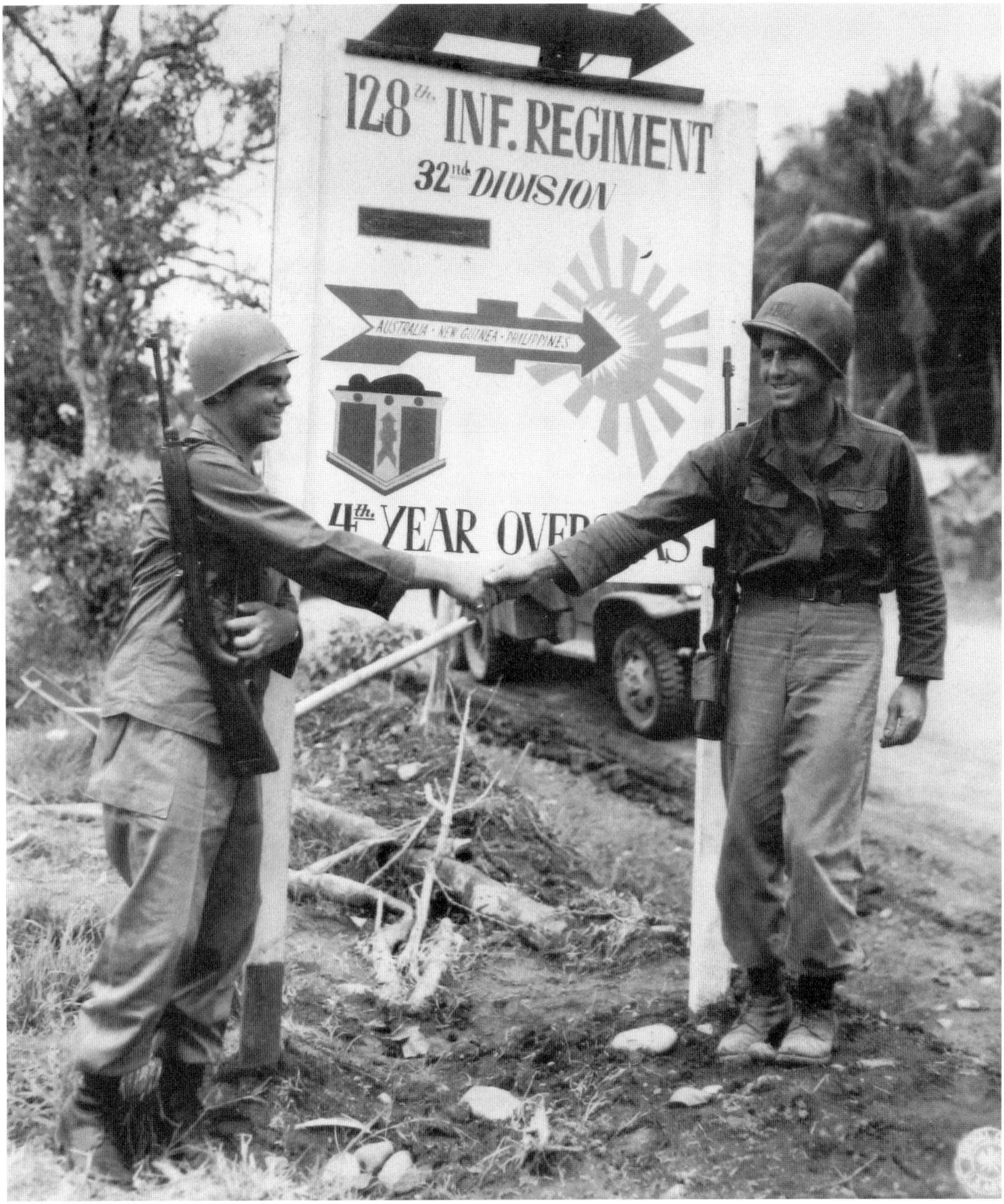
128th INF. REGIMENT
32nd DIVISION
AUSTRALIA · NEW GUINEA · PHILIPPINES

Soldiers of the 32nd Division's 128th IR are shown proudly standing next to their regimental signpost in northern Luzon during the summer of 1945. The sign displayed '4th Year Overseas'. The 32nd Division was hastily deployed to Australia in early 1942 prior to being sent by MacArthur to Papua in the autumn of 1942 to move through the jungle terrain and attack the Japanese defences at Buna, which produced a staggering casualty list due to combat wounds and disease. *(NARA)*

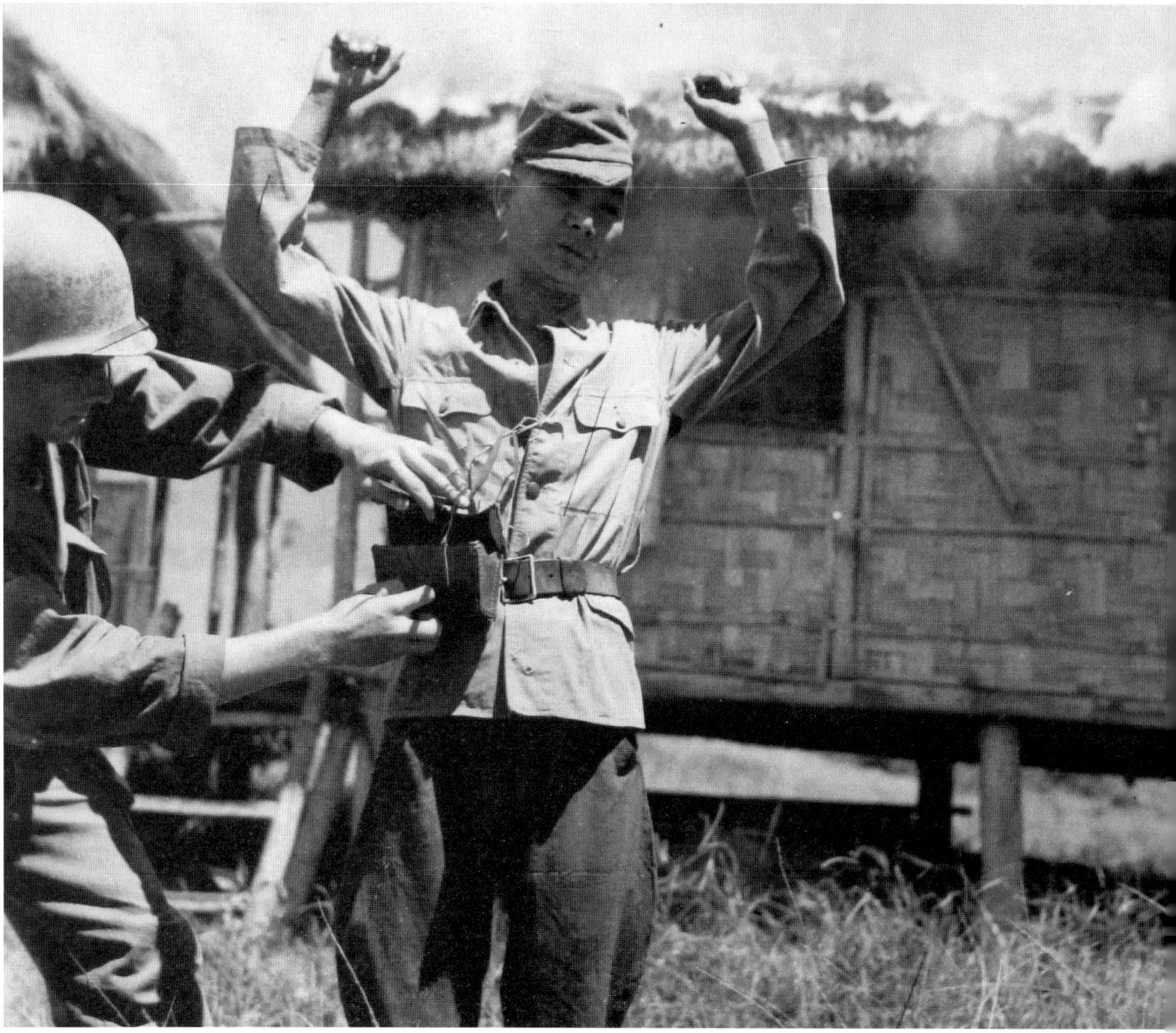

(**Above**) A well-fed and properly-kempt Japanese soldier is shown being searched by a member of I Company, 126th IR, 32nd Division after surrendering to American troops. Other Japanese soldiers chose death rather than surrender according to their *bushido* code after firing on the advancing American infantry from a shack (rear) in northern Luzon's Cagayan Valley on 13 July 1945. *(NARA)*

(**Opposite, above**) Soldiers of the Sixth Army's 43rd Infantry Division are shown here watching over captured Japanese PoWs. They were given tins of American C-rations and some were informally questioned. Surrender was unusual; however, several of these Japanese soldiers being taken captive in May 1945 were showing signs of malnutrition and disease which decreased their élan. *(NARA)*

(**Opposite, below**) A Japanese PoW who was brought to the top of Hill 700 in the Cabaruan Hills sector of Luzon is pointing out enemy strongpoints to American officers of the 1st IR of the 6th Infantry Division on 29 January 1945. The enemy pledged a suicidal defence in this sector with camouflage and were entrenched with pillboxes, foxholes and prepared earthworks. The 6th Division units moved forward, often unable to observe the Japanese strongpoints, and incurred almost 300 casualties. This was part of the 6th Division's 'Purple Heart Campaign'. *(NARA)*

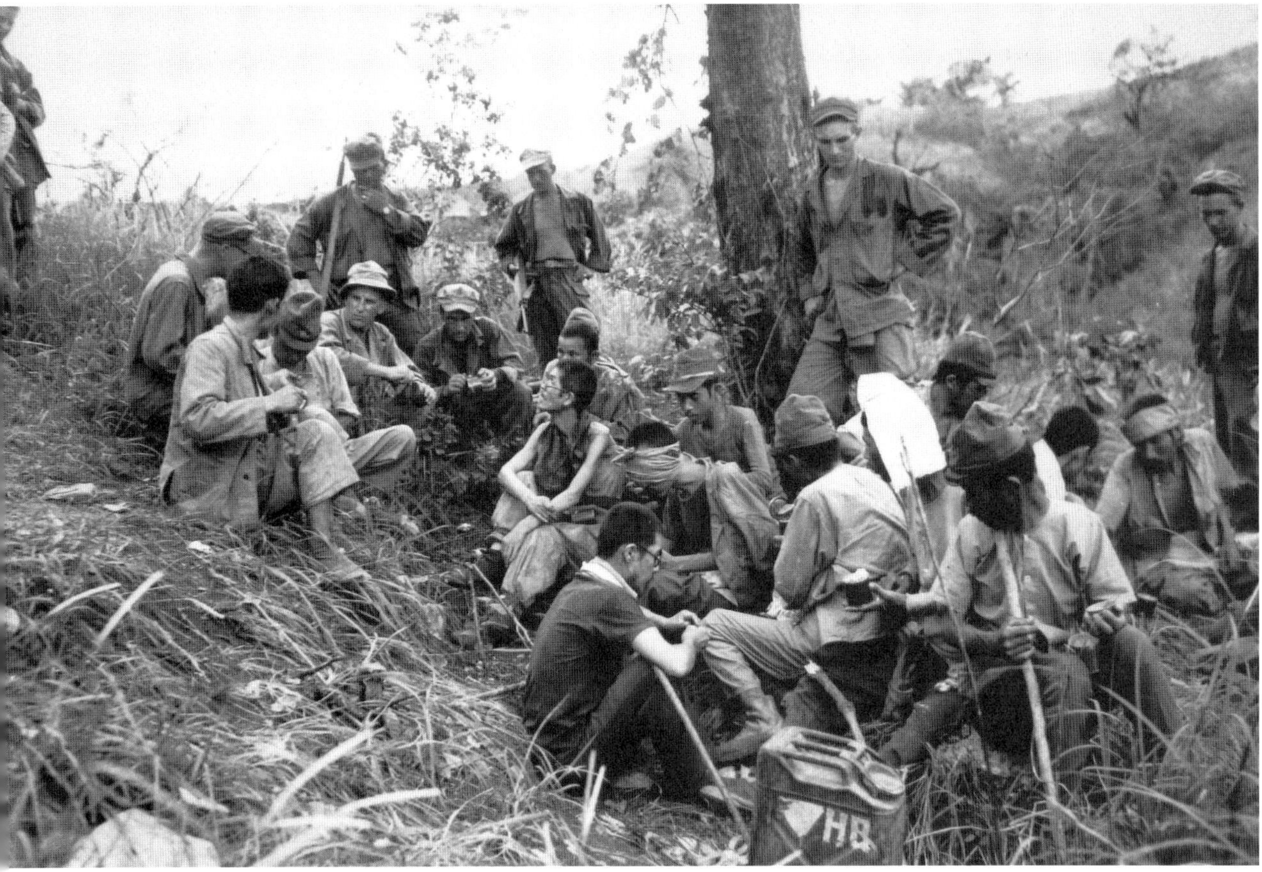
HB

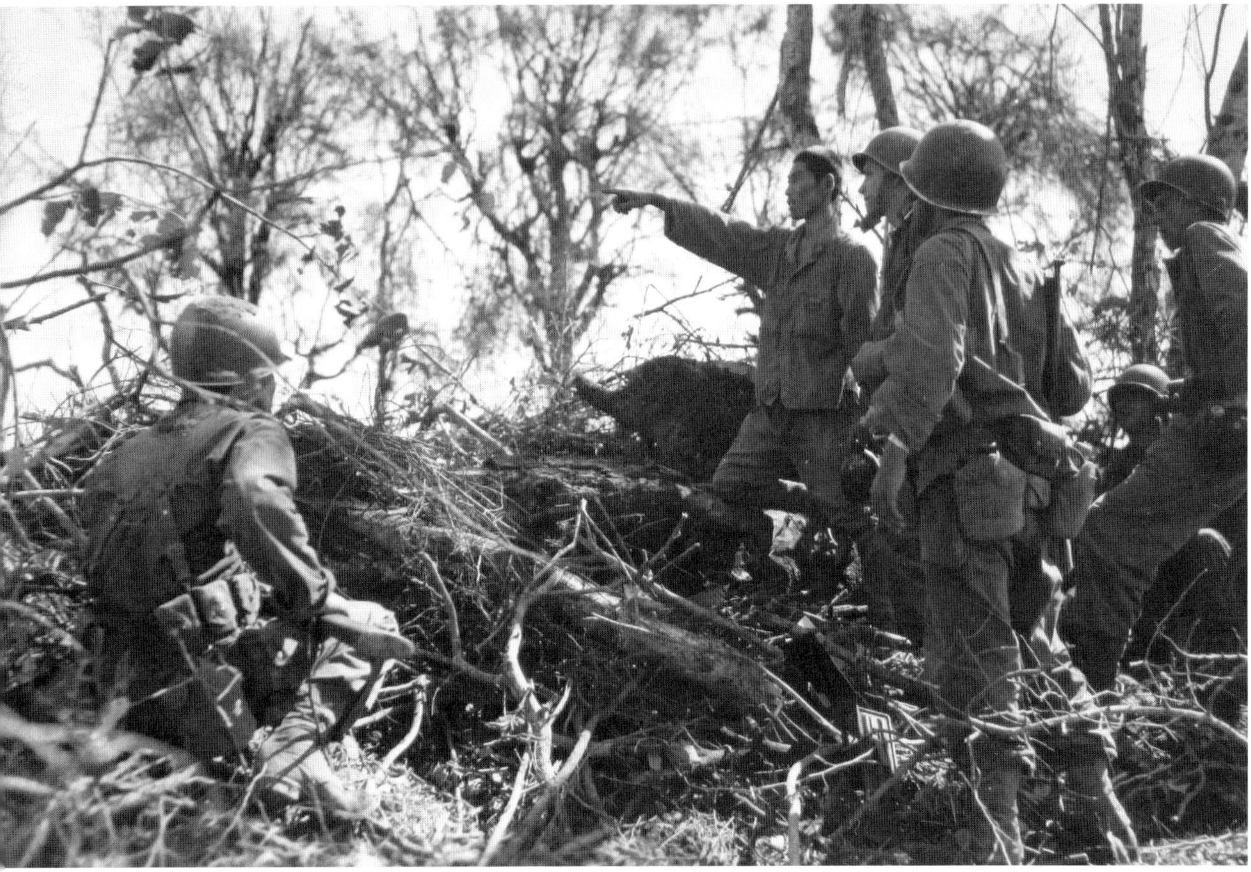

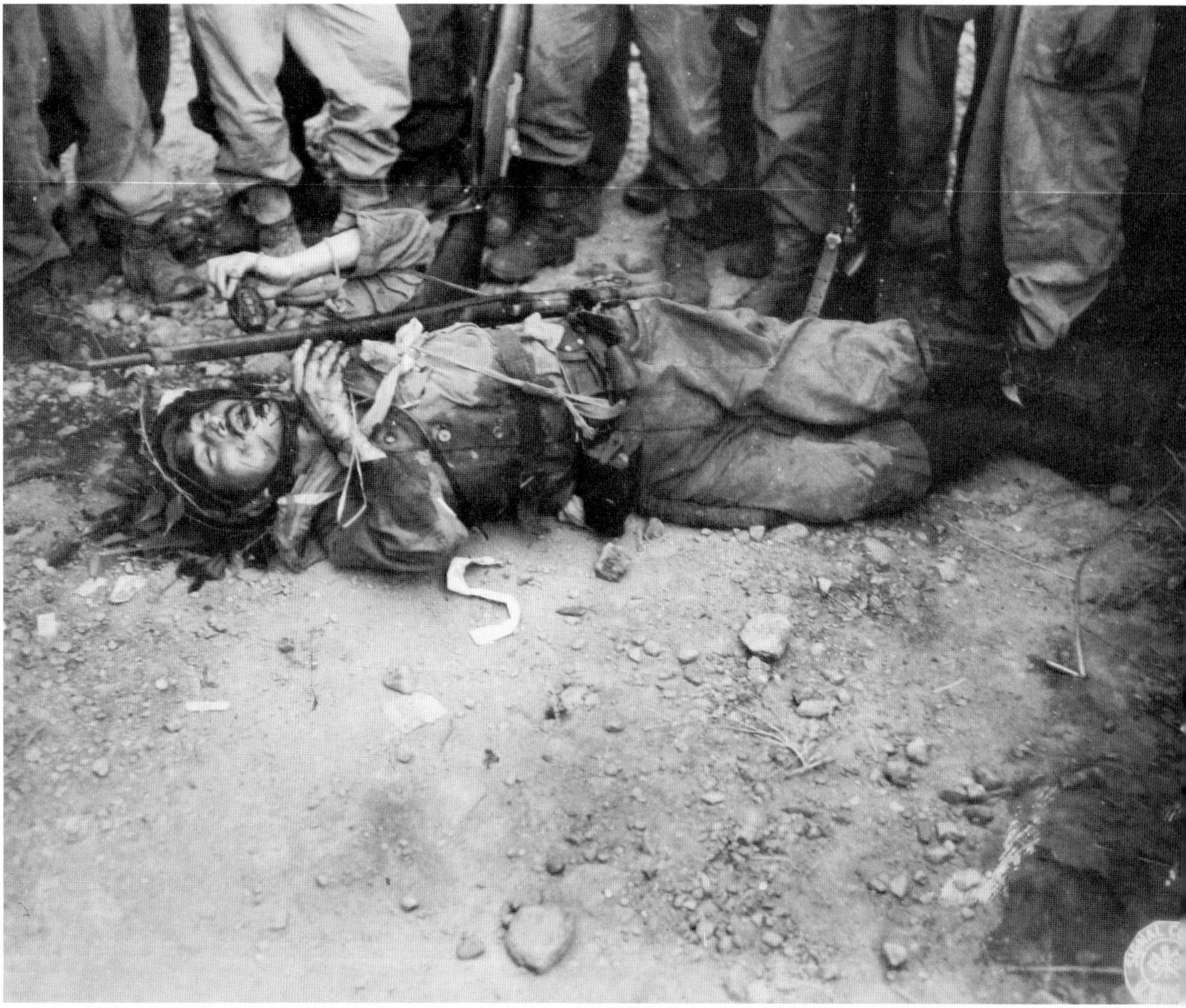

A dead Japanese officer with a hand grenade in one hand and carrying a satchel full of explosives is shown here near Luzon's Port Royal Tayabas. The officer was killed in a suicidal rush in front of A Battery, 139th FA attached to the 38th Infantry Division on 20 July 1945. Even at this late stage of the campaign, Japanese soldiers abided by their *bushido* code and preferred death to surrender. (*NARA*)

Chapter Four

The American Invasion of Leyte 20 October 1944

Leyte Invasion, 20 October 1944 (see Map 5)

The US Sixth Army's X and XXIV Corps achieved surprise at their respective landing zones to seize the vital airfields for Kenney's air forces. X Corps, comprising the 1st Cavalry and 24th Infantry divisions, landed at White Beach (near San Jose) and Red Beach (north of Palo) respectively. The White Beach landings were largely unopposed, with the 7th Cavalry Regiment heading north towards Tacloban Airfield. The 24th Division's 19th and 34th IRs landed at Red Beach under Japanese artillery and mortar fire as well as light opposition from elements of the IJA 33rd IR, which was overcome. The 19th IR seized Hill 533 and repelled Japanese resistance in field fortifications to seize Palo. Then 19th IR units moved south of Palo to seize Hill 85, and then west by 26 October to begin securing Leyte Valley's northern end.

The US Sixth Army's XXIV Corps, comprising the 7th and 96th Infantry divisions, landed south of X Corps. The Dulag airfield, inland and to the west of the landing zones, was an objective. The 382nd and 383rd IRs of the 96th Division landed at Blue and Orange Beaches respectively. The 382nd IR received Japanese mortar and artillery fire at Blue Beach, while the 383rd IR met with minimal enemy resistance. To the south, the 32nd IR of the 7th Division landed at Violet Beach, with the 184th IR landing unopposed at Yellow Beach. Elements of the 184th IR reached the eastern edge of the Dulag Airfield by the end of 20 October.

From 21 to 30 October, units of the 96th Division's battalions moved northward towards Kiling after combating more than 6,000 IJA troops at Labiranan and at Catmon Hill, while other divisional elements moved north up coastal Highway 1 towards Tanauan to clear out the southern end of the Leyte Valley. The clearance of Catmon Hill required the 96th Division's 381st IR with more than forty tanks to attack an entrenched IJA 9th IR, which was defeated on 29 October after clearing scores of pillboxes and caves on 31 October.

The 7th Division's 17th, 32nd and 184th IRs moved westward to seize enemy airfields at San Pablo, Buri and Bayug before reaching Burauen's outskirts on 23 October, which was cleared of Japanese defenders the next day. Buri Airfield also proved to be a difficult position to take as 1,000 IJA 20th IR troops along with Japanese airfield personnel fought from trenches and pillboxes. By 27 October, the 7th Division's 32nd IR dispersed the enemy defenders, killing several hundred in the process. During the fight for Buri Airfield, the 7th Division's 17th IR moved north against determined Japanese resistance from 1,500 to 2,000 enemy defenders. Four days were needed for the 7th Division's 17th IR to advance 5 to 6 miles to reach Dagami on 29 October. The Japanese withdrew the next day. Other 7th Division units fared much better, heading south from near Dulag towards Abuyog. Encountering limited enemy resistance, elements of the 7th Division were nearing Baybay on Leyte's west coast on 2 November.

With almost 35in of rainfall over forty days, US engineers could not level the airfields' muddy runways for operations. A new US Fifth Air Force airstrip was constructed on relatively dry ground with good drainage at Tanauan, 9 miles south of Tacloban's airfield.

In Manila, Yamashita wanted to maintain his troop strength on Luzon for a future American invasion and he had doubts about the ultimate defence of Leyte. Yamashita was overruled and Japanese HQ ordered the IJA 1st Division to alter its transit from Manchuria to Leyte instead of Luzon.

The IJA 16th Division was steadily pushed back to different defensive lines. Japanese convoys from Luzon kept feeding reinforcements into Leyte via the port city of Ormoc on the island's western coast from 23 October to 1 November. The IJA 1st Division (approximately 13,000 troops) disembarked at Ormoc on 1 November during darkness as Suzuki had now transferred his personal HQ from Cebu to Leyte. Upon disembarking, these IJA troops headed north up Highway 2 towards Carigara Bay to bolster a defensive line spanning from Jaro in the south-east to Limon just south of the bay.

Naval Battle of Leyte Gulf (see Map 4 for Locales)

IJN General Staff, after learning of the dispositions of the US Third and Seventh Fleets, rapidly formed a plan to destroy the American anchorage in Leyte Gulf soon after the US Sixth Army's 200,000 troops were ashore. Vice Admiral Takeo Kurita was to lead a Centre Striking Force of seven battleships (including the *Yamato* and *Musashi*), thirteen heavy cruisers and three light cruisers steaming north from Singapore. Kurita was ordered to divide his force in two with the smaller detachment (Southern Force), under Vice Admiral Teiji Nishimura, to enter Leyte Gulf through the Surigao Strait to the south-west. Kurita's main body was to steam through the San Bernadino Strait to the north-west where both naval groups were to converge on Kinkaid's transports, older battleships, escort carriers, destroyer and destroyer escorts. The 18in guns of the *Yamato* and *Musashi* were to sink the Allied transport and pound the new beachhead into submission, compromising the Sixth Army's beachhead.

Admiral Halsey's Task Force 34, the major component of the US Third Fleet, was guarding the San Bernardino Strait. A third Japanese naval flotilla (Northern Force) was to lure Halsey and his fleet carriers away from the strait. This force steaming south from the Home Islands was under the command of Vice Admiral Jisaburō Ozawa. It comprised four older carriers and two battleships converted into carriers, all with a total of fewer than 100 planes with inexperienced IJN pilots. Halsey had been briefed that while he was to provide air cover for MacArthur's beachhead, he could engage a major portion of Japanese naval strength if the opportunity arose.

Two US submarines sighted Kurita's Centre Striking Force off the coast of Borneo on Monday, 23 October 1944. The following day, 24 October, the two submarines torpedoed three of Kurita's cruisers, sinking two of them. Later that day, Halsey's carrier-based bombers, in search of Kurita's force, found the *Musashi* and sank this massive battleship, compelling Kurita to turn his fleet away from Leyte Gulf's north-western entrance, the San Bernardino Strait, and Halsey's carrier-based planes. In the late afternoon of Tuesday, 24 October, Halsey found Ozawa's Northern Force and raced after it, leaving the San Bernardino Strait unguarded.

During the nocturnal hours of 24 October, Nishimura's Southern Force entered the Surigao Strait. Rear Admiral Jesse Oldendorf's Seventh Fleet battleline 'crossed the Japanese T' and devastated Nishimura's vessels with 16in and 18in guns during a nighttime engagement. The Southern Force was destroyed, with Nishimura drowning. While the Battle of Surigao Strait was under way, Kurita turned back towards the San Bernardino Strait as Halsey's Task Force 34 had already steamed north in pursuit of Ozawa believing that his carrier-based planes had destroyed Kurita's fleet when, in fact, only the *Musashi* was sunk.

On Wednesday, 25 October, Kurita's Centre Striking Force passed through the San Bernardino Strait and soon engaged only six USN escort carriers and a group of destroyers and destroyer escorts covering the US Sixth Army's beachhead in the Battle off Samar Island. US destroyers and escorts made smoke and attacked Kurita's battleships and cruisers, while the escort carriers launched all their planes in successive sorties. As a result of the valour of the US surface vessels, the escort carrier attacks, and Kurita's belief from intercepted radio traffic that Halsey's Task Force 34 was rapidly returning to the San Bernardino Strait, the Centre Striking Force admiral with the largest fleet since Midway retired through the strait at 10.00pm on 25 October a few hours before Halsey's fast battleships and cruisers would arrive.

The USN lost one light carrier, two escort carriers and three destroyers. However, Halsey's and Kinkaid's vessels sunk four Japanese carriers, three battleships, six heavy cruisers, three light cruisers and eight destroyers.

Leyte Ground Combat, 24 October to 25 December

X Corps' 1st Cavalry Division units advanced up the north-eastern shore of Leyte, securing Tacloban on 24 October. The cavalrymen then amphibiously assaulted and captured Babatngon from units of the IJA 9th IR on the Janabatas Channel that connects Carigara Bay to San Pedro Bay via the San Juanico Strait.

The X Corps' other division, the 24th Infantry, moved west by north-west across the Leyte Valley from Palo towards Carigara with the 1st Cavalry Division advancing westward along Carigara Bay. There were 5,000 IJA troops in Carigara. As the 24th Division moved on Carigara from the south after it had captured Jaro on 29 October, the 1st Cavalry Division moved west towards Barugo on that day. However, Suzuki's forces stalled the 24th Division's further northern movement up the Leyte Valley. The US 24th Division, in order to save lives against the Japanese resistance lines around Jaro, utilized their advantage in artillery and armour rather than making frontal assaults.

Suzuki began to receive reinforcements via Ormoc as early as 23–25 October and he wanted to counterattack X Corps' units in the Leyte Valley by having the Ormoc-bound reinforcements head north upon their arrival up Highway 2 and then move east along Carigara Bay to strike at the American forces at Carigara. The IJA 41st IR passed through Carigara on 28 October as other enemy units moved there too. Despite the reinforcements, the IJA withdrew westward along the bay from Carigara to Capoocan on 1 November and then to just south of Limon on 6 November.

To clear the Ormoc valley, Krueger had to move his X Corps' divisions (the 24th Infantry and 1st Cavalry) west from Carigara over extremely steep terrain known as 'Breakneck Ridge' towards heavily-defended Limon during the first week of November. The 24th Division's 34th IR had already moved to the west of Capoocan on 3 November, but encountered intricate Japanese entrenchments amid the steep terrain just to the north of Limon. Elements of the IJA 1st Division began counter-attacking the American probing force, but US FA 155mm cannons forced an enemy retreat. Krueger needed to bolster his Carigara defences from a now-reinforced Japanese counterattack before taking on the IJA 1st Division on and in the vicinity of Breakneck Ridge and then moving south to the port of Ormoc. To keep casualties down from frontal assaults, Krueger used enveloping tactics over the rough terrain.

The initial attacks against the Japanese on Breakneck Ridge started on 5 November with X Corps' 24th Division's 21st IR, which made a slow advance against enemy fortified positions and local counterattacks over several days. Enveloping amphibious and overland movements to the south of Limon by the elements of the 34th IR on 13 November and the 19th IR on 15 November respectively compressed the Japanese positions on Breakneck Ridge with high casualties to both combatant forces. The US 32nd Infantry Division, which was slated to attack Samar, had to relieve the battered 24th Infantry Division on 18 November. The 32nd Infantry Division captured Limon on 22 November after a series of ground assaults with strong preparatory heavy artillery bombardment (105mm and 155mm guns). The capture of Limon enabled the Sixth Army to control Breakneck Ridge.

The US 7th Infantry Division, which easily captured Baybay on Luzon's west coast, started a northern coastal move on 14 November to seize Ormoc. The Japanese reacted to this American movement by sending elements of the IJA 26th Division to block the 7th Infantry Division's advance. On 23 November, elements of the 7th Infantry Division's 32nd IR, which were situated along hilly terrain ('Shoestring Ridge') south of the Palanas River in the vicinity of Damulaan, were first shelled and then attacked by the IJA 13th IR. The battle raged through 26 November with the Americans preventing the Japanese from capturing Damulaan. The 32nd IR was relieved by the 184th IR on 28 November. Limon was captured by the Americans two days later.

Battle of Ormoc Bay, 9 November

As the Breakneck Ridge battle was under way, Yamashita shipped the IJA 26th Division and remaining elements of the IJA 1st Division from Manila to Ormoc in two IJN-organized convoys on 8 and 9 November.

The Fifth Air Force's B-25 and A-20 medium bombers and Halsey's carrier-based planes, along with USN PT boats, interdicted the first main IJN convoy on 9–10 November, sinking two large transports and an escort vessel with many other ships damaged in Ormoc Bay. On 11 November, more than 300 of Halsey's TF 38 carrier-borne aircraft sank three IJN transports and five escort vessels of the second smaller convoy with more than 3,000 IJA troops lost in the attacks.

Despite these devastating Japanese convoy and personnel losses at Ormoc Bay, Field Marshal Terauchi, the Southern Army Commander, ordered Yamashita to continue sending reinforcements to enable Suzuki to mount counterattacks. Other IJA divisions were scheduled to sail for Leyte in December.

On 23 November, Suzuki and Yamashita planned a future counterattack to seize the airfields (at Buri, Bayug and San Pablo) near Burauen with a coordinated attack by ground forces (dwindling remaining elements of the IJA 16th and 26th Divisions) and the parachute regiments of the 2nd Parachute Group. The IJA leaders believed that if Kenney's captured airfields could be retaken, grounding American air power, then the Japanese could hold on to Leyte. Additional attacks by Japanese parachute troops were also to be launched at Dulag and Tacloban airfields. On 6 December, 300 IJA parachute troops landed at San Pablo Airfield with some initial control, but like the paratrooper assault at Buri Airfield, the Japanese retired into the hills after US forces mounted attacks to reclaim the airfields. The enemy attacks were disjointed and disrupted by adverse weather. These operations had ended in failure by 11 December.

MacArthur wanted Ormoc captured, so Krueger landed the 77th Infantry Division at Deposito to Ormoc's south on 7 December. The 77th moved north up Highway 2 to Ormoc against resistance from the remnants of the IJA 26th Division. Ormoc fell to the American force on 10 December, thereby preventing any likelihood of reinforcements for Suzuki's poorly-supplied troops. In mid-December, Yamashita was ordered not to send three divisions to Leyte but to keep them for Luzon's defence.

Subsequent operations of Krueger's forces were to secure the Ormoc Valley against dwindling Japanese resistance. The US 24th Infantry Division moved to the San Isidro area of north-west Leyte. On 12 December, the US 32nd Infantry Division moved onto enemy positions south of Limon and the Japanese began to withdraw from that heavily-contested area near Carigara Bay. Final US land and amphibious movements centred on the IJA redoubt of Palompon on Leyte's west coast, which Krueger's forces occupied on 25 December leading MacArthur to proclaim that organized resistance on Leyte was over. The following day, Eichelberger's Eighth Army relieved Krueger's Sixth Army for mopping-up operations on the island.

Approximately 250,000 US Army troops participated in the campaign for Leyte. The Sixth Army incurred more than 3,000 troops KIA and another 12,000 wounded. Of the 65,000 Japanese 35th Army troops that fought on Leyte, almost 60,000 of them were lost combating the US Sixth Army through to 26 December. From 26 December 1944 to 8 May 1945, the US Eighth Army killed an additional 24,000 IJA troops.

(**Opposite, above**) A Grumman TBM Avenger torpedo-bomber flies above the US Seventh Fleet's amphibious force against Leyte on 20 October 1944. The US Sixth Army landed two corps along an 18-mile front of Leyte's eastern coast with the specific intent of securing airfields at Tacloban (X Corps) and Dulag (XXIV Corps). (*NARA*)

(**Opposite, below**) US Sixth Army soldiers anxiously observe plumes of smoke emanating from Leyte's beaches following naval gunfire from the 7th Fleet's Bombardment Group as well as aerial sorties against Japanese positions on 20 October 1944. The pre-landing bombardment in the Dulag area started at 0600 hours, while the northern beaches in the X Corps sector around Tacloban were shelled commencing at 0900. (*NARA*)

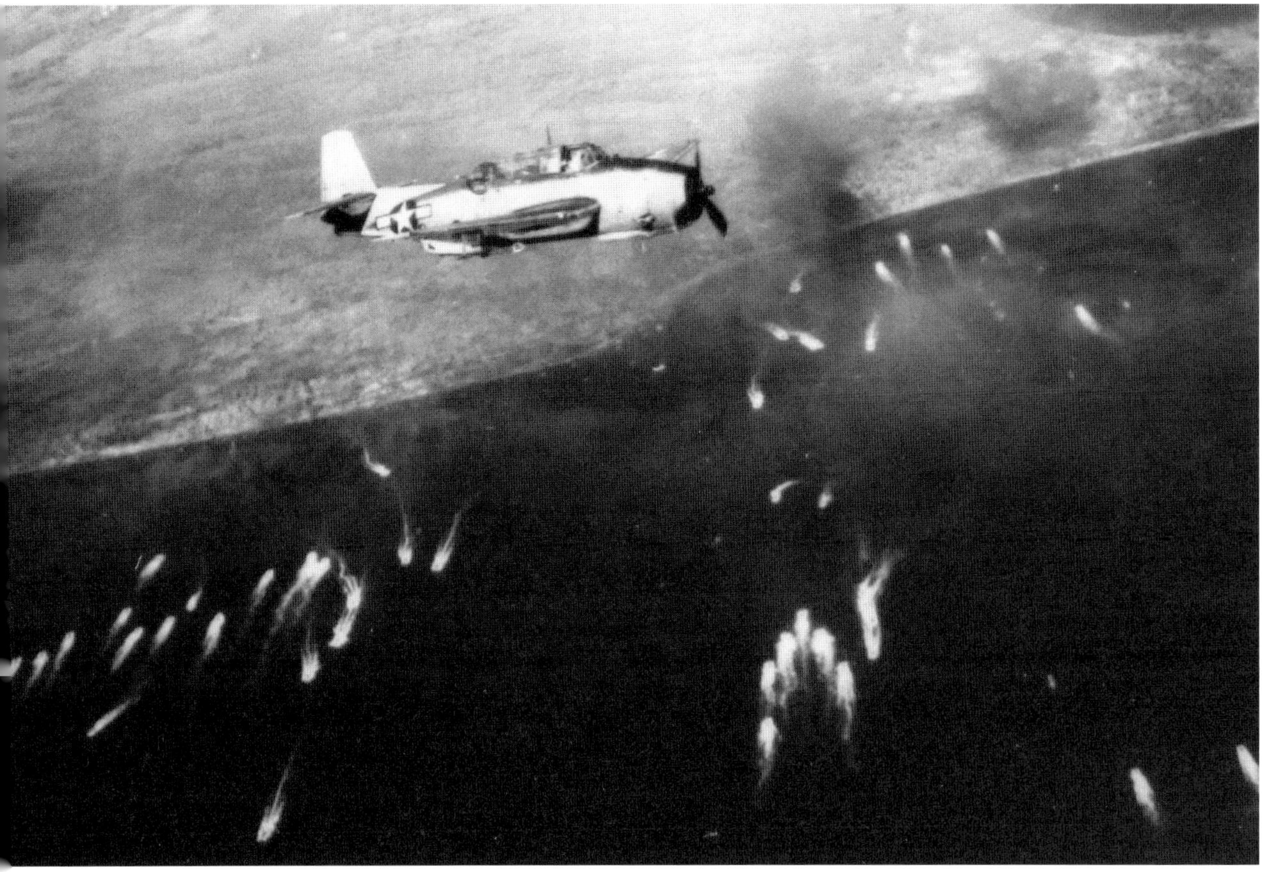

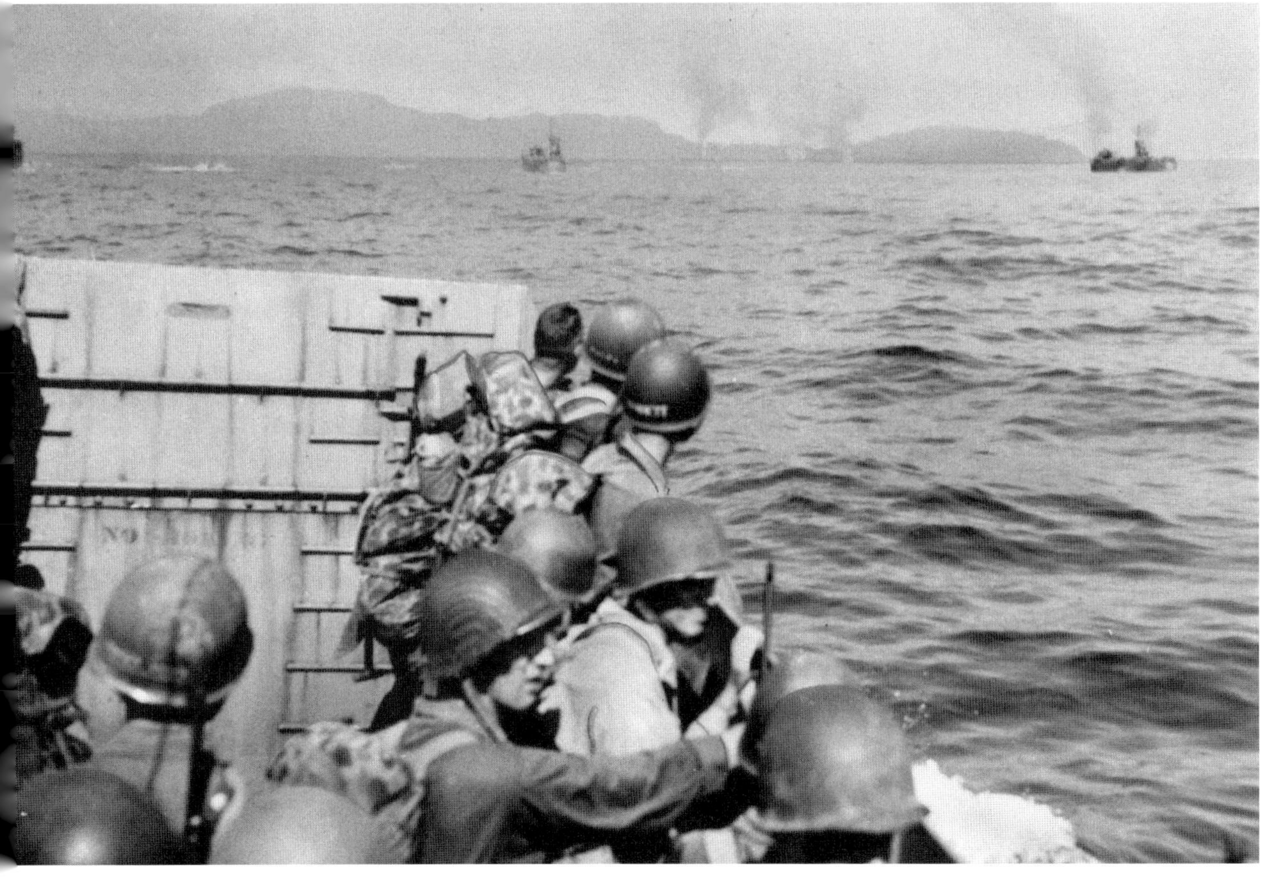

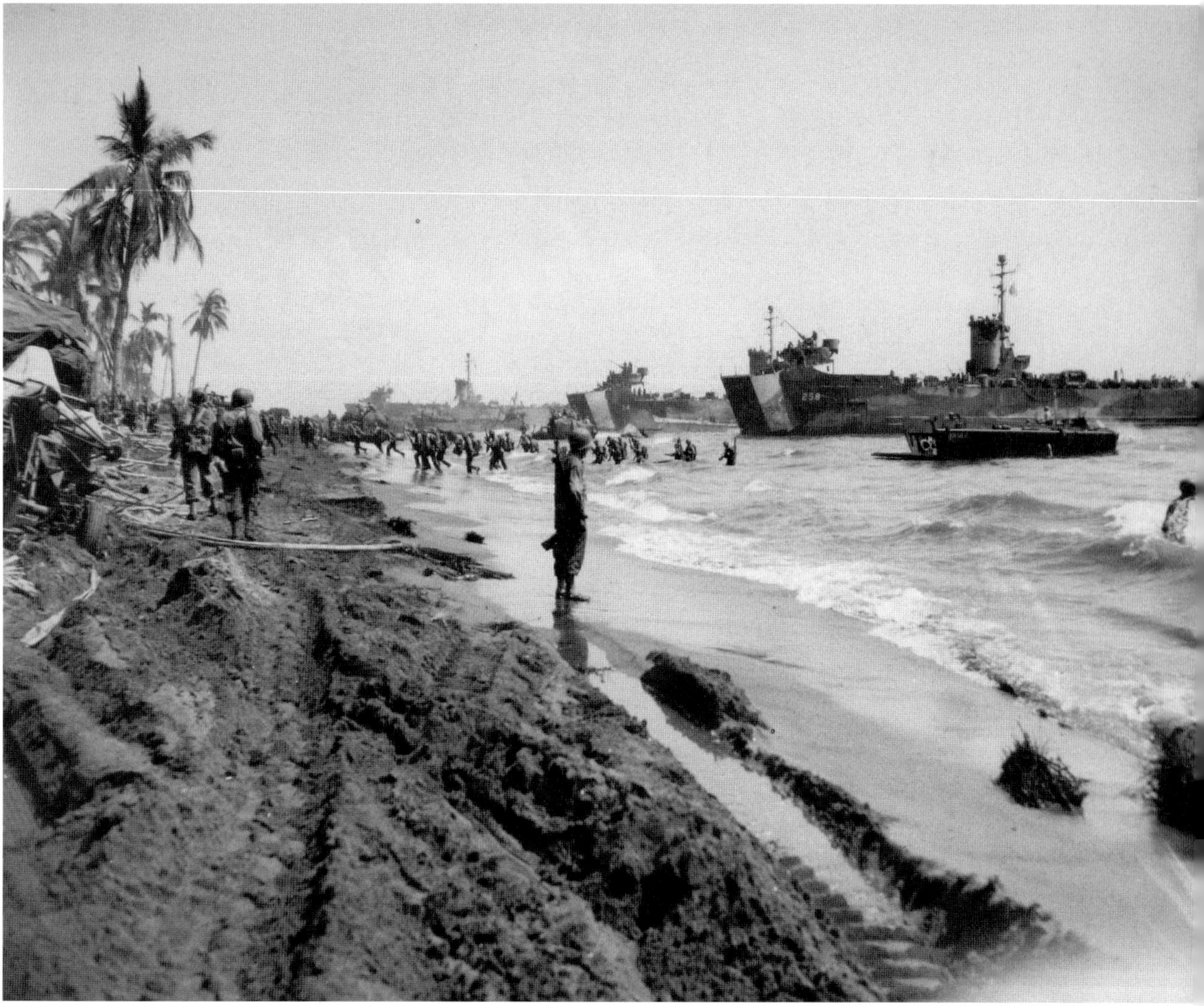

(**Above**) LSTs and LCVPs land armour and soldiers respectively at Leyte on 20 October 1944. X Corps' 1st Cavalry and 24th Infantry divisions came ashore at Red and White Beaches around Tacloban Airfield near Cataisan Point. The aim of those near-perfect landings was to seize Tacloban Airfield and Palo which would enable the Seventh Fleet's control of San Pedro Bay and the San Juanico Strait. XXIV Corps' two divisions, the 7th and 96th Infantry divisions with an attached 767th TB, landed at Yellow, Violet, Blue and Orange Beaches. Their task was to capture Dulag Airfield and three others further inland: San Pablo, Bayug and Buri Airfields. These American formations met more stout IJA 35th Army formations, the 9th and 20th IRs, at Catmon Hill, Labiranan Head and the Dulag area as the Japanese army commander, Lieutenant General Sōsaku Suzuki, believed the landings would occur there. *(NARA)*

(**Opposite, above**) US Sixth Army soldiers landing at Leyte on 20 October 1944 haul a two-wheeled cart through soft sand. An LST with its bow ramps open (background) is seen here. Soldiers moved inland quickly in order to seize vital airfields for army planes, which were needed to augment the escort carriers' air umbrellas over the beachhead. *(NARA)*

(**Opposite, below**) A heavy weapons unit of X Corps' 1st Cavalry Division moves off White Beach near San Jose in their northern inland movement to seize Tacloban Airfield. The cavalrymen fortunately faced limited Japanese resistance at their beachhead. *(NARA)*

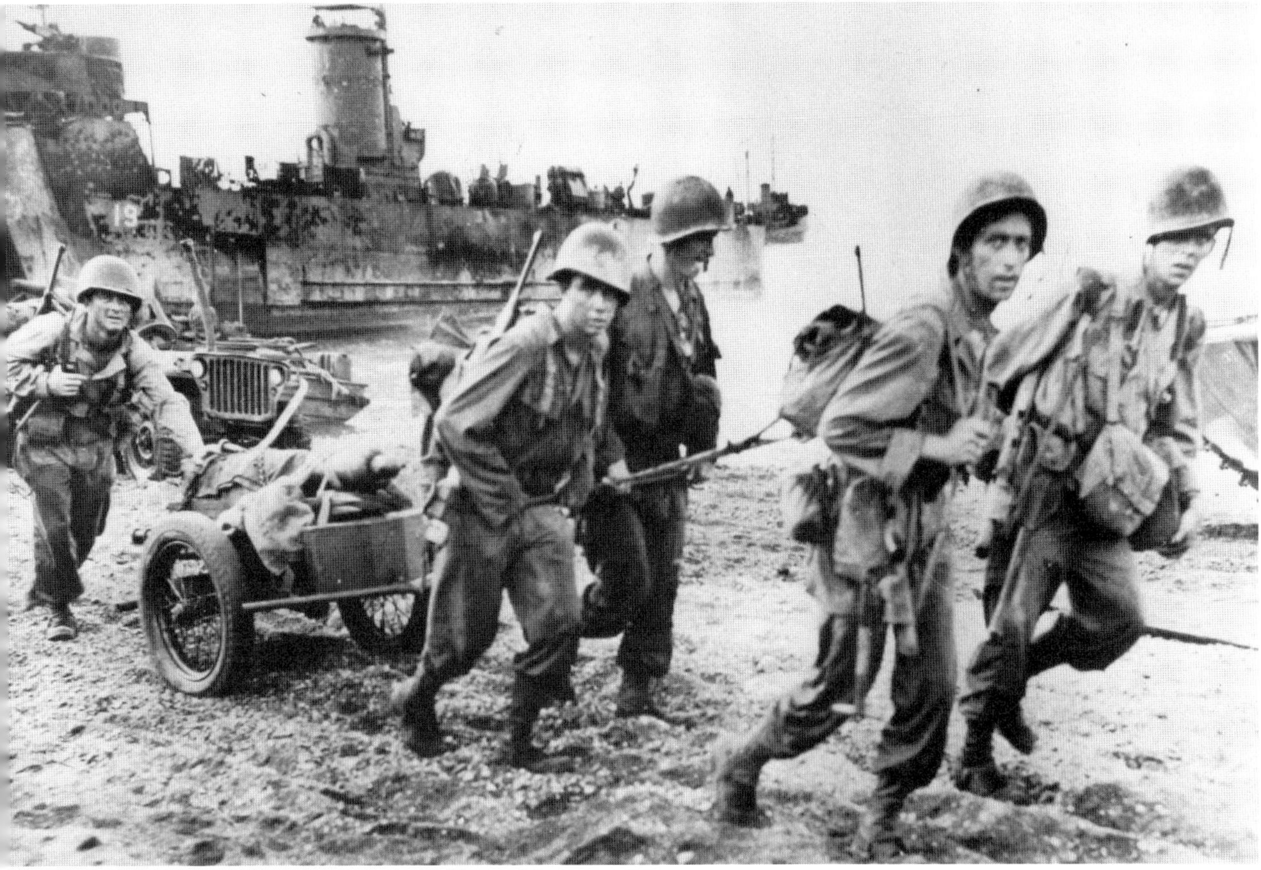
19

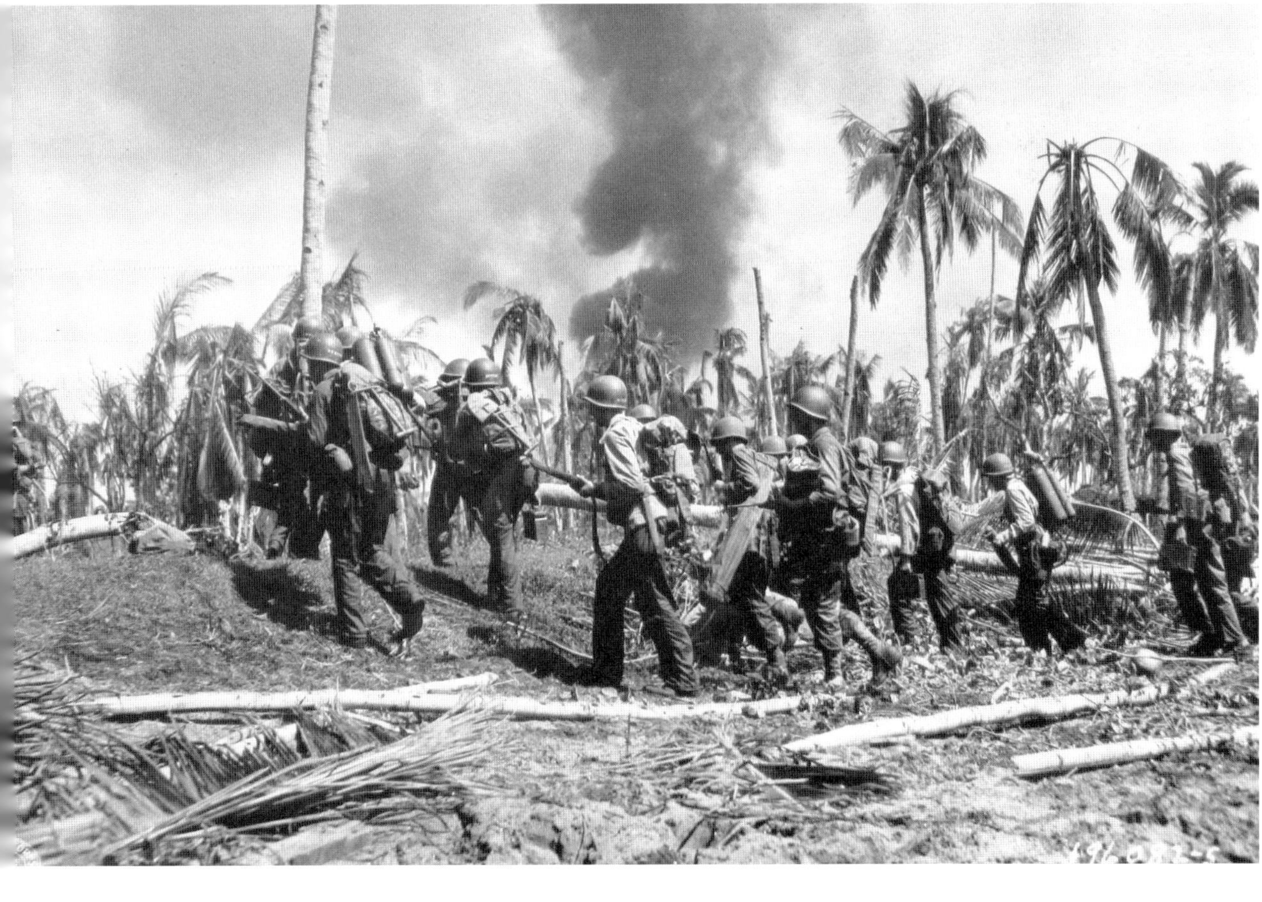

(**Left**) A USN Bos'n Mate 1st Class member of a Leyte Beach Landing Party is shown here hauling up the 'Stars and Stripes' onto the remnants of a palm tree that survived the naval and aerial bombardments on 20 October 1944. Resistance was light at the northern X Corps beaches defended by elements of the IJA 33rd IR, but much stiffer at the southern beaches contested by US XXIV Corps against IJA 9th and 20th IRs of the 35th Army's 16th Division. (*NARA*)

(**Opposite, above**) In an iconic photograph, General Douglas MacArthur and his entourage wade ashore at Palo (Red Beach) from an LCM after a run-in from the USS *Nashville* at 1430 hours on 20 October 1944. Red Beach was just seized by X Corps' 24th Infantry Division. MacArthur was accompanied by the president of the Philippines Sergio Osmeña (far left), his COS Lieutenant General Richard Sunderland (to the right of MacArthur), CBS news correspondent Bill Dunn (next to Sunderland) and Staff Officer Colonel Courtney Whitney (behind MacArthur), who commanded an extensive Filipino guerrilla network. Shortly after coming ashore, MacArthur broadcast: 'People of the Philippines, I have returned.' (*NARA*)

(**Opposite, below**) Sixth Army's XXIV Corps' 96th Division infantrymen attack Japanese snipers in a Filipino village on 29 October 1944. The 96th Division encountered swamps and intense IJA 16th Division resistance north of Dulag. After landing, the 96th Division's 3rd Battalion of the 381st IR moved north up the coastal Highway 1 to capture Tanauan on 26 October. Then this unit wheeled east to attack Kiling two days later. The 381st's 1st and 2nd battalions battled the Japanese 9th IR at Catmon Hill, which they secured on 29 October. Elements of the 383rd IR advanced westward around the Japanese defences at Catmon Hill and also moved onto Kiling on 31 October after capturing San Vicente the day before. From its Dulag area beachhead, part of the 96th Division's 382nd IR drove inland to reach Tabontabon and Digahongan on 26 and 28 October respectively. All three of the division's regiments met in the vicinity of Kiling by the end of October. (*NARA*)

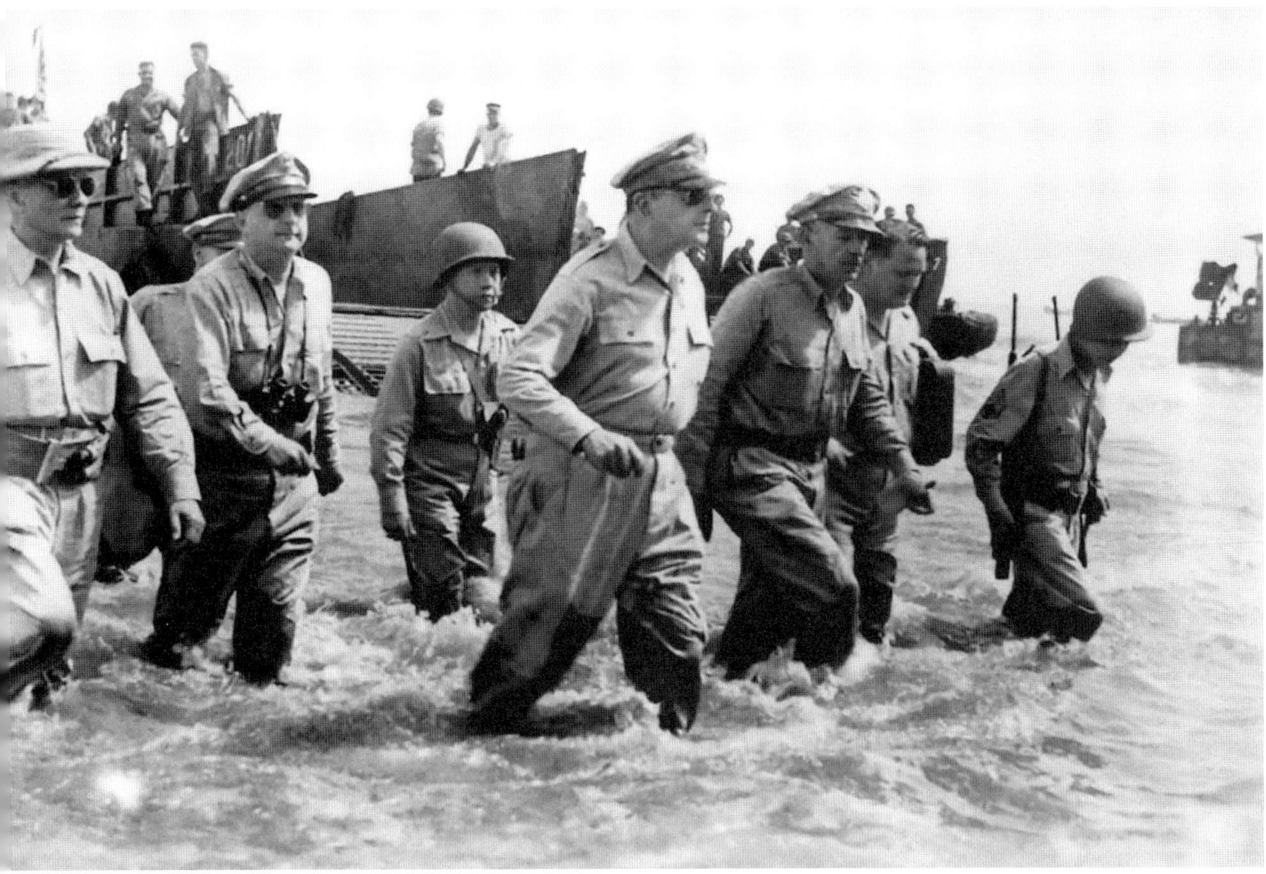

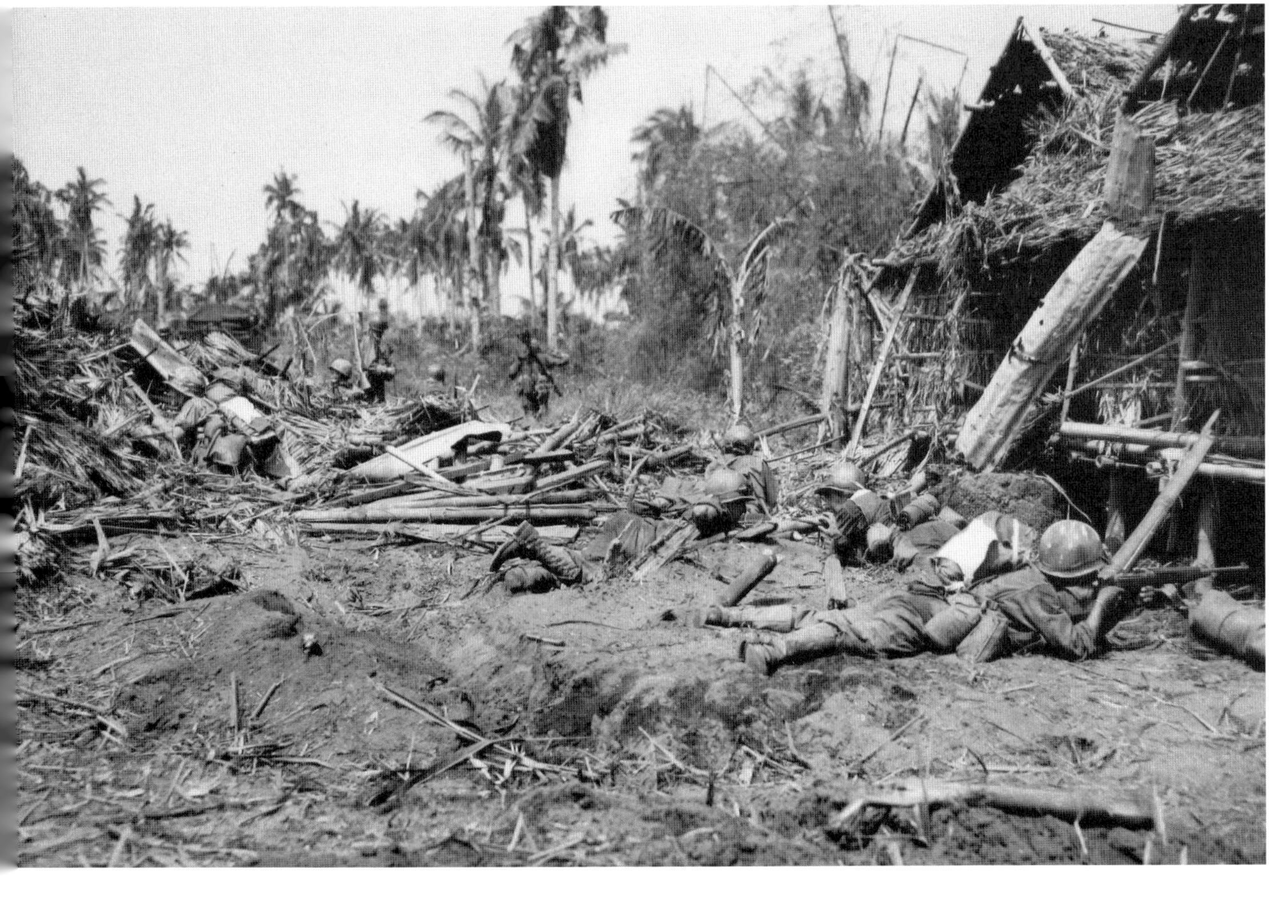

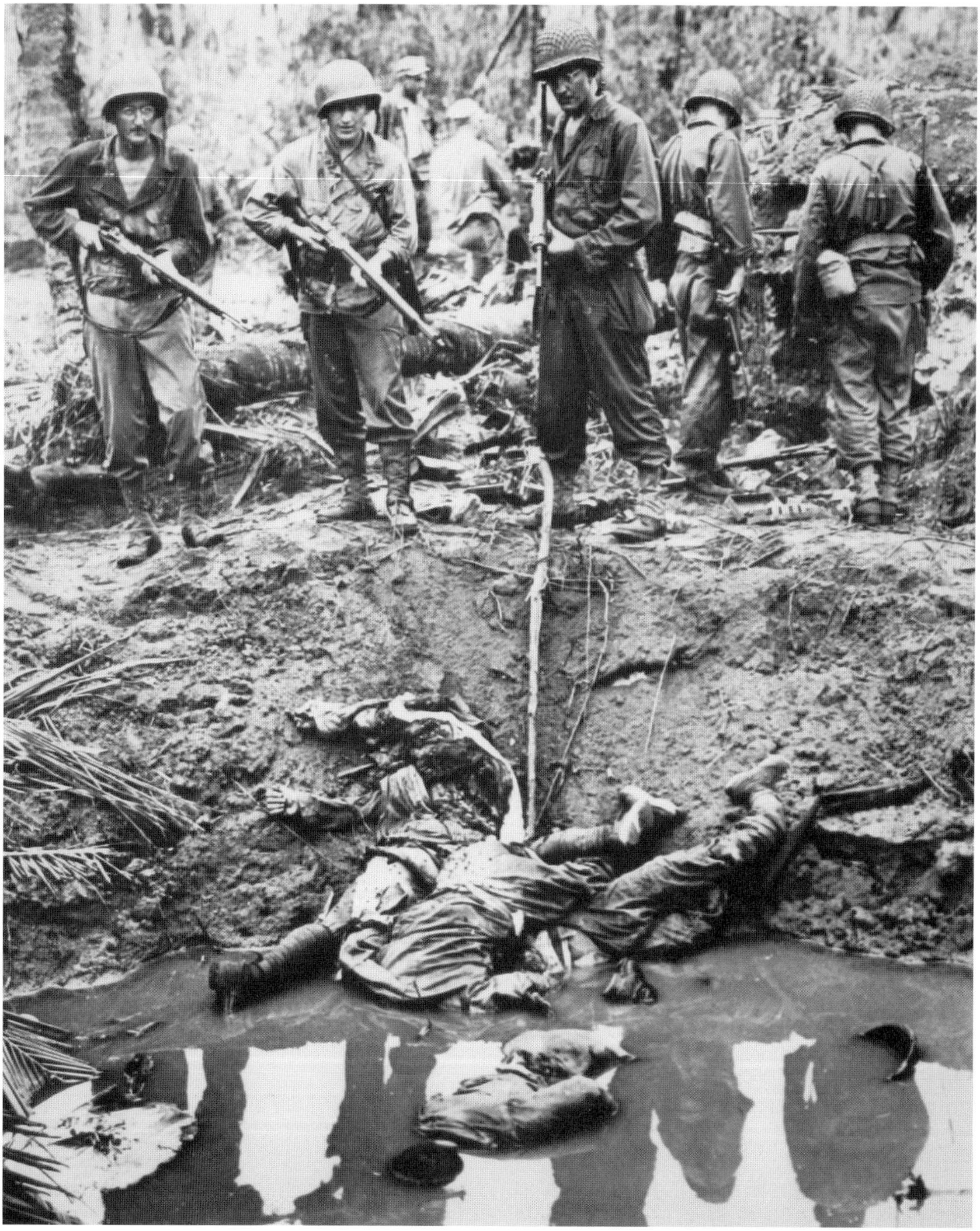

Dead Japanese snipers are seen here in a water-filled shell-hole after firing on advancing US Sixth Army troops. The furthest right infantryman is holding an M3 SMG ('Grease Gun'). This SMG was developed to replace the more intricately-assembled and expensive M1928 Thompson SMG. The M3 did not enter service until late 1944. It was as heavy as the M1928 at just over 10lb loaded, utilized a thirty-round detachable box magazine and had a cyclic rate of fire of 450 rounds per minute (rpm), which was below the Thompson's rate of 700 rpm. The range of the M3 was 100ft less than the M1928. *(NARA)*

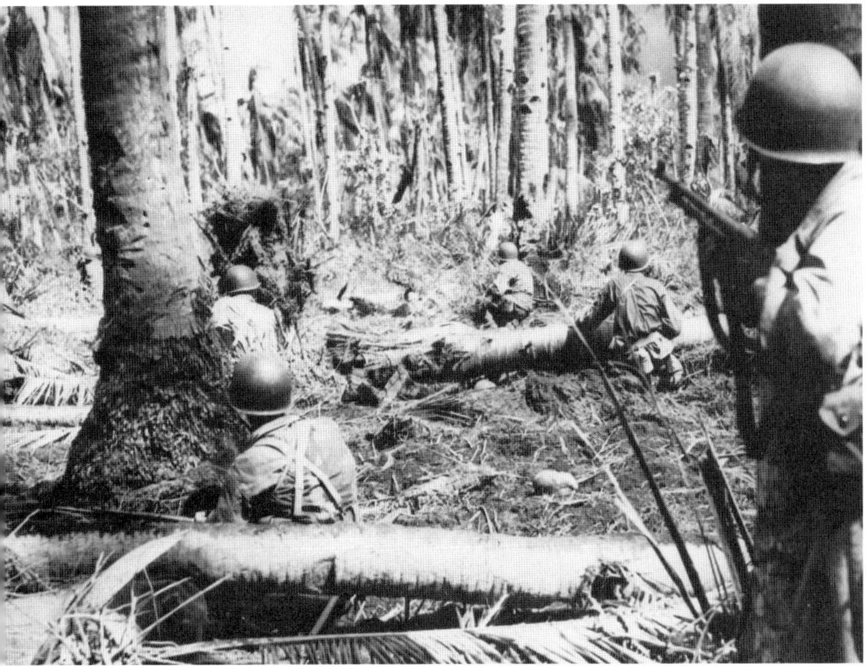

Soldiers from X Corps' 24th Infantry Division move inland through jungle palm tree vegetation from Red Beach onto Palo against a Japanese MG position. From 23–26 October 1944, battalion-size movements of the 24th Division's 19th IR approached Castilla, inland to the west, capturing Hills 85 (south of Palo) and B (west of Palo), both defended by elements of the IJA 33rd IR. *(NARA)*

A 24th Infantry Division jeep towing a 37mm AT gun is examined by three Sixth Army soldiers on Leyte. The jeep's driver (right) was killed by a Japanese sniper with an M4 medium tank (left) on the road north of Jaro on 30 October 1944. The 24th Division's 34th IR seized Jaro on 29 October; however, IJA troops comprising snipers, artillery and mortars delayed the advance of the 24th Division troops toward Carigara situated to the north-west of Jaro on Leyte's northern coast of Carigara Bay. The Japanese had recently reinforced Leyte with troop arrivals at Ormoc on 25 October. The IJA 41st IR moved north from Ormoc, through Carigara to contest the US 24th Division's 34th IR movement onto that latter locale on 29 October. *(NARA)*

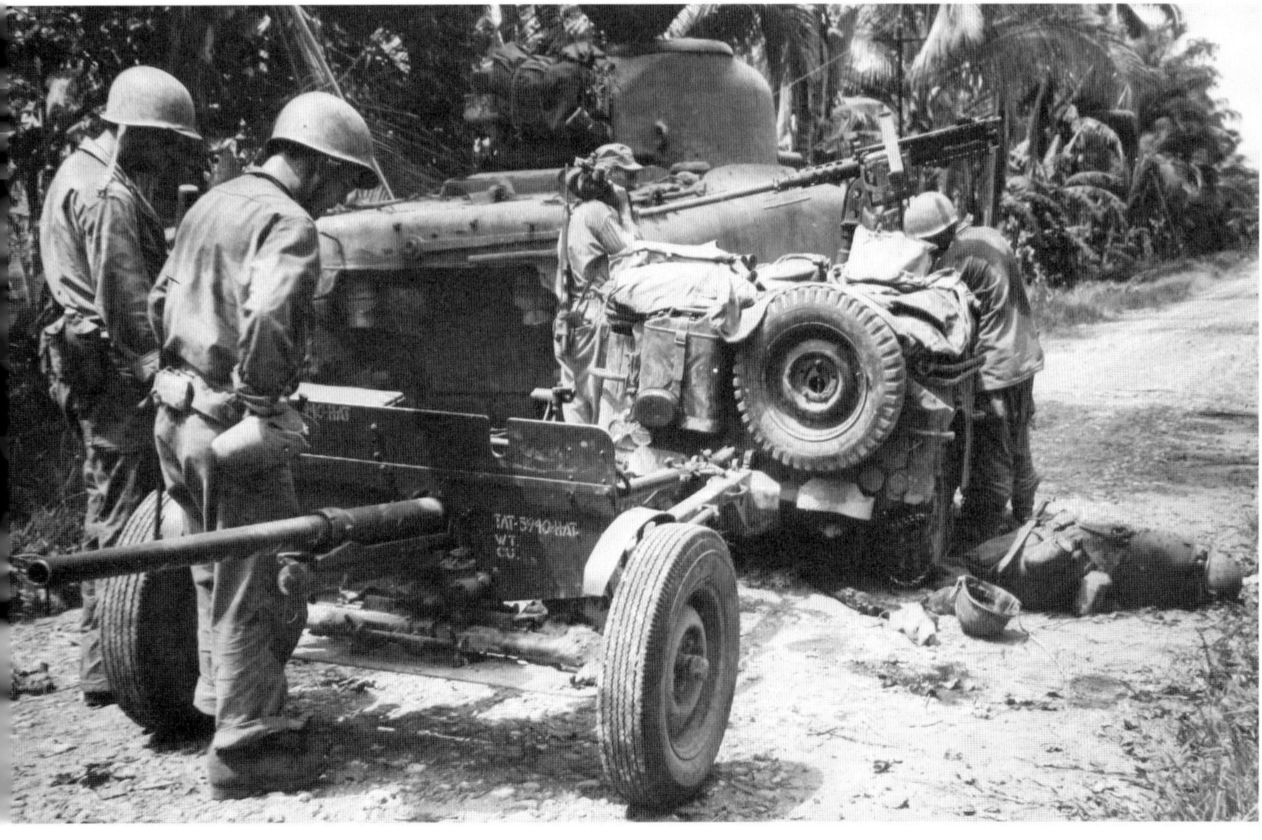

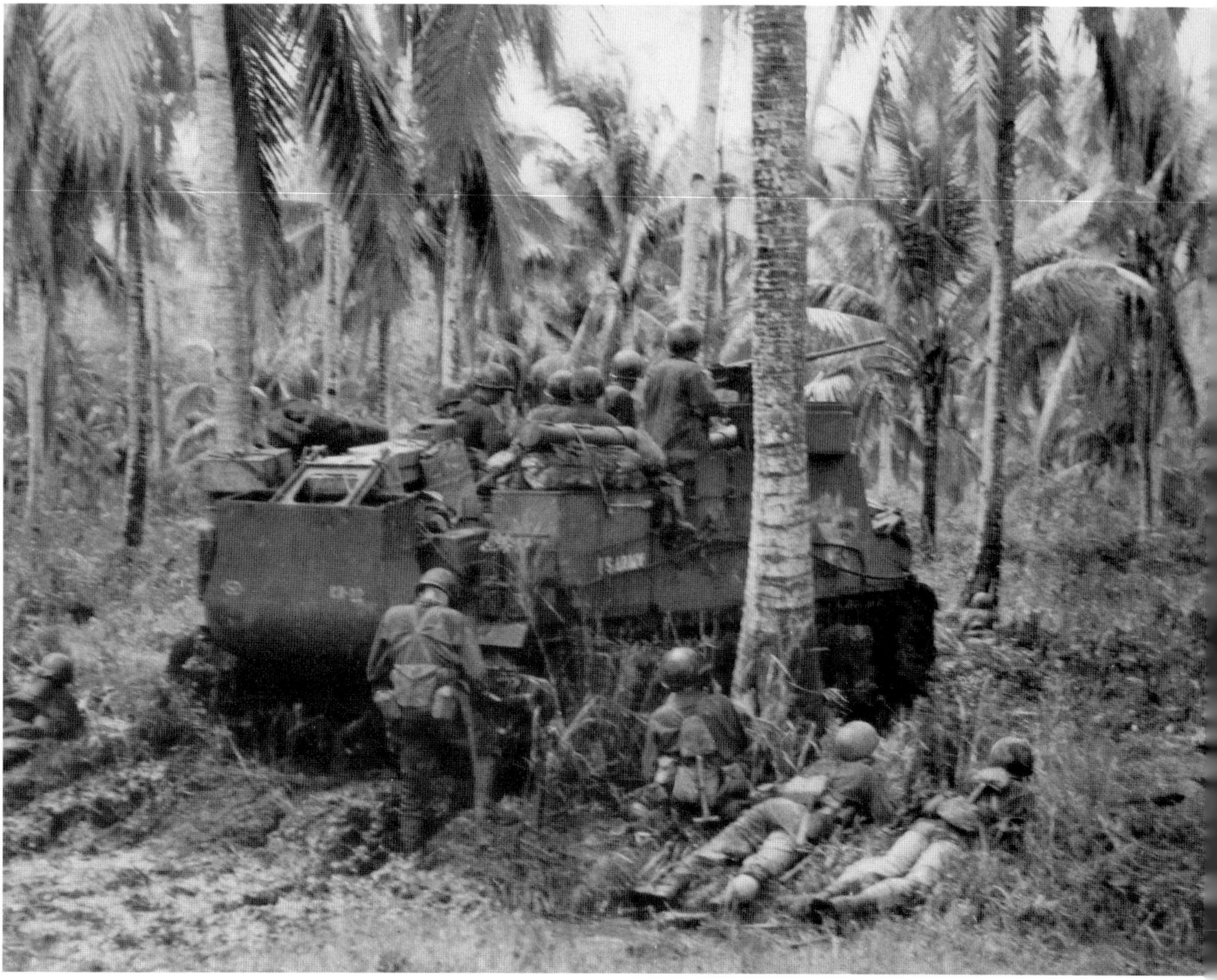

(**Above**) X Corps' 24th Division infantrymen are lying prone next to an M7 SPA, which had a 105mm howitzer, to knock out Japanese pillboxes 3 miles north of Jaro during the movement towards Carigara. The M7 had a Browning 0.50in-calibre HMG in its ring turret on the hull's right front. *(NARA)*

(**Opposite, above**) The USS *Gambier Bay*, a *Casablanca*-class escort carrier (foreground) is seen making smoke as a fighter prepares for take-off during the Battle off Samar Island on 25 October 1944. Two other destroyer escorts are also seen making smoke (left background) for concealment from Kurita's Centre Striking Force of four battleships and six heavy and two light cruisers intent on attacking American transports in Leyte Gulf. The *Gambier Bay* was sunk during this engagement, the only American carrier sunk by enemy ship gunfire during the war. *(NARA)*

(**Opposite, below**) The USS *Heerman*, a *Fletcher*-class destroyer demonstrates its camouflage scheme as it makes smoke for concealment against the IJN Centre Striking Force at the Battle off Samar Island on 25 October 1944. The *Heerman* with two other destroyers, four destroyer escorts and six escort carriers of Taffy 3, under Rear Admiral Clifton Sprague, attacked the Japanese battleships and cruisers and eventually turned them back with torpedoes and their 5in guns as the escort carriers launched fighter sorties against the IJN vessels. The *Heerman* survived the engagement; however, two American escort carriers, two destroyers and one destroyer escort were sunk. Three IJN heavy cruisers were sunk along with three others damaged by the aggressive under-gunned USN surface and carrier aircraft force. *(NARA)*

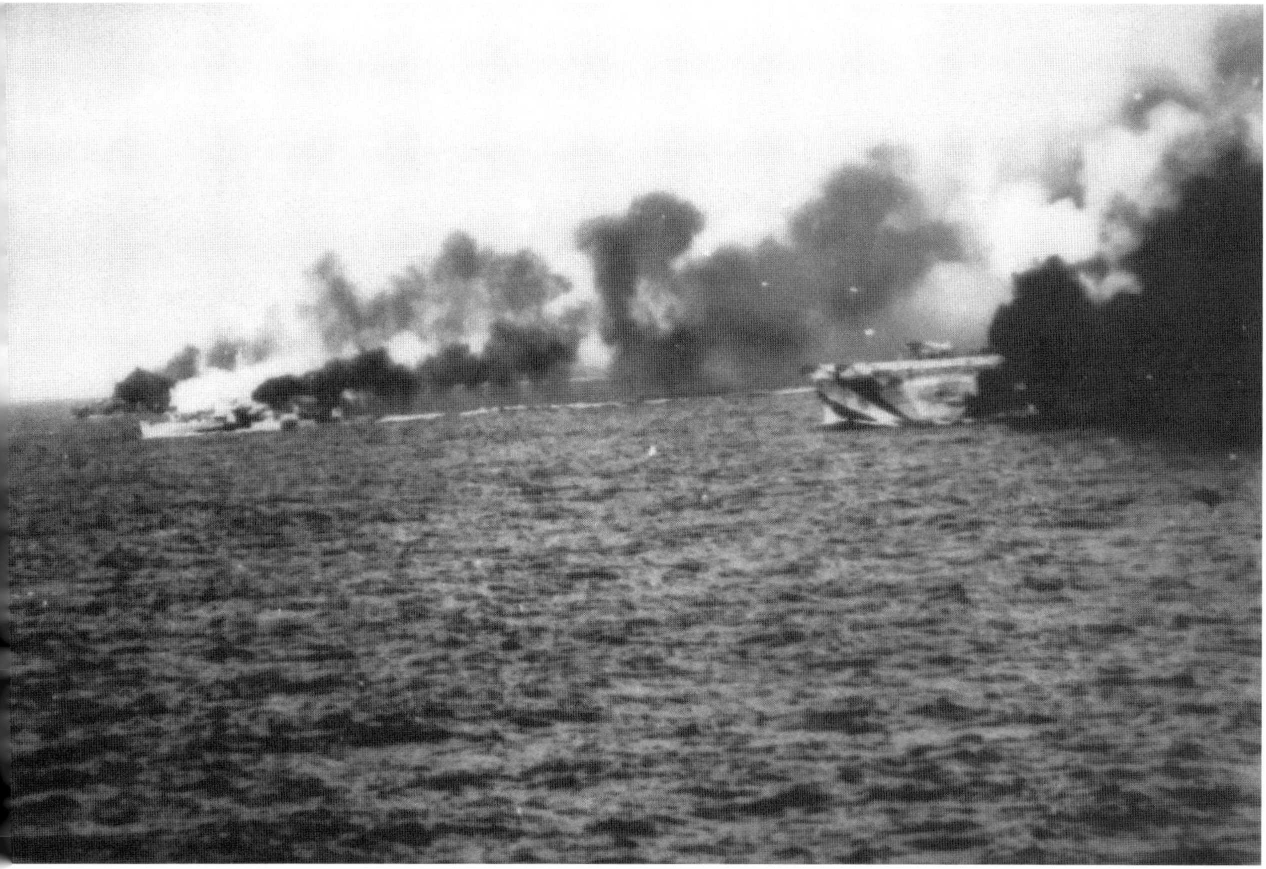

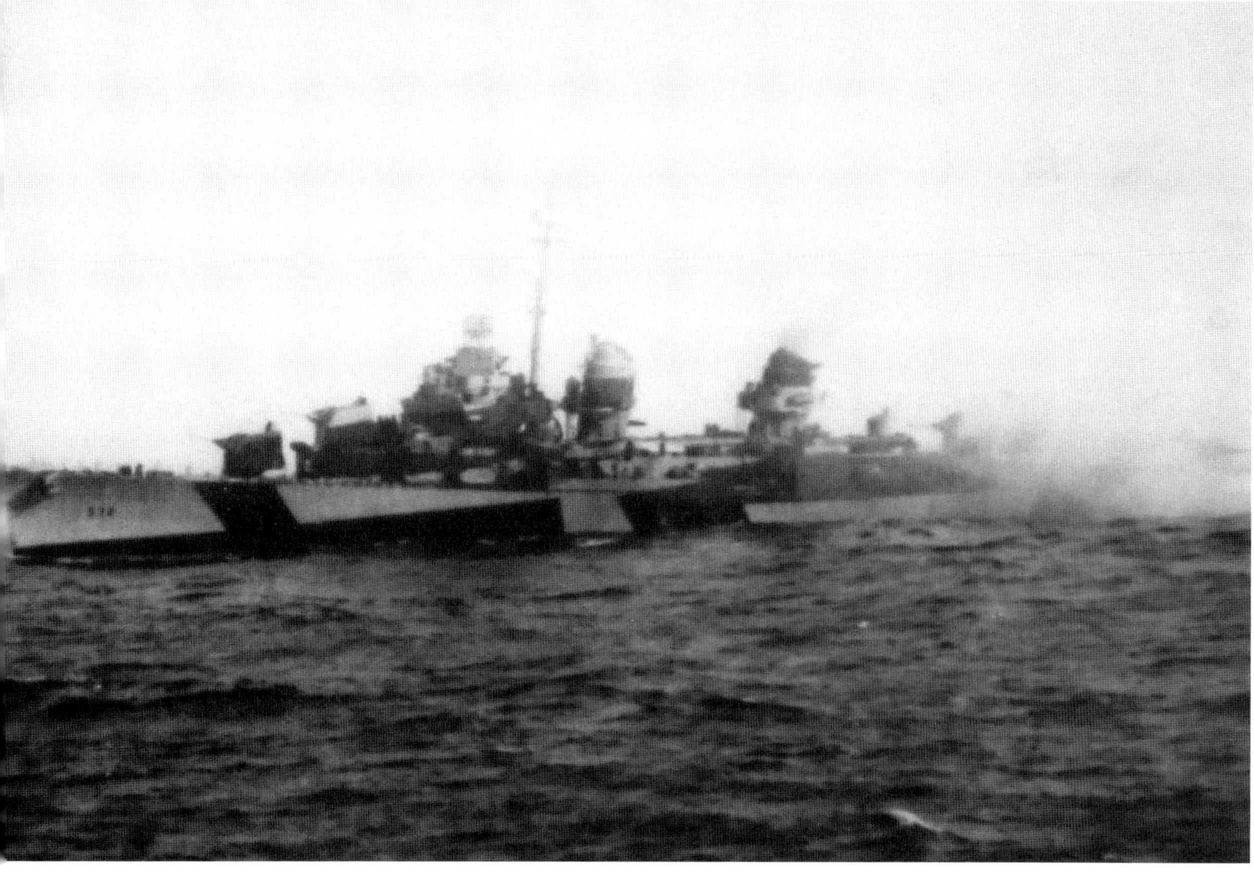

(**Above**) The Japanese heavy cruiser *Tone*, a scouting vessel with six *Aichi* E13A float-planes takes evasive action from a USN escort carrier aerial attack during the Battle off Samar Island on 25 October 1944. The *Tone*, along with three other heavy cruisers, sortied from Brunei to join Kurita's Centre Striking Force. Two other heavy cruisers in this IJN surface force, the *Atago* and *Maya*, were sunk and the cruiser *Takao* was damaged by USN submarines (*Darter* and *Dace*) while sailing through the Palawan Passage on 23 October 1944. As the Centre Striking Force entered the Sibuyan Sea on 24 October, it was assaulted by aircraft from carriers of Task Force 38.2. The cruiser *Musashi* was sunk and the *Tone* was hit by bombs. The following day, at the Battle off Samar Island, the battleships *Yamato*, *Nagato*, *Haruna* and the cruiser *Myoko* were damaged. During that naval battle, the *Tone* engaged the American destroyer USS *Heerman*, but was turned back by USN aircraft launched from Taffy 3's escort carriers. The *Tone* escaped through the San Bernardino Strait, but the *Chikuma* was sunk along with the cruisers *Chokai* and *Suzuya*. (*NARA*)

(**Opposite, above**) The IJN battleship *Yamashiro* (foreground) and the cruiser *Mogami* (background) are shown here under USN aerial attack at the Battle of the Sulu Sea on 24 October 1944. During the Battles of the Sulu Sea and the Sibuyan Sea, USN carrier aircraft from Halsey's Third Fleet, Task Force (TF) 38, attacked the IJN Centre Striking Force under Kurita and the smaller Southern Force under Vice Admiral Shoji Nishimura. The smaller but potent Southern Force, comprising the battleships *Yamashiro* and *Fuso*, the heavy cruiser *Mogami* and four destroyers, had started to cross the Sulu Sea. There, the battleships *Yamashiro* and *Fuso* along with the destroyer *Shigure* were damaged, but Nishimura's force continued towards the Surigao Strait, situated between Leyte and Dinagat Islands, in an effort to attack American transports in Leyte Gulf. During the ensuing Battle of Surigao Strait (24–25 October), Nishimura's Southern Force was engaged by Rear Admiral Jesse Oldendorf's Task Group (TG) 77.2, comprising six battleships, eight cruisers, twenty-nine destroyers and forty PT boats. Nishimura's Southern Force was crushed when Oldendorf's vessels 'crossed the Japanese T'. Nishimura drowned when his flagship *Yamashiro* sank after multiple USN battleship gunfire hits. (*NARA*)

(**Opposite, below**) IJN surface vessels' gunfire is seen here falling near the USS *White Plains* (background), a *Casablanca*-class escort carrier with twenty-four aircraft at the Battle off Samar Island on 25 October 1944. USN fighter planes prepare for take-off from the USS *Kitkun Bay* (foreground), another *Casablanca*-class escort carrier with 860 men and 27 aircraft, to attack the IJN Centre Striking Force. (*NARA*)

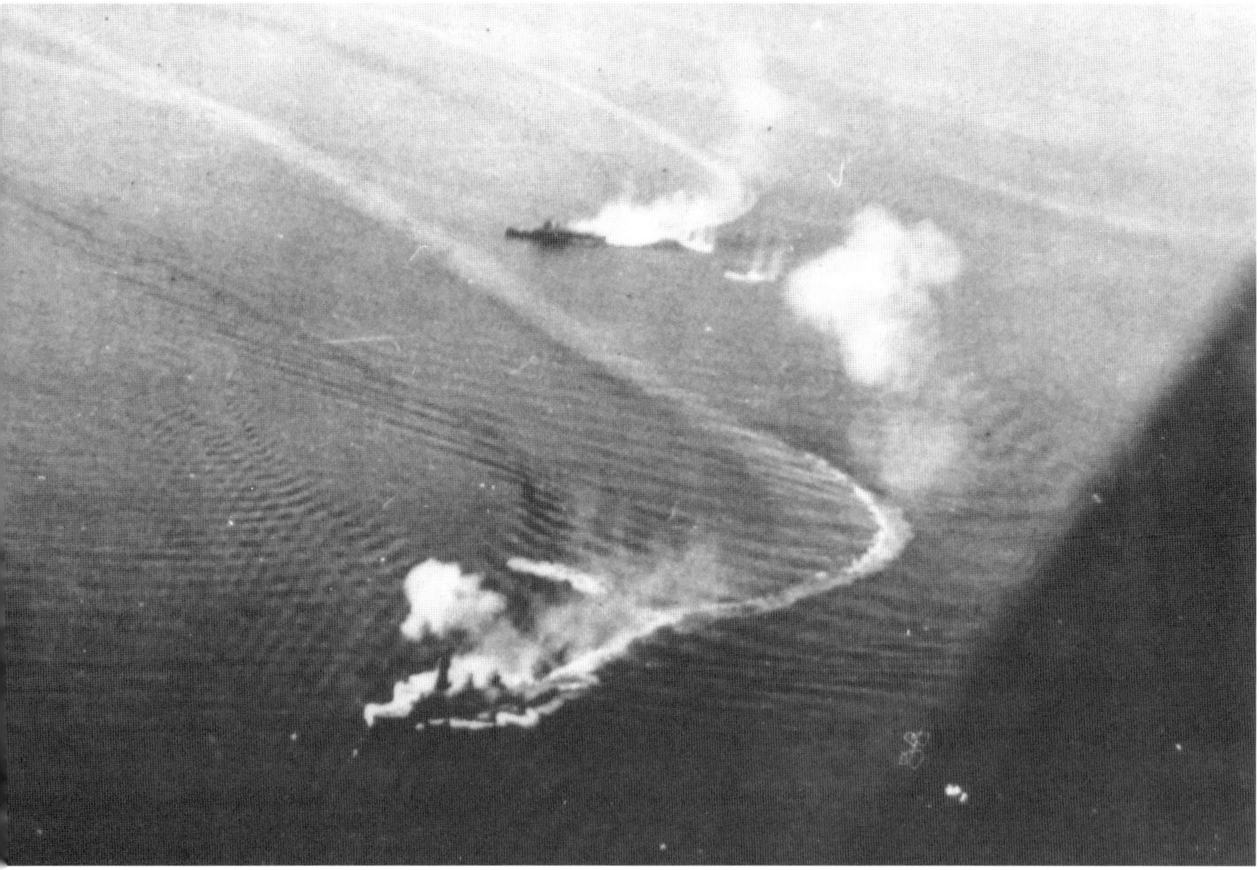

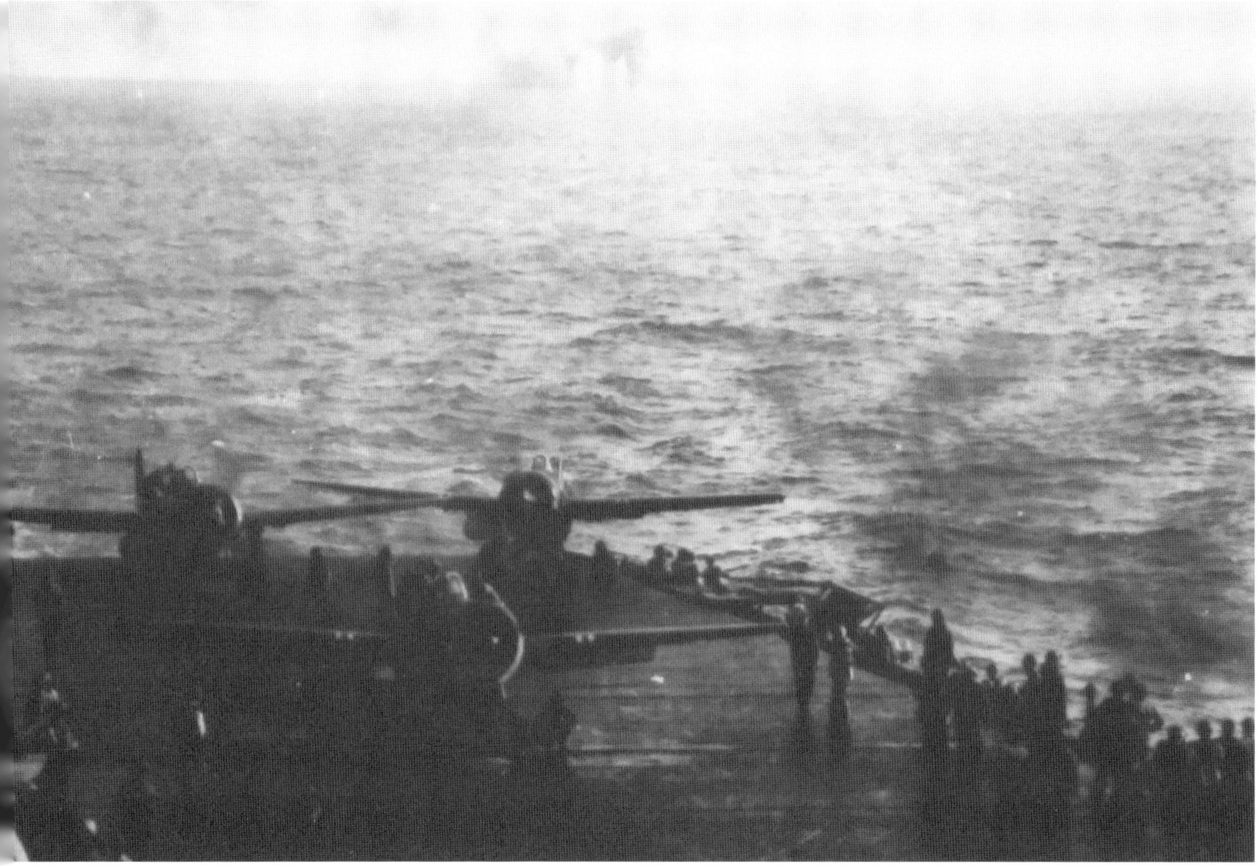

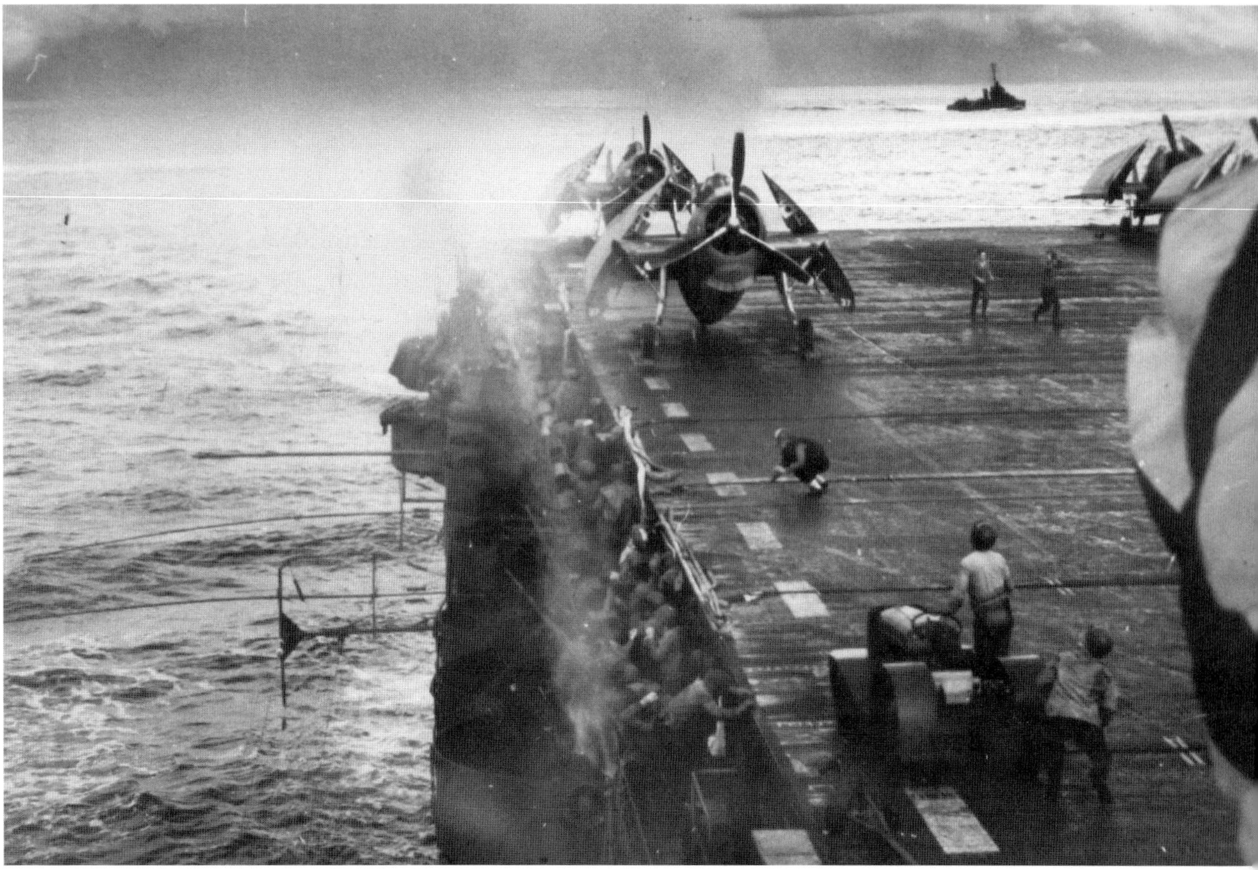

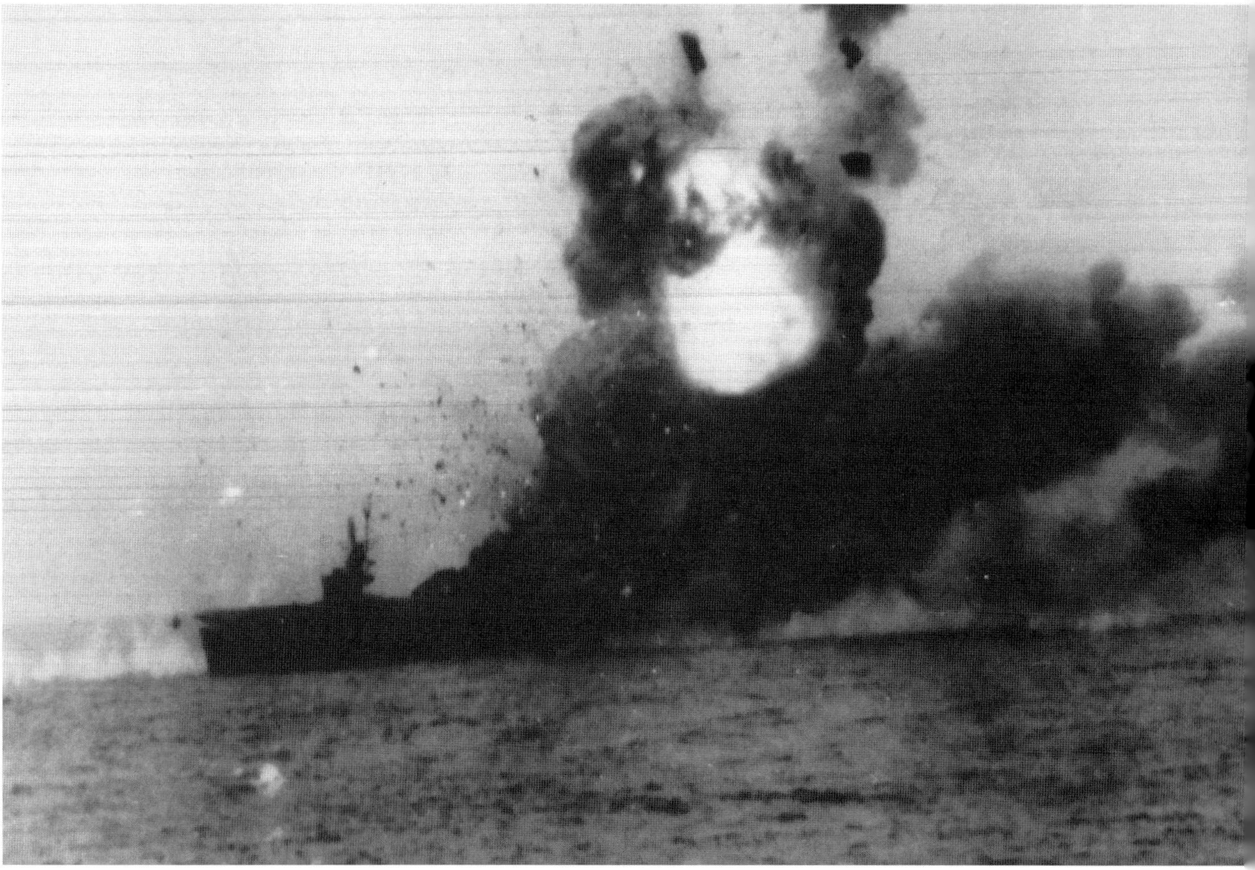

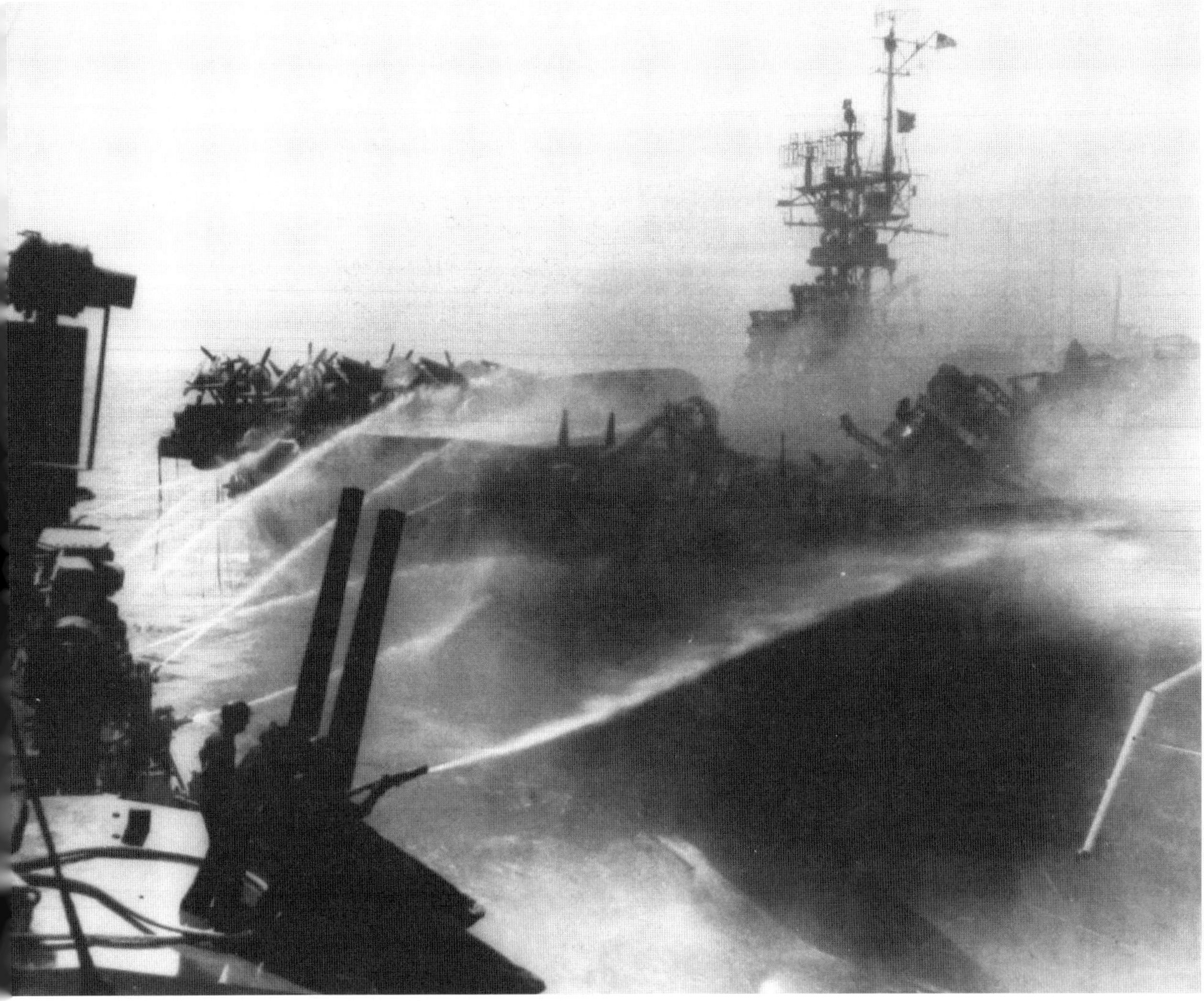

(**Opposite, above**) After the naval Battle of Leyte Gulf, USN warships had to contend with another Japanese menace, *kamikaze* suicidal aerial attacks. A US carrier's AAA guns in the gallery beside and below the flight deck mount defensive fire against a Japanese kamikaze attack on 6 December 1944. A picket destroyer or destroyer escort is seen manoeuvring in the background. (*NARA*)

(**Opposite, below**) The USS *St. Lo*, a *Casablanca*-class escort carrier in Rear Admiral Clifton Sprague's unit (Taffy 3), explodes following a *kamikaze* strike at the Battle off Samar Island on 25 October 1944. The *St. Lo* was the first major warship to sink following a *kamikaze* attack. All of Taffy 3's escort carriers, with the exception of Sprague's flagship, the USS *Fanshaw Bay*, were damaged in a forty-minute engagement with enemy *kamikazes*. (*NARA*)

(**Above**) The USS *Birmingham*, a *Cleveland*-class light cruiser, is shown here with its fire hoses trying to quell the flames of the light carrier USS *Princeton* during the Battle of the Sulu Sea on 24 October. The *Princeton* was set ablaze by an AP bomb from an enemy aircraft. The *Birmingham* suffered great topside damage from explosions aboard the *Princeton* while extinguishing the carrier's flames. Numerous sailors of the *Birmingham* died or were wounded. With many dead and casualties, along with continued fires aboard the *Princeton*, this carrier was later scuttled by a torpedo from the light cruiser USS *Reno*. (*NARA*)

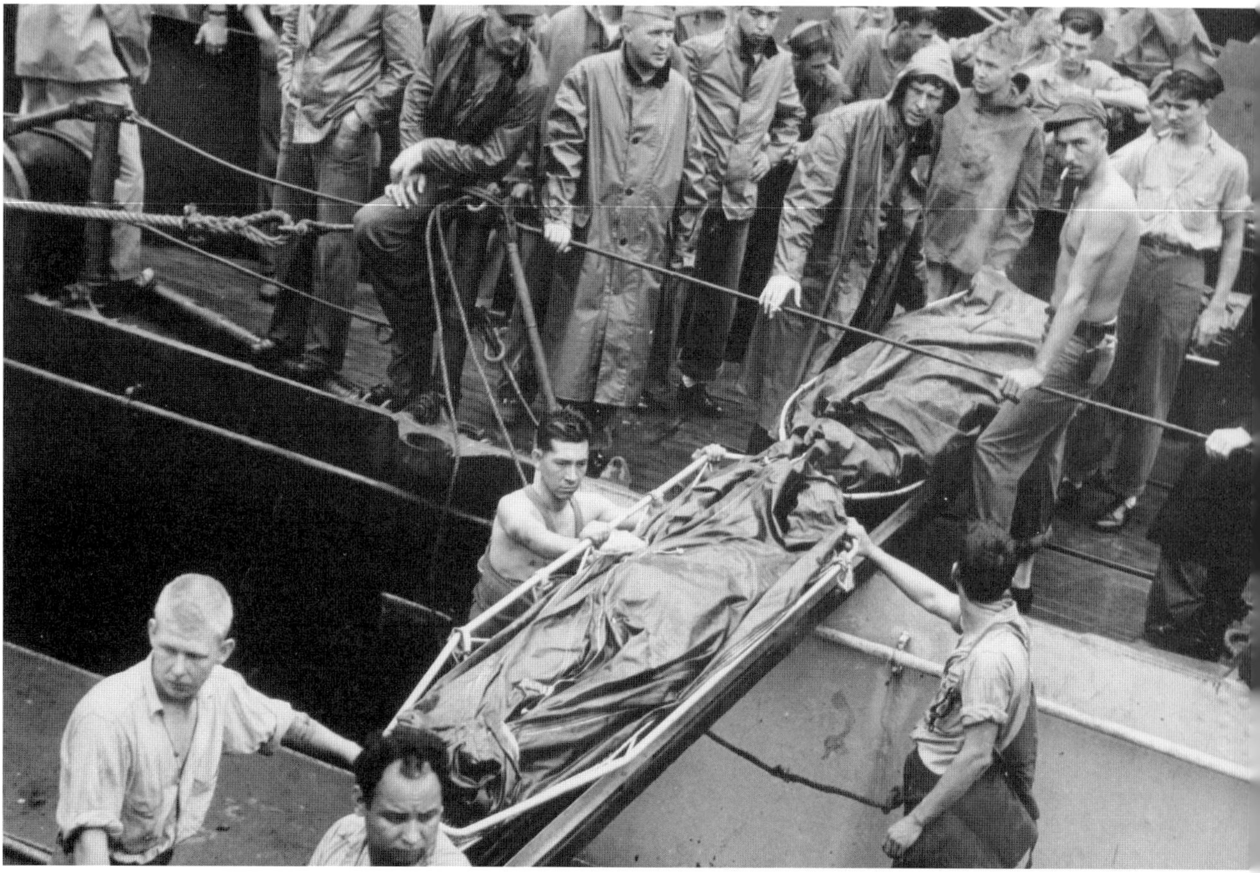

USN sailors that died aboard one of the American vessels damaged by action during the overall Battle of Leyte Gulf are transferred to another vessel for burial. The solemn facial expressions on the faces of the surviving crew members are clearly evident. *(NARA)*

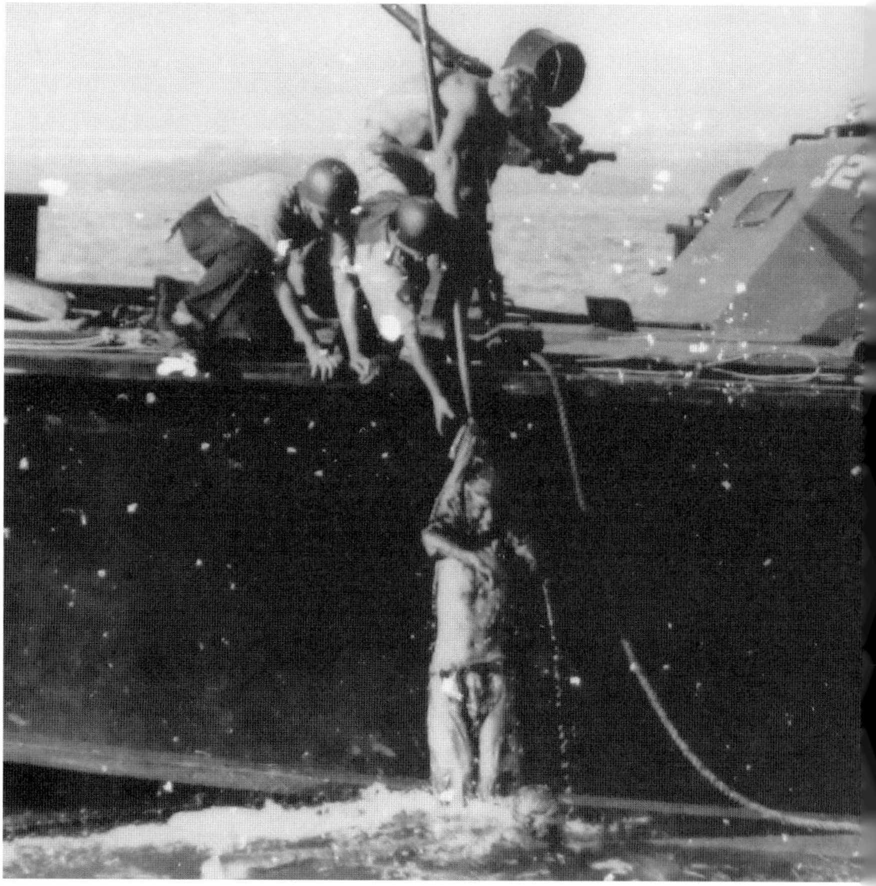

Crew members of USN *PT 321* pull a surviving Japanese sailor out of the water after the Battle of Surigao Strait on 24 October 1944. Vice Admiral Shoji Nishimura's Southern Force was crushed by Rear Admiral Jesse Oldendorf's battleships and cruisers during this naval engagement. *(NARA)*

Chapter Five

Luzon's Recapture and the Liberation of Manila

The Americans required vast logistical and air superiority proximate to Luzon's assault beaches. At Leyte, Kenney's air forces were unable to use the muddy airfield there. The aerial fighter umbrella over Leyte came from distant aerodromes, limiting time over the Sixth Army battlefields, and Third Fleet carriers.

MacArthur and his staff selected Mindoro as a closer island that could provide airfields for pre-invasion sorties against Japanese targets on Luzon as well as protect Kinkaid's convoys manoeuvring towards Lingayen Gulf. On 15 December 1944, Mindoro was invaded by elements of the 24th Infantry Division and the 11th Airborne's 503rd PIR to seize two airfields near San Jose and anchorage in Mangarin Bay. The IJA offered limited resistance. Once Kenney's aircraft were operational on Mindoro, Luzon targets could be attacked and local American air superiority achieved. Additionally, American air strength was augmented by Halsey's Third Fleet carrier-borne aircraft and Kinkaid's escort carriers. All were needed to deal with the mounting deadly Japanese *kamikaze* threat.

For Luzon's Lingayen Gulf invasion, MacArthur had 1,000 ships, accompanied by 3,000 landing craft and 280,000 men. Although Kinkaid's Seventh Fleet suffered forty ships sunk or damaged from *kamikaze* attacks in their transit north to Lingayen Gulf, the landing beaches there offered Krueger's armoured and mechanized forces access to the Central Luzon Plain's excellent terrain for an advance on Manila. Yamashita did not vigorously defend all the Lingayen Gulf's beaches but waited inland in three separate mountainous redoubts with a total of 275,000 troops.

US Sixth Army Landings at Lingayen Gulf, 9 January 1945

The US 43rd Infantry Division of Major General Ennis Swift's I Corps landed on White 1, 2 and 3 Beaches near San Fabian at Lingayen Gulf's eastern end on the morning of 9 January 1944. The IJA 53rd IMB and elements of the 64th Division, in the nearby Ilocos Mountains, mounted stiff resistance from the southern defensive positions of the *Shobu* Group against the 43rd Division's 169th and 172nd IRs. However, the 43rd Division's 103rd IR captured San Fabian unopposed. I Corps' other division, the 6th Infantry, landed to the west of San Fabian at Blue 1 and 2 Beaches.

Opposite the locale of Lingayen, Major General Oscar Griswold's XIV Corps' 40th Infantry Division landed at Orange and Green Beaches with the 185th and 160th IRs, easily capturing Lingayen airfield. The other XIV Corps' division, the 37th Infantry's 148th and 129th IRs landed at Yellow Beach, to the east of the 40th Division. The 37th Division slowly moved 6,000 yards inland while repairing demolished bridges.

The Sixth Army's I Corps expanded its beachhead towards Urdaneta. Yamashita committed some of his 2nd Armoured Division tanks, but I Corps' 6th Infantry Division took Urdaneta on 17 January. The US 43rd Infantry Division (now reinforced with the 158th RCT) moved on to the Damortis-Rosario Road, a key road and railroad centre to Lingayen Gulf's north-east. The 158th RCT captured Damortis on 13 January and the 43rd Division's 172nd IR simultaneously moved north of Rosario. With Rosario to the south of the *Shobu* Group's headquarters at Baguio, the IJA 23rd Division contested any US 43rd Infantry Division move from Damortis-Rosario area through to 31 January. On 16 January, two 25th Infantry Division IRs were added to the 43rd Division.

After landing, Griswold's XIV Corps drove south through the Central Luzon Plain towards Manila. Yamashita decided not to contest the American drive for Manila as he was more concerned with preventing Swift's I Corps breaking through the southern *Shobu* Group positions and driving towards Baguio through the Cagayan Valley, which was the 'breadbasket' for the northern Luzon IJA troops.

San Jose, south of the Balete Pass, was a critical town and road junction for Yamashita to hold as it led north to the *Shobu* Group's northern Luzon mountainous stronghold. Yamashita had stockpiled supplies in San Jose for his northern Luzon force. The Balete Pass was to be a heavily-contested conduit north to Santa Fe.

On 17 January, MacArthur pressured Krueger to move XIV Corps to capture Clark Field. On 21 January, XIV Corps moved south against Tarlac and then on to Clark Field, even though the *Kembu* Group was on his flank. Another dilemma was that when XIV Corps drove on Clark Field, the *Kembu* Group could move south into the Bataan Peninsula and establish strong defensive positions.

By 23 January, Griswold's XIV Corps, which skirted the Zambales Mountains, was in position to attack Clark Field and Fort Stotsenburg with the 37th and 40th Infantry divisions.

US Eighth Army Landings on Luzon's West Coast near Olongapo, 29 January 1945

To prevent the *Kembu* Group from entering the Bataan Peninsula south of Clark Field, MacArthur directed Eichelberger's 38th Infantry Division (reinforced with the 34th IR from the 24th Infantry Division) from the Eighth Army's XI Corps to land at San Antonio on Luzon's west coast and seize the airfield at San Marcelino.

On 29 January 1945, the assault was unopposed and the airfield was immediately restored for American air sorties. Eichelberger's troops then attacked Olongapo and captured the former USN base at Subic Bay, providing Kinkaid with a port closer to Manila and unburdening Lingayen Gulf as Luzon's only beachhead for supply and troop disembarkation.

The movement of Griswold's XIV Corps on to Clark Field and Fort Stotsenburg along with Eichelberger's XI Corps landing on the west coast of the Bataan Peninsula compelled the *Kembu* Group to head towards the Zambales Mountains. Japanese resistance stiffened along the US 38th Infantry Division's front near the Zigzag Pass, preventing that locale's capture until 14 February. The *Kembu* Group was now isolated from Yamashita's other two groups.

The Seizure of Clark Field and Fort Stotsenburg

On 27 January, XIVth Corps' 37th Infantry Division commenced its attack against limited IJA opposition, principally with minefields and local counterattacks. One IJA detachment manned the defences near Clark Field, while another was west of the runway complex. A third IJA detachment, held in reserve, was garrisoned in Angeles, a city south-east of Clark Field. The 37th Division's 129th IR captured the airfield complex on 28 January. Fort Stotsenburg was captured by 37th Division units on 29 January as retreating Japanese troops headed into the Zambales Mountains to the west, which prevented American air operations from Clark Field's runway complex for some time.

Combat in Southern and Northern Luzon

After the capture of Clark Field, Fort Stotsenburg and Manila, the *Kembu* Group was isolated in the Zambales Mountains on Luzon's west coast and offered limited resistance but did make Clark Field inoperable for some time. East of Manila and within southern Luzon, the *Shimbu* Group was isolated. Yamashita's *Shobu* Group was situated in northern Luzon.

Griswold's XIV Corps' divisions were to clear Manila's water reservoirs and dams east of the capital. The US 6th Infantry and 1st Cavalry divisions led the assaults against the *Shimbu* Group's resistance which, having failed by 5 March, necessitated the 43rd Division replacing those units of the 1st Cavalry Division. After initial success by the 43rd Division, the Japanese counterattacked but American artillery and air power stopped it. The 6th Infantry Division continued its eastward movement 12–26 March; however, American casualties were high including the death of its division commander, Major General Edward Patrick. The *Shimbu* Group also incurred heavy casualties. Additional moves on Luzon's Wawa Dam from 27 to 28 March caused attrition within the 6th Division, necessitating its replacement by the 38th Division to continue the assault against the *Shimbu* Group's defence of the dam.

Units from the 1st Cavalry and 11th Airborne Divisions units, along with the 158th RCT, were all assigned to XIV Corps to move south-west of Laguna de Bay to seize Batangas on the Sibuyan Sea from units of the IJA 8th Division, and then clear the Bicol Peninsula on south-east Luzon across from Samar Island. Japanese resistance was fierce; however, the US 8th Cavalry captured a key road junction on 29 March. The 158th RCT landed unopposed at Legazpi on the east coast of the Bicol Peninsula on 1 April. Six days later the Japanese retreated, which ended enemy resistance there.

The *Shobu* Group was in the last major IJA Japanese redoubt in northern Luzon. Swift's I Corps was engaged with the *Shobu* Group's southern forces since the Lingayen Gulf landings. Yamashita concentrated his 150,000 IJA troops near Baguio and east to Bambang, anticipating that Krueger would move through San Jose and then up the highway through the Balete Pass towards Santa Fe and the Cagayan Valley. Yamashita never mounted a concerted counterattack with his entire *Shobu* Group against the advancing US 37th and 25th Infantry divisions. Instead, the Japanese commander defended the mountainous redoubt which had few passes and adequate roads, thereby limiting the Sixth Army's advantage in armour and motorized units.

The 1st IR of I Corps' 6th Division seized San Jose on 4 February. Then the US 32nd Infantry Division advanced along the Villa Verde Trail towards Santa Fe, but the assault stalled on 23 March with IJA resistance in the mountain passes. On 6 March Krueger added the 25th Division, which advanced amid adverse terrain and weather against strong local enemy resistance. Krueger then tasked his 33rd Division to drive on Baguio from Rosario and then on to San Fernando to the north along Luzon's west coast; however, this division's attack halted on 20 March, 10 miles to Baguio's south. Filipino guerrilla formations of 8,000 men along with two IRs from the 37th Division on 7 April added much-needed troop strength to Krueger's Baguio assault. Elements of the 37th Division broke through on 21 April compelling Yamashita's north-eastward retreat to Bambang while the IJA Baguio defenders held out until 27 April.

The US 25th and 32nd Divisions continued advancing towards Santa Fe and then on to Bambang despite IJA heavy artillery and the remnants of their 2nd Armoured Division. American artillery and air strikes enabled these Sixth Army formations to capture the Balete Pass on 13 May. After a two-week delay before Santa Fe, these two divisions now resumed their offensives into the Cagayan Valley.

On 5 June, along Luzon's west coast between Vigan and Laoag, Krueger assembled a force of the 32nd Division's 127th IR, the 6th Ranger Battalion and Filipino guerrilla units to move onto Luzon's northern coast and attack the IJA 103rd Division at Aparri, which eventually fell to the American ad hoc formation on 21 June. Yamashita was trapped within the Central Cordillera Range at Kiangan, while other enemy units fled into the Sierra Madre Range east of the Cagayan Valley along Luzon's east coast.

Mopping up enemy pockets in northern Luzon continued throughout the summer of 1945. By V-J Day, when Yamashita surrendered, scattered groups of the enemy were at large, usually amid mountainous terrain, and numbered almost 50,000. Some Japanese soldiers evaded capture for several years. The cost in combatant lives to liberate Luzon was large. The Japanese had more than 200,000 troops killed in action or from starvation, with several thousand enemy soldiers captured, a rarity during the Pacific War. US casualties were approximately 40,000 with more than 8,100 killed in action and almost 30,000 wounded. An estimated 140,000 Filipinos perished, primarily during the month-long struggle to liberate the capital city of Manila (see Chapter 6).

Vice Admiral Thomas Kinkaid's Seventh Fleet Bombardment and Fire Support Group (TG 77.2) with its line of battleships, now under Vice Admiral Jesse Oldendorf, is seen here moving towards Luzon's Lingayen Gulf for the US Sixth Army's invasion on 9 January 1945. Kinkaid planned and executed the amphibious assault from his flagship, the USS *Wasatch*. He commanded the Luzon Attack Force (TF 77), comprising both the Lingayen Attack Force (TF 79) with XIV Corps and the San Fabian Attack Force (TF 78) with I Corps. *(NARA)*

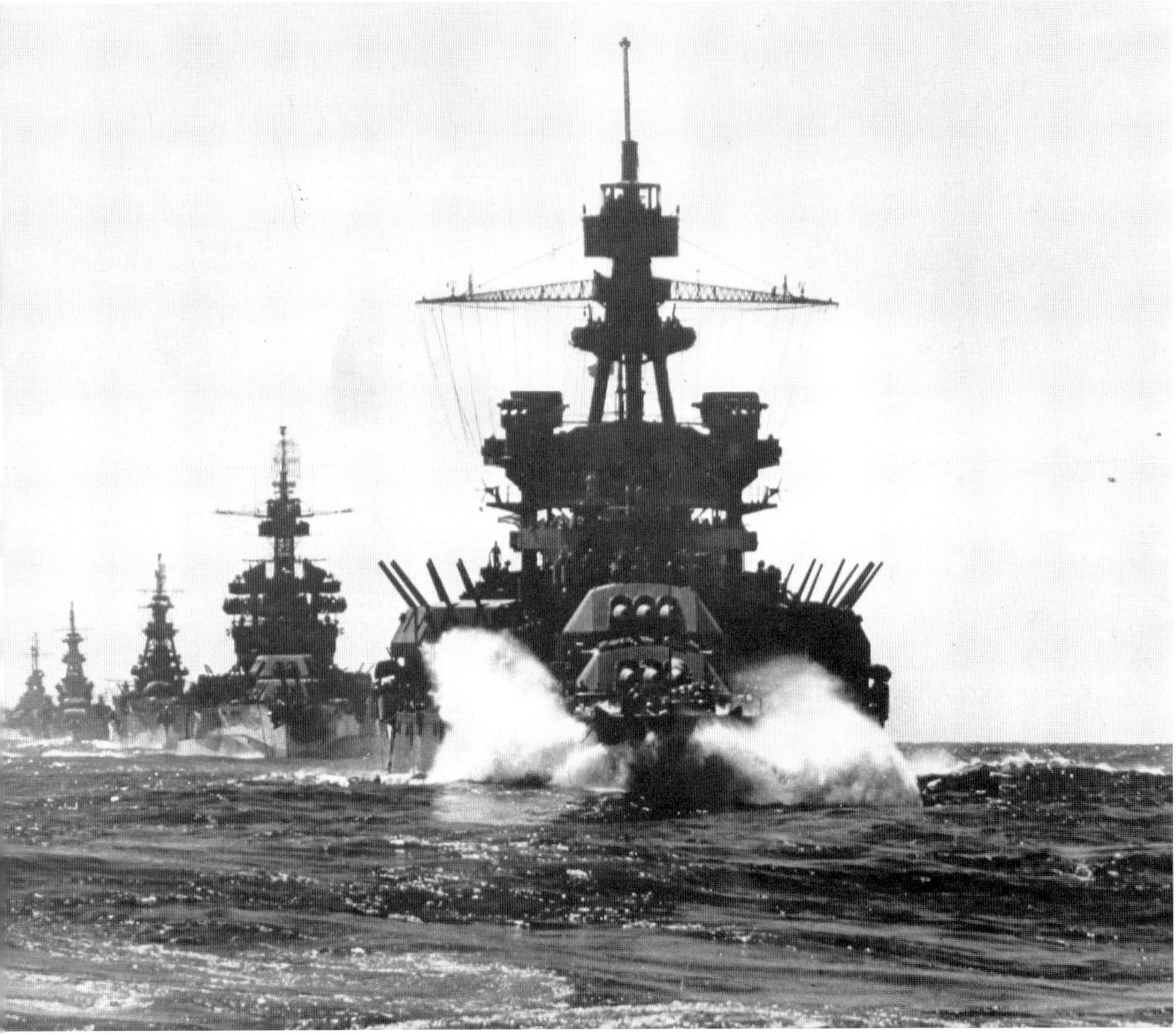

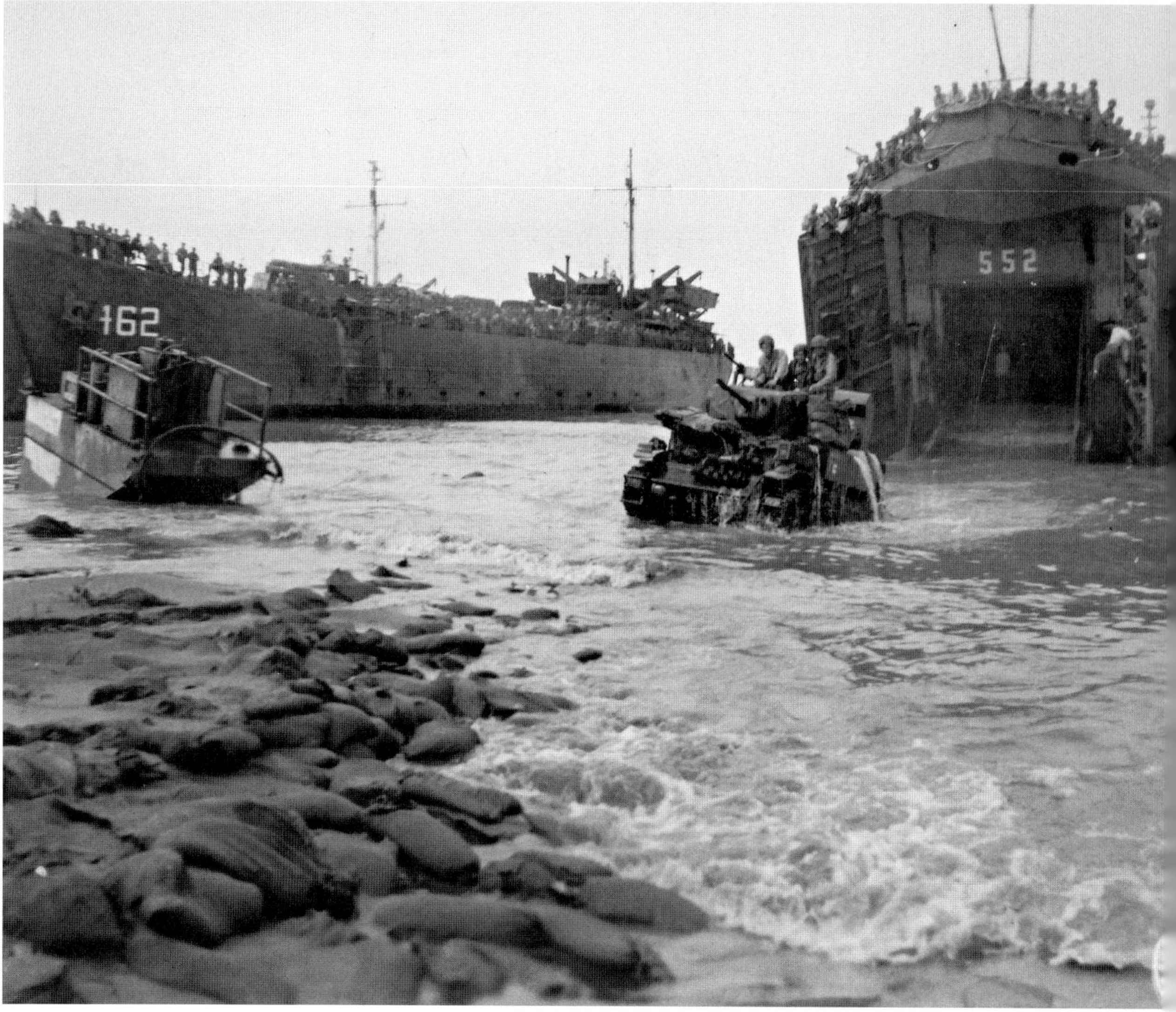
162
552

(**Above**) An M4 medium tank leaves LST 552 (from TF 78) via its downed bow ramp to wade ashore at Lingayen Gulf on 9 January 1945 with its specially-designed exhaust system at the armoured vehicle's rear. The M4 tank was from the 13th Armoured Group which provided follow-up armoured support for I Corps' 43rd Infantry Division, which assaulted White 1, White 2 and White 3 Beaches at 0930 hours near San Fabian. Japanese opposition was limited to some shelling and sniping. *(NARA)*

(**Opposite, above**) Infantrymen from the 38th Division of Lieutenant General Eichelberger's Eighth Army's XI Corps land at San Antonio on Luzon's western coast on 29 January 1945. This division was reinforced with the 34th IR from the 24th Division as they were to seize the San Marcelino airfield and strike against Olongapo and Subic Bay to block a Japanese retreat into the Bataan Peninsula via the Zigzag Pass. *(NARA)*

(**Opposite, below**) Eighth Army infantrymen disembark unopposed at 0830 hours on 29 January 1945 from an LCI between the towns of San Antonio and San Marcelino on Luzon's western coast. USAAF personnel quickly made the airfield there operational. XI Corps was to envelop the stiffening resistance of the IJA's *Kembu* Group's *Nagayoshi* Detachment. *(NARA)*

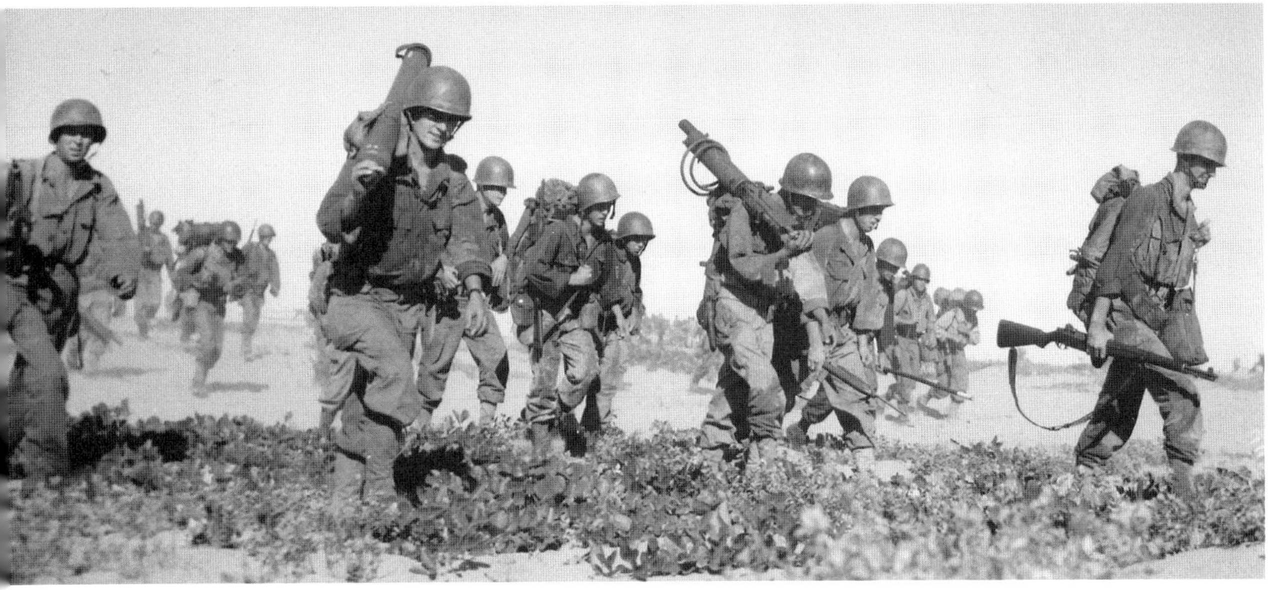

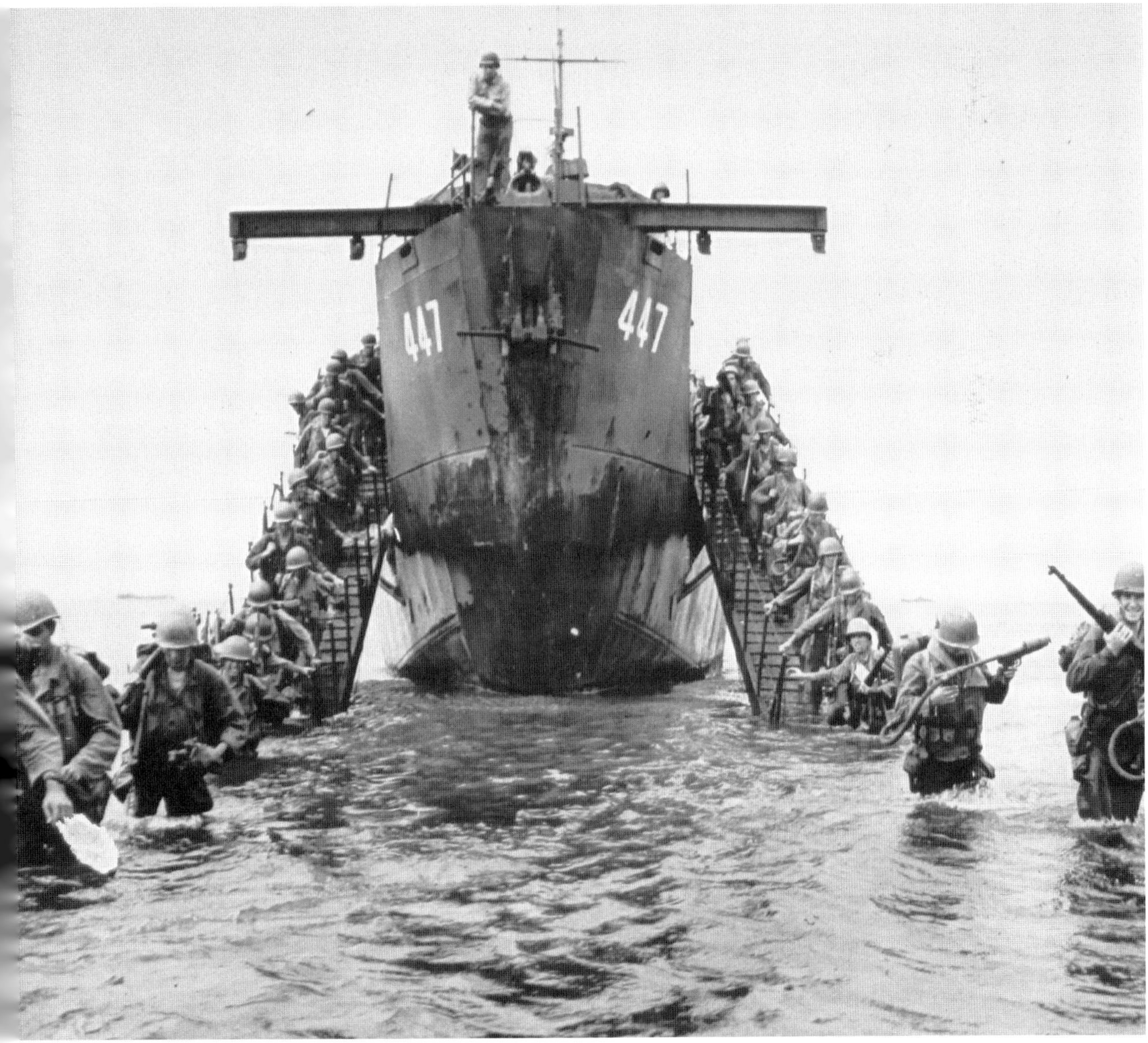
447
447

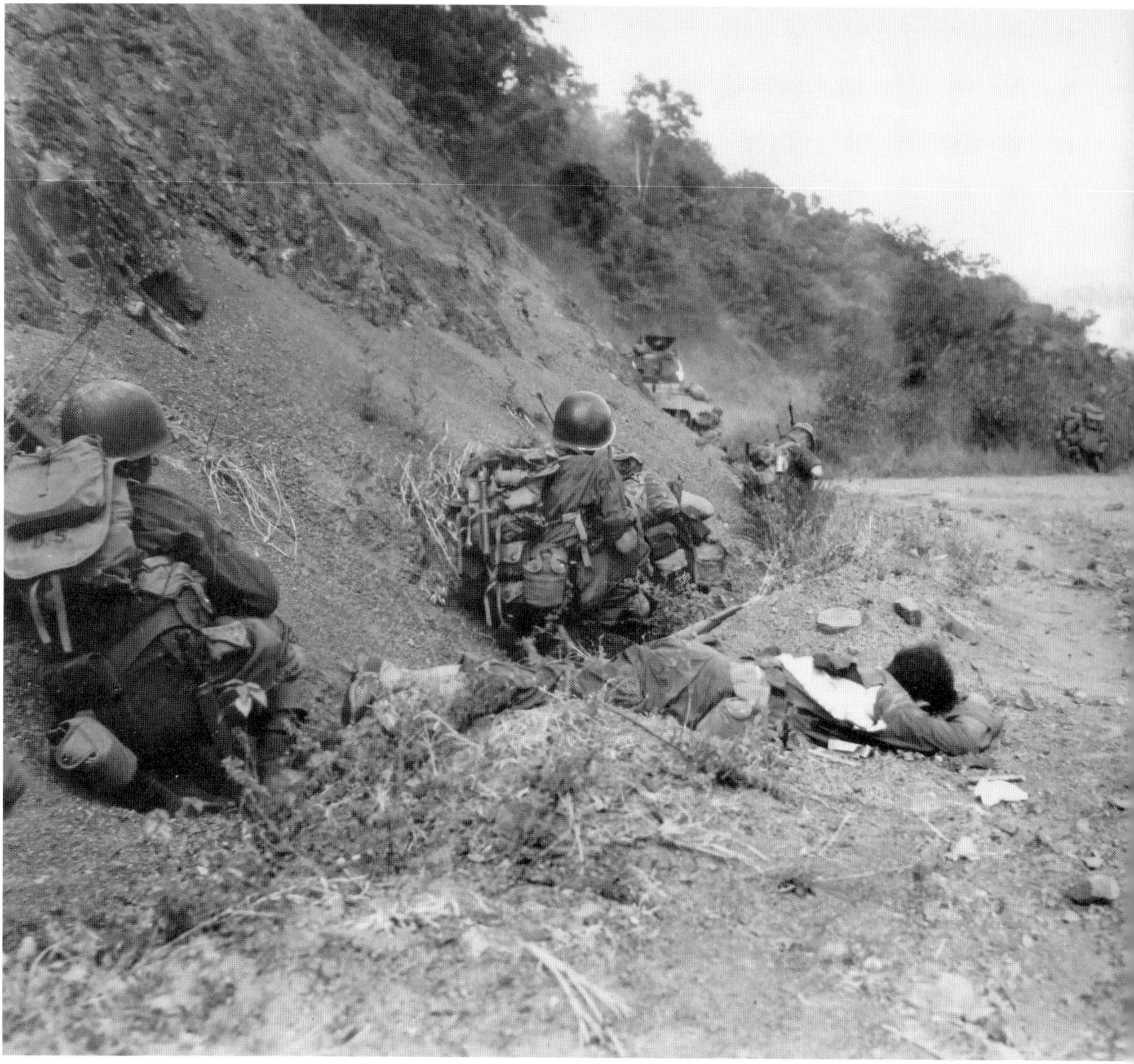

(**Above**) American infantrymen take cover from an enemy MG nest which claimed the life of one US soldier along a hillside with an M4 medium tank ahead (background). US armoured vehicles provided an abundance of turret gunfire and MG rounds to neutralize enemy pillboxes and strongpoints that brought infantry advances to abrupt halts. *(NARA)*

(**Opposite**) Paratroopers from the 11th Airborne Division's 511th PIR descend after jumping from their Mindoro-based, twin-engined C-47 transports with other planes flying abreast over a Luzon drop zone on 3 February 1945 near Nichols Field south of Manila. Filipino guerrillas neutralized any Japanese opposition at the landing zone. On 31 January, the 11th Airborne's 187th Glider Infantry Regiment (GIR) amphibiously landed at Nasugbu Bay under Lieutenant General Eichelberger's direction. The 187th GIR hit strong enemy resistance from Japanese pillboxes and strongpoints as the glidermen fought for several days in their drive to Nichols Field against the enemy's 3rd Naval Defence Battalion and the Southern Flank Detachment of IJA Major General Takashi Kobayashi's Manila Defence Force. The 511th PIR linked up with the glidermen to clear the enemy positions around Nichols Field on 12–13 February. *(NARA)*

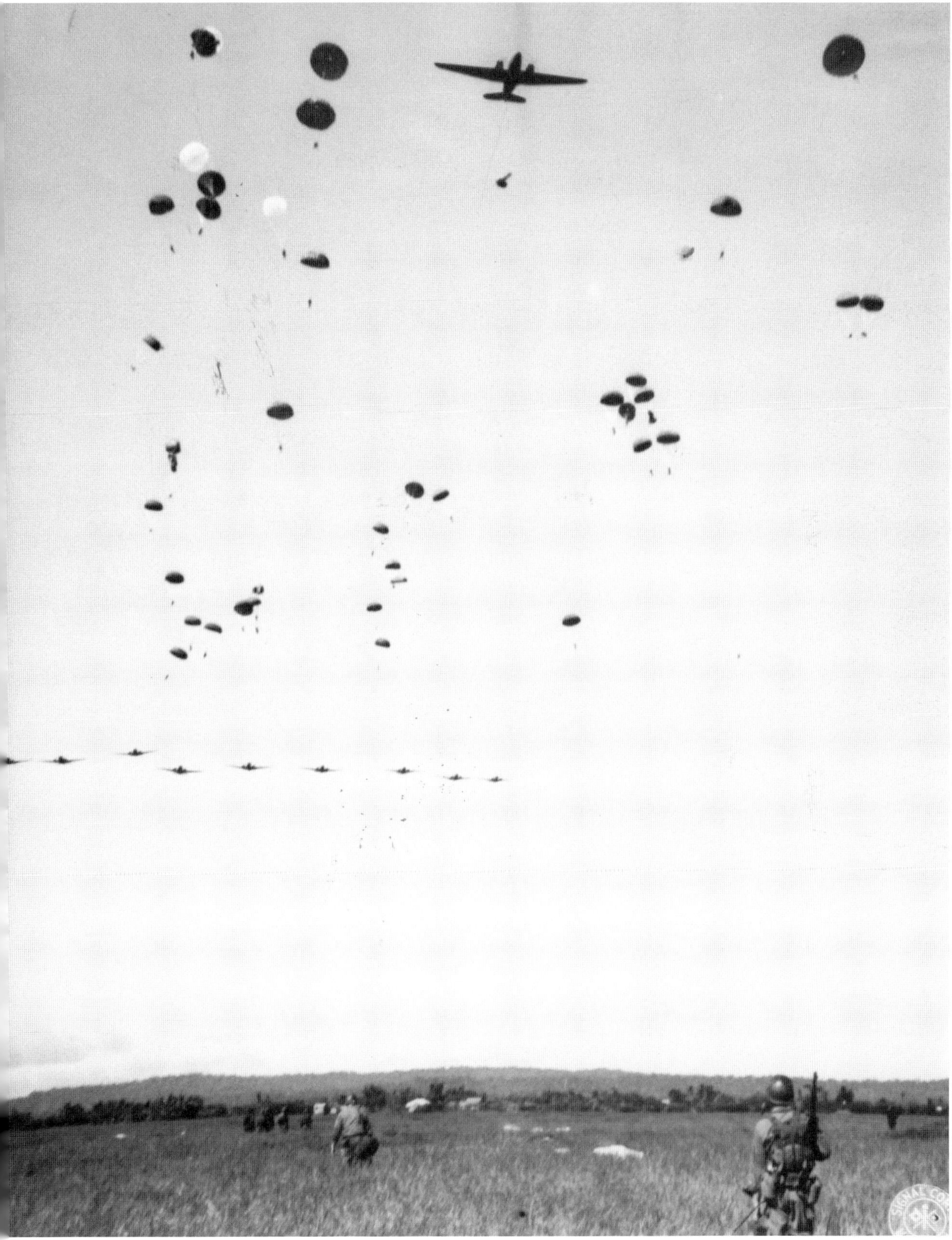

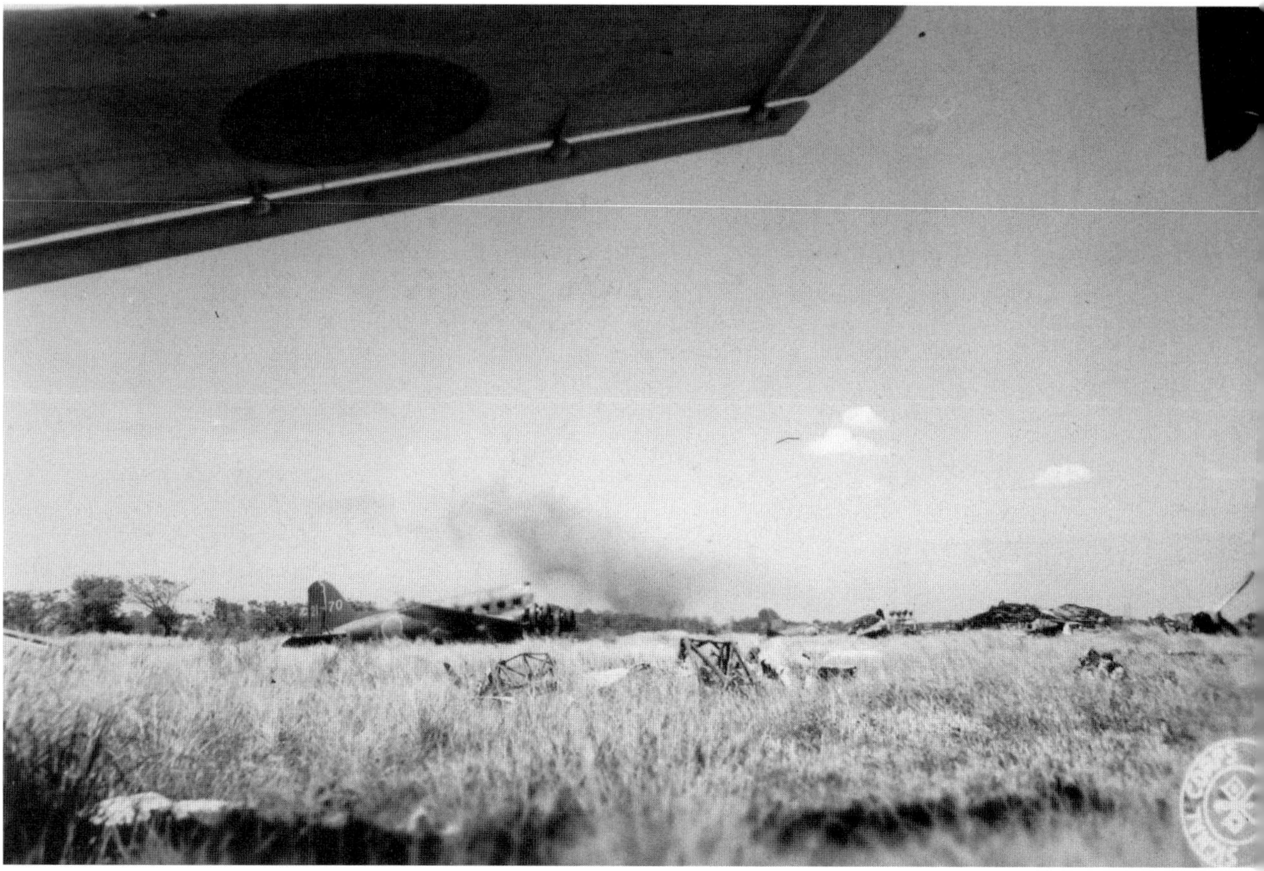

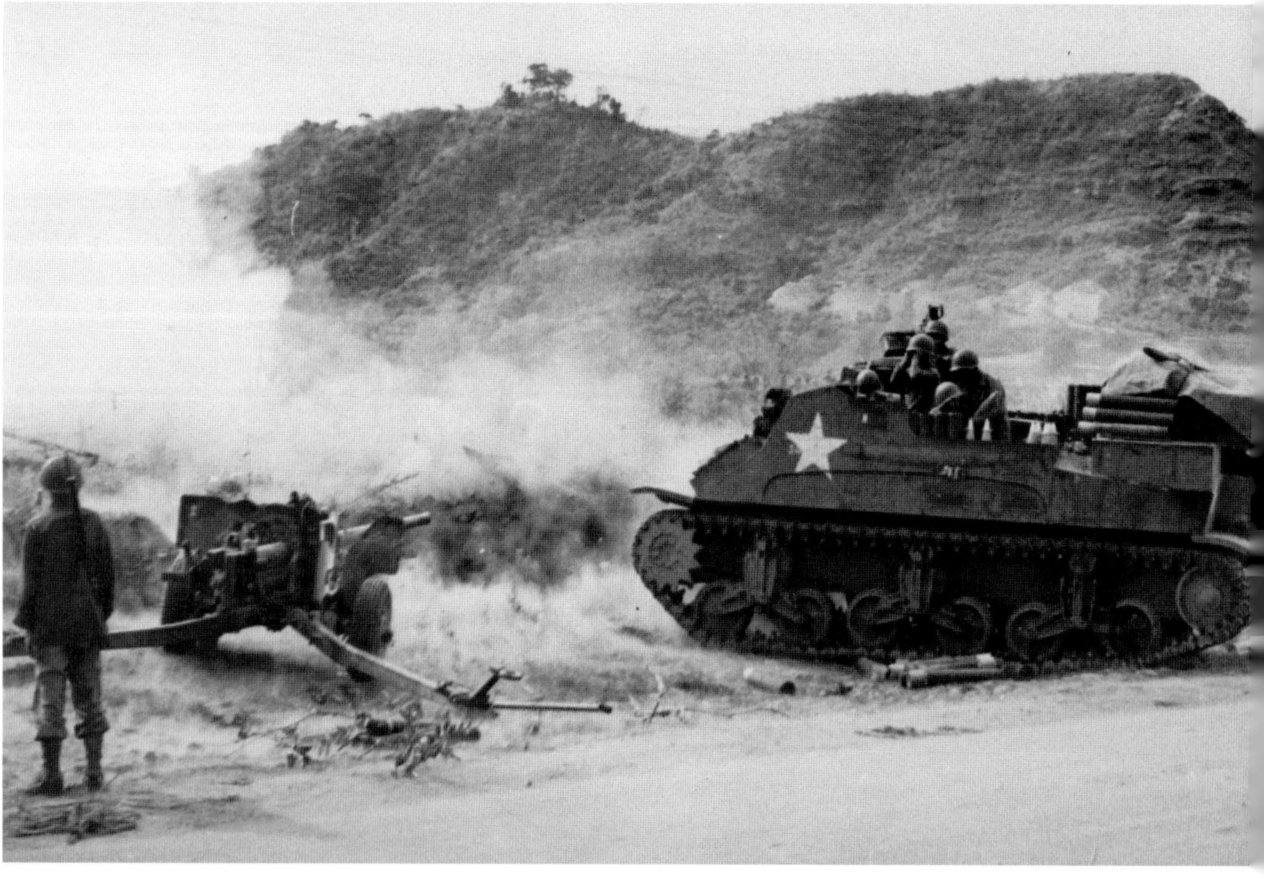

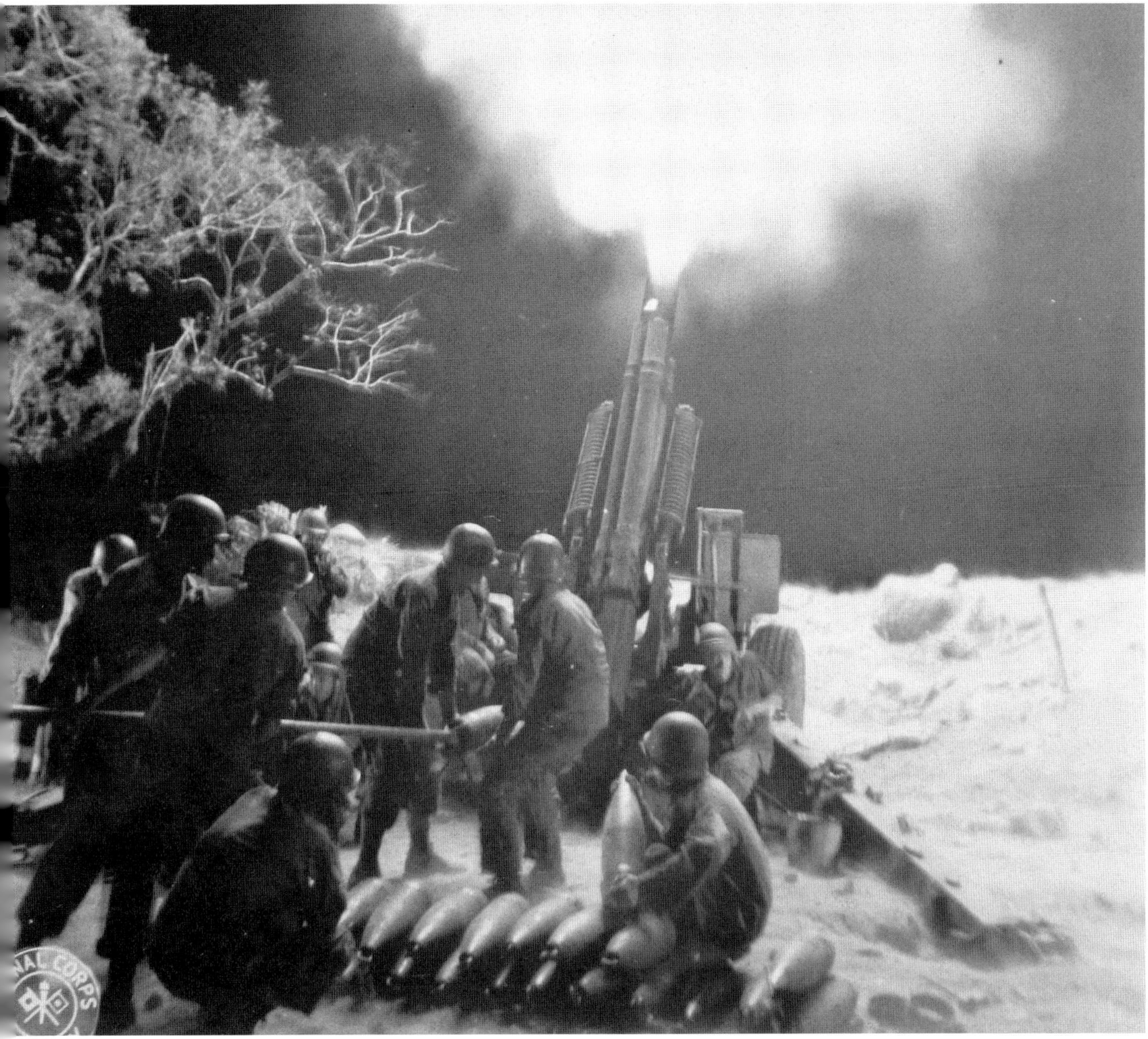

(**Opposite, above**) Wrecked Japanese aircraft are seen here on a bombed runway at Nichols Field in early February 1945. The smoke (background) emanated from Manila to the north. *(NARA)*

(**Above**) A 90th FA's 155mm howitzer attached to the US 25th Infantry Division is fired during a night mission against Japanese 150mm artillery positions that were under the direction of enemy observers on Mount Imugan near the Villa Verde Trail on 19 April 1945. Yamashita just relocated his forces to another defensive line at Bambang to the north-west of the Balete Pass. After Baguio fell to American forces on 27 April, the US 25th and 32nd Divisions continued their drive through the Balete Pass to Santa Fe and then north-west towards Bambang. *(NARA)*

(**Opposite, below**) An M7 SPA ('Priest') and a 57mm AT cannon attached to the US 37th Infantry Division bombard Japanese positions in the hills overlooking Clark Field. Even after Clark Field was recaptured on 28 January 1945 by the 129th IR of the 37th Infantry Division, enemy light artillery in the caves of the Zambales Mountains fired on the US XIV Corps soldiers as they moved towards Fort Stotsenburg. *(NARA)*

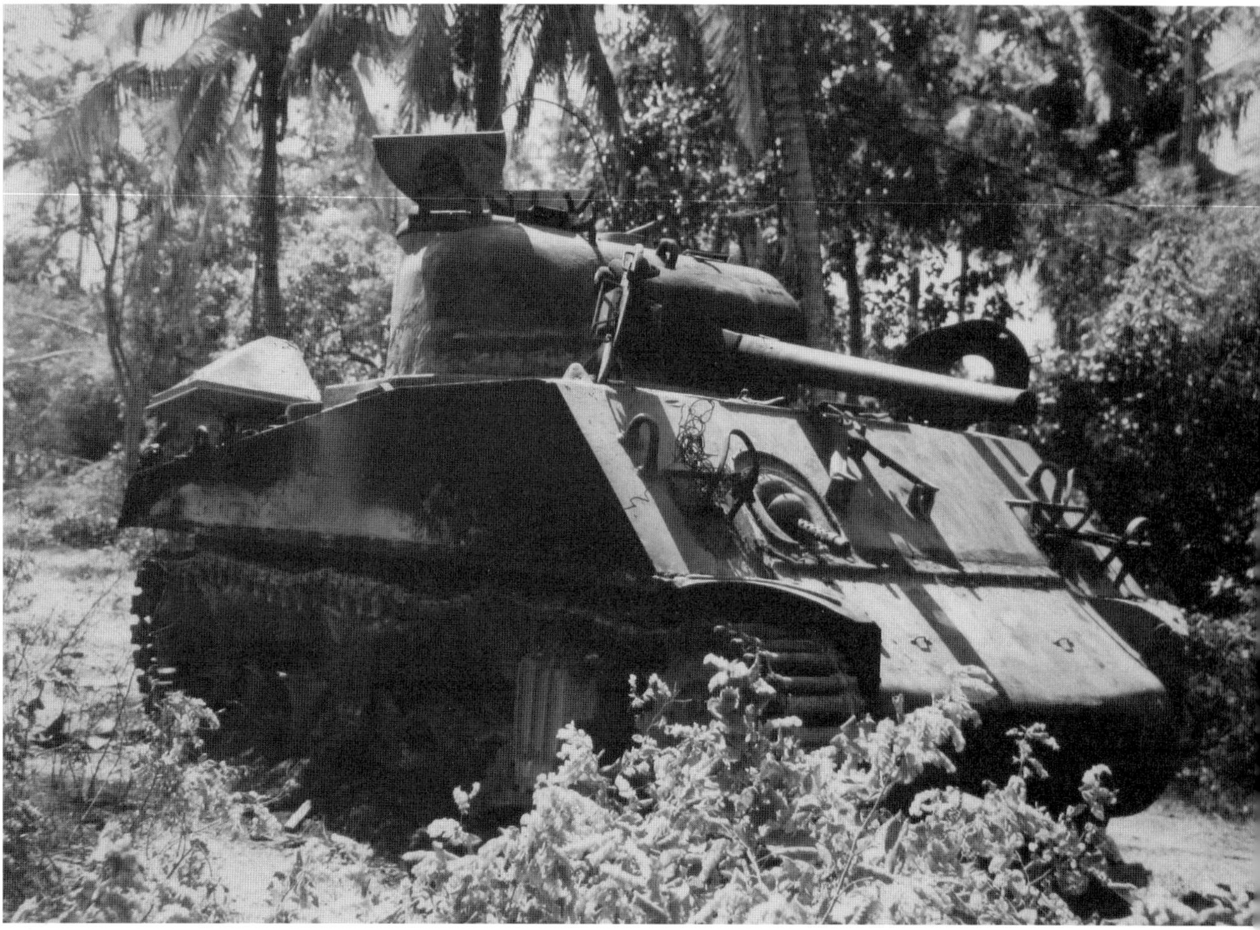

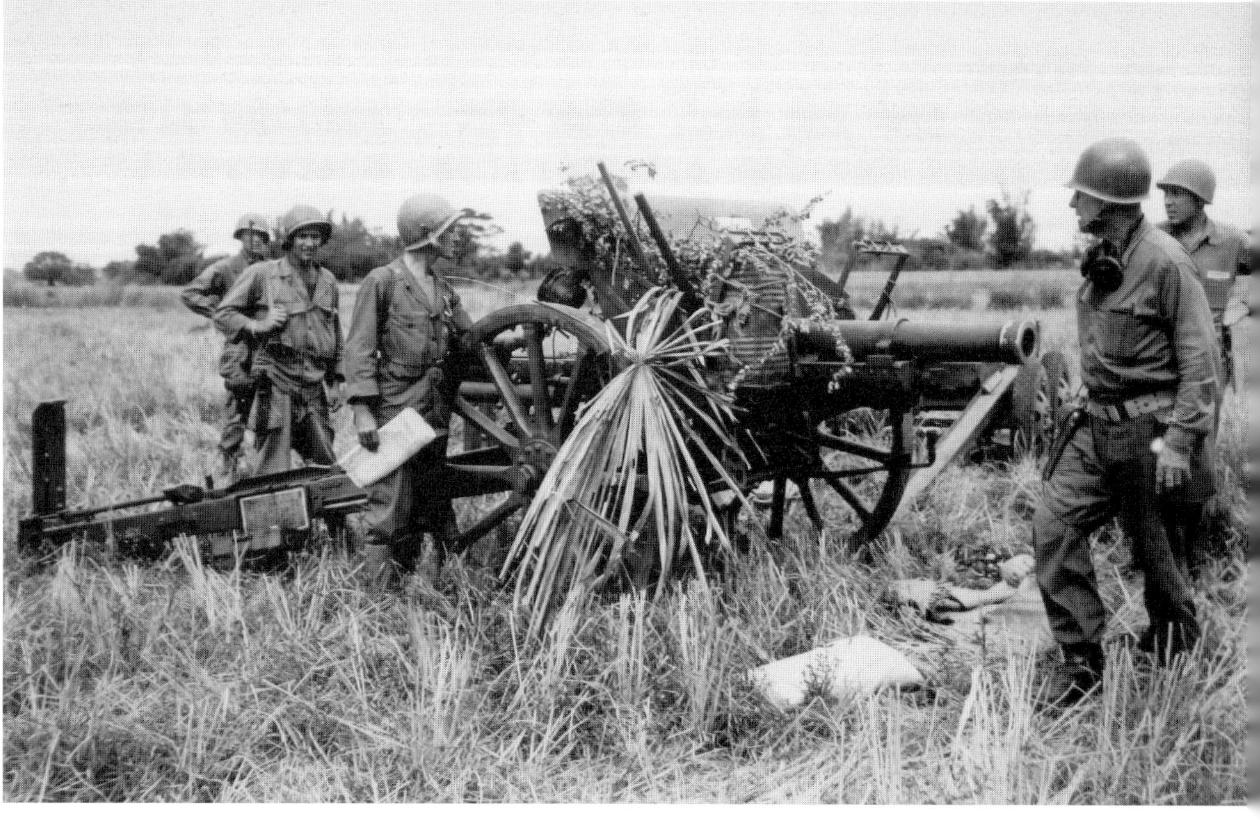

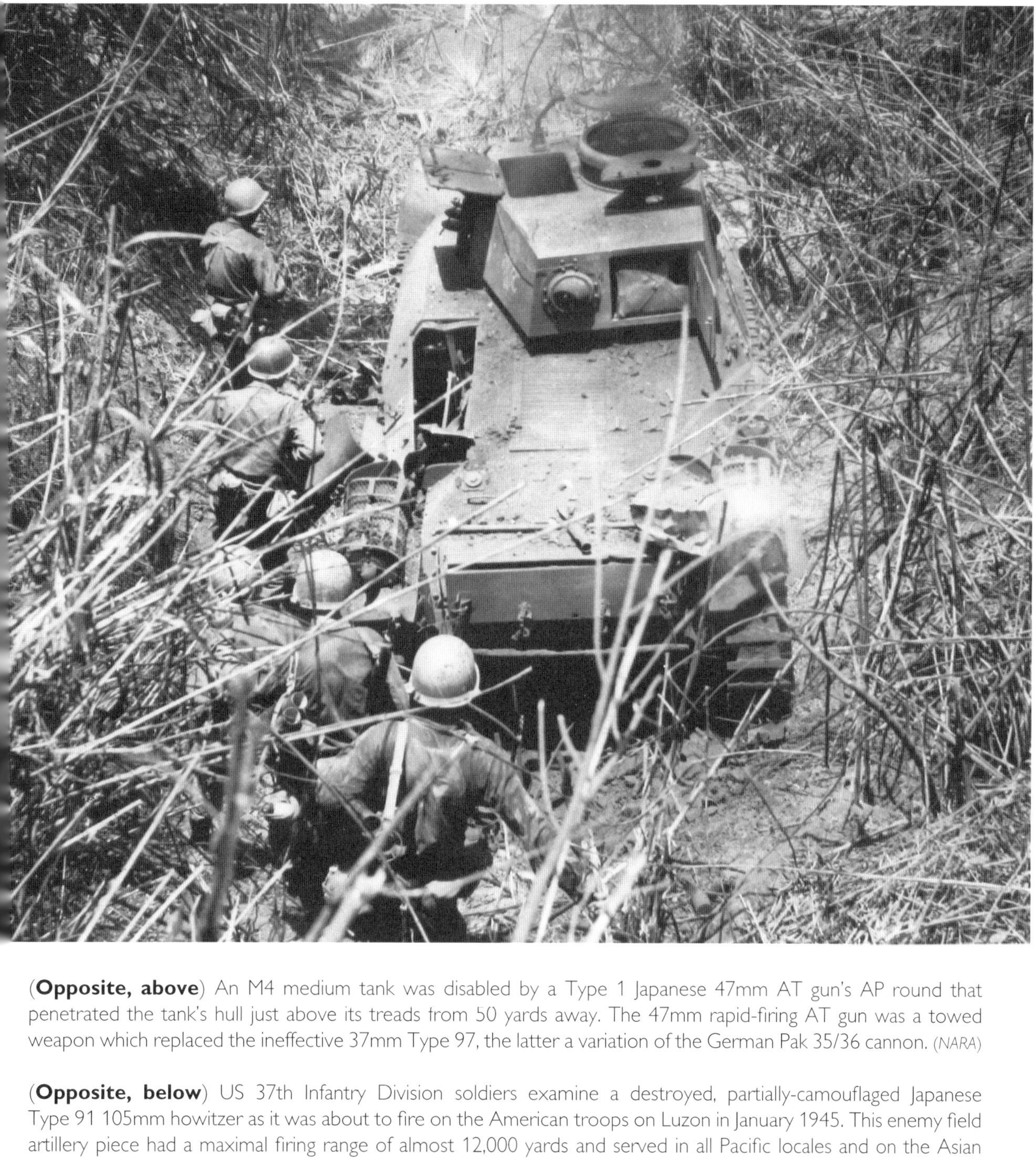

(**Opposite, above**) An M4 medium tank was disabled by a Type 1 Japanese 47mm AT gun's AP round that penetrated the tank's hull just above its treads from 50 yards away. The 47mm rapid-firing AT gun was a towed weapon which replaced the ineffective 37mm Type 97, the latter a variation of the German Pak 35/36 cannon. *(NARA)*

(**Opposite, below**) US 37th Infantry Division soldiers examine a destroyed, partially-camouflaged Japanese Type 91 105mm howitzer as it was about to fire on the American troops on Luzon in January 1945. This enemy field artillery piece had a maximal firing range of almost 12,000 yards and served in all Pacific locales and on the Asian mainland. *(NARA)*

(**Above**) A patrol of US 37th Infantry Division soldiers traverses dense brush and encounters a disabled Type 89 *I-Go* medium Japanese tank of the IJA 2nd Armoured Division in northern Luzon in June 1945. The Type 89 had a short-barrelled 57mm Type 90 turret for knocking out pillboxes and enemy fortifications as well two 6.5mm Type 91 MGs, one in the hull and one in the turret's rear. *(NARA)*

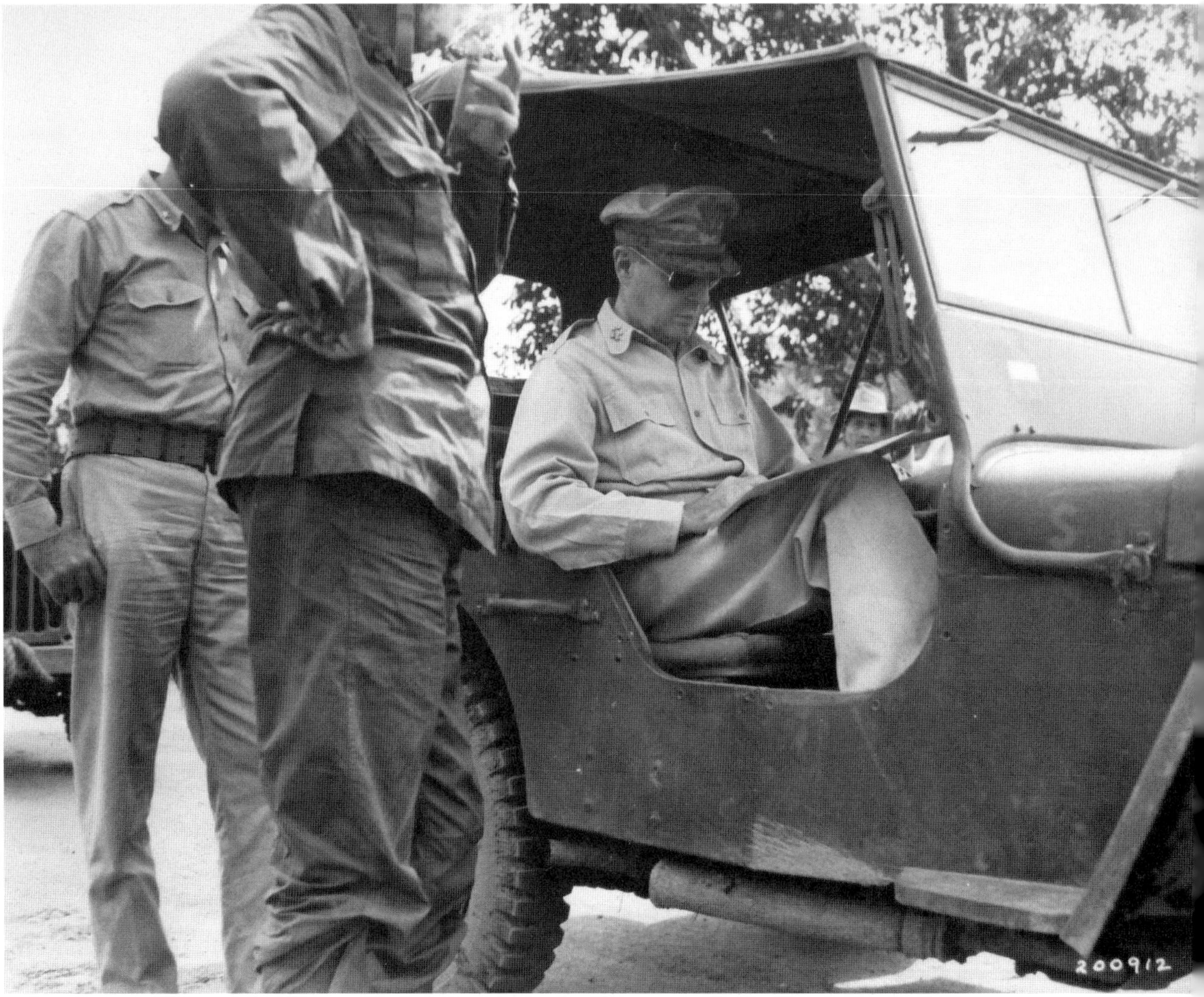
200912

(**Above**) General MacArthur is seen here reviewing maps in his jeep at Camiling on Luzon on 20 January 1945. Days later, intelligence reports emerged of massacred American PoWs at the Puerto Princesa camp on Palawan Island from a handful of prisoners that escaped the atrocity. MacArthur and Krueger feared that a similar fate awaited the estimated 500 American PoWs in the Cabanatuan camp in eastern Luzon. On 28 January, Lieutenant Colonel Henry Mucci, commander of the 6th Ranger Battalion, led Company C reinforced with the 2nd Platoon of Company F on a behind-the-lines march towards the camp and a rendezvous with Filipino guerrillas. At dusk on 30 January, Mucci's force attacked the camp and liberated 512 PoWs for the loss of two Rangers killed and one wounded. *(NARA)*

(**Opposite, above**) The Cabanatuan PoW camp is shown here with gardens cultivated by the American prisoners. In 1942 Jim Geary, a West Point graduate, stands next to a well that served as the gardens' water source. Geary was later shipped with other able-bodied PoWs to Japan to either work on the docks or in mines on the Home Islands. *(NARA)*

(**Opposite, above**) Some of the 512 Cabanatuan PoW camp's American prisoners, who were well enough to walk, are seen here marching to rear area medical facilities and transport centres after being liberated by units of the US 6th Raider Battalion and Filipino guerrillas on 30 January 1945. Those too sick were transported in carabao-pulled carts or carried by Rangers. *(NARA)*

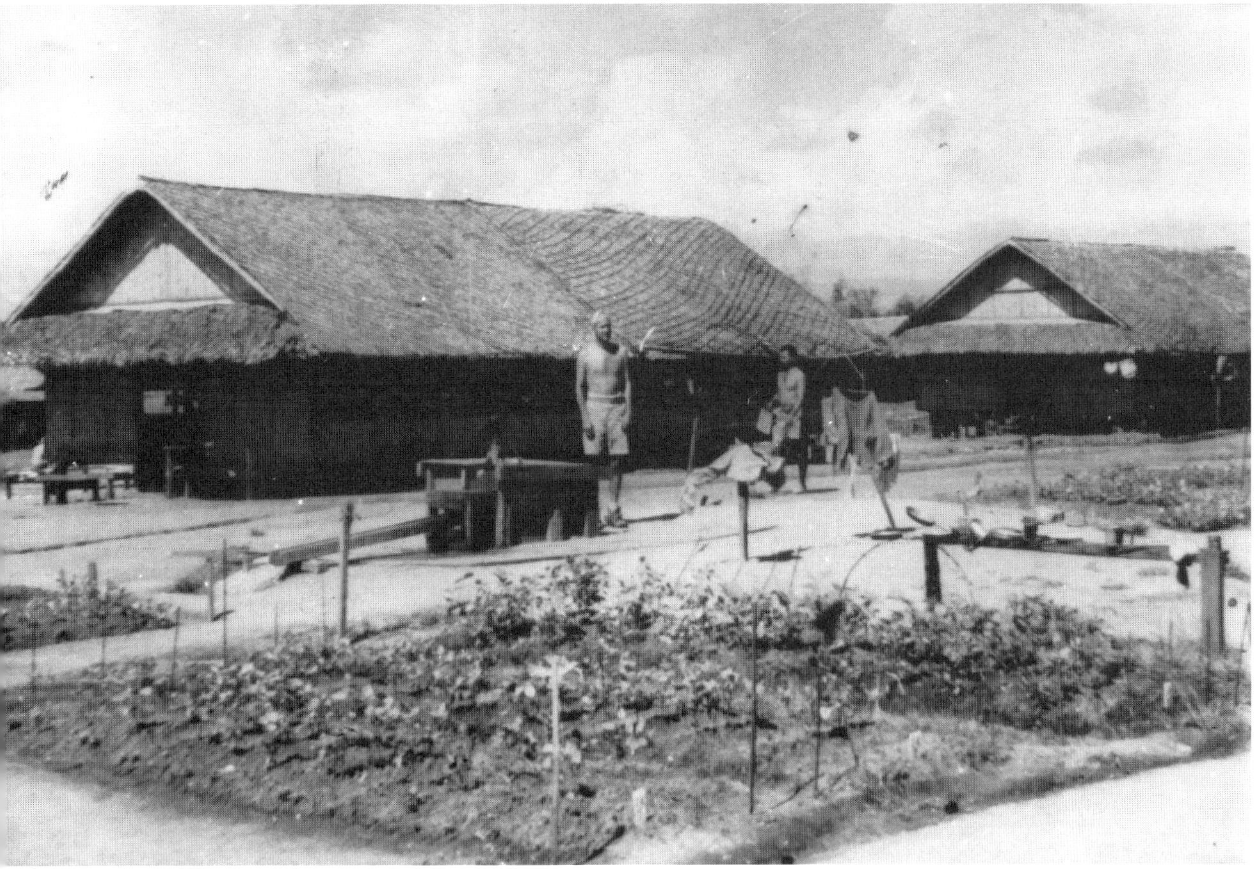

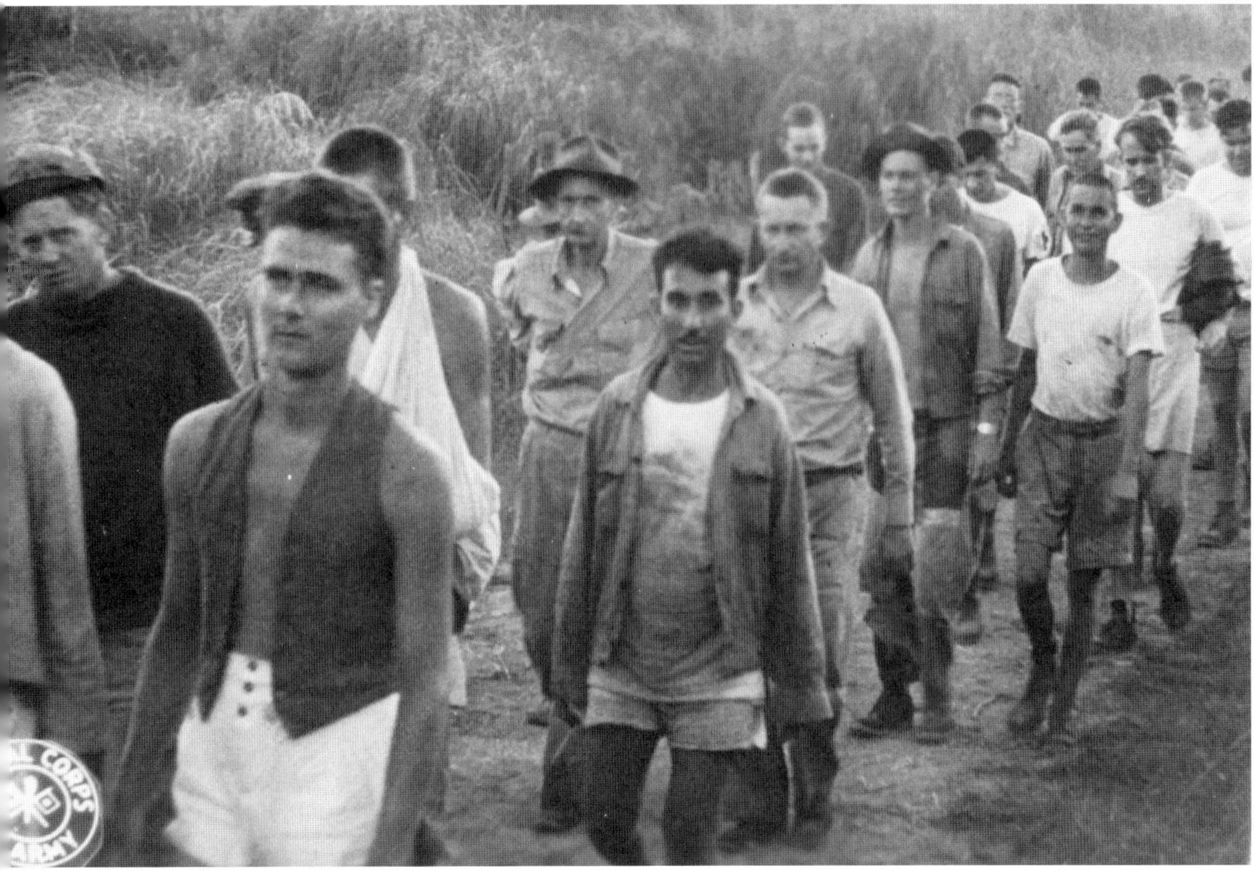

Chapter Six

Battles for Manila, Bataan and Corregidor 1945

After Sixth Army's I Corps blocked Yamashita's threat to Luzon's Central Plain and Eighth Army's XI Corps prevented the *Kembu* Group from moving south into the Bataan Peninsula, MacArthur urged Krueger to move on Manila with his XIV Corps' 37th Infantry Division on 1 February. The 1st Cavalry Division with attached armour also advanced south on 31 January. In Manila, there were approximately 13,000 IJN sailors of the Manila Defence Force under Rear Admiral Sanji Iwabuchi, in addition to the Southern Flank Detachment of IJA Major General Takashi Kobayashi's Manila Defence. Although Yamashita wanted a withdrawal of Japanese troops from Manila into the hills east of the city to add to the *Shimbu* Group, Iwabuchi decided to defend the capital on both sides of the Pasig River with pillboxes, mines and barricades, especially within the *Intramuros* section, comprising vastly thickened reinforced concrete walls of the old Spanish quarter that contained universities, commercial buildings and a stadium.

Two 1st Cavalry Division reinforced motorized regiments, the 5th and 8th Cavalry, rapidly moved south from Cabanatuan and entered Manila during the evening of 3 February. The 37th Infantry Division's 148th IR arrived the following day. Elements of Eichelberger's 11th Airborne Division were amphibiously landed at Nasugbu Bay 40 miles to Manila's south on 31 January. This Eighth Army force was to move north towards Manila and fight through enemy fortifications manned by IJN sailors and IJA soldiers of the Southern Flank Detachment to capture Nichols Field, which was accomplished on 12–13 February.

Sixth Army soldiers were amid urban, booby-trapped terrain with numerous hidden enemy low-calibre artillery and sniper positions. The 37th Division made an amphibious crossing of the Pasig River beginning on 7 February and five days later the 129th and 148th IRs reached the *Intramuros* after tenacious house-to-house fighting. Other crossings of the Pasig by the 129th IR along with the 37th Division's 145th IR entering the fortress were also conducted utilizing heavy-calibre FA ordnance and armour; however, Iwabuchi's *Intramuros* redoubt held out until 25 February.

Coincident with the combat in the capital city, the Eighth Army's 38th Division sealed off the Bataan Peninsula on 14 February. Movements by this division's 151st, 149th and 152nd IRs completed the capture of Bataan by 21 February. Following Manila's capture, Corregidor Island was amphibiously assaulted by the 3rd Battalion of the 34th Infantry Division and also attacked during a daytime 503rd PIR parachute drop, both on 16 February. Fighting on the island ended on 27 February and MacArthur returned on 7 March for flag-raising ceremonies. XI Corps then reduced three Manila Bay islands: Caballo, El Fraile and Carabao, all housing heavy-calibre naval guns. Cavite, situated on Manila Bay's southern shore, was also seized as it was bypassed by the 11th Airborne Division earlier in its drive towards Manila and Nichols Field.

American infantrymen cross over tram tracks in Manila on 7 February 1945 with many Filipinos among them. Fighting erupted in the capital city when Rear Admiral Sanji Iwabuchi, the commander of the IJN Manila Naval Defence Force, disobeyed Yamashita's order and contested the US Sixth Army's entry into Manila. Iwabuchi's forces committed numerous atrocities, killing thousands of Manila's civilians. *(NARA)*

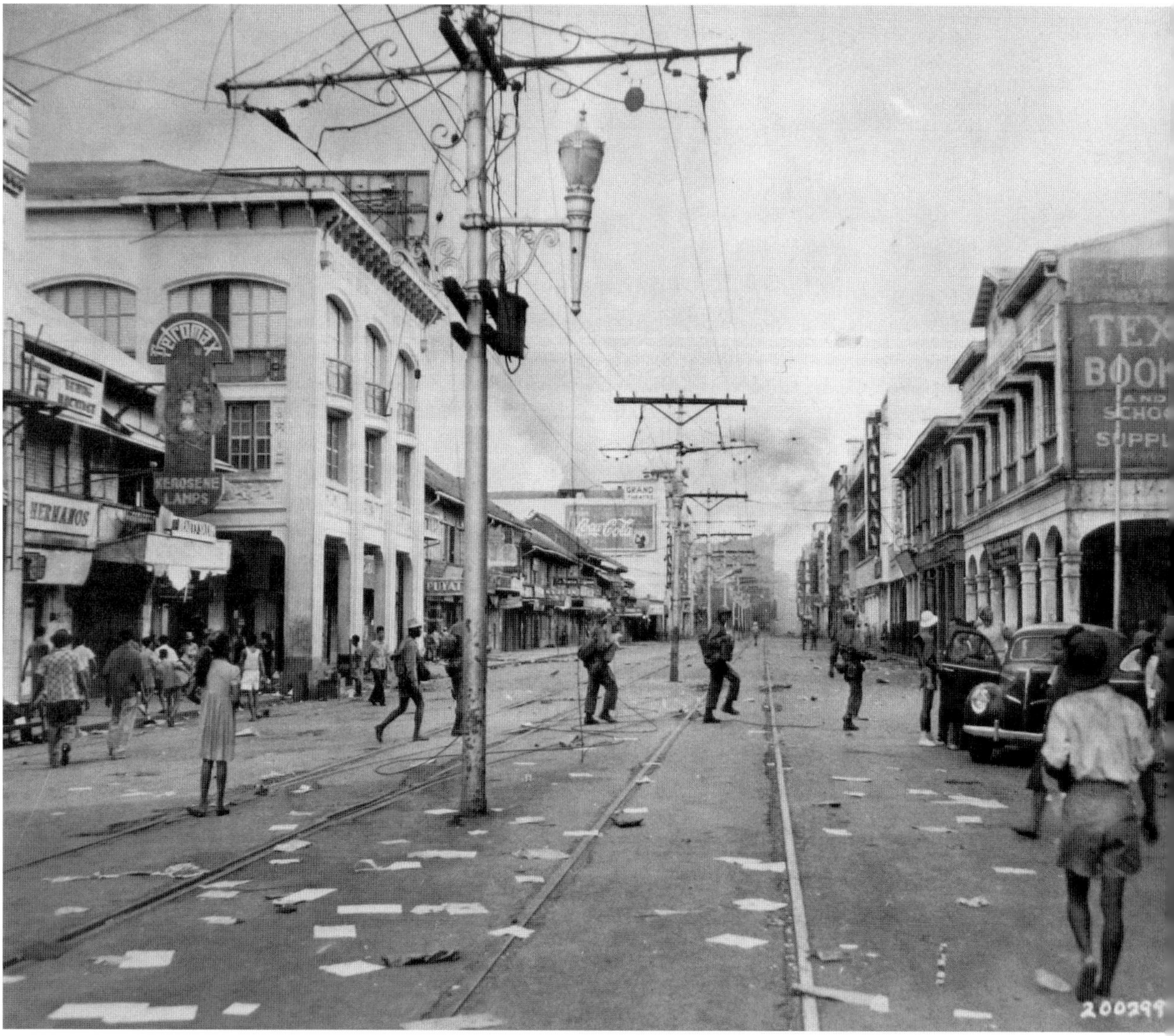
KEROSENE LAMPS
HERMANOS
200299

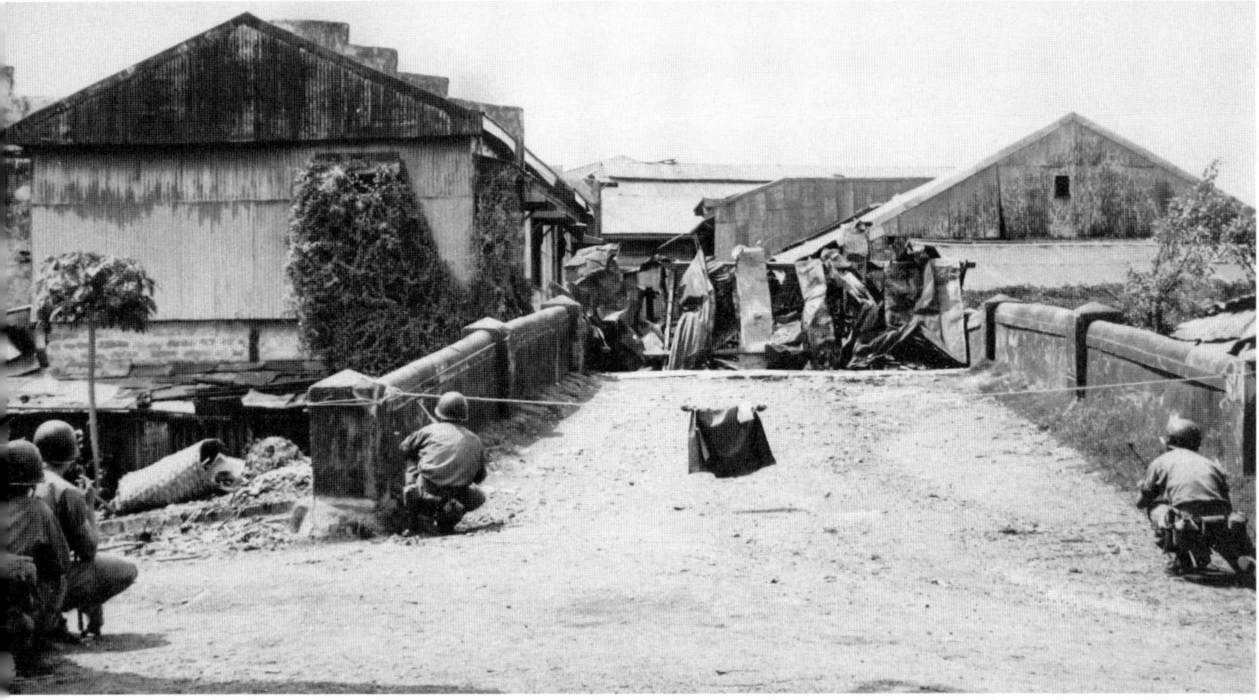

US 37th Infantry Division soldiers reconnoitre a barricaded Manila road bridge on 6 February 1945. Obstructed roads and bridges as well as Japanese sniping delayed this division's entry into Manila; however, the Pasig River was reached and the Bilibid Prison liberated to set free more than 1,000 Allied internees held captive there since early 1942. *(NARA)*

An American 37mm AT gun crew fires an HE round at a Japanese MG position in the church tower (far background) on 20 February 1945. Although this weapon was obsolete in the ETO, its portability and array of HE, AP and canister made it a useful piece of ordnance in the Pacific against Japanese fortified positions and massed infantry. *(NARA)*

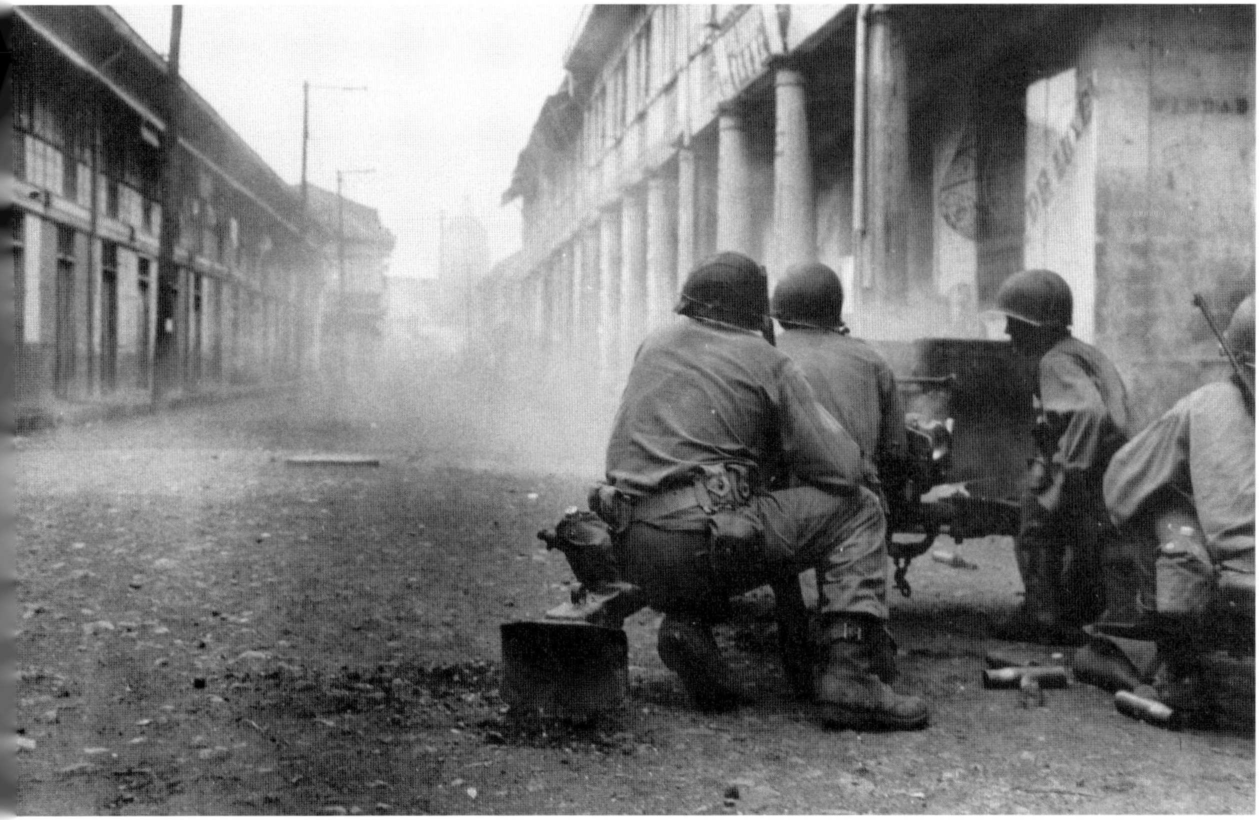

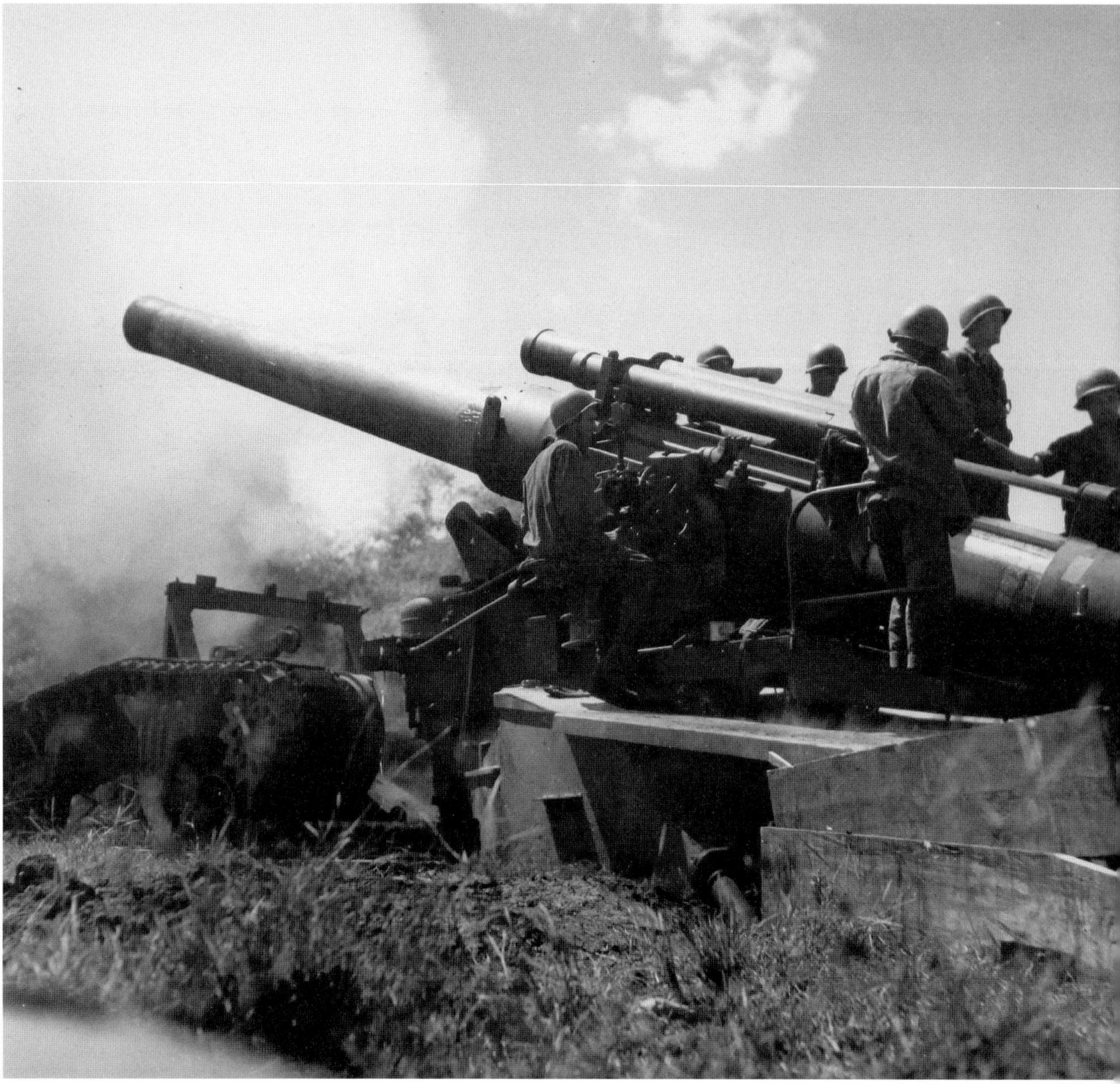

(**Above**) A US FA 240mm M1 howitzer blasts a Manila earthquake-proof building as Sixth Army troops prepare to storm the *Intramuros* section of the capital across the Pasig River from the city. The 240mm M1 howitzer was the most powerful piece of ordnance deployed by American FA units during the war. Its crew of fourteen was able to fire a 360lb HE shell over 25,000 yards and was useful against heavily-fortified enemy targets in both the ETO and Pacific.

(**Opposite, above**) A US 155mm shell explodes in front of the Tetran Building within Manila's *Intramuros* section on 17 February 1945. The Pasig River is seen in the foreground. *(NARA)*

(**Opposite, below**) Elements of the 37th Division's 148th IR amphibiously cross the Pasig River on 7 February 1945 as the Japanese destroyed all usable bridges. The division's 129th IR crossed at another site. The two IRs participated in a house-to-house struggle to reach the *Intramuros* section by 12 February 1945. *(NARA)*

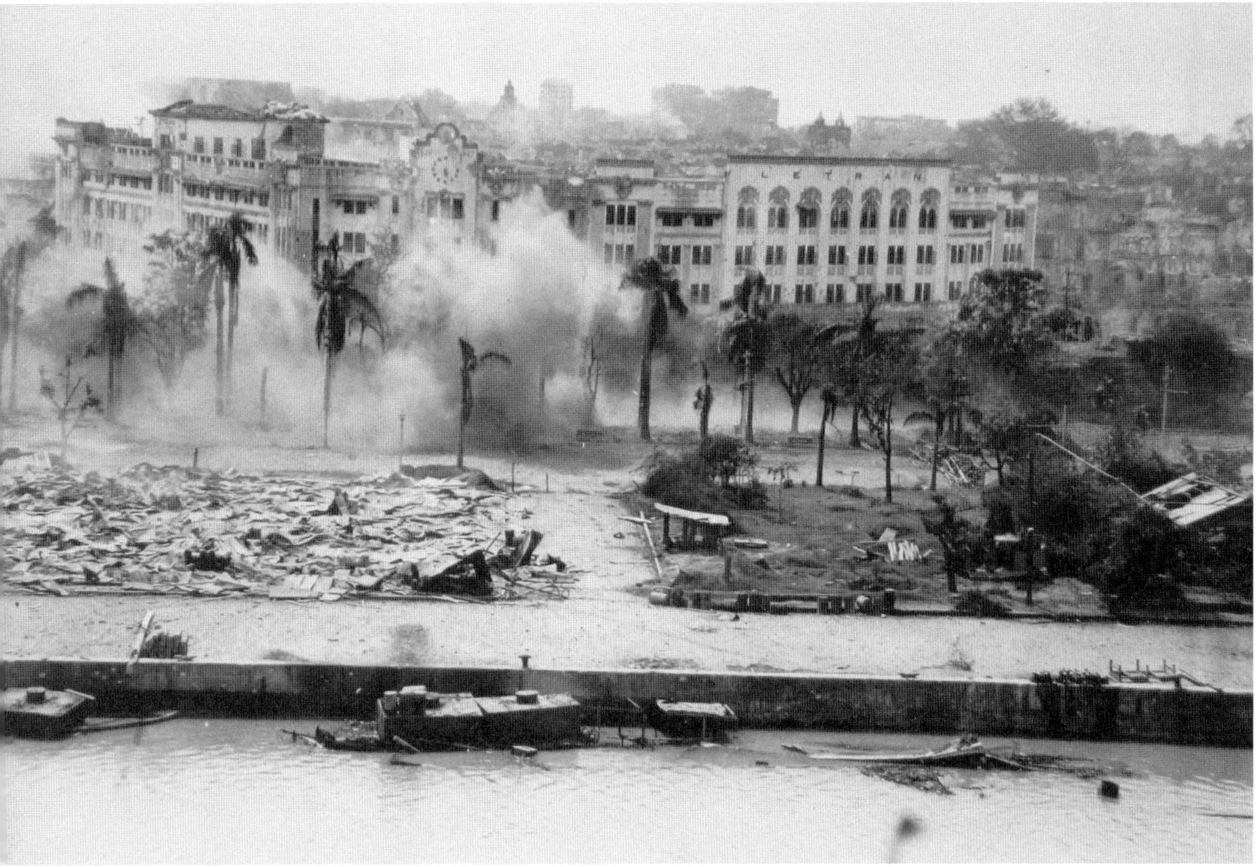
LETRAN
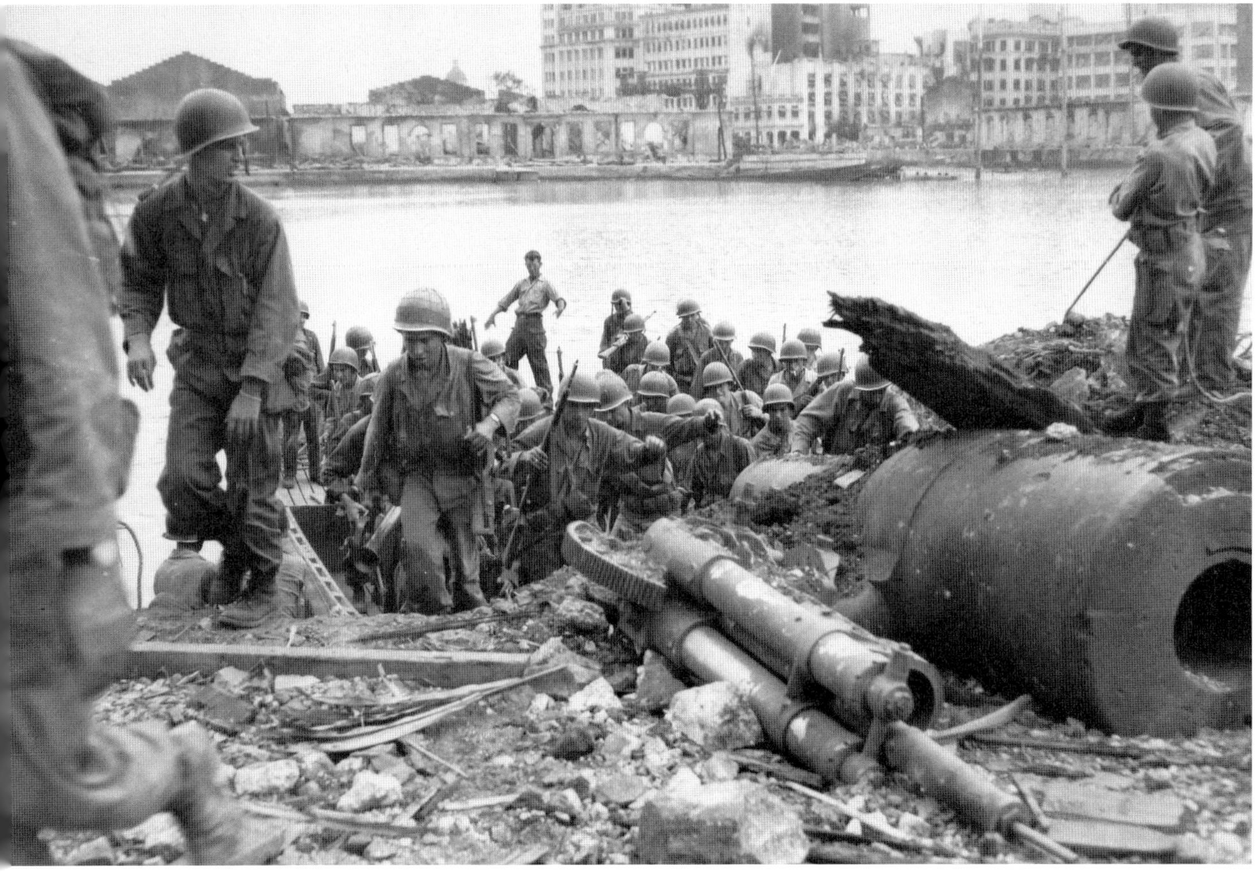

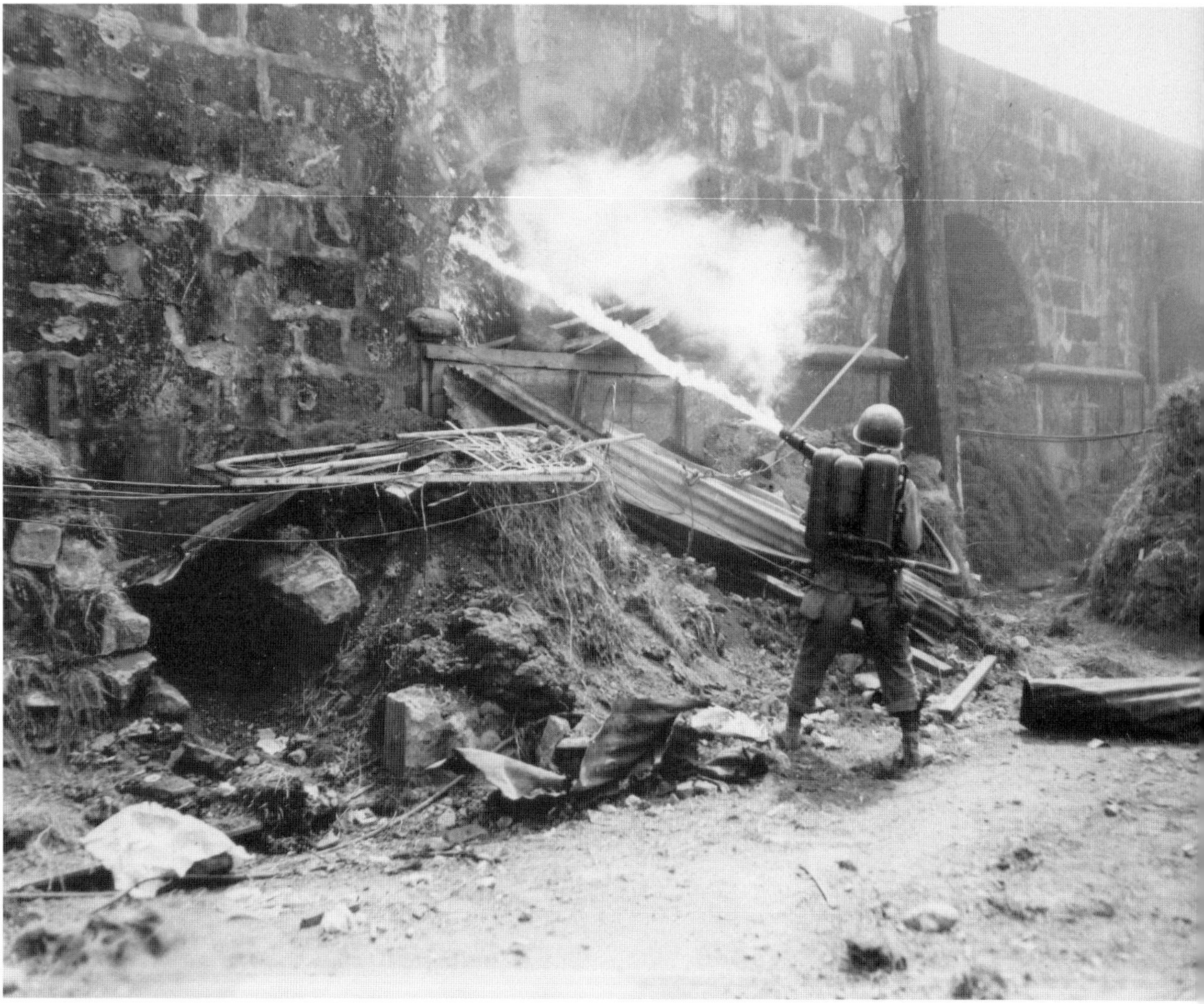

(**Above**) An American soldier is seen here wearing a three-tank M2-2 flame-thrower. Two tanks housed 4 gallons of combustible fuel, while the third contained nitrogen propellant. The soldier shoots a burst of flame into a barricaded archway of the *Intramuros* section. All three regiments of the 37th Infantry Division attacked Rear Admiral Iwabuchi's final redoubt from different tangents. The 145th IR with tank and FA support attacked the north-west corner of the *Intramuros* while the 129th IR crossed the Pasig River near the Government Mint to attack the northern sector. The 148th IR combated the suicidal IJN defenders near the Legislative and Finance buildings near the *Intramuros*' south-east, which fell on 25 February. *(NARA)*

(**Opposite, above**) A 37th Division's 129th IR soldier runs towards a Manila building in the Ermita District, which was a centre for finance and higher education, on 14 February 1945. Ermita was the scene of horrific massacres of Filipinos with more than 75 per cent of this area destroyed during the Battle of Manila. The 37th Division cleared southern Manila from the Pasig River south and then turned west and moved towards Manila Bay, seizing the districts of Pandacan, Paco and Ermita. *(NARA)*

(**Opposite, below**) US 37th Division riflemen pour gunfire into Japanese positions across the Pasig River from a partially-destroyed rooftop parapet. Their weapons included BARs, 0.30in M1 carbines and 0.30-06 M1 Garand rifles. *(NARA)*

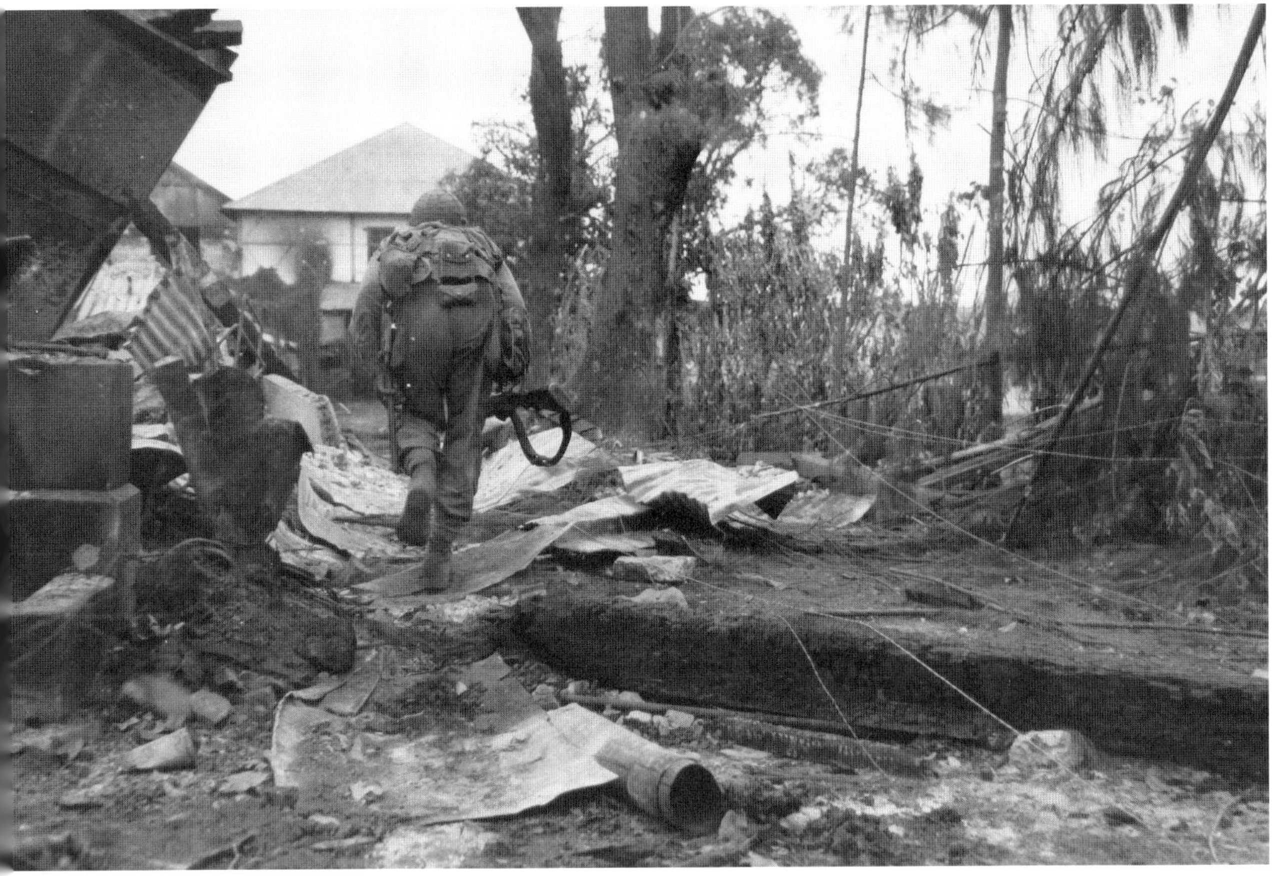

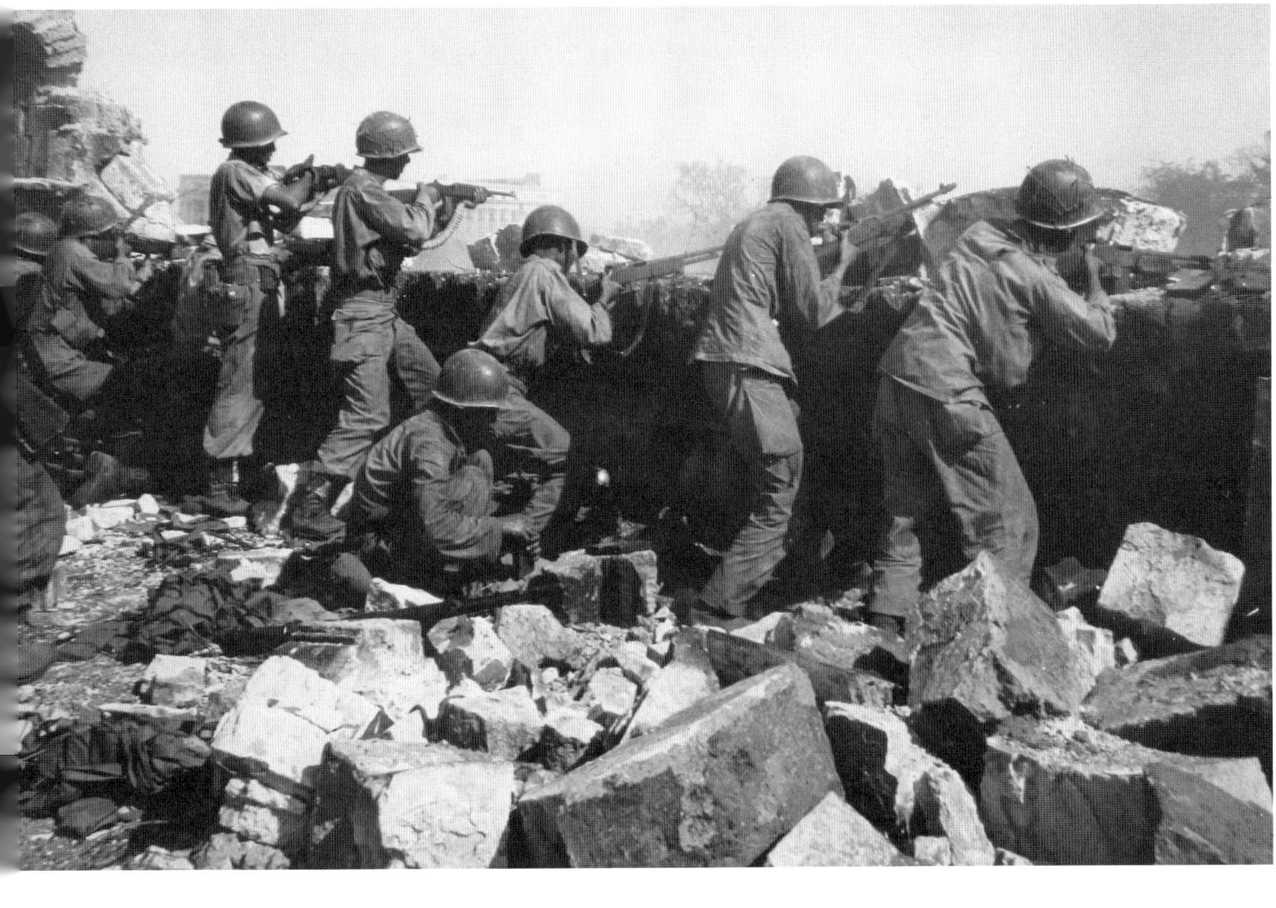

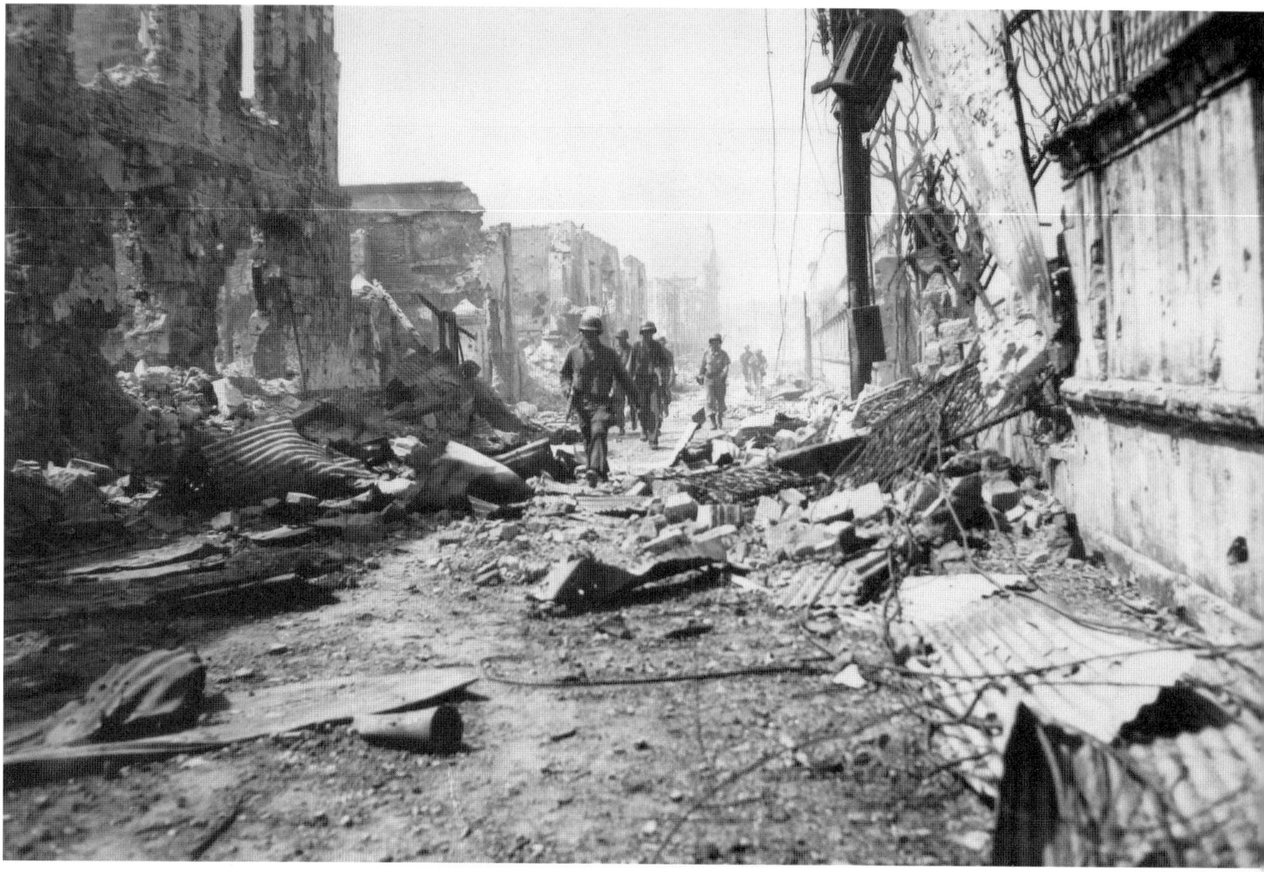

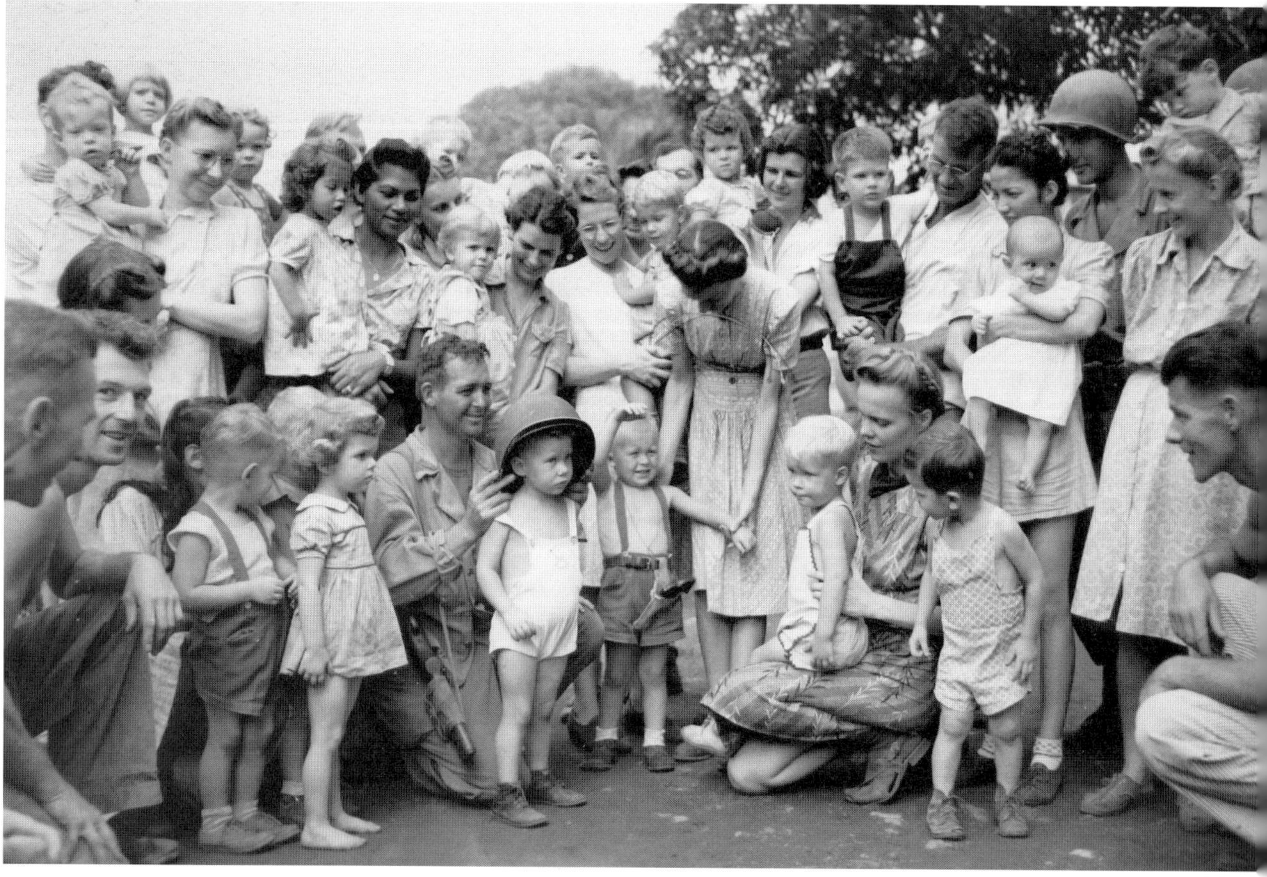

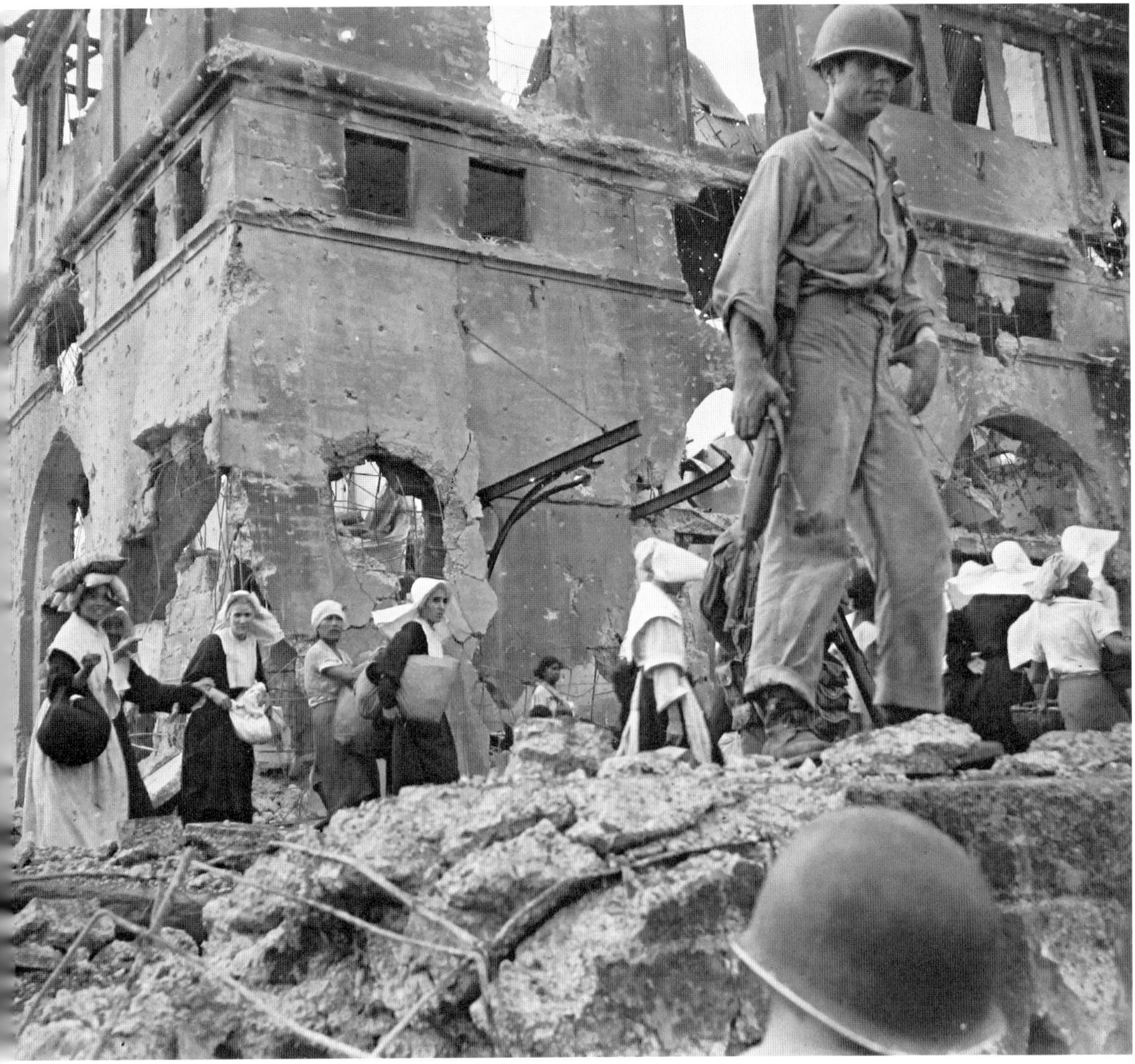

(**Opposite, above**) A platoon of American soldiers moves into the *Intramuros* section on 23 February 1945, two days before the final Japanese Manila redoubts fell. Near-complete devastation of this section's buildings is evident. *(NARA)*

(**Opposite, below**) Some 37th Division's 148th IR soldiers mingle on 5 February 1945 with some of the more than 1,000 Allied internees liberated from Manila's Bilibid Prison. The very young children were born in captivity. Also on 5 February, the 1st Cavalry Division's 8th Cavalry Regiment freed more than 3,500 internees from Santo Tomas University. *(NARA)*

(**Above**) American infantrymen escort nuns through Manila's rubble during the street fighting on 23 February 1945. The nuns and other Filipino refugees moved towards a boat landing on the Pasig River for evacuation from the *Intramuros* section. *(NARA)*

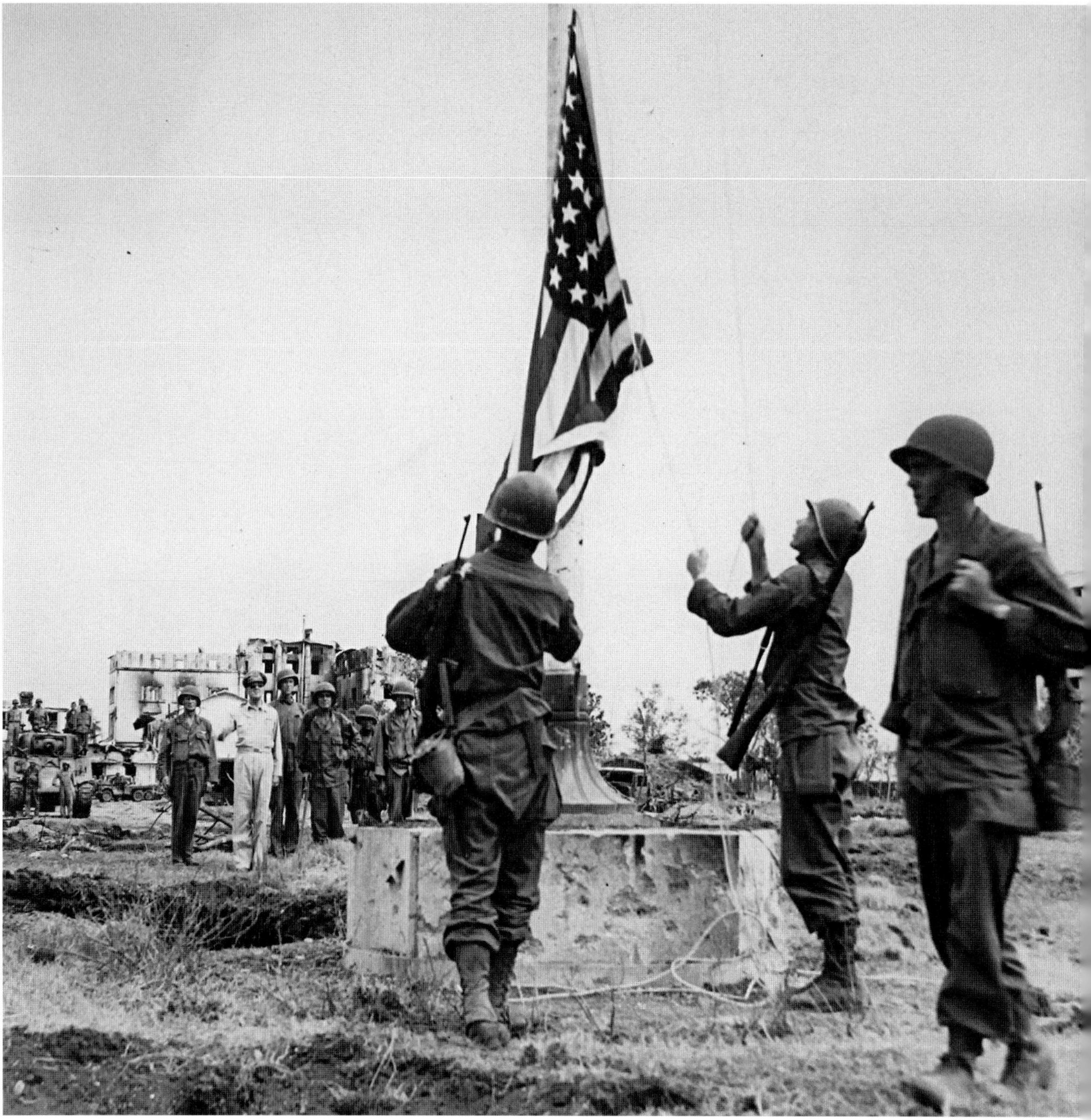

(**Opposite, above**) General MacArthur attends a flag-raising ceremony on the site of the Manila Hotel. MacArthur and his family lived in a luxurious penthouse atop the hotel before his evacuation to Corregidor on 24 December 1941. Manila was declared an 'Open City' in the hope that the 'Pearl of the Orient' would avoid destruction. *(NARA)*

(**Opposite, below**) Corregidor, the 1,735-acre island in Manila Bay, is under an 11th Airborne Division's 503rd PIR paratroop attack on 16 February 1945 with numerous white parachutes over the island's 'Topside' area. The destroyed American barracks – which the Japanese never rebuilt – and adjacent parade ground are visible (background left). From 23 January through to 16 February, Lieutenant General George Kenney's Fifth Air Force pummelled Corregidor with more than 3,000 tons of bombs. *(NARA)*

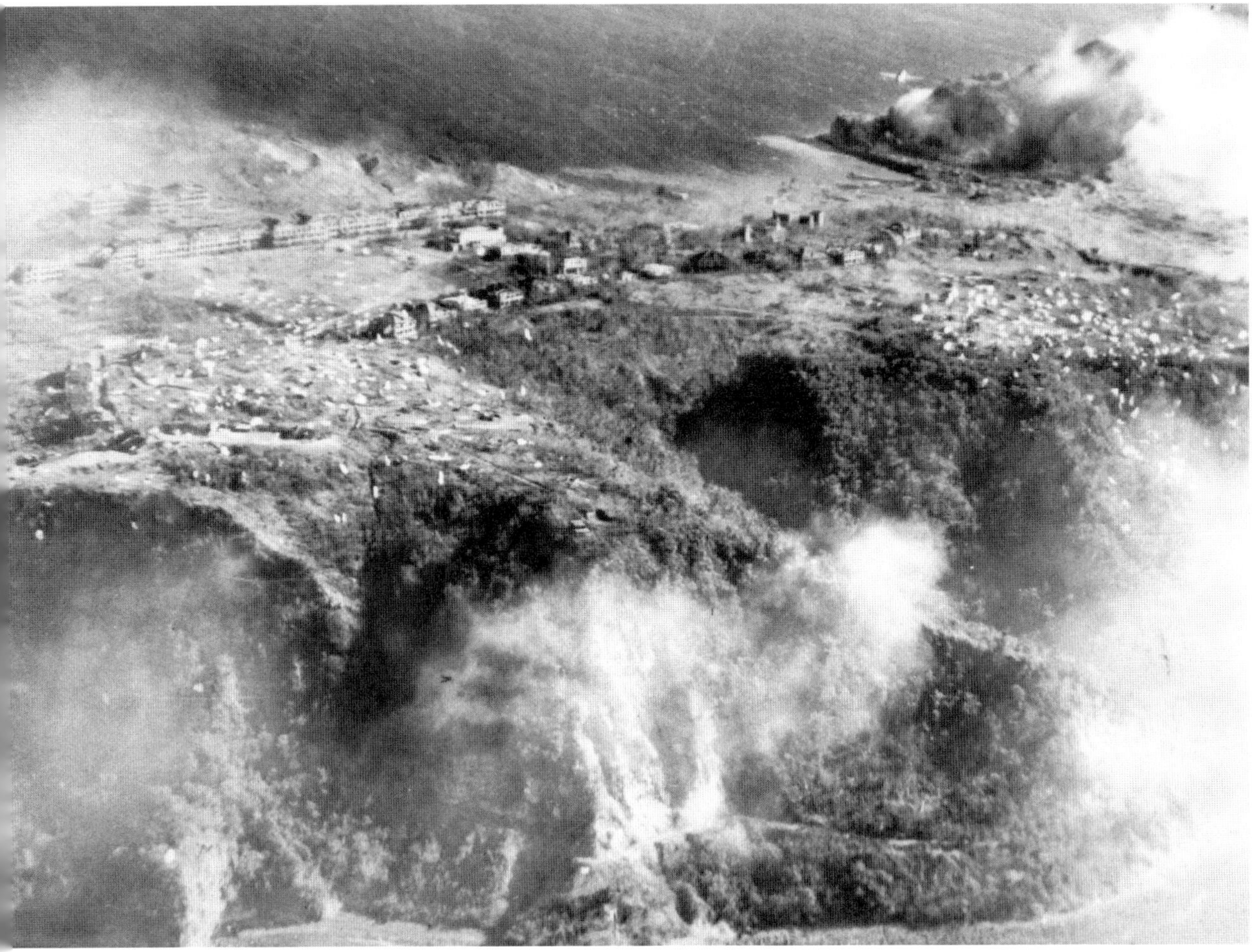

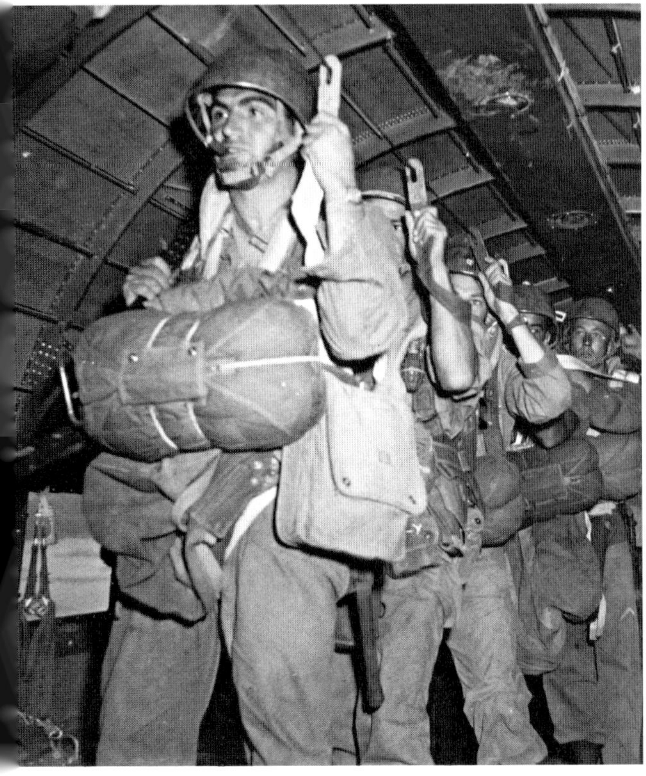

(**Left**) A C-47 twin-engined plane's interior transports members of the 503rd PIR to jump out onto Corregidor Island on 16 February 1945. The paratroopers' main parachute is connected to a metal line, which opened the parachute upon exiting the aircraft. An auxiliary parachute can be seen worn at waist level on each paratrooper. The heavy kit contains the paratroopers' weapons and gear to confront the enemy as light infantry upon landing. Army intelligence vastly underestimated that there were only 850 enemy IJA soldiers on Corregidor. More than 2,000 paratroopers of the 503rd PIR assaulted Corregidor that day with the regiment's 2nd Battalion making the initial drop onto the 'Topside' area at 1250 hours. In light of the successful aerial and amphibious landings, a third drop was cancelled and the 503rd PIR's third battalion would be brought in by boat on 17 February. *(NARA)*

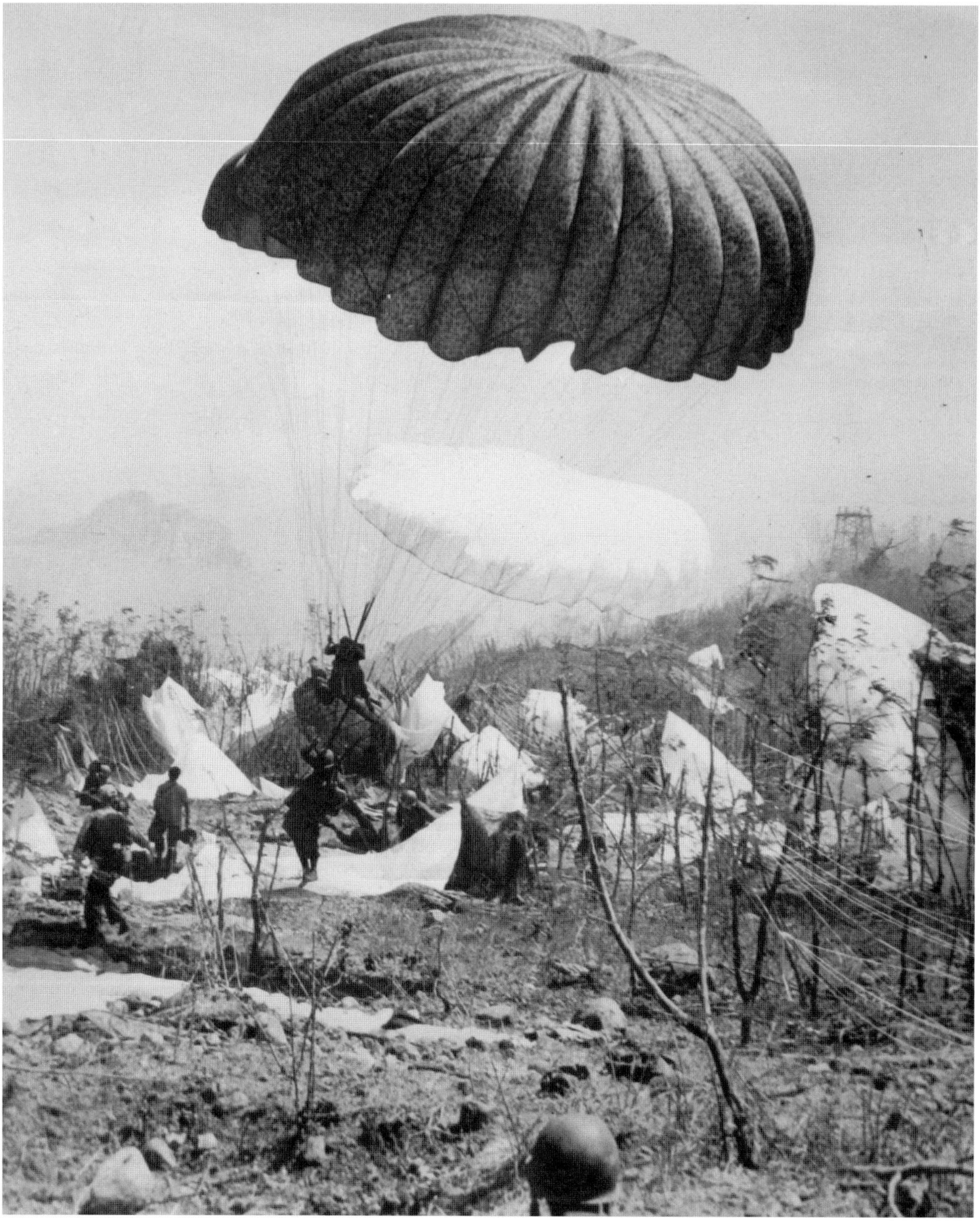

Parachutes festoon Topside's landscape where elements of the 11th Airborne Division's 503rd PIR descended from their transports during one of the two 'lifts' on 16 February 1945. After re-forming their units, the paratroopers found concealed Japanese pockets in caves and other fortified areas, causing a protracted battle. *(NARA)*

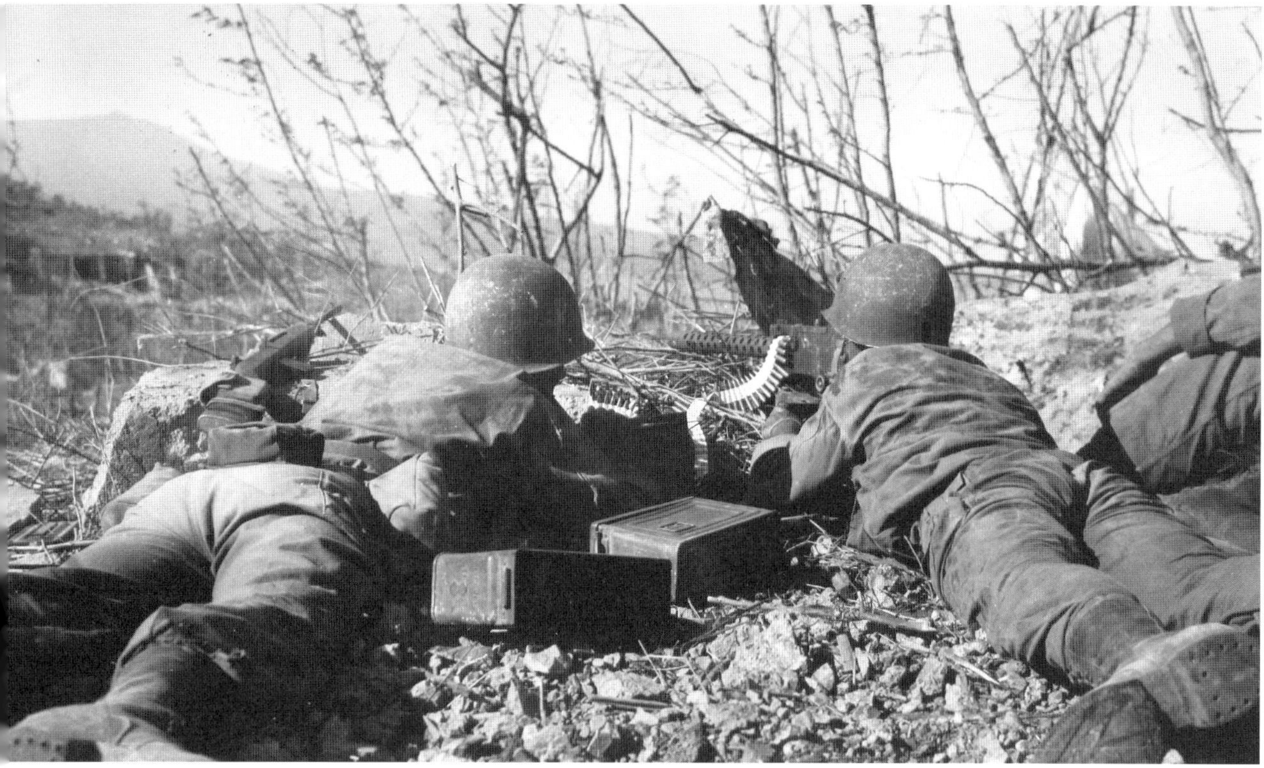

A 503rd PIR 0.30in-calibre LMG crew fires their weapon at Japanese soldiers within a fortified position (left background) in late February 1945. These paratroopers were combat veterans of the New Guinea, Leyte and Luzon campaigns. *(NARA)*

A USN attack transport approaches Corregidor Island's beach to simultaneously correspond with the 503rd PIR attack. At 1030 hours on 16 February 1945, the 24th Division's 34th IR's 3rd Battalion amphibiously assaulted Corregidor against no opposition on the island's south dock near Malinta Hill (background). *(NARA)*

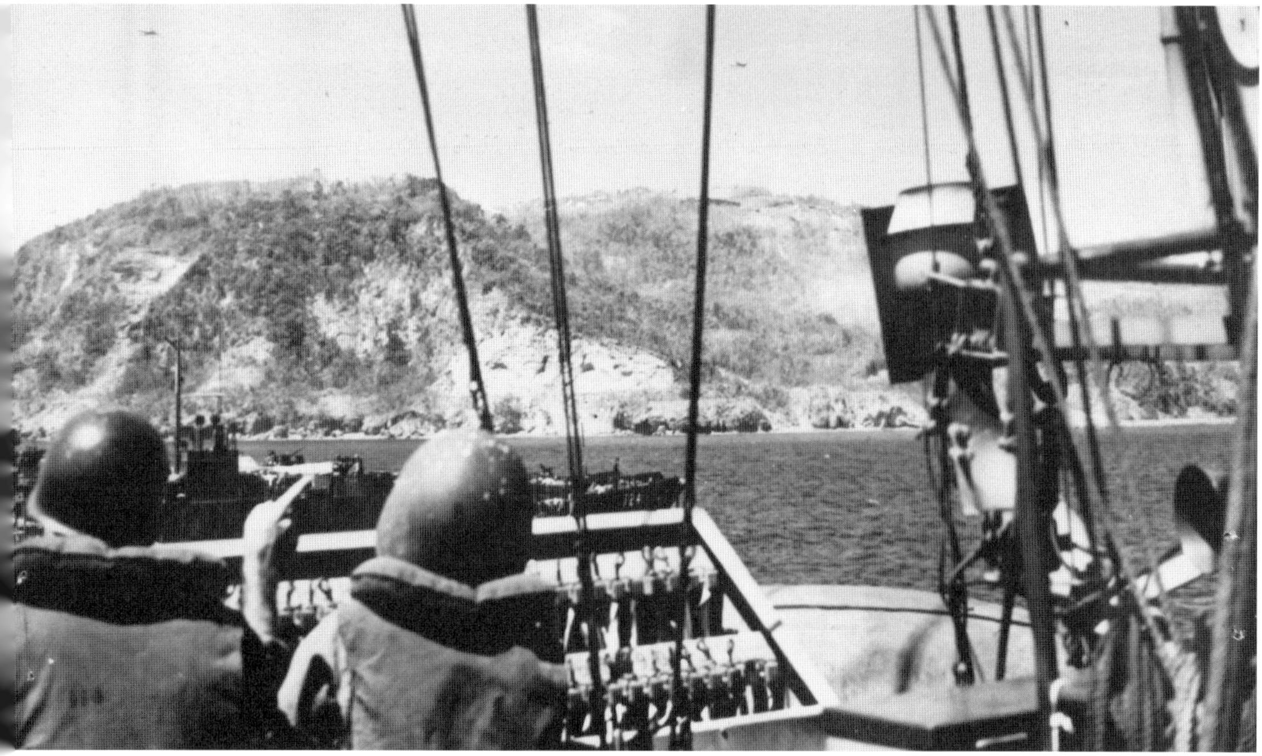

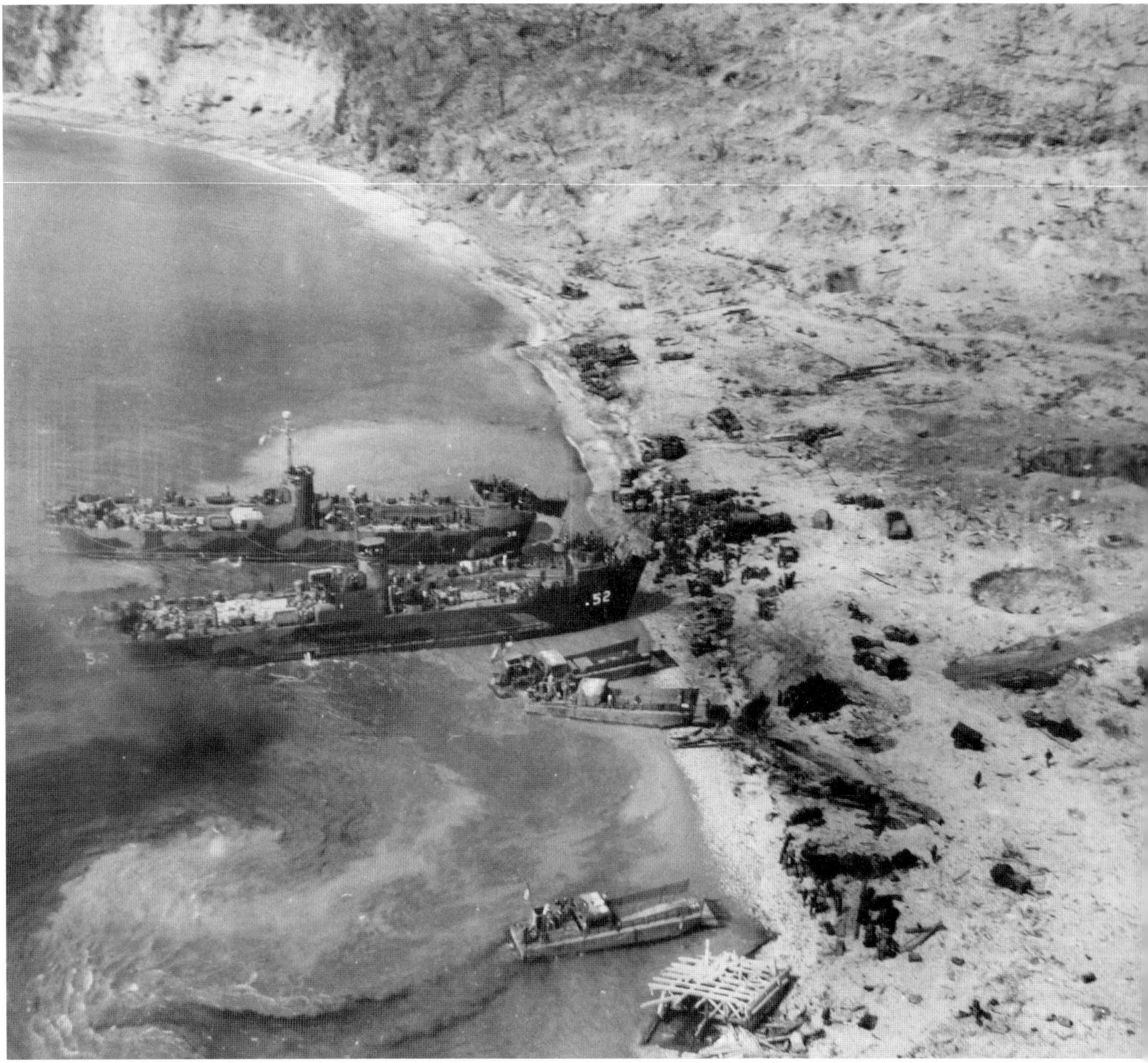

(**Above**) Two USN attack transports and smaller landing craft are seen here unloading matériel after the successful amphibious assault on Corregidor's south dock. The 1,000-man 3rd Battalion of the 34th IR quickly engaged the Japanese defenders hiding in their fortified positions. *(NARA)*

(**Opposite, above**) Soldiers from the 34th IR, 25th Division advance and fire their rifles at Japanese troops hiding in caves and rocky crevices on Corregidor during the third week of February 1945. Enemy sniping continued even up until MacArthur's arrival on the island on 2 March. *(NARA)*

(**Opposite, below**) A squad of 34th IR soldiers takes cover amid masonry debris inland from their landing area on Corregidor on 16 February 1945. The Japanese did not resist the amphibious assault, but many of the island's 5,000 defenders chose to sequester themselves in natural and man-made fortifications. However, some of the Japanese defenders attempted to re-take Topside with a *banzai* charge early on 17 February during which 500 enemy soldiers died in the five-hour fire-fight. *(NARA)*

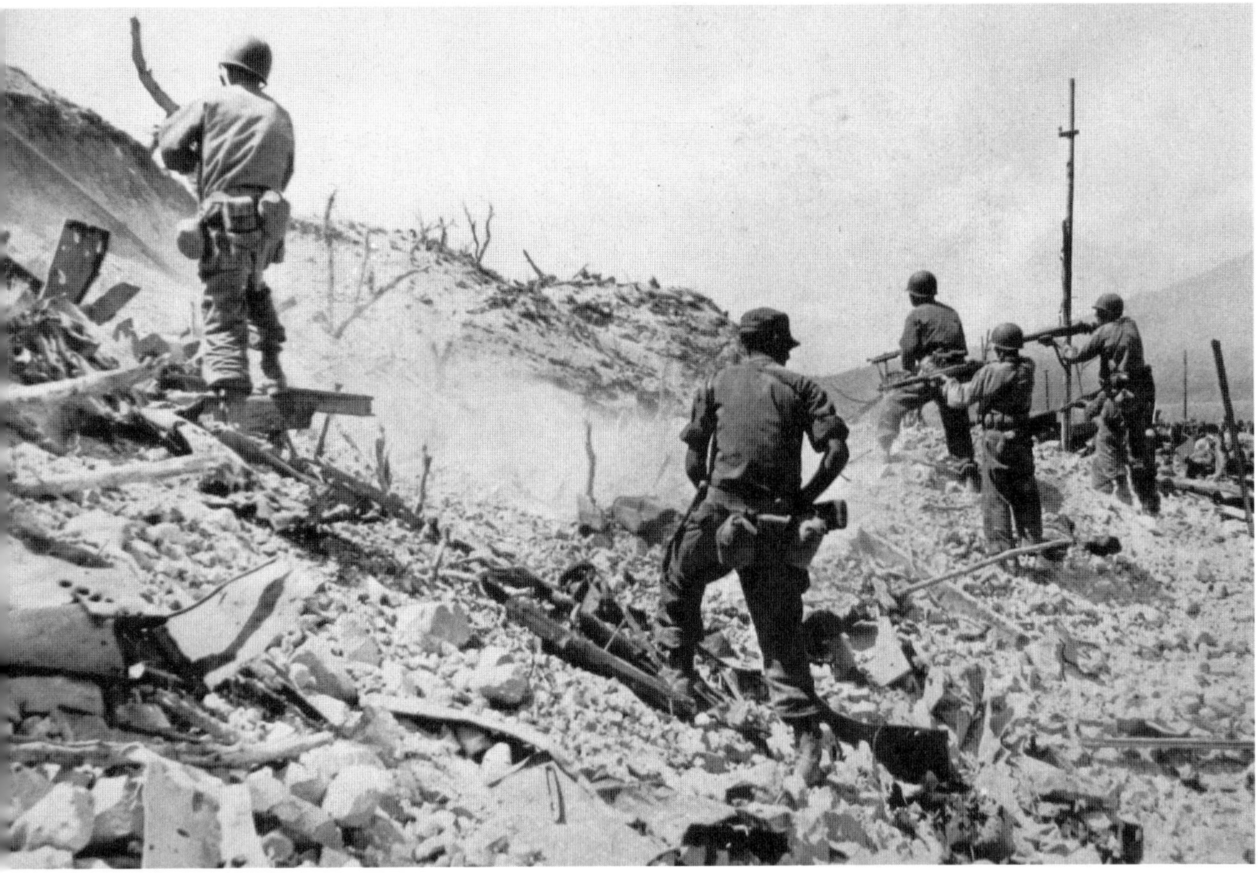

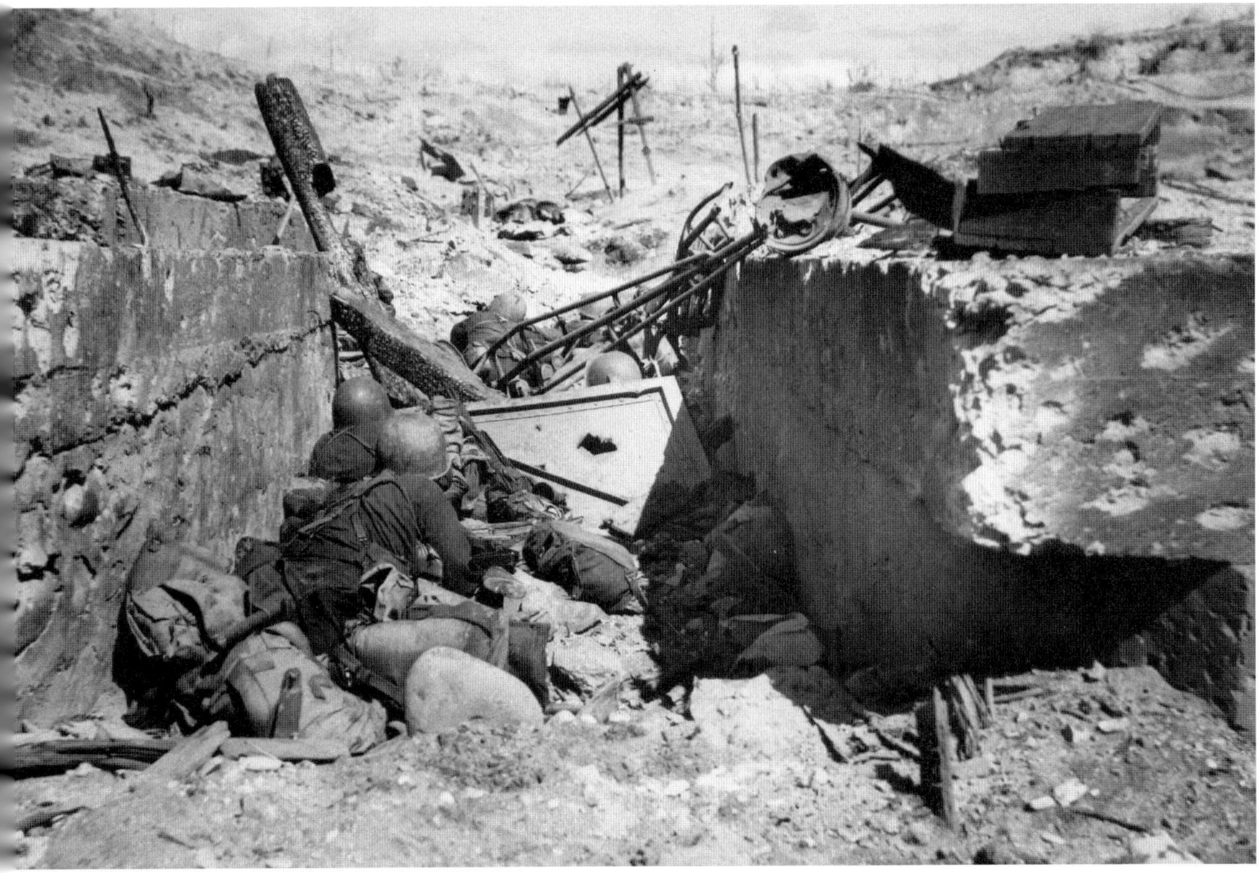

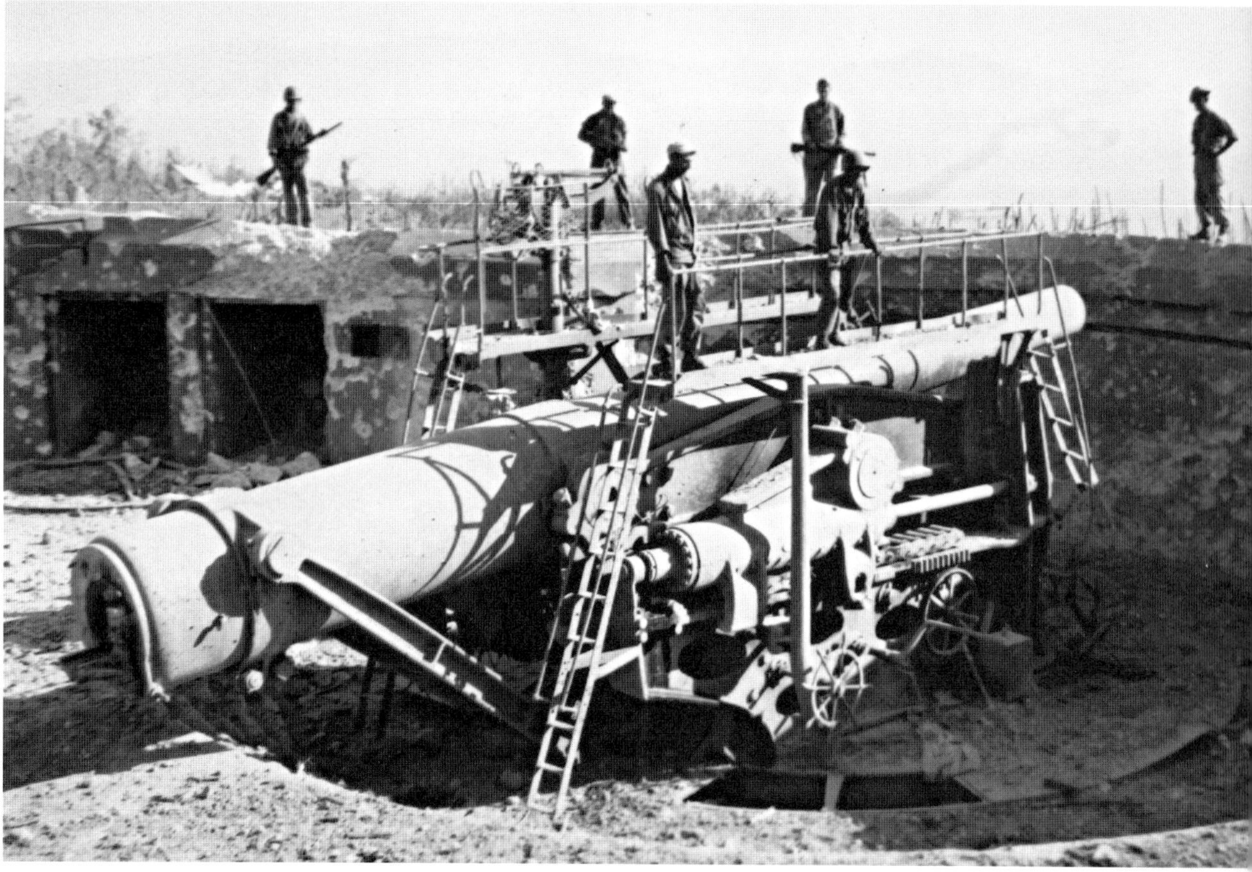

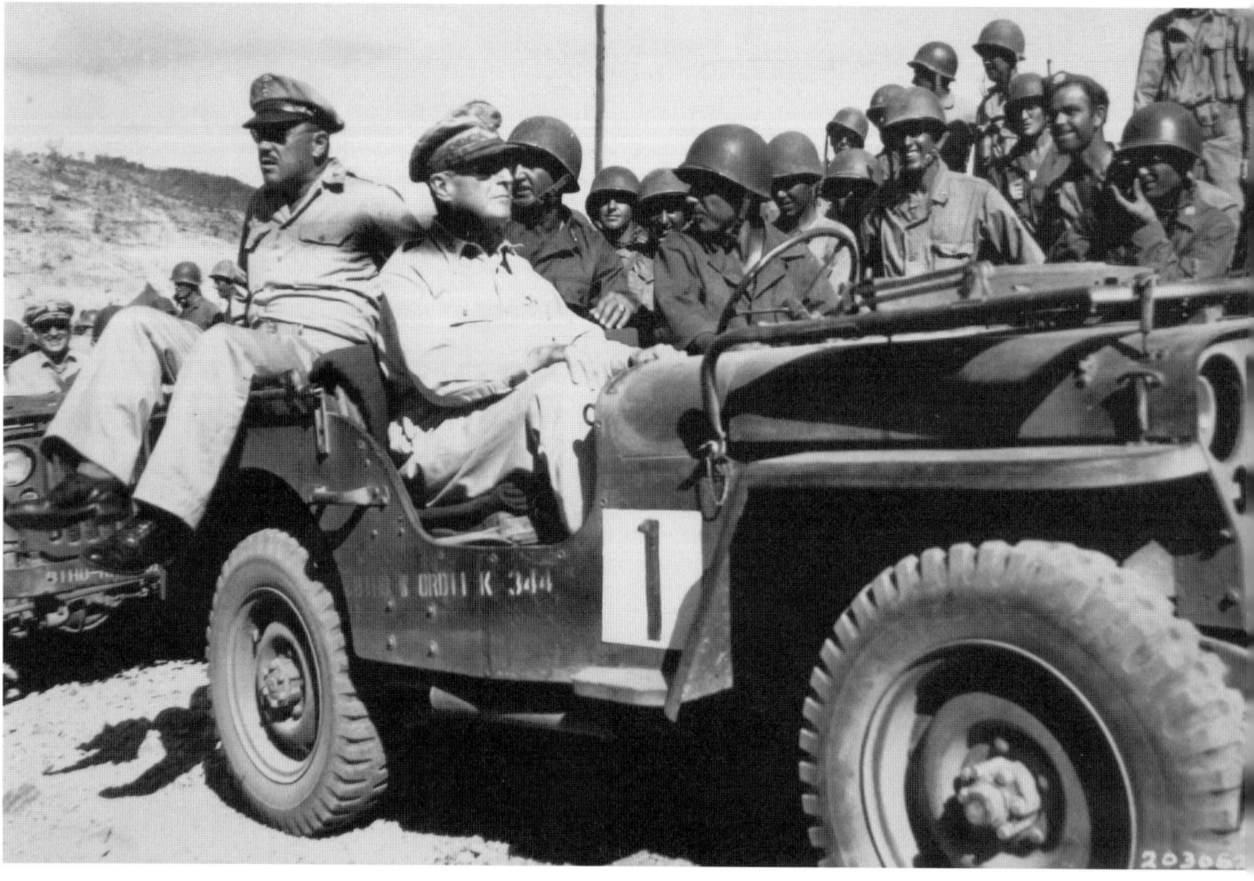
1

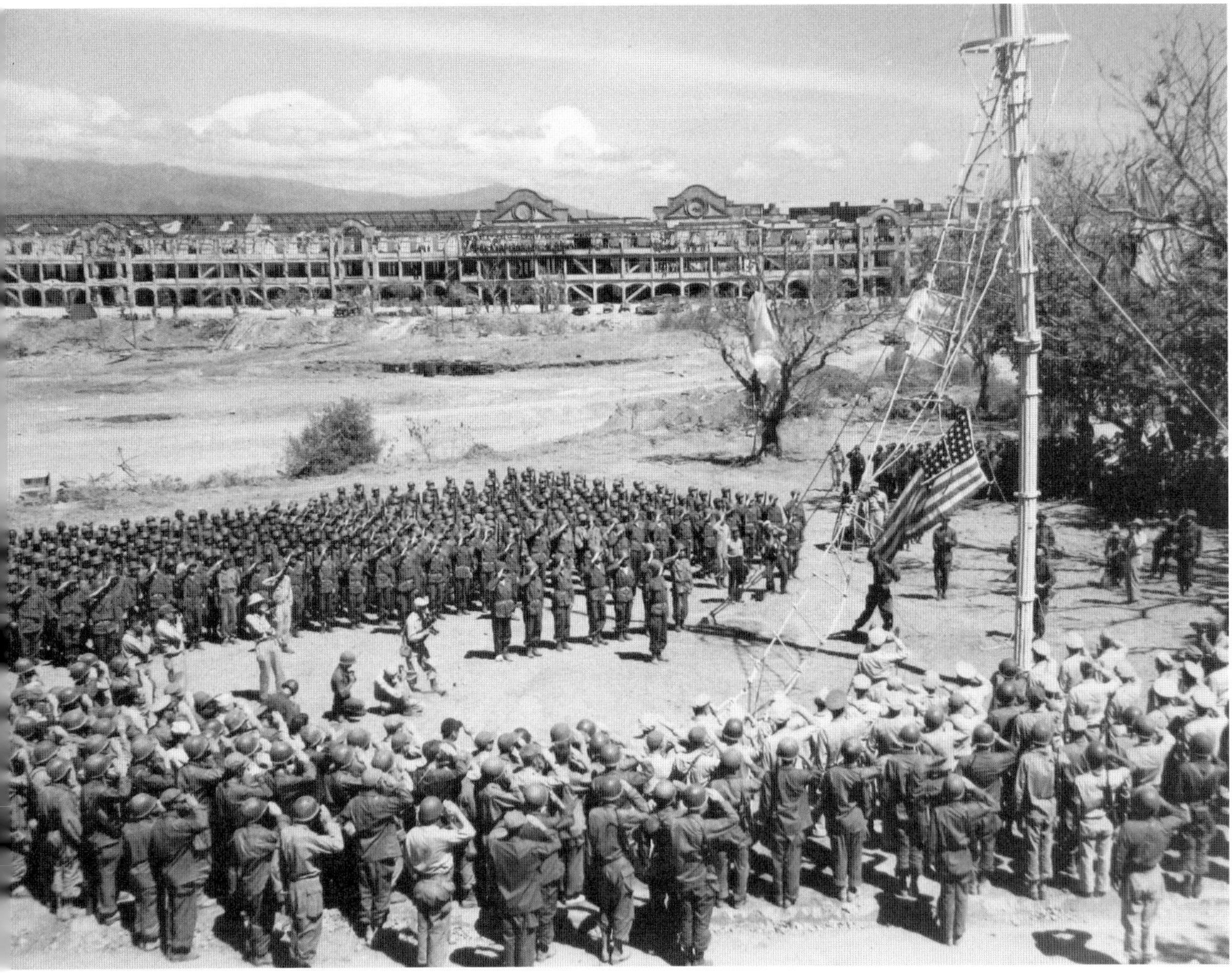

(**Opposite, above**) Soldiers from the 34th IR inspect a 12in heavy coastal gun at Battery Wheeler at Corregidor's south-western tip on 2 March 1945. The Japanese had captured this position shortly before Lieutenant General Wainwright's surrender in May 1942. Lieutenant General Homma amphibiously landed his Japanese forces on the eastern 'tail' of Corregidor between Kindley Field and Battery Denver on 6 May 1942 before advancing with some armour towards Malinta Tunnel, precipitating the American surrender to prevent a slaughter that same day. *(NARA)*

(**Opposite, below**) General MacArthur is shown here during his jeep tour of the recaptured Corregidor Island on 2 March 1945. He visited Battery Wheeler and the jeep convoy began its ascent up Corregidor to the Topside area, reaching it near noon. On the way towards Topside, MacArthur was greeted by victorious 503rd PIR paratroopers and soldiers of the 34th IR's 3rd Battalion as well as burning pyres of Japanese corpses. Enemy losses were 4,500 killed and 19 captured, which again reflected the *bushido* code of the Japanese soldier. American casualties were 200 killed and more than 700 wounded. *(NARA)*

(**Above**) General MacArthur salutes the American flag with elements of the 503rd PIR as it is raised up the flagpole on 2 March 1945 on Topside's parade ground near the destroyed army barracks (background). MacArthur addressed Colonel George Jones, a class of 1936 West Point graduate: 'Have your troops hoist the colors to its peak and let no enemy ever haul them down again.' It was almost three years since the Japanese had pulled down the 'Stars and Stripes' after Wainwright surrendered the island fortress in May 1942. *(NARA)*

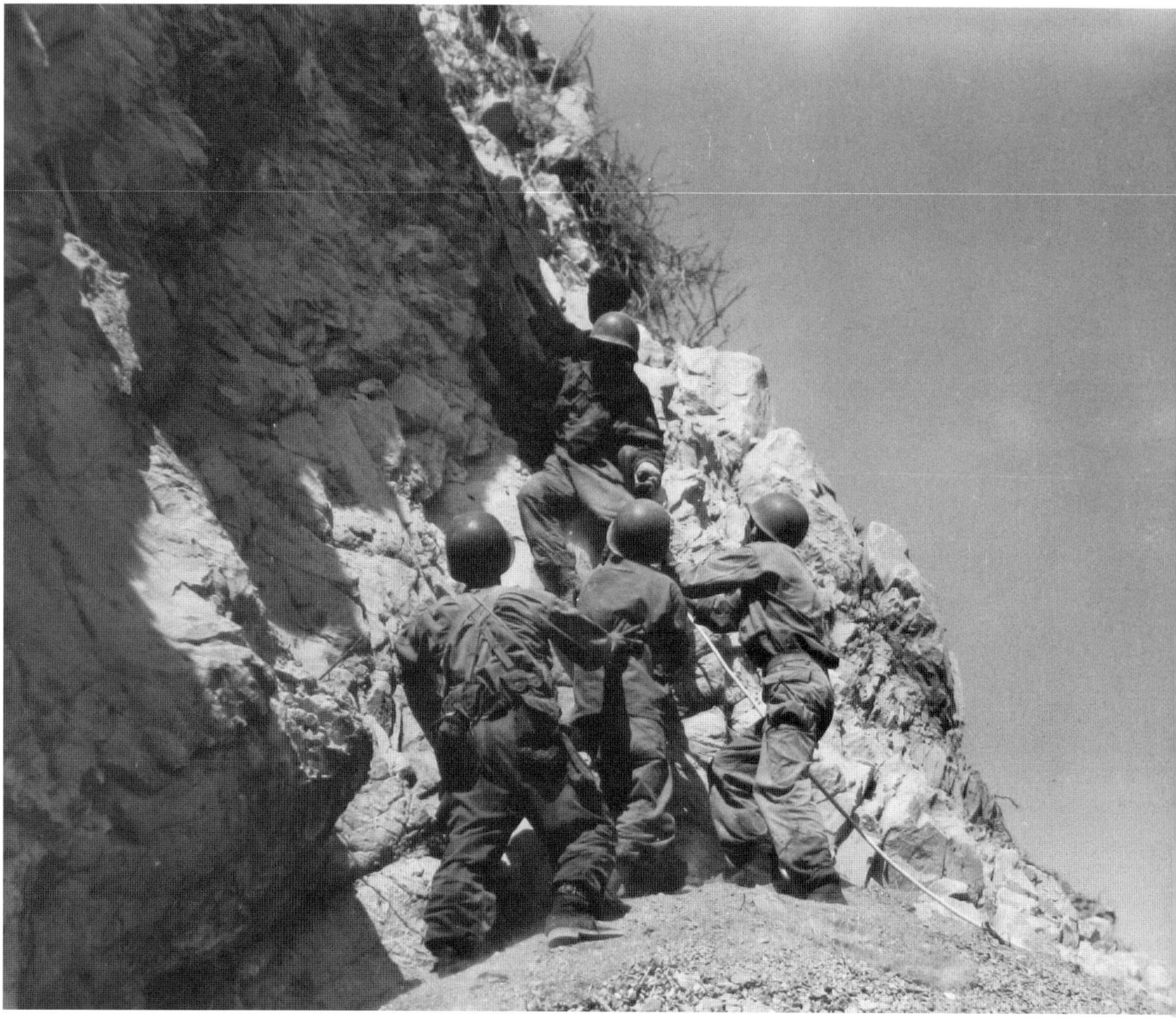

(**Above**) Soldiers of the 38th Division's 2nd Battalion, 151st IR climb sheer rock faces to fight entrenched Japanese soldiers on Caballo Island (also known as Fort Hughes) in Manila Bay on 27 March 1945. US Army engineers ignited diesel oil with WP grenades to destroy enemy-held caves. The Japanese occupying Caballo Island were wiped out by 13 April. *(NARA)*

(**Opposite, above**) A 0.30in-calibre LMG of the 3rd Battalion, 158th RCT ('The Bushmasters') covers a Luzon bridge at Batangas on the island's southern portion on 13 March 1945. This formation landed at Lingayen Gulf on 11 January and occupied Damortis on 13 January while attached to the 43rd Infantry Division (3 January to 3 March). On 4 March the 158th RCT was attached to the 11th Airborne Division and was responsible for taking Lipa and Batangas. *(NARA)*

(**Opposite, below**) A member of a bazooka team from Company K, 3rd Battalion, 161st RCT, 25th Infantry Division fires his rocket to blast out Japanese soldiers from their fortified positions. This action took place on 23 March 1945 near the Balete Pass, a key point on the road to Baguio, the Philippines summer capital. Baguio was where Yamashita headquartered his Fourteenth Area Army. The US Sixth Army's 33rd and 37th Divisions, with attached armour, converged on Baguio on 27 April. *(NARA)*

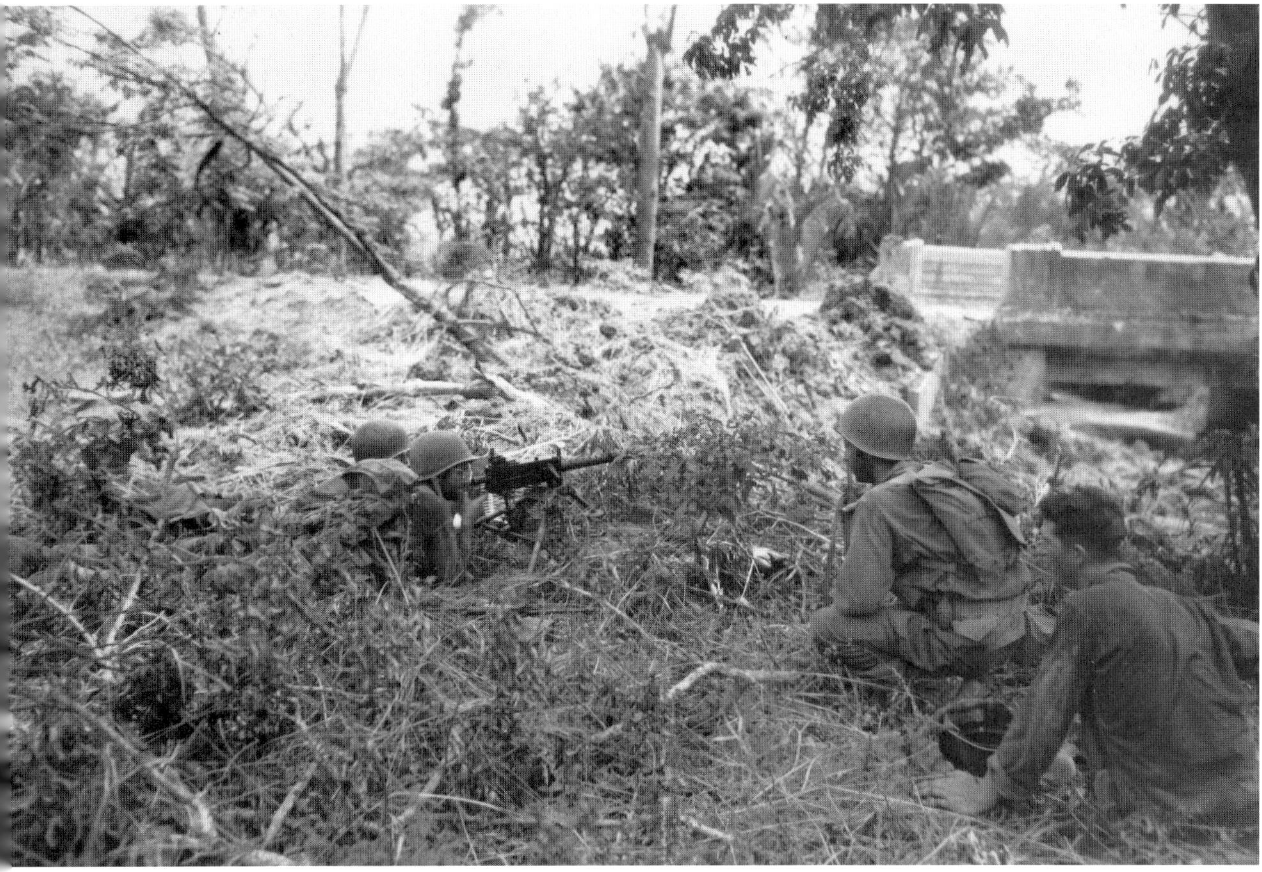

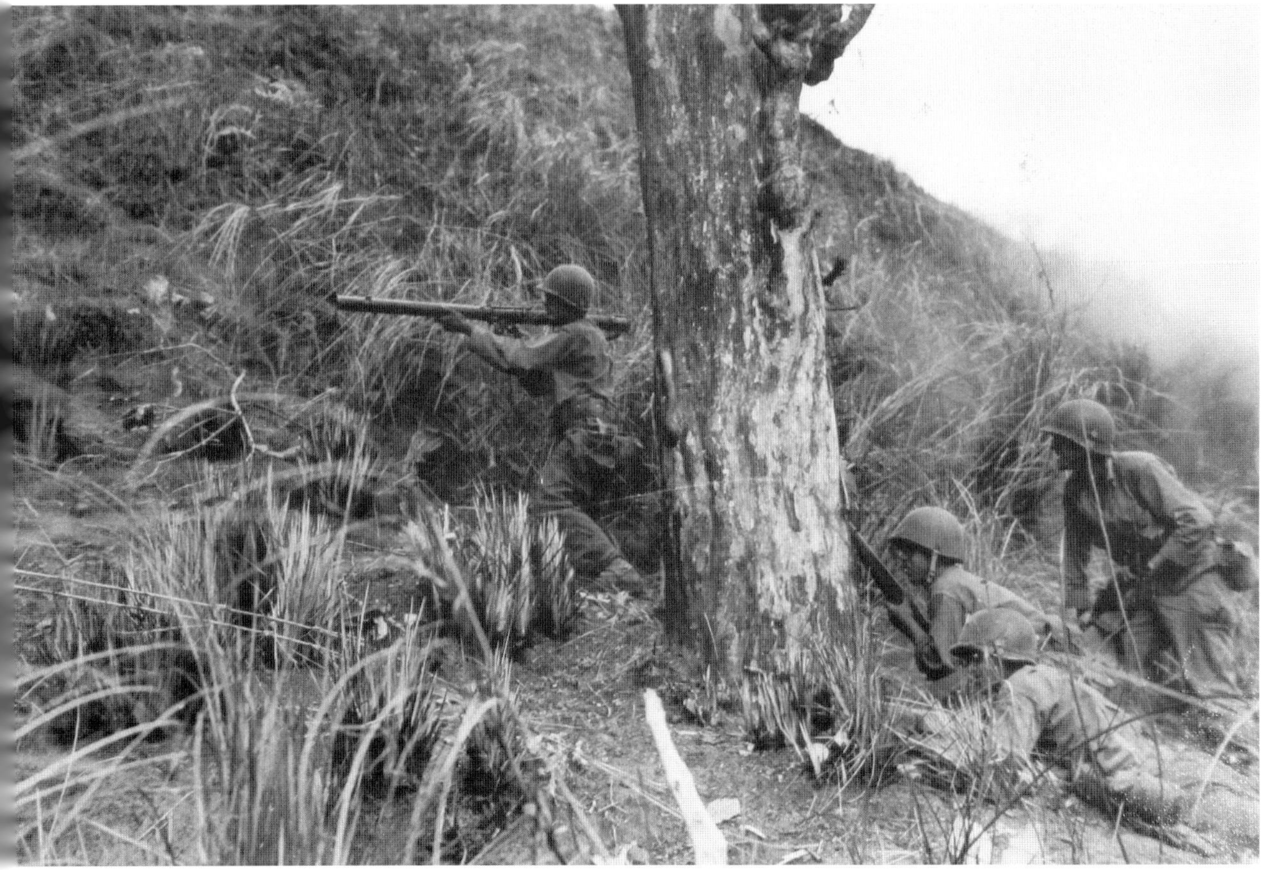

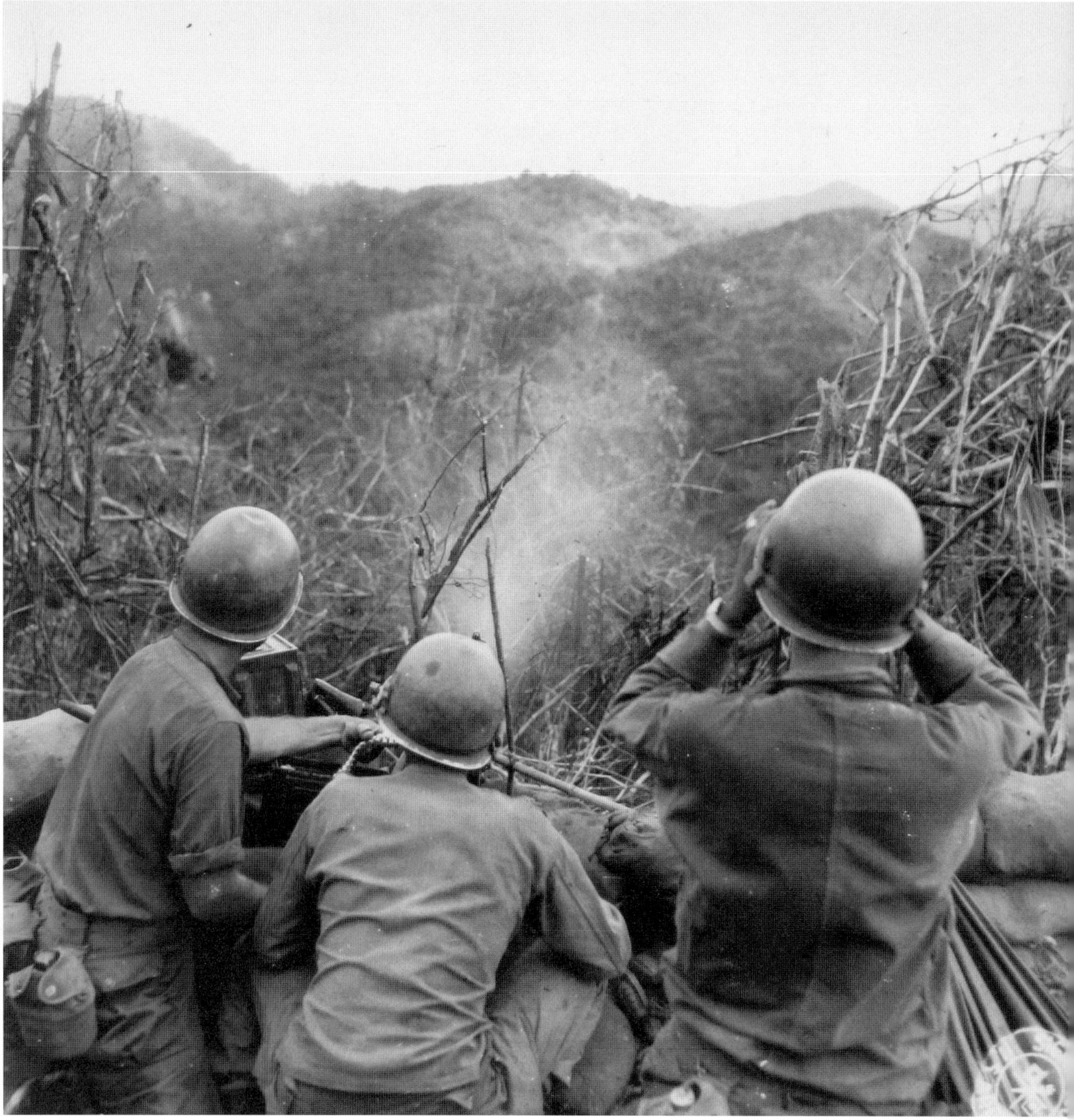

A 0.30in-calibre LMG position of the 2nd Platoon of the 2nd Battalion's Heavy Weapons Company in the 32nd Division's 127th IR provides overhead covering fire for infantrymen ascending Hill 506 on the Villa Verde Trail on 2 May 1945. Both the 25th and 32nd Infantry divisions were heavily engaged in combat along the Villa Verde Trail throughout March and April to capture Santa Fe. These US Sixth Army divisions had to confront suicidal Japanese resistance and the mountainous terrain. *(NARA)*

Chapter Seven

Invasions of the Visayan Group, Mindanao and the Sulu Archipelago 1945

Victor I was the code-name for Lieutenant General Robert Eichelberger's Eighth Army assault on the western portion of the Visayan Group of central Philippine islands and it included assaults on north-western Negros and Panay Island. On 18 March 1945, the 40th Infantry Division's 185th IR landed unopposed several miles south of Iloilo City on Panay Island. The Japanese were concentrated in Iloilo City, which fell to the American and Filipino guerrilla forces on 20 March. Mopping-up operations continued until the war's end with more than 1,000 Japanese troops surrendering.

On 29 March elements of the 40th Division's 185th IR invaded Bacolod City on Negros Island's north-western corner as part of Victor I. By 2 April, the coastal plain of Negros was in Allied hands. On 9 April, all three of the 40th Division's regiments pushed east into the mountainous interior of Negros against strong Japanese defences. By 4 June, the Japanese withdrew further into the mountains, taking the 40th Division eight weeks to overcome the enemy.

The Americal Division assaulted Cebu Island, Bohol and the south-eastern tip of Negros Island in the Visayan Group of central Philippine islands as part of Eichelberger's Victor II. On 26 March 1945, the Americal Division's 182nd and 132nd IRs landed undetected to the south-west and north-east of Cebu City, meeting no opposition but incurring casualties inland from enemy mines and 'booby-traps', which required clearance by army engineers.

More than 15,000 IJA troops were on Cebu, under the command of Major General Takeo Manjome; however, Filipino guerrillas isolated 2,000 enemy soldiers in northern Cebu. On 27 March, American forces moved into an almost destroyed Cebu City. On 28 March, more significant fighting occurred as the Americal Division's regiments seized Lahug Airfield 2 miles to the north-west of Cebu City. In early April, the division's third regiment, the 164th, was sent to the island as reinforcements. More than 400 American soldiers were killed and another 1,700 wounded. Although Cebu City was officially liberated early in the campaign, Manjome's troops resisted to the city's north. More than 9,000 Japanese were killed, with an estimated 2,000 committing suicide.

On 7 April, a small-scale American invasion of Masbate Island in the central Philippines, situated between Panay Island to the south-west and Samar Island to the east, was conducted in order to liberate the last of the major islands of the Visayan Group.

Victor III comprised Palawan Island's (situated across the Sulu Sea from Mindanao) capture by the 41st Infantry Division's 186th IR and lasted from 28 February to 22 April 1945. Remnants of Lieutenant General Sōsaku Suzuki's 35th Army withdrew into the hills to the north-west of Puerto Princesa on the island's east coast and mounted a tenacious defence. In December 1944, an atrocity was committed against American PoWs at a Puerto Princesa stockade, resulting in the massacre of 150. A few American PoWs escaped to eventually reach American lines to recount their details of the mass murder, which spawned the 6th Raider Battalion's liberation of Luzon's Cabanatuan PoW camp in late January 1945.

On 9 March 1945, as part of Victor IV, elements of the 41st Division's 162nd and 163rd IRs assaulted Zamboanga City, located at the southern tip of western Mindanao's same-named peninsula. Zamboanga City, defended by IJA Lieutenant General Tokichi Hojo's 8,900-man force of the 54th Independent Mixed Brigade (IMB), was the scene of heavy fighting until the Japanese centre broke and the heavily-bombed city was occupied on 10 March. The Japanese retreated into fixed highland fortifications and on 11 March, American forces encountered stiffening Japanese resistance there, resulting in two weeks of heavy combat. Basilan Island and Tawi-Tawi were assaulted on 16 March and rapidly captured.

On 23 March, the 41st Division's 186th IR replaced the 163rd to press the remnants of IJA 54th IMB to retreat through the peninsula's jungles with Filipino guerrillas in pursuit. In all, 220 soldiers from the 41st Division were killed in action compared to IJA Hojo's 6,400 dead from his original brigade strength.

On 2 April 1945, during Victor IV, the 2nd Battalion of the 41st Division's 163rd IR landed at Sanga-Sanga and Bongao in the Sulu Archipelago, which stretched from Zamboanga City to British Northern Borneo. A week later, Jolo Island in the archipelago was invaded by the 163rd IR's other two battalions, along with Filipino guerrillas. Stiff Japanese resistance was encountered through 22 April with more than 2,000 Japanese killed, while the 163rd IR suffered fewer than 50 killed in action and approximately 200 wounded. Normal for the Pacific War, only eighty-seven Japanese soldiers surrendered on Jolo, with many IJA troops hiding in the jungles until after the war's end only to be killed by local island fighters.

During Victor V, the 24th Division landed at Parang on Mindanao's west coast on 17 April and pushed inland into the large island's central portion. On 22 April, the other X Corps Division, the 31st, landed as the 24th Division was ordered to move on Davao City, situated at the top of a bay in south-eastern Mindanao. The 24th Division entered Davao City, the last major Philippine city, on 3 May against light opposition with the enemy withdrawing inland after destroying the locale. However, heavy fighting in mid-May continued between the 24th Division and the Japanese positioned in bunkers built in dense sugar cane fields costing 350 Americans killed and 1,600 wounded. The IJA 100th Division incurred 5,000 casualties. On 12 July, the 24th Division's 21st IR arrived at the north-west shore of Sarangani Bay. The Japanese retreated into General Santos City, making a last stand until mid-August when organized enemy resistance on Mindanao ceased.

Eighth Army assault troops of the 3rd Battalion, 132nd IR, Americal Division make a surprise amphibious landing north-east of Cebu City on 26 March 1945. The division's other IR, the 182nd, also landed that day but to Cebu City's south-west. *(NARA)*

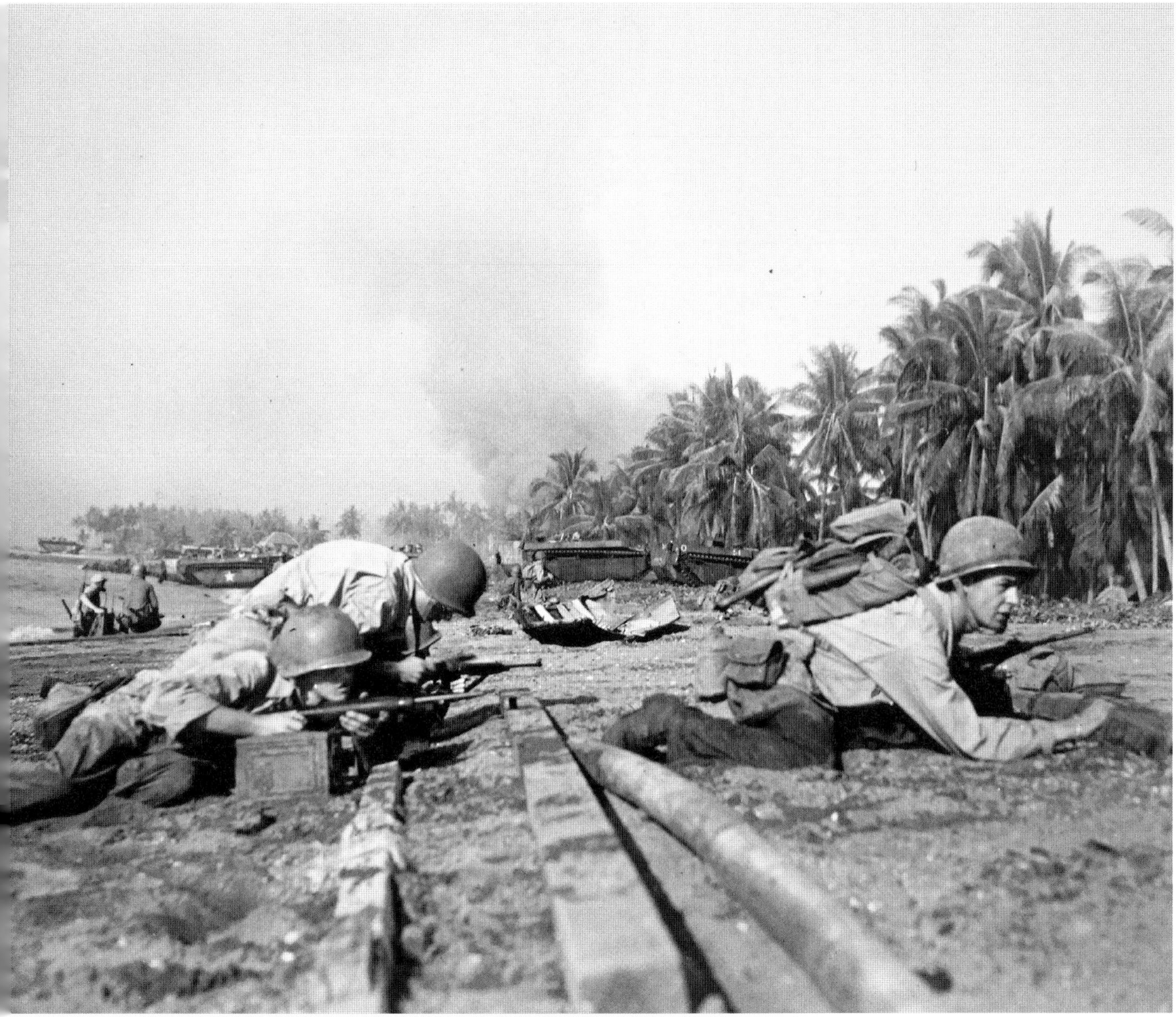

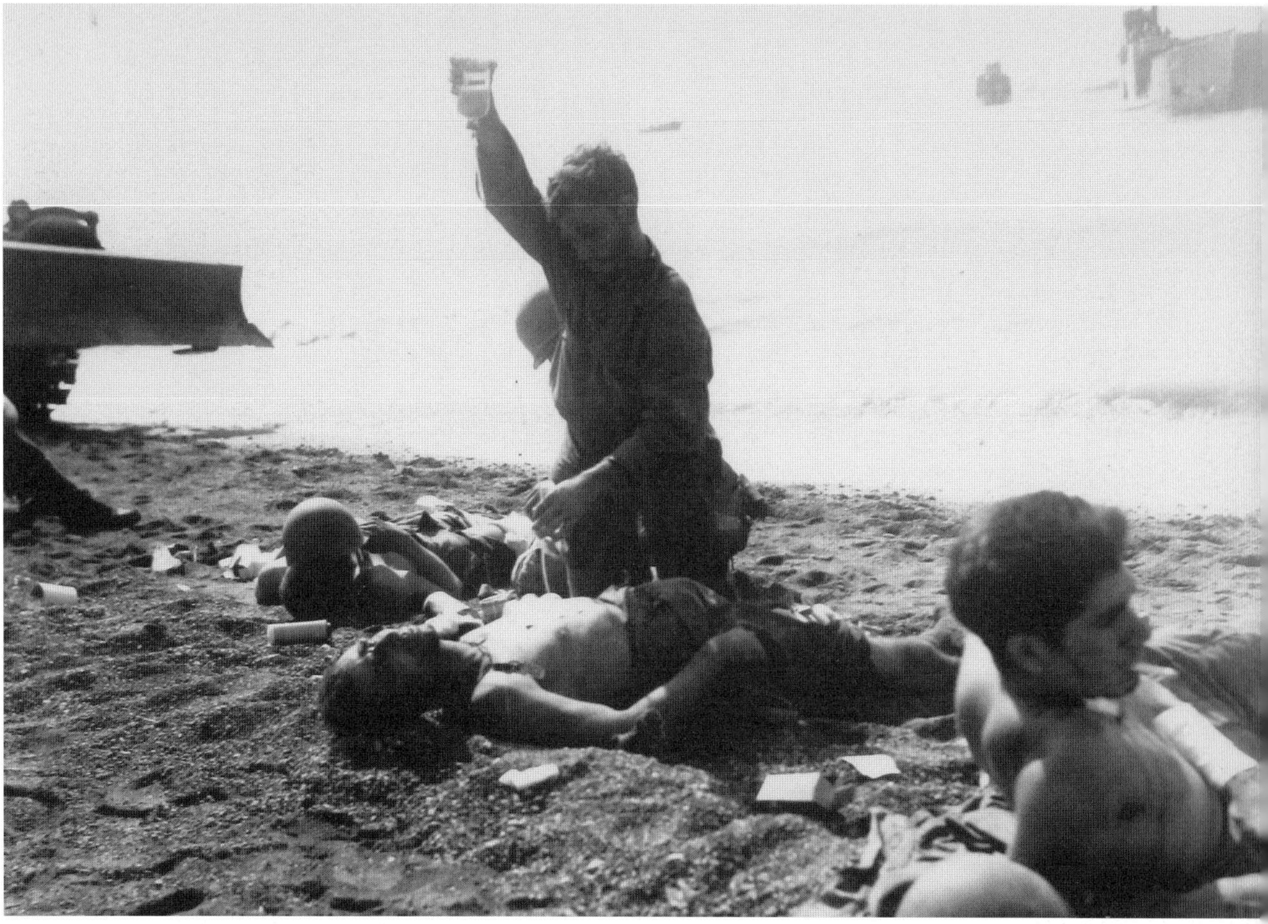

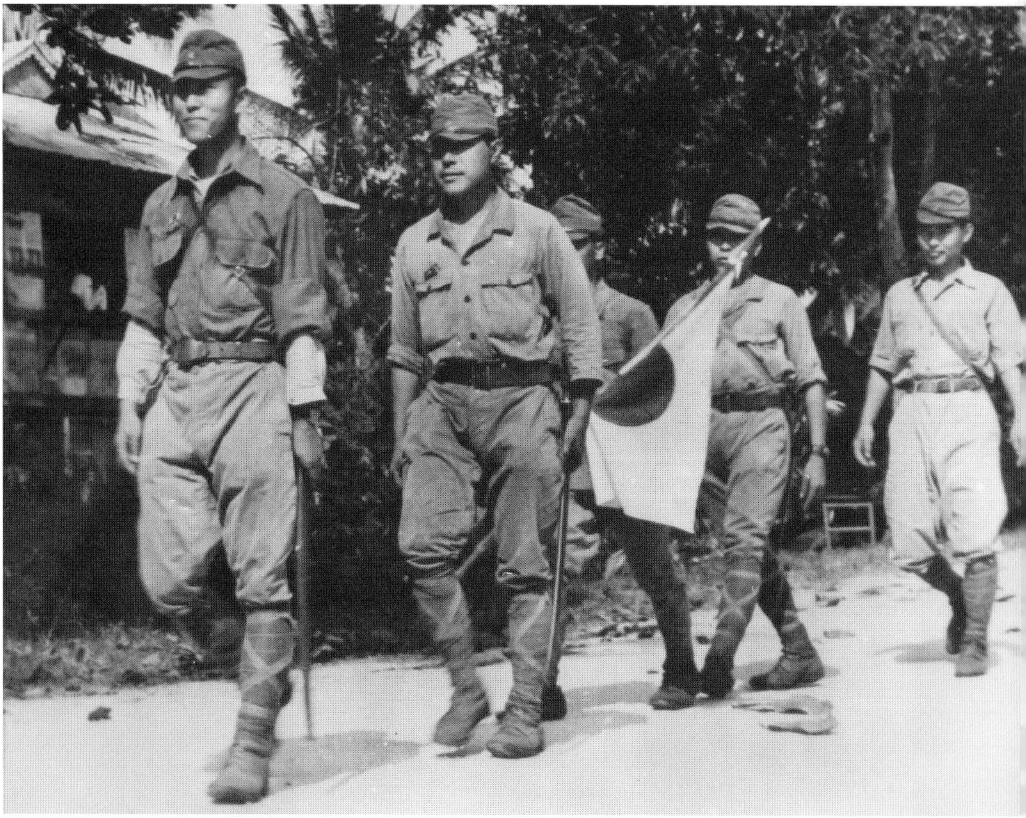

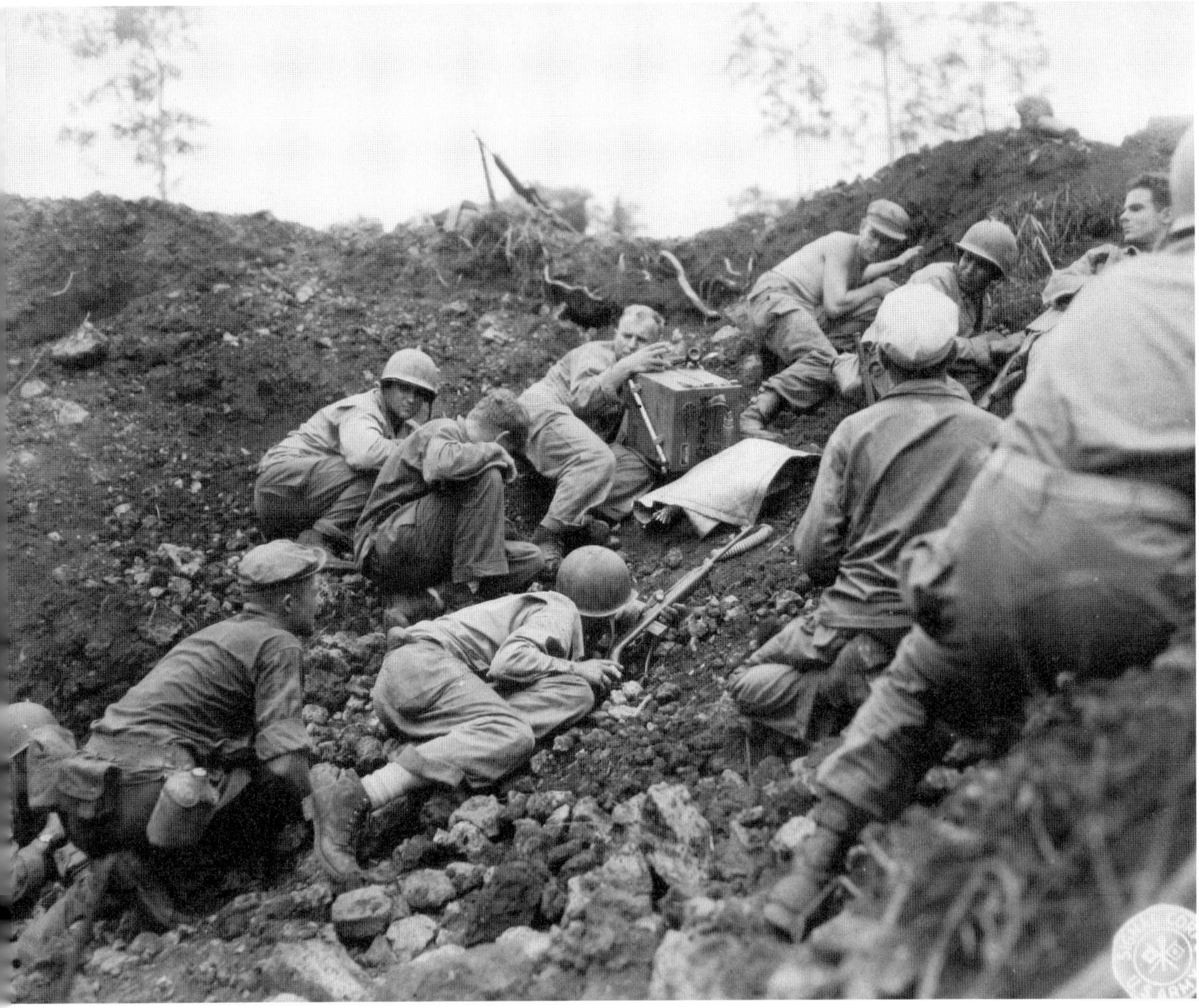

(**Opposite, above**) The Americal Division's 132nd IR wounded receive plasma from medics on Cebu's assault beach on 26 March 1945. There was no organized Japanese landing area resistance at Cebu; however, casualties resulted from inland enemy mines and booby-traps. On 28 March, more significant fighting occurred as the Americal Division's regiments seized Lahug Airfield 2 miles north-west of Cebu City. In early April, the division's third regiment, the 164th, arrived as reinforcements. *(NARA)*

(**Opposite, below**) Japanese officers, among 2,000 surrendering enemy soldiers, walk in procession to meet Americal Division representatives on 8 April 1945. Although Cebu City was officially liberated early in the campaign, Japanese troops maintained strong pockets of resistance to the north of the city. *(NARA)*

(**Above**) Advance troops of the US 41st Infantry Division direct air strikes against Japanese 20mm cannon and other MG positions on Jolo Island in the Sulu Archipelago on 20 April 1945. On 2 April, the 2nd Battalion of that division's 163rd IR landed at Sanga-Sanga and Bongao in the Sulu Archipelago. One week later, the regiment's other two battalions left Mindanao and landed at Jolo. Aided by the Muslim population leader, the 163rd IR killed more than 2,500 Japanese troops on the island while suffering fewer than 50 killed in action and approximately 200 wounded. *(NARA)*

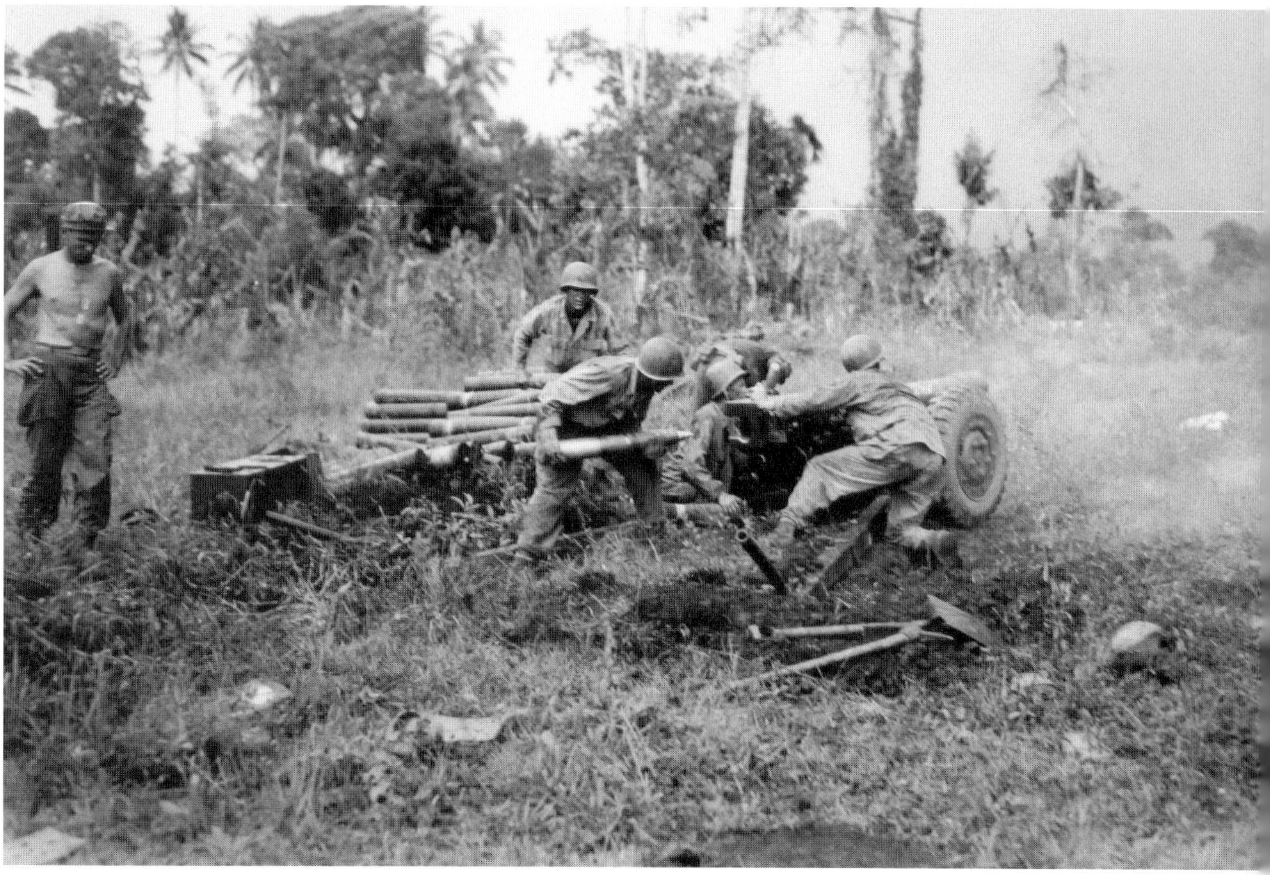

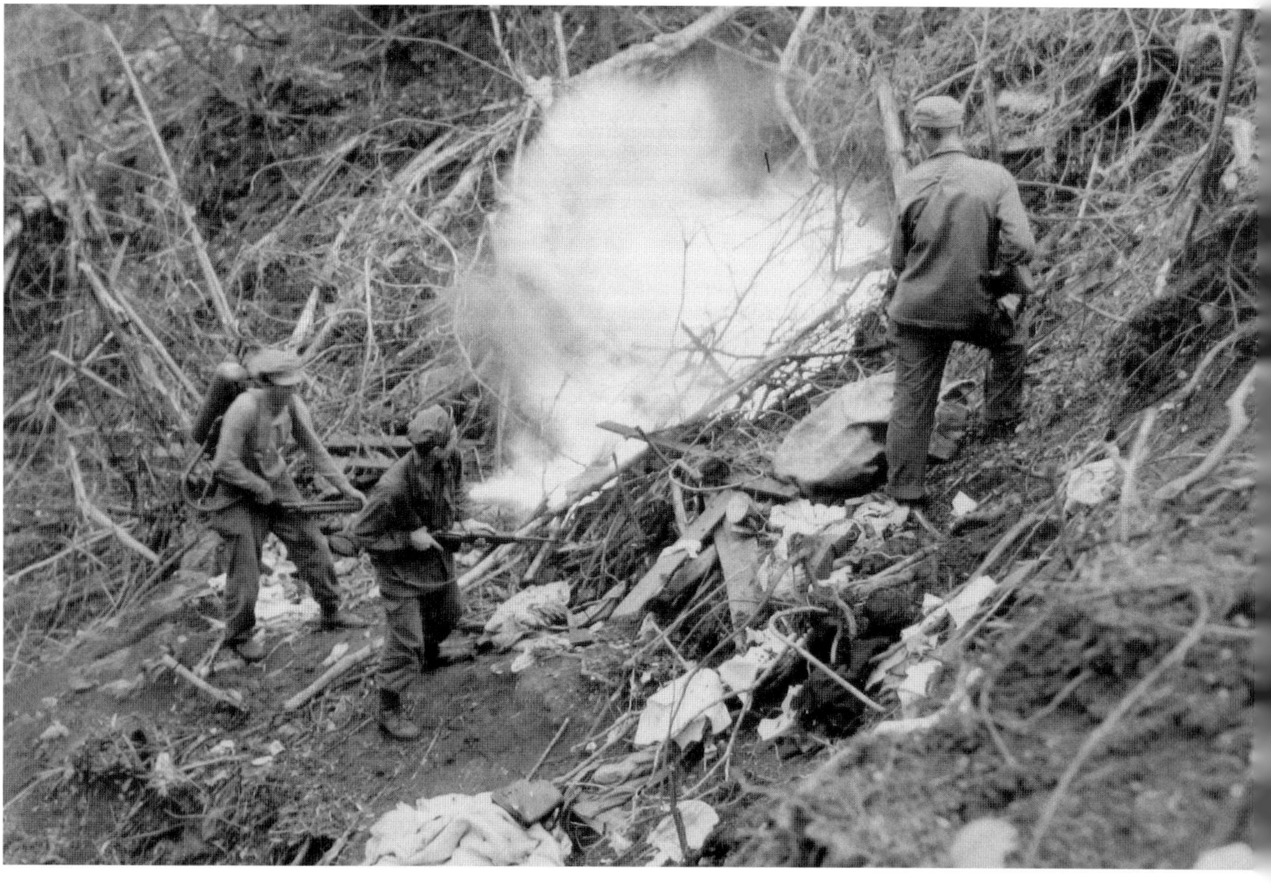

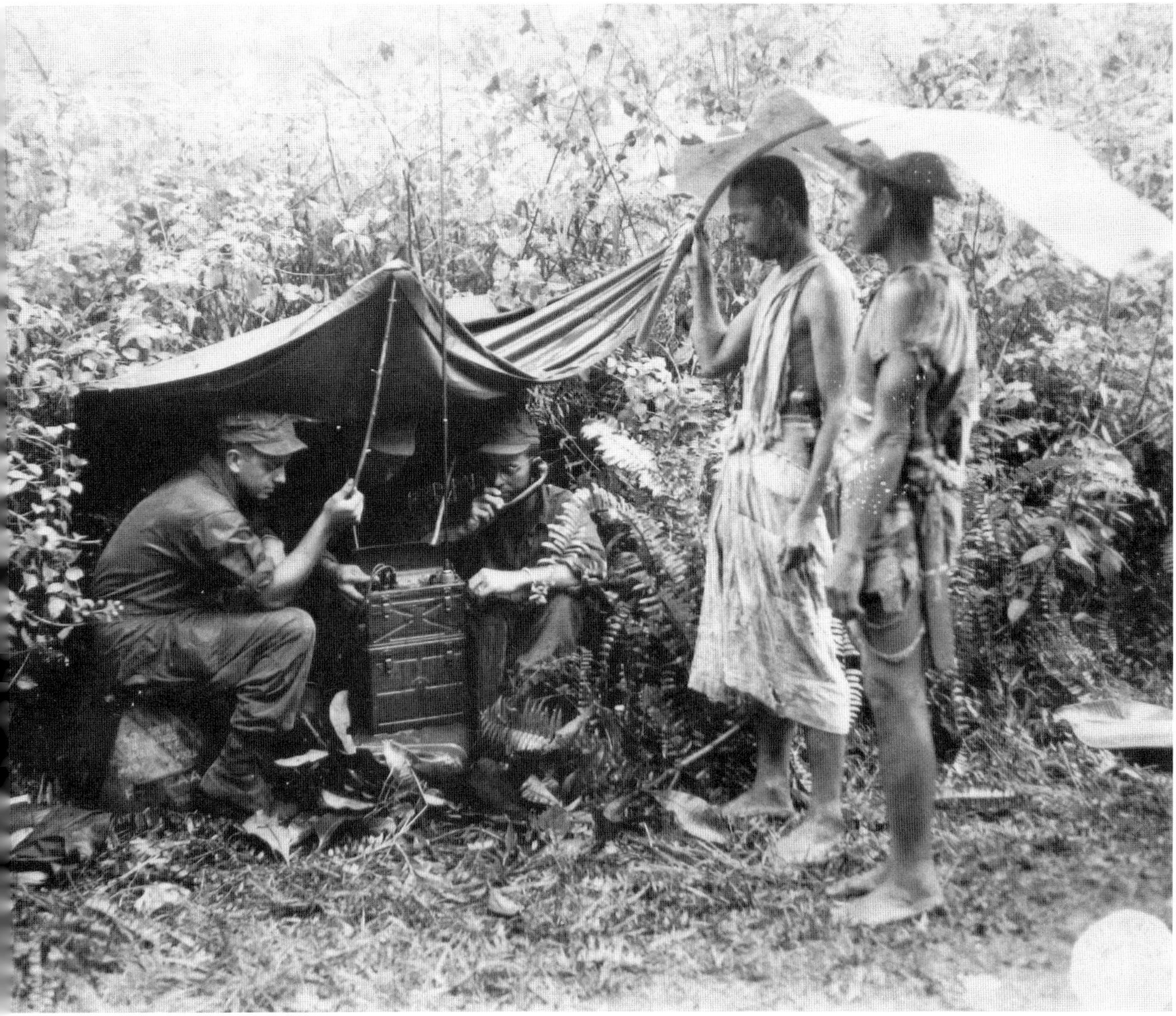

(**Opposite, above**) A 105mm howitzer crew of a 41st Division's Cannon Company fire their weapon point-blank at a Japanese pillbox on Jolo on 18 April 1945. This was unusual as the 105mm howitzer had excellent range and was often used for 'plunging' fire on enemy strongpoints. *(NARA)*

(**Opposite, below**) A 41st Infantry Division flame-thrower team eliminates a Japanese position on heavily-defended Mount Daho, the highest point on Jolo Island, on 25 April 1945. More than 3,500 Japanese troops had held off the 163rd IR supported by Filipino guerrillas. By 22 April the enemy held only isolated pockets or had fled into the jungle. *(NARA)*

(**Above**) Two Moros view a 41st Division's infantry company command post on Jolo near Mount Daho on 17 April 1945. The Moros' attire had not changed since the previous American military expedition, which was led in part by General John J. Pershing and Leonard Wood. Both Moros are wearing their bolos, which were large cutting knives similar to machetes. The hilts of the bolos were usually made of hardwood or carabao horn. Several different types of bolos were used in the Philippines for martial purposes and agriculture, as well as for cutting and marching through thick jungle vegetation. *(NARA)*

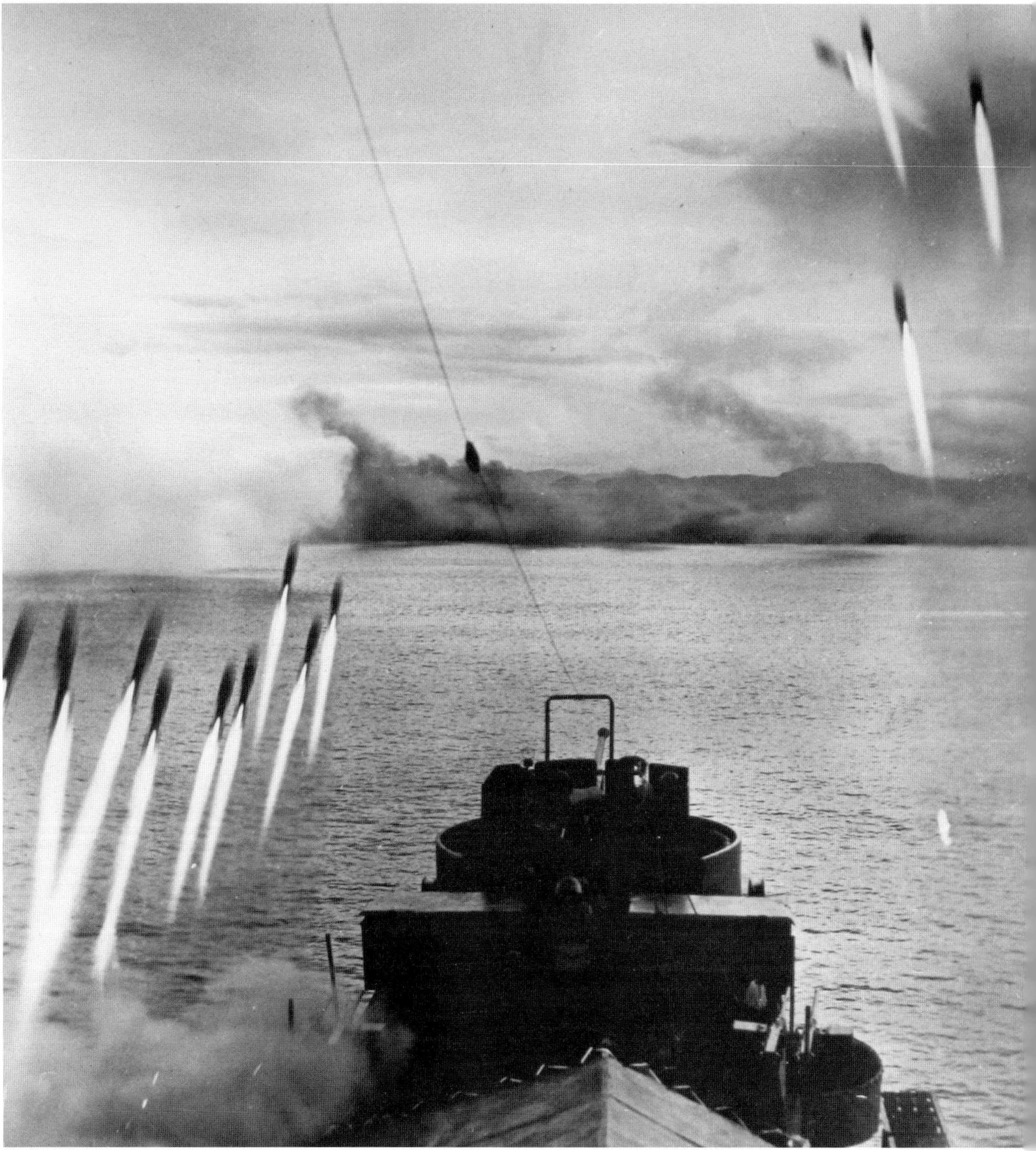

An assault craft fires rockets onto a Mindanao landing beach on 9 March 1945. The invasion, a part of Operation Victor V by Eichelberger's Eighth Army, was covered by Vice Admiral Thomas Kinkaid's Seventh Fleet to clear the large southern Philippine island. Eichelberger's plan called for landing at undefended Illana Bay on the island's western coast and then striking Japanese forces from the rear after a jungle and mountain trek. Major General Franklin Sibert led the X Corps' ground operations with Major General Roscoe Woodruff commanding the 24th Infantry Division and Major General Clarence Martin leading the 31st Infantry Division. *(NARA)*

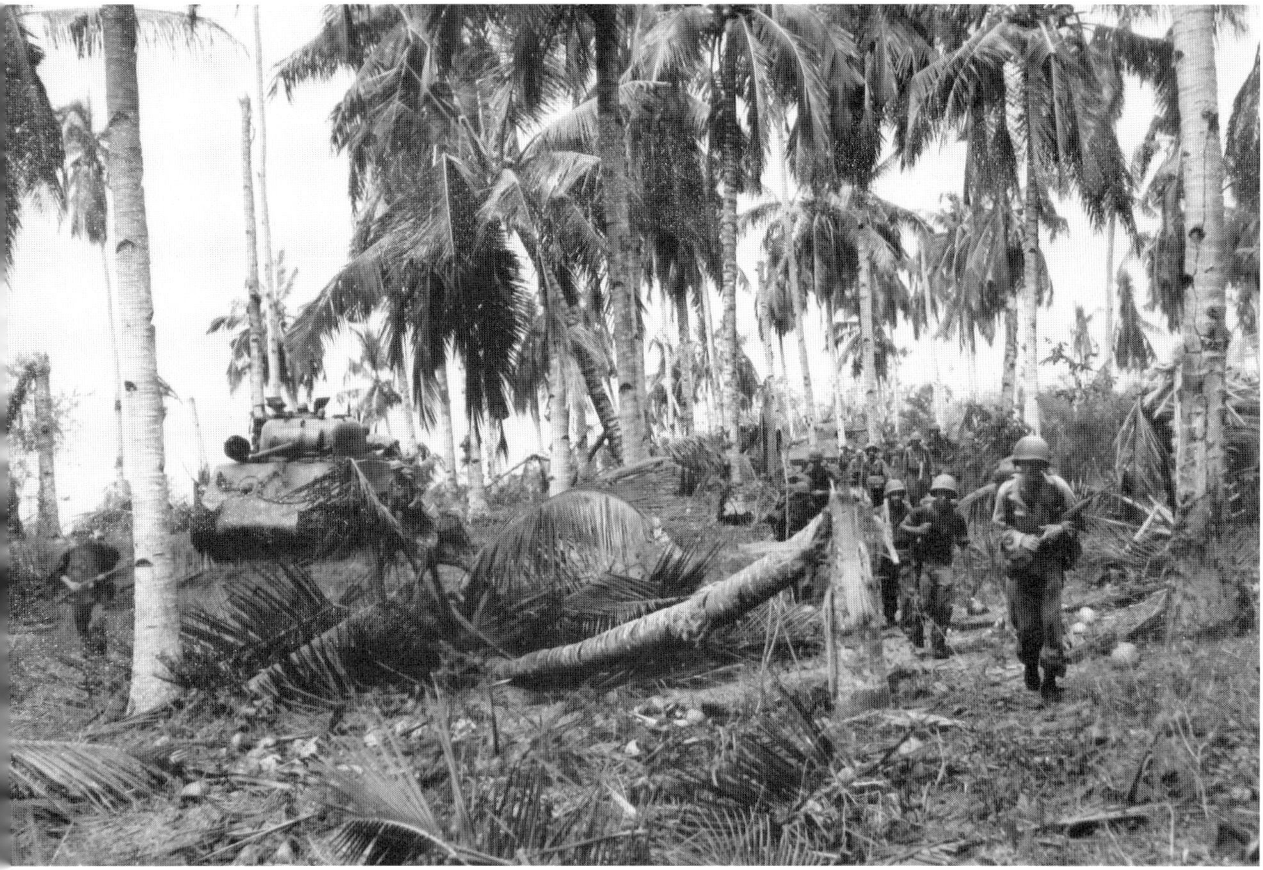

Soldiers of the 41st Division's 163rd IR move inland through thick jungle of Mindanao's Zamboanga Peninsula with an M4 medium tank. On 9 March 1945, Major General Jens Doe's 162nd and 163rd IRs, 41st Infantry Division executed Operation Victor IV, the seizure of Zamboanga, the large peninsula that extended to Mindanao's south-west. Concurrent with this assault was Victor III, the recapture of Palawan Island across the Sulu Sea from Mindanao by other 41st Infantry Division units. Defending Zamboanga City, located at the southern tip of the peninsula, was IJA Lieutenant General Tokichi Hojo's 8,900-man force of the 54th Independent Mixed Brigade (IMB). *(NARA)*

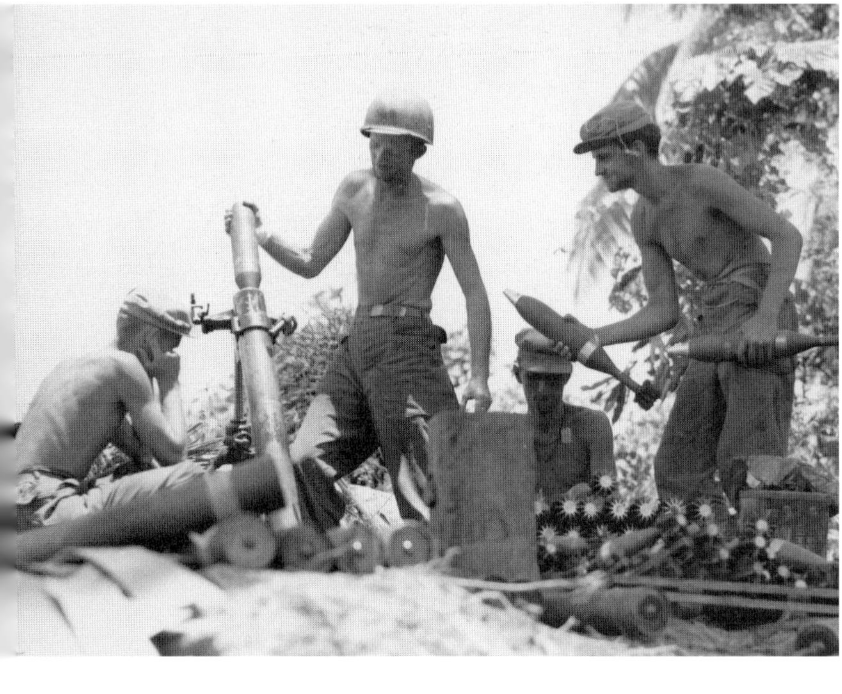

An 81mm mortar crew of the 41st Infantry Division's 163rd IR fires rounds on 23 March 1945 against Japanese positions near Zamboanga City on Mindanao's similarly-named south-western peninsula. On 23 March, the Japanese centre broke after heavy fighting. The 41st Division's 186th IR replaced the 163rd to press the remnants of IJA 54th IMB to retreat through the peninsula's jungles with Filipino guerrillas in pursuit. *(NARA)*

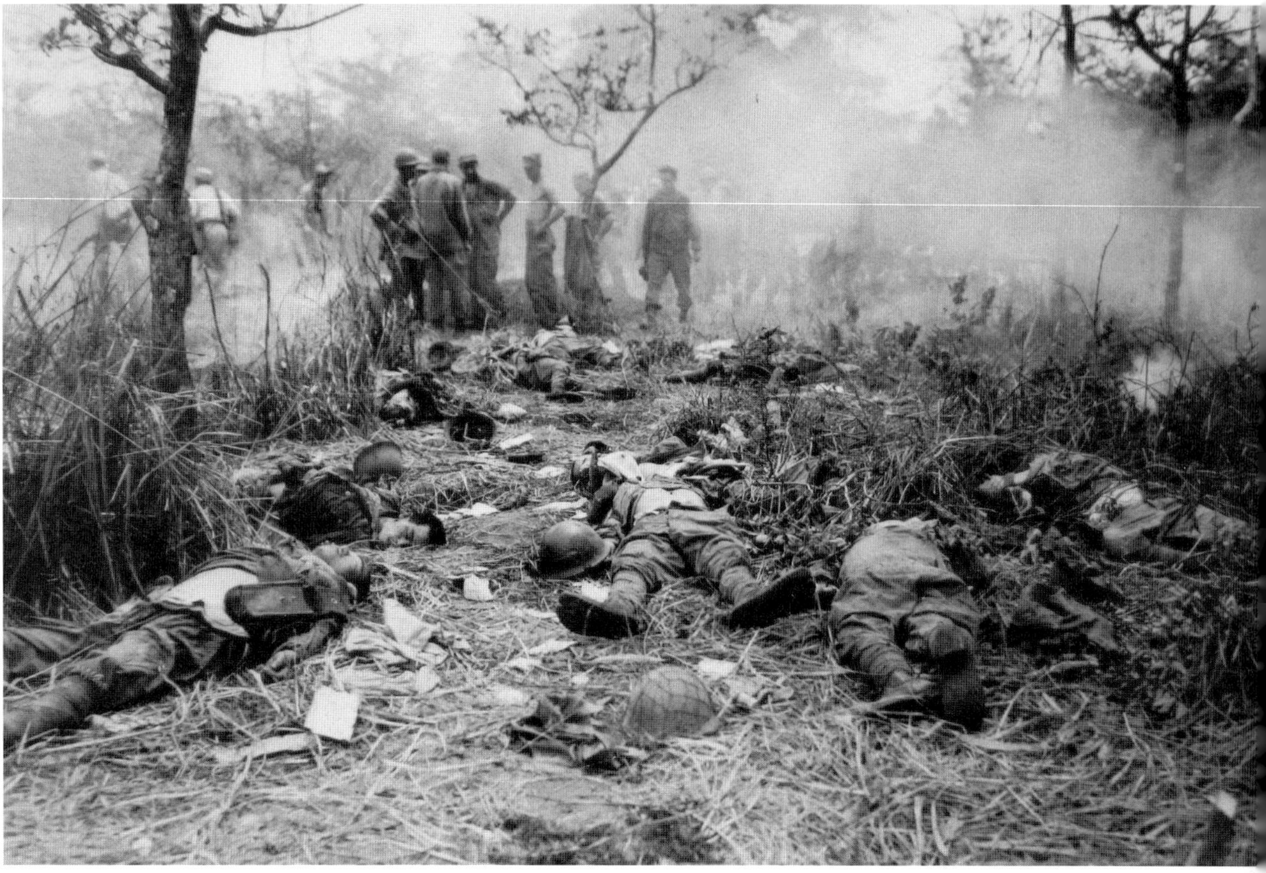

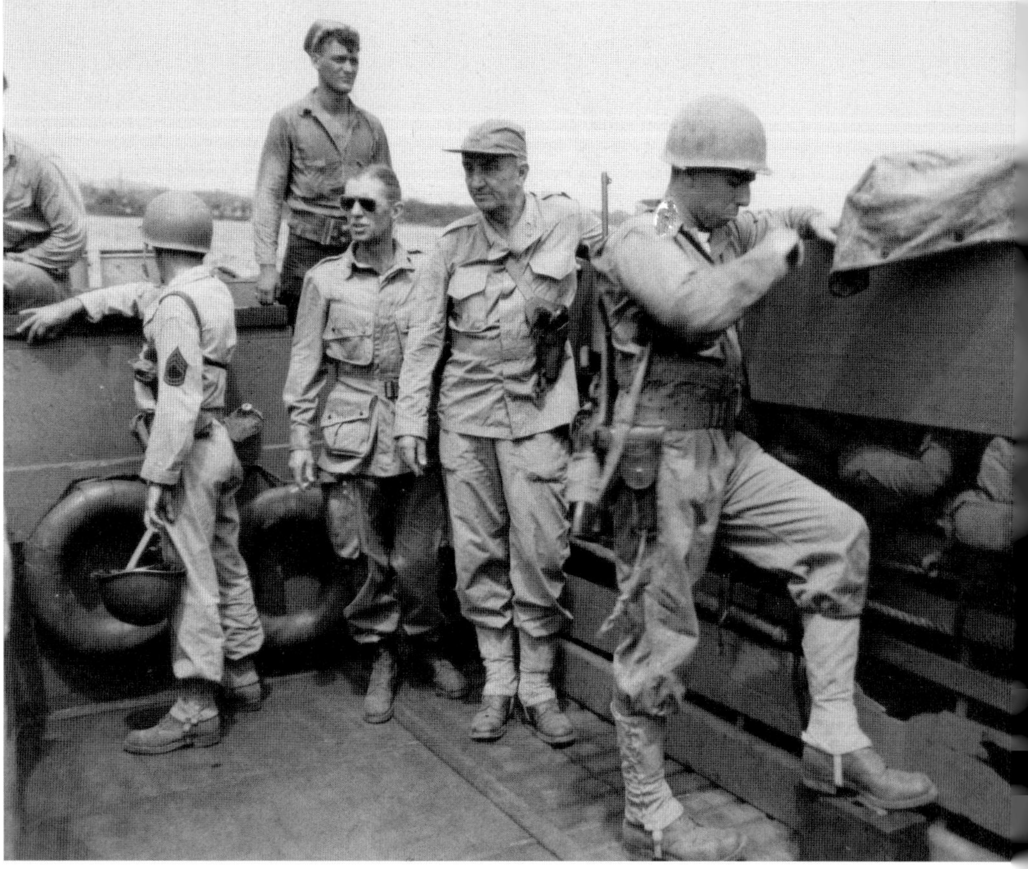

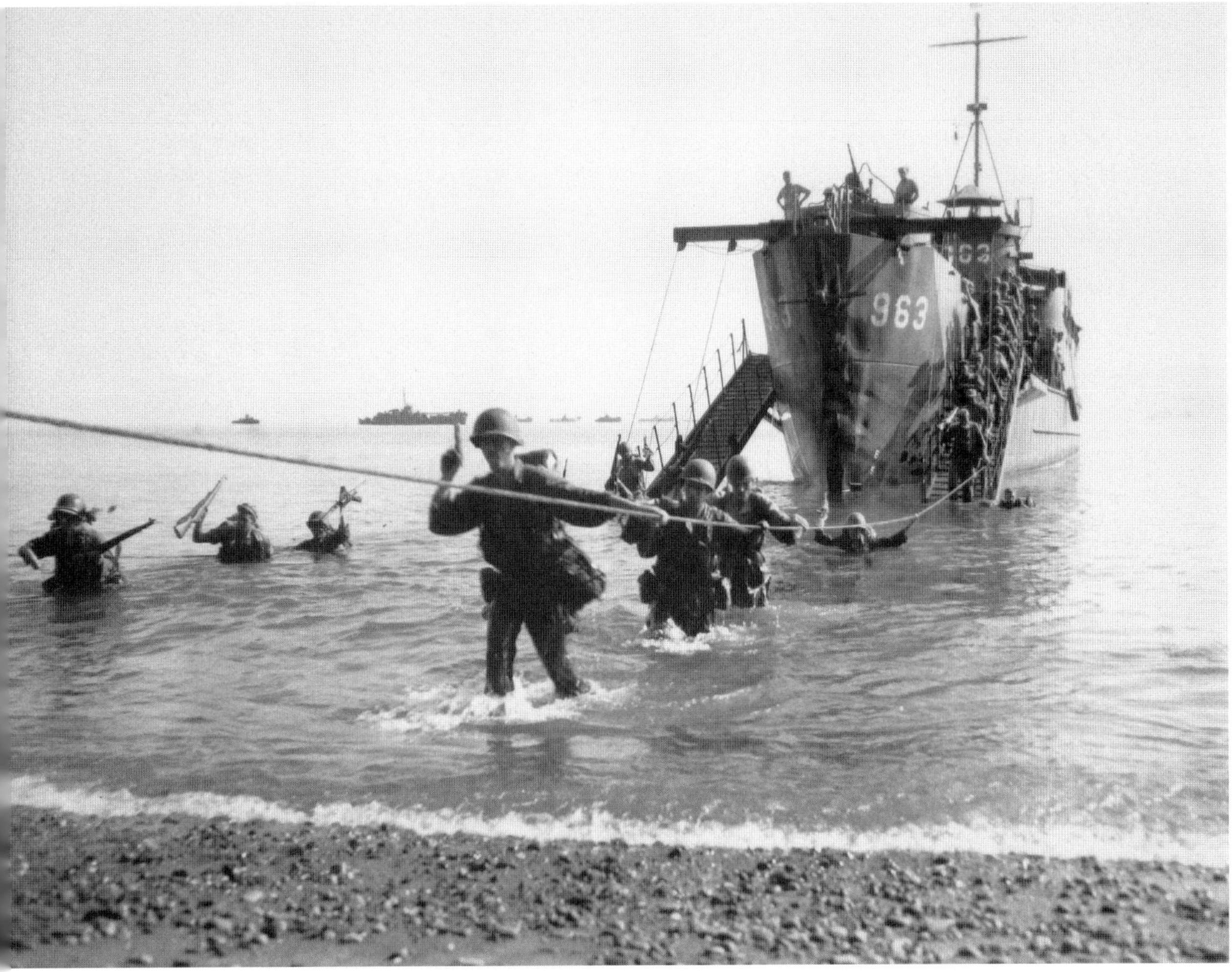

(**Opposite, above**) More than seventy dead enemy soldiers of a failed Japanese *banzai* charge near Maramag on Mindanao on the night of 14 May 1945 are graphically seen here. An earlier *banzai* charge occurred on 7 May. The suicidal rushes were repelled by Companies C and H of the 124th IR of X Corps' 31st Infantry Division. The 124th IR lost 60 men killed and 120 wounded from 7–14 May. The X Corps' other division, the 24th, was ordered to seize Davao City, situated at the top of a bay towards Mindanao's eastern part. *(NARA)*

(**Opposite, below**) Lieutenant General Robert Eichelberger, the US Eighth Army commander, is seen here standing in a landing craft on 10 March 1945. He was heading to the command post of the 163rd IR, 41st Division that had started its Zamboanga Peninsula campaign on Mindanao the previous day. *(NARA)*

(**Above**) Elements of the Americal Division's 164th IR wade ashore holding guide ropes after descending from the bow ramps of an LCI on 26 April 1945 onto the beaches of south-eastern Negros, an island situated between Cebu and Panay Islands in the Visayan group. The Battles of the Visayas from 18 March to 30 July 1945 were code-named Victor I and II involving Eichelberger's Eighth Army. Victor I entailed the seizure of north-western Negros and Panay Islands. These assaults were led by the US 40th Infantry Division under Major General Rapp Brush and the 11th Airborne Division's 503rd PIR as a reserve force. Elements of the 185th IR, 40th Division seized Bacolod on 30 March on Negros' north-western coast. Victor II involved the Americal Division's seizure of south-eastern Negros, Cebu and Bohol. *(NARA)*

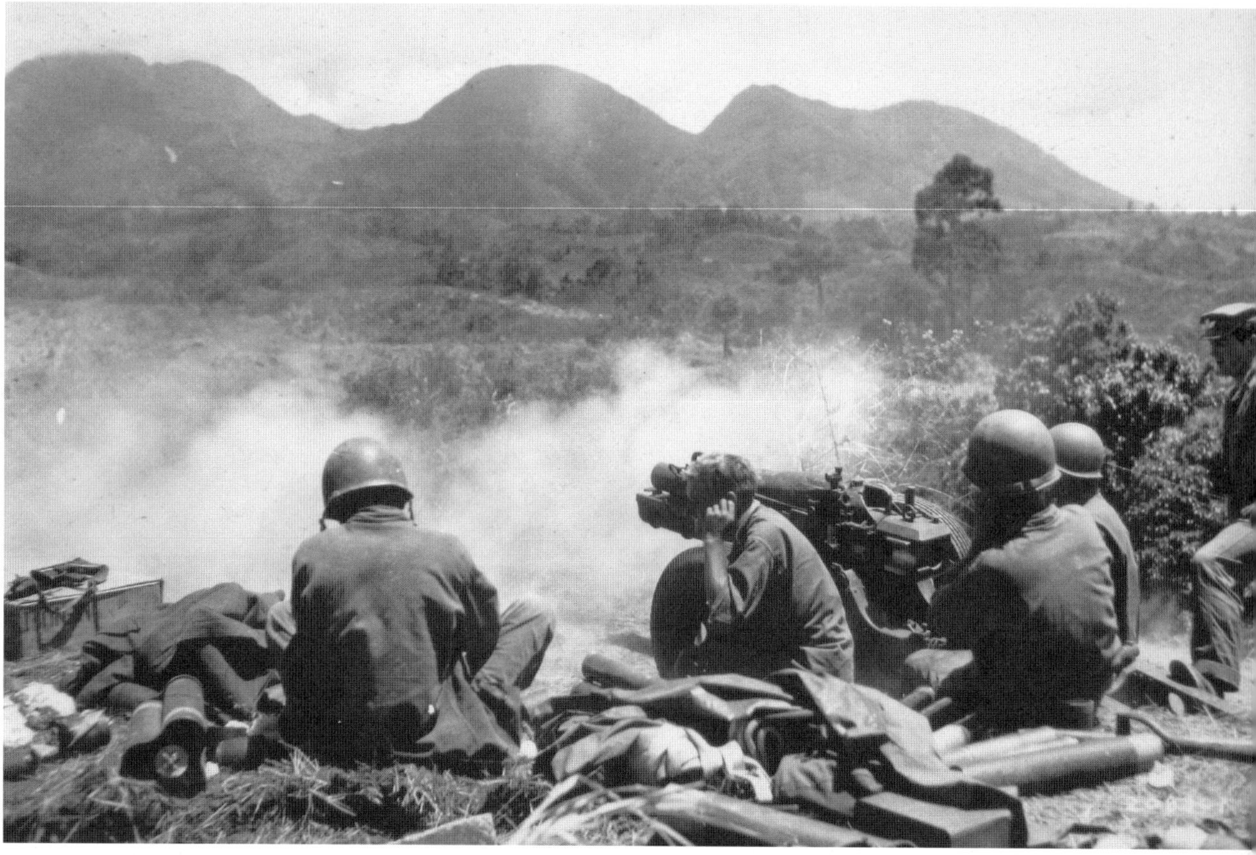

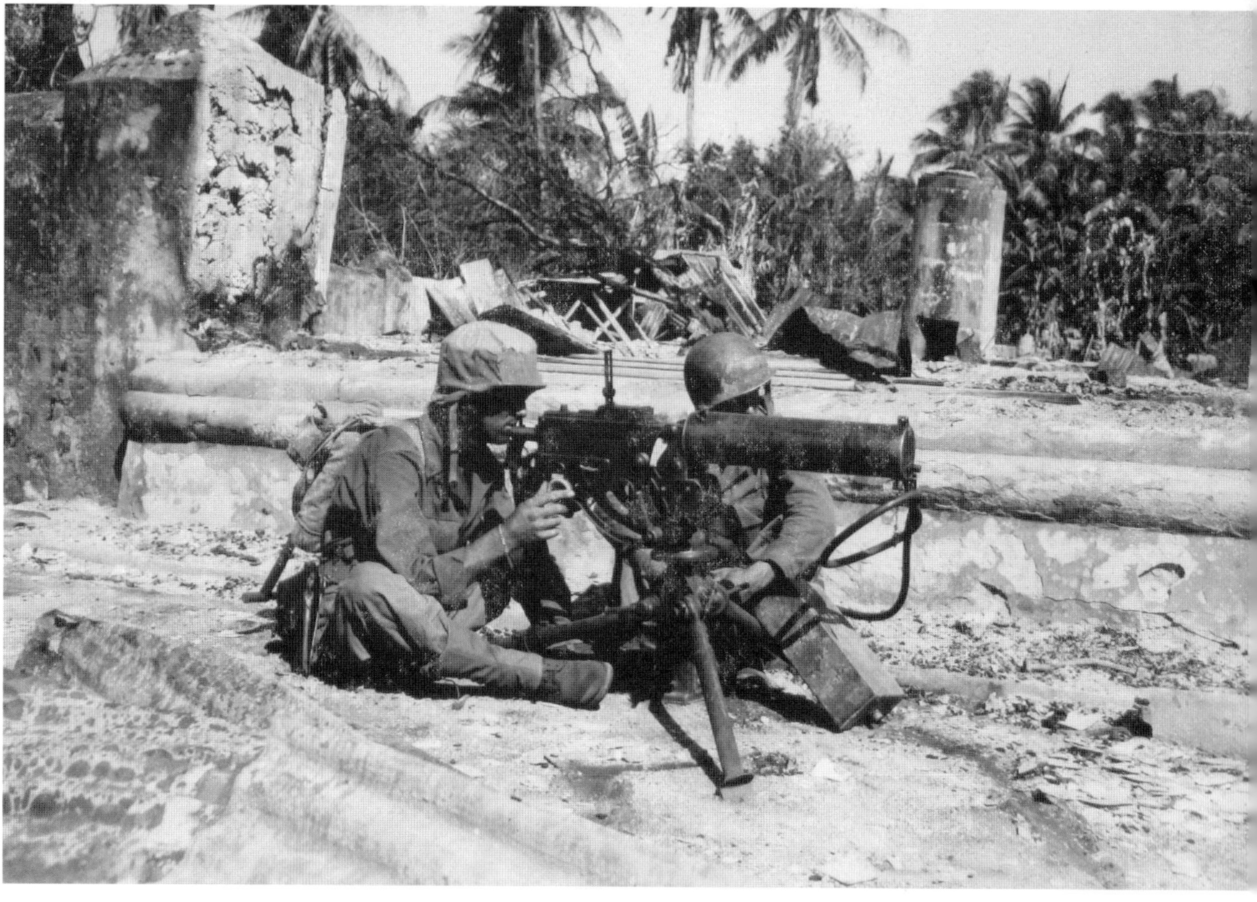

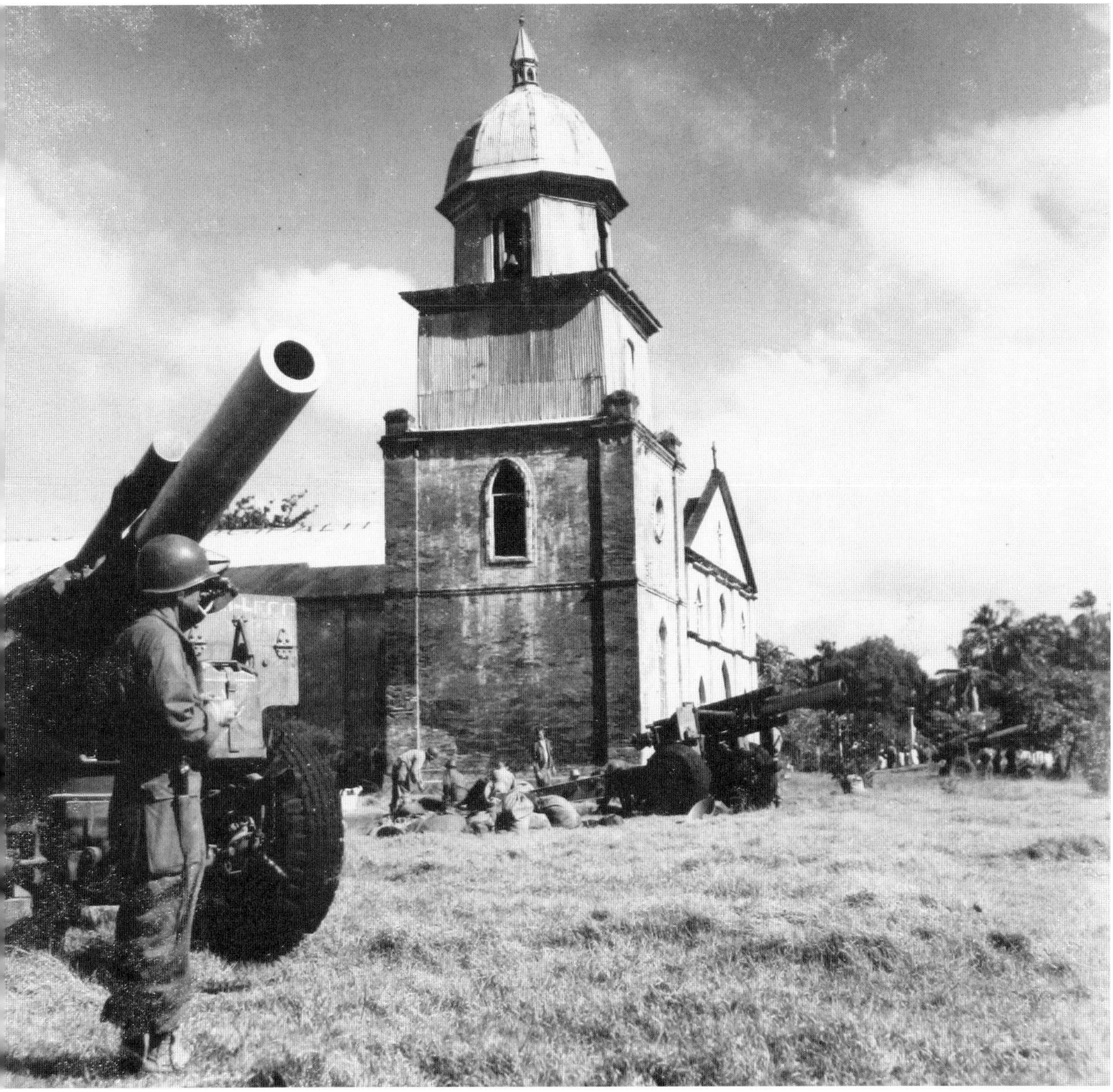

(**Opposite, above**) Paratroopers from the 11th Airborne Division's 503rd PIR fire their 75mm pack howitzer on Japanese positions on north-western Negros on 19 April 1945. This gun and its crew were from Battery A. *(NARA)*

(**Above**) A battery of 155mm howitzers is situated in a churchyard on Panay Island on 19 March 1945. The guns were readied for fire missions on Japanese positions. The assault on Panay Island in the Visayan group was the first objective in Victor I. On 18 March 1945, the 185th IR of the 40th Infantry Division landed unopposed. Japanese opposition was concentrated in Iloilo City, which was overcome in two days. *(NARA)*

(**Opposite, below**) A venerable 0.30in-calibre, water-cooled M1917 Browning MMG mounted on a tripod is ready for action here with two of its crew from Company D, 185th IR, 40th Division on 19 March 1945 as part of the offensive on Japanese positions in Iloilo City. *(NARA)*

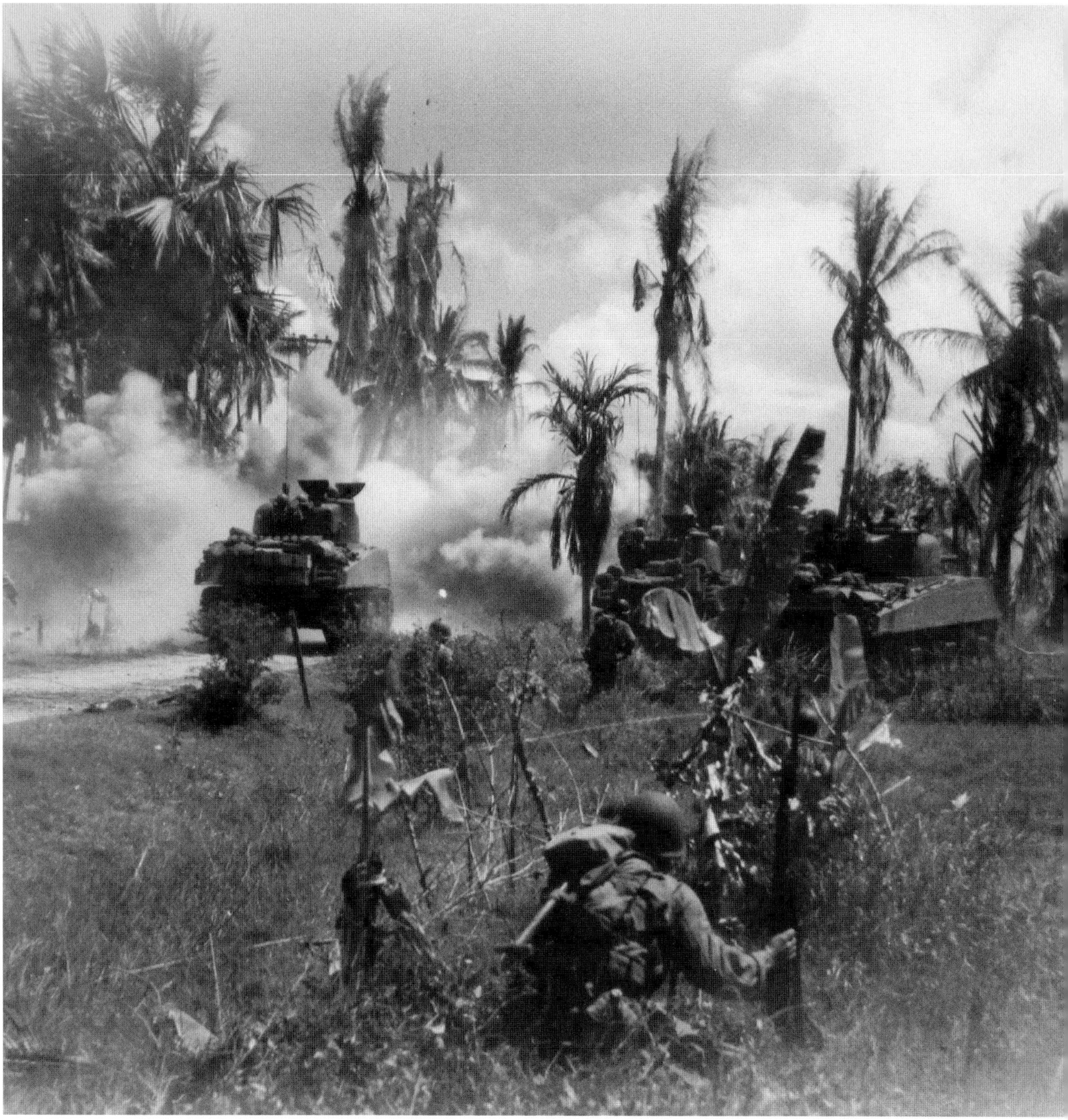

Infantrymen of the 185th IR, 40th Division with attached M4 medium tanks advance against Japanese outposts on the road to Iloilo City on Panay Island as part of the Eighth Army's Victor I on 18 March 1945. Shortly after he took this photograph, combat photographer Robert Fields was killed in action. *(NARA)*

Epilogue

After the two atomic detonations on Hiroshima and Nagasaki on 6 and 9 August 1945 respectively by B-29 crews of the 509th Composite Group, there were still 115,000 Japanese troops at large on Luzon as well as on the central and southern Philippine islands. Yamashita's *Shobu* Group, combating three American infantry divisions, did not surrender until 2 September at Kiangan, although most of their troops were starving.

MacArthur's SWPA command tied down or vanquished 400,000 Japanese troops that might have been used for the defence of the Home Islands. Leyte cost the Japanese 70,000 troops and the great naval battle at Leyte Gulf destroyed the remainder of the Imperial Japanese Combined Fleet that launched the Pacific blitzkrieg from December 1941 to June 1942. Japanese air power was decimated by General Kenney's combined air forces, but the *kamikaze* attacks wreaked havoc on Vice Admiral Kinkaid's Seventh Fleet at Leyte and Luzon.

American casualties for Luzon and the campaign in the Visayan Group and southern Philippine islands cost the US Sixth and Eighth armies more than 10,000 killed in action and 37,000 wounded. This does not include almost 100,000 non-battle casualties from disease or injury.

By 30 June, Yamashita had lost more than 170,000 troops killed in action on Luzon with 4,000 enemy captured. More than 50,000 Japanese were bottled up in mountainous positions until Yamashita's surrender at Kiangan in northern Luzon on 2 September 1945.

In contrast to other Pacific campaigns, the liberation of the Philippines saw the implementation of a large organized Filipino guerrilla force generally supported by the local population. Their participation tied down numerous Japanese units as well as saving innumerable American lives.

Ultimately, Emperor Hirohito accepted the Potsdam Declaration's terms of unconditional surrender on 14 August. Twelve days later, an initial detachment of the US 11th Airborne Division arrived at Atsugi Air Base near Tokyo, with the formal surrender ceremony aboard the USS *Missouri* on 2 September under the supervision of MacArthur, now Supreme Commander for the Allied Powers in the Pacific.

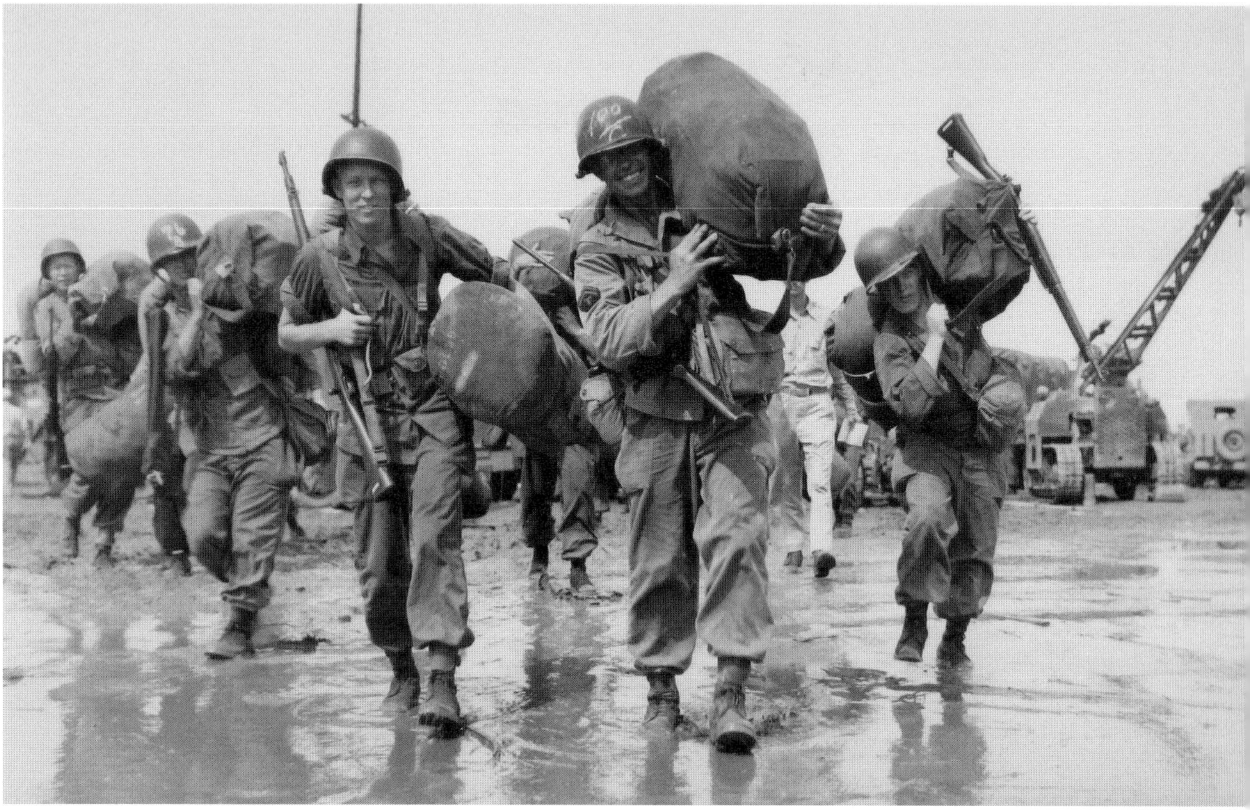

US Army engineers arrive on Luzon on 22 July 1945 from the ETO to help rebuild Manila. With the urban combat that had lasted from 3 February to 3 March with thousands of Filipino citizens killed, there was much reconstruction to be done. *(NARA)*

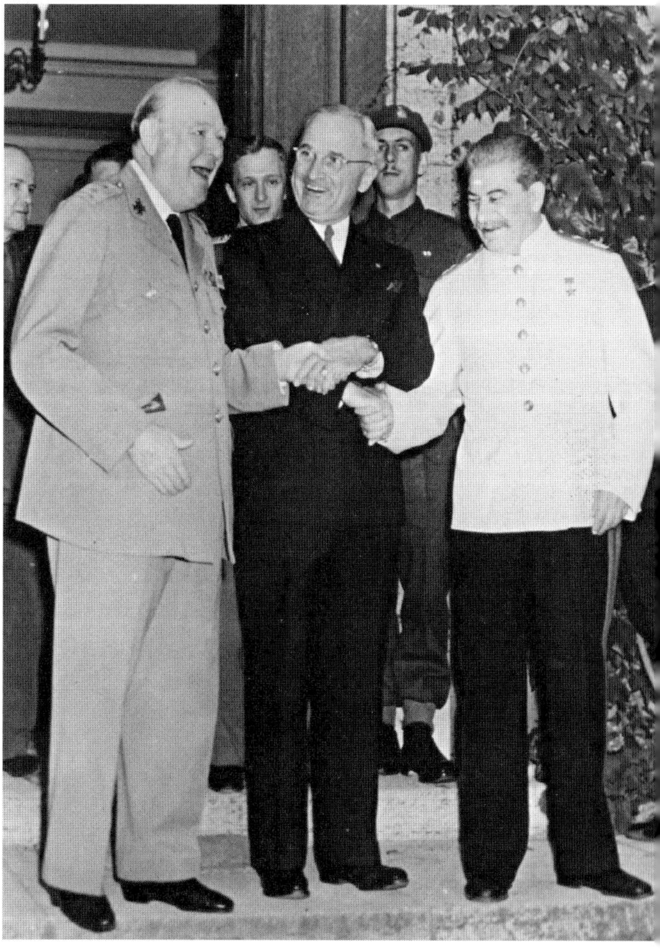

At the Potsdam Conference (also known as the Berlin Conference), which ran from 17 July to 2 August 1945, the three Allied heads of state shake hands on 23 July and are (from left to right) British Prime Minister Winston Churchill, American President Harry Truman and Soviet General Secretary of the Communist Party Joseph Stalin. The outcome of Britain's 5 July 1945 general election became known after votes from the armed forces were counted in their home constituencies with British Labour Party leader Clement Atlee becoming the new prime minister and replacing Churchill. On 26 July Churchill, Truman and Generalissimo Chiang Kai-shek issued the Potsdam Declaration compelling Imperial Japan to unconditional surrender. The Soviets did not participate since they were not yet at war with Japan. *(NARA)*

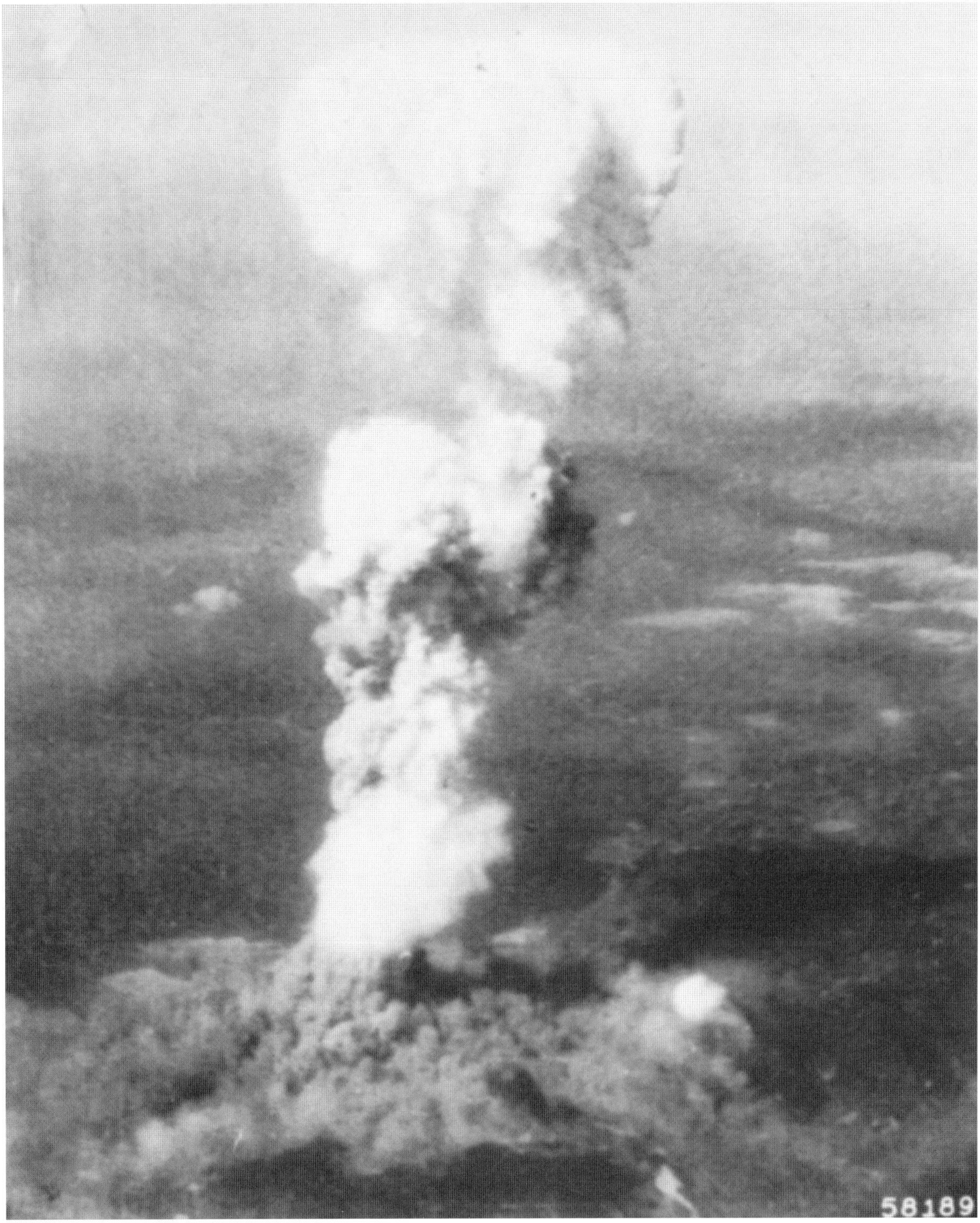
58189

The atomic bomb's 'mushroom' cloud looms over Hiroshima after the American 'Manhattan Project's' weapon was dropped by a Tinian-based B-29 Superfortress called 'Enola Gay' on 6 August 1945. After another atomic detonation on Nagasaki on 9 August, Imperial Japan sought peace. *(NARA)*

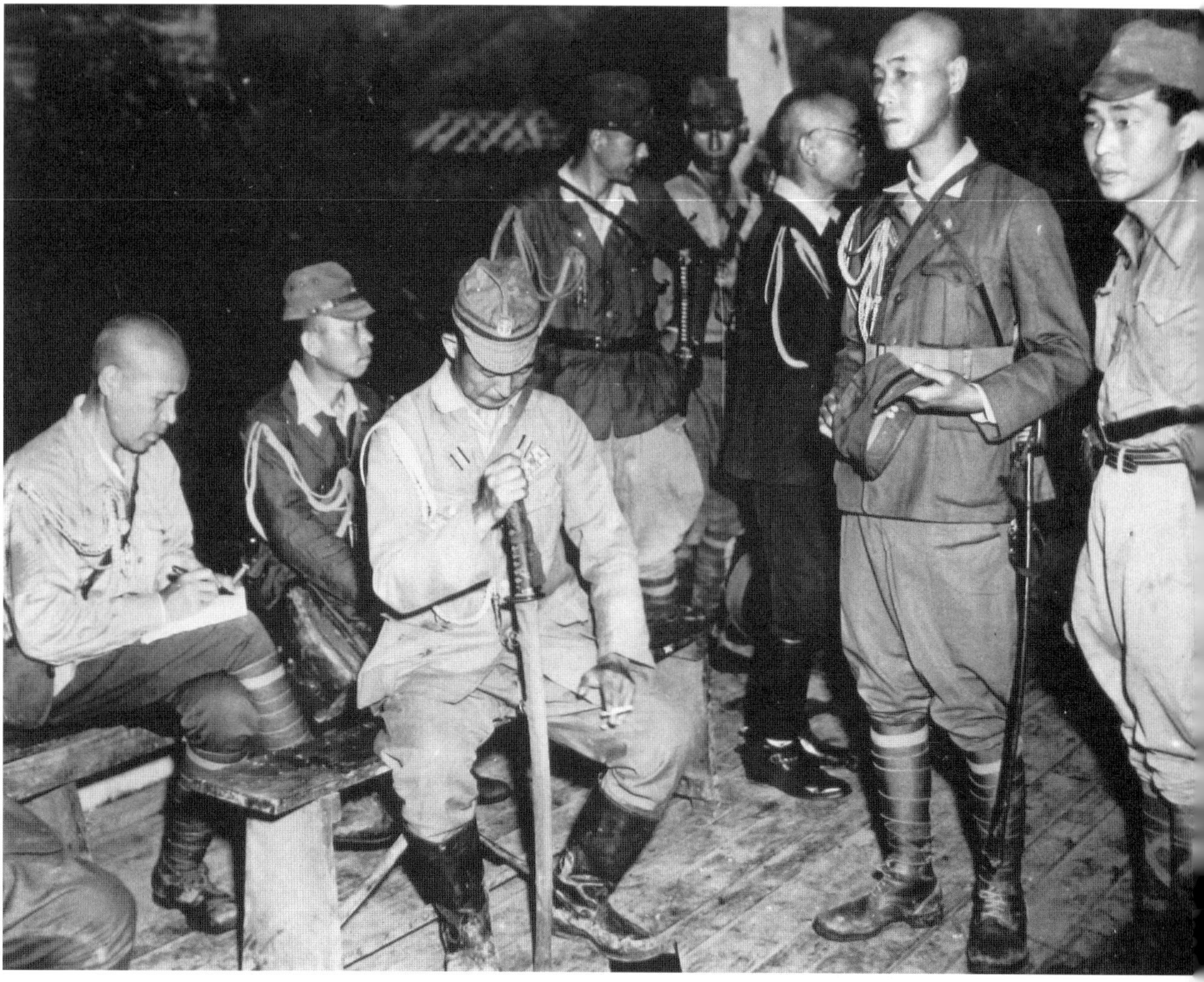

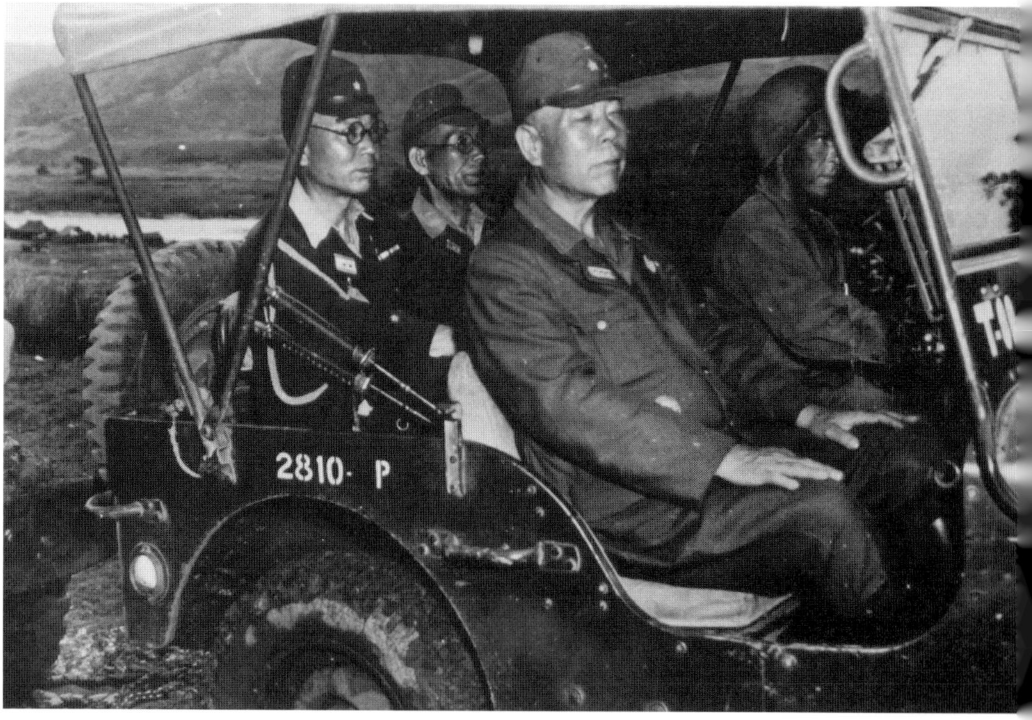
2810- P

IJN pilots at a Saigon air base are shown here being ushered into captivity by French soldiers. This was in sharp contrast to the élan that these Japanese airmen displayed prior to their successful aerial attacks which sank the HMS *Prince of Wales* and *Repulse* on 10 December off the Malayan coast in the South China Sea, as well as the concurrent devastating air-raids on Luzon's Cavite Navy Base, Clark Field and Nichols Field. (*NARA*)

(**Opposite, above**) Japanese generals comprising Lieutenant General Yamashita's staff are shown here looking despondent after having surrendered to elements of the US 37th Infantry Division, led by Major General Robert Beightler, in Kiangan Mountain Province in Northern Luzon on 2 September 1945. (*NARA*)

(**Opposite, below**) Lieutenant General Yamashita sits in the front passenger seat of an American jeep in Kiangan on 2 September 1945. Yamashita was air-ferried to Baguio and then on to Manila, where he was tried by an American Military Tribunal in the ballroom of the US High Commissioner's residence in downtown Manila. He was charged with failing to prevent his troops from committing atrocities against American and Filipino citizens. The trial focused on the massacres and rapes in Manila rather than on those committed by Yamashita's IJA Twenty-Fifth Army in Malaya and Singapore in 1942. He was convicted and hung on 23 February 1946 at Los Baños, 45 miles south of Manila. (*NARA*)

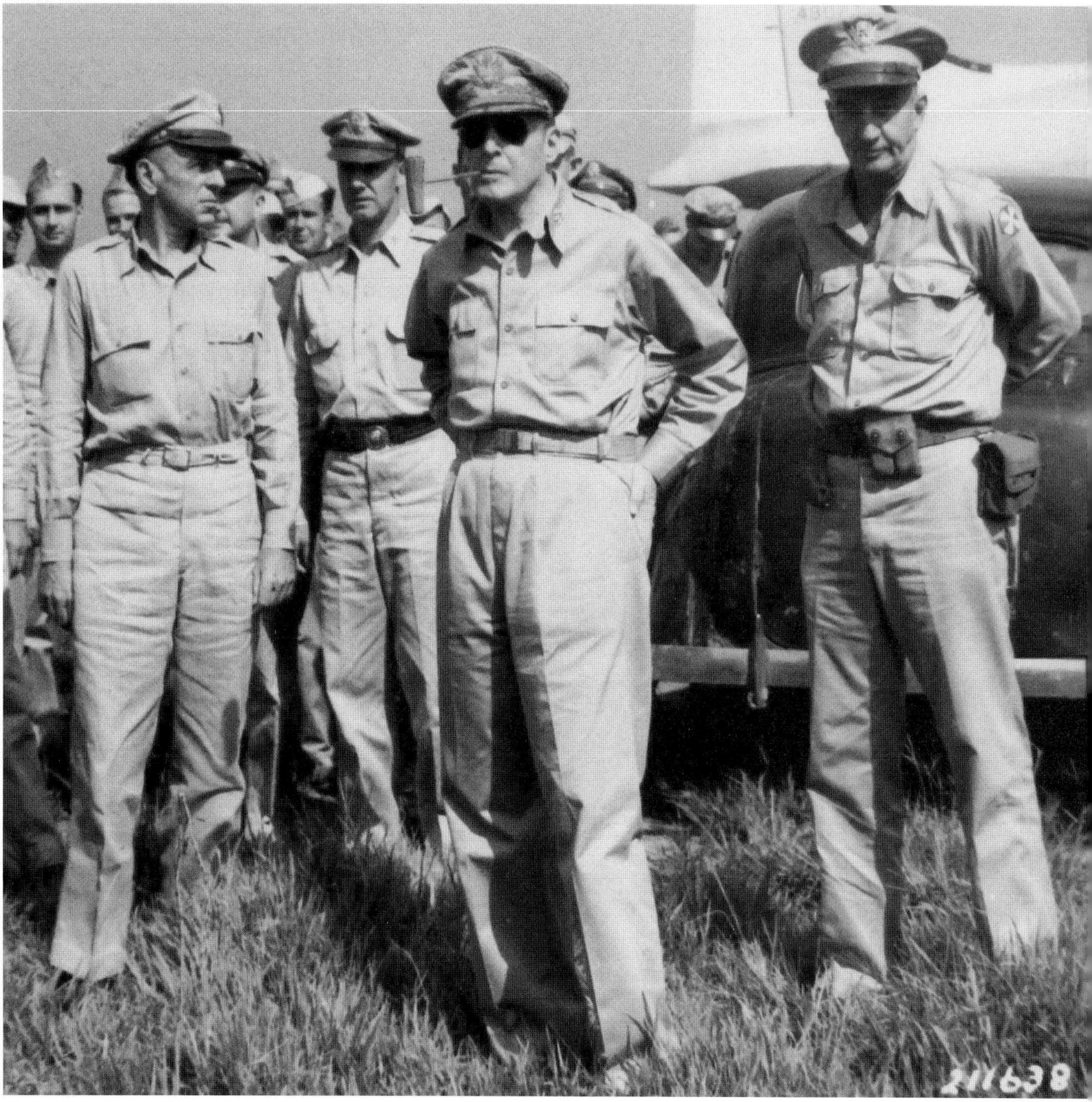
211638

General Douglas MacArthur (centre), COS Lieutenant General Sutherland (left) and Lieutenant General Robert Eichelberger (right) pose for photographers upon their arrival at Atsugi Airfield on 30 August 1945. MacArthur displayed both his trademark 'hands-on-hips' pose and the oversized corncob pipe. Soon to follow was the official signing of the document representing Imperial Japan's surrender to the Allies aboard the USS *Missouri* anchored in Tokyo Bay on 2 September 1945. *(NARA)*

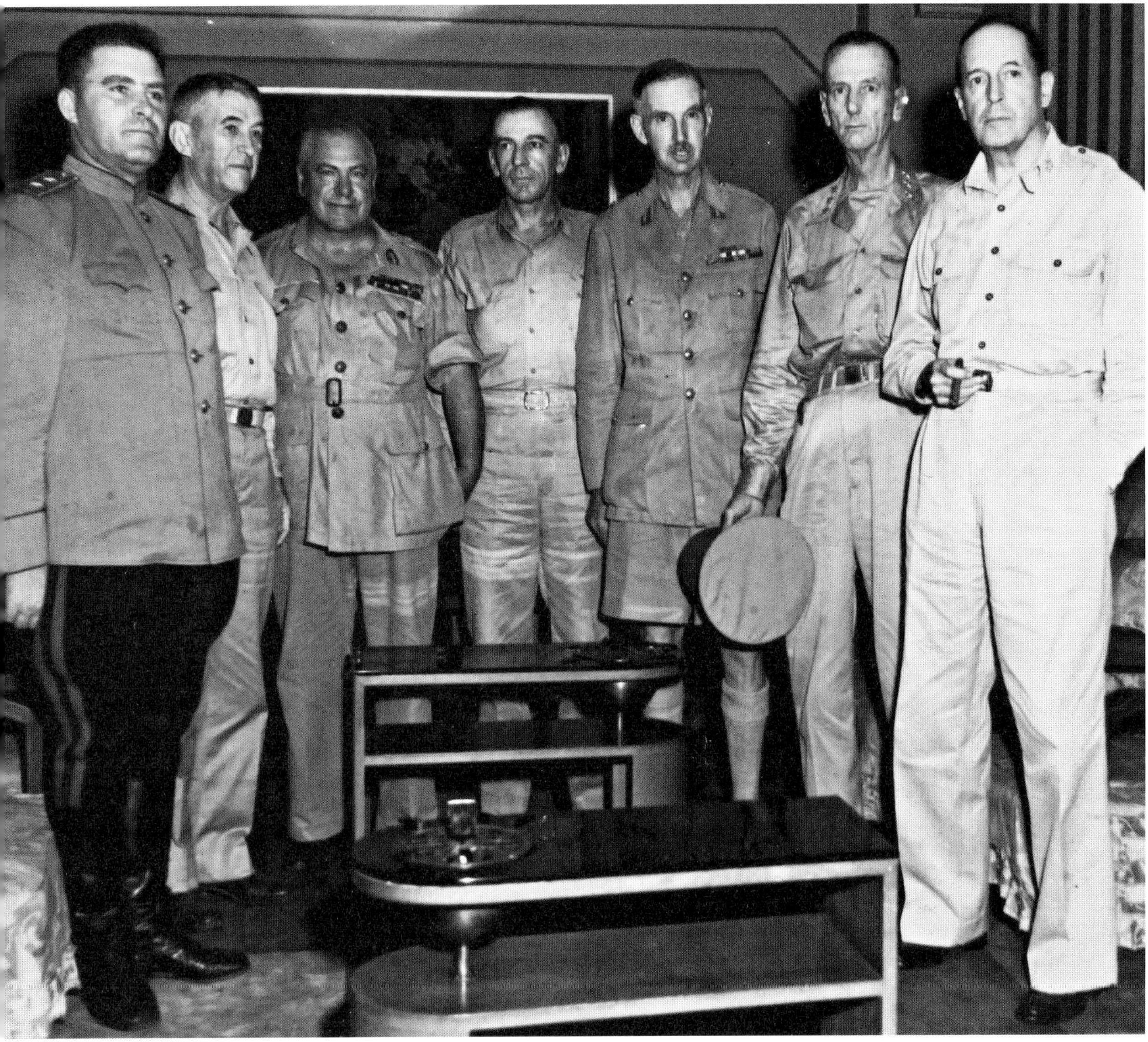

General Douglas MacArthur (right) stands relaxed holding a cigar with some Allied military leaders on 31 August 1945 that were congregating in Tokyo for the formal surrender ceremony on 2 September. From left to right were Soviet Lieutenant General Kuzma Derevyanko (Stalin opportunistically declared war on Japan on 8 August 1945), US Sixth Army commander Lieutenant General Walter Krueger, Australia's General Sir Thomas Blamey, COS Lieutenant General Richard Sutherland, Britain's Lieutenant General Arthur Percival who surrendered Singapore on 15 February 1942 and was recently released from Japanese captivity, and an emaciated Lieutenant General Jonathan Wainwright who was also a Japanese PoW. *(NARA)*

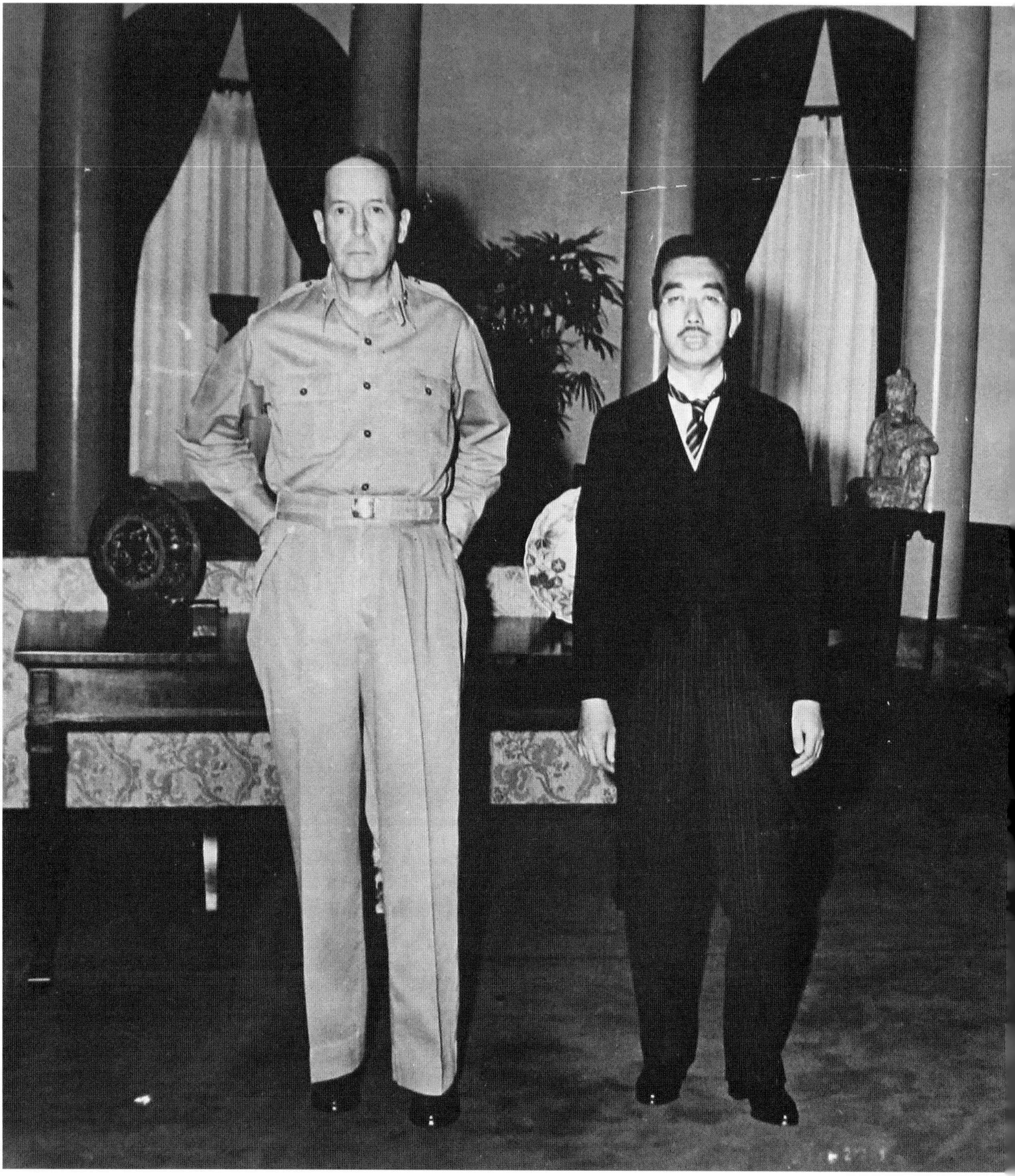

General Douglas MacArthur sets the tone of who would rule post-war Japan as he towers over Emperor Hirohito. MacArthur was the Supreme Commander of the Allied Powers and functioned from his *Dai-Ichi Seimei* building's HQ as a de facto emperor to demilitarize, reorganize and democratize Japan. MacArthur stated his intent to 'restore security, dignity and self-respect' to the Japanese citizenry. *(NARA)*

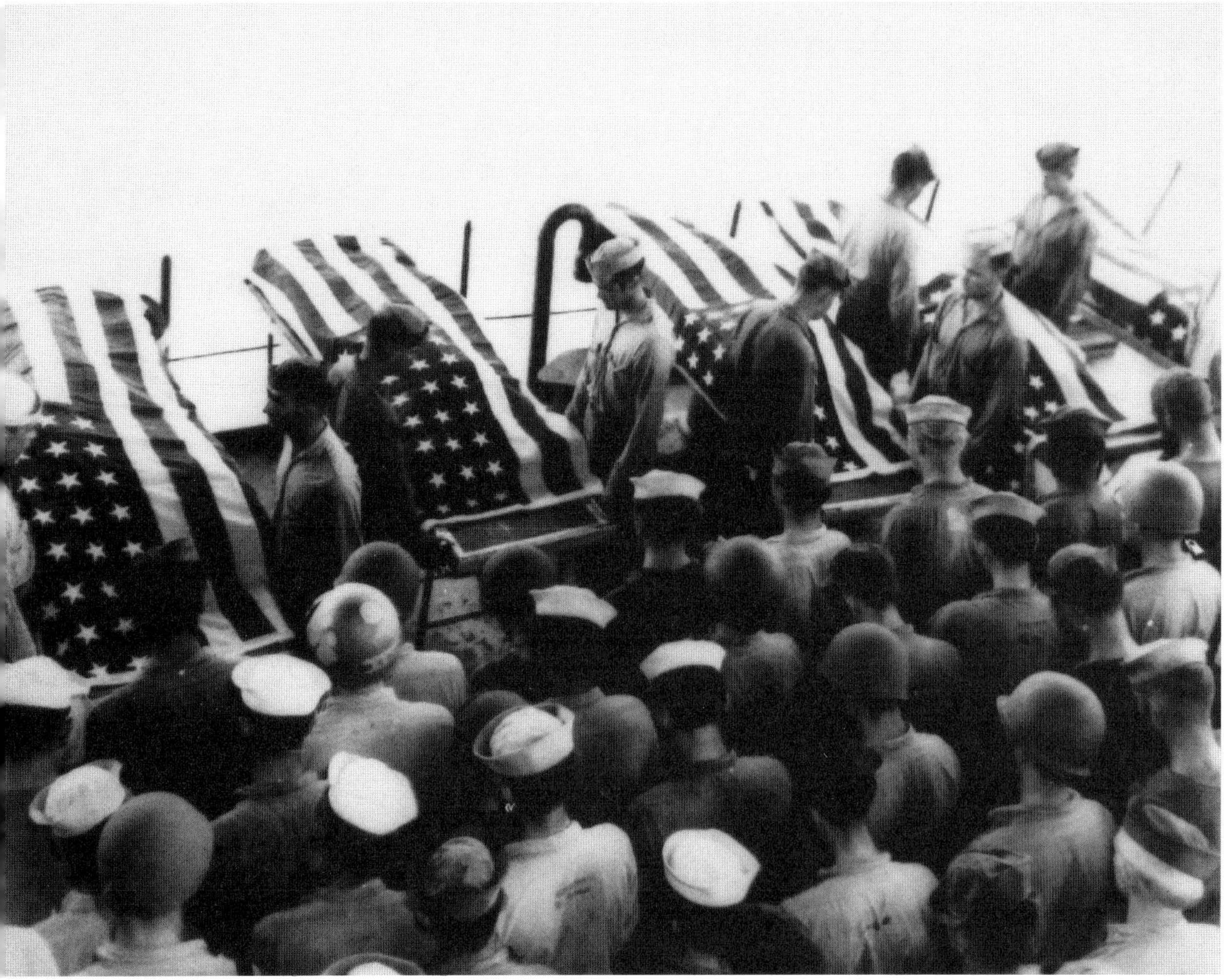

As an upsetting reminder of the cost of war, USN sailors and officers killed at the Battle off Samar Island on 25 October 1944 during the larger naval Battle of Leyte Gulf are buried at sea from the deck of the *Casablanca*-class escort carrier USS *Kalinin Bay*. This was but one isolated, solemn and grim ceremony to commemorate, lest we forget, all the Allied soldiers, seamen and airmen that perished, were grievously wounded or went missing in action during the Second World War's Pacific and Asian conflicts to free the Philippine Islands and so many other Far Eastern countries from Japanese hegemony. *(NARA)*

Bibliography

Breuer, William, *The Great Raid* (Hyperion, New York, 2002).

Cannon, M. Hamlin, *Leyte: The Return to the Philippines* (Center for Military History, Washington, 1993).

Chun, Clay, *The Fall of the Philippines 1941–42* (Osprey Publishing, Oxford, 2012).

Chun, Clay, *Leyte 1944* (Osprey Publishing, Oxford, 2015).

Chun, Clay, *Luzon 1945* (Osprey Publishing, Oxford, 2017).

Diamond, Jon, *New Guinea. The Allied Jungle Campaign in World War II* (Stackpole Books, Guildford, 2015).

Diamond, Jon, *The War in the South Pacific* (Pen & Sword Books, Barnsley, 2017).

Diamond, Jon, *MacArthur's Papua New Guinea Offensive 1942–1943* (Pen & Sword Books, Barnsley, 2020).

Duffy, James P., *War at the End of the World: Douglas MacArthur and the Forgotten Fight for New Guinea, 1942–1945* (NAL Caliber, New York, 2016).

Eichelberger, Robert L., *Our Jungle Road to Tokyo* (Battery Classics, Nashville, 1989).

Falk, Stanley, *Liberation of the Philippines* (Ballantine Books, Inc., New York, 1971).

Frank, Richard, *Tower of Skulls* (Norton, New York, 2020).

Gailey, Harry, *MacArthur Strikes Back: Decision at Buna, New Guinea, 1942–1943* (Presidio, Novato, 2000).

McManus, John, *Fire and Fortitude* (Caliber, New York, 2019).

Milner, Samuel, *Victory in Papua* (Center of Military History, United States Army, Washington D.C., 1989).

Rutherford, Ward, *Fall of the Philippines* (Ballantine Books, Inc., New York, 1971).

Scott, James, *Rampage* (W.W. Norton & Company, New York, 2018).

Sides, Hampton, *Ghost Soldiers* (Anchor Books, New York, 2002).

Smith, Robert, *Triumph in the Philippines* (Center for Military History, Washington, 1984).

Vader, John, *New Guinea: The Tide is Stemmed* (Ballantine Books, Inc., New York, 1971).

Notes